EVENTS IN PSYCHOLOGY		EVENTS IN HISTORY
		Clinton Elected U.S. President
		Persian Gulf War
	19—90	
APS Founded		Berlin Wall Topples: Cold War Ends
		Bush Elected U.S. President
PDP Research Group's *Explorations in Parallel Distributed Processing*		Space Shuttle Challenger Explodes
		Wreck of Titanic Discovered
		Invasion of Grenada
Sperry's and Hubel & Wiesel's Noble Prizes		President Reagan Shot
Searle's "Minds, Brains, and Programs"	19—80	Reagan Elected U.S. President
Simon's Nobel Prize/Cognitive Science Society		Jonestown Massacre
		Carter Elected U.S. President
Wilson's *Sociobiology*		U.S. Abandons S. Vietnam/Nixon Resigns
Vail Conference		
Skinner's *Beyond Freedom and Dignity*		Watergate Arrests
Journal *Cognitive Psychology* Founded	19—70	
		Moon Landing/King, R. Kennedy Assassinated/Nixon Elected U.S. President
		Arab-Israeli 8-Day War
Neisser's *Cognitive Psychology*		
		Project Camelot Uncovered
		Johnson Elected U.S. President
		J. Kennedy Assassinated
Kuhn's *Structure of Scientific Revolutions*		
		Berlin Wall Constructed
Hebb's "Second American Revolution"	19—60	J. Kennedy Elected U.S. President
Chomsky's Review of *Verbal Behavior*		
Newell, Shaw, & Simon's General Problem Solver		Stereo Recordings
Skinner's *Verbal Behavior*		Soviet *Sputnik* Launch
Colorado Symposium on Cognition		Montgomery, Alabama, Bus Boycott
Skinner's *Science and Human Behavior*		Armistice in Korea
		Eisenhower Elected U.S. President
Turing Test for AI Proposed/Dartmouth Conference on Learning Theory	19—50	Korean War Begins
Boulder Conference		
Tolman's "Cognitive Maps in Rats and Men"		*Sexual Behavior of the Human Male* (Kinsey)
		Cold War Begins: Churchill's "Iron Curtain" Speech
"New" APA Created		World War II Ends
Hull's *Principles of Behavior*		Effectiveness of Penicillin Demonstrated
		First "Electronic Brain" or Computer
OPP Established		Pearl Harbor/U.S. Enters WWII
	19—40	
		World War II Begins
Skinner's *Behavior of Organisms*/AAAP Founded		
Hull's "Mind, Mechanism, and Adaptive Behavior"		Spanish Civil War
		Boulder Dam Completed
		Hitler Becomes *Führer*
Tolman's *Purposive Behavior in Animals and Men*		"New Deal" Declared
Association of Consulting Psychologists		Smoot-Hawley Tariff
	19—30	

Second Edition

A History of Modern Psychology

Thomas Hardy Leahey

Virginia Commonwealth University

PRENTICE HALL   Englewood Cliffs, New Jersey   07632

Library of Congress Cataloging-in-Publication

LEAHEY, THOMAS HARDY.
    A history of modern psychology / Thomas Hardy Leahey. —2nd ed.
      p. cm.
    Includes bibliographical references and index.
    ISBN 0-13-501271-6

    1. Psychology—History—20th century. 2. Psychology—
History—19th century.   I. Title.
BF105.L43 1994
150′.9—dc20   93-34463
                                                CIP

ACQUISITIONS EDITOR: Peter Janzow
MANAGING EDITOR: Heidi Freund
PRODUCTION EDITOR: Hilda Tauber
PRODUCTION COORDINATOR: Herb Klein, Tricia Kenny
COVER DESIGN: Carol Ceraldi

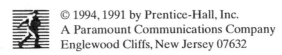 © 1994, 1991 by Prentice-Hall, Inc.
A Paramount Communications Company
Englewood Cliffs, New Jersey 07632

Printed in the United States of America
10 9 8 7 6 5 4 3 2 1

ISBN 0-13-501271-6

Prentice-Hall International (UK) Limited, *London*
Prentice-Hall of Australia Pty. Limited, *Sydney*
Prentice-Hall Canada Inc., *Toronto*
Prentice-Hall Hispanoamericana, S.A., *Mexico*
Prentice-Hall of India Private Limited, *New Delhi*
Prentice-Hall of Japan, Inc., *Tokyo*
Simon & Schuster Asia Pte. Ltd., *Singapore*
Editora Prentice-Hall do Brasil, Ltda., *Rio de Janeiro*

CONTENTS

Contents

Contents

PREFACE

I am gratified that enough professors and students used the first edition of *A History of Modern Psychology* to warrant publication of a second edition. By and large this second edition is based on the third edition of *A History of Psychology* that appeared in 1992. Minor changes have been made throughout the text, with major revisions to four chapters.

Chapter 1 on psychology, science, and history has been completely rewritten. The chapter in *A History of Psychology,* third edition, was rewritten and expanded to reflect important developments in the philosophy of science. However, length considerations required me to greatly shorten Chapter 1 in this *A History of Modern Psychology*. Teachers wishing full treatment of scientific explanation, the nature of theories, and the naturalistic approach to science will need to use or lecture from Chapter 1 of *A History of Modern Psychology,* third edition. The chapter in the present book omits everything not directly discussed later in the historical portion of the text, focusing on controversial issues in science that are important in psychology.

Two chapters on the founding of psychology have been reworked to include recent scholarship. Chapter 2 on the psychology of consciousness has been expanded to include the institutional setting in which German psychology was founded and a fuller treatment of the changes Wundt made to his system of psychology as he moved from Heidelberg to Leipzig. With the exception of the "Three Masterpieces" section, Chapter 3 on Freud and psychoanalysis is entirely new. Freud has been the object of renewed scholarly interest, and some publications such as the complete translation of the Freud/Fliess letters—long awaited by historians and psychologists—have provoked a great deal of controversy and at least one lawsuit. The development of Freud's thought has been revealed in ways not always flattering to him, and to a degree my chapter is a now a debunking by a disappointed follower.

Chapters 14 and 15, which bring the story of scientific psychology down to the present have been updated, though not rewritten. Chapter 15 in particular has been updated since its appearance in *A History of Psychology*, third edition.

I hope that readers find the second edition of *A History of Modern Psychology* an improvement on its predecessor. Please feel free to write me or e-mail me (tleahey@cabell.vcu.edu, on Internet) about anything in it you particularly like or dislike. In that way you may help shape the third edition.

THOMAS HARDY LEAHEY
Richmond, Virginia

CHAPTER 1

Psychology, Science, and History

INTRODUCTION
PSYCHOLOGY AND SCIENCE
  Psychology Without Science
  Psychology as a Science
  Perspectives and Issues About Science
  The Scientific Challenges to Psychology
PSYCHOLOGY AND HISTORY
  History of Science
  Historiography of Psychology

INTRODUCTION

Psychology is a sprawling, confusing, and important human undertaking practiced by scientific psychologists, professional psychologists, and lay people. Scientific psychologists the researchers of psychology—study a breadth of topics greater than that of any other discipline. Some of them study the structure and function of single nerve cells. Others study how information is stored in memory, how children develop, how attitudes are formed, or how people act in groups. Professional psychology constitutes the applied branch of psychology, and the breadth of the problems professional psychologists try to solve is likewise great. Some professional psychologists try to help people overcome their personal problems. Others advise people on the sort of work for which they are suited, help construct effective advertisements, improve industrial productivity, or teach children how to cope with surgical pain.

Lay people are psychologists, too. Everyone uses psychology every day. Some is borrowed from organized psychology, but most is folk psychology, the informal language we use to talk about ourselves and others. In folk psychology we explain human actions in terms of beliefs and desires, and by and large folk psychology works well for us. Sometimes we borrow ideas from technical psychology: Freudian terms such as *ego* and *libido*, and behavioristic terms such as *conditioning* and *reflex*. Meanwhile, scientific and professional psychologists use folk psychology in their day-to-day interactions with friends, families, and colleagues.

Not only is psychology diverse in its subject matter, it is diverse in the ways psychologists approach and explain psychological phenomena. Within organized psychology there is widespread disagreement among psychologists about many issues. Some psychologists believe in free will, others do not. Some psychologists think it is acceptable to use mentalistic concepts in explaining behavior, others do not. Some psychologists think that all psychology ultimately will be translatable into neuroscience, others do not.

Finally, psychology is socially important. Psychologists work in business and industry, in advertising, in schools, in companies that devise tests, in government, and in private practice helping people adjust to life. They appear on TV talk shows to explain unusual behavior and give advice to viewers. Even if you never consult a psychologist, you are shaped by psychology, because psychological concepts have become part of our everyday means of understanding ourselves and others.

At the undergraduate level, only two courses treat the full range of psychology and attempt to view the field as a whole. Introductory courses survey what psychology is doing and has discovered. The course for which you are using this book, probably called History and Systems of Psychology, takes a more analytical and synthetic approach to seeing psychology in its entirety. Our main tool in this book will be history; we will try to understand psychology as part of the history of Western civilization since the middle of the nineteenth century, when psychology as a science was founded.

Like all sciences, psychology began in philosophy and then branched off from it. All sciences maintain some contact with philosophy. For example, when modern physicists discuss the nature of causality in the world of subatomic particles and quantum mechanics, they get embroiled in deep philosophical questions about the fundamental nature of reality (d'Espagnet, 1979; Herbert, 1985). In psychology, however, the connection with philosophy has been, and remains, more direct. This is only partly because psychology became independent so recently. Philosophers who inquire into how people know the world raise questions about human perception, thinking, and learning; and when they begin to address these questions empirically, they become psychologists in practice, if not in name. Psychology, therefore, is intimately entangled with philosophy. Nor is epistemology, the study of human knowledge, the only area of philosophy involved in psychology. Psychology is also involved in ethics. Psychology is concerned with how people behave, and ethics is concerned with how people ought to behave. Understanding how people should behave cannot be entirely divorced from describing how people do behave. Prohibition failed because, despite strenuous and earnest efforts by moralists to keep people from drinking, people would not give up consciousness-altering booze—a triumph of real psychology over ideal ethics. Psychology also connects with ethics and law in real life, as when murderers are found not guilty because of evidence, usually presented by a psychologist or psychiatrist, about their psychological state at the time they committed the crime. The fundamental psychological question of how we know another person has a mind arises when physicians decide whether or not to keep a comatose patient alive.

Scientific psychology began in the last quarter of the nineteenth century when Wilhelm Wundt and the other founders of experimental psychology sought to make psychology a science by bringing the techniques and concepts of experimental science to bear on the traditional philosophical problems of mind. They drew heavily on physiology, using techniques and concepts of nervous functioning to illumine the workings of consciousness, continuing a tradition of philosophical physiology dating back to ancient Greece. However, until physiology matured as a discipline in the nineteenth century, such efforts, however well intended, serious, and even heroic, remained speculative. Today, midway through the Decade of the Brain, with neuroscience one of the most rapidly advancing fields in all of science, the connections between brain and mind and behavior are becoming clearer, fulfilling the initial hopes of psychology's founders.

I have spoken about history; what about systems? Psychologists, like philosophers and others in the humanities and social sciences, tend to divide themselves into ideologically definable groups based on systematically different ways of doing psychology. As we shall see, psychologists inherited their systematic viewpoints from philosophy, and systematic disagreements have produced theoretical debate and empirical research.

PSYCHOLOGY AND SCIENCE

Psychology Without Science

For thousands of years men and women got along without benefit of scientific psychology. People effectively describe, predict, explain, and even control their behavior without knowing any so-called science at all. More than other sciences, therefore, scientific psychology meets existing rivals on the field it hopes to conquer. Two of these rivals deserve special attention. One, *dualism*, is deeply appealing and lies at the heart of religious conceptions of behavior, and the other, *folk psychology*, is a powerful theory we use every day to explain our own behavior as well as others'. Each presents a distinct challenge to the possibility of scientific psychology.

Dualism is the psychology of most religions. In addition to the natural material world, religions typically posit a supernatural world populated by nonmaterial beings such as a god or gods, angels, and demons. Human beings, and sometimes animals, are regarded as composite creatures, composed of a nonmaterial supernatural soul contained within and controlling a material natural body. Dualists explain experience and behavior as the result of interaction between the body and its ruling soul.

Despite its appeal, dualism is incompatible with science. Although science is usually defined in terms of its method, science is also committed to one central dogma, *naturalism*, the thesis that no supernatural or non-natural causes are at work in nature (Leahey & Leahey, 1976). Religions explain much of what happens in the world supernaturally, as the result of God's will, demonic possession, or the decisions of the soul. By contrast, the aim of science is to explain every event as the result of natural causes. Psychology as a science is committed to naturalism and thus must reject dualism. Wherever the dualist sees the operation of the soul the psychologist must see the operation of natural causes. Beginning with the battle between the Old (religious) Psychology and the New (scientific) Psychology a century ago, psychology as science has been profoundly at odds with psychology as *psyche-logos*, the study (Greek *logos*, word) of the soul (Greek *psyche*, soul). So deep and thorough is psychology's commitment to naturalism that its indifference, even hostility, to religion is scarcely noticed, save by a small group of religiously inclined psychologists. To a large degree, the history of scientific psychology is the history of the rejection of dualist conceptions of mind and behavior and their replacement by naturalistic ones.

The other framework for explaining behavior before and outside scientific psychology is the simple but powerful system of folk psychology. In everyday life people explain behavior in a framework of *beliefs* and *desires*. So a student will explain her taking a course on History and Systems of Psychology by saying she *desires* to do well on the Graduate Record Examination and *believes* that taking History and Systems just before taking the exam will help her do well on it. Folk psychology works very well and finds little it cannot explain, but it is not clear whether or not it can be regarded as a scientific or even potentially scientific theory of behavior.

One problem concerns the nature of reasons. When we justify an action we cite reasons for doing it, but reasons are statements connecting beliefs, and it is controversial if reasons cause behavior in a scientific sense, because reasons connect beliefs logically and conceptually, not by a natural, causal process in the brain.

A second reason for doubting that folk psychology is or can be a scientific theory of behavior concerns the fact that reasons have to do mainly with the *meanings* of events rather than their causal structure. The reasoning of our imaginary student makes sense only in a cultural place and time with graduate schools, assessment procedures, and formal classroom teaching, embedded in a larger set of cultural practices and beliefs such as the high prestige assigned professionals with graduate degrees and the salary they command, the idea of employment for pay, the idea of money, its importance, and so on in an enormously large web of concepts. Science, however, is supposed to be about causal patterns that transcend time and place and are part of nature, not culture. Because folk psychology depends on historically and culturally constrained reasons, rather than natural causes, it is not a scientific theory, despite its usefulness in everyday life. These considerations are the focus of much current debate in philosophical psychology, and we will return to them in Chapter 15. The distinction between reasons and causes was first raised in the context of historical explanation and will be discussed again in the section on historiography in this chapter.

Closely connected with its concern for meanings rather than causes is folk psychology's concern with justifying behavior rather than explaining it. When we discuss the reasons for our behavior or the behavior of others, we are usually concerned to decide if a certain course of action was or would be morally right. When natural causes enter folk psychological explanations they are usually put forward as excuses, placing a behavior outside moral evaluation, as when an accused criminal pleads not guilty by reason of insanity. The accused admits that the behavior occurred, but maintains it was irrational—caused rather than willed. Science, however, is value neutral, taking nature as she finds it, looking for causal laws that make events happen rather than moral laws that justify or condemn human actions. Folk psychology's concern with right and wrong sets it outside science.

A final problem with folk psychology is its invocation of purposes, known technically as *teleology*, from the Greek word *telos*, meaning goal or desired end. Our student's argument is teleological: It cites a future state (going to graduate school) as a cause of a current behavior (taking History and Systems). However, it is generally accepted in science that causes must precede effects. In the first system of science, the Greek philosopher Aristotle's final (teleological) causes could be legitimately invoked to explain not only human behavior but animal behavior, plant growth, and the fall of a rock toward the surface of the earth; all these events were seen by Aristotle as resulting from a striving for perfection. However, since the time of Newton science has relentlessly replaced purposive explanations with mechanical ones in which causes precede effects, leaving teleological explanation of human behavior a strange anomaly in a discipline that calls itself a science. Citing future events as causes of present ones is automatically suspect in modern science. Along with purging dualism, purging teleology from psychology has been a driving force in the century or so psychology has been a science. Indeed, the two ideas are connected because it is to the soul that purposes are most usually attributed.

Psychology as a Science

For just over a hundred years—the period covered by this book—psychology has claimed to be a science. There are three main reasons for this. First, human beings are part of the natural world, so it seems reasonable that natural science should encompass them. Second, by the nineteenth century, when scientific psychology was founded, the authority of science was growing daily, and it seemed no discipline could be respectable were it not a science. Finally, and this was especially true in the United States, scientific status was important to making plausible professional psychology's pretensions to solve social and personal problems. Only a discipline that was a science could claim to control behavior, providing applied psychologists with professional expertise. Thus while mentalists defined psychology as the science of conscious experience, and behavioralists defined it as the science of behavior, they agreed that psychology was, or at least ought to be, a science.

The science psychologists emulated was physics. One of the most influential voices urging the creation of genuine social sciences, John Stuart Mill, wrote in the nineteenth century that "the backward state of the Moral [social] Sciences can only be remedied by applying to them the methods of Physical Science, duly extended and generalized." By Mill's time physical science in the tradition of Isaac Newton had proven itself the one reliably successful human enterprise, moving from triumph to triumph. Religion was a shambles of sects, political order dissolved into revolution, war, and tyranny, while philosophers still debated Plato's problems. Scientists, by contrast, seemed to know what they were about, solving problem after problem with increasing elegance and precision. Science alone seemed to progress. So it seemed to Mill and others that human affairs, including psychology, the study of the individual, should be subjected to the same scrutiny physical science had applied to nature. Mill's impulse gave rise to the founding of psychology as an autonomous discipline applying laboratory methods to the human mind. Although psychology today is likely to define itself as the science of behavior, it still considers itself a science on a conceptual par with the natural sciences, though not quite as developed.

Perspectives and Issues About Science

Since at least Mill's day the authority of science derives from its success at answering questions, while artistic, religious, political, and philosophical institutions appear to be mired in controversy and awash in uncertainty. However, while scientists have succeeded in explaining the world, observers of science have had a hard time explaining science. Certain approaches and issues concerning the nature of science have been quite important in the struggle to make psychology a science.

The Newtonian Style.   Science today derives from the achievements of the Scientific Revolution of the seventeenth century, above all from the intellectual style of Sir Isaac Newton (1642–1727). Newton defined the scientific enterprise as the search for a small number of mathematical laws from which one could deduce observed regularities in nature. His domain was the physics of motion, which he proposed to explain in terms of three laws of motion and a law of gravity, and he showed how his laws could precisely account for the movement of the bodies in the solar system. As an example of the *Newtonian style* of explanation (Cohen, 1980) let us take the law of gravity: Between any two material bodies there is a mutually attracting force—gravity—whose strength is inversely proportional to the square of the distance between them.

Newton was roundly criticized by his contemporaries for failing to provide any mechanism to explain *how* gravity worked; to them, action at a distance between two objects smacked of magic. Critics preferred the rival view of Descartes which explained gravitational attraction as resulting from vacuum-like vortices whirling in space about the stars and planets. Newton, however, replied *"hypotheses non fingo,"* "I do not feign [propose] hypotheses." Newton refused, in other words, to explain his principle of gravity; for him it was sufficient to postulate a force from which one could predict the motions of the heavenly bodies. Newton realized that all explanations must come to a stop with a few principles—*ideals of natural order* (Toulmin, 1961)—that science accepts as ultimate and beyond explanation themselves. The job of science is then to explain the complexities of nature and behavior as resulting from the operations of a deeper, simpler, mathematical reality.

The prestige of Newtonian physics was such that many psychologists developed physics envy. Psychologists tried to apply the methods and aims of physics to their subject matter and felt inadequate when they did not succeed. Physics envy is a hallmark of twentieth-century psychology, especially in America. Psychologists engage in a Newtonian fantasy (Leahey, 1990). One day, their faith says, a Newton will arise among psychologists and propound a rigorous theory of behavior, delivering psychology unto the promised land of science. In Samuel Beckett's play *Waiting for Godot*, two characters wait for a third who never arrives. Psychologists have been waiting for their Newton for over a century (Leahey, 1990). Will he or she ever arrive? The Newtonian fantasy assumes that a natural science of human beings is possible and that the model of that science is physics. In Chapter 15 we will ask if these assumptions are reasonable.

Positivism.   With Newton, a new philosophy for understanding nature began that was later codified in an extreme form by Auguste Comte (1798–1857) and his followers the *positivists*. Comte agreed with his friend Mill that science's success demonstrated that its methodology should be adopted by other forms of human endeavor, and Comte founded the philosophy of science by attempting to distill the essence of science into a formula others could use.

For Comte and the positivists who followed him, science worked because of the Newtonian style of remaining as close as possible to the observable facts and as far as possible from hypothetical explanations. For positivism, then, the basic job of science is *description* rather than explanation. Scientists were supposed to observe nature closely, looking for regular occurrences and reliable correlations. On the basis of their observations, scientists would propose scientific *laws*, such as Newton's law of gravity. Extending Newton's reluctance to frame hypotheses, positivists understood scientific laws to be mathematical summaries of past observations rather than truths of nature.

From the first function of science, description, ideally summarized as laws, came the second function, *prediction*. Using Newton's law of gravity and his three laws of motion, scientists could predict future events such as eclipses and the return of comets. Finally, prediction from laws made *control* of nature possible. Using Newton's laws, engineers could calculate the thrust required to throw satellites into precise orbits around the earth and send probes to the distant planets. Knowledge, as Francis Bacon said, is power, and control was the ultimate rationale for science in the positivist's philosophy. Comte looked forward to the scientific rule of society, and the desire to apply scientific psychological expertise to Comte's project played an important role in shaping twentieth-century psychology.

Science vs. Pseudoscience. Astronomy is a genuine science; astrology is a pretend science, a *pseudoscience*. In this case, the difference between the two is clear and obvious, but other cases remain uncertain. Is the theory of cold fusion science or pseudoscience? Is psychoanalysis science or pseudoscience? Sir Karl Popper (1902–), originally of Vienna and later of the London School of Economics, has devoted his long career to formulating a rule by which to separate real from pretend science.

In Vienna, when Popper was a young man, many systems of thought put themselves forward as sciences, including relativity theory and psychoanalysis. Popper wanted to know which claims to take seriously and which to dismiss. He approached the problem by looking at clear-cut cases of science, such as Newtonian physics, and clear-cut cases of pseudosciences, such as astrology, trying to figure out the difference between them. Positivists stressed the *confirmability* of theories as the test of their scientific status. That is, from a well-formulated theory, such as Newton's, we can deduce predictions whose confirmation lends credence to the theory.

Popper saw, however, that things were not so simple. Pseudosciences can claim many confirmations. The astrologer can point to predictions verified—raises gotten, girlfriends won—and can defend failed predictions by employing escape clauses such as neglected influences from minor planets. Nor did confirmability help with the uncertain cases such as relativity or psychoanalysis, since both could claim confirmation of their theories in case after case.

It was, in fact, listening to psychoanalysts and comparing them to Einstein that led Popper to formulate his *demarcation criterion* for detecting pseudoscience. Popper discovered that no matter what difficulties a case seemed to raise for psychoanalysis, a good analyst, like a good astrologer, could always reinterpret it to fit analytic theory. At the same time, shortly after World War I, an expedition was mounted to test one of relativity's predictions: that light bends in the presence of a gravitational field. Taking photographs of stars near the edge of the sun during a total eclipse, astronomers found that light rays from them were bent as Einstein's theory required.

Although at first glance this successful test appeared consistent with the logical positivists' confirmation requirement, Popper found in it a decisive difference between relativity and psychoanalysis: Although both could claim confirmation of their theory, only relativity risked *falsification*. The important thing about Einstein's prediction was not that it might prove true, but that it might prove false. There were some events relativity admitted it could not explain, while in contrast psychoanalysis—like astrology—could readily explain everything. In other words, according to Popper, scientific rationality consists not in seeking to be proved right but to be proved wrong, to stick one's neck out and risk being beheaded by a fact.

For many scientists, including psychologists, Popper's standard of falsifiability is the touchstone of good science. When a new theory is proposed, scientists ask what falsifiable predictions it makes, and proceed to test them. If a theory cannot make falsifiable predictions, it is dismissed as speculation at best, fraud at worst. As we shall see in Chapter 4, Popper's criterion has played a large role in the scientific evaluation of psychoanalysis.

The Iron Law of Explanation. Another measure of a theory's worth in science is its conformance to what I call the Iron Law of Explanation. Science seeks to explain the world with its theories, which means that scientists must carefully separate the principles and concepts of their theories from the phenomena that they wish to explain, keeping the two absolutely separate. An explanation in which the phenomenon to be explained is already in the theory is *circular*, and is no explanation at all.

An example borrowed from Molière may be used to illustrate a circular explanation. Imagine asking "Why does *Somitol* make me sleepy?" and receiving the reply, "Because it possesses the soporific power!" This appears to be an explanation of one thing (sleepiness) in terms of another (soporific power), and indeed stated forcefully in an advertisement it might be able to pass itself off as one. However, when we learn that "soporific" means "sleep-inducing," we see that the proffered explanation is empty, because it says in effect "Somitol makes you sleepy because it makes you sleepy." The explanation is circular, because the phenomenon to be explained was contained in the principle which explained it.

Although the Iron Law of Explanation may seem straightforward, following it is not easy. It is tempting to label a phenomenon—especially one with a fancy-sounding name like "soporific power"—and then think one has gained an explanation. Ancient doctors, having observed the sleep-inducing properties of various substances, may have inferred the presence of a "soporific power" capable of putting people to sleep. Now while this may be a first step toward understanding the pharmacology of sleep, it is not an explanation. People often invent names for things and think they have explained them.

To be a science, psychologists must guard against this temptation. Psychologists reject dualism in part because the concept of the soul already contains features of behavior such as intelligence and purposiveness that they wish to explain scientifically. The soul is a mere Ghost in the bodily Machine, as Gilbert Ryle will argue in Chapter 10. If one is going to explain purpose or intelligence, those terms cannot be part of scientific theories. In Chapter 7 we will see that the status of purpose—Is it an ideal of natural order or a phenomenon to be explained?—divided the great behaviorists

Tolman and Hull. In Chapters 10 and 15 we will see that B. F. Skinner castigates folk psychology, mentalistic psychology, psychoanalysis, and cognitive psychology for violating the Iron Law of Explanation.

Realism. A lively issue in the study of science, and one with enduring importance for psychology, is how to interpret scientific theories. Most theories in science—Skinner's radical, positivistic, behaviorism being a conspicuous exception—cite unseen entities and forces as the underlying causes of observable phenomena. But do these forces and entities which we never see really exist? At stake is the possibility of attaining truth in science, because only if they exist can a scientific theory be true. On one side of this question stand the *realists*, who say "science aims to give us, in its theories, a literally true story of what the world is like; and acceptance of a scientific theory involves the belief that it is true" (van Frassen, 1980, p. 8); on the other side stand the *antirealists*, saying, "science aims to give us theories which are empirically adequate [the laws cover the phenomena]; and the acceptance of a theory involves as belief only that it is empirically adequate" (van Frassen, 1980, italics deleted, p. 12). Antirealists come in agnostic and atheistic brands (Newton-Smith, 1981; Salmon, 1989). The atheists are *instrumentalists*, who regard all inferred entities as false, while the agnostics are *constructive empiricists* (van Frassen, 1980), who say we simply cannot tell if our inferences are correct or not.

The dispute may be historically illustrated by the late nineteenth-century debate between atomists and antiatomists. Since the late eighteenth century, widespread acceptance had been gained by the theory that various observable phenomena such as the behavior of gases and the regularities governing the combination of chemical elements could best be explained by supposing that objects were composed of infinitesimally small particles called *atoms*. Yet how to interpret the concept of atoms remained unclear. In one camp were the positivists, led in this battle by the distinguished physicist Ernst Mach (1838–1916). Mach argued that since atoms could not be seen, belief in their existence was faith, not science; he said atoms should be regarded at best as hypothetical fictions whose postulation made sense of data but whose existence could not be confirmed. The atomic camp was led by Russian chemist Dmitri Mendeleev (1834–1907), who believed atoms were real things whose properties and interactions explained the regularities of the periodic table he had invented.

Mendeleev's view is a realist conception of atoms: Behind observations lies a realm of unseen but real things about which science theorizes; observations are regarded as evidence for the underlying causal structure of the universe. Mach's positivist view is an antirealist view of atoms, regarding observations themselves as the only things science need explain.

In psychology, the realism-antirealism issue is an important one, although sometimes it is hidden from view. From the founding of psychology there have been realists and antirealists among psychologists. Wundt believed that mental forces such as attention existed; his student Titchener thought attention a myth; the American William James couldn't make up his mind. In the 1930s and 1940s behaviorists realistically argued over what changed inside an animal when it learned; by the 1950s antirealist psychologists said there was no way to tell. Today, as we will see in Chapters 14 and 15, psychologists argue about the status of the unseen information processes posited by cognitive psychology.

Relations Between Theories. Scientists frequently propose more than one theory applying to the same domain of natural phenomena. When this happens, two outcomes can occur, *reduction* of one theory to another, or *replacement* of one theory by another.

Intertheoretic reduction is related to the issue of realism. If theories are not true—if they are only useful fictions—then any two theories can be related only by seeing how well each accounts for observable phenomena. On the other hand, if theories are true—if there are layers of deeper and deeper causal structures in nature that theories can capture—then some theories are more basic, capturing deeper levels of reality than others. Less deep theories may then be reduced by more basic or fundamental theories, the deeper theory explaining why the higher theory works.

The process of reduction may be illustrated by the reduction of the classical gas laws to the kinetic theory of gases and the reduction of Mendelian genetics to molecular genetics. Physicists in the eighteenth century determined that the pressure, volume, and temperature of gases were interrelated by a mathematical equation called the *ideal gas law*: $P = V \times T$. Using this law, physicists could describe, predict, control, and explain the behavior of gases in precise and useful ways.

One of the early triumphs of the atomic hypothesis was the kinetic theory of gases, which gave a causal explanation of the ideal gas law. The kinetic theory held that gases (like everything else) were made up of billiard-ball-like atoms, whose degree of excitation—movement—was a function of energy. The ideal gas law predicted, for example, that if we heat the air in a balloon it will expand, while if we cool the air it will deflate (placed in liquid nitrogen it deflates to nothing), and the kinetic theory explains why. As we heat air, the particles that compose it move around more, bouncing into the skin of the balloon, pushing it outward in expansion. As we cool the air the atoms slow down, striking the balloon's skin less vigorously, and if they slow down enough, there will be no pressure at all. The kinetic theory is deeper and more basic than the ideal gas law, showing why the ideal gas law works by revealing underlying causal mechanisms of the behavior of gases. Thus, the ideal gas law was *reduced* to the kinetic theory. In principle, we could do away with the gas law, but we keep it as valid and useful in its range of application.

A similar story may be told about Mendelian genetics. In the 1860s, Gregor Mendel (1822–1884) proposed the existence of a unit of hereditary transmission, the *gene*, which was entirely hypothetical. Mendel's concept provided the basis for population genetics, but no one ever saw a gene or knew what one might look like. However, in the early 1950s the structure of DNA began to be revealed, and it emerged that DNA was the bearer of hereditary traits. As molecular genetics has progressed, we have learned that coding sequences of DNA are the real "genes," and that they do not always behave in the simple ways that Mendel thought. Nevertheless, Mendelian genetics remains valid for its purposes—population genetics—but, like the ideal gas law, has been reduced to and unified with molecular genetics.

In the case of reduction, the older theory is recognized as still scientific and as usefully valid within its sphere of application; it simply takes a subsidiary place in the grand scheme of science. The fate of a replaced theory, on the other hand, is very different. Often it turns out that an old theory is simply wrong (on the realist account), or inferior in descriptive power (on the antirealist account) and cannot be woven into the extending tapestry of scientific theory. In this case, it is abandoned and replaced by a better theory. The Ptolemaic theory of the heavens, which placed the earth at the center of the universe and described the sun, moon, and stars as revolving in complex and unlikely circles around it, was accepted by astronomers for centuries because it gave a usefully precise account of the motions of heavenly objects. Using it they could describe, predict, and explain events such as eclipses. Despite its descriptive and predictive powers, after a long struggle the Ptolemaic view was shown to be hopelessly wrong, and it was replaced with the Copernican system that placed the sun at the center with everything else revolving around it.

The founders of psychology supported their claim that psychology was a real science by linking it to neurophysiology. Wundt proclaimed an "alliance" between psychology and physiology, Freud wrote a "psychology for neurologists," and James declared that psychology must be "cerebralist." At least early in their careers, all three worked to link mind and behavior to their physiological causes. Doing so, however, meant that in the long run psychology might disappear, being reduced to or replaced by, neurophysiology, and Wundt, Freud, and James abandoned, in different ways, their enthusiasm for the alliance. Today, however, as physiologists discover the physiological bases of processes such as memory and disorders such as depression, the threat—or promise—of unifying psychology with physiology has returned.

Naturalistic Studies of Science. The approaches to and issues in science we have discussed so far are philosophical in nature. However, it is also possible to study science itself scientifically. Science is a human institution practiced by human beings, possessed of a 300 year history. It is therefore possible to study science using the methods of the social sciences, sociology, anthropology, psychology, and history.

The naturalistic approach to science emerged powerfully and controversially in the 1960s in the work of Thomas Kuhn (1962/1970), who inspired a whole generation of students of science tired of mere philosophy. Drawing on history, sociology, and psychology, Kuhn depicted science as a human institution not very different from politics or art. Gone was the image of the scientist as a disinterested, objective observer of nature, replaced by an image of the scientist as a combative, even heroic, theorist, observing nature under the spell of a largely unconscious framework, a *paradigm*, that guided and shaped his or her work. Scientific history became high drama in periods of scientific revolution, when conservative adherents of an old paradigm were challenged and defeated by young revolutionaries conquering their science under the banner of a new paradigm.

Psychology in the 1960s would be heavily influenced by Kuhn. Bored by the positivism of behaviorism and its use of animal research to illuminate human behavior, and inflamed by the revolutionary rhetoric of 1960s political radicals, young experimental psychologists proclaimed a Kuhnian revolution against behaviorism in the name of a new paradigm, cognitive psychology. Later, Kuhn would retract his more radical theses, and historians would show that revolutions in science are, at best, extremely rare. Whether or not there was a cognitive "revolution" in psychology will occupy us in Chapter 14.

A less heroic naturalistic approach to science has been proposed by Gerald Holton's (1973, 1978, 1984) analysis of *themata* in the history of science. Somewhat like paradigms, themata are metatheoretical, even metaphysical commitments that motivate and guide scientists' work and often come in pairs. In physics, for example, one ancient opposing pair of themata is the belief that the universe can be analyzed into a small number of discrete parts versus the belief that there are no ultimate parts, that the universe is a continuum. Each theme can be traced back at least to ancient Greece, and neither is yet triumphant (Herbert, 1985).

In Holton's scheme there is no constant underlying scientific process beyond physicist Percy Bridgman's formulation: "The scientific method is doing one's damnedest, no holds barred" (Holton, 1984, p. 1232). Rather, science is shaped by the beliefs scientists hold about the nature of the world. Holton's story of science is less heroic than Kuhn's, dispensing with revolutions. Sometimes opposing themata come into sharp conflict, and sometimes one is overwhelmingly dominant for a time, giving a picture of ordinary science punctuated by revolutions. On the other hand, themata endure; so there are no real revolutions, ensuring that the science of today is entirely continuous with the science of yesterday and even of the distant past.

The most recent discipline to contribute to the study of science is psychology (Tweney, Mynatt, & Dougherty, 1981; Gholson, Shadish, Niemeyer, & Houts, 1989). The field of psychology of science is new, embracing approaches from traditional psychology, such as describing the personality of the creative scientist (e.g., Simonton, 1989), to recent psychology, such as applying to science the program evaluation techniques developed for business and government (Shadish, 1989). Without doubt, however, the most active area in the psychology of science is in applying concepts of cognitive psychology to understanding the research and theorizing of scientists (e.g., Giere, 1988; Thagard, 1988; Tweney, 1989).

No overarching perspective has emerged from the cognitive study of science, but the work of Ryan Tweney (e.g., 1989) may be taken as an example. Tweney has experimentally studied scientific reasoning in nonscientists and historically studied case studies of actual science. In the first line of research (e.g., Mynatt, Doherty, & Tweney, 1978), subjects interact with a computer-generated reality, conducting experiments to discover the laws governing motion in an alternate universe. The main object is to find out what strategies people use to solve scientific problems, and to what degree they are similar to strategies used by working scientists or suggested by philosophers of science. In 1989, Tweney examined the reasoning of the physicist Michael Faraday as he formulated his theory of magnetic fields. Various concepts from cognitive science, including schemas, scripts, heuristics, and production systems were employed to represent how Faraday tested hypotheses and gradually built up the body of knowledge about magnetism and electricity that culminated in his postulation of magnetic fields and the description of their behavior. Tweney would like to write a computer program that emulates Faraday the scientist.

The Scientific Challenges to Psychology

Given the problems of incorporating traditional modes of explaining human mind and behavior within the framework of modern science, it is not surprising that psychology is a confusing enterprise, comprising not only of a broad array of research areas, but also a diversity of approaches to researching and explaining each one. Listed below are several key problems that will occupy us in the chapters to follow.

- *The challenge of **naturalism**.* The goal of science is to explain natural things in a natural way, without resorting to supernatural entities or processes, and within a universalizing framework that transcends time, location, history, and culture. Is it possible to explain human mind and behavior this way?
- *The challenge of **realism**.* Many theories in psychology such as those of Freud and information processing infer from behavior unconscious underlying states and processes, such as id and schemas, repression and schema instantiation. Do these states and processes really exist in a realm of the mind that is inaccessible to introspection, or are they convenient fictions?
- *The challenge of **autonomy**.* Many thinkers believe the ultimate nature of reality is material, and the ultimate causes of human consciousness and behavior must therefore be physiological. Is psychology autonomous from biology, or are psychological theories doomed to be reduced one day to neurophysiological theories, or, worse, replaced outright, thrown on the scrap heap of history with alchemy and astrology? What fate awaits folk psychology? teleological explanation? explanation by reasons?
- *The challenge of **explanation**.* Scientific explanation stops when we reach laws of nature—ideals of natural order—such as rectilinear motion, that are considered to be ultimate, requiring no explanation themselves. What are psychology's ideals of natural order? What should psychologists accept as ultimate and what should they define as problems to be solved?

PSYCHOLOGY AND HISTORY

History of Science

History is a well-developed discipline with its own professional norms and controversies. I will discuss here only those issues that bear directly on writing a history of psychology.

The most general problem in writing history, especially scientific history, is the tension between *reasons* and *causes* in explaining human action. Imagine the investigation of a murder. The police first determine the *cause* of death; that is, they must find out what physical process (for example, the ingestion of arsenic) caused the victim to die. Then investigators must determine the *reason* for the victim's death. They might discover that the victim's husband was having an affair with his secretary, had taken out an insurance policy on his wife, and had bought two air tickets to Rio—suggesting that the husband killed his wife in order to live in luxury with his mistress (who had better watch out). Any historical event may be explained in either or both of two ways: as a series of physical causes or of reasons. In our example the series of physical causes is placing arsenic in coffee, its ingestion by the victim, and its effect on the nervous system. The series of reasons, of rational acts carried out with intention and foresight, is purchasing arsenic, putting it in one's intended victim's drink, setting up an alibi, and planning an escape.

Tension arises between rational and causal accounts of human action when it is unclear how much explanatory force to attribute to each. So far in our example the causal story is relatively trivial, because we know the cause of death, and fixing the guilt seems clear. However, causal considerations may enter into our evaluations of an actor's behavior. During his first term, President Ronald Reagan was shot and wounded by a young man, John Hinckley. There was no doubt that Hinckley fired the bullet and was thereby part of the cause of Reagan's wound, but there were serious doubts about whether Hinckley's act could be explained rationally. The reason advanced for his attack on the president was to win the love of actress Jodie Foster, but this reason seems strange, certainly stranger than murdering one's wife to run off with one's mistress. Moreover, testimony was offered by psychiatrists that Hinckley was psychotic, showing abnormal brain X-rays. Taken together, such evidence convinced the jury that Hinckley's shooting of the president had no reasons, only causes involving Hinckley's diseased brain. Thus he was found not guilty, because where there is no reason there can be no guilt. In cases such as John Hinckley's we feel the tension between rational and causal explanation at its highest pitch. We want to condemn a proven criminal, but we know we may only direct moral outrage at someone who chose to act as he or she did, who could have done otherwise. We recognize that a person with a diseased brain cannot choose what to do and so deserves no blame.

In history of science the tension between reasons and causes is perennial. Science professes to be a wholly rational enterprise, in sharp contrast to other human practices. Scientific theories are supposed to be proposed, tested, accepted, or rejected on rational grounds alone. Yet, since scientists are human beings, it is impossible to exempt scientists from the causal forces that play a part in determining human behavior. Scientists crave fame, fortune, and love as much as anyone else, and they may choose one hypothesis over another, one line of research among many, because of inner personal causes or outer sociological causes that cannot be rationally defended, that may even be entirely unconscious. In every instance the historian, including the historian of science, must consider both reasons and causes, weighing both the rational merits of a scientific idea and the causes that may have contributed to its proposal, and to its acceptance or rejection.

Traditionally, history of science has tended to overestimate reasons, producing *Whig* history and *presentism*. These failings are shared by other branches of history, too, but are most tempting to the historian of science. A Whig account of history sees history as a series of progressive steps leading up to our current state of enlightenment. A Whig history of science assumes that present-day science is essentially correct, or at least superior to that of the past, and tells the story of science in terms of how brilliant scientists discovered the truth known to us today. Error is condemned in a Whig account as an aberration of reason, and scientists whose ideas do not conform to present wisdom are either ignored or dismissed as fools.

Whig history is comforting to scientists and therefore is inevitably found in scientific textbooks. However, Whig history is fairy-tale history and is increasingly being supplanted by more adequate history of science, at least among professional historians of science. Unfortunately, because it shows scientists as human beings and science as upon occasion irrationally influenced by social and personal causes, good history of science is sometimes seen by practicing scientists as undermining the norms of their discipline, and therefore as dangerous. I have written this book in the spirit of the new history of science, trusting, with historian of physics Stephen Brush (1974), that instead of harming science good history can help young scientists by liberating them from positivist and Whiggish dogma, making them more receptive to unusual and even radical ideas. A large-scale historical survey of the sort I am writing must be to some degree presentist—that is, concerned with how psychology got to be the way it is. This is not because I think psychology today is for the best, as a Whig historian would, but because I wish to use history to understand psychology's current condition. As we shall find, psychology could have taken other paths than it did, but it is beyond the scope of this book to explore what might have been.

An important dimension in history of science is *internalism-externalism*. Whig histories of science are typically internal, seeing science as a self-contained discipline solving well-defined problems by rational use of the scientific method, unaffected by whatever social changes may be occurring at the same time. An internal history of science could be written with few references to kings and presidents, wars and revolutions, economics and social structure. Recent history of science recognizes that while scientists might wish themselves free of influence by society and social change, they cannot achieve it. Science is a social institution with particular needs and goals within the larger society, and scientists are human beings socialized within a given culture and striving for success within a certain social setting. Recent history of science is therefore externalist in orientation, considering science within the larger social context of which it is a part and within which it acts. In this text, I will try to show how historical forces external to psychology have powerfully shaped its development.

An old historical dispute, tied up with reasons vs. causes, Whig vs. new history of science, and internalism vs. externalism, is the dispute between those who see Great Men as the makers of history, and those who see history made by large impersonal forces outside human control. In the latter, *Zeitgeist* (German for *spirit of the times*) view of history, people are sometimes depicted as little more than puppets.

The Great Man view was eloquently stated by the English writer Thomas Carlyle (1795–1881):

> For, as I take it, Universal History, the history of what man has accomplished in this world, is at bottom the History of the Great Men who have worked here. They were the leaders of men, these great ones; the modellers, patterns, and in a wide sense creators, of whatsoever the general mass of men contrived to do or attain; all things that we see standing accomplished in the world are properly the outer material result, the practical realization and embodiment, of Thoughts that dwelt in the Great Men sent into the world: the soul of the world's history, it may justly be considered, were the history of these. (Carlyle, 1841/1966, p. 1)

Great Man history is often stirring, for it tells of individual struggle and triumph. In science, Great Man history is the story of the research and theorizing of brilliant scientists unlocking the secrets of nature. Because Great Men are revered by later ages for their accomplishments, Great Man history is usually Whiggish and internalist, precisely because it stresses rationality and success, downplaying cultural and social causes of human thought and action.

The opposing view was essentially invented by the German philosopher Georg Wilhelm Friedrich Hegel (1770–1831):

> [O]nly the study of world history itself can show that it has proceeded rationally, that it represents the rationally necessary course of the World Spirit, the Spirit whose nature is indeed always one and the same, but whose nature unfolds in the course of the world. ... [W]orld history goes on in the realm of the Spirit. ... Spirit, and the course of its development, is the substance of history. (Hegel, 1837/1953, p. 12)

Zeitgeist history tends to ignore the actions of human beings, because people are believed to be living preordained lives controlled by hidden forces working themselves out through historical process. In Hegel's original formulation the hidden force was the Absolute Spirit (often identified with God) developing through human history. Spirit has gone out of fashion, but *Zeitgeist* histories remain. Hegel's student Karl Marx materialized Hegel's Spirit into economics and saw human history as the development of modes of economic production. Modern externalist history of science tends to emphasize forces in the *Zeitgeist* over the heroics of individuals.

Because of its emphasis on the inevitability of progress, in Hegel's or Marx's conception *Zeitgeist* conception of history was Whiggish. Both Hegel and Marx saw human history directed toward some final end, the ultimate realization of the Spirit or God, or the ultimate achievement of socialism, the perfect economic order, and both viewed historical development as a rational process. Their history is not, however, internalist, because it places the determination of history outside the actions of men and women. The contribution of Hegel and Marx was inventing externalism, directing historians' attention to the larger context in which people work, discovering that the context of action shapes action in ways at best dimly seen by historical actors themselves. Taking this broad perspective, externalism provides a greater understanding of history. However, contrary to Hegel or Marx, history has no discernible direction. The history of the world, or of psychology, could have been other than it has been. We humans struggle in a semidarkness of social and personal causes, yet, as Freud observed, the still small voice of human reason, not some abstract Reason or economic plan, is finally heard.

Historiography of Psychology

The history and methodology of the field of history is called *historiography*. The historiography of science—of which history of psychology is a part—has passed through two stages (Brush, 1974). In the earlier stage, from the nineteenth century until the 1950s, history of science was mostly written by scientists themselves, typically older scientists no longer active at the forefront of research. This is not surprising, since one of the special difficulties of writing history of science is that one must be able to understand the details of scientific theory and research in order to chronicle its story. However, beginning in the 1950s, and gaining momentum in the 1960s, a "New History of science" emerged as the field was professionalized. History of science was taken over by men and women trained as historians, although in many cases they had scientific backgrounds.

History of psychology underwent the same change, although a little later and still incompletely. The classic Old History of psychology is Edwin G. Boring's magisterial *History of Experimental Psychology,* first published in 1929, with a revised edition in 1950. Boring was a psychologist, a student of introspectionist E. B. Titchener, and the psychology which Boring knew was being superseded by behaviorism and the rise of applied psychology. So while Boring was by no means retired, he wrote his *History* as an internalist, Whiggish justification of his tradition (O'Donnel, 1979).

Boring's book was the standard text for decades, but beginning in the mid-1960s the new professional history of psychology began to replace the old. In 1965 a specialized journal appeared, *Journal of the History of the Behavioral Sciences*, and the American Psychological Association approved formation of a Division (26) for the History of Psychology. In 1967 the first graduate program in history of psychology was begun at the University of New Hampshire, under the direction of Robert I. Watson, founder of the *Journal* (Watson, 1975; Furomoto, 1989). The development of the "New History of psychology" gathered steam in the 1970s and 1980s, until in 1988 Laurel Furomoto could declare it fully matured and demand its incorporation into the psychological curriculum. We should note that the change is incomplete: Although the text you are reading is one of the few to be influenced by the new history of psychology (Furomoto, 1989), I am a cognitive psychologist with no formal training in history.

There is much more involved in the change from the old history of science (and psychology) to the new than who writes it. This change coincides with a longer-term movement in historiography from "Old History" to "New History" (Himmelfarb, 1987; Furomoto, 1989). "Old History" was "history from above"; it was primarily political, diplomatic, and military, concentrating on great people and great events. Its form was the narrative, telling readable stories—frequently written for a broadly educated public, not just other historians—of nations, men, and women. New History is history from below; it attempts to describe, even recreate in words, the intimate lives of the anonymous mass of people neglected by the old history. As Peter Stearns has put it, "When the history of menarche is widely recognized as equal in importance to the history of monarchy, we [new historians] will have arrived" (quoted by Himmelfarb, 1987, p. 13). Its form is analytic rather than narrative, often incorporating statistics and analytic techniques borrowed from sociology, psychology, and other social sciences.

The New History is very much *Zeitgeist* history, depreciating the role of the individual and seeing history as made by impersonal forces, not the actions of men and women. Although the new history focuses on ordinary lives, it depicts men and women as victims of forces they do not control. Contingency is denied, as the new history is described by perhaps its foremost practitioner, French historian Fernand Braudel:

> So when I think of the individual, I am always inclined to see him imprisoned within a destiny in which he himself has little hand, fixed in a landscape in which the infinite perspectives of the long term stretch into the distance both behind him and before. In historical analysis, as I see it, rightly or wrongly, the long term always wins in the end. Annihilating innumerable events—all those which cannot be accommodated in the main ongoing current and which are therefore ruthlessly swept to one side—it indubitably limits both the freedom of the individual and even the role of chance. (Quoted by Himmelfarb, 1987, p. 12)

The new history of psychology is described by Furomoto:

> The new history tends to be critical rather than ceremonial, contextual rather than simply the history of ideas, and more inclusive, going beyond the study of "great men." The new history utilizes primary sources and archival documents rather than relying on secondary sources, which can lead to the passing down of anecdotes and myths from one generation of textbook writers to the next. And finally, the new history tries to get inside the thought of a period to see issues as they appeared at the time, instead of looking for antecedents of current ideas or writing history backwards from the present context of the field. (1989, p. 16)

Apart from its call for greater inclusiveness in writing history, Furomoto's description of the new history of psychology actually describes good traditional history as well.

Although the New History has become mainstream history, it has provoked, and continues to provoke, controversy (Himmelfarb, 1987). Most upsetting to traditional historians is the abandonment of narrative for analysis, the denial of contingency, and the rejection of the efficacy of human action. A backlash in favor of narrative and in appreciation of contingency and the importance of individuals has recently appeared. For example, James M. McPherson, in his splendid *Battle Cry of Freedom*, adopted narrative as the only mode of history that could do justice to his topic, the American Civil War, and in the end concludes that human will and leadership—Lincoln's political skill and Grant's and Sherman's generalship—won the war for the North.

Where in the spectrum of Old to New history does the present book fit? While it is true that I have been influenced by and have used the new history of psychology in writing my book, it is not entirely *of* the new history. I feel the greatest affinity for the traditional history of ideas and have not generally sought to find the causes of psychology's development in the biographies of psychologists. I believe that history is a humanity, not a science, and that when historians lean on the social sciences they are leaning on weak reeds. I agree with Matthew Arnold that the humanities should concern themselves with the best (and most important) that has been said and done. Finally, I agree with English historian G. R. Elton that history "can instruct in the use of reason." I have tried, then, to write as narrative a history as the material allows, focusing on the leading ideas in psychological thought and aiming to instruct the young psychologist in the use of reason in psychology.

BIBLIOGRAPHY

The literature on philosophy of science is large. A good recent survey is David Oldroyd, *The arch of knowledge* (New York: Methuen, 1986). A slightly older and more technical survey, but one that was widely cited as a definitive is Frederick Suppe's long introduction to F. Suppe (Ed.), *The structure of scientific theories*, 2nd. ed. (Urbana: University of Illinois Press, 1977). *Science and philosophy: The process of science* (Dordrecht: Martinus Nijhoff, 1987) edited by Nancy J. Nersessian contains a selection of papers by leading philosophers of science written for nonspecialists. Many of the issues and approaches mentioned in the text are discussed and represented in Nersessian's volume.

The realism-antirealism issue is treated from both points of view in Wesley Salmon (Ed.), *Scientific explanation* (Minneapolis, MN: University of Minnesota Press, 1989). Salmon provides a comprehensive history of the problem of scientific explanation by one of the area's leading lights; Salmon is a realist, and in the same volume his friend Kitcher gives a lengthy summation of the antirealist perspective. The realism-antirealism issue is given an interesting treatment by Arthur Fine in "Unnatural attitudes: Realist and instrumentalist attachments to science," *Mind* (1986, 95, 149–179), who argues that both viewpoints are flawed by mirror-image failings: "metaphysical inflationism" and "epistemological inflationism," respectively. For realism in physics, see Nick Herbert, *Quantum reality* (New York: Doubleday, 1985), a wonderful introduction to modern quantum physics and its many puzzles.

W. H. Newton-Smith, *The rationality of science* (London: Routledge & Kegan Paul, 1981) provides a general treatment of and argument in favor of the view of science as a uniquely rational enterprise, in contrast to the heroic, revolutionary naturalism of Kuhn. Ronald N. Giere, on the other hand, in "Philosophy of science naturalized," *Philosophy of Science* (1985, *52*, 331–356), argues for the opposite point of view. One approach to science not discussed in the text sees it as working like Darwinian evolution; see David Hull, *Science as a process: The evolutionary account of the social and conceptual development of science* (Chicago: University of Chicago Press, 1988).

Empirical studies of science, including psychology of science, from the seventeenth century to the present are collected in R. Tweney, C. Mynatt, & D. Doherty, *On scientific thinking* (New York: Columbia University Press, 1981). A forceful set of arguments for, plus case studies of, psychology of science may be found in Gholson et al. (1989). Essays applying philosophy of science to psychology include Barry Gholson & Peter Barker, "Kuhn, Lakatos and Laudan: Applications in the history of physics and psychology," *American Psychologist* (1985, *40*, 744–769); Peter Manicas & Paul Secord, "Implications for psychology of the new philosophy of science," *American Psychologist* (1983, *38,* 399–414); and Joseph Margolis, Peter Manicas, Rom Harre, & Paul Secord, *Psychology: Designing the discipline* (Oxford: Basil Blackwell, 1986).

Useful studies in philosophy of psychology include several surveys: Neil Bolton (Ed.), *Philosophical problems in psychology* (New York: Methuen, 1979); Mario Bunge & Ruben Ardila, *Philosophy of psychology* (New York: Springer, 1987); Paul Churchland, *Matter and consciousness* (Cambridge, MA: Bradford/MIT, 1988), who focuses on materialism and reductionism/replacement); Fred Dretske, *Explaining behavior: Reasons in a world of causes* (Cambridge, MA: Bradford/MIT, 1988), focusing on reasons and causes; Peter Smith & O. R. Jones, *The philosophy of mind* (Cambridge, England: Cambridge University Press, 1986); and Jenny Teichman, *Philosophy and the mind* (Oxford: Basil Blackwell, 1988).

REFERENCES

Brush, S. G. (1974). Should the history of psychology be rated X? *Science, 183*, 1164–1172.

Carlyle, T. (1841/1966). *On heroes, hero-worship and the heroic in history*. Lincoln, NE: University of Nebraska Press.

Cohen, I. B. (1980). *The Newtonian revolution*. Cambridge, England: Cambridge University Press.

Cohen, I. B. (1985). *Revolution in science*. Cambridge, MA: The Belknap Press of Harvard University Press.

D'Espagnet, B. (1979, November). The quantum theory and reality. *Scientific American, 241*, 158–181.

Furomoto, L. (1989). The new history of psychology. In T. S. Cohen (Ed.), *The G. Stanley Hall Lecture Series* (Vol. 9). Washington, DC: American Psychological Association.

Gholson, B., Shadish, W. R., Jr., Niemeyer, R. A., & Houts, A. (Eds.). (1989). *Psychology of science*. Cambridge, England: Cambridge University Press.

Giere, R. N. (1988). *Explaining science*. Chicago: University of Chicago Press.

Hegel, G. W. F. (1837/1953). *Reason in history: A general introduction to the philosophy of history* (R. Hartmann, Trans.). Indianapolis, IN: Bobbs-Merrill.

Herbert, N. (1985). *Quantum reality: Beyond the new physics*. New York: Anchor Press/Doubleday.

Heyes, C. M. (1989). Uneasy chapters in the relationship between psychology and epistemology. In B. Gholson et al. (Eds.), *Psychology of science*. Cambridge, England: Cambridge University Press.

Himmelfarb, G. (1987). *The new history and the old*. Cambridge, MA: Belknap Press of Harvard University Press.

Holton, G. (1973). *Thematic origins of scientific thought: Kepler to Einstein*. Cambridge, MA: Harvard University Press.

Holton, G. (1978). *The scientific imagination: Case studies*. Cambridge, England: Cambridge University Press.

Holton, G. (1984, November 2). Do scientists need a philosophy? *Times Literary Supplement,* 1231–1234.

Kuhn, T. S. (1962/1970). *The structure of scientific revolutions*, rev. ed. Chicago: University of Chicago Press.

Leahey, T. H. (1990, August). Waiting for Newton. Paper presented at the annual meeting of the American Psychological Association, Boston.

Leahey, T. H. & Leahey, G. E. (1983). *Psychology's occult doubles: Psychology and the problem of pseudoscience*. Chicago: Nelson-Hall.

McPherson, J. L. (1988). *The battle cry of freedom: The Civil War era*. New York: Oxford University Press.

Mynatt, C. R., Doherty, M. E., & Tweney, R. D. (1978). Consequences of confirmation and disconfirmation in a simulated research environment. *Quarterly Journal of Experimental Psychology, 30,* 395–406. Partially reprinted in Tweney, Doherty & Mynatt (1981).

Newton-Smith, W. H. (1981). *The rationality of science*. London: Routledge & Kegan Paul.

O'Donnel, J. M. (1979). The crisis of experimentalism in the 1920s: E. G. Boring and his uses of history. *American Psychologist, 34,* 289–295.

Popper, Karl. (1963). *Conjectures and refutations: The growth of scientific knowledge*. London: Routledge & Kegan Paul.

Salmon, W. S. (1984). *Scientific explanation and the causal structure of the world*. Princeton, NJ: Princeton University Press.

Salmon, W. (1989). Four decades of scientific explanation. In P. Kitcher and W. S. Salmon (Eds.). (1989). *Scientific explanation. Minnesota studies in the philosophy of science* (Vol. 13). Minneapolis, MN: University of Minnesota Press.

Salmon, W. (1990). *Scientific theories. Minnesota studies in the philosophy of science.* (Vol. 14). Minneapolis, MN: University of Minnesota Press.

Shadish, W. R., Jr. (1989). The perception and evaluation of quality in science. In B. Gholson et al. (Eds.), *Psychology of science*. Cambridge, England: Cambridge University Press.

Simonton, D. K. (1989). The chance-configuration theory of scientific creativity. In B. Gholson et al. (Eds.), *Psychology of science*. Cambridge, England: Cambridge University Press.

Thagard, P. (1988). *Computational philosophy of science*. Cambridge, MA: Bradford Books/MIT Press.

Toulmin, S. (1961). *Foresight and understanding*. Princeton, NJ: Princeton University Press.

Tweney, R. D. (1989). A framework for the cognitive psychology of science. In B. Gholson et al. (Eds.), *Psychology of science*. Cambridge, England: Cambridge University Press.

Tweney, R. D., Mynatt, C. R., & Doherty, M. E. (Eds.). (1981). *On scientific thinking*. New York: Columbia University Press.

van Frassen, B. C. (1980). *The scientific image*. Oxford: Clarendon Press of Oxford University Press.

Watson, R. I. (1975). The history of psychology as a specialty: A personal view of its first 15 years. *Journal of the History of the Behavioral Sciences, 11,* 5–14.

PART I

FOUNDING SCIENTIFIC PSYCHOLOGY

Although psychologists traditionally revere one man, Wilhelm Wundt, as the founder of psychology, and one date, 1879, as the founding year of psychology, their faith is misleadingly simple. Wundt's long-term importance for psychology has proven to be institutional, for it was he who created a socially recognized and independent science and a new social role for its practitioners. Conceptually, psychology was founded three times. Each founding gave rise to a distinctive way of thinking about psychology's problems.

The most traditional founding psychology was the psychology of consciousness, the introspective study of the normal, adult human mind. This psychology directly continued traditional philosophical psychology and made it more rigorous. Wundt stands at the head of this tradition, although many others took part. The most important rival of psychology of consciousness was Gestalt psychology, which rejected many of Wundt's premises and drifted into a kind of science of behavior. The psychology of consciousness proved to be the least durable form of psychology.

The most famous, and in its own time notorious, founding psychology was Sigmund Freud's psychology of the unconscious. Freud attempted to plumb the hidden and threatening dark side of human nature, and what he found there offended some and inspired others. Freud's psychology of the unconscious is less a rival of Wundt's psychology than its complement. It has, however, been much more influential and durable than Wundt's psychology. Freud's ideas have profoundly affected Western thought in the twentieth century, and Freudian psychoanalysis has spawned innumerable variants into our own time.

Among academic psychologists, the most important founding psychology has been the psychology of adaptation. Its founding was the work of many hands, first among them being William James. The psychology of adaptation does not see the problem of psychology to be the philosophically motivated dissection of consciousness or the therapeutic exploration of the unconscious, but instead the biological study of the evolutionary utility of mind and behavior. The psychology of adaptation began as an introspective study of mental activity, but it soon became the study of activity itself—that is, the study of behavior.

CHAPTER 2

The Psychology of Consciousness

PROLOGUE: FOUNDATION STONES FOR PSYCHOLOGY

First Stone: Physiology and Mind

For millennia, religions and philosophies mostly taught that mind and body were separate substances. According to this *dualism*, a human being was composed of a spiritual supernatural soul and a material body-machine. However, beginning in the eighteenth century and with increasing force in the nineteenth, some philosophers and scientists embraced materialism, maintaining that the soul is a myth, that human beings and animals are just machines. This step was necessary for psychology to become a science. Science's guiding idea is naturalism, the attempt to explain the makeup and behavior of the universe in exclusively natural terms, eschewing all reference to supernatural entities and forces such as gods, demons, and souls. For psychology to become a natural science, then, it had to dispense with the soul and look to the study of the body—specifically the brain and nervous system—as revealing the causes of consciousness, mind, and behavior. Indeed, despite the dominance of dualism, since Greek times there had been thinkers—primarily physicians interested in the mind—who had tried to unite the physiological and philosophical approaches to mind and behavior. However, their efforts remained speculative until the nineteenth century, when advances in the study of brain and nervous system made a real naturalistic psychology seem plausible.

THE PHYSIOLOGY OF THE BRAIN AND THE NERVOUS SYSTEM

The First Physiological Psychology: Phrenology and Localization of Brain Functions. Franz Joseph Gall (1758–1828) reversed this relationship. Gall may fairly be regarded as the founder of neuropsychology because he was the first to take seriously the idea that the brain is the seat of the soul. The idea was hardly new: Plato believed it; the Hellenistic scientists of Alexandria demonstrated it; the medieval faculty psychologists located each faculty in a different portion of the brain. However, beyond encouraging materialism, the concept had little effect on psychological thought. The locations assigned to the medieval faculties were based on prior analysis of mind, not brain, and philosophical psychology had done nothing to change this. Gall, however, stated that the brain was the specific organ of mental activity in the same way that the stomach is the organ of digestion and the lungs the organ of respiration. Therefore the study of human nature should begin with those functions of the brain that give rise to thought and action, rather than with abstract and introspective inquiries into mind.

The philosophical background against which Gall reacted was French empiricism and associationism, especially Condillac's sensationism. Gall offered several reproaches to that philosophical approach to psychology (Young, 1970). To begin with, the empiricists claimed that experience was the proper basis of science, yet their own psychology, Hume's science of human nature, was wholly speculative, having no reference to objective behavior or to the brain that controls it. Furthermore, the categories of analysis used by the philosophers were "mere abstractions." None of the faculties proposed by philosophers—such as memory, attention, and imagination—were specific enough to explain actual human behavior and concrete individual differences. In *On the Functions of the Brain,* Gall wrote: "How are we to explain, by sensation in general, by attention [etc.] … the origin and exercise of the principle of propagation; that of the love of offspring, of the instinct of attachment? How explain by all these generalities, the talents for music, for mechanics, for a sense of the relations of space, for painting, poetry, etc." The philosophers' faculties exist but "they are not applicable to the detailed study of a species, or an individual. Every man, except an idiot, enjoys all these faculties. Yet all men have not the same intellectual or moral character. We need faculties, the different distribution of which shall determine the different species of animals, and the different proportions of which explain the differences in individuals" (Young, 1970, p. 18). In short, the philosophers' concepts are useless for the specific empirical investigations that science requires.

Gall's ideas brought him into conflict with empiricist philosophers in a final way. Condillac had attempted to derive every faculty of mind from sensation and association. Gall, however, believing the brain to be the organ of the mind, concluded that each of his proposed faculties was innate, based in a particular region of the brain. Gall's approach also implies a comparative psychology. Since the brains of species differ up and down the Great Chain of Being (Gall wrote before Darwin), so should the corresponding faculties differ. In fact, Gall carried out comparative anatomical studies to support this argument.

The problem for Gall, then, was to correlate specific behavioral functions with particular regions of the brain. Although he carried out detailed anatomical studies of the brain and nervous system, he found the techniques of his time too crude to answer the questions he posed, and he had moral scruples about experimenting on living but "martyrized" animals. Gall's method, therefore, was different. He assumed that well-developed faculties would correspond to well-developed parts of the brain. Those "organs" corresponding to the well-developed faculties in the brain would be larger than those organs corresponding to less-developed faculties, and their relative size would be registered on the skull as bumps overlying the developed organ. Empirically, then, Gall's method was to show that people possessing certain striking traits would possess skulls with bumps over the corresponding organs of the brain, and that weak traits would go with undeveloped brain organs and skull regions. Although Gall's specific hypothesis was new, the idea that personality traits reveal themselves in physique and face was as old as antiquity.

Gall's theory has been schematized by Young (1970), as in Figure 2–1. Thus Gall could observe an individual's unique behaviors and correlate them with cranial prominences. On the basis of such observations Gall drew up a long list of faculties,

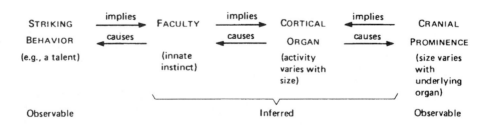

FIGURE 2-1 Gall's theory of mind, brain, and behavior. (Adapted from Young, 1970)

PART I FOUNDING SCIENTIFIC PSYCHOLOGY

including destructiveness, friendship, and language, each located in a particular region of the brain. Destructiveness, for example, was located just above the ear. Later followers of Gall expanded his list to include such faculties as veneration, whose existence was believed to show that God must exist to be the object of veneration.

Certain conceptual features of Gall's approach have been mentioned: It was nativistic; it compared humans with other animals; it was materialistic, although Gall himself struggled against this tendency. Gall's psychology was also behavioristic rather than introspectionistic. His system rested on the observation of behaviors and of bumps on the skull rather than on the introspection of his own mind. Gall's psychology was therefore the first objective, rather than subjective, psychology. More broadly, Gall's was a functional psychology concerned with how the mind and its organ, the brain, actually adapt a person or animal to everyday demands. Philosophical psychology was more concerned with grand problems of epistemology. Finally, Gall's psychology was a psychology of individual differences. He explicitly rejected the study of the generalized adult mind in favor of a study of how people differ.

Gall, in his system of phrenology, had been the first to take seriously the idea that the brain is the organ of the mind. He therefore investigated the detailed relationship of brain organ and mental faculty. Gall's researches raised a storm of controversy in physiology, helping to push physiologists to experiment on the brain to discover exactly how it works and what it does. These experiments first led away from phrenology and then back to a "new phrenology" as physiologists discounted, and then discovered, the localization of brain functions.

Gall's major critic was a leading French physiologist, Jean-Pierre-Marie Flourens (1794–1867), a pioneer in experimental brain research. Flourens discovered the functions of the various lower parts of the brain, but when it came to the cerebral hemispheres, he parted company with Gall. Flourens ridiculed phrenology and argued on the basis of his own researches—which involved lesioning or ablating parts of the brain—that the cerebral hemispheres act as a unit, containing no specialized organs for special mental faculties. In his conclusions, Flourens was more dominated by philosophical ideas than Gall was. Flourens was a Cartesian dualist who viewed the soul as residing in the cerebral hemispheres, and since the soul is unitary, the action of the hemispheres must be so too. He believed there was no organic connection between the sensory and motor functions of the lower parts of the brain and the cerebrum. Flourens's stature assured the success of his attack on Gall, and his view of the unitary action of the cerebrum remained orthodox dogma for decades.

Alongside experimental methods for studying the brain and nervous system is the clinical method, which proceeds by examining the effects of damage and disease on thought and behavior. An important discovery in this tradition was made by Pierre Paul Broca (1824–1880), who observed that patients with speech disorders showed, when autopsied, damage to the same area of the left frontal lobe of the brain. Broca, who rejected the study of bumps on the head, viewed his finding as limited support for Gall, although the faculty of language had not been found where Gall had predicted. Certainly Broca's finding supported the assertion that mental functions are located in different parts of the brain instead of being uniformly distributed throughout it, as Flourens had claimed.

Understanding the Nervous System. As Gall, Flourens, and Broca were debating and advancing the understanding of the brain, progress was also being made in understanding how nerves and neurons work. That nerves (bundles of neurons) conduct sensory and motor impulses had been known since Greek times. However, the nature of nervous transmission remained unclear until the nineteenth century. First, Luigi Galvani (1737–1798) showed that nervous impulses are electrical in nature.

Second, it had always been assumed that nerves carry impulses indifferently in either direction, towards the brain as sensory impulses and away from the brain as motor control impulses. However, in 1822, a discovery of momentous long-term implications (Cranefield, 1974) was announced by François Magendie (1783–1855). Earlier, on the basis of postmortem dissections, the English physiologist Charles Bell (1774–1842) had distinguished two sets of nerves at the base of the spinal column. Bell suggested that one set carried information to the brain (sensory nerves), while the other carried information from the brain to the muscles (motor nerves). Magendie discovered the same thing independently and more conclusively, because he demonstrated the different functions of the nerves in the spinal column by direct experiment on living animals. The next decade in brain physiology saw the extension of the sensorimotor distinctions up the spinal column.

Brain and Nervous System Unified: The Reflex Theory. As physiologists extended their investigations of nervous functions into the brain, they began to develop a unified theory for the whole neural network of the body: that the nervous system is a sensorimotor reflex device at whose center is the brain, responsible for connecting sensory input with motor output. As early as 1845, one English physician wrote: "The brain ... is subject to the laws of reflex action, and that, in this respect it does not differ from the other ganglia of the nervous system ... [and] must necessarily be regulated ... by laws identical with those governing the spinal ganglia and their analogues in the lower animals" (Young, 1970, p. 204).

Against the view that the nervous tissue of the brain was identical to that outside the brain was the observation that the cerebral hemispheres seemed insensitive to the sorts of stimulation that excite other nerves. The cerebral hemispheres had been poked, prodded, pressed, and pricked in living animals, but no movement resulted. This supported Flourens's view that the hemispheres were not involved in action. However, in 1870, two German researchers, Gustav Fritsch and Eduard Hitzig, announced that microvoltage electrical excitation of parts of the cerebrum elicited movements in a dog, and that different areas of what we now call the motor cortex seemed, when stimulated, to regulate different movements.

This finding encouraged others to map out the brain, locating each sensory and motor function. Today such maps are remarkably precise and allow tumors to be located with great accuracy. A "new phrenology" was thus born, in which each part of the brain was assigned a discrete sensory or behavioral function. But the new localizations were different from Gall's, for they resulted from an extension of the sensorimotor nerve distinction to the cerebrum. Some parts of the brain receive sensations, others govern specific actions, and the association of sensation and action produces behavior. In this view, the brain is a complex reflex machine. It should be pointed out here that not all neurophysiologists accepted then, or accept now, the localization of brain functions. Some maintain that the brain acts at least in some respects as a unit and that information present in one part of the brain is at least potentially present in others.

The formulation of the brain as a reflex device associating sensory input with motor action was powerfully summarized in 1876 in British physiologist David Ferrer's *The Functions of the Brain*. Thus a sound basis was laid for the integration of philosophy of mind with the physiology of the nervous system.

TOWARD NATURALISTIC PSYCHOLOGY

England: Alexander Bain (1818–1903) and Association Psychology. In 1851, Bain wrote to his friend and colleague John Stuart Mill: "There is nothing I wish more than so to unite psychology and physiology that physiologists may be made to appreciate the true ends and drift of their researches into the nervous system." Bain fulfilled his desire in two massive volumes, *The Senses and the Intellect* (1855) and *The Emotions and the Will* (1859), a comprehensive survey of psychology from the standpoints of associationism and physiology and embracing every psychological topic from simple sensation to aesthetics and ethics.

Bain offered few new ideas. His associationism derived from the earlier association psychologies of David Hartley and James and John Stuart Mill. His physiology was drawn from leading texts and lectures of his time. The idea of uniting physiology and philosophical psychology was ancient. Bain's physiology, however, was based on experimental research, not on speculation. Bain's wish to unite psychology and physiology probably came from his early exposure to phrenology, which he later rejected in favor of Mill's associationism and Flourens's physiology.

What is most important about Bain is the attitude he adopted toward his material. The aim of the earlier associationists was to give an adequate empiricist epistemology. Bain, however, wrote as a psychologist. He assumed the associationist epistemology and inquired instead into how to account for human action, not just conception. Bain was not concerned to justify human knowledge, but to explain human thinking and behavior. Bain's concern with behavior greatly influenced American pragmatism.

To this end Bain adopted the sensorimotor physiology of the German physiologist Johannes Müller (1801–58). In his *Elements of Physiology* (1842), Müller had already proposed that the role of the brain is to associate incoming sensory information with appropriate motor responses. Bain knew the *Elements* and incorporated Müller's conception of the role of the brain into his psychology. Thus Bain united the philosophy of associationism with sensorimotor physiology to give a unified human psychology. Even today most general psychology texts are organized like Bain's, beginning with simple nerve function in sensation and working up to thinking and social relations. Bain's integration was quite influential. He wrote before the functions of the cerebrum were known, and his uncompromising associative view of physiology guided later English investigators to press their studies into the mysterious cerebral hemispheres.

Thus Bain had a considerable effect on psychology. The journal *Mind*, which he founded in 1874, is still in existence as an organ of philosophical psychology. He was, however, too philosophical in his outlook; his conception of mind was soon out of date.

Despite his use of physiological data, he did no experiments, and while he recognized the importance of Darwin's work, his associationism remained preevolutionary. The future of association psychology lay more in its integration with evolution than with physiology.

France: Ideology, Spiritualism, and Positivism.   During and after the French Revolution, French philosophical psychology was carried on by the "ideologists," named by their founder, Destutt de Tracy (1754–1836). *Ideology* means here the study of ideas and their origin, and it continued the Enlightenment tradition of French empiricism. De Tracy returned to a conventional faculty psychology consistent with Locke. As heirs to the Enlightenment, the ideologists had as their real goal social reform. They favored a moderate democracy based on personal property and were particularly interested in improving education as the foundation for the new society.

The best known of the ideologists is Pierre Jean Georges Cabanis (1757–1808), a physician who is sometimes called the "father of physiological psychology." Cabanis is the epitome of Enlightenment empiricism and materialism. Stating what could have been Condillac's motto, Cabanis said, "We sense; we are." He compared the function of the brain to the function of the stomach. Wrote Cabanis (1824): "The brain digests the impressions; [and] organically produces the secretion of thought." Although Cabanis detested the Reign of Terror—when ideologists had been imprisoned—he used the "experiments" of the guillotine to argue that mental activity and action are multileveled: The body may twitch after the head is severed, but this is simply unconscious reflex activity. Consciousness resides in the brain and disappears at the moment of execution. Cabanis never performed physiological researches and avoided any precise speculation on the relation of nervous activity to mind, although he was clearly a materialist. Consequently, his ideas remained more philosophical than those of Gall or the later experimental physiologists, although he did tend in their direction.

One interesting figure began as an ideologist but then swam against the prevailing empiricist-materialist stream toward Catholicism. He was François-Pierre Maine de Biran (1766–1824). Although Maine de Biran was not afraid to take a physiological approach to the study of the mind—and always insisted that psychology should study the whole person—he felt that there was more to human nature than mere matter. He possessed an intensely introspective disposition and argued that the fundamental method of psychology should be reflection, or the scrutiny of one's own mind. Maine de Biran called this enterprise "experimental psychology." Upon such reflection, the central psychological fact he discovered was will, or the feeling of effort we experience as we carry out a voluntary action. Like Wundt, Maine de Biran was a voluntarist, with the important distinction that Maine de Biran's experimental psychology used an intense Cartesian form of introspection rather than Wundt's simple self-observation. Maine de Biran's one direct influence on psychology was on Freud, who knew of Maine de Biran's belief that many important influences on mental life are marginally conscious at best and that only careful reflection could reveal them. As Maine de Biran grew older, he moved further still from French naturalism and toward religion. He finally believed in a separate immortal soul whose relation to God needed investigation. This last direction of his thinking helped found the later French school of spiritualism, which opposed materialism and insisted on humankind's spiritual nature but did not involve psychic phenomena. Maine de Biran completed his retreat from the naturalism of ideology by dying a Catholic. He represents an attempt, ultimately unsuccessful, to reassert the reflective Platonic-Cartesian rationalist psychology against the rising tide of naturalism and positivism.

The last French philosophical psychologist, Hippolyte-Adolphe Taine (1828–1893), expounded these new positions. Although most of his works are on history and literature, he was most proud of his psychological book, *On Intelligence* (1870, 1875), which William James used as his text when he first taught psychology at Harvard. In *On Intelligence*, Taine presents an integration of association psychology similar to Bain's, arguing that all ideas, no matter how apparently abstract, may be reduced to a collection of sensations associated with the idea's name. The business of psychology is thus similar to chemistry's—"to decompose [compounds] into their elements to show the different groupings these elements are capable of, and to construct different compounds with them" (Taine, 1875). Following Leibniz, Taine proposed that conscious sensations are simply aggregates of weaker, more fleeting sensations that are only marginally conscious at best. Thus Taine, like so many others in the nineteenth century, believed in the unconscious.

Taine then discussed the physiological substrate of sensation. He maintained a dual-aspect psychophysical parallelism, holding that every event in consciousness has a corresponding neural event. According to Taine, the reverse is not true, for some neural events give rise only to unconscious sensations. Taine's neurophysiology presents the brain as an unspecialized organ associating stimulus and response: "The brain, then, is the *repeater* of the sensory centers." That is, the brain simply copies incoming neural information, as mental images copy sensations. Mind and brain are both seen in terms similar to Hume's or Hartley's.

Taine, then, may be regarded as a French Bain, although he had less systematic effect on later psychology than Bain, since his later writings abandoned psychology. Nevertheless, he integrated physiology and philosophical association psychology and is followed historically by the earliest French psychologists. In his philosophy, he even pointed beyond Bain toward behaviorism. His approach to science resembled that of the later logical positivists. In this view, the first task of a science is to gather firm observational data from which simple generalizations are drawn. Then a logically organized, deductive, theoretical edifice is to be erected on the observational foundation. Finally, new phenomena may be predicted from the theoretical system and these predictions checked against observation. Biran had tried to return French psychology to reflective rationalism, but Taine put it back on course as an objective, empiricistic science integrated with biology.

Germany: Struggle Toward Science. The dominant philosophical system in Germany following Kant was idealism in one form or another. Certain concepts of the idealists found a place in early German psychology. Wundt studied individual consciousness, proposed a historical, genetic approach to the investigation of the higher mental processes, and stressed human will as the unifying force in mental life. All of these ideas are part of idealist philosophy. Freud, too, was influenced by Schopenhauer's concept of unconscious primitive forces lurking in the personality. Nevertheless, the German idealists, following Kant, took a dim view of psychology as a would-be science. Psychology studies only a concrete individual, or a set of individuals, whereas what the idealists sought was transcendent Platonic knowledge of a godlike Absolute Spirit, which they took to be the noumenal reality behind physical appearances and the individual mind. Although Wundt retained a bias toward the study of the general human mind, he did not believe in an Absolute Mind. Empirical research seems trivial in the idealist context, and the idealists—most forcefully Hegel—actively opposed the development of empirical psychology (Leary, 1978b).

However, there were those in Germany who did seek a scientific psychology, taking Kant's negative analysis of psychology as a challenge (Leary, 1978a). The most important of them was Johann Friedrich Herbart (1776–1841), who attempted to mathematicize psychology. Herbart viewed psychology as applied metaphysics. His extremely complex psychological system formed only a small part of an even more complex metaphysics, developed largely out of Leibniz's monadology.

Herbart pictured the mind as a collection of elementary ideas of varying intensity. Some ideas are strong enough to cross the threshold of consciousness; others reside in unconsciousness. In fact, Herbart prefigured Freud by maintaining that no idea is ever completely destroyed. Ideas struggle with one another for access to consciousness, as dissonant ideas repel one another and associated ideas help pull each other into consciousness or drag each other down into unconsciousness. Herbart's real aim was to formulate a Newtonian mathematics of the mind. Just as Newton described the mathematically exact interaction of objects in space, so Herbart tried to describe the mathematically exact interaction of ideas in the mind. In equation after equation, Herbart proposed exact formulas for the mechanics of ideas entering and leaving consciousness.

The difficulty of Herbart's system was that there was no way to connect it to empirical reality. To begin with, Herbart himself argued that the mind could not be subject to experiment because each mind is unique and can shed no light on general mental functioning. Furthermore, he admitted that his calculations were wholly fictional, based on hypothetical assumptions incapable of proof. Finally, Herbart said that in his psychology for an idea to be "in consciousness" doesn't mean that its possessor is conscious of it! This seems to cut Herbart's psychology off from science as ordinarily understood, and Wundt continually attacked Herbart's metaphysical, unscientific psychology. It was a common criticism of Herbart that he failed to measure mind, as Fechner was able to do later.

We must bear in mind, however, that mental measurement and experiment were not Herbart's aim. It is best to view him as proposing a mental algebra or geometry in Plato's realm of mathematics. When you solve the quadratic equation or prove the Pythagorean theorem, you are concerned wholly with abstract entities. Algebra and Euclidean geometry are, like Herbart's psychology, hypothetical systems based on *a priori* rules for manipulating symbols, rules that may be changed to create a different system (such as non-Euclidean geometry). Algebra can be used to compute the price of apples or the force of gravity; geometry can be used to survey roads or map the stars. Each is also an autonomous study in its own right. So Herbart would have thought his laws of the rise and fall of ideas could be applied equally to dissonant musical notes or dissonant Oedipal attitudes toward one's father.

Viewed this way, Herbart resembles the later psychological school of twentieth-century structuralism, associated with Chomsky and Piaget. Piaget, for example, treated thinking as an abstract activity which can be described in the language of formal logic. *What* a child thinks about is less important to Piaget than the logical *structure* of his thinking. The Western child may think about classifying sports cars, the African child about classifying species of antelope, but the logic of classification is universal. Herbart seems to have held the same position. Each person's mind is absolutely unique, for the experiences giving us our ideas are unique; but common to all people are the mathematics of how ideas are related.

Herbart's direct influence in psychology was limited. His idea that ideas continuously vary in intensity helped Fechner formulate psychophysics, using a version of Leibniz's concept of apperception which was greatly stressed by Wundt. He contributed to the idea of the unconscious and, against the idealists, proclaimed psychology a science. Yet Wundt, Fechner, and all experimental psychologists repudiated Herbart's metaphysical, vaguely introspective, fictional mathematics of mind. They had to if they were to establish psychology as an independent science. Herbart was much interested in pedagogy, and several decades after his death "Herbartianism" enjoyed a vogue in educational circles. But Herbartianism was more the creation of others who picked up and reshaped Herbart's ideas, and even in modified form it exerted no long-term influence. Herbart's most lasting effect was his determination to make psychology a science despite the strictures of Kant and the opposition of the idealists.

Another important German philosophical psychologist was Hermann Lotze (1817–1881). Before he turned to philosophy, Lotze received his M.D., and he was Fechner's friend and physician. In one respect, Lotze appears to be German psychology's Bain or Taine. In his *Outlines of Psychology* (1881), Lotze proposed an empiricist view of consciousness, saying that depth perception is learned, not innate, and experience is compounded out of simple ideas. This empiricism he integrated with the growing sensorimotor concept of brain function.

However, Lotze was not wholly dedicated to empiricism and naturalism. He insisted that although physiology offered a valid approach to the material aspects of mind and behavior, human beings and animals each possessed divinely given souls. As was typical of German philosophers, Lotze (and Herbart) emphatically rejected materialism in favor of Cartesian dualism. By insisting on the human spiritual nature, Lotze earned the admiration of English-speaking psychologists dissatisfied with the associationistic and reductive psychologies they found around them. Among them were James Ward, the English psychologist who bitterly attacked naturalism, and William James, the tender-minded psychologist who took part in psychical research.

A more eminent and consistent exponent of naturalism and empiricism was Hermann von Helmholtz (1821–1894), probably the greatest natural scientist of the nineteenth century. For much of his career he was occupied with physiology. Soon, we will discuss his research on the speed of nerve conduction; he also conducted definitive studies of physiological optics and acoustics. But he was also a leading physicist, formulating the law of conservation of energy when he was only twenty-six.

Helmholtz's approach to the mind is essentially that of a Lockean empiricism in which ideas are interpreted as mental content. Helmholtz argued that all we know for certain are our ideas, or images of the world gathered by experience. He strikes a pragmatic note by acknowledging that we cannot know if our ideas are true, but argues that this does not matter as long as they lead to effective action in the real world. Science was an example of such effective action. Although he followed Kant in holding causality to be an innate principle, Helmholtz, like the empiricists, maintained that the other Kantian categories of knowledge are acquired.

Of particular interest to psychology is Helmholtz's theory of unconscious inference. If, for example, visual perception of space is not an innate intuition, then in the course of development we must learn to calculate the distance of objects from us, as George Berkeley proposed in the early eighteenth century. Yet we are not aware of performing such calculations. Helmholtz theorized that these kinds of calculations, or inferences, must be unconscious, and moreover must be unconsciously learned, as happens in language acquisition. Like words, ideas (including sensations) are mental contents that represent reality. Just as children learn language spontaneously and with no direct instruction, so too they spontaneously and unconsciously learn the meanings of ideas. Helmholtz's theory of the unconscious differs from other views. For Herbart, the unconscious was just a place where ideas reside when they are not conscious. For the romantics, it was a repository of ancient and irrational forces. For Helmholtz, it was an agency autonomous of consciousness, but essentially rational; unconscious inferences were of the same form as conscious ones.

As we would expect of a physicist and physiologist, Helmholtz was a forceful advocate of the natural sciences. He welcomed their growth in the German universities and heaped scorn on the idealist philosophers for whom natural science was the trivial study of physical reality, which was of no consequence compared to the spirit behind physical reality. Furthermore, Helmholtz's own researches supported materialism. His physiological studies of sensation established the dependence of perception on mere fleshly matter. His theory of conservation of energy inspired some young physiologists to swear, as Helmholtz's friend Emil du Bois-Reymond put it in a letter, "a solemn oath to put in effect this truth: no other forces than the common physical-chemical ones are active within the organism" (Kahl, 1971). This attitude encouraged the young Freud to compose his first systematic psychology, one that was entirely materialistic.

Helmholtz, however, was aware of the dangers of too much materialism when he wrote in "Thought in Medicine" (1877, pp. 355–56): "Our generation has had to suffer under the tyranny of spiritualistic metaphysics; the younger generation will probably have to guard against materialistic metaphysics." He continues, "Please do not forget that materialism is a metaphysical hypothesis ... If one forgets this, materialism becomes a dogma [compare this to the "solemn oath" above] which hinders the progress of science and, like all dogmas, leads to violent intolerance." While he could not accept spiritualism or vitalism, neither could he accept extreme materialism. He preferred to maintain an open mind and let the facts decide.

Second Stone: Experimental Research Methods

The great German philosopher Immanual Kant (1724–1804), whose influence in German universities was immense, had argued that no science of the mind was possible, in part because no aspect of mental life could be measured or investigated experimentally. Thus while linking physiology to the philosophy of mind made the idea of a naturalistic psychology plausible, actually creating a working scientific psychology required practical methods for overcoming Kant's objections. Two very different methods for quantitative experimental study of consciousness had been developed by the middle of the nineteenth century.

Psychophysics: Psychology's First Research Program. The dean of historians of psychology, E. G. Boring, dates the founding of experimental psychology to 1860, the year in which a book called *Elements of Psychophysics* was published, written by a retired physicist, Gustav Theodore Fechner (1801–1887). Boring's claim rests on the fact that Fechner conceived and carried out the first systematic research in experimental psychology—research, moreover, that produced mathematical laws. Before Fechner, philosophers had widely assumed, following Kant, that the mind can neither be experimented on nor subjected to mathematical scrutiny. Fechner showed these assumptions to be false. The difficulties do at first seem to be immense. In physics, we can manipulate objects and observe what they do, and we can measure their position and momentum, writing mathematical laws interrelating these variables (such as Newton's inverse-square law of gravitation). However, minds are private, and no instruments can be applied to conscious experiences.

Fechner's greatness was to overcome these problems. He saw that the content of consciousness can be manipulated by controlling the stimuli to which a person is exposed. This control makes mental experiment possible. We can have a person lift objects of known weight, listen to tones of known pitch and volume, and so on. Even so, how do we measure the resulting conscious experiences, or sensations? We can assign no number to a tone or weight sensation. Fechner perceived the difficulty and got around it by quantifying sensations indirectly. We can ask a subject to say which of two weights is heavier, which of two tones is louder. By systematically varying both the absolute values of the pairs of stimuli and the difference between them, and by observing when subjects can and cannot distinguish the pairs, sensation can be indirectly quantified. Hence we can mathematically relate stimulus magnitude (R) with the resulting strength of sensation (S). One might expect that sensation would vary directly with stimulus, but Fechner found it did not. Instead, he found that $S = k$ log R (where k is a constant). That is, stimulus differences are easier to detect when both stimuli are of moderate absolute intensity than of high absolute intensity (for example, it would be easier to distinguish a 10-ounce weight from an 11-ounce weight than a 10-pound weight from a 10-pound, 1-ounce weight).

Fechner's approach was not without antecedents. The basic method of asking subjects to distinguish stimulus differences had been pioneered by the physiologist E. H. Weber (1795–1878). The concept of treating sensations as quantitatively varying conscious states goes back to philosopher G. W. Leibniz's distinction between *petite perception*—sensations too weak to enter consciousness—and *apperception*—consciously experienced sensations. This line of thinking had been developed further by the German philosopher, Herbart. Fechner followed both in admitting the existence of unconscious—or, as he called them, negative—sensations, which do not cross the threshold of consciousness. The immediate motivation of Fechner's work was the mind-body problem. Fechner held a dual-aspect position, believing that mind and brain were simply two aspects of the same underlying reality, and therefore that physical stimuli and subjective sensations ought to be functionally related. Fechner hoped his psychophysics would solve the mind-body problem.

Fechner is not the founder of the science of psychology because, unlike Wundt, he carved out no societally recognized role for psychologists to take. Nevertheless, Fechner founded experimental psychology, for his methods, broadened to encompass more than sensations, were basic to Wundt's experimental psychology of consciousness. In Wundt's experiments, antecedent stimulus conditions were controlled, as in Fechner's, and data were provided as subjects reported the resulting conscious content. It was not Wundt's only method, but it was an important one, and it was the one most of his students carried away with them from his laboratory.

Chronometric Analysis of Mental Processes. Another method that made possible the founding of scientific experimental psychology was the measurement of the speed of mental processes. One historical source for the development of mental chronometry is in astronomy, a field far removed from psychology. For their own reasons, astronomers were the first scientists to attempt to quantify the mind's speed. An important function of astronomy is to precisely map the stars. Until the advent of modern mechanical and photographic methods in which an astronomer rarely looks through a telescope, accurately locating stars depended on the ability of an astronomer to note the exact moment when a star passed directly overhead, marked by a single cross-hair in the telescope's field of vision. In one common early method, the astronomer noted the exact time on a clock as the star entered the field of vision and then counted as the clock beat seconds until the star crossed the cross-hair. Accurately noting the exact moment of transit was critical, for slight errors would be translated into immense interstellar distances in calculating the exact positions of stars in the galaxy.

In 1795, an assistant astronomer at Greenwich observatory lost his job when his superior discovered that his own transit times were about 0.5 second faster than his assistant's. Of course, the head astronomer assumed his own times to be correct and his assistant's in error. Years later, this event came to the attention of the German astronomer F. W. Bessel (1784–1846), who began systematically to compare the transit times of different astronomers. Bessel discovered that all astronomers differed in the speed with which they reported transits. To correct this grave situation, Bessel constructed "personal equations" so that the differences among astronomers could be canceled out in astronomical calculations. For example, the "personal equation" of the two Greenwich astronomers would be Junior − Superior = 0.5 sec. The observations of any pair of astronomers could be compared by these equations reflecting their personal reaction times, and calculations of star positions could be corrected accordingly. Unfortunately for astronomers, use of the personal equations assumed that individual differences were stable, which proved to be false. Indeed, experiments with artificial stars with known transit times showed that sometimes observers "saw" the star intersect the cross-hair before it occurred. Only the increasing automation of observation was able to eliminate these problems.

The second source of mental chronometry lies in the efforts of physiologists to measure the speed at which action potentials move along the axons of neurons. The pioneer was the great physicist and physiologist Hermann von Helmholtz, with whom Wundt would later study. In 1850, Helmholtz stimulated the motor nerve of a frog's leg at points near and far from the muscle itself, measuring the time it took for the muscle to respond. Before Helmholtz's investigation, it had been widely assumed that nerve impulses traveled at infinite or at least immeasurably fast speeds. Helmholtz estimated the speed to be only 26 meters per second.

These two lines of research on reaction time came together in the work of F. C. Donders (1818–1889), a Dutch physiologist, the founder of mental chronometry. Donders saw that the time between a stimulus and its response could be used to objectively quantify the speed of mental processes. Helmholtz had measured the simplest sort of stimulus-response (S-R) reaction, while astronomers had, for another purpose, investigated mental processes such as judgment. It was Donders's especial contribution to use reaction time to infer the action of complex mental processes. So, for example, one could measure a person's simple key-press response to a single stimulus—a mild shock to the foot. This is *simple reaction time.* However, one might ask the subject to press a key with the left hand when the left foot is shocked and with the right hand when the right is shocked. Obviously, a simple reaction is involved, but in addition, the subject must discriminate which foot is shocked and choose which response to make. If simple reaction takes, for example, 150 msec to complete, and the discrimination and choice experiment takes 230 msec to complete, Donders reasoned that the mental actions of choice and discrimination inserted into the simple reaction must take 230 msec − 150 msec, or 80 msec. This seemed to offer an objective way of measuring physiological and mental processes and was called *mental chronometry.*

The method was taken up early by Wundt and extensively used by the early mentalistic psychologists. Precisely because it was a quantitative method, it helped assure the scientific stature of experimental psychology as apart from qualitative philosophical psychology. It took the mind out of the armchair and into the laboratory. Unfortunately, numerous difficulties in the application of mental chronometry cropped up, and it ran into a dead end early in the twentieth century. One of the difficulties was implicit in its original discovery by astronomers—the problem of individual differences. These differences troubled Wundt, the psychologist of the general mind, but they fascinated his American student, J. M. Cattell. With the advent of behaviorism, psychologists largely turned away from reaction-time experiments in their attention to learning. However, when cognitive psychology arose in the 1960s, mental chronometry was reborn, for cognitivists wanted ways to infer the temporal nature of inferred mental processes such as judgment, reasoning, memory, and pattern matching.

THE FOUNDING OF PSYCHOLOGY IN GERMANY

By the last quarter of the nineteenth century, conditions were ripe for psychology to emerge as an autonomous science. As we have seen, scientific psychology was fated to be born as the hybrid offspring of philosophy of mind—called psychology by the middle of the century—and physiology. Wilhelm Wundt (1832–1920) was the philosopher-physician who established psychology as an academic discipline. Like Moses, he did not follow his people—the future generations of psychologists—entirely into the land of science, but he made possible psychology's recognition as a science.

The Path Through Physiology

In the work that first defined scientific psychology, *Principles of Physiological Psychology,* Wundt (1873) proclaimed "an alliance between two sciences." The first was physiology, which "informs us about those life phenomena that we perceive by our external senses," and psychology, in which "the person looks upon himself from *within.*" The result of the alliance was to be a new science, *physiological psychology,* whose tasks were two:

> [*F*]*irst,* to investigate those life processes [consciousness] that, standing midway between external and internal experience, require the simultaneous application of both methods of observation, the external and the internal; and *second,* to throw light upon the totality of life processes from the points of view gained by investigations of this area and in this way perhaps to mediate a total comprehension of human existence. [This new science] begins with physiological processes and seeks to demonstrate how these influence the domain of internal observation.... The name *physiological psychology* ... points to psychology as the real subject of our science.... If one wishes to place emphasis on methodological characteristics, our sciences might be called *experimental psychology* in distinction from the usual science of mind based purely on introspection. (Wundt, 1873, pp. 157–58)

Besides being a culmination of the ideas of centuries of philosopher-physicians, the alliance of physiology and psychology served several important functions for the fledgling science of psychology. The first concerned methodology both broadly and narrowly defined. Although in Wundt's time the word *physiology* was acquiring the biological meaning it has today, it still possessed a broader and different meaning. The Greek root of *physiology* is the same as of physics, *physis,* and in the nineteenth century, the word was often used simply to designate taking an experimental approach to a subject. More specifically, in the case of psychology, apparatus and techniques such as reaction-time measurement were taken over from physiology and put to use in psychology laboratories. Because of the important methodological aspect of the alliance, Wundt also called physiological psychology "experimental psychology."

A second set of functions of the alliance between physiology and psychology is only alluded to by Wundt in the quoted passage and concerned the content of the new science. At a philosophical level, the alliance helped psychology become part of the aggressively emerging naturalistic world-view of science. Traditionally, psychology meant *psyche-logos,* the study of the soul. But the supernatural soul had no place in naturalistic science, so to continue pursuing psychology along traditional lines would bar it from science on the grounds of unscientific dualism. However, by insisting that the nervous system is the basis of all mentality, and defining psychology as the investigation of the physiological conditions of conscious events, the new field of physiological psychology could establish itself as a science. For example, the most important mental process in Wundt's psychology was apperception, and Wundt proposed the existence of an "apperception center" in the brain. In addition, psychologists could borrow established physiological concepts such as neural excitation and inhibition and use them in psychological theories.

One theoretical possibility opened up by creating physiological psychology was reductionism: not simply borrowing physiological concepts for psychological usage, but explaining mental and behavioral events in terms of physiological causes. To take a familiar modern example, it appears that the cause of long-term depression is depletion of catecholamines in the brain rather than repressed psychological conflicts. All three of the main founders of psychology—Wundt, Freud, and James—were attracted by the idea of jettisoning psychological theory altogether in favor of explaining consciousness as the outcome of neural causes, without positing a level of unconscious mediating psychological processes. All three found the idea of reducing psychology to neurophysiology initially attractive but ultimately repellant. At the very least, if physiology could explain mind and behavior, psychology's status as a discipline was threatened, since physiological psychology would become simply physiology. Wundt and Freud moved away from reductionism, while James struggled mightily with it and eventually gave up psychology altogether for philosophy. Nevertheless, the idea of reduction lived on in the succeeding generations of psychologists, sometimes hidden but never dying, and today it is reasserting itself with new vigor (see Chapter 15).

The last function of the alliance between physiology and psychology was institutional. In Germany, physiology was the most recently established scientific discipline. Its practitioners, such as Hermann von Helmholtz, with whom Wundt studied, were among the leading scientists, and its rapid progress soon gave it enormous prestige. For an ambitious academic like Wundt, the champion of a new field seeking funds, space, and students, alliance with physiology was a shrewd move in the game of academic politics (Ben-David & Collins, 1966).

Cultural and Intellectual Setting: The German Mandarins

Ancient Confucian China was largely ruled by an intellectual elite called the Mandarins. Theoretically, the Mandarin class was open to all who received a classical education and could pass the civil service examinations, but in practice, few besides the established Mandarin families could afford the private tutoring needed to enter the ruling elite. The Mandarins made up the bureaucracy that governed China through the rise and fall of emperors and imperial dynasties. They ruled by controlling the life of the emperor, establishing endless and exacting rounds of rituals and duties for the emperor to perform according to carefully prepared rules. Often it was difficult if not impossible for the emperor to leave the Forbidden City or do anything on his own. The historian Fritz Ringer (1969) has described German intellectuals as comprising a Mandarin class of their own, based on classical education of the personality—*Bildung*—and governmental control through bureaucracy and education. Wilhelm Wundt was the very model of a modern German Mandarin, and his career reveals the Mandarin mind that shaped German psychology before the rise of Nazism.

Wilhelm Maximilian Wundt was born on August 16, 1832, in Neckarau, Baden, Germany—the fourth child of a minister, Maximilian Wundt, and his wife, Marie Frederike. Many ancestors on both sides of Wundt's family were intellectuals, scientists, professors, government officials, and physicians. At the age of thirteen, Wundt began his formal education at a Catholic *Gymnasium*.[1] He disliked school and failed, but he transferred to a school in Heidelberg, from which he graduated in 1851. Wundt decided to go into medicine, and after an initially poor start, he applied himself and

---

[1]The German *Gymnasium* was a college-preparatory high school; entrance was generally restricted to the sons of middle-class intellectuals.

excelled in his studies. His scientific interests emerged in physiological research. He got his M.D. in 1855, *summa cum laude,* and after some study with the physiologist Johannes Müller received in 1857 the second doctorate German universities required of lecturers. He immediately gave his first course in experimental physiology—to four students in his mother's apartment in Heidelberg.[2] These courses were interrupted by an acute illness from which he almost died.

During his convalescence Wundt applied for and received an assistantship with Hermann von Helmholtz. Although Wundt admired Helmholtz, they were never close, and Wundt rejected Helmholtz's materialism. While with Helmholtz, Wundt gave his first course in "Psychology as a Natural Science" in 1862, and his first important writings began to appear.

He worked his way up the academic ladder at Heidelberg while dabbling in politics, for the first and last time, as an idealistic socialist. He got married in 1872. His publications continued, including the first edition of his fundamental work, *Grundzüge der Physiologischen Psychologie,* in 1873 and 1874. This work in its many editions propounded the central tenets of his experimental psychology.

After a year in a "waiting room" position in Zürich, Wundt received a chair in philosophy at Leipzig, where he taught from 1875 to 1917. It was at Leipzig that Wundt won a degree of independence for psychology by founding his Psychological Institute. Beginning as a purely private institute in 1879, it was supported out of his own pocket until 1881. Finally, in 1885, it was officially recognized by the university and listed in the catalogue. It began as a primitive, one-room affair and expanded over the years; in 1897, it moved to its own specially designed building, later destroyed during World War II.

During the years at Leipzig, Wundt continued his extraordinary output—supervising at least 200 dissertations, teaching over 24,000 students, and writing or revising volume after volume, as well as overseeing and writing for the psychological journal he founded, *Philosophische Studien.* He trained the first generation of psychologists, many of them Americans.

In 1900, he began a massive undertaking, the publication of his *Völkerpsychologie,* which was completed only in 1920, the year of his death. In it, Wundt developed what he believed was the other half of psychology, the study of the individual in society as opposed to the individual in the laboratory. Wundt's work continued to the last. His final undertaking was his reminiscences, *Erlebtes und Erkanntes,* which he completed only a few days before he died on August 31, 1920, at the age of eighty-eight.

During World War I, Wundt, like almost all German intellectuals, was fervently nationalistic. He, like many other "patriots of the lectern," wrote violently anti-English and anti-American tracts that can be read only with embarrassment today. They are interesting, however, as they reveal the gulf between the German and the Anglo-French-American world-views. For Wundt and other German intellectuals, the English were—in the words of Werner Sombart—mere "traders" who regarded

---

[2]The German university system in the nineteenth century was very different from the modern American system. One had to obtain the usual doctorate and then a second, higher-level doctorate before one could teach—and even then one had no regular salary and could only give private, fee-supported courses. Only after years of private teaching and a life of relative poverty could one obtain a salaried professorship.

"the whole existence of man on earth as a sum of commercial transactions which everyone makes as favorably as possible for himself" (Ringer, 1969). The English were excoriated by Wundt for their "egotistic utilitarianism," "materialism," "positivism," and "pragmatism" (Ringer, 1969). The German ideal, on the other hand, was "the hero," a warrior whose ideals were "sacrifice, faithfulness, openness, respect, courage, religiosity, charity and willingness to obey" (Ringer, 1969). The goal of the Englishman was seen as personal comfort, while that of the German was seen as sacrifice and service. Germans also had a long-standing contempt for French "civilization," which they considered a superficial veneer of manners as opposed to the true German, organic "culture."

Such polemics illustrate the German intellectual climate in the nineteenth century. The Germans as a whole, and despite Kant, followed Herder in openly rejecting the Enlightenment. They were romantic intellectuals who valued things of the heart, spirit, and soul rather than things of the cold intellect. They saw Germany as midway between the intellectualism of the countries west of the Rhine and the anti-intellectual, religious culture of Holy Mother Russia to the east. They rejected the atomism and utilitarianism of British philosophy and were anti-individualistic. In place of atomism, the German intellectuals constantly sought synthesis, to reconcile opposites into a higher truth. Wundt and the other elitist intellectuals of the German "Mandarin" tradition perceived, maintained, and strengthened an immense intellectual gulf between themselves and the West (Ringer, 1969). Wundt held himself to be the heir of Kant, Fichte, and Hegel, and he rejected the philosophies of Locke, the Mills, Spencer, and William James. He rejected association of static ideas, atomism, and reductionism in favor of psychological synthesis. His view sought no practical results, although it did not exclude them. Finally, it rejected the study of individual differences in favor of an almost Platonic investigation of *the* human mind.

Institutional Setting: The German Research Universities

Throughout the nineteenth century, German universities were unique both in quality and organization, especially with regard to science. In Britain and France, for different reasons, scientists worked outside the educational system, and British universities were moribund backwaters of no distinction. The United States had colleges devoted to undergraduate learning rather than universities offering graduate training. Higher education in the United States was largely a private, rather than government-supported enterprise as was the case in Europe. Most colleges were established by religious denominations to educate and build character among their members and to train their clergy. Faculty were generalists whose primary vocation was teaching; they were not specialists in research teaching in specialized fields. German universities, however, combined research and teaching functions and established the world's leading programs of graduate education. Moreover, the governments of the separate German principalities, and the Central Imperial German government after the unification of Germany in 1870, strongly supported German universities with money and resources.

This setting affected the establishment of psychology as a science. Germany was then at the forefront of the Industrial Revolution, and Richard Littman (1979, p. 51) argues that in its universities, "Germany had industrialized the process of acquiring and applying knowledge." Thus, Littman argues, Germany was uniquely open to the creation of new scientific disciplines promising more production of world-leading research. If the German system was well suited to give birth to psychology, however, it also possessed features that would slow its growth and shape its form (Ash, 1980, 1981). First of all, although German universities valued research, their primary function remained the *Bildung* of the Mandarin elite, and the bureaucrats who ran the education ministry never lost sight of that fact. After its establishment by Wundt as a research specialty, psychology had a hard time making a case that aspiring lawyers, doctors, and teachers—the Mandarin elite—needed physiological psychology to build their characters.

Related to this primary educational mission of the university was the concept of *Wissenschaft* that guided *Bildung*. Today *Wissenschaft* is translated as "science," suggesting natural experimental science. However, in the nineteenth century, *Wissenschaft* meant systematically organized knowledge along philosophical lines, and philosophy and other humanistic studies were the controlling models of organized thought. Natural science was gaining prestige, but experimentation was still to many intellectuals an untested, unreliable, unorganized way to procure truth. When Wundt was called to Leipzig, he was called as a philosopher, and he never sought autonomous status for psychology outside philosophy. From his arrival at Leipzig onward, Wundt regarded physiological psychology as a continuation of traditional philosophical psychology with new means and with new concepts taken over from physiology. Philosophers came to resent the intrusion of rude experiments into their hallowed field and did much to slow the growth of psychology in Germany.

WILHELM WUNDT'S PSYCHOLOGY OF CONSCIOUSNESS

Will to System

Today hardly anyone expects the theories and findings of various disciplines to have a systematic and logical relation to those of other disciplines; we do not expect, for example, that the work of a neurophysiologist should have any formal and logical bearing on the conclusions of a moral philosopher. Yet for the Mandarins of the nineteenth century, finding such connections, coordinating the ideas of different disciplines, and subsuming them all into a single comprehensive scheme of human life was the highest end for which a philosopher—James (1875) called them "heaven-scaling Titans"—might strive. We see just a hint of Wundt as a "heaven-scaling Titan" in the opening of the 1873 edition of *Principles of Physiological Psychology,* when he offered the hope that physiological psychology might "mediate a total comprehension of human existence."

As a good Mandarin, Wundt was thoroughly in the grasp of the "Will to System" (Woodward, 1982) and conceived of psychology as but one component in a grand scheme of human knowledge. Although the personalities of Wundt and Freud are in other respects as different as night and day, they shared a trait necessary to the founder of a general system of thought: They were both ambitious hedgehogs.[3] Freud, as we shall see, called himself a conquistador; William James observed that Wundt "aims at being a sort of Napoleon of the mind." Freud in large measure succeeded in conquering the world in the name of a few salient ideas. Wundt, however, seemed to have no central theme; James called him "a Napoleon without genius and with no central idea which, if defeated, brings down the whole fabric in ruins.... Cut him up like a worm and each fragment crawls; there is no *noeud vital* [vital node] in his medulla oblongata, so you can't kill him all at once" (quoted by van Hoorn & Verhave, 1980, p. 72).

Wundt offered to the world at least two different systems of psychology. He formulated the first at Heidelberg but came to repudiate it later as a "sin of my youthful days" (quoted by van Hoorn & Verhave, 1980, p. 78), as Freud later repudiated his early "Project for a Scientific Psychology." The second program was propounded shortly after Wundt's arrival in Leipzig, and it changed significantly over the years (Diamond, 1980; Graumann, 1980; Richards, 1980; van Hoorn & Verhave, 1980; but see Danziger, 1980a,b; Blumenthal 1980, 1986a).

What remained constant across the years was Wundt's definition of psychology as the study of consciousness and the search for distinct laws governing the mind, but Wundt's assumptions about the mind and the methods he used to investigate it changed dramatically. Wundt's youthful program was conceived at Heidelberg and, like Freud's, conceived of psychology as a natural science. Echoing John Stuart Mill's sentiments, Wundt wrote that the mind could be brought within the ambit of natural science by experimental method: "It has been the experiment only that has made progress in the natural sciences possible; let us then apply the experiment to the nature of the mind" (quoted by van Hoorn & Verhave, 1980, p. 86). In his early definition of psychology, Wundt did not identify the mind with consciousness, as he was to do later. Rather, the goal of experimentation was to gather data permitting inferences about unconscious processes: "The experiment in psychology is the major means which guides us from the facts of consciousness to those processes which in the dark background of our mind prepare conscious life" (quoted by Graumann, 1980, p. 37).

Wundt was called to Leipzig, however, as a philosopher, to lecture in philosophy, build a philosophical system, and conduct psychology as part of philosophy. In the Mandarin German university system, philosophy held sway, and Wundt had to find a new place for psychology in the Mandarin scheme of knowledge. In the spirit of Herder and Vico, German intellectuals typically distinguished between *Naturwissenschaft* and *Geisteswissenschaft*. *Naturwissenschaft* translates straightforwardly as "natural science," the study of the physical world and the search for the laws that govern it. *Geisteswissenschaft* is a more difficult concept. A literal translation is "spiritual (*Geist* means spirit) science," but what was meant was a study of the human world created by human history, and the search for laws governing human life, human development, and human history.

In the medieval Neoplatonic conception of the universe, human beings stood betwixt the material and spiritual worlds, half bodily animal and half divine soul. In the Mandarin conception, human beings occupied a similar position, betwixt the material world and the social world. In each case, the human body and the elementary

---

[3]Sir Isiah Berlin (1954) calls hedgehogs thinkers driven and guided by a single overarching idea. Foxes are thinkers who have no system of thought, but many unrelated and tentative ideas.

mental functions humans share with animals belong to the world of matter and natural science, while the higher reaches of the human mind—the soul for Christians, the higher mental processes for scientific psychology—belong to the world of *Geist* and the *Geisteswissenschaften*. Thus "psychology forms … the transition from the *Natur-* to the *Geisteswissenschaften*." The experimental methods of physiological psychology, which study those aspects of consciousness close to sensation and motor response, lead to an approach that "is related to the methodology of the physical sciences." On the other hand, above these elementary phenomena "rise the higher mental processes, which are the ruling forces in history as well as in society. Thus, they, on their side, require a scientific analysis, which approaches those of the special *Geisteswiss-enschaften*" (Wundt, quoted by van Hoorn & Verhave, 1980, p. 93).

Over the years, the Leipzig program also changed. Solomon Diamond has translated the introductory argument of Wundt's *Principles of Physiological Psychology* from its first edition in 1873 to its last edition in 1908–1911. As edition supplanted edition, Wundt's declared the alliance between physiology and psychology was weakened. In the earliest versions, psychology was linked, as we have seen, substantively as well as methodologically to physiology. The study of the nervous system was expected to shed light on the nature of human consciousness. However, by the fourth edition of 1893, only the methodological link remained, and *physiological psychology* had come to mean only *experimental psychology* (Wundt, 1873–1908). Like Freud and James, Wundt moved away from seeing psychology as a simple extension of physiology.

Methods

Wundt's conceptions of the methods to be used by psychology changed, too. However, in one central and fundamental respect, Wundt's conception of psychology's central method, introspection, did not change. Old-fashioned philosophical psychology had used armchair introspection to reveal the contents and workings of the mind, but it had fallen into bad odor among some scientists and philosophers as unreliable and subjective. Wundt agreed with these critiques of introspection, recognizing that a science of consciousness could only be erected on objective, replicable results based on standardized conditions capable of duplication and systematic variation (Wundt, 1907). It was precisely in order to achieve these aims that he introduced physiological techniques into the hitherto philosophical realm of psychology.

Wundt distinguished between two means of psychological observation whose German names are unfortunately rendered into English as "introspection," giving rise to passages in which Wundt both condemns introspection and commends it as the fundamental method of psychology (Blumenthal, 1980, 1986a). *Innere Wahrnehmung,* or "internal perception," referred to the prescientific method of armchair, subjective, introspection, as practiced, for example, by Descartes or Locke. This kind of introspection is carried out in a haphazard, uncontrolled way and cannot hope to yield results useful to a scientific psychology. On the other hand, *Experimentelle Selbstbeobachtung,* experimental self-observation, designates a scientifically valid form of introspection. In it, subjects are exposed to standard, repeatable situations and are asked to respond with simple, quantifiable responses. Conducting armchair introspection, philosophers contemplated the depths of their mental processes; in experimental introspection, experimental subjects do not reflect on their minds at all, but simply respond to stimuli.

The rationale and limits of experimental introspection changed as Wundt's systematic definition of psychology changed. In the Heidelberg years, when Wundt believed in unconscious psychological processes, traditional introspection was rejected because it was limited to observation of consciousness and could not, by definition, reveal the workings of the unconscious. Careful experimentation, Wundt held, might reveal phenomena from which the workings of unconscious mental processes might be deduced. During this period, Wundt assigned introspective method a wider scope of application than he would later. In his Heidelberg years, Wundt stated that it is mere "prejudice" to regard as "futile to attempt to penetrate into the realm of the higher mental processes by means of experimental methods" (quoted by van Hoorn & Verhave, 1980). Later, when Wundt rejected the existence of the unconscious, experimentation was valued as making it possible to recreate the same experience in different subjects or the same subjects at different times. This emphasis on exact duplication of experiences severely limited the realm of experimental introspection to the simplest mental processes, and Wundt duly excluded the study of the higher mental processes from physiological psychology, completely reversing his Heidelberg stance.

Alongside experimental introspection, Wundt recognized other methods of psychological investigation. The method of experimental introspection was by its nature limited to the study of normal, adult, human minds, that is, the minds of experimental subjects. In addition, then, to experimental introspection, Wundt recognized *vergleichend psychologische* (comparative-psychological) and *historisch-psychologische* (historical-psychological) methods (van Hoorn & Verhave, 1980). Both these methods involved the study of mental differences. The comparative method applied to the study of consciousness in animals, children, and the "disturbed." The historical method applied to "mental differences as determined by *race* and *nationality*" (quoted by van Hoorn & Verhave, 1980, p. 92). The relations between the study of normal adult, animal, disturbed, and historically conditioned consciousness shifted over the years (van Hoorn & Verhave, 1980), but the most general change was in the importance Wundt assigned to the historical method, or *Völkerpsychologie*.

Wundt always believed, as would Freud, in the biogenetic law, that the development of the individual recapitulated the evolution of the species. In keeping with this notion, Wundt held that the best way to construct a theory of psychological development in individuals was to study the historical development of the human race. In his earliest program of psychology, the historical method was put forward as an adjunct to the main method of psychology, experimental introspection. However, when Wundt repositioned psychology as the crucial discipline lying between *Naturwissenschaft* and *Geisteswissenschaft,* the historical method was elevated to parity with the experimental method. The experimental method faced toward *Naturwissenschaft,* applying to the more strictly physiological aspects of the mind, while the historical method faced toward *Geisteswissenschaft,* applying to the inner processes of mental creativity revealed in history, especially language, myth, and custom. Thus, when Wundt withdrew experimental introspection from the study of the higher mental processes, he replaced it with the historical method of *Völkerpsychologie*.

Theory and Research

In order to illustrate the nature of Wundt's psychology, we shall consider two topics taken up in the two branches of his psychology of consciousness. The first applies the experimental method of physiological psychology to an old question in philosophical psychology, how many ideas can consciousness contain at a given moment? The second applies the method of the *Völkerpsychologie* to the question of how human beings create and understand sentences.

PHYSIOLOGICAL PSYCHOLOGY

For Wundt, psychology was the scientific study of immediate experience—and thus the study of human consciousness or the mind, as long as mind is understood as the totality of conscious experience at a given moment and not as a mental substance. The natural sciences are also based on experience, but of a kind Wundt called *mediate* experience, because the experience is regarded as dependent on external objects and all subjective elements are removed. Psychology studies all experience—including subjective elements such as feelings—directly as it is given in consciousness, and as dependent on the psychological state of the observer.

To the question, "How many ideas can the mind hold at once?" traditional philosophical introspection could provide no reliable answers, Wundt held. Without experimental control, attempting to introspect the number of ideas in one's mind is futile, since their content varies from time to time, and we must rely on fallible memories to give us the facts that introspection reports.

Therefore an experiment was called for, one that would complement and perfect introspection and yield quantitative results. The following is an updated and simplified version of Wundt's experiment. Imagine sitting in a darkened room facing a projection screen. For an instant, about 0.09 sec, a stimulus is flashed on the screen. This stimulus is a four-column by four-row array of randomly chosen letters, and your task is to recall as many letters as possible. What is recalled provides a measure of how many simple ideas can be grasped in an instant of time and so may give an answer to the original question. Wundt found that unpracticed subjects could recall about four letters; subjects who have practiced could recall up to six but no more. These figures agree remarkably well with modern results on the capacity of short-term memory.

Two further important phenomena can be observed in this experiment. First, imagine an experiment in which each line of four letters forms a word, for example, *work, many, room, idea.* Under these conditions one could probably recall all four words, or at least three, for a total of twelve to sixteen letters. Similarly, one could quickly read and recall the word "miscellaneousness," which contains seventeen letters. Letters as isolated elements quickly fill up consciousness so that only four to six can be perceived in a given moment, but if these elements are organized, many more can be grasped. In Wundt's term, the letter-elements are *synthesized* into a greater whole, which is understood as a single complex idea and grasped as one new element.

This phenomenon shows in what sense Wundt was an atomist and in what sense he was not. The word *work* is in fact made up of four simpler elementary idea-processes, *w, o, r,* and *k,* but it cannot be reduced to these elements. The word is a *synthesis* of the elements and the whole word functions as an element. Complex ideas derive from elements; they are not compounded out of them or reducible to them. Wundt rejected the atomism of the British associationists, including the mental chemistry of J. S. Mill.

A second phenomenon can be observed in this memory experiment. The subject in the original experiment very easily notices that some letters—the ones the subject names—are perceived clearly and distinctly, but that other letters are only dimly and hazily perceived. Consciousness seems to be a large field populated with ideational elements. One area of this field is in the focus of *attention,* and the ideas within it are clearly perceived. The elements lying outside the focal area are only faintly felt as present and cannot be identified.

Attention, like synthesis, played a key role in Wundt's theory. In fact, attention was the process that could actively synthesize elements into larger units. Wundt's ideas on attention were derived from Leibniz, and Wundt used Leibniz's terms. An idea that enters the large field of consciousness was said to be *apprehended,* and one that enters the focal area of attention was said to be *apperceived.*

Apperception was especially important in Wundt's system. Not only was it responsible for the active synthesis of elements into wholes, but it also accounted for the higher mental activities of analysis (revealing the parts of a whole) and of judgment. It was responsible for the activities of relating and comparing, which are simpler forms of synthesis and analysis. Synthesis itself took two forms: imagination and understanding. Apperception was the basis for all higher forms of thought, such as reasoning and use of language, and was central to Wundt's psychology in both its individual and social divisions.

Finally, Wundt's emphasis on apperception displays the *voluntaristic* nature of his system. Since neither *mind* nor *self* referred to a special substance for Wundt, to what did he attribute our sense of self and the feeling that we have a mind? It is this *feeling* that provides the answer. Apperception is a voluntary act of the will by which we control and give synthetic unity to our mind. It is the feeling of activity, control, and unity that defined the self. Wundt wrote (1896, p. 234): "What we call our 'self' is simply the unity of volition plus the universal control of our mental life which it renders possible."

Wundt did not neglect feelings and emotions, for they are an obvious part of our conscious experience. He often used introspectively reported feelings as clues to what processes were going on in the mind at a given moment. Apperception, for instance, he thought to be marked by a feeling of mental effort. He also studied feelings and emotions in their own right, and his tridimensional theory of feeling became a source of controversy, especially with Titchener. Wundt proposed that feelings could be defined along three dimensions: pleasant vs. unpleasant, high vs. low arousal, and concentrated vs. relaxed attention. He conducted a long series of studies designed to establish a physiological basis for each dimension, but the results were inconclusive, and other laboratories produced conflicting findings. Recent factor-analyses of affect, however, have arrived at similar three-dimensional systems (Blumenthal, 1975). While Wundt emphasized the active, synthesizing power of apperception, he recognized the existence of passive processes as well, which he classified as various forms of association or "passive" apperception. There were, for example, *assimilations,* in which a current sensation is associated to an older element. When one looks at a chair, one knows immediately what it is by assimilation, for the current image of the perceived chair is immediately associated with the older universal element *chair*. Recognition is a form of assimilation, stretched out into two steps—a vague feeling of familiarity followed by the act of recognition proper. Recollection, on the other hand, was for Wundt, as for some contemporary psychologists, an act of reconstruction rather than reactivation of old elements. One cannot reexperience an earlier event, for ideas are not permanent. Rather one reconstructs it from current cues and certain general rules.

Finally, Wundt did not fail to notice abnormal states of consciousness. He discussed hallucinations, depressions, hypnosis, and dreams. Of particular interest was his discussion of what we now call *schizophrenia*. He observed that this disease involves a breakdown in attentional processes. The schizophrenic loses the apperceptive control of thoughts characteristic of normal consciousness and surrenders instead to passive associative processes, so that thought becomes a simple train of associations rather than coordinated processes directed by volition. This theory was developed by Wundt's student and friend, the great psychiatrist Emil Kraepelin, and it has been revived by modern students of schizophrenia and autism.

VÖLKERPSYCHOLOGIE

Wundt believed that experimental individual psychology could not be a complete psychology. The minds of living individuals are the products of a long course of species development of which each person is ignorant. Therefore, to understand the development of the mind, we must have recourse to history. The study of animals and children is limited by their inability to introspect. History expands the range of the individual consciousness. In particular, the range of existing human cultures represents the various stages in cultural and mental evolution, from primitive tribes to civilized nation-states. *Völkerpsychologie* is thus the study of the products of collective life—especially of language, myth, and custom—that provide clues to the higher operations of mind. Wundt said that experimental psychology penetrates only the "outworks" of the mind; *Völkerpsychologie* reaches deeper.

Emphasis on historical development, a legacy from Vico and Herder, was typical of German intellectuals in the nineteenth century. In the German view, every individual springs from, and has an organic relationship with, his or her natal culture. Further, cultures have complex histories which determine their forms and contents. Thus it was generally believed that history could be used as a method for arriving at an intuitive understanding of human psychology.

Wundt's remarks on myth and custom were typical of his time. He saw history as going through a series of stages from primitive tribes to an age of heroes and then to the formation of states, culminating in a world state based on the concept of humanity as a whole. It was, however, in the study of language (which early in his career Wundt almost pursued instead of psychology) that he made his most substantial contribution, articulating a theory of psycholinguistics that reaches conclusions being rediscovered today. Language was a part of *Völkerpsychologie* for Wundt because, like myth and custom, it is a product of collective life.

Wundt divided language into two aspects: *outer phenomena,* consisting of actually produced or perceived utterances, and *inner phenomena,* the cognitive processes that underlie the outer string of words. This division of psychological phenomena into inner and outer aspects is central to Wundt's psychology and has come up before in the contrast between the "outworks" of the mind that can be reached by experimentation and the deeper processes that cannot. The distinction between inner and outer phenomena is easiest to understand with regard to language. It is possible to describe language as an organized, associated system of sounds that we speak or hear; this constitutes the outer form of language. However, this outer form is the surface expression of deeper cognitive processes that organize a speaker's thoughts and prepare them for utterance and enable the listener to extract meaning from what she or he hears. These cognitive processes constitute the inner mental form of speech.

Sentence production, according to Wundt, begins with a unified idea that one wishes to express, the *Gesamtvorstellung,* or whole mental configuration.[4] The analytic function of apperception prepares the unified idea for speech, for it must be analyzed into component parts and a structure that retains the relationship between the parts and the whole. Consider the simple sentence, "The cat is orange." The basic structural division in such a sentence is between the subject and predicate and can be represented with the *tree-diagram* introduced by Wundt. If we let G = *Gesamtvorstellung,* S = subject, and P = predicate, then we have

The idea of an orange cat has now been divided into its two fundamental ideas and can be expressed verbally as "the cat is orange" with the addition of the function words (*the, is*) required in our particular language. More complex ideas require more analysis and must be represented by more complex diagrams. The entire process in all cases can be described as the transformation of an inexpressible organized whole thought into an expressible sequential structure of words organized in a sentence.

The process is reversed in comprehension of speech. Here the synthesizing rather than the analytic function of apperception is called on. The words and grammatical structure in a heard sentence must be used by the hearer to reconstruct in his or her own mind the whole mental configuration that the speaker is attempting to communicate. Wundt supported his view of comprehension by pointing out that we remember the gist of what we hear, but only rarely the surface (outer) form, which tends to disappear in the process of constructing the *Gesamtvorstellung.*

We have touched on only a small portion of Wundt's discussion of language. He also wrote on gesture-language; the origin of language from involuntary, expressive sounds; primitive language (based more on association than on apperception); phonology; and meaning-change. Wundt has a fair claim to be the founder of psycholinguistics as well as psychology.

---

[4]*Gesamtvorstellung* was misleadingly translated by Titchener, Wundt's leading translator, as "aggregate idea," but Blumenthal (1970) has shown Titchener's error and proposed the phrase used here: "whole mental configuration." The mistranslation reveals Titchener's misperception of Wundt's psychology.

AFTER LEIPZIG: NEW METHODS, NEW MOVEMENTS

The Next Generation

Wundt established psychology as a discipline, but he could not and did not retain a monopoly on it, as new psychologists founded new laboratories and new movements in Germany and around the world. Indeed, Wundt had surprisingly little effect on the next generation of psychologists. The younger German generation established new journals and the Society for Experimental Psychology, but Wundt was conspicuous by his absence and lack of participation (Ash, 1981). At the founding of the society in 1904, Wundt was honored in a telegram, but he was called the "Nestor of experimental psychology" (Ash, 1981 p. 266). In the *Iliad,* Nestor was an allegedly wise but pompous old windbag whose advice was usually ignored.

Foremost among the Wundtian strictures ignored by the new generation of psychologists was Wundt's limitation on the introspective method. The generation after Wundt was much influenced by positivism (Danziger, 1979) and believed that if psychology was going to be a science erected on positive facts, the higher mental processes would have to be observed directly. So, Wundt's simple and rigorously controlled method of introspection was replaced by "systematic introspection," a looser, more retrospective, probing of consciousness that in some respects resembled psychoanalysis more than experimental psychology. In both, mental events were analyzed in detail after the fact by subjects responding to questions posed by another person. The accuracy of the introspective reports of both thus suffered from the limitations of memory and the human tendency to invent memories upon suggestion.

At the same time, theories in psychology moved away from Wundt. Structural psychology recast the psychology of consciousness in terms defined by British associationism. Gestalt psychology redefined the study of experience, rejecting the analysis of experience into theoretically defined atoms of experience, replacing it with the study of meaningful objects given directly in consciousness. Act psychology proposed a system of mind built around mental acts rather than the contents of experience.

Systematic Introspection: The Würzburg School (1901–1909)

One of Wundt's most outstanding and successful students was Oswald Külpe (1862–1915). Although his early psychology was even more conservative than Wundt's, during his brief professorial tenure at the University of Würzburg, he helped develop a new approach to psychological experiment, one which claimed that thinking could be studied experimentally. Two important sets of results emerged from this research. The first indicated, contrary to Wundt, that some thoughts are imageless, while the second undermined associationism as an account of thinking.

As early as 1879, Hermann Ebbinghaus undertook to study the higher mental process of memory, his results appearing in 1885. Shortly after leaving Wundt, Külpe seems to have decided that the highest mental process of all, thinking, could be experimentally studied and could be introspected—if only Wundt's methods were changed. Wundt's experiments were quite simple, involving little more than reaction to, or a brief description of, a stimulus. Fechner's psychophysics, Donders's mental chronometry, and Wundt's apperception experiments are examples of this procedure. Under Külpe (who never published an experiment from his Würzburg days but participated in others' experiments), the tasks were made more difficult and the job of introspection more elaborate.

During the years of the Würzburg school, the complexity of the experimental tasks increased from giving free associations to single stimulus words to agreeing or disagreeing with difficult metaphysical theses or Nietzsche's aphorisms. These tasks, whether simple or difficult, required thinking, whereas Wundtian tasks did not. Subjects had to respond to the problem and then describe the thought-processes leading to the response. As the method developed, the subject would be asked to concentrate introspective attention on different parts of the subjective experience— that is, the subjects would focus on their mental state while awaiting the stimulus word, or on the appearance of the answer in consciousness. In these experiments, the Würzburgers hoped to directly observe thinking as it happened.

The first results were a shock to almost all psychologists: Thoughts can be imageless. This finding emerged in the first Würzburg paper by A. M. Mayer and J. Orth, published in 1901. In this experiment, the subject was instructed to respond with the first word that came to mind after hearing a stimulus word. The experimenter gave a ready signal, called out the stimulus word, and started a stopwatch; the subject gave a response and the experimenter stopped the watch. The subject then described the thinking process. Mayer and Orth reported that most thinking involved definite images or feelings associated with acts of will. However, wrote Mayer and Orth (1901), "apart from these two classes of conscious processes, we must introduce a third group … The subjects very frequently reported that they experienced certain conscious processes which they could describe neither as definite images nor as acts of will." For example, while serving as a subject, Mayer "made the observation that following the stimulus word 'meter' there occurred a peculiar conscious process, not further definable, which was followed by the spoken word 'trochee.'" So Wundt was wrong, according to Mayer and Orth; nonimaginal events in consciousness had been found.

The Würzburgers refined their methods over the years, but the results remained: There are imageless thoughts. Moreover, the finding was made independently in Paris by Alfred Binet in his studies of children's thinking, and in New York by Robert Woodworth. Both studies were reported in 1903, but the investigators did not know the Würzburg work. In fact, Binet later claimed that the new method should be called the "method of Paris." In any event, the finding of imageless thought was a challenge to psychological orthodoxy and provoked a controversy that aided and abetted the birth of behaviorism.

What was to be made of imageless thought? The Würzburgers own interpretation changed during the life of the school. Mayer and Orth did no more than discover imageless thoughts—vague, impalpable, almost indescribable "conscious states." Later on they were identified simply as "thoughts" themselves. The final interpretation was that thought is actually an unconscious process, reducing the imageless thought elements to conscious indicators of thinking rather than thinking itself. However, on both sides of the Atlantic many psychologists found the Würzburg methods, results, and interpretations to be unacceptable or at least suspect.

Writing in 1907, Wundt tried to falsify the Würzburg results by attacking the method. He argued that the Würzburg experiments were sham experiments, merely reversions to unreliable armchair introspection that happened to be conducted in a laboratory. According to Wundt, experimental control was entirely lacking in the thought experiments. The subject did not know exactly what task would be set. The ensuing mental process would vary from subject to subject and from trial to trial, so the results could not be replicated. Finally, said Wundt, it is difficult if not impossible for a subject to both think about the set problem and watch that process at the same time. Consequently, Wundt said, the so-called findings of imageless thought are invalid. Properly conducted experiments would show that, properly analyzed, "imageless" content was imaginal after all.

Titchener undertook the experimental refutation of the Würzburg findings. Methodologically, Titchener echoed Wundt by claiming that subjects' reports of "imageless" thought were not descriptions of consciousness at all, but fabrications based on beliefs about how one would solve the problems set in the experiments. Experimentally, Titchener's students performed thought experiments and reported that they could find no evidence of imageless thought elements; they successfully traced all conscious content to sensations or feelings (Clark, 1911). Titchener concluded that the Würzburgers had failed as introspectors by declining to analyze a mental content and then calling it "imageless thought."

Other commentators offered alternative interpretations of the Würzburg results. It was suggested by some that certain types of minds possess imageless thought while others do not, reducing the Titchener-Külpe controversy to one of individual differences. This hypothesis was criticized as unparsimonious; why should nature create two types of mind to attain the same end—accurate thinking? The hypothesis of unconscious thinking was rejected on the grounds that what is not conscious is not mental but physiological, and therefore not a part of psychology. A similar criticism greeted Freud's hypothesis of the unconscious.

Perhaps the most important consequence of the debate about imageless thought was the suspicion that introspection was a fragile and unreliable tool, easily prejudiced by theoretical expectations. The Würzburg subjects believed in imageless thought, and they found it. Titchener's subjects believed only in sensations and feelings, and they found only those. R. M. Ogden, an American supporter of imageless thought, wrote that if Wundt's and Titchener's criticisms of the Würzburg methods were valid, "may we not carry the point a step farther and deny the value of *all* introspection. Indeed, in a recent discussion among psychologists, this position was vigorously maintained by two among those present" (1911a). Ogden himself suggested that the differential results from Titchener's laboratory in Cornell and Külpe's in Würzburg betray "unconscious bias" based on different training (Ogden, 1911b, p. 193). The imageless thought controversy revealed difficulties with the introspective method and by 1911, the year of Ogden's papers, we find some psychologists ready to discard it altogether. Two years later Watson, the founder of behaviorism, included this controversy in his indictment of mentalism.

The imageless thought results represented a budding anomaly for certain forms of mentalism. Woodworth wrote as late as 1938 that "the whole question may well be shelved as permanently debatable and insoluble" (p. 788). This is one fate of anomalies, according to Kuhn. The debate over imageless thought showed signs of developing into a Kuhnian paradigm clash. In 1911, J. R. Angell wrote: "One feels that the differences which divide certain of the writers are largely those of mutual misunderstanding as to the precise phenomenon under discussion" (p. 306). Angell was disturbed that the combatants in the dispute had been "largely reduced to mere assertion and denial ..." "It is!" or "It isn't!" (p. 305). However, the anomaly and paradigm clash were incipient only; their development was cut short by the advent of behaviorism. Woodworth found the problem being shelved in 1938 not because the problem had been exhausted, but because no one cared anymore. By the second (1954) edition of Woodworth's *Experimental Psychology,* this controversy which had occupied many pages in the 1938 edition had shriveled to four paragraphs.

The Würzburgers' second shock for the psychological establishment arose when they studied the process of thinking. Their results led them to reject traditional associationism as an adequate account of mind. Their problem was this: What makes one idea rather than another follow a given idea? For free association, as in Mayer and Orth's experiment, associationism has a plausible answer. If the stimulus word is "bird" the subject may respond "canary," then the associationist can say simply that the bird-canary bond was the strongest in the subject's associative network. However, this situation is complicated if we use a method of constrained association, as Henry J. Watt did in 1905. In this method, we set a specific task for the subject to carry out, such as "give a subordinate category" or "give a superordinate category." To the former task the subject may still reply "canary." To the second task the correct response cannot be "canary" but instead should be "animal." However, these tasks are no longer free associations, but rather acts of directed thinking that produce propositions that may be true or false—unlike free association. So the simple associative bond, bird-canary, is overridden in directed thinking.

The Würzburgers argued that associationism fails to explain thinking, for something must direct thought along the proper lines in the associative network in order for a subject to respond correctly to such tasks as Watt's. The Würzburgers proposed that it was the task itself that directed thinking. In their later terminology, they said that the task establishes a mental set—or determining tendency—in the mind that properly directs the subject's use of his or her associative network. It was these experiments that suggested unconscious thinking, for subjects found that given the task "Give superordinate to canary," the response "bird" popped into their heads with little experienced mental activity. The Würzburgers concluded that the mental set accomplishes thinking even before the problem is given; the subject is so prepared to give a superordinate that the actual response occurs automatically.

Their investigations of the process of thinking took the Würzburg psychologists toward a psychology of function instead of content. They found that laboratory work could reveal something about how the mind functions in addition to what it contains. We will find that American psychology was predominantly functional, and the reception of the idea of the mental set was much more favorable in America than the reception given imageless thought. While the discussion of imageless thought in Woodworth's authoritative *Experimental Psychology* shrank between 1938 and 1954, index references to *set* increased from nineteen to thirty-five, with more extended discussions. The concept of *set* made sense to American functional psychologists interested in mental operations, and the behaviorists found that they could reinterpret *set* as establishing determining tendencies in behavior instead of in mind.

Although Würzburg-inspired work continued after 1909 (especially by Otto Selz, who had worked there), the school essentially dissolved when Külpe left for the

University of Bonn. No systematic theory based on the Würzburg studies was ever published, although there is evidence Külpe was working on such a theory when he died. It is puzzling that from 1909 until his death Külpe said almost nothing about the dramatic Würzburg results. Therefore no alternative psychology arose from the Würzburg school. Their methods were innovative, their findings stimulating and anomalous, and in the concept of the mental set they made a permanent contribution. But the Würzburg school remained a school, a research program cut off prematurely.

Structural Psychology

Edward Bradford Titchener (1867–1927) was an Englishman who brought German psychology to America. He thus played an important role in the founding of American psychology, for he was the foe of both functionalism and behaviorism, while on the European front he was the enemy of act psychology and of imageless thought. In this section, we will examine his system, structuralism, especially in its relation to Wundt's psychology, with which it is often confused.

Titchener has usually been taken by historians to be a faithful reflection of Wundt, the two systems being seen as identical. A recent history of psychology says this: "Titchener's system was so close to Wundt's and so much easier to describe, that we shall not here dwell on" Wundt (Keller, 1973, p. 19). This attitude naturally led American psychologists who rejected Titchener's system to reject Wundt's at the same time. We shall see to what degree this identification and simultaneous rejection was justified.

TITCHENER'S BACKGROUND

E. B. Titchener was born in 1867 at Chichester, England. His ancestors included a mayor of Chichester, a school headmaster, and a distinguished lawyer. He attended a prestigious secondary school and went to Oxford from 1885 to 1890. His educational record was outstanding. During his Oxford years, his interests shifted from classics and philosophy to physiology. The conjunction of interests in philosophy and physiology naturally predisposed Titchener to psychology, and while at Oxford he translated the third edition of Wundt's massive *Principles of Physiological Psychology*. Titchener could find no one in England to train him in psychology, so in 1890 he went to Leipzig, taking his doctorate in 1892. Titchener was impressed by Wundt, but they were never close.

As an Englishman, Titchener arrived in Leipzig from the other side of the intellectual gulf separating Germany from the West. He was thoroughly versed in philosophy and was much impressed by English philosopher James Mill, remarking that Mill's association psychology could be empirically demonstrated. In his first systematic book, *An Outline of Psychology* (1897), he wrote: "The general standpoint of [my] book is that of the traditional English psychology." It is reasonable to expect, therefore, that Titchener may well have assimilated Wundt's German psychology into the "traditional English psychology" that Wundt rejected. Titchener's personality was reputedly "German," but his psychology is more a mixture of German and English.

After a short stint as a lecturer in biology in England—a country long unreceptive to psychology—Titchener left for America to teach at Cornell. He remained at

Cornell until his death in 1927. He transformed Cornell into a bastion of mentalistic psychology, even as America's focus went first functionalist and, after 1913, behaviorist. Titchener never compromised with these movements, despite his friendships with the functionalist J. R. Angell and with Watson, the founder of behaviorism. He published almost exclusively in the *American Journal of Psychology,* which he edited, shunning rival journals like *Psychological Review* and *Journal of Experimental Psychology.* He did not participate actively in the American Psychological Association, even when it met at Cornell, preferring instead his own group, the Experimental Psychologists, which he kept true to his version of psychology. It was clear that structuralism depended upon one man, Titchener, and when he unexpectedly died in 1927, the school collapsed.

TITCHENER'S PSYCHOLOGY

Titchener apparently possessed a mind in which everything had imaginal-sensational character. His mind even had an image for such an abstract word as *meaning.* Titchener (1904, p. 19) wrote: "I see meaning as the blue-grey tip of a kind of scoop, which has a bit of yellow above it ... and which is just digging into a dank mass of ... plastic material." Even though he recognized that not everyone had an imaginal mind, as he called it, he built his psychology on the premise that the mind was made up of sensations or images of sensation and *nothing else.* This led to his rejection of various Wundtian concepts such as apperception, which is not directly observed. Titchener's system was thus explicitly sensationistic as opposed to Wundt's, which was voluntaristic.

The first task of Titchener's sensationistic psychology was the discovery of the basic sensation-elements to which all complex processes could be reduced. As early as 1897, he drew up a catalogue of elements found in the different sense-departments. There were, for instance, 30,500 visual elements, four taste elements, and three sensations in the alimentary canal.

Elements were defined by Titchener as the simplest sensations to be found in experience. They were to be discovered through the systematic dissection by introspection of the contents of consciousness; when an experience could not be dissected into parts, it was declared *elemental.* Titchener's method of introspection was much more elaborate than Wundt's, for it was not a simple report of an experience, but a complicated retrospective analysis of that experience. Wrote Titchener (1909): "Be as attentive as possible to the object or process which gives rise to the sensation, and, when the object is removed or the process completed, recall the sensation by an act of memory as vividly and completely as you can." Persistent application of this method would in Titchener's view eventually produce a complete description of the elements of human experience. It was an unfinished (and, as many thought, unfinishable) task when Titchener died.

The second task of Titchener's sensationistic approach was to determine how the elementary sensations are connected together to form complex perceptions, ideas, and images. These connections were not all associations, because for Titchener an association was a connection of elements that persisted even when the original conditions for the connection could no longer be obtained. Titchener rejected the label of associationism, not only for this reason, but also because the associationists spoke of association of meaningful ideas, not of simple meaningless sensations, which was all that concerned Titchener.

The third task of Titchener's psychology was to explain the workings of mind. Introspection, according to Titchener, could yield only a description of mind. At least until about 1925, he believed that a scientific psychology required more than mere description. Explanation for Titchener was to be sought in physiology, which would explain why the sensory elements arise and become connected. Titchener rejected Wundt's attempt to psychologically explain the operation of the mind. According to Titchener's system, all that can be found in experience are sensory elements rather than processes such as attention. Appeal to such an unobservable entity as apperception was illegitimate in Titchener's eyes, which betrays his positivism. He therefore sought to explain mind by reference to observable nerve-physiology.

How did Titchener treat a mental process such as attention that was so central to Wundt's psychology? He rejected as wholly unnecessary the term *apperception,* which in Wundt's psychology gave rise to attention. Attention itself Titchener reduced to sensation. One obvious attribute of any sensation is clarity, and Titchener said that "attended" sensations are simply the clearest ones. Attention was not for him a mental process, but simply an attribute of sensation—clearness—produced by certain nerve-processes. What of the mental effort that Wundt says goes along with attention? This, too, Titchener reduced to sensations. Wrote Titchener in *Experimental Psychology: A Manual of Laboratory Practice* (1897, p. 4): "When I am trying to attend I ... find myself frowning, wrinkling my forehead etc. All such ... bodily sets and movements give rise to characteristic ... sensations. Why should not these sensations be what we call 'attention.'"

Was Titchener a more comprehensible, English-speaking double for Wundt, as is so often assumed? We must conclude not: Titchener is "so much easier" than Wundt because Titchener discarded so much of his teacher's theory. He took the complex voluntaristic psychology of Wundt and filtered it through his own positivism and atomism to produce a reductive sensationism for which mind consists of nothing but complexes of elements found in experience. He proposed nothing similar to Wundt's *Völkerpsychologie.* Wundt's psychology has resonances with modern cognitive psychology; Titchener's structuralism has none. However, as we will see, it does have resonances with the most extreme form of behaviorism—B. F. Skinner's descriptive behaviorism.

A word should be said about the direction Titchener's thought was taking at his death. His last work was *Systematic Psychology: Prologemena,* which appeared posthumously in 1929. In this book, he was becoming even more positivistic than before. He abandoned explanation as a goal of science in favor of pure description. He abandoned the notion of analytically discovered sensory elements in favor of phenomenologically described dimensions of sensory attributes. He departed even further from Wundt's attempt to penetrate the hidden mental processes underneath the outer, sensory phenomena.

Gestalt Psychology

Atomism is a useful dimension on which to classify psychologists. The most atomistic psychology was James Mill's association psychology, in which consciousness is depicted as a tinkertoy-like assemblage of sensations connected by associative links; Titchener's catalogue of sensory atoms is not much different. Moving toward holism, we find John Stuart Mill's mental chemistry and Wundt's theory of apperceptive synthesis. Both recognized the emergence of new properties as mental elements combine, but both still believed psychology should analyze complexes into elements, just as chemists do. More holistic still was Thomas Reid, who maintained that complex ideas are not built up out of elements by any process, but are immediately given in experience as meaningful wholes. Introspection can break them down into elements, but this is artificial and does not imply that the mind starts with atoms and forms wholes; according to Reid, the wholes are there from the beginning.

The Gestalt psychologists went even further, arguing that decomposing wholes into parts is not only artificial, but pointless and scientifically sterile, revealing nothing about the mind whatsoever. The philosophical root of their protest was *phenomenology,* whose proponents argued that experience should be simply described as given, never analyzed. Presented with a triangle, a good Titchenerian introspector would report, "I see three lines"; the report would contain only meaningless sensory atoms. The phenomenologist would say, "I see a triangle," reporting a meaningful mental whole transcending the atomic elements.

Some elementalists were moving in this direction. Christian Ehrenfels (1859–1932) discussed "Gestalt qualities" in 1890. Ehrenfels wanted to know how certain experiences maintain their character despite sensory changes. This is most apparent in hearing tunes. Despite transposition of keys, and thus its sensory elements, we always hear the same tune as the same. Ehrenfels was dealing with the problem of organized perceptions, not elements, and arguing for a new mental element. A tune is made up of sensory elements—its specific notes—but it possesses in addition a Gestalt (or form) quality that represents the organization. Similarly, a triangle is made up of three sensory elements, the lines, plus a form-quality element of triangularity. Ehrenfel's former teacher, the philosopher Alexius Meinong (1853–1920), tried to specify the source of the form-quality. Sensory elements are given by experience, and then the mind in a mental act adds the structuring form-quality. This theory of an additional mental act derived from the act psychology of Franz Brentano, whom we shall consider next. Both Ehrenfels's and Meinong's theories remained elementalistic, merely adding a mental element of organization to the accepted list of sensory elements.

Both atomistic elementalism and the act interpretation of form-qualities were rejected by the phenomenologically oriented Gestalt psychologists, as is shown by the following Gestalt experiment. A subject is seated in a darkened room and two spots of light are flashed off and on alternately. When the interval between flashes is more than 0.2 sec, the subject sees two flashing lights; but when the interval is less than 0.2 sec, the subject sees one light in continuous motion. The subject perceives apparent motion where in fact there is none. This phenomenon underlies our experience of movies, which are actually a rapidly displayed series of still photographs. Such experiments indicated that more than a mental element was needed. Such apparent motion undermines the atomistic account of consciousness, for sensational "atoms" given on the retina are not perceived, but instead give rise to a qualitatively different experience. Apparent motion is an experience that emerges from simple sensations but cannot plausibly be reduced to them. It is, in short, a perceptual whole (*Gestalt,* in German), given immediately to consciousness and deserving direct study. The Gestalt psychologists advocated a holistic psychology based on the mind's perception of complete forms.

This experimental demonstration (called the *phi phenomenon*), which shows that conscious experience is not usefully reducible to bundles of discrete sensations, was the starting point of the Gestalt movement. Its inspiration, however, had deeper and more general sources. We have already seen how German culture rejected the tide of associationism, atomism, and mechanism that flowed from traditional British and French philosophies. Wundt's psychology was a partial reaction to this tide, but the young men of the next generation reacted even more strongly. Even more than Wundt they looked for wholeness and transcendence as a way out of the post–World War I crisis of German culture. They fought against all philosophies or sciences that saw creatures or cultures as machines, as no more than collections of simpler parts.

The leader of this movement in psychology was Max Wertheimer (1880–1943), who carried out the phi phenomena research in 1912 using the other two great Gestalt psychologists, Wolfgang Köhler (1887–1967) and Kurt Koffka (1887–1941), as the main subjects. Wertheimer was by nature a prophet for whom the idea of the Gestalt was "not only a theory of perception or of thinking, or a theory of psychology, or even an entire philosophy; it was, rather, a *Weltanschauung*—indeed, an all-encompassing religion. The core of this religion is the hope that the world is a sensible coherent whole, that reality is organized into meaningful parts, that natural units have their own structure" (Wertheimer, 1978).

The phi phenomenon demonstrated a faith that Wertheimer held before 1912. Despite being a Jew, he received an education "typical of the elite of his day" including studies with Ehrenfels at Prague and Külpe at Würzburg (Wertheimer, 1978). In all his studies, he was immersed in the reaction against traditional atomism and traditional psychology, but Wertheimer moved in a more holistic direction than either of his teachers. His Gestalt ideas appeared first in a 1910 paper on the primitive music of a Ceylonese tribe, in which he concluded that their compositions were organized by "*Gestalten* that are rhythmically and melodically strict" (Wertheimer, 1978).

Central to the Gestalt movement was the "Gestalt vision," Wertheimer's holistic *Weltanschauung*. In 1924, Wertheimer declared that "Gestalt theory is neither more nor less" than the belief that "there are wholes, the behavior of which is not determined by that of their individual elements, but where the part processes are themselves determined by the intrinsic nature of the whole. It is the hope of Gestalt theory to determine the nature of such wholes." So Wundt's halfway holism in which wholes are constructed by the mind was unacceptable. Wertheimer condemned traditional—Wundtian—psychology for containing what he called an abundance of "things arid, poor and inessential" and for having "alien, wooden, monstrous" implications (1925). He argued that traditional psychology rested on two erroneous assumptions. The first is *the mosaic or bundle hypothesis,* which is Wertheimer's term for sensationism. The second is *the association hypothesis,* by which Wertheimer means the tinker-toy theory. Nor could Wertheimer accept Wundt's idea that the mind's power of apperception unites elements into greater wholes, for this still concedes the fundamental status of sensational elements. Wrote Wertheimer (1922): "Gestalten" are not "the sums of aggregated contents erected subjectively upon primarily given pieces.... Instead, we are dealing with wholes and whole-processes possessed of inner intrinsic laws.

'Elements' are determined as parts by the intrinsic conditions of their wholes and are to be understood 'as parts' relative to such wholes." This is the central formula of Gestalt psychology.

Two important new concepts were used by the Gestalt psychologists to put their formula into practice. The first is the concept of the psychological field, consciously borrowed from field theory in physics. Gestaltists deny that experience is like a mosaic, a collection of inert, noninteracting, discrete units, or sensations. Instead, they see experience as a field of dynamically interacting parts. In the phi phenomenon, the "parts" of the field, the two flashing lights, interact to give rise to the perception of motion. Thus a visual illusion such as the Müller-Lyer is produced by interactions among the visual elements. The central lines are the same size, but because of the context in which they are viewed (the arrowheads), they seem to be different lengths.

The Gestalt psychologists extended the field concept to refer not only to the phenomenal field of immediate experience involved in the phi phenomenon or illusions, but also to the behavioral field in which our actions take place. For the Gestalt psychologists, a problem to be solved defined a behavioral field in stress. An animal or child, for example, might be prevented from reaching visible food by a barrier. The "stress" in such a field is obvious. The problem is resolved when the field is reorganized by "insight," that is, when the subject sees that the barrier may be walked around. The solution allows access to the food and relieves the stress in the behavioral field; the problem no longer exists. An important implication is that the subject must be aware of all elements in a problem situation before a real psychological problem exists. Should the subject not be able to see the food, no problem would exist, for no psychological field stress would exist, even if the subject were hungry. For this reason, the Gestalt psychologists criticized animal-learning experiments, such as E. L. Thorndike's, in which the animal could not perceive all elements of the situation. How can an animal exhibit its intelligence unless the relevant factors are available for intelligence to consider? According to Gestaltists, animals are reduced to trial-and-error conditioning if this is the only kind of behavior allowed in an experiment.

The field concept proved capable of indefinite extension to psychological problems. It could be applied not only to simple visual experiences and problem solving, but also to creativity (by Wertheimer himself) and social psychology (by Kurt Lewin, 1890–1947). However, the concept of the experiential field was insufficient. The two flashing lights do not by themselves create apparent motion; it is a psychological phenomenon. Problems do not solve themselves, they only pose themselves. The Gestalt psychologists, however, were unwilling to posit an active mind "which is able to grasp intrinsic relations and utilize such understanding," just as they did not recognize active apperception as a unifying force behind the creation of whole ideas. In their view, this alternative would lead to "vitalistic or spiritualistic dualism which we … have refused to accept" (Koffka, 1935/1963, p. 63). Instead, he said, "the dynamics of the process [of perceiving or thinking] are determined by the intrinsic properties of the data."

These "intrinsic properties" must act on the organism to produce experience or behavior. If there is no mind to act on, the action must be directly on the nervous system. This leads us to the second important concept of Gestalt psychology, the principle of *isomorphism*. This principle has given rise to numerous misconceptions. The Gestalt psychologists held that the brain is not the sensorimotor association machine that most believed it to be, but instead is a complex electrical field. The idea of isomorphism is that the structural relationships in the behavioral field create in the individual who experiences them a pattern of brain-fields isomorphic to themselves. So in the phi phenomenon, the flashing lights create two brain-fields that overlap and create the experience of motion. In a problem situation, the stresses in the behavioral field are represented in the brain as stresses in its electrical field. Insight is the resolution of the brain-field stresses that leads to resolution of the real problem.

The concept of isomorphism is difficult to grasp. A good analogy was suggested by Woodworth (1938). Functional isomorphism exists between the United States and a map of the United States. The two things are not the same, but structural relations in the former are directly related to structural relations in the latter. So the problem of driving from Chicago to Los Angeles can be experienced and solved through the map. The "stresses" of the trip can be seen and resolved on the map. But Woodworth's analogy is simplified. The Gestalt psychologists did not maintain that a picture of the behavioral-field exists in the brain. Exactly what they did mean remains obscure; it is only certain that they maintained a functional isomorphism between behavioral- and brain-fields. It was only through isomorphism and the electric-field picture of the brain that the Gestalt psychologists could uphold their holistic dynamic-field explanations of experience and behavior without falling into dualism.

The Gestalt movement thus attempted to avoid both atomism and dualism by considering people as perceiving organisms that respond to whole perceptual fields. The Gestalt experiments uncovered several interesting quirks of perception, such as the phi phenomenon, that had to be included in any later perceptual psychology. The Gestalt psychologists' almost mystical theory, however, did not travel well. It was far too German to do well in England and America, where psychology has been most studied since World War II.

Act Psychology

By and large, all the psychologies we have considered so far may be regarded primarily as psychologies of content. That is, they are concerned with discovering and describing the contents of consciousness. The imageless thought debate, for example, is a controversy about mental content: Do sensations, feelings, and images exhaustively describe all possible mental contents, or must we add "conscious states" to the list?

Franz Brentano (1878–1917), however, insisted that what is most important and characteristic of the mind is that it *acts*. Mental acts are directed at contents, Brentano said, but more important than the content is the act. Brentano divided mental acts into three classes: *ideating* (I see, I hear, I imagine), *judging* (I reject, I believe, I recall), and *loving-hating* (I wish, I intend, I desire). Acts are always directed at mental contents, and here arises Brentano's most significant concept, *intentionality,* as the criterion of mind. Rather than advocating a Cartesian dualism of substances, Brentano argued that only mental states—his "acts"—possess intentionality. Mental states are always directed at, or represent, something. So my idea of my cat Freya is directed at, is about, Freya; I possess a mental representation of her. The direction of thought on object Brentano called intentionality, and it should not be confused with the idea of purpose, for it is much broader. Purposes possess intentionality, for they are directed at something, a goal. However, Brentano said that all mental states are directed, even those that are purely cognitive. Intentionality separates mind from brain because only mental states are intentional. A neuron can never refer to, be about, intend anything, because it is mere matter and can no more refer to something outside itself than can a rock.

In his own time, Brentano's influence on psychology was limited. He was sympathetic to experimental psychology and tried, but failed, to establish an experimental laboratory at the University of Vienna. Psychologists, among them Titchener, tended to regard him as an armchair functional psychologist and paid little heed to his doctrine of intentionality. His influence was much greater in philosophy, especially through his student Edmund Husserl's phenomenology.

THE FATE OF THE PSYCHOLOGY OF CONSCIOUSNESS

Unlike psychoanalysis and the psychology of adaptation, the psychology of consciousness is no longer with us. Some of its methods, such as reaction time measurement, and ideas, such as mental set, endure, but the enterprise of the psychology of consciousness is dead. In its home, the psychology of consciousness met heavy weather attempting to establish itself as an autonomous discipline, while in the United States—psychology's future home—it was an alien Mandarin presence in a distinctly practical country.

Slow Growth in Germany

In Germany, the growth of psychology was greatly inhibited by the Mandarin culture of philosophical *Bildung.* As long as psychology remained where Wundt left it, in philosophy, psychologists had to compete with philosophers for professorships and resources. Especially as psychology became more completely experimental, it seemed to philosophers to be a rude intrusion upon their traditional concerns, and they banded together to oppose its growth within philosophy. However, efforts to move it elsewhere—to medicine, for example, as Külpe proposed—were unsuccessful.

The coming of the Nazis to power in 1933 complicated matters. They destroyed the old Mandarin system and drove from Germany its best minds. Jews and others sickened by Nazi oppression left Germany in a remarkable emigration that included outstanding intellectuals of every type, from writers such as Thomas Mann to physicists such as Einstein. Important psychologists were among their number, most notably the Gestalt psychologists, who moved to the United States, and Sigmund Freud, who spent his last months in England. Appallingly, many psychologists who remained in Germany turned with rapidity in the Nazi direction, in some cases providing "scientific" justification for Nazi racial policies.

On the other hand, psychology won its autonomy under the Nazi regime. One route to independence for psychology had been rejected by the Mandarins, that of making psychology a practical, applied discipline, which, for example, the mayor of Berlin asked for as early as 1912 (Ash, 1981). Applied psychology was called "psychotechnics" in Germany, and in 1941 German psychotechnic psychology won bureaucratic recognition as an independent field of study "because the Wehrmacht required trained psychologists to assist in the selection of officers" (Ash, 1981, p. 286). This proved a Faustian bargain, of course, when the Nazi regime brought upon Germany the destruction of World War II and the subsequent division of Germany into East and West. It was not until the 1950s that psychology in Germany got on its feet again (Ash, 1981) in an entirely new environment, dominated by American ideas.

Transplantation to America

In one respect, German psychology flourished in America. As we shall see in Chapters 4 and 5, growth of psychology in America quickly outpaced growth in Germany. For example, the American Psychological Association was founded a decade before the German Society for Experimental Psychology. In other respects, however, the psychology of consciousness in its German form could not be carried beyond the borders of Mandarin Germany. G. Stanley Hall wrote in 1912, "We need a psychology that is usable, that is dietetic, efficient for thinking, living, and working, and although Wundtian thoughts are now so successfully cultivated in academic gardens, they can never be acclimated here, as they are antipathetic to the American spirit and temper" (quoted by Blumenthal, 1986b).

Of all the early psychologies of consciousness, Wundt's was the most Mandarin and the most liable to rejection by practical-minded Americans. But the other psychologies of consciousness did not fare much better. Although Titchener created a psychology of consciousness along the lines of English-speaking philosophy, his adamant rejection of applied psychology, his prickly personality, and his cultivation of arcane research problems left him decisively outside the mainstream of psychology in America. The Würzburg movement was too short-lived to create a systematic approach to psychology. Brentano's act psychology possessed similarities to the functional psychology that came to dominate psychological theorizing after 1900, but his direct influence in psychology was limited by obscurity and by his lack of a psychological laboratory. Ironically, Brentano's significance lay in the future, when his concept of *intentionality* posed a fundamental challenge to the computer model of the mind (see Chapter 14).

The influence of Gestalt psychology in the United States is the hardest to evaluate. There is no question that the Gestalt psychologists were well received and honored in America. Wertheimer, Koffka, Köhler, and Lewin all settled in the United States either before or during the German intellectual migration. All of them were listened to respectfully, and Köhler was eventually elected president of the American Psychological Association. Some of their findings, such as those on insight learning, and some of their ideas, such as the principles of object perception, are found in textbooks to the present day. Nevertheless, the depth of their influence remains unclear.

Their greatest contribution, perhaps, lay in reformulating the study of perception so that it "carved nature at the joints," as philosophers today put it. The image is unpleasant, but vividly meaningful. When we buy precut chicken parts at the supermarket, they are often not carved at the joints: The chicken is divided into pieces by a saw that imposes arbitrary divisions on the chicken skeleton. When we carve a chicken at home, however, the parts into which we cut it conform to the structure of the skeleton: We carve the chicken at the joints and the pieces we create respect the lineaments of nature. If they could have used this metaphor, the Gestalt psychologists would have maintained that traditional, atomistic psychology did not carve perception at the joints, but imposed on experience an arbitrary atomism of simple sensations, the way the saw imposes on the chicken carcass arbitrary sectioning. They did not object to analyzing experience into parts (Henle, 1985), but analyzing it into arbitrary parts. In place of analysis of experience into meaningless sensations, they proposed it be analyzed into meaningful phenomenal objects (Henle, 1985), and in fact perceptual psychology no longer insists on a Titchenerian analysis of experience into theoretical atoms of basic sensations.

Gestalt psychologists may be said, therefore, to have reoriented the study of experience, but the influence of their own theories on psychology seems to have remained limited. Perhaps the most balanced summary of Gestalt psychology's impact is offered by one of the last surviving Gestalt psychologists, A. S. Luchins. Luchins (1975) acknowledges that Gestalt terminology is often used in contemporary—especially American—psychology but denies that the concepts to which the terms refer have been assimilated. With its emphasis on wholes, on synthesis, and on placing psychology within a larger "total comprehension of human existence," Gestalt psychology, like Wundt's, may have been too Mandarin for export.

BIBLIOGRAPHY

Largely because of psychology's centennial celebration in 1979, a great deal has been written about psychology's founding, about the psychology of consciousness, and about Wundt and his psychology in particular. In this bibliography, I will indicate only some of the literature on Wundt and the founding of psychology, trying to highlight the more important and accessible new work.

First, there are several edited volumes on psychology's beginnings: Wolfgang Bringmann & Ryan D. Tweney (1980); Josef Brozek & Ludwig Pongratz (Eds.), *Historiography of modern psychology* (Toronto: C. J. Hogrefe, 1980); Buxton (1986); Eliot Hearst (Ed.), *The first century of experimental psychology* (Hillsdale, NJ: Erlbaum, 1979); Sigmund Koch & David Leary (Eds.), *A century of psychology as science* (New York: McGraw-Hill, 1985); Rieber (Ed.), (1980); and William W. Woodward & Mitchell G. Ash (Eds.), *The problematic science: Psychology in nineteenth-century thought* (New York: Praeger, 1982).

An excellent introduction to the intellectual climate in nineteenth-century Germany is provided by Ringer (1969). Three papers discuss the conditions of psychology's founding. Richard Littman (1979) provides a general account of psychology's emergence as a discipline. Ash (1981) discusses psychology's difficulties in the Mandarin University system. Kurt Danziger, *Historical construction of social roles in the psychological experiment,* paper presented at the annual meeting of the American Psychological Association, 1981, uses sociological techniques to analyze the emergence of the human psychology experiment. Finally, an older but still useful account of psychology's beginning, written soon after it happened, is found in J. Mark Baldwin, "Sketch of the history of psychology," *Psychological Review* (1905, *12:* 144–65).

A great deal of work has been done on Wundt and his psychology. Besides Wundt (1896), the following works of his are available in English: *Outlines of psychology* (1897; reprinted St. Clair Shores: Michigan Scholarly Press, 1969); *Principles of physiological psychology,* Vol. 1, 5th ed. (New York: Macmillan, 1910); *An introduction to psychology* (1912; reprinted New York: Arno, 1973); *Elements of folk psychology* (London: Allen & Unwin, 1916); and *The language of gestures,* an excerpt from his *Völkerpsychologie* of 1900–1920 (The Hague: Mouton, 1973). For Wundt's biography, see Wolfgang Bringmann, William Balance, & Rand Evans, "Wilhelm Wundt, 1832–1920: A brief biographical sketch," *Journal of the History of the Behavioral Sciences* (1975, *11:* 287–97); Wolfgang Bringmann, Norma J. Bringmann, & William Balance, "Wilhelm Maximilian Wundt 1832–74: The formative years," in Bringmann & Tweney (1980); and Solomon Diamond, "Wundt before Leipzig," in Rieber (1980).

Other sources on Wundt include Joseph Jastrow, "Experimental psychology in Leipzig," *Science* (1886, 7 [198, Supplement]: 459–62), which describes in detail a few of Wundt's experiments, some of which are startlingly similar to current work in cognitive psychology. These parallels are discussed in my own "Something old, something new: Attention in Wundt and modern cognitive psychology," *Journal of the History of the Behavioral Sciences* (1979, *15:* 242–52). Theodore Mischel discusses "Wundt and the conceptual foundations of psychology," *Philosophical and Phenomenological Research* (1970, *31:* 1–26). William R. Woodward, "Wundt's program for the new psychology: Vicissitudes of experiment, theory, and system" (in Woodward & Ash, 1982, listed above), presents Wundt as a typical German intellectual with a Will to System. Two papers by Kurt Danziger (1979, 1980a) correct errors in the older picture of Wundt and examine his fate in Germany. Arthur Blumenthal (1986a) provides a good general orientation to Wundt's psychology in "Wilhelm Wundt: Psychology as the propaedeutic science."

Titchener was a prolific writer. Important works in addition to those cited in the chapter include *Experimental psychology: A manual of laboratory practice* (New York: Macmillan, 1901–1905); *Lectures on the elementary psychology of feeling and attention* (New York: Macmillan, 1908); "The past decade in experimental psychology," *American Journal of Psychology* (1910, *21:* 404–21); "The scheme of introspection," *American Journal of Psychology* (1912, *23:* 485–508; "Experimental psychology: A retrospect," *American Journal of Psychology* (1925, *36:* 313–23); and *A text-book of psychology* (New York: Macmillan, 1913). In my article "The mistaken mirror: On Wundt's and Titchener's psychologies," *Journal of the History of the Behavioral Sciences* (1981, *17:* 273–82), I show that Titchener was not, as is usually assumed, a simple follower of Wundt faithfully reflecting the master's views.

Some of the Würzburg school's papers are translated and excerpted in George Mandler & Jean Mandler (Eds.), *The psychology of thinking: From association to Gestalt* (New York: Wiley, 1964). Besides the references in the text, there were two important contemporary discussions of imageless thought: J. R. Angell, "Imageless thought," *Psychological Review* (1911, *18:* 295–323); and Robert S. Woodworth, "Imageless thought," *Journal of Philosophy, Psychology, and Scientific Methods* (1906, *3:* 701–8). A recent discussion is David Lindenfield, "Oswald Külpe and the Wurzburg school," *Journal of the History of the Behavioral Sciences* (1978, *14:* 132–41). George Humphrey, in part of his *Thinking* (New York: Science Editions, 1963), discusses the Würzburg findings, although he overestimates their damage to Wundt's psychology.

Besides the references, Köhler's important works include *The mentality of apes* (New York: Liveright, 1938); *The place of value in a world of facts* (New York: Liveright, 1938); *Dynamics in psychology* (New York: Liveright, 1940); *Gestalt psychology* (New York: Mentor, 1947); and *Selected papers of Wolfgang Köhler* (New York: Liveright, 1971); Wertheimer's best known book is *Productive thinking* (New York: Harper & Row, 1959). Mary Henle has edited a selection of papers by the Gestaltists, *Documents of Gestalt psychology* (Berkeley: University of California Press, 1961). The most influential Gestalt psychologist in the United States was Kurt Lewin, who for some time affected social, personality, and, to a lesser extent, learning, psychology; for example, his *Principles of topological psychology* (New York: McGraw-Hill, 1936). Julian Hochberg, "Organization and the Gestalt tradition," in E. Carterette & M. Friedman (Eds.), *Handbook of perception,* vol. 1: *Historical and philosophical roots of perception* (New York: Academic Press, 1974), discusses their influence on perception. Mary Henle tries to explain isomorphism in "Isomorphism: Setting the record straight," *Psychological Research* (1984, *46:* 317–27). The roots of Wertheimer's ideas are discussed in Abraham S. & Edith H. Luchins, "An introduction to the origins of Wertheimer's Gestalt Psychologie," *Gestalt Theory* (1982, *4:* 145–71). In a massive doctoral dissertation, Mitchell Graham Ash thoroughly documents and discusses the origin and development of Gestalt psychology in Germany in *The emergence of Gestalt theory: Experimental psychology in Germany 1890–1920,* unpublished doctoral dissertation (Harvard University, 1982). The reception of Gestalt psychology in the United States is discussed by Michael Sokal (1984).

Brentano's basic work is *Psychology from an empirical standpoint* (New York: The Humanities Press, 1973). For discussions of Brentano, see L. McAlister (Ed.), *The philosophy of Brentano* (Atlantic Highlands, NJ: Humanities Press, 1976).

REFERENCES

Angell, S. R. (1911). On the imageless thought controversy. *Psychological Review*, *18,* 295–323.

Ash, M. G. (1980). Wilhelm Wundt and Oswald Külpe on the institutional status of psychology: An academic controversy in historical context. In W. Bringmann & R. D. Tweney (Eds.), *Wundt studies.* Toronto: Hogrefe.

Ash, M. G. (1981). Academic politics in the history of science: Experimental psychology in Germany, 1879–1941. *Central European History, 13,* 255–286.

Ben-David, J. & Collins, R. (1966). Social factors in the origins of a new science: The case of psychology. *American Sociological Review, 31,* 451–465.

Berlin, I. (1954). *The fox and the hedgehog.* New York: Touchstone.

Blumenthal, A. L. (1970). *Language and psychology: Historical aspects of psycholinguistics.* New York: John Wiley.

Blumenthal, A. L. (1975). A reappraisal of Wilhelm Wundt. *American Psychologist, 30,* 1081–1088.

Blumenthal, A. L. (1980a). Wilhelm Wundt and early American psychology: A clash of cultures. In R. W. Rieber (Ed.), *Wilhelm Wundt and the making of a scientific psychology.* New York: Plenum.

Blumenthal, A. L. (1980b). Wilhelm Wundt: Problems of interpretation. In W. Bringmann & R. D. Tweney (Eds.), *Wundt studies.* Toronto: Hogrefe.

Blumenthal, A. L. (1986a). Wilhelm Wundt: Psychology as the propaedeutic science. In C. Buxton (Ed.), *Points of view in the history of psychology.* New York: Academic Press.

Blumenthal, A. L. (1986b). Shaping a tradition: Experimentalism begins. In C. Buxton (Ed.), *Points of view in the history of psychology.* New York: Academic Press.

Bringmann, W. & Tweney, R. D. (Eds.), (1980). *Wundt studies.* Toronto: Hogrefe.

Buxton, C. (Ed.), (1986). *Points of view in the history of psychology.* New York: Academic Press.

Clark, H. M. (1911). Conscious attitudes. *American Journal of Psychology, 22,* 214–249.

Danziger, K. (1979). The positivist repudiation of Wundt. *Journal of the History of the Behavioral Sciences, 15,* 205–230.

Danziger, K. (1980a). The history of introspection reconsidered. *Journal of the History of the Behavioral Sciences, 16,* 241–262.

Danziger, K. (1980b). Wundt and the two traditions of psychology. In R. W. Rieber (Ed.), *Wilhelm Wundt and the making of a scientific psychology.* New York: Plenum.

Diamond, S. (1980). Wundt before Leipzig. In R. W. Rieber (Ed.), *Wilhelm Wundt and the making of a scientific psychology.* New York: Plenum.

Ellis, W. D. (Ed.), (1938). *A sourcebook of Gestalt psychology.* London: Routledge & Kegan Paul.

Graumann, C. (1980). Experiment, statistics, history: Wundt's first program of psychology. In W. Bringmann & R. D. Tweney (Eds.), *Wundt studies.* Toronto: Hogrefe.

Henle, M. (1977). The influence of Gestalt psychology in America. *Annals of the New York Academy of Sciences, 291,* 3–12.

Henle, M. (1985). Rediscovering Gestalt psychology. In S. Koch & D. Leary (Eds.), *A century of psychology as science.* New York: McGraw-Hill.

Hilgard, E. R. & Bower, G. (1975). *Theories of learning,* 4th ed. Englewood Cliffs, NJ: Prentice-Hall.

James, W. (1875). Review of *Grundzüge der physiologischen psychologie. North American Review, 121,* 195–201. (Reprinted in Bringmann & Tweney, 1980; and Rieber, 1980).

Keller, F. S. (1973). *The definition of psychology.* Englewood Cliffs, NJ: Prentice-Hall.

Koffka, K. (1922). Perception: An introduction to Gestalt-theorie. *Psychological Bulletin, 19,* 531–585.

Koffka, K. (1935/1963). *Principles of Gestalt psychology.* San Diego, CA: Harcourt Brace Jovanovich.

Littman, R. (1979). Social and intellectual origins of experimental psychology. In E. Hearst (Ed.), *The first century of experimental psychology.* Hillsdale, NJ: Erlbaum.

Luchins, A. S. (1975). The place of Gestalt theory in American psychology. In S. Ertel, L. Kemmler, & M. Sadler (Eds.), *Gestalt-theorie in der modernen psychologie.* Darmstadt, Germany: Dietrich Steinfopf Verlag.

Mayer, A. & Orth, J. (1901). Experimental studies of association. Partially reprinted in G. Mandler & J. Mandler (Eds.), (1964). *The psychology of thinking: From associationism to Gestalt.* New York: John Wiley.

Ogden, R. M. (1911a). Imageless thought. *Psychological Bulletin, 8,* 183–197.

Ogden, R. M. (1911b). The unconscious bias of laboratories. *Psychological Bulletin, 8,* 330–331.

Richards, R. J. (1980). Wundt's early theories of unconscious inference and cognitive evolution in their relation to Darwinian biopsychology. In W. Bringmann & R. D. Tweney (Eds.), *Wundt studies.* Toronto: Hogrefe.

Rieber, R. W. (Ed.), (1980). *Wilhelm Wundt and the making of a scientific psychology.* New York: Plenum.

Ringer, F. K. (1969). *The decline of German Mandarins: The German academic community 1890–1933.* Cambridge: Harvard University Press.

Sokal, M. (1984). The Gestalt psychologists in behaviorist America. *American Historical Review, 89,* 1240–1263.

Steffens, L. (1938). *The letters of Lincoln Steffens.* New York: Harcourt Brace.

Titchener, E. B. (1897). *An outline of psychology.* New York: Macmillan.

Titchener, E. B. (1901–1905). *Experimental psychology: A manual of laboratory practice,* 4 vols. New York: Macmillan.

Titchener, E. B. (1904). *Lectures on the experimental psychology of the thought processes.* New York: Macmillan.

Titchener, E. B. (1929/1972). *Systematic psychology: Prologemena.* Ithaca: Cornell University Press.

Van Hoorn, W. & Verhave, T. (1980). Wundt's changing conception of a general and theoretical psychology. In W. Bringmann & R. D. Tweney (Eds.), *Wundt studies.* Toronto: Hogrefe.

PART I FOUNDING SCIENTIFIC PSYCHOLOGY

Washburn, M. F. (1961). Some recollections. In C. Murchison (Ed.), *History of psychology in autobiography,* Vol. 2. New York: Russell & Russell.

Wertheimer, Max. (1922). The general theoretical situation. In W. D. Ellis (Ed.). (1938), *A sourcebook of Gestalt psychology.* London: Routledge & Kegan Paul.

Wertheimer, Max. (1925). Gestalt theory. In W. D. Ellis (Ed.). (1938), *A sourcebook of Gestalt psychology.* London: Routledge & Kegan Paul.

Wertheimer, Michael. (1978, Aug. 31). Max Wertheimer: Gestalt prophet. Presidential Address to Division 26 (History), annual meeting of the American Psychological Association, Toronto, Canada.

Woodward, W. W. (1982). Wundt's program for the new psychology: Vicissitudes of experiment, theory, and system. In W. Woodward & M. Ash (Eds.), *The problematic science: Psychology in nineteenth century thought.* New York: Praeger.

Woodworth, R. S. (1938). *Experimental psychology.* New York: Holt, Rinehart & Winston.

Woodworth, R. S. & Schlosberg, H. (1954). *Experimental psychology,* 2nd ed. New York: Holt, Rinehart & Winston.

Wundt, W. M. (1896). *Lectures on human and animal psychology.* New York: Macmillan.

Wundt, W. M. (1873). *Principles of physiological psychology.* Portions reprinted in Rieber (1980), trans. S. Diamond.

Wundt, W. M. (1907–1908). Über Ausfrageexperimenten und über die Methoden zur Psychologie des Denkens. *Psychologischen Studien, 3,* 301–360.

CHAPTER 3

The Psychology of the Unconscious Mind

INTRODUCTION

The Significance of Psychoanalysis

The psychology of the unconscious was markedly different from the psychology of consciousness. Wundt and the other psychologists of consciousness focused on the normal, human, adult mind known through introspection, attempting to make an experimental science out of philosophers' traditional questions and theories. The fields of sensation and perception and cognitive psychology largely defined the field, although some attention was given to social, developmental, and animal psychology. Freud's psychology, in contrast, focused on abnormal minds and claimed to unmask consciousnesss—including normal consciousness—as a self-deceiving puppet of disgusting primal impulses it dared not acknowledge. Instead of conducting experiments, Freud investigated the mind by clinically probing it, looking for the concealed springs of human conduct in unconscious, primitive residues of childhood and evolution. Freud and psychoanalysis rounded out what psychology was to be, adding the fields of personality, motivation, and psychopathology, and strengthening interest in developmental and social psychology.

Freud's character, too, was different from that of the other German founders of psychology. Wundt, his students, and the Gestalt psychologists were, for all their differences, products of Mandarin Germany, cautious and circumspect scholars and scientists. Freud, however, rejected the Mandarin outlook, "scorn[ing] to distinguish culture and civilization" (Freud, 1930/1961). He was born a Jew—but was an atheist proud of his Jewish heritage—and lived in the shadow of centuries of oppression by the Mandarin class. Freud created psychoanalysis in part as a political challenge to the rulers of Austria-Hungary (Schorske, 1980; McGrath, 1986).

Freud wanted to be a conquering hero in the mold of Moses, bringer of disagreeable commandments to a disbelieving people. Possibly under the influence of cocaine—he used it regularly in the late 1880s and 1890s (Crews, 1986)—Freud (1960, p. 202, letter 94) described himself to his fiancée, Minna Bernays (February 2, 1886):

> Breuer [sometime friend and collaborator] told me he had discovered that hidden under the surface of timidity there lay in me an extremely daring and fearless human being. I had always thought so, but never dared tell anyone. I have often felt as though I had inherited all the defiance and all the passions with which our ancestors defended their temple and could gladly sacrifice my life for one great moment in history.

On February 1, 1900, awaiting the reception of *The Interpretation of Dreams,* Freud wrote to his intimate friend Wilhelm Fliess:

> For I am actually not at all a man of science, not an observer, not an experimenter, not a thinker. I am by temperament nothing but a conquistador—an adventurer, if you want it translated—with all the curiosity, daring, and tenacity characteristic of a man of this sort. Such people are customarily esteemed only if they have been successful, have really discovered something; otherwise they are dropped by the wayside. And that is not altogether unjust.[1] (Freud, 1985, p. 398)

To the world he aimed to conquer, Freud presented psychoanalysis as a revolution. Psychoanalysis, he often said (Gay, 1989), represented the third great blow to human self-esteem. The first blow was Copernicus's demonstration that human beings did not live at the center of the universe. The second blow was Darwin's demonstration

---

[1]From *The Complete Letters of Sigmund Freud to Wilhelm Fliess,* 1887–1904, by J. M. Masson, ed., Cambridge, MA: Harvard University Press, Copyright © 1985 and under the Bern Convention Sigmund Freud Copyrights, Ltd.; translation and editorial matter © 1985 by J. M. Masson.

that human beings were part of nature—being animals like any other. The third blow, Freud claimed, was his own demonstration that the human ego is not master in its own house.

Foundation Stones: Freud and Scientific Psychology

FREUD AND ACADEMIC PSYCHOLOGY

"Freud is inescapable": Peter Gay (1989) thus summarizes the conquistador's achievement. There can be no doubt that "we all speak Freud whether we know it or not.... Freud's terminology and his essential ideas pervade contemporary ways of thinking about human feelings and conduct" (Gay, 1989, p. xii). Nevertheless, it is both ironic and inevitable that Freud's influence should have been less in academic psychology than in any other field concerned with human affairs save perhaps economics. Psychologists of consciousness rejected the existence of the unconscious, Freud's indispensable hypothesis. Behaviorists rejected the existence of mind altogether. So it is unsurprising that apart from occasional recognition of Freud's somewhat literary insights into human motives, academic psychology has largely ignored or rejected psychoanalysis. Rapprochements between academic psychology and psychoanalysis have sometimes been sought (Erdelyi, 1985; Sears, 1985) but never achieved.

Moreover, the isolation of psychoanalysis from academic psychology has been abetted by the development—over Freud's own objections—of psychoanalysis as a branch of medicine. Especially in the United States, an M.D. degree with specialization in psychiatry became the prerequisite for undertaking training as a psychoanalyst. Isolation became enmity with the professional rivalry that arose between psychiatry and clinical psychology. Psychiatrists have always tended to look upon clinical psychologists as poorly trained interlopers in the business of medicine, and in the case of psychoanalysis this resulted in exclusion of Ph.D. psychologists from training in schools of psychoanalysis, a policy that remains bitterly contentious to the present day.

FOUNDATION STONE: THERAPEUTIC SUCCESS, NOT EXPERIMENTAL TEST

While Freud may have regarded himself as a conquistador rather than a scientist, there is no doubt that Freud shared the goal of the other founders of psychology—to create a psychology that was a science like any other. Freud rejected the suggestion that psychoanalysis offered anything other than a scientific view of the world: "Psycho-analysis, in my opinion, is incapable of creating a *Weltanschauung* of its own. It does not need one; it is a part of science" (Freud, 1932, in Gay, 1989, p. 796). Yet Freud did not undertake to construct an experimental psychology of the unconscious, nor did he welcome attempts to experimentally verify his ideas. In the 1930s, an American psychologist, Saul Rosenzweig, wrote to Freud about his attempts at experimental testing of psychoanalysis. Freud replied very briefly (February 28, 1934): "I have examined your experimental studies for the verification of psychoanalytic propositions with interest. I cannot put much value on such confirmation because the abundance of reliable observations on which these propositions rest makes them independent of experimental verification. Still, it can do no harm" (quoted by Rosenzweig, 1985, pp. 171–72).

The "abundance of reliable observations" on which Freud erected psychoanalysis consisted of his clinical cases. We are apt to think today of psychoanalysis as primarily a therapy; but even though Freud certainly valued therapeutic success, he intended psychoanalytic psychology to be a science. He therefore regarded the talk of his patients as scientific data and the analytic session as a scientifically valid method of investigation. Indeed, his remarks to Rosenzweig suggest that he regarded analysis as more than the equal of experimentation as a scientific method. For Freud, successful therapy was not an end in itself, but constituted evidence that psychoanalytic theory was true.

Obviously, such dismissal of experimental methodology served to further isolate psychoanalysis from mainstream psychology. Psychoanalysts said that only someone who had been through psychoanalysis was fit to criticize it, leading academic psychologists to regard psychoanalysis more as a cult with an initiation rite than as a science open to all (Sulloway, 1991). Furthermore, reliance on clinical evidence raised more than political difficulties for psychoanalysis as a science. Fechner, Donders, Wundt, and others had introduced experiment to psychology in order to rid it of unscientific subjectivity, replacing armchair introspection with experimental rigor. Psychoanalysis sought to replace armchair introspection with couch introspection, and it could be reasonably asked if Freud had replaced a bad method with a worse one. After all, the introspective observer in psychoanalysis is a patient: a sick individual wishing to be cured of neurosis, rather than a trained observer committed to the advancement of science. These were not and are not idle concerns, and as we shall see they may have played a subterranean role in Freud's greatest challenge, his seduction mistake.

FOUNDATION STONE: FREUD AND THE PATH THROUGH PHYSIOLOGY

Like the other founding psychologists, Freud was attracted to the idea of approaching psychology through physiology, but he struggled with it as well. Allying the infant psychology with physiology was attractive to psychologists for several reasons. Six were especially important to experimental psychologists of consciousness, as we have seen:

- The founders of psychology were trained in physiology as physicians, and like the ancient philosopher-physicians, their psychology represented an extension of their science into questions of mind.
- Wundt regarded psychological experimentation as grounded in physiological experimentation and in fact borrowed important methods such as reaction-time measurement directly from physiology.
- Psychologists often borrowed concepts from physiology; for example, Frederick Bartlett's (1932) conception of the *schema* as a mental organizing principle was borrowed from neurologist Henry Head's concept of schema as a neurological organizing principle (Brewer & Nakamura, 1984).
- Linking psychology to physiology helped defend the new science against charges of unscientific dualism.
- Physiology was an established and prestigious discipline, and by defining psychology as physiological, psychologists helped win it academic recognition and respect.
- Some psychologists, including Titchener, some of the Gestalt psychologists, and

William James, hoped to find in physiology the theoretical principles by which to explain mind and behavior.

Freud's situation and ambition as a founder were in large degree the same as the other founders'. He had a medical degree and carried out important work in anatomy and physiology. Ernst Brücke, a distinguished physiologist of a reductive temper, had taught Freud and influenced him considerably. Thus Freud's psychology was likely to be physiological for the same reasons as Wundt's, but once Freud took up clinical practice and began to create psychoanalysis as both science and therapy, the path through physiology also exerted two special attractions for him.

First, one charge that could reasonably be leveled against a science built upon the talk of neurotic patients was *cultural parochialism*. Science is supposed to discover universal truths: laws of nature that hold good across time and space. In the case of psychology, this means finding laws of human behavior that transcend any particular culture or historical era. Living up to this standard of science was vexing enough for experimental psychologists, who could at least point to the rigor and simplicity of their experiments as warrant of their universal character, but such a claim could not be made for psychoanalytic therapy. However, if therapeutic findings were used to elaborate a neurophysiological *theory* of mind and behavior, then charges of cultural parochialism might be deflected (Sulloway, 1979). After all, human nervous systems exist apart from culture, so that a theory pitched at the neural level could stake a claim to universal truth.

The most unique attraction for Freud of the path to science through physiology, however, lay in his situation as a clinical neurologist. Today the term "neurosis" is virtually synonymous with a disorder that is entirely mental ("all in your head"), but in Freud's time, neuroses were viewed as primarily *neural* disorders. By far the most common neurosis of the time was hysteria. In our post-Freudian world, hysteria is called *dissociative disorder*, defined as a physical symptom having a psychological cause, but in Freud's time, the physical symptoms of hysteria—such things as paralyses and failures of sense perception—were thought to stem from an unknown disorder of the nervous system (Macmillan, 1991).

Before the advent of scientific medicine, hysteria had been viewed as a moral failing, whether a weakness of will or a possession by evil spirits. William James, who suffered from "nervous" diseases himself, spoke for enlightened medical opinion and long-suffering patients when he said in his 1896 Lowell Lectures on abnormal mental states, "Poor hysterics! First treated as victims of sexual trouble … then of moral perversity and mendacity … then of imagination … honest disease not thought of" (quoted by Myers, 1986, ellipses in original, p. 5). Ironically, in the same year, Freud gave a paper on hysteria before the Society for Psychiatry and Neurology in which he broached for the first time his view that hysteria had a psychological—specifically sexual—etiology. Chairing the session was the greatest student of sexual psychopathology of the day, Richard von Krafft-Ebing, who pronounced it a "scientific fairytale." With James, Krafft-Ebing and the rest of the medical establishment—Freud called them "donkeys"—regarded the strictly medical view of hysteria as a great advance (Sulloway, 1979).

Patients treated for hysteria would probably have disagreed. For a physical etiology for hysteria prescribed physical treatments, no matter how mysterious the malady. The nosological term "hysteria" derived from the Greek word *hyster*, meaning womb, reflecting the prevailing belief that hysteria was suffered almost only by women. Physicians were always male, so that the doctor-patient relationship was defined by the norms of a patriarchal social order. Doctors expected all patients to be quietly submissive, an expectation doubled for women. Moreover, there could be a hidden sexual element in male-female doctor-patient relationships. Freud had trouble handling his own feelings for at least one patient (Decker, 1981, 1991). These factors made the physical treatments for hysteria especially unpleasant for women.

Treatments for hysteria were often "heroic" in the extreme, bordering on torture. The leading treatment was "electrotherapy." Its milder form was "faradization," for which Freud bought the needed equipment in 1886. The patient, naked or lightly covered, was seated in water with her feet on a negative electrode, while the physician probed her body from head to foot with a positive electrode or (for "sensitive" patients) with his "electrical hand," the current passing through his own body. Treatment sessions lasted ten to twenty minutes and were frequently repeated. Many patients had severe adverse reactions, ranging from burns to dizziness or defecation.

Other therapies included suffocation, beating with wet towels, ridicule, hard icy showers, insertion of tubes in the rectum, application of hot irons to the spine, and in "intractable" cases, ovariectomies and cauterization of the clitoris. Such treatments may fairly be regarded as abuse of women by powerful men, but it should also be noted that treatment for some male disorders was equally "heroic," involving, for example, cauterization of parts of the genitalia (Decker, 1991). Whether or not psychoanalysis worked, it could not have worked worse than such "heroic" treatments and must have been regarded with relief by experienced hysterics.

In Freud's case, the physiological path to scientific psychology found fullest expression in a manuscript he never completed, the "Project for a Scientific Psychology." It was written in a white heat of Newtonian passion (Solomon, 1974) in the fall of 1894 and the spring of 1895. On April 27, Freud wrote to Fliess, "Scientifically, I am in a bad way; namely caught up in the 'Psychology for neurologists' [Freud's working title], which regularly consumes me totally…. "(p. 127). On May 25: " … a man like me cannot live without a hobbyhorse, without a consuming passion, without—in Schiller's words—a tyrant. I have found one. In its service I know no limits. It is psychology" (p. 129).

Freud was "tormented by two aims: first, to examine what shape the theory of mental functioning takes if one introduces quantitative considerations, a sort of economics of nerve forces; and second, to peel off from psychopathology a gain for normal psychology" (letter to Fliess of May 25, p. 129). In the "Project" itself, Freud defined his Newtonian "intention … to furnish a psychology that shall be a natural science: that is, to represent psychical processes as quantitatively determinate states of specifiable material particles." He went on to develop a general theory of mind and behavior in entirely physiological and quantitative terms. For example, motivation is described as resulting from the buildup of tension at "barriers"—today called synapses—between neurons. This buildup is felt as unpleasure, and its eventual discharge across the barrier is felt as pleasure. Memory is explained (as it is in most neural models today) as changes to the permeability of neuronal barriers (changes in synaptic strength) resulting from repeated firing of connected neurons. In similarly quantitative-neurological ways, Freud explained the full range of "mental" functions from hallucinations to cognition.

Freud's "Project" remains one of the most fascinating but troublesome documents in the history of psychoanalysis. It is fascinating because so much of Freud's psychological theory is introduced in the "Project" in neurological guise, but it is troublesome because it is hard to evaluate Freud's final attitude to it, or properly place it in the history of psychoanalytic thought. Since he abandoned writing it and later resisted its publication, it is fair to conclude that Freud regarded the "Project" as fatally flawed, but the question remains why. The standard account accepted by later Freudians is that shortly after working on the "Project" Freud undertook a "heroic" self-analysis in which he discovered that the causes of behavior are psychological events occurring in a psychological unconscious, and he consequently abandoned the "Project" as a young man's foolishness. Certainly he remained driven by his "tyrant," psychology, but his later theories, like Wundt's, became more psychological. In his clinical work, he came to distinguish between "actual neuroses" and "psychoneuroses." The actual neuroses were true physical diseases, caused by "excess or deficiency of certain nerve-poisons" (Freud, 1908/1953, p. 81); the psychoneuroses, including hysteria, have causes that "are psychogenic, and depend upon the operation of unconscious (repressed) ideational complexes" (Freud, 1908/1953, p. 81).

On the other hand, Sulloway (1979) has persuasively argued that regarding Freud's self-analysis as the critical event in the history of psychoanalysis was a myth put out by Freud and his followers to turn Freud into a heroic conqueror of pure psychology and to obscure Freud's continued reliance on biology as the secret foundation of psychoanalytic theory. Freud gave up the "Project" because he could not construct a mechanism compatible with his main guiding thesis about the origin of neurosis. Whether in the seduction theory or later, Freud always held that adult neurotic symptoms find their ultimate cause in a childhood trauma or disgusting thought. At the time, this event or thought has no pathological effect, but lies dormant, and is unconsciously reawakened years later, expressed as a symptom.

This view of the etiology of symptoms was so dear to Freud that he gave up neurologizing, but he did not give up biology. According to Sulloway (1979), Freud turned from mechanistic physiological biology to Lamarckian evolutionary biology to explain human development. For example, most scientists of the day (including Wundt) accepted the "biogenetic law" of Ernst Haeckel (1834–1919), Germany's leading Darwinian. According to the biogenetic law—which we now know to be false—"ontogeny recapitulates phylogeny," that is, the embryological development of any creature repeats its species' evolutionary path. Thus to casual inspection a human fetus passes through an amphibian stage, a reptile stage, a simple mammal stage, and so on until it resembles a miniature human being. Freud simply extended the biogenetic law to include psychological development. The stages of psychosexual development he regarded as recapitulations of the sex life of our predecessor species, including latency as a recapitulation of the ice ages! Lamarckian inheritance became a convenient way out of many difficulties. Thus in order for a child to develop castration anxiety, he or she did not have to see that opposite-sexed people have different genitals; the knowledge was written in the genes. In Sulloway's view, then, Freud ceased to seek the cause of psychoneuroses in the physiochemical mechanics of the nervous system, but he never gave up the search for an organic basis for neurotic and normal psychological development.

Central to Freud's new biological conception of human development and behavior was the sex instinct. Sex provided a basis for constructing a truly universal and naturalistic scientific psychology because it was neither species- nor culture-specific. Following the path of the Enlightenment and going against the German Mandarins, Freud wanted a psychology shorn of scientifically irrelevant cultural factors. The ubiquity of the sex drive provided its foundation. Freud always supposed that the list of biological needs was short: hunger, thirst, self-preservation, and sex (and later, aggression). If one accepts this list as exhaustive, then one has a problem explaining much of human behavior. It is clear that animal behavior always seems to serve one of these needs, but it is equally clear that human behavior does not. Humans build cathedrals, paint pictures, write novels, think of philosophies, and conduct science, none of which immediately meets any biological need. Most writers on human affairs were not faced with Freud's problem, because they supposed that human beings have special motives that lead to religion, art, philosophy, and science.

Freud, however, by taking a biologically reductive and simplifying view of motivation, accepted a short list of drives and needed to show that behavior not directly caused by them was in reality indirectly caused by them. It had to be the case that instincts could be redirected from their innately determined channels into other, less biological ones. Hunger, thirst, and self-preservation are poor candidates for rechanneling, since satisfying them is necessary for the survival of the organism. Sexuality, on the other hand, is a powerful motive whose satisfaction can be postponed or even abandoned; the animal may be unhappy, but it lives. Sexuality, then, is the biological motive most capable of displacement from direct satisfaction into more socially acceptable and creative activity, or into neurosis. Freud was not the first to find in sex the hidden cause of human achievement; romantic poets and philosophers such as Schopenhauer talked about the sublimation of sexuality into higher things, as did Freud's friend Fliess (Sulloway, 1979). Only Freud, however, made sublimation part of a general theory of human mind and behavior.

Moreover, the sexual drive is the one human societies take the greatest interest in regulating. Societies universally regulate the sort of person one may take as a sex partner and marry, while taking no interest in one's dining companions. It appeared to Freud then, that society actively seeks to rechannel sex away from its native goal toward more civilized ones but often succeeds in making neuroses instead.

Sex played the key role in the formation of neuroses, giving Freud's science a biological foundation (Sulloway, 1979). In the case of the actual neuroses, "the sexual factor is the essential one in [their] causation" (Freud, 1908/1953), since the "nerve poisons" that cause actual neuroses are generated by wrong sexual practices such as adult masturbation or sexual abstinence (Sulloway, 1979). The situation with regard to psychoneuroses was different, with sexuality playing a more psychological role. The most purely biological factor in psychoneurosis was the prior state of the nervous system, since "hereditary influence is more marked" than in the actual neuroses (Freud, 1908/1953). Sexuality came into play as the factor working on the nervous system to cause the symptoms of hysteria. In Freud's early theorizing, sexual seduction as a child provided the trauma that would later blossom into neurosis. In his later theory, it was childhood sexual fantasies that provided the kernels of adult neuroses.

By 1905, Freud had written the founding works of psychoanalysis, *Interpretation of Dreams* and *Three Essays on the Theory of Sexuality,* and had sorted out what was biological and what was psychological in psychoanalysis:

> Some of my medical colleagues have looked upon my theory of hysteria as a purely psychological one, and have for that reason pronounced it *ipso facto* incapable of solving a pathological problem.... [But] it is the therapeutic technique alone which is purely psychological; the theory does not by any means fail to point out that neuroses have an organic basis—though it is true that it does not look for that basis in any pathological anatomical changes.... No one, probably, will be inclined to deny the sexual function the character of an organic factor, and it is the sexual function that I look upon as the foundation of hysteria and of the psychoneuroses in general. (1905b in Gay, 1989, p. 372)

Issues and Concepts

Freud always regarded two concepts as fundamental to psychoanalysis. One is the concept of the *psychological unconscious.* To give a psychological explanation of hysteria, Freud was led to posit the existence of a willfully hidden part of the mind. This unconscious contained ancient wishes and thoughts from the racial or personal past, thoughts too terrible to allow into consciousness. Although hidden, these thoughts still found expression as symptoms in hysterics, and in dreams and slips of the tongue in allegedly "normal" people. The other cornerstone of psychoanalysis is Freud's insistence that what was repressed into the unconscious was primarily sexual in nature, so that sexual wishes—most importantly childhood sexual wishes—lay at the root of neurotic symptoms and modern nervousness as well as much of the rest of human behavior. Yet both concepts were and remain controversial in scientific psychology. Not all psychologists have believed in the unconscious—nor do all value sex so highly or agree with Freud's interpretation of childhood sexuality.

THE UNCONSCIOUS

Issue: Does the Unconscious Exist?

Positing the existence of unconscious mental states was not new with Freud. Leibniz's *petite perceptions* are unconscious. Like Freud, Herbart divided the mind into conscious and unconscious areas and viewed mental life as a competition between ideas competing for access to consciousness. Helmholtz believed that the construction of the experienced world from the atoms of sensation required the existence of unconscious inferences. The hypnotic trance and the power of posthypnotic suggestion, with which Freud was familiar from his studies with Charcot and his own use of hypnosis in therapy, seemed to point to a realm of mind apart from consciousness. Schopenhauer spoke of the "wild beast" within the human soul, and Nietzsche said "Consciousness is a surface" (Kaufmann, 1985). Freud acknowledged Nietzsche's grasp of unconscious dynamics in *Psychopathology of Everyday Life* when he quoted Nietzsche's pithy aphorism "*'I have done that,' says my memory. 'I could not have done that,' says my pride and remains inexorable. Finally, my memory yields*" (Kaufmann, 1985; italics in Kaufmann). By the turn of the century, students of human affairs were increasingly regarding human behavior as being caused by factors and motives lying outside awareness (Hughes, 1958; Ellenberger, 1970).

Nevertheless, the hypothesis of unconscious mental states was not the dominant one among academic psychologists, who viewed mind as coextensive with consciousness. For them, the science of mind—psychology—was the science of consciousness. Freud's most important instructor in philosophy, Franz Brentano, rejected the unconscious (Krantz, 1990), and he was joined in his views by the preeminent American psychologist, William James (1890). Brentano and James were united in holding the doctrine called by Brentano the "infallibility of inner perception" and by James *esse est sentiri*. According to this view, ideas in consciousness were (*esse est*) exactly what they appeared to be (*sentiri*). That is, ideas in consciousness were not compounded up by what James called "the Kantian machine shop of the unconscious" out of simpler mental elements. The Gestalt view was similar, arguing that complex wholes were given directly in consciousness without hidden mental machinery behind the stage of experience.

It is important to realize that neither Brentano nor James denied the validity of a purely *descriptive* use of the term "unconscious." They fully recognized that behavior or experience may be determined by factors of which we are not aware, but they believed that the existence of unconscious causes of experience and behavior did not require the positing of unconscious mental states. They proposed a number of alternative mechanisms by which mind and behavior might be unconsciously shaped. James fully treated the problem in his *Principles of Psychology* (1890).

As James points out, consciousness is a brain process, and we are not aware of the states of our brain. Our cerebellum keeps us balanced upright, for example, but to explain upright posture we need not suppose that the cerebellum is unconsciously computing the laws of physics. So memories not now recalled need not be supposed to exist psychologically at all, but to exist as traces in the brain, dispositions toward consciousness awaiting activation (James, 1890).

Other apparently unconscious mental states may be explained as lapses in attention and memory. Apprehended stimuli, to use Wundt's terms, are conscious, but because they are not apperceived may not be remembered. If we are influenced by them, we might be disposed to think they influenced us "unconsciously," when in fact their presence in consciousness was merely no longer recollected. In 1960, George Sperling would show that in Wundt's letter-perception experiment, apprehended letters were perceived briefly but forgotten during the time it took the subject to pronounce the letters they had seen. A dream or memory we cannot recover need not be thought to be unconscious because repressed, but "unconscious" because forgotten (James, 1890). Finally, phenomena such as hypnotism and the existence of multiple personalities may be explained by dissociation of consciousness rather than the existence of an unconscious. That is, within the brain of a single individual two distinct consciousnesses may be present, unknown to each other, rather than a single consciousness beset by unconscious forces.

Positing an unconscious seemed to James and other psychologists to be scientifically dangerous. Since the unconscious by definition lies outside inspection, it can easily become a convenient vehicle by which to construct untestable theories. As James (1890, p. 163) wrote, the unconscious "is the sovereign means for believing what one likes in psychology, and of turning what might become a science into a tumbling-ground for whimsies."

Nevertheless, Freud cast his lot with the party of the unconscious, and it is the one truly indispensable shibboleth of psychoanalysis (Gay, 1989), the "consummation of psychoanalytic research" (Freud, 1915b). Unconscious causes of hysterical symptoms make their first psychoanalytic appearance in *Studies in Hysteria,* published by Freud and Joseph Breuer (1842–1925) in 1895. Breuer was a distinguished general physician and physiologist who in 1880 first treated the patient whose case starts the story of psychoanalytic therapy. Called Anna O. in *Studies,* Bertha von Pappenheim was a young middle-class woman who, like many others, had to nurse a sick father (as Anna Freud later nursed Sigmund). She fell prey to hysteria, primarily minor paralyses and difficulties speaking and hearing. Treating her over a period of time, Breuer found that she gained some symptomatic relief by falling into autohypnosis and talking about her symptoms, recovering while doing so forgotten events that had caused them. For example, her inability to drink water from a glass was traced to having seen a dog licking water from a glass, and when she recovered this memory, she immediately drank again. Despite continued treatment, Anna O. showed no continued improvement and in fact had to be hospitalized at one point. The statement in *Studies* that she got well was false, nor did she experience a hysterical pregnancy naming Breuer as the father, as analytic legend has it.

In some respects, Anna invented psychotherapy, for she was one of a number of reported cases in the nineteenth century in which hysterical patients guided doctors to their cures (Macmillan, 1991). In Anna's case, she set her own timetable for therapy, placed herself in hypnosis, and led herself to the precipitating causes of her symptoms, a procedure she named "the talking cure." She was an intelligent and forceful woman who went on to an important, influential, and successful career as the founder of social work in Germany. Despite being present at the creation, however, she never had kind words for psychoanalysis.

Freud had nothing to do with the case of Anna O., but later collaborated with Breuer in applying the talking cure to hysterics and formulating a general theory of hysteria. The case of Anna O. was tidied up, and Freud contributed the rest of the case histories which together with a theoretical chapter comprise *Studies in Hysteria.* In the theoretical chapter, Breuer and Freud argued that hysterics fall ill because they "suffer mainly from reminiscences." That is, they experience an emotional trauma that is repressed. Instead of working through the negative emotions aroused by the event, the affect is "strangulated"—repressed—along with the memory itself, but the affect survives in the unconscious and manifests itself as a symptom. Under hypnosis the experience is relived fully: The affect is unstrangulated, or "abreacted," and the symptom connected with the event disappears. Macmillan (1991) points out that in Anna O.'s case, the abreaction described in the book never took place. Breuer's rediscovered clinical notes showed that Anna got relief from simply remembering events, not reliving them.

In *Studies in Hysteria,* Breuer and Freud began to move away from a purely medical-physiological view of hysteria and toward a psychological view involving unconscious processes. Freud soon found that hypnosis was not the only way to tap unconscious wishes and ideas. Patients could slowly plumb their unconscious during sessions of uninhibited talk guided by the interpretations of the therapist. In 1896, Freud first used the term "psychoanalysis" to describe his new, nonhypnotic technique (Sulloway, 1979). In the same year, Freud's rejection of Breuer began. Breuer the scientist was too cautious for Freud the conquistador. Freud rejected Breuer because

Freud was a hedgehog and Breuer a fox; Freud confided to Fliess on March 1, 1896 (p. 175):

> According to him [Breuer] I should have to ask myself every day whether I am suffering from moral insanity or paranoia scientifica. Yet, I regard myself as the more normal one. I believe that he will never forgive that in the *Studies* I dragged him along and involved him in something where he unfailingly knows three candidates for the position of *one* truth and abhors all generalizations, regarding them as presumptuous.... Will the two of us experience the same thing with each other?

For his part, Breuer agreed: "Freud is a man given to absolute and exclusive formulations; this is a psychical need which, in my opinion, leads to excessive generalization" (quoted by Crews, 1986). Breuer was the first of several friend-collaborators used and then discarded by Freud. Years later, when Breuer was an old man hobbling along the street with his daughter, they saw Freud; Breuer threw his arms out in greeting, but Freud hurried past, giving no sign of recognition (Roazen, 1974). An even more bitter estrangement awaited Wilhelm Fliess.

Changing Conceptions of the Unconscious

Freud spelled out his conception of the unconscious mind in detail in "The Unconscious" (1915b). To counter arguments such as James's, Freud began by justifying his positing of unconscious mind. Part of the dispute over the unconscious seemed to Freud merely verbal: To say that memories are brain traces, not unconscious mental states, simply restates the definition of psychology as the study of consciousness and defines unconscious states out of existence rather than disproving their existence. As Freud saw it, equating mind and consciousness was "inexpedient," primarily because physiological explanations of experience were not available (a likely reason for giving up the "Project") and represented an abandoning of psychology altogether.

Beyond arguing that psychological theorizing in terms of unconscious processes is thus more satisfying than theorizing in terms of physiology, Freud offered two main arguments for the unconscious. The first "incontrovertible proof" was the therapeutic success of psychoanalysis: Only therapy based on true theory can cure. Opponents of the unconscious might have reasoned that cures may be spontaneous, having nothing to do with the physician's treatments as modern studies of psychotherapy have shown. Moreover, critics could continue, even if the therapy works, the theory may not be true, since effective action may be based on wrong theory, as ancient mariners sailed the seas by the principles of Ptolemaic astronomy. Modern critics may challenge the efficacy of psychoanalysis, as we will see later in the chapter.

The second argument in defense of the unconscious is based on the philosophical issue of other minds raised by Descartes. Freud built from Descartes's argument that we infer consciousness in others to the conclusion of an inferred unconscious within us. Freud argued that just as we infer the presence of mind in other people, and perhaps animals, from "observable utterances and actions," so we should in our own individual case as well. "[A]ll the acts and manifestations which I notice in myself must be judged as if they belonged to someone else," another mind within me. Freud acknowledged that this argument "leads logically to the assumption of another, second consciousness" within oneself, but notwithstanding James's espousal of this very hypothesis, Freud thought it unlikely to win approval from psychologists of consciousness. Moreover, Freud asserted, this other consciousness possesses characteristics "which seem alien to us, even incredible," to the point that it is preferable to regard them as possessed not by a second consciousness but by unconscious mental processes (Gay, 1989, p. 576).

Freud proceeded to distinguish several senses of the term "unconscious." We have already recognized a *descriptive* usage on which Freud and psychologists of consciousness agreed—namely, that we are not always fully conscious of the causes of our behavior. Disagreement began with Freud's *topographical* conception of an unconscious mental space—*the* unconscious—where ideas and wishes live when they are not present to consciousness. Freud's scheme is like Nietzsche's: Consciousness is a surface lying over a vast and unknown realm sensed dimly, if at all. In Freud's description of the mind, all mental events begin in the unconscious, where they are tested for acceptability to consciousness. Thoughts that pass the censorship test may become conscious; if they fail, they will not be allowed into consciousness. Applied to perception, this analysis provided the foundation for the important "New Look in Perception" movement of the 1950s. Passing the test of censorship does not directly lead to consciousness but only makes an idea *"capable of becoming conscious."* Ideas that are available to consciousness in this way reside in the *preconscious,* which Freud did not regard as importantly different from consciousness.

More important and psychoanalytically interesting was the fate of ideas or wishes that did not pass muster with the mental censor. These ideas and wishes are often very powerful, constantly seeking expression. Because they are repugnant, however, they must continually be forced to remain unconscious. This *dynamic unconscious* is created by *repression,* the act of actively and forcefully opposing the entrance to consciousness of unacceptable thoughts. When, as is sometimes the case in modern textbooks, the dynamic unconscious is presented as a mental dungeon, its dynamic character is lost, and one of Freud's crucial theses is ignored. Repression is a dynamic act, not a locking-away. Repressed thoughts and wishes live on and, blocked by censorship and repression, find indirect expression in neurotic symptoms, dreams, mental errors, and rechanneling—*sublimation*—into more acceptable forms of thought and behavior.

To the descriptive, topographical, and dynamic usages of the unconscious, Freud added a *systematic* usage. The unconscious is not simply a place in space (topographical use) containing readily available thoughts (the preconscious) and repressed thoughts (the dynamic unconscious). It is also a separate system of mind from consciousness, following its own fantastical principles. In contrast to consciousness, it is exempt from logic, emotionally unstable, lives as much in the past as the present, and is wholly out of touch with external reality.

The systematic conception of the unconscious became increasingly important to Freud and became central to the later restructuring of his picture of the mind (Freud, 1923/1960). The topographical model of the mind as a collection of spaces (conscious, preconscious, dynamic unconscious) was replaced by a *structural* model in which the mind comprised three distinct mental systems: the innate, irrational, and gratification-oriented *id* (the old systematic conception of the unconscious); the learned, rational, reality-oriented *ego* (consciousness plus the preconscious); and the moralistically irrational *superego* (the censor), composed of moral imperatives inherited by Lamarckian evolution. The old dichotomy of consciousness and unconsciousness, Freud said, "begins to lose significance" with the adoption of the systematic viewpoint.

The id represents the biological basis of the mind, the source of all motives, and thus is the ultimate engine of behavior. The desires of the id usually lie hidden behind all that is best and worst in human history, behind tragedy and achievement, war and art, religion and science, health and neurosis, and all of human civilization. The study of the instincts of the id is the heart of Freudian psychoanalysis.

THE INSTINCTS

Freud took a narrow view of animal and human motivation, believing that animals had only a few instincts, and that humans had none they did not share with the animals. In the original formulation of psychoanalysis, the most important instinct by far was sex. After World War I, it was joined, in Freud's estimation, by death.

In his time and our own, Freud is best known—even notorious—for tracing every symptom, every dream, every apparently noble act back to sex. Some of Freud's readers have always regarded psychoanalysis as a sewer, and psychoanalytic writings as "pornography gone to seed" (Cioffi, 1973). Others found Freud's explicit treatment of sexuality refreshing in an antisexual age and an important recognition of a major human drive. The founder of behaviorism, John B. Watson, had no use for Freud's hypothesized mental apparatus, but he applauded Freud's attention to the biological side of the mind so neglected by traditional psychologists of consciousness. It should be remembered, however, that Freud, while sometimes shocking, was not a lone voice in a sexually repressive wilderness. Just as he did not invent the concept of the unconscious, so he was not the only thinker to draw attention to sexuality and attack sexual hypocrisy. In Britain, for example, the path of sexual openness was blazed by Havelock Ellis (1859–1939), whose works were sometimes banned but always read. In Germany, Richard von Krafft-Ebing may have branded one of Freud's early ideas a "fairytale," but his *Psychopathia Sexualis* was a best-selling compendium of abnormal sexual practices whose decorous use of Latin was transparent to his educated readers. Nevertheless, although Ellis and Krafft-Ebing may have prophesied its coming, ours is truly a post-*Freudian* age, because it was Freud who not only brought sex into the open but also built upon it a theory of human nature.

Issue: Why Sex? Historical Factors

Freud came to find in sex the main motive in human life for several reasons. As we have seen, sex furnished an organic basis for neurosis and a universal biological basis for his theoretical psychology. Another reason was his "discovery" of childhood sexuality as the root cause of neuroses (see later discussion). A third is found in social history: Men and women of Freud's day really did find sexuality hard to cope with.

Freud and other physicians found themselves presented with problems rooted in the nineteenth century's struggles with sexuality. The cause of the problem is straightforward. As societies develop economically, they experience an important demographic transition from large families to small ones. In rural and village societies, children are economic resources, hands to be put to work as soon as possible and the main support for parents in their old age. In industrially developed societies, children turn into economic liabilities. Costly to raise and educate before they can join the work force, they become drains on parents' income. As standards of living rise, children become increasingly less attractive economically, and parents begin to have fewer children.

It was the middle classes of Victorian Europe who most acutely felt the problem of controlling reproduction without modern contraceptives. To succeed economically, they had to work hard and exert enormous self-control, including control of potentially costly reproduction. They looked on the large families of rural and laboring classes, for whom children were still exploitable resources, with a mixture of horror and sometimes salacious envy. The middle class was horrified by the squalor and misery of lower-class lives, but envious of their sexual freedom. Poet George Meredith expressed both attitudes: "You burly lovers on the village green/Yours is a lower and a happier star!" (quoted by Gay, 1986). Freud, too, saw greater sexual happiness among the poor without wishing to join them. Describing for a lecture audience two imagined case histories, he said, "sexual activity appeared to the caretaker's daughter just as natural and unproblematic in later life as it had in childhood" and is "free from neurosis," while the landlord's daughter "experienced the impact of education and acknowledged its claims," turned from sex with "distaste," and became neurotic (quoted by Gay, 1986). Yet Freud, like most educated and agnostic or atheistic Victorians, continued to live on nerve, never prescribing sex. He wrote to his fiancée, Martha Bernays (August 29, 1883; Freud, 1960, letter 18; p. 50): "The rabble live without constraint while we deprive ourselves." We bourgeois do so "to maintain our integrity.... We keep ourselves for something, we know not what, and this habit of constantly suppressing our natural drives gives us the character of refinement" (quoted by Gay, 1986, p. 400).

There is abundant evidence that the struggle for integrity by the middle classes—from which Freud drew most of his patients—was intense and was fought in an environment that we today would find shocking.

> Where should we find that reverence for the female sex, that tenderness towards their feelings, that deep devotion of the heart to them, which is the beautiful and purifying part of love? Is it not certain that all of the delicate, the chivalric which still pervades our sentiments, may be traced to the *repressed,* and therefore hallowed and elevated passion?

So wrote W. R. Greg in 1850 (quoted by Houghton, 1957, p. 380). The Victorians did not accept the animal part of their nature, whether sexual or simply sensual. Wrote the anonymous author of an antismoking pamphlet: "Smoking ... is liked because it gives agreeable sensations. Now it is a positive objection to a thing that it gives agreeable sensations. An earnest man will expressly avoid what gives agreeable sensations" (Houghton, 1957, p. 236). (Earnestness was a cardinal virtue to Victorians.) Victorian culture and religion thundered against pleasure, especially sexual pleasure, and Victorians were burdened by an oppressive sense of guilt. Like a medieval saint, British Liberal Prime Minister William Gladstone recorded his least sin and grieved over it. Guilt was heightened by constant temptation. Prostitution was rampant; men and women, boys and girls—all could be had for a price. The anonymous author of *My Secret Life,* a sexual autobiography, claimed to have seduced over two thousand people of all ages and sexual orientations and engaged in every vice. Boys at the finest private schools were sexually abused. The Victorians were caught between stern conscience and compelling temptation.

Freud (1912/1953) named as the most common cause of impotence the inability of men to love where they lusted and lust where they loved, and not only because sleeping with one's wife might beget children. Physicians often taught, and men came to believe, that women, at least middle-class women, had no sexual feelings, and men felt guilty about thrusting brutish sexuality on their wives, resulting in impotence at worst and greatly inhibited sex at best. Men could fully lust after prostitutes, but these women were degraded by their very sexuality, made unworthy of love. Middle-class women, for their part, were trapped and inhibited by being idealized and idolized. Writing to his fiancée on November 15, 1883, Freud (1960, letter 28, p. 76) wrote against feminism: "Am I to think of my delicate, sweet girl as a competitor? ... Women's delicate natures ... are so much in need of protection. [Emancipation would take away] the most lovely thing the world has to offer us: our ideal of womanhood." Perhaps Freud was typical of many men of his day. On October 3, 1897, at age 41, Freud wrote Fliess, "Sexual excitement, too, is no longer of use for someone like me." From about 1900, the year *Interpretation of Dreams* came out, Freud ceased having sex with his wife (Decker, 1981), but there is little evidence he took up with anyone else (Gay, 1988).

Notwithstanding, or perhaps because of, his own situation, Freud sided with the movement of sexual reform led by people such as Havelock Ellis. In 1905, Freud gave a deposition before a commission looking into liberalization of Austria's laws on marriage and sexuality. Freud testified in favor of "...legalization of relations between the sexes outside of marriage, according a greater measure of sexual freedom and curtailing restrictions on that freedom" (Boyer, 1978, p. 100, original German; p. 92, English translation). Ten years later, Freud repeated this sentiment in a letter to one of his leading American supporters, the neurologist J. J. Putnam: "Sexual morality—as society, in its most extreme form, the American, defines it—seems to me very contemptible. I advocate an incomparably freer sexual life" (quoted by Gay, 1988, p. 143). In "'Civilized' sexual morality and modern nervousness" (1908/1953), Freud paints a devastating portrait of the effects of civilized marriage. Men become impotent, as we've seen, or "undesirably immoral" by finding sex outside marriage, but women, suffering from a double standard, are made ill.

> [Can] sexual intercourse in legitimate marriage offer full compensation for the restraint before marriage[?] The abundance of material supporting a reply in the negative is ... overwhelming. We must above all keep in mind that our civilized sexual morality restricts sexual intercourse in marriage itself.... and all the contraceptives available hitherto impair sexual enjoyment.... [The "physical tenderness" and "mental affection" between husband and wife disappear] and under the disappointments of matrimony women succumb to severe, lifelong neurosis.... Marital unfaithfulness would ... be a ... probable cure for the neurosis resulting from marriage.... [But] the more earnestly [a wife] has submitted to the demands of civilization, the more does she fear this way of escape, and in conflict between her desires and her sense of duty she again will seek refuge in neurosis. Nothing protects her virtue so securely as illness. (pp. 89–90)

Freud the clinician found sex at the root of his patients' problems because at that time and place sex had a hard time fitting in with people's economic and moral aspirations. If Freud's emphasis on sexuality sometimes seems outrageously alien and implausible, it may be because the sexual reforms he championed (but did not gain from) came about and because technology improved contraception. Sex is still a problem for us, but not in the way it was for Freud's civilized sufferers.

Issue: Why Sex? The "Discovery" of Childhood Sexuality

It was not just sexuality that Freud claimed to find at the root of neuroses, but *childhood* sexuality. If many of Freud's contemporaries found his emphasis on sex shocking, many more found shocking his postulation of childhood sexuality. Asserting the existence of sexual feelings in childhood was central to the psychoanalytic strategy for explaining human behavior. For without childhood sexual drives there could be no Oedipus complex, whose happy or unhappy resolution held the key to later normality or neurosis. Childhood sexuality and the Oedipus complex are also crucial to the whole idea of depth psychology. Freud located the causes of neurosis—and, by implication, happiness—entirely in the minds of his patients. Their personal situations were not the ultimate cause of sufferer's problems, Freud said. The feelings they had had as children were. Consequently, therapy consisted of adjusting a patient's inner life, not changing the circumstances in which she or he lived. Health would come when one resolved the difficulties one had when one was five years old, not the difficulties one faced today.

The central episode in the history of psychoanalysis is the abandonment of Freud's seduction theory of hysteria—in which he asserted that hysteria was caused by childhood sexual seductions—and its replacement by the Oedipus complex. In recent years, especially following the publication of the complete and unexpurgated letters of Freud to Fliess, the seduction mistake has occupied center stage in Freud scholarship, and the ensuing controversies have generated at times more heat than light. I will first recount the "Official Story": Freud's own account of the seduction mistake, the account followed by loyal Freudians unto the present day, and then present several alternative accounts of the same events.

We begin with the Official Story. As he was writing the "Project," Freud was equally excited by making apparent progress on the cause and cure of hysteria. Writing to Fliess on October 15, 1895, "in the throes of writing fever," he asked, "Have I revealed the great clinical secret to you …? Hysteria is the consequence of a presexual *sexual shock*" The shock is "… later transformed into [self-] *reproach*" hidden in the unconscious, "effective only as *memories*" (p. 144). Five days later Freud exclaimed, "Other confirmations concerning the neuroses are pouring in on me. The thing is really true and genuine" (p. 147). On October 31, he told Fliess that "I perpetrated three lectures on hysteria in which I was very imprudent. I am now inclined to be arrogant" (p. 148).

So, in April 1896, Freud delivered the paper that Krafft-Ebing (1840–1902) called a "scientific fairytale," containing his seduction theory of hysteria. As we have seen, in *Studies in Hysteria,* Freud and Breuer had proposed that the kernel of every hysterical symptom is a repressed traumatic event. Freud now claimed, based on the psychoanalytic recollections of his patients, that there was a single traumatic event at the heart of hysteria: seduction of sexually innocent children by their fathers. Krafft-Ebing and the other "donkeys" of the medical establishment hooted at the theory for being a reversion to the prescientific conceptions of hysteria they had worked so hard to escape.

However, Freud's enthusiasm for the seduction theory turned to ashes. On September 21, 1897, Freud confessed to his friend Fliess that perhaps the seduction theory was a fairy tale after all: "I want to confide in you immediately the great secret that has been slowly dawning on me in the last few months. I no longer believe my *neurotica* [theory of the neuroses]." The stories of seduction told by his patients were untrue; they had not been seduced after all. Freud advanced four reasons for giving up the seduction theory. The first was therapeutic failure: "disappointment in my efforts to bring a single analysis to a real conclusion; the running away [of previously successful patients]; the absence of the complete successes on which I had counted." The second was "the surprise that in all cases, the *father,* not excluding my own, had to be accused of being perverse" when "surely such widespread perversions are not very probable." Third, there was "the certain insight that there are no indications of reality in the unconscious, so that one cannot distinguish between truth and [emotionally believed] fiction.... (Accordingly there would remain the solution that the sexual fantasy invariably seizes upon the theme of the parents)." Fourth and finally, such stories are not found in delirium, when all mental defenses break down. Freud was so shaken that "I was ready to give up two things: the complete resolution of neurosis and the certain knowledge of its etiology in childhood." Nevertheless, the conquistador felt no sense of "weakness" or "shame." Instead, Freud wrote: "I have more the feeling of a victory than a defeat" and hoped that "this doubt merely represents an episode in the advance toward further insight.... In spite of all this I am in very good spirits" (pp. 264–66).

It is at this point that Freud's self-analysis plays its dramatic role in the tale of psychoanalysis. The critical revelation, the discovery of his own childhood sexuality, is reported by Freud to Fliess on October 3, 1897. Freud claimed to have remembered an event on a train trip when he was 2½ years old: "[M]y libido towards *matrem* was awakened ... we must have spent the night together and there must have been an opportunity of seeing her *nudam* (p. 268)." On October 15, Freud announces, "My self analysis is the most essential thing I have at present and promises to become of the greatest value to me if it reaches its end" (p. 270). Further, he declared his own experience to be universal. In his "own case," Freud had learned of "being in love with my mother and jealous of my father, and I now consider it a universal event in early childhood" (p. 272). Now, Freud concluded, we can understand the power of *Oedipus Rex* and *Hamlet.* As he suggested in his letter to Fliess, Freud now regarded the seduction stories as Oedipal fantasies from childhood falsely recalled as memories. This resolution allowed Freud to retain his treasured view that neuroses result from the unconscious reawakening of childhood events. In the old theory, the events were real childhood sexual seductions; in the new theory, the events were real childhood sexual fantasies.

In this way, the Official Story concludes, Freud heroically discovered the existence of childhood sexuality and the Oedipus complex by giving up his old theory and constructing the new out of his own unsparingly honest self-interrogation. Before evaluating the Official Story, it is important to observe how much is at stake: the very foundations of psychoanalysis. Anna Freud, daughter and loyal disciple, wrote to Jeffrey Masson, controversial critic of the seduction episode: "Keeping up the seduction theory would mean to abandon the Oedipus complex, and with it the whole importance of phantasy life, conscious or unconscious phantasy. In fact, I think there would have been no psychoanalysis afterwards" (quoted by Masson, 1984a, p. 59).

Every claim of the Official Story has been disputed, often bitterly, by Freud's critics, and important Unofficial Stories abound. I shall discuss three. One is Sulloway's (1979) contention that the Official Story has served to obscure the influence of Fliess on Freud, and that Freud's insistence on having heroically "discovered" childhood sexuality all by himself led to the breakup of their deep friendship. Fliess is, in retrospect, a man with odd ideas from which later psychoanalysis wanted to distance itself. He believed in a theory of biorhythms, based on twenty-three–day male and twenty-eight–day female cycles whose combination in complex permutations could explain events such as births and deaths. Freud for a time believed Fliess's theory wholeheartedly; his letters to Fliess often contain calculations concerning himself, and calculations concerning the birth of Anna (under a pseudonym) were used in a publication by Fliess. Fliess believed that the nose plays an important role in the regulation of human sexual life, and that surgery on the nose could cure sexual problems like masturbation. Freud himself submitted at least once to Fliess's knife. While Fliess may appear today to be a quack and a pseudoscientist, Sulloway has shown that his ideas were perfectly respectable in their own time.

The critical issue for understanding the development of psychoanalysis is Fliess's influence on Freud's thinking after the abandonment of the "Project." Sulloway argues that in the aftermath of the failure of the "Project," Freud adopted almost *in toto* Fliess's theories of sexuality and human development, while systematically concealing that he had done so. In Sulloway's account, Fliess conceived of the id and Freud took it over without acknowledgment. Fliess's influence on Freud was so thoroughgoing that it cannot be briefly summarized, but in the present context, the most important borrowing is the concept of childhood sexuality. Fliess campaigned for the view that children had sexual feelings, advancing, for example, observations of his own children in support. Moreover, Fliess believed in the innate bisexuality of human beings, an important component of the biorhythm theory, and later a central thesis in the psychoanalytic theory of libidinal development. At what proved to be their last personal meeting, Freud boasted of his discovery of the innate childhood bisexual nature of human beings, and Fliess tried to remind him who had the idea first. Freud persisted in claiming personal credit for the discovery, and Fliess, fearing his ideas were being stolen, withdrew from the relationship. The Official Story of Freud the hero claims Freud was little influenced by Fliess and himself withdrew from the relationship when he saw through Fliess's crazy ideas.

The second Alternative Story is Frank Cioffi's (1972, 1974, 1984). Cioffi is one of Freud's most trenchant critics, and here he focuses on why Freud was told the stories of seduction in the first place. Freud was correct, Cioffi says, to disbelieve them, but in order to protect the scientific validity of the psychoanalytic method, he adopted the implausible and wrong-headed theory of childhood sexual fantasies. It must be remembered that Freud looked with disdain on experimental verifications of psychoanalysis and held out the products of analysis as furnishing proof of psychoanalysis. However, from Freud's time to our own, critics have found doubtful the validity of therapy as a tool of scientific investigation. Patients are ill; they are motivated to get well; they will therefore eagerly seize therapists' suggestions as revealing causes and providing cures of their miserable plight. Most to the point, patients want to please their therapists and are apt to tell them what they want to hear.

Students of psychoanalysis have demonstrated that from early on Freud believed in sexual causes of neurotic disorders. It has also been shown that while Freud's later therapeutic technique may have been nondirective and noninterpretive, as is the current ideal, in his early cases, Freud was highly directive and interpretive, showering his patients with sexual interpretations of their condition, and wearing them down until they agreed with his view of their behavior (Rieff, 1979; Crews, 1986; Decker, 1991). As befits a conquistador, Freud was supremely confident of his ability to discern secrets hidden even from a patient's own consciousness: "[N]o mortal can keep a secret. If his lips are silent, he chatters with his fingertips; betrayal oozes out of him at every pore" (Freud, 1905b). Freud wrote of finding facts that "I did not hesitate to use against her" (the patient Dora; Freud, 1905b). Before conquering the world, Freud first conquered his patients.

Freud enjoyed forcing his patients to accept what he, Freud, regarded as the truth, and every resistance he interpreted as a sign that he was getting near a great secret. Given Freud's therapeutic technique, then, if he were on the path of childhood sexuality, as Cioffi says he was, surely his patients would produce stories to support it. Cioffi claims that Freud's patients invented the stories of their seductions in order to placate their conqueror, who was, no doubt, pleased to find verification of his hypotheses. It is no wonder his patients ran away.

Cioffi argues that at some point Freud came to believe that the seduction stories were false, and he was put in the position of explaining how that could be so while at the same time maintaining psychoanalytic therapy as a means for revealing scientific truth. He did so, Cioffi avers, by inventing the Oedipus complex and childhood sexuality. In the new formulation, the seduction stories are admitted to be false about patient's outer lives as children but wonderfully revealing about their inner lives, their sexual fantasies about mother or father. Psychoanalysis became a doctrine concerned only with the inner life of human beings, and psychoanalytic method was said to reveal that inner life even to the earliest days of childhood. If Cioffi is right, then even if Freudian ideas are correct, they must be tested by some other means than psychoanalytic therapy.

The last and most flamboyantly controversial student of the seduction episode is Jeffrey Moussaieff Masson (1984a,b), who says Freud was right to begin with: His patients suffered from sexual abuse. Today we have become increasingly aware of the extent of sexual abuse of children, and Masson argues that Freud discovered the reality of child abuse and then walked away from it, constructing a theory that not only denied the existence of seductions but provided a means for disbelieving children when they complained of abuse. Masson alleges two motives for Freud's abandoning the seduction theory. The first was a desire to curry favor with the medical establishment by agreeing that the seduction theory was the fairy tale they had pronounced it to be in 1896.

The second motive involves a dramatic episode deleted from the official publication of the Freud-Fliess letters (Masson, 1984a,b). Freud had a patient named Emma Eckstein, who suffered from stomach pains and menstrual irregularities. We have already seen that Freud regarded masturbation as pathogenic, and he apparently agreed with Fliess that masturbation caused menstrual problems. Moreover, Fliess taught that nasal surgery could eliminate masturbation and hence the problems it caused. Freud brought Fliess to Vienna to perform surgery on Emma Eckstein's nose. The operation may have been Fliess's first; in any event, postoperative recovery did not go well. Eckstein suffered pain, bleeding, and discharge of pus. Freud eventually called in a Viennese doctor, who removed from Eckstein's nose a half meter of gauze that had been incompetently left behind by Fliess. At this point, Eckstein hemorrhaged, turned pale, and very nearly died. Freud was so shattered by the sight of Emma Eckstein seemingly dying that he fled, revived by brandy brought by the doctor's wife.

Remarkably, I think, Eckstein stayed in therapy with Freud. She continued to suffer pain and occasional, sometimes violent, bleeding from the nose. For Masson, the critical moments in the story concern Freud's attitude to Eckstein's suffering. Following Fliess's operation, Freud came to regard her nasal problems as hysterical symptoms. The dramatic events following the removal of the gauze made Freud admit otherwise. He wrote to Fliess "So we had done her an injustice; she was not abnormal" but suffered from Fliess's mistake, and, by extension, Freud's mistake in subjecting her to Fliess.

Masson shows that Freud returned to his psychological interpretation of Eckstein's bleeding. Just over a year after her brush with death, on June 4, 1896, Freud wrote that Eckstein's continued bleeding was "due to wishes." In this way, Masson says, Freud absolved both Fliess and himself of guilt. They had not by bungled surgery nearly killed Emma Eckstein, her hysterical wishes had. Having let himself off the hook about Eckstein, Freud was "free to abandon the seduction hypothesis" (Masson, 1984a). In both cases, Freud moved from locating the causes of hysterical symptoms in real events to locating them in the unconscious wishes.

Even Freud's most outspoken detractors have found Masson's arguments as tendentious as Freud's own (Cioffi, 1984; Crews, 1986). Masson claims that Freud gave up the seduction theory in order to regain the favor of the "donkeys" of established medicine who called it a fairy tale, but the even more complex theory of childhood sexual fantasies seems ill-calculated to recoup his standing. Moreover, Freud's problem was not to explain why his patients were miserable, but why they were hysterical. By extensively canvassing the evidence for child abuse in the nineteenth century, Masson himself shows that Freud should have been aware of the extent of child abuse and should have believed his patients' stories. However, most child abuse then and now is not sexual. As Cioffi (1984 p. 743) writes: "Children [in the analytic view] may be starved, beaten, or tortured but providing they have not simultaneously been sexually stimulated the experience can have no neurotic aftermath." Thus psychoanalysts could concede that child abuse is a genuine problem yet deny that it has anything to do with the etiology of the neuroses with which they were concerned.

While Masson's criticisms of Freud's abandonment of the seduction theory are flawed, they may be regarded as part of a broader critique, often made by psychoanalysts themselves, of Freud as insensitive—sometimes brutally so—to the life problems faced by his patients (Decker, 1981, 1991; Holt, 1982; Klein and Tribich, 1982). As Freud constructed his depth psychology, he came to locate the causes of neurosis entirely in his patients' fantasies, blinding himself to how people can suffer from circumstances.

The most important document in this indictment of Freud is "Fragment of an Analysis of a Case of Hysteria" (1905b), describing Freud's admittedly unsuccessful treatment of an eighteen-year-old woman known as "Dora" (Ida Bauer). Shortly after the publication of *Interpretation of Dreams,* Dora was brought in for therapy by her father, a successful businessman and former patient of Freud's. Dora was suffering from symptoms Freud thought were neurotic, primarily shortness of breath and a cough. As therapeutic sessions proceeded day by day (Freud saw his patients six days a week), Freud discovered that Dora came from a family whose tangled intrigues would do justice to a soap opera today. Dora's father's real reason for seeking Dora's treatment was to make her less unhappy about his affair with Frau K. The K.'s were close friends of the Bauers, seeing each other regularly and vacationing together; it was on a vacation that Dora deduced the affair from her father's rearranging hotel rooms in order to have convenient access to Frau K. Dora's mother suffered, Freud opined, from "housewife's psychosis"—obsessive neatness—and had long since ceased having sexual relations with her husband. Dora objected most of all to the advances of Herr K.—whose wife had stopped sleeping with *him*—who had twice attempted to force himself on her, the first attempt coming when Dora was thirteen. Herr K. arranged to be alone in his place of business with Dora ostensibly to watch a parade, but he suddenly grabbed her, pressed himself against her, and kissed her. Dora fled in disgust, tried to avoid Herr K., but nevertheless had to turn down a proposition from him two years later.

Freud's (1905b) reaction to the scene is remarkable: "This was surely just the situation to call up a distinct feeling of sexual excitement in a girl of fourteen [Freud miscalculated the age; Decker, 1991, p. 124] who had never before been approached.... [T]he behavior of this child of fourteen was already entirely and completely hysterical. I should without question consider a person hysterical in whom an occasion for sexual excitement elicited feelings that were preponderantly or exclusively unpleasurable.... Instead of the genital sensation which would certainly have been felt by a healthy girl in such circumstances, Dora was overcome by the unpleasurable feeling" of disgust. Freud was especially puzzled since "I happen to know Herr K."—he came with Dora and Dora's father to Freud's office—"and he was still quite young and of prepossessing appearance" (Gay, 1989, p. 184). At this point in his career, Freud was an aggressive therapist, and he quickly used against Dora every interpretation he could. Playing with her purse during therapy represented desire to masturbate; her cough represented hidden thoughts of Frau K. performing fellatio on her father and, therefore, Dora's secret wish to do the same. Unsurprisingly, Dora was a patient who ran away. Freud ascribed his therapeutic failure to unanalyzed transference: Dora had transferred her sexual desires from Herr K., whom Freud was certain Dora secretly desired, to himself, and he had not taken due notice of it at the time. Freud said nothing about possible countertransference—from a middle-aged man no longer sleeping with his wife—to Dora, an attractive adolescent girl (Decker, 1981, 1991).

In Dora's case, we find Freud pushing all responsibility for hysteria onto his patient. Dora should have been sexually excited by Herr K.'s attentions; the disgust she felt was a symptom of her hysteria, not the cause of her distaste for the handsome Herr K. In 1895, when Freud still believed in the seduction theory, Freud had treated another young woman upon whom sexual advances had been made, and he wrote of "the horror by which a virginal mind is overcome when it is faced for the first time with the world of sexuality" (quoted by Decker, 1991). In sum, the Dora case is typical of Freud's dismissal of family dynamics and other current influences on patient's troubles. Depth psychology imputed to the unconscious full sovereignty over mental health and mental illness, making patients solely responsible for their health.

Changing Conceptions of the Instincts

By 1905, when he wrote *Three Essays on the Theory of Sexuality,* Freud had concluded that whether or not one became healthy, neurotic, or sexually "perverse" depended on childhood sexual thoughts, and most importantly on the resolution of the Oedipus complex. Central to his concept of the dynamic unconscious, which contained the wishes lying behind symptoms, dreams, and slips of the tongue, was repression. Yet since repression was a continuing act of denying unacceptable sexual wishes access to consciousness, there remained a problem of explaining the source of the mental energy used to carry out repression of libido. Freud (1915a) proposed as a "working hypothesis" that there exist two groups of "primal instincts": "the *ego* or *self-preservative*, instincts and the *sexual* instincts." The ego uses its ego-instinct energy to defend itself from—that is, repress—wishes driven by the sexual instincts. With this formulation, the mind as depicted by psychoanalysis became an arena of struggle, the compromised results of which were conscious thoughts and behavior.

Freud did not remain satisfied with his working hypothesis. In 1920, he published *Beyond the Pleasure Principle,* the first of two major revisions of his theory, culminating in the structural model of personality in *The Ego and the Id.* Perhaps because of his own suffering from intractable cancer of the jaw—he endured numerous operations and had to painfully replace a prosthesis in his jaw every day—and perhaps because of the carnage of World War I, Freud became increasingly pessimistic. In *Beyond the Pleasure Principle,* Freud proposed that *"The aim of all life is death."* Freud here gave psychoanalytic expression to an older truth, that we are born in order to die. In a sermon from 1630, John Donne had said, "Wee have a winding sheet in our Mother's wombe, which grows with us from our conception, and wee come into the world, wound up in that *winding sheet*, for we come *to seek a grave*" (quoted by Macmillan, 1991, p. 429).

Freud's argument is based on his conceptions of instincts as drives and behavior as motivated by drive reduction. Unsatisfied instincts give rise to states of arousal which the organism seeks to reduce by engaging in behavior that satisfies the instinct. Satisfaction is only temporary, of course, so in time the instinct must be gratified anew, causing a cyclical process of arousal and satisfaction Freud called the *repetition compulsion*. It appears, then, that the optimum state sought by every living thing is complete oblivion—freedom from arousal. The wheel of the repetition compulsion is broken by death, when the aim of living—tension reduction—is permanently reached. There lies within us, Freud concluded, a drive toward death along with drives toward life. The ego-instincts preserve the life of the individual, and the sexual instincts preserve the life of the species, so Freud bundled them together as the life instincts, named *Eros,* after the Greek word for love. Opposed to the life instincts is the death instinct, or *Thanatos*, Greek for death. Eros and Thanatos are mutually repressing. Thanatos provides the energy by which the ego, at the behest of the moralizing superego, represses sexual wishes, and Eros provides the energy to repress the death instinct from immediately fulfilling its lethal wish.

Postulation of the death wish provided a new solution for the problem of aggression. In Freud's earlier theory, aggressive acts were deemed to occur out of frustrated ego or sexual needs. Thus animals fought out of self-defense or over food, water, territory, or reproductive opportunities. In the new theory, aggression was an autonomous drive in itself. Just as sexual instincts could be rechanneled from their proper biological object, so too could the death instinct be redirected away from bringing about the death of the organism. Eros could for a time repress Thanatos's suicidal aggression, but the necessary result was aggression displaced onto others. Freud's new theory did not win universal acclaim among later analysts, many of whom preferred to accept Freud's earlier, less pessimistic, view of human nature, but both theories of aggression appear in later nonpsychoanalytic psychology. The first conception of aggression as caused by frustration surfaced in social learning theory's *frustration-aggression* hypothesis (Dollard et al., 1939), while the second conception of aggression as a necessary part of nature was reasserted by the ethologists, who stressed the adaptive value of an aggressive drive (Lorenz, 1966), if not a suicide drive.

THREE MASTERPIECES

In order to convey the flavor of Freud's arguments, I will discuss three of his works that are generally reckoned to be his most important and influential. The first two, *The Interpretation of Dreams,* and *Three Essays on the Theory of Sexuality,* were the only books Freud continued to revise as psychoanalysis developed; thus they constitute the defining documents of psychoanalysis. The third work, *Civilization and Its Discontents,* written late in Freud's life, represented the summing up of a lifetime's work and proved to be the most widely influential of Freud's books (Gay, 1989). In it, Freud took up the Enlightenment problem of reconciling human happiness with the advance of civilization, reaching a deeply pessimistic Hobbesian conclusion.

The Interpretation of Dreams (1900)

Of all his works, Freud himself believed *The Interpretation of Dreams* to be his greatest. In a letter to Fliess (Freud 1960), he hoped that a plaque would be erected someday saying, "In this House on July 24, 1895, the Secret of Dreams was revealed to Dr. Sigmund Freud." The insight Freud valued so highly was that a dream is not the meaningless collection of images it appears to be, but is "the royal road to the unconscious": a clue to the innermost recesses of the personality. That dreams have meaning was not a new idea, as Freud acknowledged, but it was out of step with the received academic opinion of his times. Most thinkers, including Wundt, assigned little importance to dreams, believing them to be only confused nighttime versions of waking mental processes. Freud sided instead with supposedly disreputable philosophers and ancient religions in valuing dreams as symbolic statements of a reality unavailable to waking experience.

Freud's basic idea is simple, but its details and ramifications are complex and far-ranging: All of us, whether neurotic or not, carry within us desires that we cannot accept consciously. In fact, we deliberately keep these desires unconscious, or *repress* them. Nevertheless, they remain active, precisely because they are repressed and not subject to conscious scrutiny and memory-decay. They constantly press for access to awareness, and hence the control of behavior. In our waking life, our *ego,* or conscious self, represses these wishes; but during sleep, consciousness lapses and repression weakens. If our repressed desires ever completely eluded repression, we would awaken and reassert control. Dreaming is a compromise that protects sleep, for dreams are hallucinatory, disguised expressions of repressed ideas. They give partial satisfaction of unacceptable wishes, but in such a way that consciousness and sleep are rarely disturbed.

Freud summarized his view by saying that every dream is a *wish-fulfillment*—that is, a disguised expression (fulfillment) of some unconscious desire, or wish. It is this characteristic of dreams that makes them the royal road to the unconscious: If we can decipher a dream and retrieve its hidden meaning, we will have recovered a piece of our unconscious mental life and be able to subject it to the light of reason. Dreams and hysteria thus have the same origin, for both are symbolic representations of unconscious needs, and both can be understood by tracing them back to their sources. The existence of dreams shows that no sharp line can be drawn between neurotic and normal mental lives. All individuals have needs of which they are unaware and whose realization they would find disturbing. In neurotics, however, the usual means of defense have broken down, and symptoms have taken their place.

The method of decoding is also the same in both hysteria and dreams—the method of free association. Just as hysterical patients were asked to freely talk about their symptoms, so we may understand dreams by free-associating to each element of the dream. Freud's assumption was that free association would reverse the process that produced the dream and bring one at last to the unconscious idea embodied in it. In both symptom analysis and dream analysis, the goal is the same: to reach rational self-understanding of the irrational unconscious, a step toward mental health.

Freud introduced technical terms as part of his theory of dreams. The actually experienced dream he called the *manifest content* of the dream. The true meaning of the dream, the repressed unconscious desires symbolized by the dream, he called the *latent content.* The process of transformation of latent to manifest content is the *dream work,* performed because of the demands of the *endopsychic censor,* which is the psychic agency that refuses direct expression to anxiety-producing desires.

The last chapter of *The Interpretation of Dreams* is a theoretical account of dream production, which appears to be an informal mentalistic version of parts of the "Project." Freud pictured the mind as a complex structure comprising several independent but related systems. Closest to the world is the *perceptual system* that receives impressions from the environment and conveys them inward, where they leave behind a series of memory-traces. At the other end of this chain of reflexes (for Freud said that all mental processes are ultimately reflexes) is the *motor system,* which produces overt behavior. The motor system is governed by the *preconscious* and its rational *secondary-process* thought, which guides realistic action. In the deepest level of the mind resides the *unconscious,* the home of repressed wishes and of the irrational *primary process.* Freud located consciousness in two places. One was the preconscious, for part of it is at any time conscious since it contains only rational and acceptable chains of thought. Consciousness is then the ultimate governor of behavior. We are also conscious of what we perceive, so consciousness is also found in the perceptual system. In the normal course of events, sensations enter the perceptual system, lay down memory-traces, and eventually progress to the preconscious, where they may be acted on in the conduct of behavior.

Dreams, however, are regressive. Unacceptable wishes, which live forever in the unconscious, seek expression but are blocked by repression during the waking hours. This control weakens during sleep, and the impulses gain strength. Sleep, however, blocks all motor activity, so these impulses cannot become behavior. Instead, they move toward the perceptual system, where they can find hallucinatory fulfillment as mock-perceptions distorted to preserve sleep.

In *The Interpretation of Dreams,* Freud quietly introduced his most famous, or infamous, concept: the *Oedipus complex.* Freud described a kind of "typical dream," which expresses infantile wishes regarding one's parents. These wishes are repressed and persist in the unconscious to later provide latent content for dreams. This infantile complex of wishes is made up of the child's sexual desire for the cross-sex parent and of the child's consequent desire that the same-sex parent, the child's rival, be eliminated. This set of feelings Freud considered universal, and named it the Oedipus complex after the mythical Greek king who unwittingly killed his father and married his mother.

It was said earlier that Freud revised *The Interpretation of Dreams* as his system evolved. The major change was in the means by which dreams may be decoded. In the early editions of the book, the only method was free association; but because of the work of a follower, Wilhelm Stekel, Freud came to believe that dreams could also be interpreted according to a more or less uniform set of symbols. That is, in most cases, certain objects or experiences could be shown to stand for the same unconscious ideas in everyone's dreams. So, for example, walking up a flight of stairs symbolizes sexual intercourse, a suitcase stands for the vagina, and a hat for the penis.

Such an approach, of course, simplified the process of dream interpretation. It also made possible a wider application of Freud's insight—namely, the interpretation of myths, legends, and works of art. Freud had already engaged in such an analysis in the early versions of the work, treating Sophocles' *Oedipus Rex* and Shakespeare's *Hamlet* as Oedipal stories, and he and other psychoanalysts would go on to do many such analyses. Psychoanalysis was never limited to a mere psychotherapy, but it was increasingly used as a general tool for understanding all of human culture. Myth, legend, and religion were seen as disguised expressions of hidden cultural conflicts; art was seen as the expression of the artist's personal conflicts—all share the same mechanism with dreams. The symbol system helped justify and make possible this extension of psychoanalysis. We cannot put Sophocles, Shakespeare, or a whole culture on the analytic couch and ask them to free-associate, but we can search their products for universal clues to the universal human unconscious.

The Interpretation of Dreams was more than an analysis of dreams as expressions of repressed wishes and thoughts, because it provided Freud with his general model of the mind as a multilayered system in which the unconscious shapes thought and behavior according to a peculiar set of rules (Sulloway, 1979). Moreover, the dream theory provided the foundation for the unmasking function of psychoanalysis so important to its hermeneutical employment by later social and literary critics. For according to psychoanalysis, dreams—and by extension neurotic symptoms, slips of the tongue, and indeed all behavior—are never what they appear to be. They all are caused by motives of which we are unaware because we find them reprehensible, and they serve by hiding us from unpleasant mental realities. In the hands of the literary critic, psychoanalysis could be used to show that works of art are never what they seem, expressing, yet hiding, the artist's—and, if the work was popular or controversial, the audience's—deepest needs and conflicts. To social critics, psychoanalysis suggested that social practices, institutions, and values existed to enforce and at the same time hide rule by reprehensible value systems (usually capitalism) and reprehensible elites (usually white males). In therapy, art, and politics, the psychoanalytic line of argument placed the therapist and critic in a privileged position, beyond the subterfuges of the unconscious, uniquely capable of revealing the truth to deluded clients, audiences, and citizens.

Throughout *The Interpretation of Dreams,* Freud made it clear that all the repressed wishes that we find in dreams have an infantile character, as in the Oedipus complex. It is during childhood that the repressions form that produce the latent material for the dreams of adulthood. The roots of personality should be sought in childhood and especially in the development of the sexual instinct during the early years of life. This brings us to Freud's second masterpiece, *Three Essays on the Theory of Sexuality.*

Three Essays on the Theory of Sexuality (1905)

There is no denying that Freud's most revolutionary impact has been on our willingness, in contrast to the Victorians, to accept sexuality as an essential part of being human. The influence and impact of Freud's discussion stems not from the details of his theory, which are anachronistic and culture-bound, but from his lack of shocked hypocrisy. By drawing attention to sexuality, he provoked the research and the culture change that transcended his own concepts.

As the title of the book says, the text consists of three short essays on different aspects of sex: "The Sexual Aberrations," "Infantile Sexuality," and "The Transformations of Puberty." Far more than *The Interpretations of Dreams,* his *Three Essays*—especially the last two—were revised after 1905 as Freud developed his later libido theory.

Freud made two important general points in the first essay on sexual aberrations. First: "There is indeed something innate lying behind the perversions but ... it is something innate in *everyone*" (p. 64). What society calls "perverse" is only a development of one component of the sexual instinct, an activity centering on an erotogenic zone other than the genitals, a zone that plays its part in "normal" sexual activity in foreplay. The second point was that "*neuroses are, so to say, the negative of perversions*" (p. 57). That is, all neuroses have a sexual basis and arise out of the patient's inability to deal with some aspect of his or her sexuality. Freud went so far as to say that a neurotic's symptoms *are* his or her sex life. The neurotic has symptoms rather than perversions or healthy sexuality.

Freud's second essay, on infantile sexuality, was the most revolutionary. When Freud said that the neurotic has difficulty with sexual needs, he meant that this difficulty began with the child's confrontation with sexual feelings in the first five years of life. Freud's basic claim was that children have sexual feelings. This shocked the

Victorians, who looked on childhood as a time free of sexual demands, a view Freud himself had echoed at one point in *The Interpretation of Dreams.*

Freud, however, believed that the child's sexual feelings are different from the adult's in that they are egocentric, or to use his term, a child is *narcissistic.* Children primarily get pleasure from the several *erotogenic zones* distributed about the human body: the mouth, the anus, and the genitals—although Freud believed the entire skin surface could be erotogenic. Pleasure from self-manipulation is narcissistic because the child chooses no other person as the object of desires but gives self-pleasure, as in masturbation or thumb-sucking. Nevertheless, these powerful feelings should later play their part in foreplay as part of adult, other-directed sexuality. The way in which the child and the parents handle these feelings early on has much to do with adult personality.

Why, Freud asked, do we usually have so little memory of our infantile sexual feelings, or indeed of any experiences before we are about six years old? Freud said that early sexual desires are strongly inhibited, or repressed, so that we do not recall them. This repression is so strong that it spreads to all early experiences and brings on a period of sexual latency, during which sexual desires are dormant, to be later activated at puberty. Freud put great value on this *primal repression* and the ensuing period of latency, for he believed them to be essential to civilization. He was, however, rather obscure as to the reason for the first repression. Although he did not deny that the most obvious source—a culture's moral teachings—may play a role, he seems to have put most emphasis on inherited "disgust" at "perverse" sexual activities and went so far as to claim that many moral taboos are inherited. Freud maintained this position throughout his life, but it was vehemently rejected by almost every later thinker, in or out of the psychoanalytic school.

We also find in the central essay Freud's most attacked hypotheses—the concepts of *penis envy* and the related *castration complex.* Freud believed that children are curious about the facts of sex and form many peculiar theories as a result of their researches—Victorian parents being loath to reveal the truth. According to Freud, the most significant of these childish ideas is that girls are castrated boys. In boys, this theory leads to fear of castration as a punishment for Oedipal desires and helps bring on latency. Girls, however, are overcome by desire for a penis and wish to be boys themselves. Freud's male Victorian valuation of the penis caused him to conclude from his analysis of childhood that an adult female's clitoral orgasm is just a childish imitation of male orgasm. He believed women should put away their hopeless emulation and locate their sexual feelings in their vaginas.

In the last essay, Freud turned to adult sexuality, which begins in puberty when maturational changes reawaken and transmute the dormant sexual instincts. At this time in the healthy person, sexual desire is directed to another person of the opposite sex, and reproductive genital intercourse becomes the goal; the instincts of childhood sexuality now serve genital drives through the kissing and caressing of foreplay that create the arousal necessary to actual coitus. In perverse individuals, the pleasure associated with some infantile instinct is great enough to replace genital activity altogether. The neurotic is overcome by adult sexual demands and converts his or her sexual needs into symptoms.

At various places in *Three Essays,* but especially in the conclusion, Freud introduced a concept that was central to the analysis of culture that occupied his later years. This was the concept of *sublimation,* the most important form of displacement. We may express our sexual desires directly; we may repress them, in which case they may find expression in dreams or neurotic symptoms; or we may employ sexual energy to motivate higher cultural activities, such as art, science, and philosophy. This last process is sublimation, and it diverts animalistic drives to the service of civilization. In *Three Essays,* Freud only discussed sublimation as an option for a person with a constitutionally strong sexual disposition; but in his later works, the alternatives of satisfying direct sexual expression, on the one hand, and repression, sublimation, and consequent residual tension on the other, were to pose a dilemma for Freud and—as he saw it—for civilization itself.

Civilization and Its Discontents (1930)

Sublimation is the conversion of sexual libido into neutral mental energy and is carried out by the child's narcissism. This unbound energy allows the ego to function, but it is an energy that serves both eros and the death instincts. On the one hand, the ego is adaptive and hence enables the person to live; but on the other hand, it opposes the id's pleasure principle, as do the death instincts. Thus a dilemma is raised for civilization. Civilized life makes increasing demands on the ego to control the immoral id, and to pursue civilized activities rather than simple animal pleasures. Yet such demands aid death and oppose pleasures, making happiness harder to achieve. The problem of civilization occupied Freud more and more as the years went by and he no longer had to establish psychoanalysis as a movement.

In *Future of an Illusion* (1927/1961), the simple precursor to the complexities to come in *Civilization and Its Discontents,* Freud used psychoanalysis as a scalpel to dissect religion, the social institution that many people cherished but which had been subjected to philosophical and scientific attack since the eighteenth century Enlightenment. The war between science and religion was well under way, and Freud hoped to strike a decisive blow for science by unmasking the infantile motives behind religious feelings. The nineteenth century appears to us to be a religiously secure age. In public, people professed strong belief in religion, holding it to be the bulwark of civilization. However, in private, these same believers were often tormented by grave doubts about the validity of what they professed. They wanted to believe, they tried to believe, they yearned for the simple untroubled faith of their childhoods—but the doubts remained. Doubt was especially frightening precisely because it appeared to be a crack in the bulwark of civilization.

Freud, however, had no doubts; *Future of an Illusion* is Freud's most polemical and assured work. He said simply that religion *is* an illusion, a massive attempt at wish-fulfillment. Religion is based on nothing more than our infantile feelings of helplessness and the consequent desire to be protected by an all-powerful parent who becomes God. Moreover, to Freud religion is a dangerous illusion, for its dogmatic teachings stunt the intellect, keeping humankind in a childish state. Religion is something to be outgrown as humans develop scientific resources and become able to stand on their own. The secret religious doubters are people who have outgrown religion but do not know it, and it was to them Freud addressed his work. His goal was, as ever, to assert the "primacy of the intellect" over infantile wishes and emotional needs.

In *Future of an Illusion,* Freud made some startlingly pessimistic statements that he took up in *Civilization and Its Discontents.* He wrote: "Every individual is virtually an enemy of civilization …" and people "feel as a heavy burden the sacrifices which civilization expects of them to make a communal life possible." In a phrase, the topic of *Civilization and Its Discontents* is the necessary unhappiness of civilized people.

At the beginning of *Civilization and Its Discontents* (p. 81), Freud wrote: "The sense of guilt [is] the most important problem in the development of civilization and … the price we pay for our advance in civilization is a loss of happiness through the heightening of a sense of guilt." Each person seeks happiness, and according to Freud, the strongest feelings of happiness come from direct satisfaction of our instinctual, especially sexual, desires. Civilization, however, demands that we renounce to a large degree such direct gratification and substitute cultural activities in their stead. Such sublimated drives provide us less pleasure than direct gratification. To add to our discontents we also internalize the demands of civilization as harsh superegos, burdening us with guilt for immoral thoughts as well as deeds. Civilized people are consequently less happy than their primitive counterparts; and as civilization grows, happiness diminishes.

On the other hand, civilization has its rewards and is necessary to human social life. Along with seventeenth century philosopher Thomas Hobbes, Freud feared that without a means of restraining aggression, society would dissolve into a war of all against all. Civilization is therefore necessary for the survival of all but the strongest, and at least partly serves eros. Moreover, in return for repression, civilization gives us not only security but also art, science, philosophy, and a more comfortable life through technology.

Civilization thus presents a dilemma from which Freud saw no way out. On the one hand, civilization is the protector and benefactor of humanity. On the other hand, it demands unhappiness and even neurosis as payment for its benefactions. Near the end of the book Freud hinted that civilizations may vary in the degree of unhappiness they produce—a question he left for others to consider.

This question has been taken up by many thinkers, for *Civilization and Its Discontents* has proven to be one of Freud's most provocative works. Some writers, such as Erich Fromm, have argued that Western civilization is neurotic and they anoint some utopia as savior, as Fromm does socialism. Others, such as Norman O. Brown, believe the only way out of Freud's dilemma is renunciation of civilization itself and a return to the simple physical pleasures of childhood. Whatever the validity of these claims, Freud's dilemma remains and is acutely felt today when the rebellion against inhibition and guilt that Freud saw beginning in his own time has achieved such large dimensions, challenged, if at all, not by repression and morality but by practical worries about death and disease.

THE FATE OF PSYCHOANALYSIS

Unlike the psychology of consciousness, psychoanalysis survives. The young Freud alienated his friends and mentors, and the older Freud, founder and keeper of psychoanalysis, alienated independent-minded followers. Otto Rank, Alfred Adler, and Carl Jung—at one time Freud's Crown Prince—were expelled from the psychoanalytic movement for disagreeing too sharply with the founder. Schism followed schism in post-Freudian psychoanalysis, too, until the field became what it remains, a Babel of competing sects. If Freud's influence on academic psychology was limited, that of his former followers was virtually nonexistent. The theoretical issues Freud raised for scientific psychology—most importantly, the concepts of the unconscious and the nature of human motivation—were not significantly changed by later psychoanalysts. But, as Peter Gay reminds us, Freud himself is inescapable. Is Freud the great hero of legend? Or is psychoanalysis "the most stupendous confidence trick of the twentieth century," as biologist Peter Medawar insists (quoted by Sulloway, 1979)? Or could Freud be a tyrant-lizard—*Tyrannosaurus*—whose time has past?

Psychoanalysis and Science

The claim of psychoanalysis to be a science like any other has been contested since the beginning. Positivists find Freudian hypotheses vague and difficult to test (Nagel, 1959). The most influential attack on the scientific status of psychoanalysis was mounted by Karl Popper, who regarded psychoanalysis as a pseudoscience. As we learned in Chapter 1, Popper formulated the falsifiability principle as the demarcation criterion separating genuine scientific viewpoints from those that merely pretended to be scientific. According to the falsifiability principle, to be worthy of science a theory must make predictions that may be proven unequivocally wrong. Popper, however, found that psychoanalysts were always able to explain any behavior, no matter how apparently inconsistent with psychoanalysis. Somewhere in the complex topography, structures, and dynamics of the mind could be found an explanation for anything at all from a woman's fiddling with her purse (symbolic masturbation) to the space race (phallic competition to build the biggest missile). In this Popperian spirit, the late philosopher Sidney Hook (1959) asked numerous psychoanalysts over a span of decades to describe what a person without an Oedipus complex would be like. He never received a satisfactory reply. Indeed, in more than one instance, he was regarded with hostility and his question met by screaming.

Although Popper's argument has been widely accepted, most analysts, unsurprisingly, reject it. Philosopher Adolf Grünbaum (1984, 1986) has agreed with them and proceeded to take Freud at his word that psychoanalysis was a science. Grünbaum argues that Freud did after all propose a test by which psychoanalysis might be falsified, a test Grünbaum calls the Tally Argument. When he offered the therapeutic success of psychoanalysis as "incontrovertible proof" of psychoanalysis, Freud said that psychoanalysis and only psychoanalysis could provide real cures for neuroses, because only psychoanalysis found the inner wishes and thoughts that "tallied" with the symptoms. As therapy recovered and eliminated the unconscious wishes, symptoms would disappear until the neurosis was completely dissolved. Other therapies, Freud argued, could achieve only partial and temporary success, since they did not go to the causes of neuroses, effecting by suggestion alone what little relief they provided.

Grünbaum accepts the Tally Argument as refutation of Popper's claim that psychoanalysis is not a science, for the Tally Argument is falsifiable. Therefore psychoanalysis is a science, and the question becomes one of determining if its claims are true or false. To be accepted as true on its own grounds, psychoanalysis must demonstrate unique therapeutic success. Unique success is vital to the Tally Argument, for if other therapeutic systems work at least as well as psychoanalysis, there is no reason to prefer the complexities of psychoanalysis to simpler theories. Behavior therapy, for example, rests on the simple principles of conditioning, and should it prove to be the equal of psychoanalysis, then by Ockham's razor, it is scientifically preferable to psychoanalysis.

When we look into the therapeutic success of psychoanalysis we find that while Freud boasted of success after success, he provided remarkably little data to support his claim. Freud reported only six cases in detail, one of which he did not treat and only two of which he claimed to be successes (Sulloway, 1991). The two successful cases were those of Rat Man and Wolf Man. The Rat Man was so-called because of his morbid fears and fantasies about rats, while the Wolf Man was named for a dream about seeing wolves. Freud's description of neither case stands up to scrutiny. Numerous distortions of the truth mark both reports, and neither patient seems to have been cured. After claiming success with the Rat Man in print, Freud confessed to Jung that the Rat Man was far from cured, and, like Dora, the Rat Man broke off therapy. The case of the Wolf Man is better known, since he outlived Freud by many years and near the end of his life told his story to a journalist. He stayed in analysis (for free) years after Freud's death. He told the reporter that he wrote a memoir about his case at the behest of one of his later analysts "[t]o show the world how Freud cured a seriously ill person," but "it's all false." He felt just as ill as when he went to Freud. In fact, he said, "The whole thing looks like a catastrophe" (quoted by Sulloway, 1991). Fisher and Greenberg (1977) wrote a largely sympathetic review of the status of psychoanalysis as science but concluded that Freud's own cases were "largely unsuccessful."

Later therapy outcome studies provide no evidence that psychoanalysis is a uniquely effective therapy. Gains from all forms of therapy are modest, and most forms of therapy have about equal success (see Chapter 15). Although Freud thought little of experimental attempts to verify psychoanalysis, many psychologists and analysts have carried out experiments, with highly variable results (for reviews of therapy and experimental studies, see Eysenck & Wilson, 1973, Fisher & Greenberg, 1977; Farrell, 1981; Kline, 1981; Grünbaum, 1984, 1986; Eysenck, 1986; Macmillan, 1991). Psychoanalysis seems to be caught on the horns of a dilemma. Either psychoanalysis cannot be tested—in which case, it is a pseudoscience—or it can be tested—in which case, it is at best a very poor science.

As a consequence, some partisans of psychoanalysis try to dissolve the dilemma by claiming that psychoanalysis is not a science at all, but a means of interpretation (Lacan, 1968; Ricoeur, 1970). This *hermeneutical* version of psychoanalysis maintains that the activity of psychoanalysis is more like literary criticism than science. A literary critic closely reads a text in order to discern its meaning, a meaning that may have been hidden even from the author who created it. Similarly, a psychoanalyst works with a patient to closely read the text of the patient's life, looking for or constructing the hidden meaning it holds. According to this version of psychoanalysis, the goal of therapy is to reach an interpretation with which the patient agrees and which can form the basis of a fuller life. Hermeneutics was originally the art of Bible interpretation, and hermeneutical psychoanalysis constitutes in part a return to the medieval conception of the world as a book containing meanings to be decoded, not causes to be discovered.

The plausibility of hermeneutic psychoanalysis is debatable (see commentary to Grünbaum, 1986). For us now, the main objection to it is that Freud clearly meant psychology to be a science (Grünbaum, 1984, 1986), even if his conception of science is now out of date (Breger, 1981). Notwithstanding Freud's intention, it is the hermeneutical Freud who has had the greatest impact on society.

Psychoanalysis and Society

Jacques Lacan (1968), one of the most influential leaders of hermeneutical psychoanalysis, places Freud among the three leaders of the Party of Suspicion—the others are Marx and Nietzsche—whose impact on twentieth-century thought has been immense. The common enemy of the Party of Suspicion is the middle class. Breuer said that Freud's emphasis on sex was motivated in part by "a desire to *épater* [shock] *le bourgeois*" (quoted by Sulloway, 1979). Marx worked for the proletarian revolution that would destroy capitalism and the bourgeoisie. Nietzsche denounced middle-class morals as unfit for the *Übermensch* (literally, "Over-man", or Superman, Nietzsche's idealized man of the future). The common weapon of the Party of Suspicion was unmasking. Freud revealed depths of sexual depravity behind the seemingly innocent screen of middle-class respectability. Marx revealed self-centered greed in the aspirations of entrepreneurial capitalists. Nietzsche revealed craven cowards behind Christian martyrs.

Today the Party of Suspicion lives on in Freudian Marxism (Geuss, 1971) and deconstructionism (Lehman, 1991). When Marx's revolution failed to appear, Marxists turned to Freud to explain why. According to this line of thinking, citizens in bourgeois societies, especially workers and the poor, are brainwashed by their culture into a state of *false consciousness*. Like neurotics unaware of the causes of their misery, the classes oppressed by the bourgeoisie are unaware of their true interests as a class. To bring about liberation, false consciousness must be raised just as a therapist raises the repressed to consciousness. In each case, a knowledgeable elite, possessing theories and powers denied the patient or the rest of the citizenry, must overcome resistance and lead a revolution. Lenin said that a vanguard elite had to awaken the masses to revolution, and the Marxist Freudians nominate themselves as the vanguard elite, using textual analysis to awaken their students to revolution. The deconstructionists continue the literary project of unmasking, sometimes showing that literature serves primarily to justify the swinish hegemony of the middle class, and sometimes taking unmasking to its natural end, showing that behind the mask of a text lies nothing, thus elevating the critic above the author (Lehmann, 1991).

To the Party of Suspicion nothing is as it seems to be, and in Freudian psychology, this means that no utterance, no action, is what it seems to be; everything requires interpretation. As Alasdair MacIntyre (1985) observes, the social sciences, especially psychology, are unique among the sciences because their theories may influence the subjects about which they write. As a result, psychology shapes the reality it describes, and the overinterpretative mode of life, as MacIntyre calls it, plays an important role in modern life.

"Freud made available the thought of the unacknowledged motive as an all-pervasive presence, so that each of us is encouraged to try and look behind the overt simplicities of the behavior of others to what is actually moving them and equally encouraged to respond to that hidden reality rather than to the surface appearance of the other" (MacIntyre, 1985, p. 899). Working within the overinterpretative mode of life, nothing can be believed; every statement, every action, requires an interpretative gloss. The interpretations no longer need be traditionally Freudian. To see the effects of overinterpretation one need only consider the oddity of modern television news in which reporters, quoting experts and anonymous "insiders," tell us, the people, how a presidential speech will "play" to the people. No longer do government officials say things, they "send messages" to be decoded by pundits. Authority and sincerity have been dissolved. What Freud and the Party of Suspicion have bequeathed us is paranoia. Perhaps Freud's contemporary, the witty journalist Karl Kraus, was right when he said "psychoanalysis is itself that mental illness of which it purports to be the cure" (Gay, 1988, p. 449).

BIBLIOGRAPHY

Trying to master the scholarly literature on Freud is like trying to drink from a fire hose: You're more likely to be blasted away and drown than get refreshed. I have listed here only a very very tiny portion of the literature. You can find much more by browsing in your library.

General Works. The standard biography of Freud is Ernest Jones's three-volume *Life and work of Sigmund Freud,* available in a one-volume abridgement (New York: Basic Books, 1961). Jones was a member of Freud's inner circle, and his biography enjoys both the benefits— privileged information—and the defects—hagiographical character—of close friendly association with its subject. Moreover, it is now out-of-date. An up-to-date biography is Peter Gay (1988). It is well written and incorporates access to some (but not all) documents hidden from the general public (some of the Freud materials held in the Library of Congress and elsewhere cannot be published until after 2100!). Gay is a historian who underwent psychoanalysis, and he writes as something of a convert; although he criticizes Freud, Freud remains a hero for Gay. Moreover, the text hides scholarly controversies about Freud, although they are discussed in the excellent and combative bibliography.

My two favorite general works on Freud are Sulloway's (1979; his 1981 may be regarded as a summary, and his 1991 as a sequel) for their elegant arguments about Freud the cryptobiologist and their dissection of the myth of Freud the hero, and Rieff (1979) for sympathetic consideration of Freud not as a doctor or a scientist or a hero, but as a moral philosopher of enormous influence. Two other biographies are philosopher Richard Wollheim's *Sigmund Freud* (New York: Viking, 1971); and professional biographer Ronald Clark's *Freud: The man and the cause* (New York: Meridian, 1980). A more critical survey, in which the cultlike nature of psychoanalysis (see also Sulloway, 1991) emerges, is Roazen (1974); one old analyst interviewed by Roazen shrieked at him, "You will never learn our secrets!" For later history of psychoanalysis, see Ellenberger (1970) and Reuben Fine, *A history of psychoanalysis* (New York: Columbia University Press, 1979). There are three collections of essays on Freud. The first two are general, S. G. M. Lee & M. Herbert (Eds.), *Freud and psychology* (Harmondsworth, England: Penguin, 1970), and the volume edited by R. Wollheim (see Solomon reference); the third, edited by Wollheim & J. Hopkins, *Philosophical essays on Freud* (Cambridge, England: Cambridge University Press, 1982), focuses on Freud as philosopher.

Various collections of Freud's letters have been published. However, due to the extraordinarily secretive nature of the keepers of the Freud archives, only two complete and unexpurgated sets of letters have been published, W. McGuire (Ed.), *The Freud-Jung letters* (Princeton,

NJ: Princeton University Press, 1974); and Freud (1985), the Freud-Fliess correspondence. Freud began the tradition of cultlike secrecy surrounding psychoanalysis, twice destroying collections of letters and manuscripts so his biographers could not get at them and tarnish his heroic image. The Freud-Fliess letters are extraordinarily revealing. Fliess was Freud's most intimate friend, and in Freud's letters to Fliess, we find revealed the early development of Freud's thought and insights into his character (the first letter was written while Freud had a woman hypnotized before him). Freud attempted to get hold of the Fliess letters when he discovered late in his life that they existed (he had destroyed Fliess's to him). The letters were published in a highly laundered edition together with the "Project" in 1954 (*The origins of psychoanalysis,* New York: Basic Books). Masson was hired to prepare Freud's complete letters for publication, but despite having been psychoanalyzed, he turned out not to be a safe choice. When he developed his version of the seduction mistake, he was fired by the Freud Archives, and only the Freud-Fliess volume was published; I fear I shall not live to see the rest. The uproar in the analytic community was considerable: See Janet Malcolm, *In the Freud Archives* (New York: Random House, 1985). Masson brought a libel suit against Malcolm and the *New Yorker,* which he won on the legal merits of the case in June, 1993. However, the trial ended with the jury deadlocked on the amount of damages to be awarded. And at press time for this book, further legal maneuvers were pending.

The best general work of Freud's is the pair of lectures, *A general introduction to psychoanalysis* (New York: Washington Square Press, 1924/1952); and its sequel, *New introductory lectures on psychoanalysis* (New York: Norton, 1933/1965). The "bible" of psychoanalysis is J. Strachey (Ed.), *The standard edition of the complete psychological works of Sigmund Freud,* 24 vols. (London: Hogarth Press, 1966–1974). Peter Gay (1989) has assembled a useful one-volume compilation of Freud's works based on the Standard Edition. Complaints have often surrounded James and Alix Strachey's translations of Freud, especially by Bruno Bettleheim, *Freud and man's soul* (New York: Vintage, 1984). Light is thrown on the difficulties of translating Freud in a delightful collection of letters by the two Freudian Bloomsburians themselves, *Bloomsbury/Freud: The letters of James and Alix Strachey* 1924–1925, P. Meisel and W. Kendrick (Eds.), (New York: Norton, 1990).

Background. The general works previously listed provide various perspectives on the background against which to view Freud. Useful for the Viennese cultural setting are Schorske (1980), a wonderful book on the whole Viennese scene; and one by his student McGrath (1986), who develops Freud's situation more fully. Decker (1991) also discusses Freud in Vienna, with special attention to the history and status of the Austrian Jewish community. David Bakan, *Sigmund Freud and the Jewish mystical tradition* (Princeton, NJ: D. van Nostrand, 1958), connects Freud's thought to Jewish theology.

For the medical background, two books on the development of the concept of neurosis are available, Jose M. Lopez Pinero, *Historical origins of the concept of neurosis* (Cambridge, England: Cambridge University Press, 1983); and George Frederick Drinka, *The birth of neurosis: Myth, malady and the Victorians* (New York: Touchstone, 1984). For no obvious reason, the scholarly study of hysteria has proliferated in just the last few years. Mark Micale has provided guides to the literature: "Hysteria and its historiography: A review of past and present writings," *History of Science* (1989, *27*: I: 223–61, II: 319–56); and "Hysteria and its historiography: The future perspective," *History of Psychiatry* (1990, *1*: 33–124).

One of the most important of Freud's self-perpetuated myths is that his ideas met with a hostile reception, but, like so many other Freud stories, it isn't true (Sulloway, 1979). See the following studies of Freud's reception and influence: Hannah S. Decker, "The interpretation of dreams: Early reception by the educated German public," *Journal of the History of the Behavioral Sciences* (1975, *11*: 129–41); Hannah S. Decker, *Freud in Germany: Revolution and reaction in science, 1893–1907* (New York: International Universities Press, 1977); *Psychological*

Issues Monographs 11 (31), Monograph 41; Nathan Hale, *Freud and the Americans* (New York: Oxford University Press, 1971); and David Shakow, *The influence of Freud on American psychology* (New York: International Universities Press, 1964).

The Path Through Physiology.   In addition to the cited works, especially Solomon's, see Karl H. Pribram & Merton Gill, *Freud's "Project" re-assessed: Preface to contemporary cognitive theory and neuropsychology* (New York: Basic Books, 1976). Pribram is a leading neuropsychologist, and he and Gill view the "Project" as pioneering and prescient.

Dora and Other Cases.   Decker (1991) provides a full account of what is now probably Freud's most studied case. For brief accounts and critical treatments of Freud's few published case studies, see Sulloway (1991).

The Unconscious.   The standard, massive history of the unconscious is Ellenberger (1970). Also useful are D. B. Klein, *The unconscious: Invention or discovery?* (Santa Monica, CA: Goodyear, 1977); and Lancelot Law Whyte, *The unconscious before Freud* (New York: Basic Books, 1960). Hughes (1958) shows how the concept of the unconscious came to grip social thought more generally. The view from continental hermeneutics is given in David Archard, *Consciousness and the unconscious* (La Salle, IL: Open Court, 1984). The concept of the unconscious is still controversial: See John R. Searle, "Consciousness, explanatory inversion, and cognitive science," *Behavioral and Brain Sciences* (1990, *13*: 585–642, with commentary), and Erdelyi (1985).

Victorian Sexuality.   How prudish and repressed the Victorians were has become a matter of controversy between a traditional picture of uptight Victorians and Peter Gay's (1984) picture of almost hedonistic Victorians (although in Gay, 1986, they seem more conservative). In the text, I try to steer a middle course, focusing on the problem as Freud saw it. Herewith is a brief introduction to the enormous literature. The traditional view is that Victorians—especially women—were intensely repressed and deeply ashamed about sex. Standard sources here include Stephen Marcus, *The other Victorians* (New York: Meridian, 1964), a work I relied on; Vern Bullough & Bonnie Bullough, *Sin, sickness, and sanity: A history of sexual attitudes* (New York: Meridian, 1977), which covers periods before and after the Victorian; G. J. Barker-Benfield, *The horrors of the half-known life: Male attitudes toward women and sexuality in nineteenth-century America* (New York: Harper Colophon, 1976), which takes a feminist perspective; Ronald Pearsall, *The worm in the bud: The world of Victorian sexuality* (Harmondsworth, England: Penguin, 1983), a social history of Victorian sexuality; John S. and Robin M. Haller, *The physician and sexuality in Victorian America* (Champaign: University of Illinois Press, 1974), a fascinating study of physicians' ideas about sex, and how they were translated into popular and professional "cures" for alleged sexual disorders; and Jeffrey Weeks, *Sex, politics and society: The regulation of sexuality since 1800* (New York: Longman, 1981). Victorians were especially alarmed by masturbation: See Arthur N. Gilbert, "Masturbation and insanity: Henry Maudsley and the ideology of sexual repression," *Albion* (1980, *12*: 268–82). However, revisionist historians have begun to assert that the traditional view of repressed Victorian sexuality is seriously mistaken. For example, a recently discovered unpublished sex survey—the first ever—of women who had grown up in the Victorian period suggests that they may have had orgasms with the same frequency as today's "liberated" women: Clelia Duel Mosher, *The Mosher survey: Sexual attitudes of Victorian women* (New York: Arno, 1980). Peter Gay (1984) has used the Mosher survey, a diary by a sexually active young American woman, and other sources to try to debunk the "myth" of the asexual Victorian; see also Cyril Pearl, *The girl with the Swansdown seat: An informal report on some aspects of mid-Victorian morality* (London: Robin Clark, 1980); and Edmund Leites, *The puritan conscience and human sexuality* (New Haven, CT: Yale University Press, 1986). How far the revisionist picture is accurate, however, is still open to question. For an evaluation, see Carol Zisowitz Sterns, "Victorian sexuality: Can historians do it better?," *Journal of Social History* (1985, *18*: 625–34). Freud himself was an advocate of sexual reform. See Boyer (1978), which contains a transcript with translation of Freud's reply to a query from a commission looking into the laws regulating marriage in Austria in 1905; and Timothy McCarthy, "Freud and the problem of sexuality," *Journal of the History of the Behavioral and Social Sciences* (1981, *17*: 332–39). Other important rebels against Victorian sexual repression, assuming it existed, are described by Paul Robinson, *The modernization of sex: Havelock Ellis, Alfred Kinsey, William Masters and Virginia Johnson* (New York: Harper Colophon, 1977); and Phyllis Grosskurth, *Havelock Ellis* (New York: Knopf, 1980). For general background, see Bernard Murstein, *Love, sex, and marriage through the ages* (New York: Springer, 1974); and Lawrence Stone, *The family, sex, and marriage in England 1500–1800* (New York: Harper & Row, 1977). Although Stone's history stops before the Victorian period, Stone shows that a cycle of sexual repression alternating with sexual freedom was a regular feature of English history.

The Standing of Psychoanalysis. The text cites the most important books evaluating psychoanalysis. It should be said that Freud's luster has tarnished over the years for myself and others. I came to psychology by reading Isaac Asimov's *Foundation* trilogy, and then Freud, and Freud was long one of my heroes. However, after writing this revised chapter, I must confess I no longer regard Freud with much affection. For similar disenchantments, see Crews (1986) and Sulloway (1991). An interesting assessment of Freud is provided by leading literary critic Harold Bloom, "Freud, Greatest modern writer," *New York Review of Books* (1986, March 23, 1, 26–27). Bloom makes his point by canvassing rival views of Freud, concluding that what Freud gave the world was great mythology—art, not science.

Hermeneutics. Key books are the Lacan and Ricoeur works cited in the text. For a remarkably readable survey of a notoriously difficult and slippery subject, see Roy J. Howard, *Three faces of hermeneutics: An introduction to current theories of understanding* (Berkeley, CA: University of California Press, 1982). See also Charles D. Axelrod, *Studies in intellectual breakthrough: Freud, Simmel, Buber* (Amherst, MA: University of Massachusetts Press, 1970); and Richard Lichtman, *The production of desire: The integration of psychoanalysis into Marxist theory* (New York: Free Press, 1982). Freud is connected to the founder of deconstructionism, Jacques Derrida, in Samuel Weber, *The legend of Freud* (Minneapolis, MN: University of Minnesota Press, 1982). For critical views of the Party of Suspicion, I recommend Geuss (1971) and Lehman (1991).

General Influence. Freud's influence has been very great in fields other than psychiatry and psychology. A collection that is especially useful for a beginner in Freud is Jonathan Miller (Ed.), *Freud: The man, his world, his influence* (Boston: Little, Brown, 1972), because it contains essays on Freud and his time, and then a set on Freud's influence in various fields. Books on specific areas of influence follow. Art: Ellen H. Spitz, *Art and Psyche: A study in psychoanalysis and aesthetics* (New Haven, CT: Yale University Press, 1985). The social sciences, including anthropology, sociology, and political science: Paul Roazen, *Freud: Political and social thought* (New York: Da Capo Press, 1986); Arthur Berliner, *Psychoanalysis and society* (Washington, DC: University Press of America, 1982); Peter Bocock, *Freud and modern society: An outline of Freud's sociology* (Sunbury on Thames, England: Nelson, 1976); H. M. Ruitenbeek (Ed.), *Psychoanalysis and social science* (New York: Dutton, 1962); Melford Spiro, *Oedipus in the Trobriands* (Chicago: University of Chicago Press, 1983); and Edwin R. Wallace, *Freud and anthropology* (New York: International Universities Press, 1983). One controversial offspring of psychoanalysis is psychohistory, which is discussed and critically examined in David E. Stannard, *Shrinking history: On Freud and the failure of psychohistory* (New York: Oxford University Press, 1980).

REFERENCES

Bartlett, F. C. (1932). *Remembering.* Cambridge: Cambridge University Press.

Boyer, J. W. (1978). Freud, marriage, and late Viennese liberalism: A commentary from 1905. *Journal of Modern History, 50,* 72–102.

Breger, L. (1981). How psychoanalysis is a science—and how it is not. *Journal of the American Academy of Psychoanalysis, 9,* 261–275.

Brewer, W. F. & Nakamura, G. V. (1984). The nature and functions of schemas. In R. S. Wyer & T. K. Srull (Eds.), *Handbook of social cognition.* Hillsdale, NJ: Erlbaum.

Cioffi, F. (1972). Wollheim on Freud. *Inquiry, 15,* 172–186.

Cioffi, F. (1973). Introduction. In F. Cioffi (Ed.), *Freud: Modern judgements.* London: Macmillan.

Cioffi, F. (1974). Was Freud a liar? *The Listener 91,* 172–174.

Cioffi, F. (1984, July 6). The cradle of neurosis. *Times Literary Supplement,* 743–744.

Crews, F. (1986). *Skeptical engagements.* New York: Oxford University Press.

Decker, H. S. (1981). Freud and Dora: Constraints on medical progress. *Journal of Social History, 14,* 445–464.

Decker, H. S. (1991). *Freud, Dora, and Vienna 1900.* New York: The Free Press.

Dollard, J., Doob, L., Miller, N., Mowrer, O., & Sears, R. (1939). *Frustration and aggression.* New Haven: Yale University Press.

Ellenberger, H. F. (1970). *The discovery of the unconscious.* New York: Basic Books.

Erdelyi, M. H. (1985). *Psychoanalysis: Freud's cognitive psychology.* San Francisco: Freeman.

Eysenck, H. J. (1986). *The decline and fall of the Freudian Empire.* Harmondsworth, England: Penguin.

Eysenck, H. J. & Wilson, G. D. (Eds.), (1973). *The experimental study of Freudian theories.* London: Methuen.

Farrell, B. A. (1981). *The standing of psychoanalysis.* Oxford: Oxford University Press.

Fisher, S. & Greenberg, R. P. (1977). *The scientific credibility of Freud's theories and therapy.* New York: Basic Books.

Freud, S. (1900/1968). *The interpretation of dreams.* New York: Avon.

Freud, S. (1905a/1962). *Three essays on the theory of sexuality.* New York: Avon.

Freud, S. (1905b). Fragments of an analysis of a case of hysteria. Partially reprinted in Gay (1989).

Freud, S. (1908/1953). 'Civilized' sexual morality and modern nervousness. *Collected Papers,* Vol. 2. London: Hogarth Press.

Freud, S. (1912/1953). Contributions to the psychology of love: The most prevalent form of degradation in erotic life. In *Collected papers,* Vol. 4. London: Hogarth Press.

Freud, S. (1915a). Instincts and their vicissitudes. Partially reprinted in Gay (1989).

Freud, S. (1915b). The unconscious. Partially reprinted in Gay (1989).

Freud, S. (1920/1961). *Beyond the pleasure principle.* New York: Norton.

Freud, S. (1923/1960). *The ego and the id.* New York: Norton.

Freud, S. (1927/1961). *Future of an illusion.* New York: Norton.

Freud, S. (1930/1961). *Civilization and its discontents.* New York: Norton.

Freud, S. (1932). The question of a *Weltanschauung.* Partially reprinted in Gay (1989).

Freud, S. (1950). Project for a scientific psychology. *Standard edition of the complete psychological works of Sigmund Freud,* Vol. 1. London: Hogarth Press.

Freud, S. (1960). *The letters of Sigmund Freud.* New York: Basic Books.

Freud, S. (1985). *The complete letters of Sigmund Freud to Wilhelm Fliess 1887–1904.* Trans. and ed. J. M. Masson. Cambridge, MA: The Belknap Press of Harvard University Press.

Freud, S. & Breuer, J. (1895/1966). *Studies in hysteria.* New York: Avon.

Gay, P. (1984). *The bourgeois experience: Victoria to Freud,* Vol. 1: *Education of the senses.* New York: Oxford University Press.

Gay, P. (1986). *The bourgeois experience: Victoria to Freud,* Vol. 2: *The tender passion.* New York: Oxford University Press.

Gay, P. (1988). *Freud: A life for our time.* New York: Norton.

Gay, P. (Ed.). (1989). *The Freud reader.* New York: Norton.

Geuss, R. (1971). *The idea of a critical theory: Habermas and the Frankfurt School.* Cambridge, England: Cambridge University Press.

Grünbaum, A. (1984). *The foundations of psychoanalysis: A philosophical critique.* Berkeley, CA: University of California Press.

Grünbaum, A. (1986). Precis of *The foundations of psychoanalysis: A philosophical critique,* with commentary. *Behavioral and Brain Sciences, 9,* 217–284.

Holt, R. R. (1982, November). Family secrets. *The Sciences, 22,* 26–28.

Hook, S. (1959). *Psychoanalysis, scientific method, and philosophy.* New York: New York University Press.

Houghton, W. E. (1957). *The Victorian frame of mind.* New Haven: Yale University Press.

Hughes, H. S. (1958). *Consciousness and society: The reorientation of European social thought 1890–1930.* New York: Vintage.

James, W. (1890). *Principles of psychology,* 2 vols. New York: Holt.

Kaufmann, W. (1985). Nietzsche as the First Great (Depth) psychologist. In S. Koch & D. Leary (Eds.), *A century of psychology as science.* New York: McGraw-Hill.

Klein, M. I. & Tribich, D. (1982, November). Blame the child. *The Sciences, 22,* 14–20.

Kline, P. (1981). *Fact and fantasy in Freudian theory,* 2nd ed. London: Methuen.

Koch, S. & Leary, D. (Eds.) (1985). *A century of psychology as science.* New York: McGraw-Hill.

Krantz, S. (1990). Brentano on "Unconscious consciousness." *Philosophy and Phenomenological Research ,1,* 745–753.

Lacan, J. (1968). *The language of the self.* Trans. A. Wilden. Baltimore: Johns Hopkins University Press.

Lehman, D. (1991). *Signs of the times.* New York: Poseidon.

Lorenz, K. (1966). *On aggression.* San Diego, CA: Harcourt Brace Jovanovich.

MacIntyre, A. (1985). How psychology makes itself true—or false. In S. Koch & D. Leary (Eds.), *A century of psychology as science.* New York: McGraw-Hill.

Macmillan, M. (1991). *Freud evaluated: The completed arc.* Amsterdam: North-Holland.

Masson, J. M. (1984a, February). Freud and the seduction theory. *Atlantic Monthly:* 33–60.

Masson, J. M. (1984b). *The assault on truth: Freud's suppression of the seduction theory.* New York: Farrar, Straus & Giroux.

McGrath, W. J. (1986). *Freud's discovery of psychoanalysis: The politics of hysteria.* Ithaca, NY: Cornell University Press.

Myers, G. E. (1986). *William James: His life and thought.* New Haven: Yale University Press.

Nagel, E. (1959). Methodological issues in psychoanalytic theory. In S. Hook (Ed.), *Psychoanalysis, scientific method, and philosophy.* New York: New York University Press.

Ricoeur, P. (1970). *Freud and philosophy.* Trans. B. Savage. New Haven: Yale University Press.

Rieff, P. (1979). *Freud: The mind of the moralist,* 3rd ed. Chicago: University of Chicago Press.

Roazen, P. (1974). *Freud and his followers.* New York: New American Library.

Rosenzweig, S. (1985). Freud and experimental psychology: The emergence of idiodynamics. In S. Koch & D. Leary (Eds.), *A century of psychology as science.* New York: McGraw-Hill.

Schorske, C. E. (1980). *Fin-de-siècle Vienna: Politics and culture.* New York: Knopf.

Sears, R. R. (1985). Psychoanalysis and behavior theory: 1907–65. In S. Koch & D. Leary (Eds.), *A century of psychology as science.* New York: McGraw-Hill.

Solomon, R. C. (1974). Freud's neurological theory of the mind. In R. Wollheim (Ed.), *Freud: A collection of critical essays.* Garden City, NY: Doubleday.

Sperling, G. A. (1960). The information available in brief visual presentation. *Psychological Monographs, 74,* Whole number 498.

Sulloway, F. J. (1979). *Freud: Biologist of the mind*. New York: Basic Books.

Sulloway, F. J. (1982). Freud and biology: The hidden legacy. In W. R. Woodward & M. J. Ash (Eds.), *The problematic science: Psychology in nineteenth-century thought*. New York: Praeger.

Sulloway, F. J. (1991). Reassessing Freud's case histories: The social construction of psychoanalysis. *Isis, 82*, 245–275.

CHAPTER 4

The Psychology of Adaptation (1855–1891)

The last founding psychology we will examine has proved the most durable and influential in academic psychology. In the twentieth century, Wundt's psychology of consciousness quickly became an anachronistic product of nineteenth-century German thought, and it survived neither transplantation to other countries nor the destruction of its intellectual ecology by the Nazis and World War II. The same is largely true of Gestalt psychology. Psychoanalysis is a living tradition, having adapted to conditions outside nineteenth-century Vienna, and its influence on modern culture has been greater than that of any other psychology. Nevertheless, psychoanalysis remains primarily a branch of medical psychiatry, and its relations with academic psychology have been ambivalent from Freud's time to our own.

The approach that academic psychologists—first in England and later in America—have found most attractive and useful is a psychology based on evolution, Lamarckian or Darwinian. With the ascendance of American psychology in the twentieth century, the psychology of adaptation in one form or another has dominated academic psychology.

Any theory of evolution raises two questions that can engender psychological research programs. The first we may call the *species question*. If the body and brain are products of organic evolution, then we may ask in what ways this inheritance shapes the thought and behavior of organisms. This question leads to comparative psychology, ethology, and sociobiology, which study species differences in mental and behavioral capacities—differences presumably created by evolution. The second psychological question raised by evolution we may call the *individual question*. As the individual creature grows up, it can be seen as adapting psychologically to the environment in a way analogous to organic evolution. This question leads to the study of learning, research designed to uncover how the individual adjusts to the environment.

The species question and the individual question are interrelated. If species differences are great, then different psychologies of individual adaptation will be needed for different species. If, on the other hand, species differences are small, then the same laws of individual learning will apply to all individuals, regardless of species. In this chapter, we will trace the development of the psychology of adaptation and will soon discover that its proponents adopt the latter line of thought. Gall's phrenology had implied a comparative psychology that looked for species differences in the possession of mental faculties. To a phrenologist, structural differences in the brain meant structural differences in mind. However, by the middle of the nineteenth century, the sensorimotor concept of the brain had vanquished phrenology among scientists, while associationism was displacing faculty psychology among philosopher-psychologists. The view of the brain as an initially formless associative machine and the view of the mind as a *tabula rasa* awaiting associations combined to cause psychologists to focus on the individual question and minimize species differences.

FOUNDATION STONE: THE DARWINIAN REVOLUTION

Background

The Newtonian-Cartesian mechanical world was as changeless as the ancient one. God, or some Creator, had constructed a marvelous machine perfect in conception and endless in time. Each object, each biological species, was fixed for eternity, changelessly perfect in obedience to fixed natural laws. On this view, change was something unusual in nature. Even the geological doctrine of uniformitarianism, which helped Darwin invent his theory of evolution, was antievolutionary in tracing the continuum of natural forces back over millions of years. In biology, the Aristotelian belief that species were fixed and immutable was a dogma supported by the highest scientific authorities right up until Darwin's time. Given the Cartesian-Newtonian concept that matter is inert, incapable of acting, and passive only, and that spontaneous change is the origin of new species, the mutation of old seemed impossible. Once the supreme Intelligence had acted creatively, dead matter could effect nothing new.

In the atmosphere of progress characteristic of the Enlightenment, however, this static view of nature began to change. Evolutionary ideas go back to a few ancient

Greek writers, but in the eighteenth century, they really began to take hold. One old Aristotelian-theological concept that helped evolution along was the Great Chain of Being, or Aristotle's *scala naturae*. The Chain was viewed by medievals as a measure of a creature's nearness to God and consequently its degree of spiritual perfection. To later naturalistic thinkers, on the other hand, it became a record of the ascent of living things toward nature's crowning perfection, humankind.

To accomplish the change from a stable but perfect universe to a changing, striving one, a different view of matter was needed; dead, stupid matter can neither change nor strive. In the eighteenth century, precisely the necessary conception arose. Matter—for some thinkers, even inorganic matter—was now endowed with vitality and a tendency to progress. It was thus possible for many writers to assert that the universe had evolved from simple beginnings, and that species had changed and progressed since the beginning of time and could go on changing and progressing forever. This view was embodied in one form or another in French transformism, vitalism, and German nature philosophy. It certainly did not abandon naturalism, for it enabled thinkers to eliminate God altogether and give a thoroughly natural account of the origin of the earth and its inhabitants. The vitalist, Romantic concept of evolution was not mechanical, however, for it endowed matter with godlike attributes. For the Newtonian, stupid matter was set in mechanical motion by an intelligent, purposeful Creator. For the vitalist, matter itself is intelligent and purposeful. Vitalism was thus a Romantic view of Nature—self-perfecting and self-directing, progressively unfolding itself throughout time.

Charles Darwin's signal contribution to the concept of evolution was to mechanize it, to deromanticize nature and capture evolution for the Newtonian world-view. However, before examining Darwin's theory, we should first consider the major romantic alternative whose appeal is strong even today—and which even Darwin himself could not entirely resist—the evolutionary theory of Jean-Baptiste Lamarck (1744–1829). Lamarck, a naturalist well known for his work in taxonomy, was the most scientific exponent of the romantic-progressive view of evolution. There were two important aspects of Lamarck's theory. The first said that organic matter is fundamentally different from inorganic, that each living species possesses an innate drive to perfect itself. Each organism strives to adapt itself to its surroundings and changes itself as it does so, developing various muscles, acquiring various habits. The second part of his theory claimed that these acquired characteristics could be passed on to an animal's offspring. Thus the results of each individual's striving for perfection were preserved and passed on, and over generations, species of plants and animals would improve themselves, fulfilling their drives for perfection. Modern genetics has destroyed the romantic-vitalist vision of nature. Organic matter is now known to be merely complexly arranged inorganic molecules; DNA is a collection of amino acids. The DNA chain is unchanged by modifications to an individual's body. (Certain external influences, such as drugs or radiation, can affect genetic information, but that is not what Lamarck meant.) In the absence of genetics, however, the inheritance of acquired characteristics was plausible and even Darwin from time to time accepted it, although he never accepted the vitalist view of matter. Later, both Wundt and Freud believed that acquired habits and experiences were capable of being passed on through heredity.

So, by Darwin's time, evolution was a widespread concept, disbelieved only by firm religionists and the biological establishment, which still accepted the fixity of species. A naturalistic but romantic conception of evolution was in place. The phrase "survival of the fittest" had already been coined in 1852 by Herbert Spencer, an English Lamarckian. And in 1849, a decade before the publication of Darwin's *Origin of Species,* Alfred, Lord Tennyson wrote in his greatest poem, *In Memoriam,* lines that foreshadowed the new view of evolution, in which the individual sacrifices for the species in the struggle for survival, a view of which Tennyson disapproved (Canto 55, l.5–8):

> Are God and Nature then at strife,
> That Nature lends such evil dreams?
> So careful of the type [species] she seems,
> So careless of the single life.

Later in the poem, in a widely quoted line, Tennyson calls nature "red in tooth and claw" (Canto 56, l. 15).

Charles Darwin (1809–1882), Victorian Revolutionary

Evolution could not long remain a poetic effusion, although Darwin's own grandfather, Erasmus Darwin, anticipated his grandson's theory in a scientific poem, *Zoonomia.* Nor could it remain a romantic fancy, inspiring but finally implausible. Darwin's achievement was to make evolution into a scientific theory by providing a mechanism—natural selection. Then a campaign to convince scientists and the public of the fact of evolution was needed. Darwin never campaigned himself. He was something of a hypochondriac—one biographer (Irvine, 1959) called him "the perfect patient"—and after his trip on the *Beagle,* he became a recluse, rarely leaving his country home. The struggle for the survival of natural selection was carried on by others, most spectacularly by Thomas Henry Huxley (1825–1895), "Darwin's bulldog."

Darwin was a young naturalist who had the good fortune to be included on a round-the-world scientific voyage aboard *HMS Beagle* from 1831 to 1836. Darwin was impressed, especially in South America, by the tremendous variation within and between species. Darwin noted that there are innumerable distinct natural forms, each of which is peculiarly suited to its particular habitat. It was easy to imagine that each subspecies had descended from a common ancestor, and that each subspecies had been selected to fit some part of the environment.

Then, sometime after his return to England, Darwin began to collect data on species—their variation and origin. In his *Autobiography,* he said that he collected facts "on a wholesale scale," on "true Baconian principles." Part of his investigation centered on artificial selection, that is, on how breeders of plants and animals improve their stocks. Darwin talked with pigeon fanciers and horticulturalists and read their pamphlets. One pamphlet he read, "The Art of Improving the Breeds of Domestic Animals," written in 1809 by John Sebright, indicated that nature, too, selected some traits and rejected others, just as breeders did: "A severe winter, or a scarcity of food, by destroying the weak and unhealthful, has all the good effects of the most skillful selection" (Ruse, 1975, p. 347). So, by the 1830s, Darwin already had a rudimentary theory of natural selection: Nature produces innumerable variations among living things, and some of these variations are selected for perpetuation. Over time, isolated populations become adapted to their surroundings. What was entirely unclear was what maintained the system of selection. Why should there be improvement in species? In the case of artificial selection, the answer is clear. Selection is made by the breeder to produce a desirable kind of plant or animal. But what force in nature parallels the breeder's ideal? Darwin could not accept Lamarck's innate drive to perfection. The cause of selection must reside outside the organism, he insisted, but where?

Darwin got his answer in 1838 while reading Thomas Malthus's (1766–1834) *Essay on the Principle of Population as It Affects the Future Improvement of Society* (1798). Malthus attacked the utopian fantasies of certain writers by arguing that population growth necessarily exceeds growth in the food supply, with the consequence that life is a struggle of too many people for too few resources. The mass of humanity is necessarily kept at a subsistence-level economy, at best. In his *Autobiography,* Darwin stated he had at last "got a theory on which he could work." It was the struggle for survival that motivated natural selection. Too many creatures struggled over too few resources, and those who were "weak and unhealthful" could not support themselves and died without offspring. The strong and healthy survived and procreated. In this way, favorable variations were preserved and unfavorable ones eliminated. Struggle for survival was the engine of evolution.

Darwin need not have gone to Malthus for the concept of individual struggle for survival. As William Irvine (1959) points out, in her evolutionary aspects, nature is almost tritely mid-Victorian. Darwin's theory "delighted…mid-century optimists" who learned that "nature moved forward on the sound business principles of laissez-faire" (p. 346). Natural selection may have offended the pious, but not the Victorian businessman of the Industrial Revolution, who knew that life was a constant struggle that rewarded failure with poverty and disgrace. The improvement of the species from the struggle of individuals was merely Adam Smith's "invisible hand" all over again.

Darwin had formulated the essentials of his theory by 1842, at which time he first set them on paper with no thought of publication. His theory may be summarized as a logical argument (Vorzimmer, 1970). First, from Malthus, Darwin holds that there is a constant struggle for existence resulting from the tendency of animals to outgrow their food sources. Second, nature constantly produces variant forms within and between species. Some variants are better adapted to the struggle for survival than others. Consequently, organisms possessing unfavorable traits will not reproduce, causing their traits to disappear. Finally, as small adaptive change follows small adaptive change over eons, species will differentiate from a common stock as each form adapts to its peculiar environment. Furthermore, environments will change, selecting new traits for perpetuation, and as environment succeeds environment, species will diverge ever more from their parent forms. Thus the observed diversity of nature can be explained as the result of a few mechanical principles operating over millions of years, as species evolve from species.

The theory as it stood was deficient. Without our knowledge of genetics, the origin of variations and the nature of their transmission could not be explained. Darwin was never able to overcome these difficulties and was in fact pushed closer and closer to Lamarckism as he defended his theories against critics. It is an irony of history that while Darwin was writing and defending his *Origin of Species,* an obscure

Polish monk, Gregor Mendel (1822–1884), was doing the work on heredity that eventually supplied the answer to Darwin's difficulties. It was not until 1900 that Mendel's work, published and ignored in 1865, was rediscovered and hailed as the foundation of modern genetics. By the time Darwin died, he had earned burial in Westminster Abbey and his thought had revolutionized the Western world-view, but it was not until the twentieth century that evolution seriously affected biology, following the synthesis of genetics and natural selection into modern neo-Darwinian theory in the 1930s.

Darwin set his ideas down in 1842, but he did not publish his *Origin of Species* until 1859. Why? It appears that even for its discoverer, evolution was too threatening a thought. In a letter, Darwin said that admitting that species are not fixed "is like confessing a murder" (Irvine, 1959). It has been suggested that Darwin's hypochondria and various physical symptoms resulted from a neurotic crisis over the enormity of the idea of natural selection. In any event, Darwin pursued other things, spending eight years, for example, studying barnacles. Then, on June 18, 1858, Darwin was shocked to discover that someone was about to publish his theory. Evolution was truly in the air. Alfred Russell Wallace (1823–1913) had also been to South America, had been impressed by natural variation, and had read Malthus. Younger than Darwin, he was less hesitant to publish his conclusions. In fact, in later years, Wallace was faithful to natural selection after Darwin retreated to Lamarckism.

It was arranged that Darwin and Wallace would each write a paper on natural selection. These were read on July 1, 1858, in their absence, to the Linnean Society of London, thus establishing Darwin and Wallace as codiscoverers of natural selection. Darwin rushed through a short version of his projected work on evolution, which appeared in 1859 as *The Origin of Species by Means of Natural Selection or the Preservation of Favored Races in the Struggle for Life*. It presented his theory backed by a mass of supporting detail. It was revised until its sixth edition in 1872, as Darwin tried to answer his scientific critics—unsuccessfully, as it turned out—in ignorance of genetics. Darwin wrote numerous other works, including two on the descent of humans and the expression of emotion in humans and the animals.

Reception and Influence

The world was well prepared for Darwin's theory. The idea of evolution was already around well before 1859, and when the *Origin* was published, it was taken seriously by learned men in all quarters. Biologists and naturalists greeted the work with varying degrees of criticism. Part of Darwin's thesis, that all living things descend from one common ancestor in the remote past, was scarcely novel and was widely accepted. Great difficulties were seen with the theory of natural selection, however, and it was still easy for scientists to hang on to some form of Lamarckism, to see the hand of God in progressive evolution (as did Charles Lyell, the great geologist, even though he was a powerful proponent of Darwin's ideas), or to exempt humans from natural selection (as did nearly everyone).

If the reception of the *Origin* was so calm, how can we speak of a Darwinian revolution? To begin with, an appearance of revolution is given by the vituperative reception given evolution by Christian fundamentalists. Beginning with Bishop Wilberforce and continuing with William Jennings Bryan, defenders of the Bible attacked evolution, only to be crushed by such powerful personalities as T. H. Huxley and Clarence Darrow. Such clashes are the stuff of drama and give an appearance of revolution to the situation. The biblical literalists, however, were already well behind the times. The Bible had received two hundred years of historical scrutiny and had been found wanting as a historical document. Even the Catholic *Dublin Review* was not shocked by Darwin's ideas.

To consider Darwinism as an intellectual revolution we must distinguish Darwinism as a scientific hypothesis and Darwinism as the fulfillment of Enlightenment naturalism. Darwin himself cared only for the first, his intellectual child, but was alive to the possibilities of the second. Darwinism as a naturalistic metaphysics was the creation of others. Herbert Spencer, who had believed in the survival of the fittest before Darwin and applied it ruthlessly to humans and society, was one forceful proponent of metaphysical Darwinism. Another was T. H. Huxley (1825–1895), who used evolution to batter the Bible, miracles, and the church generally.

Huxley did much to popularize Darwinism as a naturalistic, even scientistic metaphysics. Darwin's theory did not begin the modern crisis of conscience. Profound doubts about the existence of God and about the meaning of life go back to the eighteenth century. Darwinism was not the beginning of the scientific challenge to the old medieval-Renaissance world-view. It was the culmination of this challenge, making it most difficult to exempt human beings from immutable, determinate natural law. In *Man's Place in Nature* (1863), Huxley carefully related mankind to the living apes, lower animals, and fossil ancestors, showing that we did indeed evolve from lower forms of life, that no Creation was needed. In the hands of people like Huxley, science then became not just the destroyer of illusions, but also a new metaphysics offering a new kind of salvation through science itself. Huxley wrote that:

> This new nature begotten by science upon fact … [constitutes] the foundation of our wealth and the condition of our safety … it is the bond which unites into a solid whole, regions larger than any empire of antiquity; it secures us from the recurrence of pestilences and famines of former times; it is the source of endless comforts and conveniences, which are not mere luxuries, but conduce to physical and moral well being.

More effusively, Winwood Reade wrote in *The Martyrdom of Man:* "The God of Light, the Spirit of Knowledge, the Divine Intellect is gradually spreading over the planet … Hunger and starvation will then be unknown … Disease will be extirpated … immortality will be invented … Man will then be perfect … he will therefore be what the vulgar worship as a God" (Houghton, 1957, p. 152). This hope is similar to Comte's positivism, which Huxley called "Catholicism *minus* Christianity." Clearly for some, the new religion of scientific humanity was at hand. Huxley also boasted of science's practical fruits: "Every chemically pure substance employed in manufacture, every abnormally fertile race of plants, or rapidly growing and fattening breed of animals …" This immediately brings to mind today's cancerous chemicals, tasteless tomatoes, and steroid-stuffed steers.

Darwinism did not instigate modern doubt, but it did intensify it. Darwin effected a Newtonian revolution in biology, robbing nature of her romantic capital *N,* reducing evolution to random variation and happenstance victory in the struggle for survival. The beginning of the reduction of biological nature to chemical nature that was completed with the discovery of DNA had begun. In psychology, Darwinism led to the psychology of adaptation. Assuming evolution, one may ask how mind and behavior, as distinct from bodily organs, help each creature adapt to its surroundings. Behaviorism is the ultimate heir to Darwinism in psychology; Skinner carefully modeled his account of animal learning on Darwinian variation, selection, and retention. Darwinism also contributed to the mechanization of human nature. In one of his more effusive moments, Huxley proclaimed that he would willingly be a clockwork mechanism if it were set to think and act correctly. Just such an image becomes the justification for Skinner's projection of a scientific utopia.

BEGINNINGS OF THE PSYCHOLOGY OF ADAPTATION IN BRITAIN

Lamarckian Psychology: Herbert Spencer (1820–1903)

In the summer of 1854, Herbert Spencer began to write a psychology whose "lines of thought had scarcely anything in common with lines of thought previously pursued" (Spencer, 1904). His work appeared the following year, 1855, as *Principles of Psychology*. This book gives Spencer a good claim to be the founder of the psychology of adaptation. Bain had integrated associationism and the sensorimotor conception of brain function; but although he acknowledged the validity of Darwinian evolution, his psychology remained part of classical, pre-evolutionary associationism. Writing before Darwin, Spencer integrated associationism and sensorimotor physiology with Lamarckian evolution. Consequently, he anticipated the psychology of adaptation. Furthermore, not only did he raise the two evolutionary questions, but he also answered them in the ways basic to Anglo-American psychology ever since.

Spencer's *Principles of Psychology* was just one part of his all-embracing *synthetic philosophy*. Spencer was the greatest systematizer since Aquinas, although he thought of himself as the new Newton. Another part of his system was the *Principles of Sociology*, and Spencer is regarded as a founder of that field, too. Aquinas organized all philosophy around the Christian God. Spencer organized it around Lamarckian evolution, in which he believed as early as 1852. He referred all questions, metaphysical or otherwise, to the principle of evolution and presented it as a cosmic process, embracing not only organic evolution but also the evolution of mind and societies.

In 1854, Spencer wrote: "If the doctrine of Evolution is true, the inevitable implication is that Mind can be understood only by observing how Mind is evolved." Here is the starting point of the psychology of adaptation. Spencer proceeded to discuss both evolutionary psychological questions. Considering the individual, Spencer viewed development as a process by which the connections between ideas come to mirror accurately the connections between events prevailing in the environment. The connections between ideas are built up by contiguity. Wrote Spencer (1897): "The growth of intelligence at large depends upon the law, that when any two psychical states occur in immediate succession, an effect is produced such that if the first subsequently recurs there is a certain tendency for the second to follow it." This tendency is strengthened as ideas are more frequently associated together. Like Bain, Spencer attempted to "deduce" the laws of mental association from the sensorimotor constitution of the nervous system and brain. In general, then, Spencer's analysis of the individual mind is that of atomistic associationism. He carried out the "successive decomposition of the more complex phenomena of intelligence into simpler ones … down to the simplest … element." What Spencer adds to Bain is the evolutionary conception, viewing the development of the mind as an adaptive adjustment to environmental conditions.

Spencer pictured the brain as a sensorimotor associational device, stating (1897) that "the human brain is an organized register of infinitely numerous experiences." His view has two important consequences. Given the Lamarckian idea of the heritability of acquired characteristics, instinct can be made acceptable to associationists and empiricists. Following the passage just quoted, Spencer described how the brain accumulates experiences "during the evolution of that series of organisms through which the human organism has been reached." Thus innate reflexes and instincts are simply associative habits so well learned they became part of a species' genetic legacy. Such habits may not be acquired during an individual's life, but they are still acquired following the laws of association in the life of the species. Innate ideas need no longer terrify the empiricist.

The second consequence of Spencer's integration of evolution and the sensorimotor concept of nervous function is more portentous: Differences in the mental processes of different species reduce to the number of associations the brains are able to make. All brains work the same way, by association, and differ only quantitatively in the richness of their associations. As Spencer (1897) put it, "The impressions received by inferior intelligences, even down to the very lowest, are dealt with after a like model." Thus his answer to the species question is to deny qualitative differences between species and admit only quantitative, associational differences. This idea extends to differences within, as well as between, species; the "European inherits from twenty to thirty cubic inches more brain than the Papuan," he said. This implies that the "civilized man has also a more complex or heterogeneous nervous system than the uncivilized man," as he wrote in *First Principles* (1880).

Spencer's conclusions are of tremendous importance for the development of the psychology of adaptation. Given his framework, comparative psychology would be directed toward studying species differences in simple associative learning, studies aimed at quantifying a single dimension of "intelligence" along which species can be arranged. Moreover, such studies could be performed in the laboratory, ignoring an organism's native environment. If the brain is no more than an initially empty stimulus-response associating mechanism, then it is irrelevant whether the associations are natural or contrived; in fact, the laboratory offers greater control of the process than naturalistic observation.

It also follows that if all organisms learn the same way, then the results of studies of simple animal learning, with their precision, replicability, and rigor, can be extended without serious modification to human learning. We will find that all of these conclusions are of fundamental importance to behavioralism, the twentieth-century psychology of adaptation. Behavioralists seek laws of learning valid for at least all mammals and assume the extension of animal findings to human psychology—often without supporting data.

Finally, the quantitative conception of associative mental function would help develop intelligence testing, which purports to assign a number to a person's intelligence. Although it is not demanded by the theory, the connection of associational ability with brain mass and complexity of association would push mental testing in a racist direction. We have already seen Spencer denigrate "uncivilized" people for having low brain mass and a simple nervous system, and in *First Principles* he implies that the "lower human races" are children: "In the infant European we see sundry resemblances to the lower human races."

One application of the theory of evolution to human society is to see it as an arena for the struggle for existence. This attitude is called *social Darwinism*, although it began before Darwin with Herbert Spencer. Spencer argued that natural selection should be allowed to take its course on the human species. Government should do nothing to save the poor, weak, and helpless. In nature, poor, weak, helpless animals, and their poor hereditary traits, are weeded out by natural selection. This should be the way in human society as well, said Spencer. Government should leave the cosmic process alone, for it will perfect humanity by the selection of the fittest. To help human failures would only serve to degrade the species by allowing them to have children and thus pass on their hereditary tendency to fail.

When Spencer toured America in 1882, he was lionized. Social Darwinism had great appeal in a *laissez-faire* capitalist society where it could justify even cutthroat competition on the grounds that such competition perfected humanity. Although it promised eventual perfection of the species, social Darwinism was profoundly conservative, for all reform was seen as tampering with nature's laws. The American social Darwinist Edward Youmans complained bitterly about the evils of the robber barons, but when asked what he proposed to do about them replied, "Nothing" (Hofstadter, 1955). Only centuries of evolution could relieve human problems.

Darwinian Psychology

Spencer's evolutionary principles, while inspired by Lamarck, are not inconsistent with Darwin's theory of natural selection. The only new assumption needed is that natural selection has produced the sensorimotor nervous system believed to exist in all animals, which justifies an associationist theory of mind, or later of behavior. Many naturalistic thinkers, including Darwin himself, consciously or unconsciously adhered to the Lamarckian view of progressive evolution, however, and sometimes even accepted the heritability of acquired characteristics. Thus Spencer's Lamarckian psychology shades insensibly into a Darwinian psychology.

Darwin on Humans. The central challenge of Darwin's *Origin of Species* concerned what Huxley called man's place in nature. In the comprehensive, naturalistic scheme of evolution, humanity was made part of nature, no longer a species that transcended it. This implication was immediately seen by all, whether they agreed with it or not. Yet *Origin* itself contains very little on human psychology. We know that in his early notebooks, dating back to the 1830s, Darwin was concerned with these topics, but he seems to have set them aside from his initial publication as too troublesome. All his life Darwin projected, but never completed, a master work on evolution in all its facets. In any event, it was not until 1871 that he finally published *The Descent of Man*, which brings human nature within the scope of natural selection.

Darwin's aim in *The Descent of Man* is to show that "man is descended from some lowly organized form," a conclusion that he regretted would "be highly distasteful to many." He broadly compared human and animal behavior and concluded that

> The difference in mind between man and the higher animals, great as it is, is certainly one of degree and not of kind. We have seen that the senses and intuitions, the various emotions and faculties, such as love, memory, attention, curiosity, imitation, reason, etc., of which man boasts may be found in an incipient, or even sometimes in a well-developed condition, in lower animals. [Even the] ennobling belief in God is not universal with man.

Descent was not primarily a work of psychology; it mainly attempted to incorporate humans fully into nature. Darwin felt that Spencer had already laid the foundations for an evolutionary psychology. Yet Darwin's work contrasts importantly with Spencer's *Principles*. Darwin followed philosophical faculty psychology, relegating association to a secondary factor in thought. Partly as a consequence, Darwin was concerned almost exclusively with the species question, for he assumed that evolution shaped the faculties. He also allowed great scope to the effects of heredity, sounding at times like an extreme nativist: For Darwin, both virtue and crime were heritable tendencies; woman is genetically inferior to man in "whatever he takes up." On the other hand, Darwin agreed with Spencer that the nature of species differences is quantitative rather than qualitative and that well-learned habits can become innate reflexes. Lamarckian psychology and Darwinian psychology differ only in emphasis, not in content. The major difference is that Darwin's psychology is only a part of a materialistic, evolutionary biology. Spencer's psychology, in contrast, was part of a grand metaphysics that tended toward dualism and postulated an "Unknowable" forever beyond the reach of science. Darwin sheared off this metaphysical growth from the psychology of adaptation.

The Spirit of Darwinian Psychology: Sir Francis Galton (1822–1911).   Galton was an outstanding example of that distinct Victorian type, the gentleman dilettante. Independently wealthy, he was able to turn his inventive mind to whatever he chose. He traveled over most of Africa and wrote a manual for travelers in wild lands. He empirically investigated the efficacy of prayer. He pioneered the use of fingerprints for personal identification. He invented composite photographic portraiture. Many of his wide-ranging investigations were psychological or sociological. He once tried to understand paranoia by suspecting everyone he met of evil intentions. He canvassed the female beauties of Great Britain trying to ascertain which county had the most beautiful women in it. He measured boredom at scientific lectures. He applied anthropomorphic tests to thousands of individuals visiting a fair in Kensington. However, Galton's researches were so eclectic that they do not add up to a research program. Consequently, Galton cannot be considered a psychologist in the same sense as Wundt, Titchener, or Freud.

Nevertheless, Galton made important contributions to the growing psychology of adaptation. He broadened psychology to encompass topics excluded by Wundt. In his *Inquires into the Human Faculty* (1883/1907, p. 47), he wrote: "No professor of ... psychology ... can claim to know the elements of what he teaches, unless he is acquainted with the ordinary phenomena of idiocy, madness, and epilepsy. He must study the manifestations of disease and congenital folly, as well as those of high intellect." Wundt wanted to understand only the normal, adult mind. Galton inquired into any human mind.

Galton devised a number of important methods used by the psychology of adaptation. He was the first to systematically apply statistics to psychological data, and he invented the correlation coefficient. He studied twins to sort out the contributions of nature and nurture to human character, intellect, and behavior. He tried to use indirect behavioral measures (rate of fidgeting) to measure a mental state (boredom). He invented the free-association technique of interrogating memory. He used questionnaires to collect data on mental processes such as mental imagery. He tried to use a psychophysical method (lifting weights) to measure acuteness of perception, and thus—he thought—intelligence. He tried to directly introspect his higher mental processes, which Wundt had said was impossible. All these techniques found a place in English and American psychology.

Spencer began the psychology of adaptation, but Galton epitomized it. His eclectic attitude concerning both method and subject matter, and his use of statistics, would strongly characterize Darwinian psychology from this point on. Above all, his interest in individual differences points to the future: In German rationalist fashion, Wundt had wanted to describe the transcendent human mind; he quite literally found the study of individual differences to be foreign and the existence of individual differences to be a nuisance. Guided by evolution—especially the concept of variation—Galton, however, was interested in all those factors that make people different. The study of individual differences is an essential part of Darwinian science, for without variation there can be no differential selection and no evolutionary improvement of the species.

Improvement of the human species was precisely Galton's aim. Underlying his various investigations was not a research program, but rather a "religious duty." He was convinced that the most important individual differences, including those of morals, character, and intellect, are not acquired. His great aim was to demonstrate that these characteristics were innate and then to measure them so that they could inform the procreative behavior of humanity. Eugenics is the selective breeding of human beings to improve the species.

In his *Hereditary Genius* of 1869, Galton

propose[d] to show that a man's natural abilities are derived by inheritance, under exactly the same limitations as are the form and physical features of the whole organic world. Consequently, as it is easy, not withstanding these limitations, to obtain by careful selection a permanent breed of dogs or horses gifted with peculiar powers of running, or of doing anything else, so it would be quite practicable to produce a highly gifted race of men by judicious marriages during several consecutive generations.

In this work, Galton endeavored to show that abilities as different as those required to be a good judge or a good wrestler are innate and heritable, which would make a eugenics program feasible. Galton's main interest was in the improvement of individuals, and he thought selective breeding would improve humanity faster than improved education. Galton's program for selective human breeding was a form of positive eugenics, attempting to get especially "fit" individuals to marry one another. Galton proposed that examinations be used to discover the ten most talented men and women in Great Britain. At a public ceremony recognizing their talent, each would be offered £5,000—a staggering sum in days when a moderately frugal person might live on a pound or so a week—as a wedding present should they choose to marry one another.

Galton's proposals gained few adherents when he first set them out in 1869. Just after the turn of the century, however, Britons were more disposed to listen. In the wake of their near defeat in the Boer War for South Africa, and the gradual recession of their empire, Britons began to worry that they were degenerating as a nation. In 1902, the Army reported that 60 percent of Englishmen were unfit for military service, setting off a furious public debate on the physical deterioration (after the name of the Army report) of the British people. In this atmosphere, worriers of all political stripes were excited by Galton's eugenic program for race improvement.

In 1901, Karl Pearson (1857–1936), an intimate of Galton's who had extended and perfected Galton's statistical approach to biology, pressed Galton to reenter the fray for eugenics. Pearson was a socialist who opposed conservative, *laissez-faire* social Darwinism and hoped to replace it with planned, politically enforced programs of eugenics. Galton agreed, despite his advanced age, again to take up the cause, and in that year he gave a public lecture on eugenics and began to work for the establishment of eugenics policies. In 1904, he gave £1,500 to establish a research fellowship in eugenics and a eugenics record office at the University of London. In 1907, he helped found the Eugenics Education Society, which began to publish a journal, *Eugenics Review*. Eugenics appealed to people all across the political spectrum. Conservative, establishment leaders used alleged "laws of heredity and development" to support their crusade for moral, especially sexual, reform. Social radicals could press eugenics into service as part of their programs for political and social reform. Eugenics was much talked about in the first decade of the twentieth century in Britain.

Despite the attention it received, British eugenics, in contrast to American eugenics, enjoyed only limited success in affecting public policy. Galton's program of rewards was never seriously considered. Some attention was given to laws enforcing negative eugenics—attempts to regulate the reproduction of the alleged "unfit"—but these were relatively mild measures that placed the socially incapacitated in institutions where they could receive care. British eugenicists were themselves divided on the need for government eugenics programs, the social radical eugenicists in particular urging education and voluntary control instead of legal compulsion. British eugenics was never fueled, as American eugenics was, by racism and race hysteria. British eugenicists were more concerned to encourage the reproduction of the middle and upper classes, whose birthrate had long been in decline, than to restrict spitefully the reproduction of allegedly inferior races. Although eugenics began in Britain, in the English-speaking world it was practiced mostly in America, as we shall see.

THE RISE OF COMPARATIVE PSYCHOLOGY

It is clear that a psychology based on evolution should call forth research aimed at comparing the various abilities of different species of animals. Simple comparison of human and animal abilities were first made by the ancient Greek philosopher Aristotle, and both René Descartes and David Hume buttressed their philosophies with such considerations. Eighteenth-century Scottish faculty psychologists argued that people had a special moral faculty that distinguished them from animals. Gall studied animals and people to discover the special mental faculties of each species. The theory of evolution, however, gave comparative psychology a powerful impetus, placing it in a wider biological context and giving it a specific rationale. In the later nineteenth century, comparative psychology grew in strength, until in the twentieth century learning theorists studied animals in preference to humans.

Modern comparative psychology may be said to have begun in 1872 with the publication of Darwin's *The Expression of the Emotions in Man and Animals* (Darwin, 1965). The new approach is heralded by Darwin's statement early in the book (p. 12): "No doubt as long as man and all other animals are viewed as independent creations, an effectual stop is put to our natural desire to investigate as far as possible the causes of Expression." However, he who admits "that the structure and habits of all animals have been gradually evolved, will look at the whole subject in a new and interesting light." In the rest of his book, Darwin surveyed the means of emotional expression possessed by humans and animals, noting the continuity between them, and demonstrating their universality among the races of humanity. Darwin's theory is very Lamarckian, it may be noted: "Actions, which were at first voluntary, soon become habitual, and at last hereditary, and may then be performed even in opposition to the will." Darwin's theory was that our involuntary emotive expressions have gone through this development.

Darwin's early work in comparative psychology was systematically carried on by his friend George John Romanes (1848–1894). In *Animal Intelligence* (1883), Romanes surveyed the mental abilities of animals from protozoa to apes. In later works, such as *Mental Evolution in Man* (1889), Romanes attempted to trace the gradual evolution of mind down the millennia. Romanes died before he could complete his comparative psychology. His literary executor was C. Lloyd Morgan (1852–1936), who in his own *Introduction to Comparative Psychology* (1894) objected to Romanes's overestimation of animal intelligence. Romanes had quite freely attributed complex thinking to animals from analogy to his own thinking. Morgan, in formulating what has since been called *Morgan's canon*, argued that inferences of animal thinking should be no more than absolutely necessary to explain some observed behavior. The last of the early founding British comparative psychologists was the philosopher Leonard T. Hobhouse (1864–1928), who used the data of comparative psychology to construct a general evolutionary metaphysics. He also carried out some experiments on animal behavior that in some respects anticipated Gestalt work on animal insight and were designed to undermine the artificiality of behaviorist animal experiments.

These comparative psychologists combined faculty psychology with associationism in their theories of development and collected some interesting facts. What proved important and controversial about their work, however, were their method and goal. What Romanes consciously introduced to psychology was an objective, behavioral method in contrast to the subjective method of introspection, since we cannot observe the minds of animals, only their behavior. Nevertheless, the theoretical goal of the British animal psychologists was never merely to describe behavior. Rather they wanted to explain the workings of animal minds, and therefore they attempted to infer mental processes from behavior. The problems involved in this research program importantly affected the development of behavioralism, which was founded by American comparative psychologists.

Methodologically, comparative psychology began with Romanes's *anecdotal method*. He collected vignettes of animal behavior from many correspondents and sifted through them for plausible and reliable information from which to reconstruct the animal mind. The anecdotal method became an object of derision among the experimentally oriented Americans, especially E. L. Thorndike. The method lacked the control available in the laboratory and was felt to overestimate animal intelligence. The anecdotal method did have the virtue, largely unappreciated at the time, of observing animals in natural, uncontrived situations. We will find that animal psychology ran into real difficulties in the 1960s because of its exclusive reliance on controlled laboratory methods that overlook the animals' ecological histories.

Theoretically, inferring mental processes from behavior presented difficulties. It is altogether too easy to attribute to animals complex mental processes they may not possess—any simple behavior can be explained (incorrectly) as the result of complex reasoning. Anyone who today reads Romanes's *Animal Intelligence* will feel that he frequently committed this error. Morgan's canon was an attempt to deal with this problem by requiring conservative inferences.

In his own treatment of animal mind, Morgan (1886) contributed a distinction that unfortunately was less known and less influential than his famous canon of simplicity. Morgan distinguished objective inferences from projective—or, as he called them in the philosophical jargon of his time, ejective—inferences from animal behavior to animal mind. Imagine watching a dog sitting at a street corner at 3:30 one afternoon. As a school bus approaches, the dog gets up, wags its tail, and watches the bus slow down and then stop. The dog looks at the children getting off the bus and, when one boy gets off, it jumps on him, licks his face, and together the boy and the dog walk off down the street. Objectively, Morgan would say, we may infer certain mental powers possessed by the dog. It must possess sufficient perceptual skills to pick one child out from the crowd getting off the bus, and it must possess at least recognition memory, as it responds differently to one child from all the others. Such inferences are objective, because they posit certain internal cognitive processes that may be further investigated by, for example, testing dogs' discriminative learning capacities. On the other hand, we are tempted to attribute a subjective mental state, happiness, to the dog on analogy with our own happiness when we greet a loved one who has been absent. Such inferences by analogy to our own subjective mental states are Morgan's projective inferences, because in making them we project our own feelings onto the animal. Objective inferences are legitimate in science, Morgan held, because they do not depend on analogy, are not emotional, and are susceptible to later verification by experiment. Projective inferences are not scientifically legitimate because they result from attributing our own feelings to animals and may not be more objectively assessed. Morgan did not claim that animals do not have feelings, only that their feelings, whatever they may be, fall outside the domain of scientific psychology.

Morgan's distinction is important, but it was neglected by later comparative psychologists. When Romanes's methods of anecdote and inference were challenged by American animal psychologists in the 1890s, the absurdities of subjective inference—calling rats "happy" and "carefree"—led to wholesale rejection of any discussion of animal mind. Had Morgan's distinction between objective and projective inferences been heeded, however, it might have been seen that although projective inferences are scientifically worthless, objective inferences are perfectly respectable.

However, no matter how conservatively and carefully mind might be reconstructed from behavior, it remained possible for the skeptic to doubt. As Romanes (1883, pp. 5–6) put it: "Skepticism of this kind is logically bound to deny evidence of mind, not only in the case of lower animals, but also in that of the higher, and even in that of men other than the skeptic himself. For all objections which could apply to the use of [inference] ... would apply with equal force to the evidence of any mind other than that of the individual objector." Such skepticism constitutes the essence of the behaviorist revolution. The behaviorist may admit that she or he possesses consciousness, if not mind, but refuses to use mental activity to explain the behavior of animals, or of other human beings.

The psychology of adaptation began in England, where the modern theory of evolution was born. However, it found more fertile ground in one of Britain's former colonies: the United States. There it became the only psychology; and, as the United States came to dominate psychology, so did the psychology of adaptation.

PSYCHOLOGY IN THE NEW WORLD

Background

General Intellectual and Social Environment. America was new. Its original inhabitants were seen by Europeans as savages, noble or brutish, who revealed original human nature untouched by civilization. The first settlers confidently expected to displace the Indians, replacing their primitive state with farms, villages, and churches. The wilderness found by the settlers opened up possibilities of erecting a new civilization in the new world. The Puritans came to establish a "city on a hill," a perfect Christian society and example to be looked up to by the rest of the world. In America, there was no feudal hierarchy, no established church, no ancient universities. Instead, each person could make his or her own way in the wilderness.

This is not to say that the European settlers brought no intellectual baggage. They did, and two traditions are particularly important: evangelical religion and Enlightenment philosophy. America was initially settled by Protestants, not Catholics. In fact, when Catholics first came to America in large numbers, they were forced to remain outside the mainstream of American life. Catholics were seen as agents of a dangerous foreign power, the pope, and anti-Catholic riots and the burning of Catholic churches were not unknown in nineteenth-century America. What emerged most strongly from the dominant American Protestantism was evangelical Christianity. This form of Christianity has little or no theological content, looking instead to the salvation of the individual soul in an emotional conversion experience when the person accepts the will of God.

An important part of the European reaction to the excessive geometric spirit of the Enlightenment was romanticism. In America, however, the reaction against the Age of Reason was a religious one. America experienced revivals in the colonial period, and another took place shortly after the French Revolution. Romanticism touched America only briefly, in the transcendental movement. Henry David Thoreau, for example, decried industry's encroachment on romantic nature. However, more important for most people was evangelical Christianity, which rejected the antireligious skepticism of the Enlightenment.

It is no accident that many early American psychologists, including John B. Watson, the founder of behaviorism, were early intended for the church. The stock in trade of the evangelical preacher is conversion, playing on an audience's emotions to change people from sinners to saints, modifying both soul and behavior. The goal of many American psychologists in both the functional and behavioral periods has been to modify behavior, to make the person of today into the new person of tomorrow. The evangelical preachers wrote about the ways to change souls through preaching; the psychologists wrote about the ways to change behavior through conditioning.

The importance of evangelical Christianity in the developing intellectual life of the United States should not be underestimated. America's tradition of freedom of religion may suggest that the founders did not care especially about religion. The contrary is true. Freedom of religion came into existence because of the demands of evangelical sects afraid of the power of established churches. Evangelical Christianity acted as a filter for Enlightenment thought, keeping out the radical skepticism and antireligious attitudes of the late Enlightenment that were unacceptable to most Americans.

In the period before 1800, America did possess some genuine philosophies. There was Benjamin Franklin, whose experiments on electricity were admired in Europe, who charmed France as the "natural man" of the new world, and who was enshrined as one of the leading figures of the Enlightenment, ranking even with Voltaire. Thomas Jefferson, another philosophe, is perhaps the best example of the geometric spirit in America. Jefferson attempted to apply numerical calculation to every subject from crop rotation to human happiness. His Newtonian mechanism even blinded him to biological facts: Arguing against the possibility of Noah's flood, he "proved" from physical calculations that in any flood the waters cannot rise more than about fifty feet above sea level, and that consequently the fossil sea shells found in the American Appalachian mountains were just unusual rock growths (Wills, 1978). Jefferson, who was skeptical of the claims of Christianity, was probably a Voltairian deist.

Ideas such as these were anathema to evangelical religion, however, and only certain moderate elements of Enlightenment thought became important in America. Foremost among these acceptable ideas were those of various thinkers of the Scottish Enlightenment, which in fact exerted more influence on Jefferson than is commonly supposed. As we have seen, the Scot's proposed a commonsense philosophy that was perfectly compatible with religion. It depicted the human mind as a collection of God-given faculties that allowed people to know the world and God's morality. In America's religious colleges, which were the vast majority of American colleges, Scottish philosophy became the established curriculum, dominating every aspect of higher education from ethics to psychology. Scottish philosophy was American orthodoxy.

In considering the intellectual climate of the United States, to the influences of evangelical Christianity and a moderate Enlightenment must be added a third element, business, which interacted with the other two in important ways. America came to be a nation of business unlike any other nation on earth. There was no feudal aristocracy, no established church, and only a distant king. What remained was individual enterprise, and the individual's struggle to survive in confrontation with the wilderness and in competition with other businessmen. The business of America was indeed business.

Out of this unique American intellectual and social environment, combined with a growing national chauvinism, several important ideas emerged. One was the supreme value placed on useful knowledge. The Enlightenment certainly held that knowledge should serve human needs, should be practical rather than metaphysical. American Protestants came to think of inventions as glorifying the ingenuity of God in creating the clever human mind. *Technology* was an American word. An unfortunate consequence of this attitude was anti-intellectualism. Abstract science was scorned as something European and degenerate. What counted was practical accomplishment that at once enriched the businessman, revealed God's principles, and advanced the American dream. The businessman valued the same hard-headed "common sense" taught in the colleges. Commonsense philosophy told the ordinary person that his or her untutored ideas were basically right, which tended to increase American anti-intellectualism.

In the use of the term "businessman" the word *man* ought to be stressed. It was the men who struggled for survival in the world of business and who valued clear-headed common sense and practical achievement. Feeling and sentiment were the special province of women, who in the nineteenth century were increasingly removed from the world of work, as such formerly domestic activities as baking, brewing, cheese making, spinning, and weaving became industrialized. This change made women of little economic importance, leaving only the realm of the emotions to female rule. In America, emotions were not romantically inspiring, but were instead taken to be feminine and weak.

Americans also tended to be radical environmentalists, greatly preferring to believe that people's circumstances, not their genes, were the primary cause of human characteristics and achievements. They believed that, contrary to the prejudices of Europeans, the American environment was the best in the world and would produce geniuses to surpass Newton. This belief reflects the empiricism of the Enlightenment and the flexible beliefs of the businessman. There would be no bounds on the perfectibility of humans in the new world, no bounds on the achievement of the free individual. Progress was the order of the day. There was even a cult of self-improvement from the early days of the American republic. In the 1830s, there was a monthly magazine called *The Cultivator,* "designed to improve the soil and the mind." Not only could a man improve his farm business, but he could improve his mind as well. In fact, it was expected that the good Christian would be a successful businessman or farmer.

All these attitudes—religious, Enlightened, and commercial—are nicely epitomized in the American attitude to the machine: the product of human ingenuity, improver of the world, and enricher of its maker. The builder of a machine became Newton's God, and the machine was made divine by association with the celestial mechanism. A writer named John Pendelton Kennedy visited an early American factory and recorded his reactions:

> When I look upon this vast enginery, this infinite complication of wheels, this exquisitely delicate adjustment of parts, and this sure, steady and invariable result shown in the operation of the perfect machine … I am lost in admiration of the genius that masters the whole. (Miller, 1965, p. 301)

One observer of the early American scene recognized these American trends. Alexis de Tocqueville wrote in *Democracy in America* following his visit to America during 1831 and 1832: "The longer a nation is democratic, enlightened and free, the greater will be the number of these interested promoters of scientific genius, and the more will discoveries immediately applicable to productive industry confer gain, fame and even power." However, Tocqueville worried that "in a community thus organized ... the human mind may be led insensibly to the neglect of theory." Aristocracies, on the other hand, "facilitate the natural impulse of the highest regions of thought." Tocqueville foresaw well. American psychology since its founding has neglected theory, even being openly hostile to theory at times. While Europeans such as Jean Piaget construct grand, almost metaphysical theories, B. F. Skinner argues that theories of learning are unnecessary.

Pre-Darwinian Background in Philosophical Psychology. The Puritans brought medieval faculty psychology with them to America. It perished in the early eighteenth century, however, when America's first great philosopher, Jonathan Edwards (1703–1758), read Locke. His enthusiasm for empiricism was such that his genius carried him independently in the direction of Berkeley and Hume. Like Berkeley, he denied the distinction between primary and secondary qualities and concluded that the mind knows only its perceptions, not the external world. Like Hume, he expanded the role of associations in the operation of the mind, finding as Hume had that contiguity, resemblance, and cause and effect are the laws of association (Jones, 1958). Finally, like Hume, he was driven toward skepticism through his recognition that generalizations about cause cannot be rationally justified, and that emotion, not reason, is the true spring of human action (Blight, 1978). Edwards, however, remained a Christian, as Hume did not, and he may be regarded as more medieval than modern in this respect (Gay, 1969).

Edwards's stress on emotion as the basis of religious conversion helped pave the way for the American form of romanticism and idealism: transcendentalism. Transcendentalism was a New England revolt against what had become a comfortable, stuffy, and dry form of Puritanism. The transcendentalists wanted to return to the lively, emotional religion of Edwards's time, and to the direct, passionate encounter with God that Edwards had believed in. Such an attitude was compatible with both romanticism and post-Kantian idealism. The former prized individual feeling and communion with nature, similar to Thoreau's report of an extended, solitary sojourn in the wilderness in *Walden*. The latter believed Kant's transcendent noumena were knowable; similarly, George Ripley, a leading transcendentalist, wrote in *A Letter Addressed to the Congressional Church in Purchase Street* that they "believe in an order of truths which transcend the sphere of the external senses" (White, 1972). Thus, in some respects, transcendentalism was in tune with European romanticism and idealism.

In other respects, however, transcendentalism appears very American. It supported, for example, an evangelical, emotional Christianity that put the individual's feelings and conscience above hierarchical authority. Ralph Waldo Emerson preached "self-reliance," always an American ideal. He derided the radical empiricists as "negative and poisonous." Whether European or American in tone, however, transcendentalism's effect on mainstream American thought was limited. Like romanticism, its chief products were artistic rather than philosophical, and even its great art, such as Melville's *Moby Dick*, was much less popular than other works totally forgotten today. The American intellectual establishment of the colleges viewed transcendentalism, Kant, and idealism with horror, so that budding scientists and philosophers had little contact with the movement.

Instead of any romantic revolt, Scottish common-sense philosophy maintained its grip on American thought. Americans, too, began to produce faculty psychology texts at an accelerating rate as the nineteenth century progressed. There were at least two attempts to integrate German and American psychology. Frederick Rauch (1806–1841) tried to Americanize Hegel in his *Psychology* (1841), only the second book to use *psychology* in its title. The theologian Laurens Perseus Hickock (1798–1888) followed both Wolff and Kant, writing a *Rational Psychology* (c. 1848) and an *Empirical Psychology* (1882). Both reveal the American tendency to make psychology serve religion by "improving" the mind. Rauch concluded his text with a discussion of religion, while Hickock appealed to Christian faith as the source of the noumenal knowledge that Kant thought unattainable. Scottish faculty psychology was so well entrenched, however, that it either overrode or assimilated outside influences.

Academic faculty psychology in America did not add anything original to European faculty psychology. The Americans simply used the Europeans' ideas to improve and indoctrinate students into proper American and religious ways of thinking. More revealing of the American temperament is the popularity of phrenology, or popular faculty psychology. Phrenology enjoyed some popularity in Europe, especially in England; but in America, where it was put on a sound business basis and decked out in the trappings of vaudeville, it became a mania.

Early in the nineteenth century, Gall's colleague Spurzheim started on a triumphal tour of the United States, and its rigors took his life after only a few weeks. Spurzheim was followed by the British phrenologist George Combe, who was well received by educators and college presidents. These lectures were too theoretical for American audiences, however, and phrenology fell into the hands of two industrious and businesslike brothers, Orson and Lorenzo Fowler. They minimized the scientific content of phrenology and maximized the practical applications. They set up an office in New York where clients could have their characters read for a fee. They wrote endlessly of the benefits of phrenology and published a phrenological journal that endured from the 1840s to 1911. They traveled around the country, concentrating on the frontiers, giving lectures and challenging skeptics. Like the great magician Houdini, they accepted any kind of test of their abilities, including blindfolded examinations of volunteers' skulls.

What made the Fowlers' phrenology so popular was its appeal to the American character. It eschewed metaphysics for practical application. It pretended to tell employers what people to hire and to tell men which wives to take. It was thus the first mental testing movement in America and was Galtonian in its scrutiny of individual differences. Furthermore, it was progressive and reformist. Gall had believed the brain's faculties to be set by heredity. The Fowlers, however, said that weak faculties could be improved by practice and overly strong ones controlled by efforts of will. Many people sought out the Fowlers for advice on how to lead their lives; the Fowlers were the first guidance counselors. They also held out the hope that the nation and the world could be improved if only every person would be "phrenologized."

Finally, the Fowlers believed they served religion and morality. They encouraged their clients to improve their moral faculties and believed that the existence of the faculty of veneration demonstrated the existence of God, because the existence of the faculty implies the existence of its object.

Mesmeric magnetism also flourished in America, and spiritualism began there as well. On his tour of America in the 1840s, George Combe reported that mediums ran a flourishing business in New York. In the early twentieth century, spiritualism was so widespread that both *Scientific American* and the United States Congress appointed committees to investigate the claims of spiritualism. Animal magnetism arrived in the United States as a music hall turn and then was assimilated to phrenology in phrenomagnetism, which joined phrenology in the business of selling advice. No one could better look out for Number One than the possessor of *Instantaneous Personal Magnetism,* a system that included diets and physical exercises to build the "magnetic mind" capable of outstanding business success.

America's Native Philosophy: Pragmatism

In 1871 and 1872, a group of young, Harvard-educated, well-to-do Bostonians—"the very topmost cream of Boston manhood," William James called them—met as the Metaphysical Club to discuss philosophy in the age of Darwin. Among the members of the club were Oliver Wendell Holmes (1841–1935), destined to become perhaps the United States' most distinguished jurist; and, more important for the history of psychology, Chauncey Wright (1830–1875), Charles S. Peirce (1839–1914), and William James (1842–1910). All three were important to the founding of psychology in America. Wright articulated an early stimulus-response theory of behavior, Peirce carried out the first psychological experiments in the new world, and James laid the foundations of American psychology with his book *Principles of Psychology* (1890). The immediate fruit of the Metaphysical Club was America's only homegrown philosophy, pragmatism, a hybrid of Bain, Darwin, and Kant. The club opposed the regnant Scottish philosophy, dualistic and closely connected to religion and creationism, and proposed a new naturalistic theory of mind.

From Bain they took the idea that beliefs were dispositions to behave; Bain defined belief as "that upon which a man is prepared to act." From Darwin they, like most intellectuals of the day, learned to treat mind as part of nature, not a gift from God. More important—this was Wright's contribution—they took the survival of the fittest as a model by which to understand mind. Wright combined Bain's definition with Darwin's theory of natural selection and proposed that a person's beliefs evolve just as species do. As one matures, one's beliefs compete for acceptance, so that adequate beliefs emerge "from the survival of the fittest among our original ... beliefs." This is the essential idea of the individual approach to the psychology of adaptation—and, if we substitute "behaviors" for "beliefs," it states the central thesis of B. F. Skinner's radical behaviorism. Wright also tried to show how self-consciousness, far from being a mystery to naturalism, evolved from sensorimotor habits. A habit, Wright held, was a relation between a class of stimuli and some response or responses. The cognition needed to link stimulus and response was rudimentary, involving recalled images of past experiences. Self-consciousness arose when one—or people, as compared with the animals—became aware of the connection between stimulus and response. Wright's ideas go a long way to making mind part of nature, and they point to the behavioral emphasis of American psychology, in which beliefs are important only insofar as they produce behavior.

Charles S. Peirce summed up the conclusions of the Metaphysical Club and in so doing invented pragmatism. Kant had, as a foundational philosopher, sought the foundation of certain knowledge. Nevertheless, he recognized that men and women must act upon beliefs that are not certain; a physician, for example, may not be absolutely certain of a diagnosis but must nevertheless proceed, believing the diagnosis is correct. Kant called "such contingent belief which still forms the basis of the actual use of means for the attainment of certain ends, *pragmatic belief.*" The upshot of the meditations of the Metaphysical Club was that beliefs could never be certain. The best that humans could hope for were beliefs that led to successful action in the world, natural selection operating to strengthen certain beliefs and weaken others as beliefs struggled for acceptance. Darwin had shown that species were not fixed, and the Metaphysical Club concluded that truth, contrary to Kant, could not be fixed either. All that remained to epistemology, then, was Kant's pragmatic belief, which Peirce refined into "the pragmatic maxim," reflecting the conclusions of the club.

In 1878, Peirce published these conclusions in a paper, "How to make our ideas clear," first read to the Metaphysical Club at the end of its life. Peirce (1878/1966) wrote that "the whole function of thought is to produce habits of action," and that what we call beliefs are "a rule of action, or, say for short, a *habit.*" "The essence of belief," Peirce argued, "is the establishment of a habit, and different beliefs are distinguished by the different modes of action to which they give rise." Habits must have a practical significance if they are to be meaningful, Peirce went on. "Now the identity of a habit depends on how it might lead us to act.... Thus we come down to what is tangible and conceivably practical as the root of every real distinction of thought ... there is no distinction so fine as to consist in anything but a possible difference in practice." In conclusion, "the rule for attaining [clear ideas] is as follows: consider what effects, which might conceivably have practical bearings, we conceive the object of our conceptions to have. Then, our conception of these effects is the whole of our conception of the object." Or, as Peirce put it more succinctly in 1905, the truth of a belief "lies exclusively in its conceivable bearing upon the conduct of life."

Peirce's pragmatic maxim is revolutionary, because it abandons the old Platonic aim of a foundational philosophy. It admits with Heraclitus that nothing can ever be certain and draws from Darwin the idea that the best beliefs are those that work in adapting us to our changing environment. The pragmatic maxim is also consistent with scientific practice. Peirce had been a working physicist and learned that a scientific concept was useless and meaningless if it could not be translated into some observable phenomenon; thus Peirce's pragmatic maxim anticipates the positivist concept of operational definition. Later, when William James allowed emotional and ethical considerations to weigh in deciding whether a belief works, Peirce, the hardheaded physicist, refused to go along. In psychology, pragmatism represents a clear articulation of the individual-question approach to the psychology of adaptation. It takes, as B. F. Skinner later would, Darwin's account of species' evolution as a model by which to understand individual learning. The pragmatic maxim also anticipates the behavioral turn in American psychology, because it says that beliefs are always (if meaningful) manifested in behavior, so that reflection upon consciousness for its own sake is idle.

While Peirce never became a psychologist, he did aid its development in the United States. He read some of Wundt's researches in 1862 and campaigned against the continued reign of Scottish common-sense psychology and for the establishment of experimental psychology in U.S. universities. In 1877, he published a psychophysical study of color, the first experimental work to come from America. A student of his, Joseph Jastrow, became one of the leading American psychologists in the first part of the twentieth century, and a president of the American Psychological Association. In 1887, Peirce asked the central question of modern cognitive science: Can a machine think like a human being? Despite all this, his influence remained remarkably limited. He was an extraordinarily difficult man to get along with. Despite the best efforts of William James, he never could hold a permanent position at Harvard and lived most of his life as a near-penniless recluse. He wrote badly, and most of his papers were not published during his lifetime. Pragmatism's great influence on philosophy and psychology came from his associate, William James.

America's Psychologist: William James

James began to work out his own version of pragmatism in the 1870s and 1880s. At first, he advanced his philosophy timidly, as psychology rather than philosophy. In 1878, he contracted with the publisher Henry Holt to write a textbook on psychology; and during the 1880s, James published a series of articles that formed the core of his new psychology and philosophy and were incorporated into the book *Principles of Psychology*. Its publication in 1890 marks a watershed in the history of American psychology, for it inspired American students as neither the Scots nor Wundt could, and it set the tone for American psychology from 1890 to 1913 and beyond. James combined the usual interests of a founding psychologist: physiology and philosophy. He began his academic career with an M.D. and held a variety of posts at Harvard. Starting as an instructor of physiology, he next saw to the establishment for himself of a Chair in Psychology; he spent his last years as a professor of philosophy. It was in the *Principles* that James began to develop his pragmatic philosophy.

"Psychology is the Science of Mental Life," James told his readers (*Principles*, vol. I, p. 1). Its primary method is ordinary introspection, accompanied by the "diabolical cunning" of German experimentalism and by comparative studies of men, animals, and savages. James rejected sensationistic atomism, the billiard-ball theory also rejected by Wundt. According to James, this theory takes the discernible parts of objects to be enduring objects of experience, falsely chopping up the flow of experience. Wrote James:

> Consciousness ... does not appear to itself chopped up in bits. Such words as "chain" or "train" do not describe it fitly, as it presents itself in the first instance. It is nothing jointed; it flows. A "river" or a "stream" are the metaphors by which it is most naturally described. *In talking of it hereafter let us call it the stream of thought, of consciousness, or of subjective life.* (*Principles*, vol. I, p. 239)

In Darwinian fashion, James found that what consciousness contains is less important than what it does; it is function, not content, that counts. The primary function of consciousness is to choose. He wrote (1890): "*It is always interested more in one part of its object than in another, and welcomes and rejects, or chooses, all the while it thinks"* (*Principles*, vol. I, p. 284). Consciousness creates and serves the ends of the organism, the first of which is survival through adaptation to the environment. For James, however, adaptation is never passive. Consciousness chooses, acting always toward some end. The ceaseless flow of choices affects perception as well as conduct: "The mind, in short, works on the data it receives very much as a sculptor works on his block of stone" (*Principles*, vol. I, p. 288). James's mind is not the passive blank slate of the sensationists. It is a "fighter for ends," actively engaged with a practical world of experience.

Although James said psychology is the Science of Mental Life, it must simultaneously be "cerebralist." It is a fundamental assumption that "the brain is the one immediate bodily condition of the mental operation," and the *Principles*, all 1,377 pages of it, is "more or less of a proof that the postulate is correct" (vol. I, p. 4). He applauded Hartley's attempt to show that the laws of association are cerebral laws, "and so far as association stands for a *cause*, it is between *processes in the brain*" (vol. I, p. 554).

This seemed to involve James in a contradiction; the brain-machine must make choices. He had said that consciousness plays a positive role in human and animal life, and explicitly rejected mechanism, or what he called the "automaton theory." For James, evolutionary naturalism demanded that consciousness exist, since it fulfilled a vital adaptive function. A dumb machine knows no direction, it is like "dice thrown forever on a table ... what chance is there that the highest number will turn up oftener than the lowest?" James argued that consciousness increases the efficiency of the cerebral machine by "loading its dice." Wrote James (*Principles of Psychology*, vol. I, p. 140): "Loading its dice would bring constant pressure to bear in favor of *those* of its performances" that serve the "interests of the brain's owner." Consciousness transforms survival from "mere hypothesis" into an "imperative decree. Survival *shall* occur and therefore organs *must* so work.... Every actually existing consciousness seems to itself at any rate to be a *fighter for ends*...." Consciousness thus possesses survival value. Association may depend on cerebral laws, but our will can, through emphasis and reinforcement, direct chains of association to serve our interests, and their direction is "all that the most eager advocate of free will need demand," for by directing association it directs thinking, and hence action, wrote James (*Principles*, vol. I, p. 141).

Although James has here proclaimed the efficacy of consciousness and will, the central doctrine of the *Principles*, on which American psychologists built for thirty years, was the "motor theory of consciousness." James's famous theory of emotion, the James-Lange theory, aptly illustrates the motor theory. On common understanding, if I see a bear in the woods, I feel afraid, and as a consequence, I run away. On James's motor account of consciousness, however, I see the bear, begin to run away, and then, finding myself fleeing, feel scared. More generally, James said that mental states have two sorts of bodily effects. First, unless some inhibition is present, the thought of an act automatically leads to the execution of the act. Second, mental states cause internal bodily changes, including covert motor responses, changes in heart rate, glandular secretions, and perhaps "processes more subtle still." Therefore, James argued, "it will be safe to lay down the general law that *no mental modification ever occurs which is not accompanied or followed by a bodily change*" (*Principles*, vol. I, p. 5). The contents of consciousness are thus determined not only by sensations coming in from outside, but by kinesthetic feedback (as we call it today) from the body's motor activity. "Our psychology must therefore take account not only of the conditions antecedent to mental states, but of their resultant consequences as well.... The whole neural organism [is] ... but a machine for converting stimuli into reactions; and the intellectual part of our life is knit up with but the middle or 'central' part of the machine's operations" (*Principles*, vol. II, p. 372).

James found himself caught in the same dilemma felt by many Romantic authors, between the heart's feeling of freedom and the intellect's scientific declaration of determinism. James was deeply committed to free will from personal experience. As a young man, he had pulled himself out of a black depression by literally willing himself to live again, and, dogged by depression his whole life, he made human will the center of his philosophy. However, in his psychology, committed to cerebralism, he found himself almost forced to accept determinism as the only scientifically acceptable view of behavior. He stoutly resisted the conclusion, denouncing mechanistic conceptions of human conduct and, as we have seen, proclaiming that consciousness decreed survival and commanded the body. After writing *Principles*, James abandoned psychology for philosophy and developed his own brand of pragmatism. There he tried to resolve the struggle between the head and the heart by setting the feelings of the heart on an equal footing with the cognitions of the head. Nevertheless, the conflict remained, and the influence of *Principles* was to lead American psychologists away from consciousness and toward behavior, and so away from James's own definition of psychology as the science of mental life.

The New Psychology

In the United States, experimental psychology was called the "new psychology," to distinguish it from the "old psychology" of the Scottish common-sense realists. The great majority of American colleges were controlled by Protestant denominations, and in the 1820s, the Scottish system was installed as a safeguard against what religious leaders took to be the skeptical and atheistic tendencies of British empiricism as described by Reid. The works of Locke, Berkeley, and Hume—and, later, the German idealists—were banished from the classroom and replaced with texts by Reid, Dugald Stewart, or their American followers. Common-sense psychology was taught as a pillar of religion and Christian behavior. For the American followers of the Scots, psychology "is the science of the soul," and its method, ordinary introspection, reveals "the soul as an emanation from the Divine, and as made in the image of God" (Dunton, 1895). "Mental science, or psychology, will therefore, be [foundational] for moral science.... The province of psychology will ... be to show what the faculties are; that of moral philosophy to show how they should be used for the attainment of their end" (Mark Hopkins 1870, quoted by Evans, 1984). Unsurprisingly, with few exceptions adherents of the old psychology looked askance at the new psychology, which brought the mind into a laboratory and investigated the connection of mental states to nervous processes.

Nevertheless, as higher education became more secular after the Civil War, the intellectual tide turned in favor of the naturalism of the new psychology. In 1875, William James established an informal psychological laboratory at Harvard in connection with a graduate course in the department of natural history called "The relations between physiology and psychology." In 1887, he began to offer a course called "Psychology" in the philosophy department; and in 1885, he obtained recognition and funds from Harvard for his laboratory, establishing the first official psychology laboratory in America (Cadwallader, 1980). At Yale the old psychology of the president, Noah Porter, yielded to George Trumball Ladd (1842-1921) who, though a Congregationalist minister and a psychological conservative, respected Wundt's experimental psychology, incorporating it into an influential text, *Elements of physiological psychology* (1887). At Princeton the president, James McCosh, was a staunch Scot but recognized that "the tendency of the day is certainly towards physiology" (Evans, 1984) and taught Wundt's psychology to his students.

Harvard minted its first Ph.D. philosopher in 1878, G. Stanley Hall (1844–1924). A student of James's, Hall was really a psychologist. He went to Johns Hopkins University—the United States' first graduate university—where he established a laboratory and a series of courses in the new psychology. Hall's psychology went well beyond Wundt, however, including, in typically American eclectic fashion, experimental studies of the higher mental processes, anthropology, and abnormal psychology, or "morbid phenomena." Hall also vigorously pursued developmental psychology, launched the child study movement, and coined the term "adolescence." Hall led the institutionalization of American psychology, starting the *American Journal of Psychology* in 1887, and organizing the founding of the American Psychological Association in 1892. One of Hall's students was James McKeen Cattell (1860–1944), who later studied with Wundt, and returned to the United States to establish laboratories at the University of Pennsylvania (1887) and Columbia University (1891).

As historians have often pointed out, however, while Americans got the methods of experimental psychology from Wundt, their ideas and theories came from elsewhere. When Cattell was in Leipzig, he proposed to study individual differences in reaction time, but Wundt disapprovingly called the subject "*ganz Amerikanisch*" (completely American). After Leipzig, Cattell studied with Francis Galton, and E. G. Boring (1950) explains American psychologists' departure from Wundtian ideals by saying "the apparatus was Wundt's, but the inspiration was Galton's." Rand Evans (1984) locates the source of American inspiration in the continuing influence of Scottish psychology. The Scots had always emphasized mind in use, mental activity, more than mental content. Their faculty psychology was, like Aristotle's, implicitly a psychology of function. And as Aristotle's was a biological psychology, the Scot's psychology of mental function, despite its religious connection, was ultimately compatible with modern Darwinian biology, as McCosh himself saw. Experiment was new in American psychology, but American psychologists have retained to the present day the Scots' concern with mental activity and with making psychology serviceable to society and the individual.

CONCLUSION: PERCEPTION AND THINKING ARE THERE FOR BEHAVIOR'S SAKE

By 1892, psychology in America was well launched. In Europe, scientific psychology was making slow headway even in Germany, the country of its birth. In the United States, by contrast, psychology expanded rapidly. In 1892, there were fourteen laboratories, including one as far west as Kansas. Half of them had been founded independently of philosophy or any other discipline. Psychology would soon be what it largely remains, an American science.

But psychology in America would not be the traditional psychology of consciousness. Once psychology met evolution, the tendency to study behavior instead of consciousness became overwhelming. Traditionally, philosophers had been concerned with human knowledge, with how we form ideas and how we know they are true or false. Action resulting from ideas formed only a tiny part of their concern. However, in a biological, evolutionary context, ideas matter only if they lead to effective action. The Metaphysical Club realized this and created the pragmatic maxim. The struggle for existence is won by successful action, and any organism "sicklied o'er with the pale cast of thought," no matter how profound, is doomed to failure. The essence of the psychology of adaptation was the idea that mind matters to evolution because it leads to successful action, and so is adaptive. As James said, "if it ever should happen that [thought] led to no active measures, it would fail of its essential function, and would have to be considered either pathological or abortive. The current of life which runs in at our eyes or ears is meant to run out at our hands, feet, or lips.... perception and thinking are only for behavior's sake" (Kuklick, 1977, p. 169).

The psychology of adaptation from Spencer to James remained nevertheless the science of mental life, not the science of behavior. However, much consciousness was tied up with behavior; no matter that it was merely a way station between stimulus and response, it was real and deserved serious study, because it was a vital way station. James said consciousness decreed survival, that it commanded the body to behave adaptively. Underneath the main current of mentalism, however, ran an undercurrent that headed toward the study of behavior instead of the study of consciousness, and in time the undercurrent became the main current, and finally a flood tide, virtually erasing the Science of Mental Life.

BIBLIOGRAPHY

Samuel Hynes, *The Edwardian turn of mind* (Princeton, NJ: Princeton University Press, 1968), provides a social history of turn-of-century Britain; he describes the impact of the Army's Physical Deterioration Report, treating it as the dividing point between the Victorian and post-Victorian eras. The changes in psychology during these years are discussed by Reba N. Soffer, *Ethics and society in England: The revolution in the social sciences 1870–1914* (Berkeley: University of California Press, 1978). Spencer's biographer is J. Peel *Herbert Spencer* (New York: Basic Books, 1971). Howard Gruber insightfully discusses *Darwin on man: A psychological study of scientific creativity,* 2nd ed. (Chicago: Chicago University Press, 1981). On Galton, see F. Forest, *Francis Galton* (New York: Taplinger, 1974). For Galton and British eugenics, see Ruth Schwartz Cowan, "Nature and nurture: The interplay of biology and politics in the work of Francis Galton," in W. Coleman & C. Limoges (Eds.), *Studies in the history of biology,* vol. 1, 133–208 (Baltimore: Johns Hopkins University Press, 1977); Robert C. Bannister, *Social Darwinism: Science and myth in Anglo-American social thought* (Philadelphia: Temple University Press, 1979); and Daniel Kevles, *In the name of eugenics: Genetics and the uses of human heredity* (New York: Knopf, 1985). Greta Jones, *Social Darwinism in English thought: The interaction between biological and social theory* (Sussex, England: The Harvester Press, 1980), discusses both social Darwinism and eugenics during the period. In addition to the cited work, an important book by Romanes is *Mental evolution in man* (New York: D. Appleton, 1889); the only biography of Romanes is Ethel Romanes, *The life and letters of George John Romanes* (New York: Longmans, Green & Co., 1898); but Frank Miller Turner, "George John Romanes, From faith to faith," in F. M. Turner, *Between science and religion: The reaction to scientific naturalism in late Victorian England* (New Haven, CT: Yale University Press, 1974), provides a fine short discussion of Romanes, focusing on his part in the Victorian crisis of conscience. Morgan's major work is *An introduction to comparative psychology* (London: Walter Scott, 1894).

For a comprehensive treatment of American life in the years before 1890, see Bernard Bailyn, "Shaping the Republic to 1760," Gordon S. Wood, "Framing the Republic 1760–1820," David Brion Davis, "Expanding the Republic 1820–1860," and David Herbert Donald, "Uniting the Republic 1860–1890," in B. Bailyn, D. B. Davis, D. H. Donald, J. L. Thomas, R. H. Wiebe, & G. S. Wood, *The great Republic: A history of the American people* (Boston: Little, Brown, 1977). Daniel Boorstin concentrates on intellectual and social history during the same years in *The Americans: The colonial experience* (New York: Vintage, 1958), and *The Americans: The national experience* (New York: Vintage, 1965); both are wonderfully readable and exciting books. The best book on the American character is still de Tocqueville (1850/1969); reporter Richard Reeves, *In search of America* (New York: Simon & Schuster, 1982), retraced de Tocqueville's itinerary, and his insights do not surpass de Tocqueville's. An important and fascinating survey of American colonial life is David Hackett Fischer, *Albion's seed: Four British folkways in America* (New York: Oxford University Press, 1989), first in a series comprising a cultural history of the United States. A valuable general intellectual history of thought in the United States is Morton White, *Science and sentiment in America: Philosophical thought from Jonathan Edwards to John Dewey* (New York: Oxford University Press, 1972). Intellectual life in the early colonial and post-revolutionary periods is discussed by Henry Steele Commager, *The empire of reason: How Europe imagined and America realized the Enlightenment* (Garden City, NY: Doubleday, 1978); Henry May, *The Enlightenment in America* (New York: Oxford University Press, 1976); and Perry Miller, *Errand into the wilderness* (New York: Harper & Row, 1956).

For specific relevant movements of the nineteenth century, see A. Douglas, *The feminization of American culture* (New York: Knopf, 1977); Richard Hofstadter, *Anti-intellectualism in American life* (New York: Vintage, 1962); and R. B. Nye, *Society and culture in America 1830–1860* (New York: Harper & Row, 1974); and for American phrenology, see Thomas H. & Grace E. Leahey, *Psychology's occult doubles* (Chicago: Nelson-Hall, 1983). For American philosophy, see A. L. Jones, *Early American philosophers* (New York: Ungar, 1958); Herbert W. Schneider, *History of American philosophy* (New York: Columbia University Press, 1963); and, especially for the post-Civil War period, Kuklick (1977), from which all quotes in the Metaphysical Club section are drawn, unless otherwise indicated. The standard biography of Jonathan Edwards is Perry Miller, *Jonathan Edwards* (New York: Meridian, 1959). On Wright, see Edward H. Madden, "Chauncy Wright's functionalism," *Journal of the History of the Behavior Sciences* (1974 *10*: 281–90). For the early philosophy of pragmatism and its influences, see Philip P. Wiener, *Evolution and the founders of pragmatism* (Cambridge, MA: Harvard University Press, 1949); J. K. Feibleman, *An introduction to the philosophy of Charles S. Peirce* (Cambridge, MA: MIT Press, 1946); and Thomas S. Knight, *Charles Peirce* (New York: Twayne, 1965). For Peirce as psychologist, see Thomas Cadwallader, "Charles S. Peirce: The first American experimental psychologist," *Journal of the History of the Behavioral Sciences* (1974, *10*: 191–98). The standard biography of William James is Ralph Barton Perry, *The thought and character of William James,* 2 vols. (Boston: Little, Brown, 1935); Perry's biography, while still the standard, suffers somewhat from Perry's attempt to make James into a realist like himself. A recent biography is Gay Wilson Allen, *William James* (Minneapolis: University of Minnesota Press, 1970). For James's lasting influence, see Don S. Browning, *Pluralism and personality: William*

James and some contemporary cultures of psychology (Lewisburg, PA: Bucknell University Press, 1980). The most important recent biography of James is Myers (1987), a full-scale evaluation of his thought (see Leahey, 1988, for an appreciation).

The only comprehensive source for the establishment of American psychology is Evans (1984); related is R. Dolby, "The transmission of two new scientific disciplines from Europe to North America in the late nineteenth century," *Annals of Science* (1977, *34:* 287–310). For psychology before the new psychology, see J. W. Fay, *American psychology before William James* (New York: Octagon Books, 1966); J. R. Fulcher, "Puritans and the passions: The faculty psychology in American Puritanism," *Journal of the History of the Behavioral Sciences* (1973, *9:* 123–39); and E. Harms, "America's first major psychologist: Laurens Perseus Hickock," *Journal of the History of the Behavioral Sciences* (1972, *8:* 120–23). Two overlapping collections edited by Robert W. Rieber and Kurt Salzinger treat American psychology primarily in the old and new periods, but also after: *The roots of American psychology: Historical influences and implications for the future* (New York: New York Academy of Sciences, *Annals of the New York Academy of Sciences* vol. 291, 1977); and *Psychology: Theoretical-historical perspectives* (New York: Academic, 1980). Josef Brozek (Ed.), *Explorations in the history of psychology in the United States* (Lewisburg, PA: Bucknell University Press, 1984) contains articles on both the old and the new psychologies. On the early psychologists mentioned in the text: Eugene S. Miller, *G. T. Ladd: Pioneer American psychologist* (Cleveland: Press of Case Western Reserve University, 1969); Dorothy Ross, *G. Stanley Hall: Psychologist as prophet* (Chicago: University of Chicago Press, 1972). Michael Sokal has spent his career writing about James McKeen Cattell—for example: "The unpublished autobiography of James McKeen Cattell," *American Psychologist* (1971, *26:* 626–35), and *An education in psychology: James McKeen Cattell's journal and letters from Germany and England, 1880–1888* (Cambridge, MA: MIT Press, 1980).

One of the landmark articles in the introduction of the new psychology to the United States is John Dewey, "The new psychology," *Andover Review* (1884, *2:* 278–89); the background and influence of the piece is discussed in Morton White, *The origin of Dewey's instrumentalism* (New York: Octagon Books, 1964). Two other contemporary or near-contemporary articles are useful for the history of the early laboratories in the United States: Anonymous, "Psychology in American universities," *American Journal of Psychology* (1892, *3:* 275–86); and Christian A. Ruckmich "The history and status of psychology in the United States," *American Journal of Psychology* (1912, *23:* 517–31). J. Mark Baldwin provides a more general account, with more background, in his "Sketch of the history of psychology," *Psychological Review* (1905, *12:* 144–65).

REFERENCES

Bartlett, F. C. (1932). *Remembering.* Cambridge, England: Cambridge University Press.
Blight, J. G. (1978). *The position of Jonathan Edwards in the history of psychology.* Paper presented at the annual meeting of the American Psychological Association, Toronto, Ontario, September 1.
Boring, E. G. (1950). *A history of experimental psychology.* Englewood Cliffs, NJ: Prentice-Hall.
Cadwallader, T. C. (1980). *William James' Harvard psychology laboratory reconsidered.* Paper presented at the annual meeting of the American Psychological Association, Montreal, Canada, September.
Darwin, C. (1896). *The descent of man and selection in relation to sex.* New York: Appleton & Co.
Darwin, C. (1872/1965). *The expression of emotion in man and animals.* Chicago: Chicago University Press.
Dunton, L. (1895). The old psychology and the new. In L. Dunton, H. Münsterberg, W. T. Harris,

& G. Stanley Hall, *The old psychology and the new: Addresses before the Massachusetts Schoolmaster's Club, April 27, 1895.* Boston: New England Publishing Co.

Emerson, R. W. (1950). *Selected prose and poetry.* New York: Holt, Rinehart & Winston.

Evans, R. (1984). The origins of American academic psychology. In J. Brozek (Ed.), *Explorations in the history of psychology in the United States.* Lewisburg, PA: Bucknell University Press.

Galton, F. (1883/1907). *Inquiries into the human faculty and its development.* London: J. M. Dent.

Galton, F. (1869/1925). *Hereditary genius.* London: Macmillian.

Gay, P. (1969). The obsolete Puritanism of Jonathan Edwards. Reprinted in J. Opie (Ed.), *Jonathan Edwards and the Enlightenment.* Lexington, MA: D. C. Heath.

Hofstadter, R. (1955). *Social Darwinism in American thought,* rev. ed. Boston: Beacon.

Hopkins, M. (1870). *Lectures on moral science.* Boston: Gould & Lincoln.

James, W. (1890). *Principles of psychology,* 2 vols. New York: Dove.

Jones, A. L. (1958). *Early American philosophers.* New York: Ungar.

Kuklick, B. (1977). *The rise of American philosophy: Cambridge, Massachusetts 1860–1930,* New Haven: Yale University Press.

Leahey, T. H. (1988). William James: Heroic metaphysician. [Review of Myers (1987)]. *Contemporary Psychology, 33,* 199–201.

Miller, P. (1965). *The life of the mind in America.* New York: Harcourt, Brace & World.

Morgan, C. L. (1886). On the study of animal intelligence. *Mind, 11,* 74–85.

Murray, D. J. (1976). Research on memory in the nineteenth century. *Canadian Journal of Psychology, 30,* 201–220.

Myers, G. (1987). *William James: His life and thought.* New Haven: Yale University Press.

Peirce, C. S. (1878/1966). How to make our ideas clear. Partially reprinted in A. Rorty (Ed.), *Pragmatic Philosophy.* Garden City, NY: Anchor Books.

Peirce, C. S. (1887). Logical machines. *American Journal of Psychology, 1,* 165–170.

Peirce, C. S. (1905/1970). What pragmatism is. In H. S. Thayer (Ed.), *Pragmatism: The classic writings.* New York: Mentor.

Romanes, G. (1883). *Animal intelligence.* New York: Appleton & Co.

Spencer, H. (1897). *The principles of psychology,* 3rd ed. New York: Appleton & Co.

Spencer, H. (1904). *An autobiography,* 2 vols. London: Williams & Norgate.

Spencer, H. (1880/1945). *First principles.* London: Watts & Co.

Tocqueville, A. de. (1850/1969). *Democracy in America.* New York: Anchor.

White, L. (1972). *Science and sentiment in America.* London: Oxford University Press.

Wills, G. (1978). *Inventing America: Jefferson's Declaration of Independence.* Garden City, NY: Doubleday.

Wyers, E. J., et al. (11) (1980). The sociobiological challenge to psychology: On the proposal to "cannibalize" comparative psychology. *American Psychologist, 35,* 955–979.

Zilbergeld, B. (1983). *The shrinking of America: Myths of psychological change.* Boston: Little, Brown.

PART II

THE CONSPIRACY OF NATURALISM (1892–1912)

The founders of psychology took psychology to be the science of mental life. For Wundt and James, psychology was the study of consciousness; for Freud, it was the study of both consciousness and the unconscious. Scientific psychologists in the twentieth century, however, have little use for conscious experience and little tolerance for Freud's cauldron of the id; instead, they take psychology to be the study of behavior. How psychology was transformed from mentalism to behavioralism, and how behavioralism became entrenched, will occupy us in Chapters 5 and 6.

Part of the reason for psychologists' increasing interest in behavior and flagging interest in introspection was their desire to be practical and succeed in business, industry, government, and among other professional providers of services such as physicians and lawyers. During World War I, psychologists established their social usefulness, and after the war, psychologists became involved in applied activities and in such social issues as eugenics and remaking the family. The trend toward applied psychology nearly tore institutional psychology apart, but the demands of World War II reunited psychologists at least temporarily. In chapters to come, we will see how social forces helped shape psychology into a behavioral science and how psychologists in turn helped shape society.

On the scientific side, the major development of the years just before and then between the world wars was the articulation and development of behaviorism. Behaviorism is a movement that has been much misunderstood by historians of psychology, primarily because their thinking has been controlled by behaviorism's own myths of origin. Behaviorism is usually seen as a dramatic break with the past largely created by one man, John B. Watson; in fact, behaviorism was part of the larger trend toward behavioralism—defining psychology as the science of behavior—with roots in the 1890s. Behaviorism is similarly seen as a reasonably coherent movement, marked by theoretical disagreements but held together by shared assumptions about the nature of science and psychology; in fact, the disagreements among behaviorists are profound, so profound that in some cases they were invisible to the behaviorists themselves and have remained so to many historians.

CHAPTER 5

The Utility of Consciousness:
The Rise of Functional Psychology (1892–1898)

INTRODUCTION

In April 1913, the philosopher Warner Fite reviewed—anonymously, as was the custom at *The Nation*—three books on "The Science of Man." One was a text on genetics, but the other two were by psychologists: Hugo Münsterberg's *Psychology and Industrial Efficiency* and Maurice Parmellee's *The Science of Human Behavior*. Fite observed that psychology in 1913 seemed little concerned with consciousness; Münsterberg explicitly stated that the psychological "way of ordinary life, in which we try to understand our neighbor by entering into his mental functions ... is not psychological analysis." Fite went on to conclude:

> Precisely. True "psychological analysis" ignores all personal experience of mentality. The science of psychology is, then, the finished result of what we may call the conspiracy of naturalism, in which each investigator has bound himself by a strange oath to obtain all his knowledge from observation of the actions of his fellows—"as a naturalist studies the

chemical elements or the stars" [Münsterberg]—and never under any circumstances to conceive them in the light of his own experience of his living. Even the psychologist's "mental states" or "objects of consciousness" are only so many hypothetical entities read from without.... [W]hat is to be expected from a science of humanity which ignores all that is most distinctive of man? (p. 370)

Clearly, psychology had changed since we left it in 1897. Wundt and James had created a science of mental life, the study of consciousness as such; Freud used introspection and inference to enter his patients' minds, both conscious and unconscious. But by 1913, Fite found a psychology aimed at behavior, not consciousness, based on treating people as things, not as conscious agents.

In twenty years, a new kind of psychology had arisen, which we will call *behavioralism.* While one might imagine that a scientific revolution had occurred, there was instead an inevitable, steady—if rapid—evolution of psychology from the science of consciousness to the science of behavior. To discuss these watershed decades we need some new terms to appreciate the major historical forces at work transforming mentalism into behavioralism.

Mentalism and Behavioralism

Traditionally (as in the first edition of this book), psychology is described as having changed from mentalism—the study of the mind—to behaviorism. However, "behaviorism" as it is usually used is becoming useless as a philosophical category and unworkable as a historical entity. Although it has always been recognized that the various behaviorists disagreed on certain points, it has only recently been shown how many and how deep these disagreements were. As we shall see in Chapter 7, it is futile to lump all of the usual behaviorists into one narrowly defined camp. Compounding this difficulty is the tendency nowadays to identify behaviorism with B. F. Skinner—and, worse, attributing to him a confused mishmash of his distinctive ideas mixed up with those of traditional 1930s behaviorists. A final motivation for redefining our usual terms is that the new and growing field of cognitive science shares many affinities with behaviorism; but simply calling it behaviorism without qualification would obscure its novel features and further distort the meaning of "behaviorism."

A new umbrella term, *behavioralism,* will denote the new psychology described by Fite. It contrasts with *mentalism,* defined in the old way as the science of consciousness as such, whose method was introspection or self-observation, augmented by objective measures of reaction times and certain other behaviors. The essential feature of mentalism was that it aimed at studying *consciousness;* even when behavior, human or animal, was brought in, the aim was always to describe, explicate, or explain what happens in consciousness.

Behavioralism turned mentalism upside down. Behavioralists seek to predict, control, explain, or model behavior, and to do so may or may not refer to conscious or unconscious mental processes. Behavioralism is aimed at behavior; consciousness—the mind—is not the object of study, although it may be called upon to explain behavior.

My proposed approach differs from an older distinction made by behaviorists and philosophers. Traditionally, two kinds of behaviorism have been distinguished, *methodological behaviorism* and *metaphysical* (or *radical*) *behaviorism.* Methodological behaviorists say that consciousness is not a fit subject for science, however real it may be; scientific *method* demands that scientists limit themselves to what is publicly observable—that is, behavior. Metaphysical behaviorists contend that mind—though not consciousness—is a myth, to be banished from the scientific understanding of the world, along with angels, demons, and spirits, while at the same time consciousness is brought into the sphere of science.

Although valuable in identifying the sorts of arguments actually made on behalf of behavioral approaches to psychology, these two categories obscure some important features of behavioralism. Methodological behaviorists refused to have anything to do with consciousness as hopelessly unscientific, but they nevertheless postulated intervening variables and hypothetical constructs: unobserved entities or processes within the organism supposed to produce behavior. Metaphysical behaviorists, on the other hand, although denying that the mind is real, nevertheless admit private, conscious events (toothaches, for example) to their science of behavior.

There is a more useful way to capture the difference between these two sets of "behaviorists." Some behavioralists, including methodological behaviorists and cognitive scientists, are willing to hypothesize and theorize about the existence and functioning of largely unconscious faculties and processes as determiners of behavior. While a given theorist of this camp may or may not be willing to call these faculties and processes "mental," they are seen as internal, causal agencies that produce behavior. These behavioralists have little to say about consciousness. Other behavioralists are true *behaviorists,* unwilling to consider any nonobservable influence on behavior or to talk about any but manifest, observable behavior. However, any influence that is observed—even if to only one person, as with a toothache—may be legitimately invoked in explaining behavior.

Psychology and Society

It is appropriate to begin the history of modern psychology in 1892, because in that year the American Psychological Association (APA) was founded, largely due to the activities of G. Stanley Hall. Our attention from now on will be fixed on American psychology, for although Germany granted the earliest degrees in psychology, it was in America that psychology became a profession; the German equivalent of the APA (see Chapter 2) was not founded until 1904 (Danziger, 1979). For better or worse, and for sometimes extraneous reasons, modern psychology is essentially American psychology. American movements and theories have been adopted overseas—so much so that in 1980 a German text in social psychology was filled with American references and made no mention of Wundt or *Völkerpsychologie.*

Society today is so professionalized—even beauticians need a license in many states—that we may overlook the impact of professionalization on the content and shape of a discipline. Before the formation of the APA, psychology was pursued by philosophers and physicians, writers and physiologists. The founders of scientific psychology necessarily began their careers in other fields, typically medicine. But professionalization brings self-consciousness about the definition of a field and control over who may call himself or herself a member of it. To establish an organization such as the APA means to establish criteria for membership, to allow some to call themselves "psychologists," to forbid the name to others. Government is then induced to enforce the rules, issuing licenses to applicants who meet the criteria for "psychologist," and prosecuting those who falsely practice psychology.

The founding of the APA took place early in a period of important change in American life, in which the professionalization of academic and practical disciplines played an important part. The years between 1890 and World War I are generally recognized as critical ones in U.S. history. America in the 1880s was, in Robert Wiebe's phrase, a nation of "island communities" scattered across the immense ocean of rural America. In these small, isolated communities, people lived lives enclosed in a web of family relations and familiar neighbors; the world outside was psychologically distant and did not—indeed, could not—intrude very often. By 1920, all this had changed. The United States had become a nation-state, united by technology and forming a common culture.

Part of the change was urbanization. In 1880, only 25 percent of the population lived in cities; by 1900, 40 percent did so. The trend has continued apace until the last few years. A city is not an island community; it is a huge collection of strangers, especially when immigration—both from our own farms and abroad—every day brings hundreds to the metropolis. Changing from farm or village dweller to urban citizen effects psychological changes and demands new psychological skills.

Changing from island community to nation-state has, as Daniel Boorstin (1974) argues, deeply affected daily lives, widening personal horizons, narrowing the range of immediate experience, and introducing a constant flow of change with which people must keep up. The railroad could take the rural immigrant to the big city. It could also bring to farmers and villagers the products of the city: frozen meat and vegetables, canned food, and above all the wonders of the Ward's and Sears-Roebuck catalogues. Previously, most men and women lived out their lives in the small radius of a few hours' walking. Now the train took them immense distances occasionally, and the trolley took them downtown every day to work and shop at the new department stores. All this freed people from what could be the stultifying confines of small-town life. It also homogenized experience. Today we can all watch the same television programs and news—even originating from a hotel room in Baghdad—buy the same brands of foods and clothes, and travel from coast to coast, staying in the same Holiday Inn motel room and eating the same McDonald's hamburger.

Psychology, as the study of people, has not been untouched by these events. As we move through this and future chapters we will see professional psychologists—no longer mere speculators about the mind—defining their job and role in society with respect to the new American scene.

The years 1892 to 1896, standing as they do at the beginning of the modern era, were especially chaotic and disquieting. The Panic of 1893 started a four-year depression of major proportions, bringing in its wake not only unemployment but also riot and insurrection. The "Année terrible" of 1894 to 1895 witnessed 1,394 strikes and a march on Washington by Coxey's Army of unemployed, dispersed by troops amid rumors of revolution. It all culminated in the crisis and election of 1896. One candidate, William Jennings Bryan, was the voice of Populism—and to established leaders he was also a leftist revolutionary, leader of "hideous and repulsive vipers." His opponent was William McKinley, a dull, solid Republican. Far from being a Marxist, Bryan was really the voice of the rural, small-town, pietistic past, a preacher of religious morality. McKinley represented the immediate future: urban, pragmatic, the voice of big business and big labor. McKinley narrowly won and revolution was averted; reform, efficiency, and progress became the watchwords of the day. After 1896, psychology would participate strongly in all three noble goals.

Read against this background of chaos and crisis, professional discussions in the APA's early years appear parochial and tedious. Nevertheless, one important theme of the times does emerge—the last defenses of the old psychology against the new. For it was in these years that the new psychology finally overthrew the old.

George Trumbull Ladd—who in his college teaching and text writing had done much to introduce the new psychology to America—rejected what it was becoming. He rejected the physiological, natural science conception of psychology he found in James and defended spiritualistic dualism (Ladd, 1892). In his APA presidential address he decried the replacement of introspection by experiment and objective measurement as "absurd" and pointed out that objective experimentation was incompetent to say anything about important parts of human psychology, including the religious sentiments. Other adherents of the old psychology, such as Larkin Dunton (before the Massachusetts School Masters' Club in 1895), defended the old psychology as "the science of the soul," "an emanation of the Divine," furnishing the key "to moral education."

Like Bryan, Ladd, Dunton, and the old psychology represented the passing world of rural, village America, based on traditional religious truths. The Scottish commonsense psychology had been created to defend religion and would continue to do so as fundamentalists clung to it against the tide of modernism. The old psychology had a soul and taught the old moral values of an American culture that were being overtaken by progress.

For the decade of the 1890s was the "age of the news"—the new education, the new ethics, the new woman, and the new psychology. The future belonged to aggressive new psychologists, professionalizers of psychology who looked to its future. Chief among them was Wundt's *ganz Amerikanisch* student Cattell, fourth president of the APA. Cattell (1896) described the new psychology as a rapidly advancing quantitative science. Moreover—and this would be a key part of professional psychology in the years to come—he claimed for experimental psychology "wide reaching practical applications" in education, medicine, the fine arts, political economy, and, indeed, in the whole conduct of life." The new psychology, not the old, was in step with the times: self-confident, self-consciously new and scientific, ready to face the challenges of urbanization, industrialization, and the unceasing ever-changing flow of American life.

Reform, efficiency, and progress were the actuating values of the major social and political movement following the crisis of 1896, Progressivism. During the nineteenth century, English middle class reformers sought to tame both the decadent aristocracy and the unruly working class (as the middle class saw them) by imposing on both its own values of frugality, self-control, and hard work. Progressivism filled the same role in America, with, of course, distinctive American touches. Progressives were middle-class professionals—including the new psychologists—who aimed to reign in the rapacious American aristocracy—the Robber Barons—and the disorderly masses of urban immigrants. Not only did the Robber Barons prey on Americans through business, but they were turning their riches to the control of politics and the living of opulent but empty lives, captured by F. Scott Fitzgerald in *The Great Gatsby.*

Progressives saw the urban masses as victims exploited by corrupt political machines, which traded votes for favors and indispensable services to hopeful immigrants building new lives in a strange but opportunity-filled land.

In place of what they defined as the greedy self-interest of the moneyed class, and the opportunistic self-interest of the political bosses, the Progressives sought to establish disinterested, expert, professional government—that is, government by themselves. There can be no doubt that, especially in the cities, living conditions were often appalling as the waves of immigrants stretched American cities beyond their old bounds and beyond their ability to cope. Urban political machines were an organic, adaptive response to urban ills, providing bewildered immigrants with a helpful intermediary between them and their new society. But because the machines' help was bought with votes, rational, middle-class Progressives, led by academics, saw only corruption and manipulation of helpless victims by self-serving politicians. The Progressives replaced corruption with the scientific management principles of the great corporations.

The philosopher of Progressivism and the prophet of twentieth-century liberalism was John Dewey, elected president of the APA for the last year of the old century. In his presidential address, "Psychology and Social Practice," Dewey examined psychology's role in modern society by focusing on the reform of education.

Educational reform was one of the central concerns of Progressivism, and John Dewey was the founder of Progressive education. According to Dewey, education as it stood was ill-suited to the needs of urban, industrial America. G. Stanley Hall had begun the reform of education with his child study movement and the idea that schools should be child-centered institutions. Nevertheless, more reforms were urgently needed, as Dewey and others recognized. Immigrants were perforce bringing with them alien customs and alien tongues; they, and especially their children, needed to be Americanized. Immigrants from the farm also needed to be educated in the habits appropriate to industrial work and in new skills unknown on the farm. Above all, the schools had to become the child's new community. America's island communities were disappearing, and immigrants had left their home communities. The school had to be a community for the child and then reform the American community through the adult it produced.

"The school is an especially favorable place in which to study the availability of psychology for social practice," Dewey told the assembled psychologists. Sounding the themes of the psychology of adaptation, Dewey argued that "mind [is] fundamentally an instrument of adaptation" to be improved by school experience, and that for "psychology to become a working hypothesis"—that is, to meet the pragmatic test—it would have to involve itself with the education of America's young minds.

Once we involve ourselves with education, Dewey continued, psychologists would inevitably be led to society at large. Above all, schools must teach values, and these values must be the values of social growth and community solidarity, the values of pragmatism and urban life. Finally, these values are not just the school's values but must become the values of every social institution; and so psychologists must naturally become engaged in the great enterprise of Progressive social reform.

Progressivism was the American New Enlightenment and as such condemned custom and replaced it with rational calculation. Dewey recognized that the island communities' values were maintained through custom, but that once values "are in any way divorced from habit and tradition" they must be "consciously proclaimed" and must find "some substitute for custom as an organ of their execution." Consequently, psychology, the study of mental adaptation, plays a special role in the reconstruction of society:

> The fact that conscious, as distinct from customary, morality and psychology have a historic parallel march, is just the concrete recognition of the necessary equivalence between ends consciously conceived, and interest in the means upon which the ends depend.... So long as custom reigns, as tradition prevails, so long as social values are determined by instinct and habit, there is no conscious question ... and hence no need of psychology.... But when once the values come to consciousness ... then the machinery by which ethical ideals are projected and manifested, comes to consciousness also. Psychology must needs be born as soon as morality becomes reflective. (Dewey, pp. 77–78)

Psychology, then, is a social analogue to consciousness. According to James, as we shall see, consciousness arises in an individual when adaptation to new circumstances is imperative. American society faced imperative changes, Dewey said, and psychology was arising to meet them. Only psychology offers an "alternative to an arbitrary and class view of society, to an aristocratic view" that would deny to some their full realization as human beings. Echoing the philosophies of the French Enlightenment, Dewey said that "we are ceasing to take existing social forms as final and unquestioned. The application of psychology to social institutions is ... just the recognition of the principle of sufficient reason in the large matters of social life." The arrangements that exist among people are the results of the working of scientific laws of human behavior, and once psychologists understand these laws, they will be able to construct a more perfect society by substituting rational planning for haphazard growth.

Individual personality would be blended into the social whole. "To save personality in all, we must all serve alike" by reducing personality to lawful scientific mechanism. "To affirm personality independent of mechanism is to restrict its full meaning to a few [the lucky aristocracy].... The entire problem," Dewey concluded, "is one of the development of science, and of its applications to life." For the capricious freedom of aristocratic society, we should look forward to a scientific society, anticipating "no other outcome than increasing control in the ethical sphere." In the new society, psychology will "enable human effort to expend itself sanely, rationally, and with assurance."

In his address, Dewey touched all the themes of Progressivism, and he deepened and developed them over the course of a long career as a public philosopher. He gave Progressivism its voice; as one Progressive said, "We were all Deweyites before we read Dewey." For not only was Progressivism the politics of the moment and of the future, it reflected America's deepest traditions: distrust of aristocrats—hereditary, moneyed, or elected—and a commitment to equal treatment of all.

Where Progressivism and Dewey broke new ground were in their conceptions of the ends to be reached by society and the means to be used to reach them. As de Tocqueville had observed, Americans distrusted intellect, which they associated with aristocracy, and still did nearly a century later. *The Saturday Evening Post* in 1912 attacked colleges for encouraging "that most un-American thing called class and culture…. There should be no such thing [in America] as a superior mind." Yet Progressivism called for government rule by a scientifically trained managerial elite. In a Progressively reformed city, the political authority of the mayor was replaced by the expertise of a university-trained city manager, whose job description was taken from big business. Progressives were obsessed by social control, the imposing of order on the disordered mass of turn-of-the-century American citizens. Progressivism's permanent legacy is government bureaucracy. The "corrupt" politicians of the urban machine knew their constituents as individuals, to be helped or harmed insofar as they supported the machine. Bureaucracy, in contrast, is rational and impersonal—rule by the expert. Questing for fairness, it imposes anonymity; people become numbers, the poor become case files, to be scientifically managed and manipulated to ensure the good of the whole.

The goal of society in the Progressive vision was the cultivation of the individual within a supportive community that nurtures him or her. Permanent achievements were replaced by growth. As Dewey later wrote, "The process of growth, of improvement and progress, rather than … the result, becomes the significant thing…. Not perfection as a final goal, but the ever-enduring process of perfecting, maturing, refining is the aim in living…. Growth itself is the only moral end" (Dewey, 1920/1948/1957). Progressivism's novel goal is Darwinian. Since there is no end to evolution, there should be no end to personal growth. Darwin had abolished God, but Dewey defined a new sin; as a Progressive enthusiast wrote: "The long disputed sin against the holy ghost has been found … the refusal to cooperate with the vital principle of betterment."

Were the goals of individual self-cultivation and the attainment of scientific social control at odds? By no means. In Dewey's view, individuals acquire their personality and thought from society. There is, in reality, no individual who preexists society, nor is society a collection of atomic individuals. Although the island communities were going, Americans still craved community, and Progressives offered a new kind of rationally planned community. A leading Progressive, Randolph Bourne, argued that in the new order of things nothing was as important as a "glowing personality"; self-cultivation "becomes almost a duty if one wants to be effective toward the great end" of reforming society. Hence deliberate social planning would bring about individual fulfillment.

So, despite its resonance with certain American values, Progressivism was at odds with America's individualistic, libertarian past. The scientific view of people and the scientific management of society on psychological principles had no room for individual freedom, for of course to naturalistic science there is no freedom. The individual should be cultivated, but in the interests of the whole state:

> Social control cannot be individually determined, but must proceed from a controlled environment which provides the individual with a uniform and constant source of stimuli…. The counter plea of "interference with individual liberty" should have no weight in court, for individuals have no liberties in opposition to a scientifically controlled society but find all their legitimate freedom in conformity to and furtherance of such social function. (Bernard, 1911)

The Progressive vision was not, of course, confined to psychology but was remaking all the social sciences along similar lines. The inevitable direction was behavioral, because ultimately social control is control of behavior. And to achieve social control psychologists would have to give up the arcane procedure of introspection for the study of how behavior is controlled by its circumstances, and finally for how control of the environment gives managers control of behavior. As the twentieth century went on, psychologists would fulfill Dewey's hopes. Psychologists would increasingly move out into society, remaking its misfits, its children, its schools, its government, its businesses, its very psyche. Psychology in the twentieth century would profoundly alter our conceptions of ourselves, our needs, our loved ones, and our neighbors. John Dewey, philosopher and psychologist, more than any other single person drew the blueprint of the twentieth-century American mind.

William James and Pragmatism

For all its influence on psychology, James's *Principles* turned out to be for him just a diversion. In 1892, he brought out a one-volume *Briefer Course* more suitable as a classroom text but pronounced himself weary of psychology. In that same year, he secured a successor to himself as Harvard's experimental psychologist and resumed his career as a philosopher, making 1892 a doubly significant year for psychology.

In response to Ladd's attack on psychology as a natural science—that is, on the new psychology—James (1892) agreed that psychology was not then a science, but "is a mass of phenomenal description, gossip and myth." He wrote the *Principles,* he said, wishing "by treating Psychology *like* a natural science to help her become one" (p. 146).

James correctly set out the new psychology's theme as a natural science. The cerebralist, reflex-action theory is invaluable because, by treating people as reaction tendencies, it works toward the "practical prediction and control" that is the aim of all natural sciences. Psychology should no longer be regarded as part of philosophy but as "a branch of biology." Finally, what is needed, said James, is a practical psychology that tells people how to act, that makes a difference to life. "The kind of psychology which could cure a case of melancholy, or charm a chronic insane delusion away, ought certainly to be preferred to the most seraphic insight into the nature of the soul" (p. 153).

Psychology should be practical, should make a difference. James not only voiced the growing desire of American psychologists as they organized and professionalized but announced his own touchstone of truth: True ideas make a real difference to life. James's next task was, then, the full development of the characteristically American philosophy, pragmatism.

By the mid-1890s, the outlines of a new psychology, distinctively American in character, were emerging. The interest of American psychologists was shifting away from what consciousness contains toward what consciousness does and how it aids an organism, human or animal, in its adaptation to a changing environment. In short, mental content was becoming less important than mental function. This new functional psychology was a natural offspring of Darwinism and the new American experience. Mind, consciousness, would not exist, James had said in the *Principles,* unless it served the adaptive needs of its host; in the America of the 1890s, it was clear that consciousness's prime function was to guide adjustment to the rapid flow of change engulfing immigrant and farmer, worker and professional. In a world of constant change, ancient truths—mental content, fixed doctrines—became more uncouth every day. The ancient Greek Heraclitus had taught that the whole universe was constantly changing, but in the middle ages and later, most people accepted a static creationist view of the world and its inhabitants. In the wake of Darwin, Heraclitus' view returned triumphant. In the Heraclitean flux, the only eternal constant was change, and therefore the only reality of experience—psychology's subject matter—is adjustment to change.

In both philosophy and psychology, America was ready to produce new doctrines to meet the challenge of the modern American experience. In philosophy, William James expanded Peirce's narrow scientific pragmatism into a broad method capable of guiding one in the flux of modern experience: pragmatism. In psychology, a new generation of young American psychologists, inspired by James's *Principles,* built a psychology of mental adjustment: functionalism.

Pragmatism had begun with the practical, scientific attitude of C. S. Peirce as a way of determining if concepts had any empirical reality. But Peirce's conception was too narrow and dry to meet fully the demands of a post-Darwinian, Heraclitean world. Virtually every nineteenth-century philosophy—romanticism, Darwinism, Hegelian idealism, Marxism—pictured a universe of change. It had become clear that there were no Platonic permanent truths; yet people will not live without some certainty, some fixed star to steer by. James found in Peirce's pragmatism a fixed star of a new sort. James offered a method for making, rather than finding, truths.

In a series of works beginning in 1895 and culminating in *Pragmatism* (1907), James developed a comprehensive pragmatic approach to the problems of science, philosophy, and life. James argued that ideas were worthless or, more precisely, meaningless, unless they *mattered* to our lives. An idea with no consequences was pointless and meaningless. As he wrote in *Pragmatism:*

> True ideas are those that we can assimilate, validate, corroborate and verify. False ideas are those that we can not. That is the practical difference it makes for us to have true ideas…. The truth of an idea is not a stagnant property inherent in it. Truth happens to an idea. It becomes true, is made true by events. Its verity is in fact an event, a process. (p. 133, italics deleted)

So far, this sounds like Peirce: a hardheaded, Darwinian approach to truth. James went beyond Peirce, however, when he said that the truth of an idea should be tested against its agreement with all of one's experience, "nothing being omitted." When Peirce had said we weigh ideas against experience, he meant experience in a narrow, cognitive sense: the scientist's apprehension of the physical world. James, however, saw no reason to value one kind of experience above another. Noncognitive experience—hopes, fears, loves, ambitions—were just as much part of a person's living reality as sensations of number, hardness, or mass. "Ideas," James said, "(which themselves are but parts of our experience) become true just in so far as they help us get into satisfactory relations with other parts of our experience" (James, 1907, p. 49, italics deleted). James's criterion of truth was thus much broader than Peirce's and could apply to any concept, no matter how seemingly fanciful or metaphysical. To the tough-minded empiricist the ideas of God or of free will were empty, meaningless, since they were devoid of sensory content. But to James these ideas could make a difference in the way we conduct our lives. If the idea of free will and its corollary, moral responsibility, lead men and women to live better, happier lives than if they believed in the automaton theory, then free will was true; or, more exactly, it was made true in the lives and experience of the people who accepted it.

James's pragmatism held no metaphysical prejudices, unlike traditional rationalism and empiricism. "Rationalism sticks to logic and the empyrean. Empiricism sticks to the external senses. Pragmatism is willing to take anything, to follow either logic or the senses and to count the humblest and most personal experiences. She will count mystical experiences if they have practical consequences" (James, 1907, p. 61). Against the cold intellectual positivism of Peirce's pragmatism, James asserted the claims of the heart, so congenial to Americans since the time of Jonathan Edwards. As James recognized, his pragmatism was anti-intellectual in setting heart and head as equals in the search for truth. Compared to the rationalist and the search for perfect Truth, James wrote (1907, p. 168), "A radical pragmatist is a happy-go-lucky anarchist sort of creature." Functional psychologists and their heirs, the behaviorists, would likewise depreciate the intellect. Learning and problem solving, as we shall see, would soon be explained in terms of blind trial and error and resulting reward and punishment, not in terms of directed cognitive activity.

Pragmatism was a functional philosophy, a method, not a doctrine. It provided a way of coping with the Heraclitean flux of experience no matter what the challenge, no matter what the topic. In the fields of theology and physics, politics and ethics, philosophy and psychology, it offered a star to navigate by. While one could not hope to find a fixed, final truth about God or matter, society or morality, metaphysics or the mind, one could at least know what questions to ask: Does this concept matter, does it make a difference to me, to my society, to my science? Pragmatism promised that even though there were no final solutions to any problem, at least there was a method of concretely resolving problems here and now.

Heretofore philosophers had searched for first principles, indubitable ideas upon which to erect a philosophical system and a philosophy of science. James's pragmatism gives up the quest for first principles, recognizing that after Darwin no truth could be fixed. Instead, James offered a philosophy that *worked* by turning away from content—fixed truths—and toward function—what ideas do for us. As James did this, psychologists were quietly developing a psychology of function, studying not the ideas a mind contained but how the mind worked in adapting its organism to a changing environment. At the same time, they hoped that psychological science would work in the modern world, meeting the challenges of immigration and education, madness and feeblemindedness, business and politics.

BUILDING ON THE PRINCIPLES: THE MOTOR THEORY OF CONSCIOUSNESS (1892–1896)

The spirit of the new psychology in America was that of James's *Principles of Psychology:* Cattell said it "has breathed the breath of life into the dust of psychology." James himself detested the professional, even commercial, attitudes overcoming academia and harbored doubts about the validity of scientific psychology. Nevertheless, it was upon his text that American psychology built itself for years to come.

Hugo Münsterberg and Action Theory

By 1892, James was weary of psychology and eager to move on to philosophy. He looked for someone to replace him as Harvard's experimental psychologist, and his attention was drawn to Hugo Münsterberg, a student of Wundt's, who nevertheless disagreed with his teacher in a way that attracted James to him.

We have already discussed James's ideo-motor theory of voluntary behavior and contrasted it to Wundt's. Münsterberg's "action theory" developed a more thorough-going motor theory of consciousness that did away with will altogether (a step James could never take) and reduced consciousness to sensation and behavior.

Anyone who, like Wundt, was a voluntarist and assigned to will an active, determining role in mind and behavior must see consciousness as deciding on actions. Information, or stimuli, are attended to, a decision is made, and behavior follows, roughly:

$$S \longleftrightarrow \text{Consciousness} \longrightarrow R$$

(the double arrow following S reflects the role of active apperception in determining what we experience).

Now, will is a tricky concept for psychology as a natural science. It seems to fly in the face of causality and determinism. It is also unphysiological—there seems no room for will in the reflex concept of the brain, then coming to full development. After the work of Fritsch and Hitzig there seemed no place to put will: The brain produced behavior simply by associating incoming stimulus nerves with outgoing response nerves. As far as physiology went, there was no need for consciousness at all:

$$S \longrightarrow \text{Physiological Process} \longrightarrow R$$

Reflex theory seemed now to be a tenable conception of how behavior is produced. As Münsterberg wrote, "For the preservation of the individual, it is obviously irrelevant whether a purposeful motion is accompanied by contents of consciousness or not" (Hale, 1980, p. 41).

However, there *are* conscious contents (the traditional subject matter of psychology) to explain: Why do we believe we have an effective will? With James, but more consistently, Münsterberg located the source in behavior—"our ideas are the product of our readiness to act, … our actions shape our knowledge" (quoted by Kuklick, 1977). Our feeling of will, the motor theory explains, comes about because we are aware of our behavior and our incipient tendencies to behave. Thus I might announce that I'm going to stand up from my chair, not because I've reached a decision to stand but because the motor processes of standing have just begun and have entered consciousness. I feel my "will" to be effective because generally the incipient tendencies to act are followed by real action, and the former trigger memories of the latter. Because the covert tendencies have usually in fact preceded overt behavior, I believe my "will" is usually carried out.

We may summarize the motor theory of consciousness (MTC) this way:

$$S \overset{\longrightarrow \text{Consciousness} \longleftarrow}{\underset{\longrightarrow \text{Physiological Process} \longrightarrow}{\Big\langle}} R$$

The contents of consciousness are determined by stimuli impinging upon us, by our overt behaviors, and by peripheral changes in muscles and glands produced by the physiological processes linking stimulus and response. As Münsterberg argued, in this account consciousness is no more than an epiphenomenon, playing no role in causing behavior. Psychology, moreover, had to be physiological in a reductive sense, explaining consciousness in terms of underlying physiological processes, especially at the periphery. Practical, applied psychology, a field in which Münsterberg was quite active, would perforce be behavioral, explaining human action as the outcome of human circumstances.

The MTC was not confined to James or Münsterberg. In one form or another, it grew in influence. We have before us now the central philosophical-psychological theme of these two decades: What, if anything, does consciousness *do?* This question surfaces over and over in place after place. In the MTC, we see a good reason for the rise of behavioralism. If the theory is true, consciousness in fact does nothing. So why, except from faith in the old definition of psychology as the study of consciousness, should we study it?

John Dewey and the Reflex Arc

After 1890, following James's *Principles,* John Dewey moved away from his earlier Hegelian idealism and began to develop what he later called *instrumentalism,* becoming the most influential of all American philosophers. In the mid-1890s, he produced a series of important but tediously written papers that, taking the *Principles* as the footings, laid the foundations of his lifelong attempt to bring together philosophy, psychology, and ethics in a harmonious whole. These papers also furnished the central conceptions of America's native psychology, functionalism.

The most influential of these papers was "The Reflex Arc Concept in Psychology" (1896). Dewey criticized the traditional associationist reflex arc concept, S→Idea→R, as artificially breaking up behavior into disjointed parts. He did not deny that stimulus, sensation (idea), and response exist. He did, however, deny that they may be regarded as separately occurring events. Instead, Dewey considered stimulus, idea, and response to be divisions of labor in an overall coordination of action—as the organism adjusts to its environment.

Developing his own motor theory of mind, Dewey regarded sensation not as the passive registration of an impression but as itself a behavior conditioned by other behaviors occurring at the same time. So, to a soldier anxiously awaiting contact with the enemy, the sound of a twig snapping has one significance; to a hiker in a peaceful woods, it has quite another. Indeed, the hiker may not even notice the snapping sound.

Dewey made here a decisive move whose significance, buried in his dry, abstract prose, is not immediately apparent. We might, with Wundt and even James, naively attribute the differences in apperception of the twig's snapping to willfully focused attention. The soldier is actively listening for sounds of approach, the hiker is attending to the songs of birds. But Dewey's motor theory, like Münsterberg's, dispensed with the individual ego and its will. It is the *current behavior,* claimed Dewey, that gives a sensation its significance, or even determines if a stimulus becomes a sensation at all. A stimulus counts as a sensation, and takes on value, only if it has a relationship with our current behavior.

James had advanced a cerebralist approach to mind but had not fully drawn out the implications of this view. Dewey saw that behavior often runs off by itself, occasioning no sensations or ideas in any significant sense of the term. It is only when behavior needs to be newly coordinated to reality—that is, needs to be adjusted—that sensation and emotion arise. The hiker's behavior need not be adjusted to the snap of a twig, and his walking continues uninterrupted. The soldier urgently needs to coordinate his behavior to the snap of a twig and its sound thus looms large in consciousness. Moreover, the soldier's emotion, fear, apprehension, and perhaps anger at the enemy are felt, Dewey argued, only because his behavior is in check; his emotions arise from feedback from his thwarted action tendencies. Emotion, said Dewey, is a sign of conflicting dispositions to act; in the soldier's case, to fight or flee. Could he do either immediately and wholeheartedly, he would feel nothing, Dewey said.

Dewey's formulation was centrally important for later American psychology; in 1943, the reflex arc paper was chosen as one of the most important articles ever published in *Psychological Review*. Dewey showed that psychology could do away with the central willing self of Wundt and James, a mysterious and unscientific being. Rather than assigning the control of perception and decision to an inaccessible ego, it became possible to account for them in terms of coordinated, ever-changing, adaptive behaviors. So hearing was one sort of behavior, attending another, and responding a third. All were coordinated toward the end of survival in a constant, fluid stream of behavior ever in motion, not unlike the daily lives of contemporary Americans. Dewey's ideas became the commonplaces of functionalism.

The new psychology had eliminated the soul; Dewey and Münsterberg eliminated the willing self, but a self, and ego, remained. What remained for psychological study were consciousness and behavior. Soon the existence of consciousness, too, would become problematic.

FROM PHILOSOPHY TO BIOLOGY: FUNCTIONAL PSYCHOLOGY (1896–1910)

Experiments Become Functional

In keeping with epistemological aims, traditional philosophy had been concerned with the ideas the mind contains and whether or not they are true. Of course, philosophers did not ignore or even neglect mental processes, but nevertheless their first concern was with mental content—that is, putative knowledge. Traditional psychology of consciousness, while naturally investigating mental processes such as apperception, retained an emphasis on conscious content as the subject matter of psychology; its primary novelty was subjecting consciousness to experimental control in order to capture psychology for science. However, as we saw in the last chapter, William James, in his *Principles of Psychology,* shifted the interest of psychology from content to process. As he pictured the mind, mental contents were evanescent, fleeting things, seen once, never to return; what endured in the mind was function, especially the function of choosing. James's new emphasis was reinforced by the new American experience of the 1890s—old truths replaced by new ones, familiar scenes by strange ones. What remained constant was the process of adjusting to the new.

The development of the motor theory of consciousness continued the process of depreciating mental content and, by implication, the method used to access it, introspection. In the motor theory, conscious content was a result of sensation and incipient motor response and seemed to play little, if any, role in actually producing behavior. While of course it remained possible to introspect and report conscious content—as Münsterberg continued to do in his laboratory—it could easily be seen as pointless, even irresponsible. American psychologists agreed with James: What was needed was a psychology that met the pragmatic test by being effective. Awash in change, Americans needed a psychology that did something to cope with the new. Introspection only revealed what *was;* Americans needed to prepare for what *is to be.* James, Münsterberg, and Dewey were preparing for the new functional psychology by turning their attention from content to adaptive process.

At the same time experimental psychologists were shifting their interest from introspective report of conscious content to an objective determination of the correlation between stimulus and response. As developed by Wundt, the experimental method had two aspects. A standardized, controlled stimulus was presented to a subject who responded to it in some way, reporting at the same time the contents of his experience. Wundt, as a mentalist, was interested in the experience produced by given conditions and used objective results as clues to the processes that produced conscious content. However, in the hands of American psychologists, emphasis shifted from conscious experience to the determination of responses by stimulus conditions.

As an example, we may take an experiment on how people locate an object in space on the basis of sound (Angell, 1903a). In this experiment, a blindfolded observer—one of them was John B. Watson, the founder of behaviorism—was seated in a chair at the center of a circular device that could present a sound at any point around the observer. After setting the sound generator at a given point, the experimenter made it produce a tone, and the observer pointed to where he believed the sound was coming from. Then the observer provided an introspective report of the conscious experience concomitant with the experimental procedure. Watson reported seeing a mental image of the apparatus surrounding him, with the sound generator located where he pointed. Now one could, as a true mentalist would, focus on the introspective report as the data of interest, aiming to describe and explain this bit of mental content. On the other hand, one could focus on the accuracy of the pointing response, correlating the position of the sound generator with the observer's indicated position.

In the present case, although both objective data—the correlation of stimulus position with the observer's response—and introspective reports were discussed, the latter were given secondary importance. The objective findings were highlighted and extensively discussed; the introspective findings were briefly mentioned at the end of the article. In the motor theory of consciousness, introspection was becoming less important, since consciousness played no causal role in determining behavior and the same attitude was infecting the experiments of the time. With the exception of reports from Titchener's laboratory—introspective reports were first isolated from the objective results and then shortened or removed altogether.

In addressing how behavior is adjusted to stimulus, American psychologists were turning from the study of mental content to the study of adaptive mental functions. Another experiment, Bryan and Harter (1897), reveals a second sense in which American psychology was becoming functional—socially functional. Bryan, an experimental psychologist, and Harter, a former railroad telegrapher turned graduate student in psychology, investigated the acquisition of telegraphic skills by new railroad telegraphers. Their report contained no introspective reports at all but instead charted the students' gradual improvement over months of practice and telegraphic work. This completely objective study was socially significant because Bryan and Harter were studying an important skill learned by people who were assuming an important role in industrialized America. As the railroads expanded and knit together the island communities of formerly rural America, railroad telegraphers were vital: They kept track of what goods were sent where, of what trains were going to what places; in short, they were the communication links that made the whole railroad system function. Their significance may be judged from the fact that Ward began his mail order business (soon rivaled by Sears) as a railroad telegrapher picking up unwanted merchandise shipped west and then selling it by advertising up and down the railroad telegraph line. Bryan and Harter, then, were bringing psychological research to bear on a topic of real social value.

Their study is significant in another respect as well. It foreshadowed the central problem of experimental psychology in the twentieth century: learning. The traditional psychology of consciousness, mentalism, had primarily investigated perception and its allied functions, because it was these that produced introspectible mental contents. But in the post-Darwinian psychology of James and his followers, consciousness was important for what it does, especially the adjustment of the organism to its environment. Gradual adjustment over time is learning—finding out about the environment and then behaving in accord with it. Bryan and Harter plotted learning curves and discussed how the novice telegraphers gradually adjusted to the demands of their jobs. In its objectivism, in its concern with a socially useful problem, and in its choice of learning as subject matter, Bryan and Harter's paper was a sign of things to come. It is no wonder, therefore, that in 1943 it was voted by leading American psychologists as the most important experimental study yet published in the *Psychological Review* and one of the five most important papers of any kind. Even today it is cited in important texts in introductory psychology.

By 1904, it was clear that the "objective" method, in which responses were correlated with stimuli, was at least as important as the introspective analysis of consciousness. Speaking before the International Congress of Arts and Science, Cattell, the American pioneer in psychology, said, "I am not convinced that psychology should be limited to the study of consciousness as such," which of course had been the definition of psychology for James and Wundt. His own work, Cattell said, "is nearly as independent of introspection as work in physics or in zoology." While introspection and experiment should "continually cooperate," it was obvious from "the brute argument of accomplished fact" that much of psychology now existed "apart from introspection." Although Cattell seemed to place introspection and objective measurement on an equal footing, it is clear from his tone, and from his later call for applied psychology, that the objective, behavioral approach to psychology was on the rise.

Functional Psychology Defined

In both theory and research, then, American psychology was moving away from the traditional psychology of conscious content and toward a psychology of mental adjustment inspired by evolutionary theory. Interestingly, it was not an American psychologist who spotted and identified this new trend but the staunchest defender of a pure psychology of content, E. B. Titchener. In his "Postulates of a Structural Psychology" (1898), Titchener cogently distinguished several kinds of psychology; and while others may have disagreed about which kind of psychology was best, his terminology endured.

Titchener drew a broad analogy among three kinds of biology and three kinds of psychology:

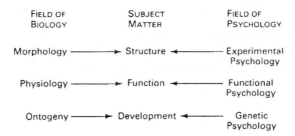

In biology the anatomist, the student of morphology, carefully dissects the body to discover the organs that compose it, revealing the body's structure. Once an organ is isolated and described, it is the job of the physiologist to figure out its function, what it does. Finally, one might study how an organ develops in the course of embryogenesis and postnatal development and how the organ came into being in the course of evolution; these studies constitute developmental biology, the study of the origin and path of change of an organ in the history of the species and of the individual.

Similarly, in psychology, the experimental psychologist—by which Titchener meant himself—dissects consciousness into its component parts; this anatomy of the mind defines structural psychology. What the revealed structures do is the province of the psychological physiologist—functional psychology. The development of mental structures and functions is the subject matter of genetic psychology, which investigates the course of individual and phylogenetic development.

In Titchener's estimation, structural psychology logically preceded functional psychology, since only after mental structures had been isolated and described could their functions be ascertained. At the same time Titchener noted the appeal of functional psychology. Its roots were ancient, its analysis of mind hewed close to common sense, as it employed faculty concepts such as "memory," "imagination," and "judgment," and it seemed to promise immediate practical application. Citing Dewey's reflex arc paper, Titchener also acknowledged that functional psychology was growing in influence. Nevertheless, Titchener urged psychologists to avoid the comfortable spaces of functional psychology and to stick to the tough, scientific job of experimental introspective psychology. Genetic psychology, while logically possible and indeed already on the scene (Baldwin, 1895; Wozniak, 1982), remained a yet more distant prospect for Titchener.

NOTE: The Bibliography for this chapter is incorporated with the Bibliography for Chapter 6.

REFERENCES

Angell, J. R. (1903). A preliminary study of the localization of sound. *Psychological Review 10,* 1–18.

Baldwin, J. M. (1895). *Mental development in the child and the race.* New York: Macmillan.

Bernard, L. L. (1911). *The transition to an objective standard of social control.* Chicago: University of Chicago Press.

Boorstin, D. J. (1974). *The Americans: The democratic experience.* New York: Vintage Books.

Bryan, W. L. & Harter, N. (1897). Studies in the psychology of the telegraphic language. *Psychological Review, 4,* 27–53.

Cattell, J. M. (1896). Address of the president. *Psychological Review, 3,* 134–148.

Danziger, K. (1979). The social origins of modern psychology. In A. Buss (Ed.), *Psychology in social context.* New York: Irvington.

Dewey, J. (1896). The reflex-arc concept in psychology. *Psychological Review, 3,* 357–370.

Dewey, J. (1900/1978). Psychology and social practice. *Psychological Review, 7,* 105–124. Reprinted in E. R. Hilgard (Ed.), *American psychology in historical perspective: Addresses of the Presidents of the American Psychological Association 1892–1977.* Washington, D.C.: APA.

Dewey, J. (1920/1948/1957). *Reconstruction in philosophy.* Boston: Beacon.

Dunton, L. (1895). The old psychology and the new. In L. Dunton, H. Munsterberg, W. T. Harris, & G. Stanley Hall, *The old psychology and the new: Addresses before the Massachusetts Schoolmaster's Club, April 27, 1895.* Boston: New England Publishing Co.

Fite, W. (1913). The science of man. *The Nation, 96,* (April 10): 368–370.

Hale, M. (1980). *Human science and social order.* Philadelphia: Temple University Press.

James, W. (1892). A plea for psychology as a natural science. *Philosophical Review, 1,* 146–153.

James, W. (1907/1955). *Pragmatism.* New York: Meridian.

Kuklick, B. (1977). *The rise of American philosophy.* New Haven: Yale University Press.

Ladd, G. T. (1892). Psychology as a so-called "natural science." *Philosophical Review, 1,* 24–53.

Titchener, E. B. (1898). Postulates of a structural psychology. *Philosophical Review, 7,* 449–465.

Wozniak, R. (1982). Metaphysics and science, reason and reality: The intellectual origins of genetic epistemology. In J. Broughton & D. Freeman Noir (Eds.), *The cognitive developmental psychology of James Mark Baldwin.* Hillsdale, NJ: Ablex.

CHAPTER 6

From Consciousness to Behavior:
BEHAVIORALISM DISCOVERED
(1898–1912)

THE TRIUMPH OF FUNCTIONAL PSYCHOLOGY (1898-1906)

From Undercurrent to Main Current

In the decade following Titchener's "Postulates," it became apparent that other psychologists found his analysis basically correct but his priorities reversed. In his December 1900 presidential address to the American Psychological Association, Peirce's one-time collaborator explored "Some Currents and Undercurrents in Psychology" (Jastrow, 1901). He declared that for him psychology is "the science of mental function," not content. The functional approach arose out of evolution; it "at once cast a blinding light" upon dark areas of psychology long held by "dogmatism, misconception and neglect" and "breathed a new life" into "the dry bones" of psychology. Jastrow correctly observed that although concern with mental function pervaded current research, it was not the central subject of investigation but rather gave a distinctive "color tone" to American psychology. Jastrow saw functional psychology as an accepted undercurrent, which he wanted to bring forward as a "main current." Functional psychology said Jastrow, is more catholic than structural psychology. It welcomes to psychology the previously excluded topics of comparative psychology, abnormal psychology, mental testing, the study of the average person, and even psychical research, although this last clearly troubled him. Jastrow predicted that functional psychology would prove of more value to practical affairs than structural psychology. Finally, he noted, as we have, that all these trends are characteristically American, and he correctly prophesied that the future would belong to functional, not structural, psychology.

A "revision" of the traditional central topic of mentalistic psychology, perception, from the functional-biological viewpoint was worked out by Thaddeus Bolton (1902). Bolton integrated theoretical developments in psychology since James, including the motor theory of consciousness and Dewey's account of the reflex arc, into a theory of perception embodying the coming behavioralist psychology. The "common view of perception held by most psychologists," according to Bolton, was Titchenerian: A percept is a complex of "all the different sensations" it produces. While not denying the reality of directly produced sensations, Bolton asserted that much more important to our perception of an object were sensations resulting from the actions provoked by that object, what Bolton, following James, called "the backstroke" in perception. We also find here the influence of Dewey (also cited by Bolton), whose reflex arc paper also pictured consciousness as largely determined by bodily response.

Perception, then, is more than a complex of sensations, argued Bolton; it is "an attitude," or, more strongly, "an act," so that "the study of perception becomes synonymous with a study of animal activity." Although Bolton did not discuss introspection, his theory naturally implies that introspection is not psychology's necessary method. If perception is to be identified with a particular adjustive response to a stimulus, as Bolton argued, then introspection is not necessary, because we can determine an organism's perceptions by observing what it does. "Only those objects ... [that] are acted towards ... are perceived." The only biologically significant percepts are those that enter into an organism's behavior; those conscious contents that are "without functional importance" are "epiphenomenal" and can be "left out of consideration." In Bolton's scheme of things, therefore, mind is not private: Anyone can determine the contents of anyone else's consciousness simply by watching that person behave—no special introspective method is necessary. As he put it, "What [an] object means, then, may be stated by describing the activity of the animal."

Consistent with his Darwinian biological orientation, Bolton stressed the continuity between humans and other "lower" animals. Humans are especially discriminating perceivers, not because of any special qualities of intellect but because we possess "an enormous variety of bodily responses" provided by language. We are able to associate with virtually any sensation some distinct motor response, or word; it is not our brains that make us unique among animals—not some central mental process—but our speech musculature. Thinking, Bolton implied, is just behavior: "Mind is to be regarded as an outgrowth of conduct, a superior and more direct means of adjusting the organism to the environment."

James Rowland Angell (1869–1949), who was about to publish a textbook written from the functional standpoint (*Psychology*, published in 1904), contrasted an admittedly inchoate functional psychology with structural psychology, while reversing Titchener's priorities. For Angell, functional psychology was more important than structural psychology. Unlike bodily organs, the structuralists' mental elements were not permanent, enduring objects but existed only at the moment of perception. That is, "the functions produce the structures," the reverse of biology, in which a given organ performs a distinct function that would not exist without it. Angell also alleged that structural psychology was socially pointless and biologically irrelevant. It studied consciousness removed from "life conditions" and could therefore tell us nothing useful about how mind works in the real world. Moreover, structuralist reductionism made of consciousness an irrelevant epiphenomenon. Functional psychology, in contrast, reveals consciousness to be "an efficient agent in the furtherance of the life activities of the organism," that is, as biologically useful and quite in accord, as Titchener himself had said, with common sense.

In several papers published in 1903 and 1904, the pragmatist philosopher H. Heath Bawden set out the new functional view of consciousness, a view that was coming to be commonly held by psychologists. Mental life, Bawden said, "is simply a name for the orderly functioning of an organism under conditions of tension in adaptation." As long as habits meet the needs of life, there is no consciousness. Consciousness only arises when there is a challenge, some novel circumstance calling for a novel behavior. Consciousness is a product of the tension produced by the need to adjust: "Consciousness never arises without a certain tension," and when new habits are devised, consciousness disappears again. In Bawden's view, like Bolton's, consciousness and behavior are closely connected: "The most fundamental statement we can make about consciousness is that it is action ... consciousness is not another realm or reality, it is simply the one world we know in its process of reconstruction."

Angell, Bawden, and Bolton were advancing James's conception of consciousness toward behavioralism. Conscious content, as such, is not very important in their functional theory of mind. For them, mind is a process whose biological value lies in its ability to be summoned forth genielike when its organism finds itself faced with a new situation. It is not needed when instincts are adequate to the stimuli at hand, or when previously learned habits are functioning smoothly. Consciousness is a sometime thing, needed only occasionally, and it would not be long before psychologists were able to go beyond Bolton and Bawden and dispense with mind altogether. As Frank Thilly (1905) pointed out, the functional view of consciousness retained James's fatal flaw. Along with just about everyone else, James and the functional psychologists following him held to mind-body parallelism while at the same time arguing that consciousness actively intervenes in the adjustive activities of the organism. Bolton was aware of the problem and tried to maintain that although consciousness does not affect nervous processes, it somehow plays a role in learning. This was not a happy position for functional psychologists to be in, and they would be rescued—or replaced—by the bolder behaviorists ready to chuck consciousness completely out of psychology. After all, if one can see conscious content in behavior, as Bolton maintained, why not just stick to talking about behavior?

By 1905, it was clear to contemporary psychologists that the functional tide was in. Edward Franklin Buchner, who for some years wrote for *Psychological Bulletin* an annual history of the year's "Psychological Progress," observed "the widespread acceptance and defense of the 'functional' as over against the 'structural' view" of psychology. The replacement of the older system by a new one did have the unfortunate effect, Buchner noted, of starting the development of the field all over again, undoing cumulative progress. In the same volume, Felix Arnold raised "the great cry" of current psychologists: "WHAT IS IT GOOD FOR?" He praised functionalists for giving up the old view of perception Bolton had attacked and replacing it with perception conceived "as a motor process ... determining serial reactions toward [an] object."

In the same year, Mary Calkins (1863–1930) took the opportunity of her APA presidential address to advance her self-psychology as a way to reconcile structural and functional psychologies. If psychology is conceived as the study of a real psychological self possessing both conscious content and mental functions, each system could be viewed as contributing part of the total psychological picture. Although Calkins aggressively pushed her self-psychology over the years in every forum she could find, it seems to have found few followers. For the time of compromise had passed. In 1907, Buchner wrote that in 1906 "the functional point of view seem[ed] to have almost completely won out"—so much so that psychology's " 'older' (and almost consecrated) terms" were about finished. Buchner awaited the framing "of a new vocabulary of psychology for the new twentieth century."

Angell seized the occasion of his APA presidential address to codify "The Province of Functional Psychology." Angell's address (given in December 1906 and published the next year) was a milestone on the road to behavioralism. In it, we can see that functionalism was mainly a bridge between mentalism and behavioralism, a way station rather than an enduring movement in its own right. As Angell conceded at the outset, functional psychology was "little more than a program" and a "protest" against the sterilities of structural psychology. Functional psychology was also not new, being found in Aristotle, in Spencer, in Darwin, and in pragmatism.

Angell repeated the already familiar distinction: Structural psychology was concerned with mental "*contents*," functionalism with mental "*operations*." Functionalism studies mental process as it is in the actual life of an organism; structuralism studies how mind "appears" in a "merely postmortem analysis." To this end, "modern investigations ... dispense with the usual direct form of introspection and concern themselves ... with a determination of what work is accomplished and what the conditions are under which it is achieved." Angell here acknowledged the trend we earlier found in his and others' research and defined the point of view of behavioralist experimentation. Repeating his argument of 1903, Angell justified this new research emphasis by quite correctly asserting that unlike physical organs dissected by the anatomist, "mental contents are evanescent and fleeting." What endures over time are mental functions: Contents come and go, but attention, memory, judgment—the mental faculties of the old psychology rehabilitated—"persist."

Functional psychology also brings with it a change in psychology's institutional relationships. Structural, mentalistic psychology grew out of philosophy and remained closely allied to it. In contrast, functional psychology "brings the psychologist cheek by jowl with the general biologist," because both study the "sum total" of an organism's "organic activities," the psychologist concentrating on the "accommodatory service" of consciousness. This new biological orientation will bring with it practical benefits as well, Angell averred. "Pedagogy and mental hygiene ... await the quickening and guiding counsel" of functional psychology. Animal psychology—"the most pregnant" movement of "our generation"—finds its "rejuvenation" in the new movement, because it is becoming "experimental ... wherever possible" and "conservatively ... non-anthropomorphic," trends we will examine in the next section. Genetic psychology and abnormal psychology—the former barely mentioned and the latter completely ignored by Titchener (1898)—will likewise be inspired by a functional approach.

Angell endorsed the view set forth by Bawden that consciousness "supervenes on certain occasions" in the life of an organism, describing the adjustment theory as "the position now held by all psychologists of repute." But he went further than Bawden or Bolton in claiming that consciousness "is no indispensable feature of the accommodatory process." Although in a footnote Angell still held that accommodation to "the novel" is "the field of conscious activity," we may still sense here a further step toward behavioralism in its suggestion that learning may take place without conscious intervention.

In conclusion, functional psychology is "functional" in a triple sense. First, it considers mind to have a distinct biological function selected by Darwinian evolution: It adapts its organism to novel circumstances. Second, it describes consciousness as itself a result of the physiological functioning of the organism: Mind, in its view, is itself a biological function. Third, functional psychology promises to be socially useful in improving education, mental hygiene, and abnormal states: Psychology will become functional in twentieth-century life. In 1906, Angell stood at a hinge in the development of modern psychology. His continued concern with consciousness, however interpreted, still linked functional psychology with the mentalism of the past. But at the same time, his emphasis on biology, on adaptation, and on applied psychology link functional psychology as a "new-old movement" whose time will someday pass with "some worthier successor [to] fill its place."

By 1907, then, functional psychology had by and large replaced structural psychology as the dominant approach to the field. However, it never became more than a program and a protest. It was finally too inconsistent to survive, clinging to a definition of psychology as the study of consciousness, while at the same time putting forth theories of perception and learning that made consciousness less and less necessary as a concept for scientific psychology. Functional theory embodied very clearly the historical forces of the time pushing psychology toward the study of behavior, and it helped psychologists change their fundamental conceptions of their profession without quite realizing that they were doing anything extraordinary.

Functional Psychology in Europe

While functional psychology was strongest in America, psychologies that could be identified with functionalism also arose in Europe. Brentano's psychology, because it was labeled an "act" psychology, was often assimilated to the functional viewpoint. Similarly, the Würzburg school could be called "functional" because of its concern with and investigations of mental processes, and its discovery of contentless (image-less) thought.

In Britain, home of modern evolutionism, functional psychology found its William James in James Ward (1843–1975), sometimes called the "father of modern British psychology" (Turner, 1974). He was for a time a minister, but after a crisis of faith turned first to physiology, then psychology, and finally philosophy, exactly as James had done. His tremendous influence in British psychology comes from his article on psychology in the *Encyclopedia Brittanica*'s ninth edition of 1886. It was the first article by that name in the *Encyclopedia,* and Ward reworked it later into a text. Ward settled at Cambridge University, where he was active in attempts to establish a psychological laboratory.

Like James, Ward rejected atomistic analysis of the continuum of consciousness. Instead of a sensationistic atomism, Ward advocated a functional view of consciousness, the brain, and the whole organism. Ward wrote (1904, p. 615): "Functionally regarded, the organism is from first to last a continuous whole … the growing complexity of psychical life is only parodied by treating it as mental chemistry." To Ward perception is not the passive reception of sensation, but active grasping of the environment. In a passage that resembles James, Ward (1904, p. 615) wrote that "not mere receptivity but creative or selective activity is the essence of subjective reality." He struck a Darwinian note when he said (1920, p. 607): "Psychologically regarded, then, the sole function of perception and intellection is, it is contended, to guide action and subserve volition—more generally to promote self-conservation and betterment."

Ward expounded the same kind of pragmatic, or functional, psychology that James did. For both men, consciousness is an active, choosing entity that adjusts the organism to the environment and so serves the struggle for survival. Ward resembled James in one more way—his *fin de siècle* concern with defending religion against the rising tide of Huxlean naturalism. Ward devoted his last great works to the refutation of naturalism and the support of Christianity.

Ward's influence endured for many years in English psychology. Britain retained a functionalist psychology that provided an orienting point for later cognitive psychology. Ward's antiatomism also endured, to be picked up by later antiassociationists. The Cambridge psychologist Frederick Bartlett, for example, explicitly rejected the attempt to study memory as the acquisition of discrete "bits" of information such as the nonsense syllables used in most memory experiments. Instead, Bartlett studied memory of everyday paragraphs. He argued that running prose is not a set of atomistic ideas, but is rather an embodiment of a larger meaning, which he called a *schema.* Bartlett (1932) showed, for example, that different cultures possess different schemas for organizing their experience, and that consequently systematic distortions are introduced into one culture's member's memory of another culture's stories. When alternatives to behaviorism were being explored in the 1960s, Bartlett's schema theory was revived and refined.

Of greater influence on later psychology was Hermann Ebbinghaus's (1850–1909) study of memory. Ebbinghaus was a young doctor of philosophy unattached to any university when he came across a copy of Fechner's *Elements Psychophysics* in a secondhand bookstore. He admired the scientific precision of Fechner's work on perception and resolved to tackle the "higher mental processes" that Wundt had excluded from experimental treatment. Using himself as his only subject, Ebbinghaus set out in 1879 to demonstrate Wundt's error. The result was his *Memory* of 1885, which was hailed even by Wundt as a first-rate contribution to psychology and which helped win him a professorship at the prestigious University of Berlin.

Memory represented a necessarily small-scale but well-thought-out research program. Ebbinghaus decided to investigate the formation of associations by learning serial lists of nonsense syllables, meaningless combinations of three letters he invented for the purpose. In electing to memorize nonsense syllables, Ebbinghaus revealed the functionalist cast of his thought. He chose nonsense syllables because they are meaningless, because the sameness of their content would not differentially affect the process of learning. He wanted to isolate and study memory as the pure *function* of learning, abstracting away any effects of content.

Ebbinghaus remained an eclectic rather than a systematic thinker, and his influence derives from his work on memory rather than from any theoretical views. But that influence was wide. In Germany, memory studies were carried on by G. E. Müller and his associates, whose distinctions, new procedures, and theories anticipated modern cognitive psychology. In America, James praised Ebbinghaus's work in *Principles,* and in 1896, Mary Calkins augmented Ebbinghaus's serial learning method with a paired-associate procedure in which the subject learns specific pairs of words or nonsense syllables. More broadly, Ebbinghaus's *Memory* prefigured the style of twentieth-century psychology. Its subject was learning, the favorite topic of functionalists, behaviorists, and cognitive psychologists. The book minimized theory while multiplying facts and looking for systematic effects on behavior of independent variables, such as list length. Ebbinghaus strove to quantify his data and apply statistical methods. In short, Ebbinghaus represents the empirical, atheoretical, research-oriented, eclectic modern psychologist.

NEW DIRECTIONS IN ANIMAL PSYCHOLOGY (1898–1909)

Animal psychology, as it had been begun by Romanes, used two methods: the anecdotal method to collect data, and the method of inference to interpret it. Although both methods had been challenged, discussed, and defended from their inception, they came under special scrutiny and criticism among American psychologists in the late nineteenth and early twentieth centuries. Anecdote was replaced by experiment, particularly by the techniques of E. L. Thorndike and I. P. Pavlov. Inference was gradually given up, at least by some animal psychologists, as it became clear that Descartes's problem of other minds had no empirical solution.

From Anecdote to Experiment

Beginning in 1898, animal psychology experienced a surge in activity and a quickening of interest. But in the new animal psychology laboratory, experiment replaced anecdotes and informal, naturalistic experiments, as psychologists investigated the behavior of species ranging from protozoa to monkeys. The aim of animal psychology, as of psychology in general, was to produce a natural science, and the young men in the field felt that gentlemanly anecdote was not the path to science; as E. L. Thorndike

(1898) wrote: "Salvation does not come from such a source." While there were many psychologists now experimenting on animal mind and behavior, two research programs deserve special attention, because their methods became enduring ones, and their theoretical conceptions embraced the whole of psychology. These programs arose at almost the same time, but in very different places and circumstances: in William James's Cambridge basement, where a young graduate student employed his mentor's children as his research assistants, and in the sophisticated laboratories of a distinguished Russian physiologist already on his way to a Nobel Prize.

THE CONNECTIONISM OF EDWARD LEE THORNDIKE (1874–1949)

Thorndike was attracted to psychology when he read James's *Principles* for a prize competition at his undergraduate school, Wesleyan (Connecticut). When Thorndike went to Harvard for graduate study, he eagerly signed up for courses with James and eventually majored in psychology. His first research interest was children and pedagogy, but no child subjects being available, Thorndike took up the study of learning in animals. James gave him a place to work in his basement after Thorndike failed to secure official research space from Harvard. Before completing his work at Harvard, Thorndike was invited to go to Columbia by Cattell; at Columbia he pursued his animal research. Upon graduation Thorndike returned to his first love, educational psychology, which—along with psychometrics—he made his field of study. Thorndike's importance for us is in his methodological and theoretical approach to animal learning and in his formulation of an S-R psychology he called *connectionism*.

Thorndike's animal researches are summarized in *Animal Intelligence,* which appeared in 1911. It includes his most important work, the report on his graduate studies, "Animal Intelligence: An Experimental Study of the Associative Processes in Animals," originally published in 1898. In the introduction, Thorndike (1911, p. 22) defined the usual problem of animal psychology, "to learn the development of mental life down through the phylum, to trace in particular the origin of the human faculty." However, he deprecated the value of previous research, for it relied on the anecdotal method, which Thorndike argued focused only on unusual animal performances, not on the typical. As a substitute Thorndike argued that the experimental approach is the only way to completely control the animal's situation. Thorndike's goal was by experiment to catch animals "using their minds."

Thorndike placed an animal in one of many "puzzle boxes," each of which could be opened by the animal in a different way. When the animal escaped, it was fed. Thorndike's subjects included cats, chicks, and dogs. Thorndike's setup is an example of what would later be called *operant conditioning* or *learning:* An animal makes some response, and if it is rewarded—in Thorndike's case with escape and food—the response is learned. If the response is not rewarded, it gradually disappears.

Thorndike's results led him to heap scorn on the older view of the anecdotal psychologists that animals reason; animals learn, he said, solely by trial and error, reward and punishment. In a passage that foreshadowed the future, Thorndike wrote that animals may have no ideas at all, no ideas to associate. There is association, but (maybe) not of ideas. Wrote Thorndike (1911, p. 98): "The effective part of the association [is] a direct bond between the situation and the impulse." In 1898, Thorndike could not quite accept this radical thesis, although he acknowledged its plausibility.

Thorndike's scorn for the old animal psychology did not escape sharp replies. Wesley Mills (1847–1915), America's senior animal psychologist, attacked Thorndike for having swept away "almost the entire fabric of comparative psychology" and for regarding his predecessors as "insane." Mills argued that animals could only be properly investigated in their natural settings, not in the artificial confines of the laboratory. Directly addressing Thorndike's studies, Mills turned sarcastic: Thorndike "placed cats in boxes only $20 \times 15 \times 12$ inches, and then expected them to act naturally. As well enclose a living man in a coffin, lower him, against his will, into the earth, and attempt to deduce normal psychology from his behavior" (Mills, 1899, p. 266). By 1904, however, Mills had to concede the ascendancy of "the laboratory school," led by Thorndike, "the chief agnostic of this school." They denied that animals reason, or plan, or imitate. But Mills, and Wolfgang Köhler, maintained that animals seemed not to reason in the laboratory because their situations did not permit it. Köhler (1925) said that animals were forced into blind trial and error by the construction of Thorndike's puzzle boxes. Since the penned-up subject could not see how the escape mechanism worked, it simply could not reason its way out; without all the relevant information, insight cannot be achieved. So instead, the poor animal is thrown back on the primitive strategy of trial and error. The method, as Flourens had said of his ablation technique, gives the results. Thorndike's method only permitted random trial and error, so that is what he found. But to go on to claim that all an animal is capable of is mere association is entirely unjustified.

Such considerations did not deter Thorndike from developing his radically simplified theory of learning. In 1911, he wrote in the introduction to *Animal Intelligence* (p. 4): Any "of the lower animals is ... obviously a bundle of original and acquired connections between situation and response." He argued that we should try to study animal behavior, not animal consciousness, because the former problem is easier. He contended that this objective method could be extended to human beings, for we can study mental states as behavior. He criticized the structuralists for fabricating a wholly artificial and imaginary picture of human consciousness. He argued that the purpose of psychology should be the control of behavior (p. 15): "There can be no moral warrant for studying man's nature unless the study will enable us to control his acts." He concluded his introduction by prophesying that psychology would become the study of behavior.

Thorndike proposed two laws of human and animal behavior. The first was the law of effect (p. 244): "Of several responses made to the same situation, those which are accompanied or closely followed by satisfaction to the animal will, other things being equal, be more firmly connected with the situation, so that, when it recurs, they will be more likely to recur." Punishment, on the other hand, reduces the strength of the connection. Further, the greater the reward or punishment, the greater the change in the connection. Later Thorndike abandoned the punishment part of the law of effect, retaining only reward. The law of effect is the basic law of operant conditioning, accepted in some form by most learning theorists. Thorndike's second law is the law of exercise (p. 244): "Any response to a situation will, all other things being equal, be more strongly connected with the situation in proportion to the number of times it has been connected with that situation, and to the average vigor and duration of the connections."

Thorndike contended that these two laws could account for all behavior, no matter how complex: It would be possible to reduce "the processes of abstraction, association by similarity and selective thinking to mere secondary consequences of the laws of exercise and effect" (p. 263). He analyzed language as a set of vocal responses learned because parents reward some of a child's sounds but not others. The rewarded ones are acquired and the nonrewarded ones are unlearned, following the law of effect.

Thorndike applied his connectionism to human behavior in *Human Learning,* a series of lectures delivered at Cornell in 1928 and 1929. He presented an elaborate S-R psychology in which many stimuli are connected to many responses in hierarchies of S-R associations. Thorndike asserted that each S-R link could be assigned a probability that S will elicit R. For example, the probability that food will elicit salivation is very near 1.00, while before conditioning the probability that a tone will elicit salivation is near 0. Learning is increasing S-R probabilities; forgetting is lowering them. Just as animal learning is automatic, unmediated by an awareness of the contingency between response and reward, so, Thorndike argues, is human learning also unconscious. One may learn an operant response without being aware that one is doing so. As he did for animals, Thorndike reduced human reasoning to automatism, custom, and habit. Thorndike held out the promise of scientific utopia, founded on eugenics and scientifically managed education.

Thorndike recognized a number of difficulties with his S-R theory that would be exploited by later critics of behaviorism. For example, he admitted that the objective psychologist, who stresses how the environment determines behavior, has a difficult time defining the situation in which an animal acts. Are all stimuli equally relevant to an act? When I am asked, for example, "What is the cube root of sixty-four?" many other stimuli are acting on me at the same time as this question. Defining the response is equally difficult. I may respond "four," but many other behaviors (such as breathing) are also occurring. How do we know what S is connected with what R without recourse to subjective, nonphysical meaning? Thorndike admitted that such questions were reasonable and that answers would have to be given eventually. About reading and listening, Thorndike (1911) wrote: "In the hearing or reading of a paragraph, the connections from the words somehow cooperate to give certain total meanings." That "somehow" conceals a mystery only partially acknowledged. He realized the complexity of language when he said that the number of connections necessary to understand a simple sentence may be well over 100,000, and he conceded that organized language is "far beyond any description given by associationist psychology."

Was Thorndike a behaviorist? His biographer (Joncich, 1968) says he was, and she can cite in support such statements as this: "Our reasons for believing in the existence of other people's minds are our experiences of their physical actions." He did formulate the basic law of operant learning, the law of effect, and the doctrine that consciousness is unnecessary for learning. Unlike Pavlov, he practiced a purely behavioral psychology without reference to physiology. On the other hand, he proposed a principle of "belongingness" that violates a basic principle of classical conditioning, that those elements most closely associated in space and time will be connected in learning. The sentences "John is a butcher, Harry is a carpenter, Jim is a doctor," presented in a list like this, would make *butcher-Harry* a stronger bond than *butcher-John* if the classical conditioning contiguity theory were correct. However, this is clearly not the case. *John* and *butcher* "belong" together (because of the structure of the sentences) and so will be associated, and recalled, together. This principle of belongingness resembled Gestalt psychology rather than behaviorism.

Historically, Thorndike is hard to place. He did not found behaviorism, though he practiced it in his animal researches. His devotion to educational psychology quickly took him outside of the mainstream of academic experimental psychology in which behaviorism developed. It might best be concluded that Thorndike was a practicing behaviorist but not a wholehearted one.

THE NEUROSCIENCE OF I. P. PAVLOV (1849–1936)

The other most important new experimental approach to animal psychology grew from Russian objective psychology, an uncompromisingly materialistic and mechanistic conception of biology. The founder of modern Russian physiology was Ivan Michailovich Sechenov (1829–1905), who studied in some of the best physiological laboratories in Europe, including Helmholtz's, and who brought back their methods and ideas to Russia. Sechenov believed that psychology, which was known to him only as a branch of philosophy, could be scientific only if it were completely taken over by physiology and adopted physiology's objective methods. Introspective psychology he dismissed as akin to primitive superstition. Sechenov (1973, pp. 350–51, translation anonymous) wrote:

> Physiology will begin by separating psychological reality from the mass of psychological fiction which even now fills the human mind. Strictly adhering to the principle of induction, physiology will begin with a detailed study of the more simple aspects of psychical life and will not rush at once into the sphere of the highest psychological phenomena. Its progress will therefore lose in rapidity, but it will gain in reliability. As an experimental science, physiology will not raise to the rank of incontrovertible truth anything that cannot be confirmed by exact experiments; this will draw a sharp boundary-line between hypotheses and positive knowledge. Psychology will thereby lose its brilliant universal theories; there will appear tremendous gaps in its supply of scientific data; many explanations will give place to a laconic "we do not know"; the essence of the psychical phenomena manifested in consciousness (and, for the matter of that, the essence of all other phenomena of nature) will remain an inexplicable enigma in all cases without exception. And yet, psychology will gain enormously, for it will be based on scientifically verifiable facts instead of the deceptive suggestions of the voice of our consciousness. Its generalizations and conclusions will be limited to actually existing analogies, they will not be subject to the influence of the personal preferences of the investigator which have so often led psychology to absurd transcendentalism, and they still thereby become really objective scientific hypotheses. The subjective, the arbitrary and the fantastic will give way to a nearer or more remote approach to truth. In a word, *psychology will become a positive science. Only physiology can do all this, for only physiology holds the key to the scientific analysis of psychical phenomena.*

Sechenov, like American functionalists, abandoned mentalism. Psychology is to be positive, concerned with objective, public facts. Starting with the simple, it will proceed to the more complex, being cautious and unspeculative. It will ignore consciousness.

Sechenov's great work was *Reflexes of the Brain* (1863/1965, p. 308), in which he wrote: "All the external manifestations of brain activity can be attributed to muscular movement.... Billions of diverse phenomena, having seemingly no relationship to each other, can be reduced to the activity of several dozen muscles." Watson's peripheralism is found in Sechenov (1863/1965, p. 321): "Thought is generally believed to be the cause of behavior ... [but this is] the greatest of falsehoods: [for] the initial cause of all behavior always lies, not in thought, but in external sensory stimulation." He also stated that all conscious, voluntary movements are reflexes. Elsewhere, he too adopted the model of language as a chain of vocal responses.

Sechenov's objectivism was popularized by Vladimir Michailovitch Bechterev (1867–1927), who called his system *reflexology,* a name that accurately describes its character. However, the greatest of Sechenov's followers, though not his student, was Ivan Petrovich Pavlov (1849–1936), one of psychology's few household names. Pavlov was a physiologist whose studies of digestion won him the Nobel Prize in 1904. In the course of this work, he discovered that stimuli other than food may produce salivation, and this led him to the study of psychology, especially to the concept of the conditioned reflex and its exhaustive investigation.

Pavlov's general attitude was uncompromisingly objective and materialistic. He had the positivist's faith in objective method as the touchstone of natural science, and consequently he rejected reference to mind. Pavlov (1957, p. 168, original paper published 1903) wrote: "For the naturalist everything lies in the method, in the chance of obtaining an unshakable, lasting truth; and solely from this point of view ... the soul ... is not only unnecessary but even harmful to his work." Pavlov rejected any appeal to an active inner agency, or mind, in favor of an analysis of the environment: It should be possible to explain behavior without reference to a "fantastic internal world," referring only to "the influence of external stimuli, their summation, etc." His analysis of thinking was atomistic and reflexive. "The entire mechanism of thinking consists in the elaboration of elementary associations and in the subsequent formation of chains of associations." His criticism of nonatomistic psychology was unremitting. He carried out replications of Köhler's ape experiments in order to show that "association is knowledge, ... thinking ... [and] insight," (Pavlov, 1957, p. 586, from Wednesday Discussion Group statements, c. 1934–1935) and he devoted many meetings of his weekly Wednesday discussion group to unfriendly analyses of Gestalt concepts. He viewed the Gestaltists as dualists who "did not understand anything" of their own experiments.

Pavlov's technical contribution to the psychology of learning was considerable. He discovered classical conditioning and inaugurated a systematic research program to discover all its mechanisms and situational determinants. In the course of his Nobel Prize–winning investigation of canine salivation, Pavlov observed that salivation could later be elicited by stimuli present at the time food was presented to an animal. He originally called these learned reactions *psychical secretions* because they were elicited by noninnate stimuli, but later he substituted the term *conditioned response.*[1]

Following the fully refined paradigm of classical conditioning, one begins with a reflex elicited by some innate stimulus, as salivation is elicited by presentation of

[1]This is the English term. However, a more accurate rendering of *ooslouny* would have been *conditional response.*

food. This connection is between an *unconditioned stimulus* (US) and an *unconditioned response* (UR). Then, while presenting the US, one presents some other stimulus that does not elicit the reflex, such as the sound of a metronome. This stimulus is called the *conditioned stimulus* (CS), for after several pairings with the US, it will come to elicit the same response (UR), now called the *conditioned response* (CR). It is also possible, although more difficult, to establish a new CS-CR relationship starting with a previously learned CS-CR relationship (for example, pairing a tone with the metronome sound to get the tone to elicit salivation). Such a procedure is known as *higher-order conditioning.*

Pavlov systematically investigated conditioned reflexes. He found that conditioned responses will occur to stimuli similar to the original CS; this is called *generalization.* Further, Pavlov found that one could require that an animal make a CR to one stimulus but not another; this is called *discrimination.* If too-fine discriminations are required of an animal, it displays neuroticlike symptoms. Pavlov also studied how to inhibit conditioned reflexes. If one repeatedly presents the CS without the US, eventually the CR will disappear; this is called *extinction.* However, if one leaves the animal alone for a while, the CS will again elicit the CR; this is called *spontaneous recovery.* There is also *conditioned inhibition,* in which one presents the CS and some new CS together without the US, although the old CS is still occasionally paired with the US. After a while the new combination will fail to elicit the CR. Pavlov's researches were meticulous and detailed, one of the best examples in psychology of a research program in Lakatos's sense.

Between them, Thorndike and Pavlov contributed important methods to psychology, methods that were to become the shared exemplars of behaviorism. At the same time, each questioned the need for psychologists and biologists to talk about animal mind. Thorndike found only blind association forming in his animals, denying that animals reason or even imitate. Pavlov, following Sechenov, proposed to substitute physiology for psychology, eliminating talk about the mind for talk about the brain. La Mettrie's vision seemed about to be fulfilled.

The Problem of Animal Mind

The trouble with animal psychology, said E. C. Sanford in his 1902 presidential address to the APA, is that it "tempts us beyond the bounds of introspection," as do the other growing elements of comparative psychology, the studies of children, the retarded, and the abnormal. But, Sanford asked, should we be "content with a purely objective science of animal or child or idiot behavior?" Sanford thought not and spelled out why, recognizing, with Romanes, the logical conclusion of an objective psychology:

> I doubt if anyone has ever seriously contemplated [a purely objective psychology] in the case of the higher animals, or could carry it to fruitful results if he should undertake it. Nor would anyone seriously propose to treat the behavior of his fellow men in the same way, i.e. to refuse to credit them with conscious experience in the main like his own, though this would seem to be required logically. (Sanford 1903, p. 105)

However, comparative psychologists still faced Descartes's problem: If they were going to infer mental processes in animals, they had to come up with some criterion of the mental. Just which behaviors could be explained as due to mechanism alone, and which ones reflected mental processes? Descartes had had a simple answer, suited to the Age of Reason: The soul, not the body, thinks; so language—the expression of thought—is the mark of the mental. Things were not so simple for comparative psychologists, though. Having accepted phylogenetic continuity and having disposed of the soul, they found Descartes's criterion no longer plausible. It seemed clear that the higher animals possess minds and that paramecia do not (although a few animal psychologists thought they did possess very low-grade intelligence), but exactly where to draw the line was intensely problematic.

They wrestled with the problem and proposed numerous criteria, thoughtfully reviewed by Robert Yerkes (1876–1956), a leading animal psychologist, in 1905. Like Sanford, Romanes, and others, Yerkes knew the problem was important for human psychology, too, since we use inference to know other human minds just as much as we do to know animal minds. Indeed, "human psychology stands or falls with comparative psychology. If the study of the mental life of lower animals is not legitimate, no more is the study of human consciousness" (Yerkes, 1905b).

As Yerkes saw it, proposed "criteria of the psychic" could be divided into two broad categories. First, there are the structural criteria: An animal might be said to have a mind if it had a sufficiently sophisticated nervous system. More important were the functional criteria, behaviors that indicated presence of mind. Among the possible functional criteria, Yerkes found that most workers took learning to be the mark of the mind and arranged their experiments to see if a given species could learn. Such a criterion was consistent with James's Darwinian psychology and with contemporary developments in functional psychology. As we have seen, functionalists, following James, viewed consciousness as above all an adjustive agency, so naturally they looked for signs of adjustment in their subjects. An animal that could not learn would be regarded as a mere automation.

Yerkes thought the search for a single criterion too simple, and he proposed three grades, or levels, of consciousness, corresponding to three classes of behavior. At the lowest level there was *discriminative* consciousness, indicated by the ability to discriminate one stimulus from another; even a sea anemone had this grade of consciousness. Next, Yerkes proposed a grade of *intelligent* consciousness, whose sign was learning. Finally, there is *rational* consciousness, which initiates behaviors rather than just responding, however flexibly, to environmental challenges.

At least one young psychologist was coming to find the whole problem a hopeless tangle. John B. Watson was a graduate student of Angell's at the University of Chicago, stronghold of Dewey's instrumentalism and psychological functionalism. Watson disliked introspection and took up animal psychology. His dissertation, "Animal Education," which was cowritten by Angell, had very little mentalism in it and was mostly an attempt to find a physiological basis for learning. As a promising animal psychologist, Watson was one of the main reviewers of the literature in animal psychology for *Psychological Bulletin,* and there we find him becoming bored by the controversy over the criterion of the mental. In 1907, he called it "the *bête noir* of the student of behavior," and asserted, "The whole contention is tedious." However, he was still at Chicago under Angell's eye, and he defended a psychology of animal mind. Mind could not be eliminated from psychology, as long as mind-body parallelism was its working hypothesis.

In the fall of 1908, Watson obtained a position at Johns Hopkins University; away from Angell and on his own, he became bolder. At a talk before the Scientific Association of Johns Hopkins, the newly arrived professor said that the study of animal behavior could be carried out purely objectively, producing facts on a par with the other natural sciences; no reference to animal mind was made (Swartz, 1908).

On December 31 of that same year, Watson (1909) spelled out "A Point of View in Comparative Psychology" for the Southern Society for Philosophy and Psychology, then meeting at Hopkins. Watson reviewed the controversy surrounding the criteria of consciousness in animals and stated (quoting E. F. Buchner, the society's secretary) "that these criteria are impossible of application and ... have been valueless to the science" of animal behavior. Watson argued that the "facts of behavior" are valuable in themselves and do not have to be "grounded in any criteria of the psychic." Human psychology too, Watson said, is coming to be more objective, seeming to abandon the use of introspection and "the speech reaction." These trends away from introspection will lead psychology toward "the perfection of technique of the physical sciences." As "criteria of the psychic ... disappear" from psychology, it will study the whole "process of adjustment" in "all of its broad biological aspects" rather than focusing narrowly on a few elements caught in a moment of introspection. While Watson would not proclaim behaviorism as such until 1913, it is clear that the "viewpoint" he described that afternoon in McCoy Hall was behaviorism in all but name. For Watson, criteria of the mental were useless in animal psychology. Grasping the nettle of the logic of his argument, he had concluded that criteria of the mental were useless in human psychology, too.

RETHINKING MIND: THE CONSCIOUSNESS DEBATE (1904–1912)

Mind's place in nature was being fundamentally revised by functional psychologists and by their colleagues in animal psychology. Mind was becoming problematic, reduced to a problem-solving genie in later functional psychology, and slowly disappearing altogether in animal psychology. In 1904 philosophers, too, began to reexamine consciousness.

Does Consciousness Exist? Radical Empiricism

Pragmatism was a method for finding the truth, not a substantive philosophical position. James, nearing the end of his life, turned to the problems of metaphysics and worked out a system he called "radical empiricism," beginning in 1904 with a paper called "Does 'Consciousness' Exist?" As always, James was provocative, setting off a debate among philosophers and psychologists that reshaped their conceptions of mind.

James argued that consciousness did not exist as a distinct, separate thing apart from experience. There simply *is* experience: hardness, redness, tones, tastes, smells. There is nothing above and beyond it called "consciousness" that possesses it and knows it. Pure experience is the stuff of which the world is made, James held. Rather than being a thing, consciousness is a function, a certain kind of relationship among portions of pure experience.

James's position is complex and difficult to grasp, involving a novel form of idealism (experience is the stuff of reality) and panpsychism (everything in the world, even a desk, is conscious). For psychology, what was important was the debate James began, because out of it arose two new conceptions of consciousness that supported behavioralism: the relational theory of consciousness and the functional theory of consciousness.

The Relational Theory of Consciousness: Neorealism

To some extent, the important place of consciousness in psychology and philosophy derived from the copy theory of knowledge. The copy theory asserts, as James put it, a "radical dualism" of object and knower. For the copy theory, consciousness contains representations of the world and knows the world only through the representations. It follows, then, that consciousness is a mental world of representations separate from the physical world of things. In this traditional definition of psychology, the science of psychology studied the world of representations with the special method of introspection, while natural sciences such as physics studied the world of objects constructed by observation. James's challenge to the copy theory surprised a group of young American philosophers to propose a form of realism that owed nothing to the old Scottish realists.

They called themselves "neorealists" and asserted what they took to be a scientific theory of mind. There is a world of physical objects that we know directly, without the mediation of internal representations. Now while this theory is epistemological in aim—asserting the knowability of a real external physical world—it carries interesting implications for psychology. For in this realist view, consciousness is not a special, inner world to be reported on by introspection. Rather, consciousness is a relationship between self and world, the relationship of knowing. This was the basic idea of the relational theory of consciousness, and it was developed in these years by Ralph Barton Perry (1876–1957), James's biographer and teacher of E. C. Tolman; by Edwin Bissel Holt (1873–1946), with Perry at Harvard, and Münsterberg's successor as Harvard's experimental psychologist; and by Edgar Singer (1873–1954), whose papers on mind would later be regarded by some as the first and best statements of behaviorism.

The development of the neorealist theory of mind began with Perry's analysis of the allegedly privileged nature of introspection. Since Descartes, philosophers had supposed that consciousness was a private, inward possession of representations, known only to itself; upon this idea much of Descartes' radical dualism of world and mind rested. In the traditional view, introspection was a special sort of observation of a special place, quite different from the usual sort of observation of external objects. Traditional mentalistic psychology accepted the radical dualism of mind and object and enshrined introspection as the observational technique peculiar to the study of consciousness. Perry argued that introspection was special only in trivial ways, and that the "mind within" of introspection was in no essential way different from the "mind without" exhibited in everyday behavior.

Asking me to introspect is certainly an easy way to enter my mind, Perry conceded. Only I have *my* memories, and only I know to what I am attending at any given moment. But in these instances, introspection is not specially privileged, nor is mind a private place. What I experienced in the past could in principle be determined by other observers present when memories were laid down; careful observation of my current behavior will reveal to what I am paying attention. In short, contents of consciousness are not exclusively my own: Anyone else may discover them. Indeed, such is the method of animal psychology, said Perry: We discover animal mind by attending to animal behavior, reading an animal's intentions and mental content by observing the way it behaves toward the objects in its environment. As Bolton had argued, an object perceived is an object acted toward, so an animal's percepts are revealed by its conduct.

Another kind of knowledge that seems to make self-consciousness and introspection special sources of knowledge is knowledge of the states of one's own body. Clearly, no one else has *my* headache. Of course, in this sense introspection is privileged. But Perry refused to see any momentous conclusion to be drawn from this circumstance. In the first place, although one does not have direct awareness of another's inner bodily states, one can easily know about them from one's own analogous states; while you do not have my headache, you do know what a headache is. Second, inner bodily processes could be better known by a properly equipped outsider. "Who is so familiar with farming as the farmer?" Perry asked. Obviously, no one; but nonetheless an expert, scientifically trained, may be able to tell the farmer how to grow more efficiently. Similarly, inner bodily processes are not one's exclusive possession, being open to physiological study. Finally, to assert special introspective access to bodily states is a very trivial defense of introspective psychology, because such contents are hardly the essence of mind.

If we follow Perry, we must conclude that mentalistic psychology is misguided. Consciousness is not a private thing known only to myself and shareable only through introspection. Rather, my consciousness is a collection of sensations derived from the external world or from my own body; with James, Perry maintained there is no entity of "consciousness" apart from experienced sensations. But since these sensations may be known by anyone else, my mind is, in fact, an open book, a public object open to scientific study. Introspection remains pragmatically useful of course, since no one has as convenient access to my sensations, past and present, as I have; so the psychologist who wishes to open my mind should simply ask me to look within and report what I find. In Perry's view, however, introspection is not the only road to the mind, since mind is always on view as behavior. In principle, then, psychology can be conducted as a purely behavioral enterprise, engaging its subjects' self-awareness when expedient, but otherwise attending only to behavior. Perry's philosophical analysis of mind coincides ultimately with the view being developed in animal psychology: Mind and behavior are, functionally, the same, and both animal and human psychology rest on the same basis—the study of behavior.

Perry claimed anyone's consciousness could be known by a sufficiently well-informed outside observer. E. B. Holt took consciousness out of a person's head and put it in the environment with his theory of *specific response*. Holt argued that the contents of consciousness were just a cross section of the objects of the universe, past or present, distant or near, to which a person is responding. To clarify his proposal Holt offered an analogy: Consciousness is like a flashlight's beam in a darkened room, revealing the things we see, while leaving others in the dark. Similarly, at any given moment, we are reacting only to some of the objects in the universe, and these are the ones of which we are conscious. So consciousness is not inside a person at all but is "out there wherever the things specifically responded to are." Even memory was treated the same way: Memory is not the recovery of some past idea stored away and recalled, but is simply the presentation before consciousness of an absent object.

Holt's view, like Perry's, rejected the alleged privacy of mind. If consciousness is no more than specific response, and its contents no more than an inventory of the objects controlling my current behavior, then anyone who turns the flashlight of consciousness on the same objects as mine will know my mind. Behavior, Holt argued, is always controlled by or directed toward some real object—that is, a goal—and behavior is to be explained by discovering the acted-toward objects. So to do psychology we need not ask our subjects to introspect, though of course we may. We may understand their minds by examining their behavior and the circumstances in which it occurs, abandoning mentalistic for behavioralistic psychology. Objects to which organisms react are those of which it is conscious, said Holt; hence the study of consciousness and the study of behavior were essentially the same.

Although he was not formally a neorealist, E. A. Singer proposed a behavioral concept of mind consistent with Perry's or Holt's. Singer applied the pragmatic test of truth to the problem of other minds: Does it matter, does it make a difference to our conduct, whether or not other people have conscious experience or not? Singer argued that pragmatically the "other minds" problem is meaningless because it cannot be resolved. It had been debated by philosophers and psychologists since Descartes with no sign of progress. So we should conclude that it is a pseudoproblem incapable of solution: It doesn't matter.

Singer then considered a possible pragmatic objection that consciousness in others does deeply matter to our everyday behavior. James once asked us to consider the "automatic sweetheart." Suppose you are deeply in love: Every adoring glance, every gentle caress, every tender sigh you will take as signs of your sweetheart's love for you; everything she does will bespeak a love for you like yours for her. Then, one day, you discover she is only a machine, cleverly constructed to exhibit tokens of love for you; but she is not conscious, being but a machine, a simulacrum of a sweetheart. Do you love her still? James thought one could not; that vital to love is not just the glances, caresses, and sighs but the conviction that behind them is a mental state called love, a subjective condition of fondness, affection, and commitment like one's own. In short, belief in other minds passes the pragmatic test, James concluded, for we will feel very differently about, and of course act very differently toward, a creature depending on whether or not we think it possesses a mind.

Singer tried to refute James's argument. He asked how terms such as "mind" or "soul" or "soulless" are used in practice. They are inferences from behaviors, constructions we erect out of another's conduct. Of course, these constructions may be wrong, and we discover our error when our expectations about a person's behavior are not fulfilled. In the case of the automatic sweetheart, Singer argued, discovering that she is "soulless" only means that you now fear that her behavior in the future will not be like her behavior in the past; that is, you have just misunderstood her, and that falling out of love with her is not due to her not having a mind, but because you no longer can predict how she will act.

Singer went on to argue that mind is an observable object. "Consciousness is not something inferred from behavior, it is behavior. Or, more accurately, our belief in consciousness is an expectation of probable behavior based on observation of actual behavior, a belief to be confirmed or refuted by more observation" (p. 183). We believe in a separate entity called consciousness only because of deeply ingrained habits of thought, most importantly reification—the tendency to think that if we can name something, it exists. So, for example, before the advent of modern physics people were tempted to think of a hot rock as a rock + heat, or of a living thing as a body + life. In these cases, we have reified into a separate entity something that merely describes behavior. Heat is not a thing, but a certain behavior; life is not a thing added to a body (for example, the Greek psyche), but the behavior of the body. Similarly, Singer maintained, "mind" is not something separate from behavior, it *is* behavior, falsely reified by us. In Singer's view, then, there is no mind for anyone to investigate: Mentalistic psychology was a delusion from the start. Psychology should abandon mind, then, and study what is real: behavior.

Whether or not you find Singer's position plausible, his debate with James raised an issue probably more important today than then. For we can now build machines that appear to think, as James's automatic sweetheart appeared to love. Do they really think? And James's own creation has been brought to life in the writings of science-fiction novelists. Can a machine, an android, love? In our age of computers and genetic engineering, these are not idle questions, and we shall meet them again in the new field of cognitive science.

Neorealism did not last long as a philosophical movement. Its primary failing was epistemological: accounting for the problem of error. If we know objects directly and without mediation by ideas, how is it that we have mistaken perceptions? With the copy theory, error is easy to explain, by saying that copies may not be accurate. Realism finds error difficult to account for. Realism did, however, have lasting influence. The neorealists professionalized philosophy. The older generations of philosophers such as James and Royce wrote for a wide audience of interested readers, and their names were well known to educated Americans. The neorealists, however, modeled their philosophy after science, making it technical and inaccessible to nonphilosophers (Kuklick, 1977). In psychology, their relational theory of consciousness aided the development of behavioralism and behaviorism, by reworking the mentalistic concept of consciousness into something knowable from behavior, and perhaps even something identical with behavior—in which case, the concept of mind need play no role in scientific psychology, however important it might remain outside the profession.

The Functional Theory of Consciousness: Instrumentalism

The neorealists developed the relational conception of mind suggested by James (1904). Dewey and his followers developed the functional conception. Dewey's emerging philosophy was called *instrumentalism,* because of his emphasis on mind as an effective actor in the world, and on knowledge as an instrument for first understanding and then changing the world. Dewey's conception of mind was thus more active than the neorealists', who still adhered to what Dewey called the "spectator theory of mind." Copy theories are spectator theories, because the world impresses itself (to use Hume's term) on a passive mind, which then simply copies the impression over into an idea. Although the neorealists rejected the copy theory, they had not, in Dewey's view, gotten away from the spectator theory, because in the relational theory consciousness is still fully determined by the objects to which one is responding. So mind is still a spectator passively viewing the world, only directly rather than through the spectacles of ideas.

Dewey (1939) got rid of the spectator theory but retained a representational theory of mind. He described mind as a function of the biological organism, adapting actively to the environment, a view going back to his 1896 reflex arc paper. As he developed his instrumentalism, Dewey became more specific about what mind actually does. Mind, he proposed, is the presence and operations of meanings, ideas—or, more specifically, is the ability to anticipate future consequences and to respond to them as stimuli to present behavior. So mind is a set of representations of the world that function instrumentally to adaptively guide the organism in its dealings with its environment. Echoing Brentano, Dewey claimed that what makes something mental rather than physical is that it points to something else—that is, it has meaning. Postulation of meanings does not require postulation of a separate realm of mind, for ideas are to be conceived as neurophysiological functions, whose total functioning we conveniently designate "mind."

Dewey also stressed the social nature of mind, even coming at times to deny that animals had minds, a change from his 1896 paper. Dewey was impressed by Watson's claim (to be described later) that thinking is just speech, or, more strongly, that vocalization is all thinking consists in, whether such vocalization is out loud or covert. Interestingly, this returns Dewey to Descartes's old view, seemingly rejected by functional psychologists, that animals do not think because they do not talk. Dewey has reversed Descartes's priorities, though. For Descartes, thinking comes first and is only expressed in speech; for Dewey, learning to speak creates the ability to think. Descartes was an individualist, investing each human with an innately given self-consciousness endowed with thought, but forever isolated from other consciousnesses.

Dewey was, generally speaking, a socialist. Humans do not possess some *a priori* consciousness; since language—speech—is acquired through social interaction, it follows that thinking, perhaps all of mind, is a social construction rather than a private possession. When we think inwardly, we just talk to ourselves rather than out loud, adjustively using our socially given speech-reactions. Dewey, the philosopher of Progressivism, always aimed at reconstructing philosophy and society on a social basis, breaking down individualism and substituting for it group-consciousness and a submerging of the individual into the greater whole. By conceiving of mind as a social construction, the Cartesian privacy of the individual mind was erased. Instead, the truly mindful entity was society itself, the larger organism of which each person was a cooperative part.

MARKED FOR SLAUGHTER: DISCARDING CONSCIOUSNESS (1910–1912)

By 1910, all the forces moving psychology from mentalism to behavioralism were well engaged. Philosophical idealism, which made the study of consciousness so important, had been replaced by pragmatism, realism, and instrumentalism, all of which denied consciousness a special, privileged place in the universe. The concept of consciousness had been reworked, becoming successively motor response, relation, and function, and could no longer be clearly differentiated from behavior. Animal psychologists were finding mind to be a problematic, even an unnecessary concept in their field. Psychology as a whole, especially in America, was shifting its concern from the structural study of mental content to the functional study of mental processes, at the same time shifting the focus of experimental technique from the introspective ascertaining of mental states to the objective determination of the influence of stimulus on behavior. Lurking behind all these changes was the desire of psychologists to be socially useful, implying the study of behavior—what people do in society—rather than the socially useless study of sensory contents. The shift from mentalism to behavioralism was inevitable, and it only needed to be discovered to be a *fait accompli*.

Change was in the air. Surveying the year 1910, E. F. Buchner confessed that "some of us are still struggling at initial clearness as to what psychology was about." A signal event of the year was Yerkes's discovery of the "low esteem" in which psychology was held by biologists, whom most psychologists now considered their closest disciplinary colleagues. Surveying leading biologists, Yerkes found that most of them were simply ignorant of psychology, or convinced it would soon disappear into biology. Yerkes concluded that "few, if any, sciences are in worse plight than psychology," attributing its "sad plight" to a lack of self-confidence, an absence of agreed-upon principles, poor training of psychologists in physical science, and a failure to teach psychology as anything more than a set of bizarre facts or as a branch of philosophy, instead of as a natural science. Yerkes's survey was widely discussed and clearly troubled psychologists, who had labored long and hard to make of psychology a dignified scientific profession.

Psychologists were casting about for a new central concept around which to organize their science, perhaps rendering it more securely a natural science. Bawden, who was continuing to push his own program of interpreting mind "in terms of hands and feet," observed that recently psychologists, without "being clearly conscious of what was happening," had begun to look at mind afresh, in terms of muscle movement, physiology, and "behavior." In any case, psychology needed a general shift in methods and attitudes away from philosophical conceptions and toward biological ones.

The APA convention of 1911 was dominated by discussion of the place of consciousness in psychology, according to an observer, M. E. Haggerty (1911). He noted with some surprise that *no one* at the convention defended the traditional definition of psychology as the study of self-consciousness. Speaking in a symposium on "Philosophical and Psychological Uses of the Terms Mind, Consciousness, and Soul," Angell (1911) put his finger on the change from mentalism to behavioralism. Soul, of course, had ceased as a psychological concept when the new psychology replaced the old. But mind, too, Angell noted, was now in "a highly precarious position," and consciousness "is likewise in danger of extinction." Angell defined behavioralism as we did at the beginning of the chapter:

> There is unquestionably a movement on foot in which interest is centered in the *results* of conscious process, rather than in the *processes* themselves. This is peculiarly true in animal psychology; it is only less true in human psychology. In these cases interest is in what may for lack of a better term be called "behavior"; and the analysis of consciousness is primarily justified by the light it throws on behavior, rather than vice-versa. (p. 47)

If this movement should go forward, Angell concluded, psychology would become "a general science of behavior," exactly the definition of the field being offered in the latest textbooks of psychology, Parmelee's (1913), C. H. Judd's (1910), and McDougall's (1912).

The year 1912 proved to be pivotal. Buchner observed further confusion about the definition of mind and noted the philosophers and their psychological allies who wanted to identify mind with behavior. Knight Dunlap, Watson's older colleague at Johns Hopkins, used the new relational theory of consciousness to make "the case against introspection." Introspection had value only under a copy theory of mind, Dunlap said, because introspection describes the privileged contents of consciousness. But on a relational view of mind, introspection loses its special character, becoming no more than a description of a real object under special conditions of attention. Introspection is thus not the reporting of an internal object, but merely the reporting of the stimulus currently controlling behavior. The term "introspection," Dunlap concluded, should be restricted to the reporting of internal stimuli, which can be gotten at no other way. Introspection was not the central method of psychology.

Elliot Frost (1912) reported on European physiologists who were taking a radical new view of consciousness. These physiologists, who included Jacques Loeb, an influence on Watson at Chicago, pronounced psychological concepts "superstitions" and found no room for animal consciousness in the explanation of animal behavior. Frost tried to refute these challenges with a functional view of mind as adaptive "consciousizing" behavior.

More important for us are the reductionistic claims of these European physiologists and certain psychologists then and soon to come. Mind may be eliminated from psychology in two ways that are distinct and should be kept separate. The program of the physiologists Frost reviewed, including Pavlov, and of psychologists such as Max Meyer, another influence on Watson, called for the reduction of mental concepts to underlying neurophysiological processes thought to cause them. Mental concepts could be eliminated from science as we learn the material causes the mentalistic terms designate. The other program for eliminating mind was inchoate as yet, and it would be often mixed up with reductionism for years to come. It claims that mental concepts are to be replaced by behavioral ones, which themselves may not be reducible to mechanical underlying physiological laws. We can see something of this view, perfected later by B. F. Skinner, in the relational theories of mind, especially Singer's; but it was not in 1912 a distinct psychological system. The historical importance of the reductionists reviewed by Frost remains—the validity of consciousness and mind as central concepts in psychology was under increasing assault from every quarter.

The December 1912 meeting of the APA in Cleveland marked the final transition of psychology, with only a few holdouts, from mentalism to behavioralism. Angell (1913) identified the behavioral view in "Behavior as a Category of Psychology." Angell began by recalling his own prophecy, made at the 1910 APA meeting, that the study of behavior was overshadowing the study of consciousness. Just two years later, consciousness had become a "victim marked for slaughter," as behavior was poised to completely replace mental life as the subject matter of psychology. In philosophy, the consciousness debate questioned consciousness's very existence. In animal psychology, researchers wanted to give up reference to mind and just study behavior, matched by a "general drift" in the same direction in human psychology. This drift,

Angell pointed out, is "not deliberate" and is thus likely to be "substantial and enduring."

Moreover, there were many flourishing fields concerned with human beings in which introspection offered "no adequate approach": social psychology, racial psychology, sociology, economics, development, individual differences, and others. The tendency to eliminate introspection is not just a product of new topics like those mentioned, but it is aided by functional psychology, which studies response more than conscious content.

Angell was not willing to completely abandon introspection. While it could no longer be psychology's premier method, it retained an important role in providing data not otherwise obtainable. It would be a "crowning absurdity," Angell said, for the new behavioral psychology to deny any significance to the "chief distinction" of human nature—mind. There was another danger in a behavioral psychology, Angell warned. By concentrating on behavior, psychologists would trespass on the territory of another science, biology; and thus there was a risk that psychology might be "swallowed up" by biology, or might become a mere vassal to biology as its "overlord."

Still, there was no mistaking Angell's message. Psychology was now the study of behavior. It was a natural science closely allied to biology, forsaking its philosophical roots. Its methods were now objective, introspection serving pragmatically when needed, but no longer at the center of the field. Concern with consciousness as such had been replaced by concern with the explanation, prediction, and control of behavior. The psychology viewed with such horror by Warner Fite had arrived.

BIBLIOGRAPHY FOR CHAPTERS 5 AND 6

A general overview of the period is given by John L. Thomas in his contribution to Bailyn et al., *The great republic* (Boston: Little, Brown, 1977), "Nationalizing the republic." The standard history of the transformation of America at the turn of the century is Robert Wiebe, *The search for order 1877–1920* (New York: Hill and Wang, 1967). Daniel Boorstin concludes his history of the United States in *The Americans: The democratic experience* (New York: Vintage, 1974), which provides a wonderfully readable, even entertaining, account of twentieth-century America, entirely dispensing with political and military history. There are several good histories of Progressivism: Richard Hofstadter, *The age of reform* (New York: Vintage, 1975); Eric Goldman, *Rendezvous with destiny* (New York: Vintage, rev. ed., 1975); and two books by David Noble, *The paradox of Progressive thought* (Minneapolis, MN: University of Minnesota Press), and *The Progressive mind* (Minneapolis, MN: Burgess, rev. ed., 1981). Works that concentrate on intellectual and social aspects of our period include Henry F. May, *The end of American innocence* (Chicago: Quadrangle, 1964); and Morton White, *Social thought in America* (London: Oxford University Press, 1976); and *Science and sentiment in America* (London: Oxford University Press, 1972).

Dewey's philosophy is central to the thought of the first part of the twentieth century. Two useful accounts of his intellectual development are Morton G. White, *The origin of Dewey's instrumentalism* (New York: Octagon, 1964); and the chapter on Dewey in E. Flower and M. Murphey, *A history of philosophy in America* (New York: Capricorn, 1977). Dewey was the leading educational philosopher in this period, which witnessed far-ranging debate about the nature and aims of education, as schools were refashioned to meet the needs of a mass, industrialized society. Merle Curti, *The social ideas of American educators* (Paterson, NJ: Littlefield, Adams, rev. ed., 1965), summarizes the views not only of Dewey, but of James and Thorndike, to mention only the psychologists. Curti's book was originally published in 1931 and reflects an apparently socialist point of view that leads to much criticism of everyone but Dewey for putting too much emphasis on the individual. For Dewey's life, see R. B. Westbrook, *John Dewey and American democracy.* (Ithaca, NY: Cornell University Press, 1991).

There are three important book-length studies of psychology in this period. Brian Mackenzie, *Behaviorism and the limits of scientific method* (London: Routledge and Kegan Paul, 1977), ties behaviorism closely to positivism, as did the first edition of the present text, and to the problem of animal mind. John M. O'Donnell's *The origins of behaviorism: American psychology 1870–1920* (New York: New York University Press, 1985) argues that behaviorism emerged gradually and inevitably out of American realist, new, and functional psychology. Reba N. Soffer's *Ethics and society in England: The revolution in the social sciences 1870–1914* (Berkeley, CA: University of California Press, 1978) covers England for the same period we've covered America and relates similar developments there to the British intellectual climate, claiming, contrary to the thesis I have argued, that a "revolution" took place during these years.

A valuable source for the history of psychology from its founding days onward is the continuing series called *A history of psychology in autobiography.* The first three volumes, which cover the period here, were edited by Carl Murchison and published by Clark University Press. Since then subsequent volumes have been published under varying editorship and by different publishers, but always under the same title.

Perhaps because of their tenuous status as scientists, psychologists were acutely conscious of the history of their discipline in its early years and often wrote historical summaries of even recent developments. Edward Franklin Buchner wrote several such reviews, including an annual piece in *Psychological Bulletin* from 1904 to 1912 called "Progress in psychology," and two general accounts, "Ten years of American psychology," *Science* (1903, *18,* 193–204) and "A quarter century of psychology in America," *American Journal of Psychology* (1903, *13,* 666–80). Another general summary from the same period is James Mark Baldwin, "A sketch of the history of psychology," *Psychological Review* (1905, *12,* 144–45). Christian Ruckmich, "The history and status of psychology in the United States," *American Journal of Psychology* (1912, *23,* 517–31), is a valuable institutional history, including not only accounts of the founding of laboratories and so on, but also a comparative economic analysis of the status within universities of psychology compared with other disciplines. Another institutional history, by a participant, is J. M. Cattell, "Early psychological laboratories," *Science* (1928, *67,* 543–48).

Perhaps the final confrontation between the old psychology and the new occurred on April 27, 1895, at the Massachusetts Schoolmaster's Club, when Larkin Dunton and W. T. Harris, educators in the old mold, confronted Hugo Münsterberg and G. Stanley Hall, new psychologists. The encounter was published as *The old psychology and the new* (Boston: New England Publishing Co., 1895).

The writings of, and some contemporary comments on, the pragmatist philosophers Peirce, James, and Dewey have been collected by Amelie Rorty, *Pragmatic philosophy* (Garden City, NY: Doubleday), and H. Standish Thayer, *Pragmatism: The classic writings* (New York: Mentor, 1970). Bruce Kuklick's *Rise of American philosophy* (New Haven, CT: Yale University Press, 1977) traces the development of pragmatism and sets it against a larger framework. Dewey's major psychological papers have been gathered up by Joseph Ratner, *John Dewey: Philosophy, psychology, and social practice* (New York: Capricorn, 1965).

The presidential addresses of the presidents of the APA have been summarized, and the more important ones reprinted, in Ernest R. Hilgard (1978), *American psychology in historical perspective* (Washington, DC: American Psychological Association).

In addition to the referenced works, students interested in animal psychology, Thorndike, and Pavlov may wish to consult the following. B. P. Babkin has written a biography of *Pavlov* (Chicago: University of Chicago Press, 1949); his experimental research program is detailed in *Conditioned reflexes,* available as a reprint paperback from Dover (New York, 1960). Thorndike's application of his learning theory may be found in his *Educational psychology*

(New York: Arno, 1964), the brief edition of which appeared almost simultaneously with Watson's behaviorism (1914). Watson wrote two popular articles for *Harper's Magazine* (1909, *120,* 346–53, and 1912, *124,* 376–82), which, while they offer few clues to his incipient behaviorism, are good accounts of early-twentieth-century animal psychology. A fine history of animal psychology is given by Robert Boakes *From Darwin to behaviorism: Psychology and the minds of animals* (New York: Cambridge University Press, 1984). Thomas Cadwallader, "Neglected aspects of the evolution of American comparative and animal psychology" (in G. Greenberg and E. Tobach [Eds.], *Behavioral evolution and integrative levels,* Hillsdale, NJ: Erlbaum, 1984), concentrates on the American scene.

There are two good places to enter the consciousness debate. The debate grew so important that the American Philosophical Association decided to devote its 1912 convention to the problem. To prepare for the meeting, the association appointed a committee to summarize the main points of the debate and to draw up a bibliography. Their report appears in *The Journal of Philosophy* (1911, *8,* 701–08). The debate continued in philosophy past 1912 and eventually inspired an excellent treatment of the problem of consciousness, including views and issues not treated in the text, by Charles Morris, *Six theories of mind* (Chicago: University of Chicago Press, 1932). Between these two, every aspect of the debate is covered, and all the relevant literature cited, with the exception (for some unknown reason) of the papers of Edgar Singer. His key paper was "Mind as an observable object," *Journal of Philosophy* (1911, *8,* 180–86), followed up in the same place with two replies the next year, "Consciousness and behavior," *Journal of Philosophy* (1912, *9,* 15–19), and "On mind as observable object," *Journal of Philosophy* (1912, *9,* 206–14).

In "The mythical revolutions of American psychology," *American Psychologist* (1992, *47,* 308-318), I provide a more detailed argument that behaviorism did not effect a revolution in psychology.

REFERENCES

Angell, J. R. (1903). The relation of structural and functional psychology to philosophy. *Philosophical Review, 12,* 243–271.

Angell, J. R. (1907). The province of functional psychology. *Psychological Review, 14,* 61–91.

Angell, J. R. (1911). Usages of the terms mind, consciousness, and soul. *Psychological Bulletin, 8,* 46–47.

Angell, J. R. (1913). Behavior as a category of psychology. *Psychological Review, 20,* 255–270.

Arnold, Felix (1905). Psychological standpoints. *Psychological Bulletin, 2,* 369–373.

Bartlett, F. C. (1932). *Remembering.* Cambridge, England: Cambridge University Press.

Bawden, H. H. (1903). The functional theory of parallelism. *Philosophical Review, 12,* 299–319.

Bawden, H. H. (1904). The meaning of the psychical in functional psychology. *Philosophical Review, 13,* 298–319.

Bawden, H. H. (1910). Mind as a category of psychology. *Psychological Bulletin, 7,* 221–225.

Bolton, T. (1902). A biological view of perception. *Psychological Review, 9,* 537–548.

Boorstin, D. J. (1974). *The Americans: The democratic experience.* New York: Vintage Books.

Calkins, M. W. (1906). A reconciliation between structural and functional psychology. *Psychological Review, 13,* 61–81.

Cattell, J. M. (1904). The conceptions and methods of psychology. *Popular Science Monthly, 66,* 176–186

Danziger, K. (1979). The social origins of modern psychology. In A. Buss (Ed.), *Psychology in social context.* New York: Irvington.

Dewey, J. (1939). *Intelligence in the modern world: The philosophy of John Dewey.* (Ed.) J. Ratner. New York: The Modern Library.

Dewey, J. (1920/1948/1957). *Reconstruction in philosophy.* Boston: Beacon.

Ebbinghaus, H. (1885/1964). *Memory.* New York: Dover.

Frost, E. P. (1912). Can biology and physiology dispense with consciousness? *Psychological Review, 3,* 246–252.

Haggerty, M. E. (1911). The nineteenth annual meeting of the A.P.A. *Journal of Philosophy, 8,* 204–217.

Herrnstein, R. & Boring, E. (Eds.), (1965). *A source book in the history of psychology.* Cambridge, MA: Harvard University Press.

James, W. (1904). Does "consciousness" exist? *Journal of Philosophy, 1,* 477–491.

Jastrow, J. (1901). Some currents and undercurrents in psychology. *Psychological Review, 8,* 1–26.

Joncich, G. (1968). *The sane positivist: A biography of E. L. Thorndike.* Middletown, CT: Wesleyan University Press.

Judd, C. H. (1910). *Psychology: General introduction.* New York: Scribner's.

Kohler, W. (1925). *The mentality of apes.* New York: Harcourt Brace.

McDougall, W. (1912). *Psychology: The study of behaviour.* New York: Holt.

Mills, W. (1899). The nature of animal intelligence. *Psychological Review, 6,* 262–274.

Mills, W. (1904). Some aspects of the development of comparative psychology. *Science, 19,* 745–757.

Parmelee, M. (1913). *The science of human behavior.* New York: Macmillan.

Pavlov, I. P. (1957). *Experimental psychology and other essays.* New York: Philosophical Library.

Sanford, E. C. (1903). Psychology and physics. *Psychological Review, 10,* 105–119.

Sechenov, I. M. (1863/1965). *Reflexes of the brain.* Reprinted in Herrnstein & Boring (1965).

Sechenov, I. M. (1973). *Biographical sketch and essays.* New York: Arno.

Singer, E. A. (1911). Mind as observable object. *Journal of Philosophy, 8,* 180–186.

Swartz, C. K. (1908). The scientific association of Johns Hopkins University. *Science, 28,* 814–815.

Thilly, F. (1905). Review of Angell's psychology. *Philosophical Review, 14,* 481–487.

Thorndike, E. L. (1898). Review of Evans' "Evolution, ethics and animal psychology." *Psychological Review, 5,* 229–230.

Thorndike, E. L. (1911/1965). *Animal intelligence.* New York: Hafner.

Thorndike, E. L. (1929/1968). *Human learning.* New York: Johnson Reprint Corporation.

Turner, F. M. (1974). *Between science and religion.* New Haven: Yale University Press.

Ward, J. (1904). The present problems of general psychology. *Philosophical Review, 13,* 603–621.

Ward, J. (1920). *Psychological principles.* Cambridge, England: Cambridge University Press.

Watson, J. B. (1907). Comparative psychology. *Psychological Bulletin, 4,* 288–302.

Watson, J. B. (1909). A point of view in comparative psychology. *Psychological Bulletin, 6,* 57–58.

Yerkes, R. (1905a). Animal psychology and the criterion of the psychic. *Journal of Philosophy, 2,* 141–149.

Yerkes, R. (1905b). Review of Claparede, "Is comparative psychology legitimate?" *Journal of Philosophy, 2,* 527–528.

PART III

PSYCHOLOGY TAKES OFF (1913–1950)

In the years encompassing World War I and leading up to World War II, psychology experienced tremendous growth. The numbers of psychologists grew dramatically, their work took them increasingly into applied areas little known to the academic founders of psychology, and psychology enjoyed popularity with ordinary people—even if it did not always command their respect. Within the field the chief developments are the rise of applied psychology, especially mental testing, and the triumph of behavioralism as the psychology of the twentieth century.

CHAPTER 7

The Golden Age of Theory: The Behaviorist Era

DEVELOPING BEHAVIORALISM (1913–1930)

Behaviorism Proclaimed

John Broadus Watson (1878–1958) was a young, ambitious animal psychologist who, as we saw in the last chapter, had by 1908 defined a purely objective, nonmentalistic approach to animal psychology shortly after graduating from the University of Chicago and taking a position at Johns Hopkins University. In his autobiography, Watson says that he had broached the idea of a purely objective human psychology to his teachers during his days as a graduate student at Chicago, but that his proposals were greeted with such horror that he kept his own counsel. After establishing himself as a leading animal psychologist in his own right, he felt emboldened to expand publicly the scope of his objective psychology. On February 13, 1913, he began a series of lectures on animal psychology at Columbia University with a lecture on "Psychology as the Behaviorist Views It." Encouraged by the editor of *Psychological Review,* Howard Warren (who for some time had been trying to get Watson to publish his new view of psychology), Watson published his lecture; in 1943, a group of eminent psychologists rated this paper as the most important one ever published in the *Review.*

From the paper's aggressive tone, it was clear that Watson was issuing a manifesto for a new kind of psychology: behaviorism. In those years, manifestos were rather more common than they are today. For example, in Watson's year of 1913, modern art came to America in the notorious Armory Show, a kind of manifesto in paint for modernism. Modern artists also issued written manifestos for various modernist movements, such as futurism and dadaism. Watson's manifesto for behaviorism shared the goals of these modernist manifestos: to repudiate the past and set out, however incoherently, a vision of life as it might be. Watson began with a ringing definition of psychology as it might be:

> Psychology as the behaviorist views it is a purely objective branch of natural science. Its theoretical goal is the prediction and control of behavior. Introspection forms no essential part of its methods, nor is the scientific value of its data dependent on the readiness with which they lend themselves to interpretation in terms of consciousness. The behaviorist, in his efforts to get a unitary scheme of animal response, recognizes no dividing line between man and brute. The behavior of man, with all of its refinement and complexity, forms only a part of the behaviorist's total scheme of investigation. (1913a, p. 158)

In the tradition of modernist manifestos, Watson went on to repudiate psychology as it had been. Watson refused to see any difference between structuralism and functionalism. Both of them adopted the traditional definition of psychology as "the science of the phenomena of consciousness," and both of them used the traditional "esoteric" method of introspection. However, psychology so conceived had "failed to make its place in the world as an undisputed natural science." As an animal psychologist, Watson felt especially constrained by mentalism. There seemed to be little room for animal work, as animals were unable to introspect, forcing psychologists to "construct" conscious contents for them on analogy to the psychologists' own minds. Moreover, traditional psychology was anthropocentric, respecting the findings of animal psychology only insofar as they bore upon questions of human psychology. Watson found this situation intolerable and aimed at reversing the traditional priorities. In 1908, he had declared the autonomy of animal psychology as the study of animal behavior; now he proposed to use "human beings as subjects and to employ methods of investigation which are exactly comparable to those now employed in animal work." Earlier comparative psychologists had warned that we should not anthropomorphize about animals; Watson urged psychologists not to anthropomorphize about human beings.

Watson faulted introspection on empirical, philosophical, and practical grounds. Empirically, it simply failed to define questions it could convincingly answer. There was as yet no answer even to the most basic question of the psychology of consciousness: how many sensations there are and the number of their attributes. Watson saw no end to a sterile discussion (1913a, p. 164): "I firmly believe that, unless the introspective method is discarded, psychology will still be divided on the question as to whether auditory sensations have the quality of 'extension' … and upon many hundreds of other [questions] of like character."

Watson's second ground for rejecting introspection was philosophical: It was not like the methods of natural science, and therefore it was not a scientific method at all. In the natural sciences, good techniques provide "reproducible results," and then, when these are not forthcoming, "the attack is made upon the experimental conditions" until reliable results are obtained. In mentalistic psychology, however, we must study the private world of an observer's consciousness. This means that instead of attacking experimental conditions when results are unclear, psychologists attack the introspective observer, saying, "Your introspection is poor" or "untrained." Watson's point seemed to be that the results of introspective psychology possess a personal element not found in the natural sciences; this contention forms the basis for methodological behaviorism.

Finally, introspection failed practical tests. In the laboratory, it demanded that animal psychologists find some behavioral criterion of consciousness, an issue we know involved Watson, as he reviewed it several times for the *Psychological Bulletin*. But he now argued that consciousness was irrelevant to animal work: "One can assume either the presence or absence of consciousness anywhere in the phylogenetic scale without affecting the problems of behavior one jot or one tittle." Experiments are in fact designed to find out what an animal will do in some novel circumstance, and its behavior is then observed; only later must the researcher attempt the "absurd," reconstructing the animal's mind as it behaved. But Watson pointed out that reconstructing the animal's consciousness added nothing at all to what had already been accomplished in the observation of behavior. In society, introspective psychology was likewise irrelevant, offering no solutions to the problems facing people in modern life. Indeed, Watson reports that it was his feeling that mentalistic psychology had "no realm of application" that early made him "dissatisfied" with it. So it is not surprising to find that the one area of existing psychology Watson praised was applied psychology: educational psychology, psychopharmacology, mental testing, psychopathology, and legal and advertising psychology. These fields were "most flourishing" because they were "less dependent on introspection." Sounding a key theme of Progressivism and of behavioralism to come, Watson lauded these "truly scientific" psychologies because they "are in search of broad generalizations which will lead to the control of human behavior."

On Watson's account, then, introspective psychology had nothing to recommend it and much to condemn it. "[P]sychology must discard all reference to consciousness." Psychology must now be defined as the science of behavior, and "never use the terms consciousness, mental states, mind, content, introspectively verifiable, imagery and the like.... It can be done in terms of stimulus and response, in terms of habit formation, habit integrations and the like. Furthermore, I believe that it is really worthwhile to make this attempt now" (pp. 166–67).

The "starting point" of Watson's new psychology would be the "fact that organisms, man and animal alike, do adjust themselves to their environment"; that is, psychology would be the study of adjustive behavior, not conscious content. Description of behavior would lead to the prediction of behavior in terms of stimulus and response (p. 167): "In a system of psychology completely worked out, given the response the stimuli can be predicted [Watson meant *retrodicted*]; given the stimuli the response can be predicted." Ultimately, Watson aimed to "learn general and particular methods by which I may control behavior." Once control techniques become available, the leaders of society will be able to "utilize our data in a practical way." While Watson did not cite Auguste Comte, his program for behaviorism—describe, predict, and control observable behavior—was clearly in the positivist tradition. The only acceptable form of explanation for both Comte and Watson was "explanation in physico-chemical terms."

The methods by which we are to achieve psychology's new goals were left rather vague, as Watson was later to admit (Watson, 1916a). The only thing made really clear about behavioral methodology in the manifesto is that under behaviorism, work "on the human being will be comparable directly with the work upon animals," because behaviorists "care as little about [a human subject's] 'conscious processes' during the conduct of the experiment as we care about such processes in the rat." He gives a few examples of how sensation and memory might be behavioristically investigated, but they are not very convincing and would soon be replaced by Pavlov's conditioned reflex method.

Watson does say some startling things about human thinking. He asserts that thinking does not involve the brain—there are no "centrally initiated processes"—but consists in "faint reinstatement of … muscular acts," specifically "motor habits in the larynx." "In other words, wherever there are thought processes there are faint contractions of the systems of musculature involved in the overt exercise of the customary act, and especially in the still finer systems of musculature involved in speech.… [I]magery becomes a mental luxury (even if it really exists) without any functional significance whatever" (p. 174). While Watson's claims may outrage the lay reader, we should see that his conclusions are the logical outcome of the motor theory of consciousness (McComas, 1916). On the motor theory, conscious content simply reflects without affecting stimulus-response connections; Watson is simply pointing out that since mental content has "no functional significance," there's no point in studying it save accumulated prejudice: "[O]ur minds have been warped by fifty odd years which have been devoted to the study of states of consciousness." Peripheralism had been gaining force as a doctrine in psychology since at least the time of Sechenov, and Watson's version of it would be found in the most influential and important forms of behavioralism until the coming of cognitive science in the 1960s.

In another Columbia lecture, "Image and Affection in Behavior," also published in 1913, Watson continued his assault on mental content. He considers, and rejects, the formula of methodological behaviorism, the view that "I care not what goes on in [a person's] so called mind" as long as his or her behavior is predictable. But for Watson, methodological behaviorism is a "partial defeat" he found unacceptable, preferring instead "to attack." He reiterated his view that "there are no centrally initiated processes." Instead, thinking is just "implicit behavior" that sometimes occurs between a stimulus and the resulting "explicit behavior." Most implicit behavior, he hypothesizes, occurs in the larynx and is open to observation, though the technique of such observation had not been developed. The important point for Watson is that there are no functional mental processes playing causal roles in determining behavior. There are only chains of behavior, some of which are difficult to observe. Should this be true—and Watson applied his thesis to both mental images and experienced emotions, as the title states—no part of psychology could escape the behaviorist's scheme, for mind would be shown to be behavior; the behaviorist would concede no subject to the mentalist. Finally, Watson suggested a theme that would emerge more vividly in his later writings, and that shows how his behaviorism was part of a larger revolt against the cultural past, not simply a revolt against a failed introspective psychology. Watson claimed that allegiance to mentalistic psychology was at root clinging to religion in a scientific age that has made religion obsolete. Those who believe that there are centrally initiated processes—that is, behaviors begun by the brain and not by some outside stimulus—really believe in the soul. Watson said that since we know nothing about the cortex, it is easy to attribute the functions of the soul to the cortex: Both are unknown mysteries. Watson's position was extremely radical: Not only did the soul not exist, neither did the cortex as anything other than a relay station connecting stimulus and response; both soul and brain could be ignored in the description, prediction, and control of behavior.

The Initial Response (1913–1918)

How did psychologists receive Watson's manifesto? One might expect that behaviorism would become the rallying cry of younger psychologists and the object of denunciation by their elders. In fact, when Watson's manifesto later took its revered place as the starting point of behaviorism, it was thought to have been received in just such fashions. However, as Samelson (1981) has shown, published responses to "Psychology as the Behaviorist Views It" were both remarkably few and remarkably restrained.

There were a few responses in 1913 itself. Watson's teacher, Angell, added some references to behaviorism in the published version of "Behavior as a Category of Psychology." He said he was "heartily sympathetic" to behaviorism and recognized it as a logical development of his own emphasis on behavior. Nevertheless, he did not think that introspection could ever be entirely eliminated from psychology, if only as providing useful reports on the processes connecting stimulus and response; Watson himself admitted such use of introspection, but he called it the "language method." Angell bid behaviorism "Godspeed" but counseled it to "forego the excesses of youth," which, like most counsel to youth, went unheeded. Without actually citing Watson, M. E. Haggerty agreed that the emerging laws of learning, or habit formation, reduced behavior to "physical terms," so there was no "longer any need to invoke ghosts in the form of consciousness" to explain thinking. Robert Yerkes criticized Watson for "throwing overboard" the method of self-observation that set psychology off from biology; under behaviorism psychology would be "merely a fragment of physiology." The philosopher Henry Marshall was afraid that psychology might be "evaporating." He observed the behavioral *Zeitgeist* of which behaviorism was the latest manifestation and concluded that it contained much of value, but that to identify behavior study with psychology was an "astounding confusion of thought," since consciousness remained to be investigated whatever the achievements of behaviorism. Mary Calkins, who had earlier proposed her self-psychology as a compromise between structural and functional psychology, now proposed it as a mediator between behaviorism and mentalism. Like most of the other commentators, she agreed with much of Watson's critique of structuralism and applauded the study of behavior; but she nevertheless found introspection to be the indispensable, if sometimes troublesome, method of psychology.

The other commentaries on behaviorism in the years before World War I interrupted the debate took much the same line as these initial responses: The deficiencies of structuralism were acknowledged, the virtues of studying behavior were conceded, but introspection was nevertheless defended as the *sine qua non* of psychology. The study of behavior was just biology; psychology, to retain its identity, had to remain introspective. A. H. Jones (1915) spoke for many when he wrote: "We may rest assured then, that whatever else psychology may be, it is at least a doctrine of awareness. To deny this … is to pour out the baby with the bath." Titchener (1914) also saw behavior study as biology rather than psychology. Since the facts of consciousness exist, he said, they can be studied, and such is the task of psychology. While behaviorism might accomplish much, since it was not psychology at all, it posed no threat to introspective psychology. One of the few substantive as opposed to methodological criticisms of Watson's behaviorism was offered by H. C. McComas (1916), who correctly saw it as a natural extension of the motor theory of consciousness. McComas showed that Watson's identification of thinking with laryngeal movements stood falsified: Some people had already lost their larynxes due to disease, without thereby losing the ability to think.

With the exception of McComas's paper, however, reactions to behaviorism in the prewar years tended to assert the same thing: That, while behavior study was valuable, it was really a form of biology rather than psychology, because psychology was by definition the study of consciousness, and must, perforce, use introspection as its method. While these critics' position was not unreasonable, they seemed not to notice that Watson might succeed in fundamentally redefining psychology altogether. As we have seen, Watson was riding the crest of behavioralism, and if enough psychologists adopted his definition of their field, it would as a matter of historical fact cease to be the study of the mind, and would become the study of behavior. While his radical peripheralism might not be accepted, behavioralism would be, and behaviorism would be its name.

Watson, of course, did not remain silent while his views were debated. He was chosen by a nominating committee and ratified by the members of the APA to be the president for 1916. In his presidential address, he tried to fill the most conspicuous gap in behaviorism: the method and theory by which it would study and explain behavior. Watson had tried for some years to show that thinking was just implicit speech, but he had failed. So he turned to the work of Karl Lashley, a student in Watson's laboratory, who had been replicating and extending Pavlov's conditioning techniques. Watson now presented the conditioned reflex work as the substance of behaviorism: Pavlov's method applied to humans would be behaviorism's tool of investigation, while the conditioned reflex theory would provide the basis for the prediction and control of behavior in animals and people. Watson's address set out in detail how the conditioned reflex method could be applied to both humans and animals, providing an objective substitute for introspection. Nor was Watson loath to apply the theory outside the laboratory. In another 1916 paper, he argued that neuroses were just "habit disturbances," most usually "disturbances of speech functions." We see again that Watson's program was not merely scientific but social; even as he was first learning about and investigating conditioned reflexes he was prepared to assert that speech, and thus neurotic symptoms, were just conditioned reflexes, poor behavior adjustments that could be corrected by the application of behavior principles.

We have noted various reactions to Watson's manifesto. However, apart from about a dozen papers, few psychologists or philosophers wrote about it. The reason is not far to seek. A manifesto is a work of rhetoric, and when we separate Watson's rhetoric from his substantive proposals, we find that he said little that was new, but said it in especially angry tones. In the last chapter, we showed that the behavioral approach had overcome psychology slowly and almost unnoticed in the years after 1892. What Watson did was to give behavioralism an aggressive voice, and to give it a name that stuck—"behaviorism," however misleading that name has since become. In its time, then, his manifesto merited little attention. Older psychologists had already admitted that psychology needed to pay attention to behavior—after all, it was they who had moved the field toward behavioralism—but remained concerned to preserve the traditional mission of psychology, the study of consciousness. Younger psychologists of Watson's generation had already accepted behavioralism, and so accepted his broad position without any sense of excitement, even if they might reject his extreme peripheralism. So no one was either outraged or inspired by Watson's manifesto of psychological modernism, for all had learned to live with modernism or were already practicing it. Watson created no revolution, but he did make clear that psychology was no longer the science of consciousness. "Psychology as the Behaviorist Views It" simply marks the moment when behavioralism became ascendant and self-conscious, creating for later behavioralists a useful "myth of origin." It provided for them a secure anchoring point in the history of psychology, and a justification for the abandonment of an introspective method they found boring and sterile. But all of these things would have happened had Watson never become a psychologist.

Behaviorism Defined (1919–1930)

Along with the rest of psychology, the discussion of behaviorism was interrupted by World War I. As we shall see, psychology was much changed by its involvement with the war; when psychologists resumed their consideration of behaviorism, the grounds of the discussion were quite different from what they had been before the war. The value of objective psychology had been proved by the tests psychologists had devised to classify soldiers, and that success had brought psychology before a wider audience. After the war the question was no longer whether behaviorism was legitimate, but what form behaviorism should take. In the 1920s, psychologists attempted to define behaviorism; but, as we shall see, they failed to make of it a coherent movement, much less a Kuhnian paradigm.

As early as 1922, it was clear that psychologists were having trouble understanding behaviorism, or formulating it in any widely agreeable way. Walter Hunter, a sympathizer of Watson's, wrote "An Open Letter to the Anti-Behaviorists." He thought behaviorism was exactly what Watson preached, the definition of psychology as the study of "stimulus and response relations." He viewed the various "new formulas" for behaviorism that by then had been offered as "illegitimate offspring" making it difficult for psychologists to see what behaviorism was. Later he (Hunter, 1925) would try to finesse the issue by defining a new science, "anthroponomy," the science of human behavior. But Hunter's new science never caught on, leaving psychologists to redefine psychology in some new, "behavioristic" way.

Some of them, most notably Albert P. Weiss (for example, 1924) and Zing Yang Kuo (1928), attempted to formulate behaviorism as Watson had, only more precisely. Kuo defined behaviorism as "a science of mechanics dealing with the mechanical movements of … organisms" and held "the duty of the behaviorist is to describe behavior in exactly the same way as the physicist describes the movements of a machine." This mechanistic, physiologically reductionist psychology, modern inheritor of La Mettrie, was most clearly and comprehensively set out by Karl Lashley (1890–1958), the student with whom Watson had studied the conditional reflex in animals and humans.

Lashley wrote that behaviorism had become "an accredited system of psychology," but that in its emphasis on "experimental method" had failed to give any satisfactory "systematic formulation" of its views. In light of behaviorism's being "so great a departure from tradition in psychology," a clearer formulation of behaviorism was needed. Heretofore, Lashley claimed, three forms of behaviorism had been advanced. The first two were scarcely distinguishable as forms of "methodological behaviorism." They allowed that "facts of conscious experience exist but are unsuited to any form of scientific treatment." It had been, according to Lashley, the beginning point of Watson's own behaviorism, but it ultimately proved unsatisfying because it conceded too much to introspective psychology. Precisely because it acknowledged the "facts of consciousness," methodological behaviorism admitted that it could never be a complete psychology and had to concede a science, or at least a study, of mind alongside the science of behavior. Opposed to methodological behaviorism was "strict behaviorism" (or, as Calkins [1921] and Wheeler [1923] named it, radical behaviorism [Schneider & Morris, 1987]), whose "extreme" view was that "the supposedly unique facts of consciousness do not exist." Such a view seems at first sight implausible, and Lashley conceded that it had not been put forward with any convincing arguments. Lashley made his own view plain:

> Let me cast off the lion's skin. My quarrel with behaviorism is not that it has gone too far, but that it has hesitated ... that it has failed to develop its premises to their logical conclusion. To me the essence of behaviorism is the belief that the study of man will reveal nothing except what is adequately describable in the concepts of mechanics and chemistry.... I believe that it is possible to construct a physiological psychology which will meet the dualist on his own ground ... and show that [his] data can be embodied in a mechanistic system.... Its physiological account of behavior will also be a complete and adequate account of all the phenomena of consciousness ... demanding that all psychological data, however obtained, shall be subjected to physical or physiological interpretation. (pp. 243–44)

Ultimately, Lashley said, the choice between behaviorism and traditional psychology comes down to a choice between two "incompatible" world-views, "scientific versus humanistic." It had been demanded of psychology heretofore that "it must leave room for human ideals and aspirations." But "other sciences have escaped this thralldom," and so must psychology escape from "metaphysics and values" and "mystical obscurantism" by turning to physiology. In physiology, it can find principles of explanation that will make of psychology a natural science, value-free, capable of addressing its "most important problems," its "most interesting and vital questions, the problems of human conduct." It would then be able to recapture the "problems of everyday life" from "sociology, education, and psychiatry," the applied fields ignored by introspective psychology. Lashley's formula for psychology was clearly La Mettrie's: the mechanistic, physiological explanation of behavior and consciousness. It was also clearly in the tradition of Comte's positivism. It preached a scientific imperialism against the humanities and questions of value, setting up instead a value-free technology claiming to solve human problems. Lashley, Weiss, Kuo, and Watson attempted to define behaviorism quite narrowly, following a behavioral version of the path through physiology, almost dismantling psychology as an independent discipline. Other psychologists and philosophical observers of psychology thought the physiologically reductive definition of behaviorism too narrow and defined a more inclusive behavioristic psychology.

The neorealist philosopher Perry (1921) saw behaviorism as nothing new, but "simply a return to the original Aristotelian view that mind and body are related as activity and organ." Adopting behaviorism did not mean denying that mind has a role in behavior. On the contrary, "If you are a behaviorist you regard the mind as something that *intervenes*" in determining behavior, and behaviorism rescues mind from the parallelistic impotence imposed on it by introspective psychology. On the other hand, the neorealist Stephen Pepper (1923), who had studied with Perry at Harvard, while similarly refusing to identify Watson's behaviorism as *the* behaviorism, nonetheless flatly contradicted Perry: For Pepper, the central contention of behaviorism was that consciousness plays no causal role in determining behavior, and that behaviorism's destiny was to bring psychology into "connection with the rest of the natural sciences." Jastrow (1927), who had been around since the beginning of psychology in America, saw nothing new in behaviorism, calling James, Peirce, and Hall "behaviorists." Psychology as the study of behavior was part of the "reconstruction" of psychology that had been taking place for the previous fifty years. It was a mistake, Jastrow argued, to confuse Watson's "radical" behaviorism with the more general and moderate behaviorism held by most American psychologists.

When we set side by side the views of Lashley, Perry, Pepper, and Jastrow, it becomes clear that "behaviorism" was a term of nearly infinite elasticity. It might signify physiological reductionism, or just the study of behavior by objective means; it might mean a significant break with the past, or it might be very old; it might mean seeing mind as a causal actor in determining behavior, or it might mean the denial of mind as causal agent. Woodworth (1924) was correct when he wrote that there is no "one great inclusive enterprise" binding together the various claimants to the title "behaviorism." Woodworth saw behaviorism's "essential program" as "behavior study, behavior concepts, laws of behavior, control of behavior," not the "neuromechanistic interpretation" of psychology associated with Watson. Woodworth observes that psychology had begun as the nonintrospective study of reaction times, memory, and psychophysics, but had been sidetracked in its development as a science by Titchener, Külpe, and others around 1900. Behaviorism—or, as we have defined it here, behavioralism—was a program for psychology, not a new method. Scientific psychology was bound to become behavioralistic; Watson had wrought nothing new.

One point of note arose in several of the papers advocating behaviorism, connecting behavioralism with its past in functionalism and its future in cognitive science: James's "automatic sweetheart." In contrasting behaviorism with humanism, Lashley noted that "the final objection to behaviorism is that it just fails to express the vital, personal quality of experience," an objection "quite evident in James's arguments concerning the "automatic sweetheart." Hunter (1923) likewise considered James's possible objection to behaviorism: It claims one's beloved is an automaton, and can one truly love a machine? With Lashley, who said descriptions of experience "belong to art, not science," Hunter dismissed worries about whether one could love, or be loved by, a machine as concerned only with the "aesthetic satisfaction" of the belief, not its scientific truth. B. H. Bode (1918) treated the problem more fully, defending the behaviorist point of view. Bode argued that upon reflection, there is no meaningful difference between a human sweetheart and a mechanical one, because no behavioral difference between them could be discerned:

> If there is no [objectively observable] difference, then the consciousness of the spiritually animated maiden plainly makes no difference in the behavior; it is a mere concomitant or epiphenomenon ... mechanism becomes the last word of explanation, and the mystery of the eternally feminine takes on much the same quality as the mystery of higher mathematics. (p. 451)

Finally, a critic of behaviorism, William McDougall, put the issue in the most up-to-date terms. The term "robot" had just been coined by Carel Capek in his science fiction play *R. U. R.*, Rossum's Universal Robots. MacDougall (1925) saw the critical question framed by behaviorism as "Men or robots?" Behaviorism rested on the claim that human beings are just machines—robots—but that claim was unproved. In Woodworth's opinion, it remained to be determined that robots could do anything human beings can do.

The concern over James's automatic, or robot, sweetheart raises the central problem of scientific psychology in the twentieth century: Can human beings be consistently conceived of as machines? This question transcends all the systems of psychology since James's (or even La Mettrie's) time, as it ties together functionalism, realism, behaviorism, and cognitive psychology. Following the development of computers in World War II, one of their creators would pose James's question in more intellectual terms: Can a machine be said to think if you can talk to it and be fooled into believing you are talking to another person? And A. M. Turing, followed by many cognitive psychologists, would give Bode's answer: If you can't tell it's just a machine, then we're just machines, too. The prospect of the automatic sweetheart filled some psychologists with excitement, but others, such as James, with revulsion. Lashley was very likely right when he saw the battle over behaviorism not just as a battle between different ways of doing psychology, but as a much deeper battle between "mechanistic explanation and finalistic valuation," between a view of human beings as robots, or as actors with purposes, values, hopes, fears, and loves.

Following World War II, in which he served unhappily in the army working up tests for aviators, Watson moved his research and his advocacy for behaviorism in a new direction. He now intensively pursued a human psychology based on the conditioned reflex by investigating the acquisition of reflexes in infants. Watson believed that nature endowed human beings with very few unconditioned reflexes, so that the complex behavior of adults might be explained as simply the acquisition of conditioned reflexes over years of Pavlovian conditioning. Contrary to eugenicists and their followers, who believed that people inherit a great deal of their intellect, personality, and morality, Watson (1930, p. 94) asserted that "there is no such thing as inheritance of *capacity, talent, temperament, mental constitution and characteristics.*" For example, Watson denied that human hand preference was innate. He could find no structural differences between babies' left and right hands and arms, nor were the different hands endowed with different strengths. So although he remained puzzled by the fact that most people were right-handed, he put the cause of it down to social training, and he said there would be no harm in trying to turn apparently left-handed children into right-handers. Nothing could better demonstrate Watson's radical peripheralism: Since he could find no peripheral differences between the hands' strength and structure, there could be, he concluded, no biological basis to handedness. He completely ignored the "mysterious" (Watson 1913b) cortex of the brain, seeing it as no more than a relay station for neural impulses. We now know that the left and right hemispheres of the human brain have very different functions, and that differences between right- and left-handers are determined there. To attempt to change a natural left-hander into a right-hander is to impose a very trying task, one well calculated to upset and make the left-handed child feel inferior.

In any event, to establish the truth of his equally radical environmentalism—"Give me a dozen healthy infants ... and my own specified world to bring them up in and I'll guarantee to take any one at random and train him to become any type of specialist I might select—doctor, lawyer, artist, merchant-chief, and, yes, even beggar-man and thief" (Watson, 1930, p. 104)—Watson turned to the nursery to show that humans are so much plastic material waiting to be molded by society. The most famous of his studies with infants is "Conditioned Emotional Reactions" (Watson and Rayner, 1920). Watson carried out an experiment on an infant known as "Albert B." designed to show that people are born with only a few "instincts"—fear, rage, and sexual response—and that all other emotions are conditioned versions of these unconditioned ones. As his US to produce fear (UR), Watson chose a loud noise, the sound of a large metal bar being struck by a hammer; this stimulus had been determined to be one of the few that would scare little Albert. He paired the noise with a CS, a rat whom Albert had liked to pet. Now, however, when Albert touched the rat, Watson struck the bar; after seven such pairings the child showed fear of the rat alone. Watson claimed to have established a "conditioned emotional reaction," and he asserted that his experimental arrangement was the prototype of emotional learning by a normal human in the normal human environment. Watson thought to have demonstrated that the rich emotional life of the adult human being was at bottom no more than a large number of conditioned responses built up over years of human development. We should point out that Watson's claims are dubious and his ethics in this experiment questionable (Samelson, 1980); furthermore, the experiment is often misdescribed by secondary sources (Harris, 1979). Watson was, at least, consistent. He fell in love with graduate student collaborator Rosalie Rayner—creating a scandal that cost him his job at Johns Hopkins in 1920—and wrote to her that "every cell I have is yours singly and collectively," and that all his emotional responses "are positive and towards you, ... likewise each and every heart response" (Cohen, 1979).

Watson had always been willing to write about psychology for a popular audience. After 1920, following his expulsion from academia, he became the first modern popular psychologist (Buckley, 1984), writing, for example, a series of articles on human psychology from the behaviorist perspective in *Harper's* from 1926 to 1928. There, Watson began by laying out behaviorism as the scientific replacement for mentalistic psychology and for psychoanalysis, which had earlier captured the popular mind. According to Watson, psychoanalysis had "too little science—real science" to long command serious attention, while the traditional psychology of consciousness "never had any right to be called a science." As he often did in his popular writings, Watson connected mentalistic psychology with religion, asserting that "mind and consciousness" were but "carryovers from the church dogma of the middle ages." The mind, or soul, was, according to Watson, one of the mysteries by whose invocation "churchmen—all medicine men in fact—have kept the public under control." Psychoanalysis was just "a substitution of demonology for science," and through such "solid walls of religious protection" science was "blasting" a new path.

Watson defied the mentalist to "prove" that "there is such a thing as consciousness." To the assertion by a mentalist that he had a mental life, Watson simply replied, "I have only your unverified and unsupported word that you have" images and sensations. So the concepts of mentalism remained "mythological, the figments of the psychologist's terminology." In place of the fantastic, secretly religious, traditional mentalistic psychology, behaviorism substituted a positivistic, scientific psychology of description, prediction, and control of behavior. Watson said that behavioral psychology began with the observation of the behavior of our fellows, and issued, suitably codified by science, in "a new weapon for controlling the individual." The social use of behavioral science was made clear by Watson: "[We] can build any man, starting at birth, into any kind of social or a-social being upon order." Elsewhere, Watson (1930) said, "It is a part of the behaviorist's scientific job to be able to state what the human machine is good for and to render serviceable predictions about its future capacities whenever society needs such information." Very much in the tradition of Comte's positivism, Watson's behaviorism rejected religion and the moral control of behavior and aimed to replace these with science and the technological control of behavior through behavioral psychology. Behaviorism was well prepared to mesh with Progressivism. Because of Progressivism's interest in establishing rational control over society through scientific means, Progressive politicians and apologists found an ally in behaviorism, which seemed to promise exactly the technology Progressivism needed to replace the outworn authority of tradition.

MAJOR FORMULATIONS OF BEHAVIORALISM (1930–1950)

By 1930, behavioralism was well established as the dominant viewpoint in experimental psychology. Watson's usage had triumphed, and psychologists called the new viewpoint "behaviorism," while recognizing that behaviorism took many forms (Williams, 1931). The stage was set for psychologists to create specific theories for predicting and explaining behavior within the new viewpoint of behavioralism. The central problem they would address in the coming decades would be learning (McGeoch, 1931). Functionalism had taken the ability to learn to be the criterion of animal mind, and the development of behavioralism had only magnified its importance. Learning was the process by which animals and humans adjusted to the environment, by which they were educated, and by which they might be changed in the interest of social control or therapy. So it is not surprising that what would later be regarded as the Golden Age of Theory in psychology—the years 1930 to 1950—would be golden only for theories of learning, rather than perception, thinking, group dynamics, or anything else.

The other major development of these decades in experimental psychology was psychologists' increasing self-consciousness about proper scientific method. Psychologists, as we have often noted, have always felt uncertain about the scientific status of their *soi-disant* "natural science" and have consequently been eager to find some methodological recipe to follow by which they could infallibly make psychology a science. Watson had, in denouncing mentalism, seen its irredeemable flaw to be the "unscientific" method of introspecting, and he had proclaimed psychology's scientific salvation to be objective method, taken over from animal study. Watson's message struck home, but his own recipe was too vague and confused to provide anything more than an attitude. In the 1930s, psychologists became aware of a very specific, prestigious recipe, logical positivism, for making science. The positivist's philosophy of science codified what psychologists already wanted to do; so they accepted the recipe and determined the goals and language of psychology for decades to come. At the same time, their own original ideas were molded so subtly by logical positivism that only today can we see the molding process at work.

Psychology and the Science of Science

We have already remarked how behavioralism reflected the image of science drawn by Comtean positivism: Its goal was the description, prediction, and control of behavior, and its techniques were to be put to use as tools of social control in a rationally managed society. The early, simple positivism of Comte and Mach had changed, however. By the early twentieth century, it was clear that positivism's extreme emphasis on talking about only what could be directly observed, excluding from science concepts such as "atom" and "electron," could not be sustained. Physicists and chemists found that their theories could not dispense with such terms, and their research results confirmed for them, albeit indirectly, the reality of atoms and electrons (Holton, 1978). So positivism changed, and its adherents found a way to admit into science terms apparently referring to unobserved entities, without giving up the basic positivist desire to expunge metaphysics from human, or at least scientific, discourse.

This new positivism came to be called *logical positivism,* because it wedded the positivist's commitment to empiricism to the logical apparatus of modern formal logic. Logical positivism was a complex and changing movement directed by many hands, but its basic idea was simple: Science had proven to be humankind's most powerful means of understanding reality, of producing knowledge, so that the task of epistemology should be to explicate and formalize the scientific method, making it available to new disciplines and improving its practice among working scientists. Thus the logical positivists purported to provide a formal recipe for doing science, offering exactly what psychologists thought they needed. Logical positivism began with a small circle of philosophers in Vienna just after World War I, but it soon became a worldwide movement aimed at the unification of science in one grand scheme of investigation orchestrated by the positivists themselves. Logical positivism had many aspects, but two have proved especially important to psychologists looking for the "scientific way," and they were adopted as talismans of scientific virtue in the 1930s: formal axiomatization of theories, and the operational definition of theoretical terms.

Scientific language, the logical positivists explained, contained two kinds of terms. Most basic were *observation terms,* which referred to directly observable properties of nature: redness, length, weight, time durations, and so on. The older positivism had stressed observation and had insisted that science should contain only observation terms. Logical positivists agreed that observations provided the bedrock of science, but they recognized that theoretical terms were necessary parts of scientific vocabulary, providing explanations in addition to descriptions of natural phenomena. Science simply could not do without terms such as "force," "mass," "field," and "electron." The problem, though, was how to admit science's theoretical vocabulary as legitimate, while excluding metaphysical and religious nonsense. The solution the logical positivists arrived at was to closely tie theoretical terms to bedrock observation terms, thereby guaranteeing their meaningfulness.

The logical positivists argued that the meaning of a theoretical term should be understood to consist in procedures linking it to observation terms. So, for example, "mass" would be defined as an object's weight at sea level. A term that could not be so defined could be dismissed as metaphysical nonsense. Such definitions were called "operational definitions," following the usage of Percy Bridgman, a physicist who had independently proposed the same idea in 1927.

The logical positivists also claimed that scientific theories consisted of theoretical axioms relating theoretical terms to one another. For example, a central axiom of Newtonian physics was "force equals mass times acceleration," or "$F = M \times A$." This theoretical sentence expresses a putative scientific law and may be tested by deriving predictions from it. Since each term has an operational definition, it is possible to take an operational measure of the mass of an object, accelerate it to a measurable speed, and then measure the resulting force generated by the object. Should the predicted force correspond to the measured force in the experiment, the axiom would be confirmed; should the values disagree, the axiom would be disconfirmed and would need to be revised. On the logical positivist account of theories, theories explained because they could predict. To explain an event was to show that it could have been predicted from the preceding circumstances combined with some scientific "covering law." So to explain why a vase broke when it was dropped on the floor, one would show that given the weight of the vase (operationally defined mass) and the height it was dropped from (operationally defined acceleration in earth gravity), the resulting force would be sufficient to crack the vase's porcelain structure.

Logical positivism formalized the ideas of the earlier Comtean and Machian positivists. For both, observation yielded unquestioned truth—both forms of positivism were empiricist. The laws of science were no more than summary statements of experiences: Theoretical axioms were complex summaries of the interactions of several theoretical variables, each of which was in turn wholly defined in terms of observations. To the logical positivist it did not matter if there were atoms or forces in reality; what counted was whether or not such concepts could be systematically related to observations. Logical positivists were thus, for all their apparently tough-minded insistence on only believing what one observes, really romantic idealists (Brush, 1980), for whom ideas—sensations, observation terms—were the only ultimate reality. Nevertheless, logical positivism seemed to offer a specific recipe for doing science in any field of study: First, operationally define one's theoretical terms, be they "mass" or "hunger"; second, state one's theory as a set of theoretical axioms from which predictions could be drawn; third, carry out experiments to test the predictions, using operational definitions to link theory and observations; and finally, revise one's theory as observations warrant.

Because the logical positivists had studied science and set out their findings in explicit logical form, S. S. Stevens (1939), the psychologist who brought operational definition to psychology (Stevens, 1935a,b), called it "the Science of Science," which promised to at last make of psychology "an undisputed natural science" (as Watson had wished), and to unify it with the other sciences in the logical positivists' scheme for the "unity of science." Operationism was exciting to psychologists because it promised to settle once and for all fruitless disputes about psychological terminology: What does "mind" mean? "Imageless thought"? "Id"? As Stevens (1935a) put it, operationism was "the revolution that will put an end to the possibility of revolution." Operationism claimed that terms that could not be operationally defined were scientifically meaningless, while scientific terms could be given operational definitions everyone could agree on. Moreover, operationism's revolution ratified behaviorism's claim to be the only scientific psychology, because only behaviorism was compatible with operationism's demand that theoretical terms be defined by linking them to observation terms (Stevens, 1939). In psychology, this meant that theoretical terms could not refer to mental entities, but only to classes of behavior. Hence mentalistic psychology was unscientific and had to be replaced by behaviorism.

By the end of the 1930s, operationism was entrenched dogma in psychology. Sigmund Koch—by 1950, an apostate from the operationist faith—wrote in his 1939 doctoral thesis that "almost every psychology sophomore knows it is bad form if reference to 'definition' is not qualified by the adjective 'operational.' " In operationism lay psychology's scientific salvation: "Hitch the constructs appearing in your postulates to a field of scientific fact [via operational definition], and only then do you get a scientific theory" (Koch, 1941, p. 127).

At a loftier professional level, the president of the APA agreed with Koch. John F. Dashiell (1939) observed that philosophy and psychology were coming together again, not to have philosophers set psychologists' agenda—from that tyranny psychology had won "emancipation"—but to work out science's proper methods. Foremost in the "rapprochement" of philosophy and psychology were two ideas of the logical positivists. The first was operationism; the other was the demand that scientific theories be collections of mathematically stated axioms. Dashiell commended one psychologist for meeting this second requirement: In "the same positivistic vein [as operationism] Hull is urging us to look to the systematic character of our thinking" by producing a rigorous, axiomatic theory. Dashiell's admiration of Clark L. Hull as the foremost logical positivist among psychologists was, as we will see, wrong. Hull was a mechanist and a realist, believing in the physiological reality of his theoretical terms. However, Dashiell's opinion became later psychologists' myth, a comforting belief that although the specifics of their theories were mistaken, Hull and E. C. Tolman had set psychology firmly on the path toward science as the logical positivists had defined it. The true natures of their theories of learning were obscured for decades, not only from the understanding of psychologists generally, but even from the understanding of Hull and Tolman themselves. Regardless of its flaws and its distorting effect on the independent ideas of Hull and Tolman, there can be no doubt that logical positivism became psychology's official philosophy of science until at least the 1960s.

Edward Chace Tolman's Purposive Behaviorism

Although it was seldom acknowledged, behaviorism's central problem was to account for mental phenomena without invoking the mind. More liberal behavioralists might—and would eventually—leave mind in psychology as an unseen, but nevertheless causal, agent that determines behavior. But at least in its early days, and in its continuing radical strain, behaviorism has aimed to oust mind from psychology. Watson, Lashley, and the other reductive, or physiological, behaviorists tried to do so by claiming that consciousness, purpose, and cognition were myths, so that the task of psychology was to describe experience and behavior as products of the mechanistic operation of the nervous system. The motor theory of consciousness could be used to good effect in such arguments, as showing that conscious contents were just sensations of bodily movements, reporting, but not causing, behavior. Different approaches to explaining behavior without invoking the mind were taken by E. C. Tolman and C. L. Hull.

Bearing a B.S. in electrochemistry, E. C. Tolman (1886–1959) arrived at Harvard in 1911 to undertake graduate study in philosophy and psychology, settling on the latter as more in tune with his capacities and interests. There he studied with the leading philosophers and psychologists of the day, Perry and Holt, Münsterberg and Yerkes. For a time, reading E. B. Titchener "almost sold [him] on structuralistic introspection," but he noticed in his courses with Münsterberg that although Münsterberg "made little opening speeches to the effect that *the* method in psychology was *introspection*," the work in his laboratory was "primarily objective in nature" and that little use could be made of introspective results in writing up experimental papers. So reading Watson's *Behavior* in Yerkes's comparative psychology course came "as a tremendous stimulus and relief" for showing that "objective measurement of behavior, not introspection, was the true method of psychology." Tolman's years at Harvard were also the great years of neorealism, just then being promulgated by Perry and Holt.

Neorealism provided the foundation for Tolman's approach to the problem of mind as he developed it after taking a position at the University of California at Berkeley in 1918. Traditionally, the evidence offered to support the existence of mind was of two sorts: introspective awareness of consciousness, and the apparent intelligence and purposefulness of behavior. Following Perry, Tolman found Watson's "muscle-twitchism" (Tolman, 1959) too simple and crude to account for either kind of evidence. Neorealism implied that there was no such thing as introspection, since there were no mental objects to observe; in the neorealist view, "introspection" was only an artificially close scrutiny of an object in one's environment, in which one reported the object's attributes in great detail. Tolman allied this analysis with the motor theory of consciousness, arguing that introspection of internal states such as emotions was just the "back action" of behavior on awareness (Tolman, 1923). In either event, introspection was of no special importance to scientific psychology; in saying this, Tolman's (1922) "A New Formula for Behaviorism" was a methodological behaviorism, conceding that awareness existed, but ruling its study out of the domain of science.

Similarly, evidence of intelligent purpose in behavior could be handled from the neorealist perspective. The leading purposive psychology of the day was William McDougall's "hormic" psychology. In "Behaviorism and Purpose," Tolman (1925) criticized McDougall for handling purpose in the traditional Cartesian way: McDougall, "being a mentalist, merely *infers* purpose from [the persistence of] behavior, while we, being behaviorists, *identify* purpose with" persistence toward a goal. Following Perry and Holt, Tolman held that "purpose ... is an objective aspect of behavior" that an observer directly perceives; it is not an inference *from* observed behavior. Tolman subjected memory to the same analysis, at once recalling the Scottish realists and anticipating B. F. Skinner: "Memory, like purpose, may be conceived ... as a purely empirical aspect of behavior." To say that one "remembers" a nonpresent object, X, is just to say that one's current behavior is "causally dependent" on X.

In summary, then, Tolman proposed a behaviorism that excised mind and consciousness from psychology as Watson wanted to do, but retained purpose and cognition, not as powers of a mysterious "mind" inferred from behavior, but as objective, observable aspects of behavior itself. In another contrast to Watson, Tolman's behaviorism was "molar" rather than "molecular" (Tolman, 1926, 1935). In Watson's molecular view, behavior was defined as muscular responses caused by triggering stimuli, so that the appropriate strategy to adopt in predicting and controlling behavior was to analyze complex behaviors into their smallest muscular components, which in turn could be understood physiologically. Tolman, viewing behavior as ineliminably purposive, studied whole, integrated, *molar* acts.

For example, according to a molecularist, a subject who has learned to withdraw her finger from an electrode when a warning signal precedes shock has learned a specific conditioned muscular reflex; according to a molar behaviorist, she has learned a global avoidance response. Now turn the subject's hand over, so that the same reflex would drive her finger into the electrode; the Watsonian predicts that a new molecular reflex will have to be learned, while Tolman predicts that the subject will immediately avoid the shock with an untrained withdrawal movement based on having learned a molar response of shock-avoidance (Wickens, 1938; the results supported Tolman, unsurprisingly).

At the same time that he was treating purpose and cognition from a neorealist perspective, Tolman hinted at a different, more traditionally mentalistic approach to the problem they presented; this approach served Tolman well following the demise of neorealism in the 1920s and is fundamental to cognitive science today. In an early paper, Tolman (1920) wrote that thoughts "can be conceived from an objective point of view as consisting in internal presentations to the organism" of stimuli not now present. Later, right alongside arguments that cognitions are "immanent" in behavior and not inferred, Tolman (1926) wrote of consciousness as providing "representations" that guide behavior. To speak of cognitions and thoughts as internal representations of the world playing a causal role in determining behavior breaks with both neorealism and behaviorism: with neorealism because representations are inferred like Lockean ideas; with behaviorism because something mental is given a place among the causes of behavior. As Tolman developed his system he relied more and more on the concept of representation, as we shall see, becoming an inferential behavioralist committed to the real existence of mind.

In 1934, Tolman traveled to Vienna, where he came under the influence of the logical positivists, particularly Rudolf Carnap, the leader of the Vienna Circle. In Carnap's treatment of psychology, the traditional terms of mentalistic folk psychology should be understood as referring not to mental objects, but to physicochemical processes in the body. So, for example, the meaning of the statement "Fred is excited" derives from the glandular, muscular, and other bodily processes that produce excitement; Carnap's analysis is a version of the motor theory of consciousness. While awaiting the full reduction of mental terms to their true physiological referents, we must, Carnap held, compromise on a sort of behaviorism. Since we do not know the physicochemical referent of "excitement," we should understand "excitement" to refer to the behaviors that lead one to attribute excitement to someone else; this compromise is acceptable, since the behaviors are "detectors" of the unknown, underlying physiology. In the long run, we should be able to eliminate behaviorism and understand mentalistic language in purely physiological terms. Carnap did recognize that in addition to its referential function, language may serve an expressive function; if I say "I feel pain," I am not just referring to some physical process within my body, I am expressing anguish. According to Carnap, the expressive function of language lies outside scientific explication and is the subject of poetry, fiction, and, more generally, art.

Carnap's psychology was not incompatible with Tolman's independently developed views, but it did give Tolman a new way to articulate his behaviorism within a philosophy of science daily growing in prestige and influence. Soon after his return to the United States, Tolman reformulated his purposive behaviorism in logical positivist language. Scientific psychology, Tolman (1935) wrote, "seeks ... the objectively statable laws and processes governing behavior." Descriptions of "immediate experience ... may be left to the arts and to metaphysics." Tolman was now able to be quite precise about behaviorism's research program. Behavior was to be regarded as a *dependent variable*, caused by environmental and internal (but not mental) *independent variables*. The ultimate goal of behaviorism, then, is "to write the form of the function *f* which connects the dependent variable [behavior] ... to the independent variables—stimulus, heredity, training, and physiological" states such as hunger. Since this goal is too ambitious to be reached all at once, behaviorists introduce *intervening variables* that connect independent and dependent variables, providing equations that allow one to predict behavior given values of the independent variables. Molar behaviorism defines independent variables "macroscopically" as purposes and cognitions defined as characteristics of behavior, but eventually molecular behaviorism will be able to explain molar independent variables "in detailed neurological and glandular terms."

Tolman (1936) expanded these remarks and redefined his behaviorism as "operational behaviorism." Operational behaviorism is cast in the mold of "the general positivistic attitude now being taken by many modern physicists and philosophers." The adjective "operational" reflects two features of his behaviorism, Tolman explained. First, it defined its intervening variables "operationally" as demanded by modern logical positivism; second, it emphasized the fact that behavior is "essentially an activity whereby the organism ... operates on its environment." There are "two main principles" of operational behaviorism. First, "it asserts that the ultimate interest of psychology is solely the prediction and control of behavior." Second, this interest is to be achieved by a functional analysis of behavior in which "psychological concepts ... may be conceived as objectively defined intervening variables ... defined wholly operationally."

In these two papers, Tolman has set out clearly and forcefully the classical program of methodological behaviorism as defined under the influence of logical positivism. However, we should observe that Tolman did not get his conception of psychology from the logical positivists. Their philosophy of science meshed with what

Tolman already thought and practiced, providing at most a sophisticated and prestigious justification for his own conceptions; his terms *independent, dependent,* and *intervening* variable are enduring contributions to psychological language. More importantly, Tolman seems quickly to have shed his operationism for psychological realism. According to operationism, theoretical terms do not refer to anything at all, but are simply convenient ways of summarizing observations. So the definition of a hungry rat's intention would be its visibly persistent orientation toward the goal box in a maze. However, in his later writings (for example, Tolman, 1948), Tolman speaks of cognitions, at least, as psychologically real entities, not just as shorthand descriptions of behavior. So "cognitive maps" were conceived as representations of the environment that a rat or person consults to guide intelligent behavior toward a goal. In the years after his return to Vienna, Tolman did not teach or even especially discuss logical positivism (Smith, 1986). It is therefore possible that his 1935 and 1936 papers, although widely read expositions of methodological behaviorism, never represented Tolman's real conception of psychology.

Finally, it is interesting to note that Tolman sometimes seemed to be fumbling for a conception of psychology that was not quite available—namely, the computational conception of cognitive science. In 1920, Tolman rejected the "slot machine" view of organisms associated with Watson. In this view, the organism was a machine in which any given stimulus elicited some reflexive response, just as putting a coin in the slot of a vending machine produces a fixed product. Rather, Tolman would prefer to think of an organism as "a complex machine capable of various adjustments such that, when one adjustment was in force," a given stimulus would produce one response, while under a different internal adjustment, the same stimulus would call out a different response. Internal adjustments would be caused either by external stimuli or by "automatic changes within the organism." The model Tolman wished for in 1920 was the computer, whose responses to input depend on its programming and its internal state. Similarly, Tolman anticipated the information-processing account of mind when in 1948 he described the mind as "a central control room" in which "incoming impulses are usually worked over and elaborated … into a cognitivelike map of the environment."

Clark Leonard Hull's Mechanistic Behaviorism

Clark Leonard Hull (1884–1952), like so many people born in the nineteenth century, lost his religious faith as a teenager and struggled ever afterward to find a substitute faith. Hull found his in mathematics and science. Just as Thomas Hobbes had been inspired by reading the book of Euclid, so Hull could say that "the study of geometry proved to be the most important event of my intellectual life." Hull also concluded, as had Hobbes, that one should conceive of thinking, reasoning, and other cognitive powers, including learning, as quite mechanical in nature, and capable of being described and understood through the elegant precision of mathematics. His infatuation with mathematics led him first to seek a career as a mining engineer, but an attack of polio forced him to make new plans. He toyed with the idea of being a minister in the Unitarian church—"a free, godless religion"—but "the prospect of attending an endless succession of ladies' teas" led him to abandon that calling. He sought "a field allied to philosophy in the sense of involving theory," which was so new that he might quickly "find recognition," and that would engage his penchant for machinery by allowing him "to design and work with automatic apparatus." Psychology met "this unique set of requirements," and Hull set out to "deliberately make a bid for a certain place in the history of science." He began by studying James's *Principles,* at first by having his mother read to him during his convalescence. Hull spent his undergraduate years at the University of Michigan, where for a course in logic he built a machine for displaying the logic of syllogisms. Turned down for graduate study by Yale—where he eventually spent most of his professional career—and Cornell, Hull took his Ph.D. from the University of Wisconsin.

Hull eventually made his mark in psychology by his theory and research on learning, and his first investigations presage the influential Hull of the 1930s. As an undergraduate, he studied learning in the insane, and he attempted to formulate mathematically precise laws to account for how they form associations (Hull, 1917). His doctoral dissertation concerned concept formation and again was very quantitative (Hull, 1920). However, circumstances led Hull to spend the next few years doing research in unrelated areas: hypnosis (an "unscientific" field, which Hull tried to improve using "quantitative methodology"); the effects of tobacco on behavior (for which Hull designed a machine through which people could smoke without inhaling tobacco's chemicals); and aptitude testing, which began to make Hull's reputation in psychology. In connection with the last, Hull designed a machine for calculating the correlations between the scores of the various tests in a test battery. Doing so confirmed for him the idea that thinking was a mechanical process that might be simulated by an actual machine; Pascal had been horrified by the same insight, but Hull found in it a hypothesis on which to work.

Like every psychologist, Hull had to grapple with Watson's behaviorism. At first, although he sympathized with Watson's attacks on introspection and call for objectivity, Hull was put off by Watson's dogmatism, and by "the semi-fanatical ardor with which some young people would espouse the Watsonian cause with ... a fanaticism more characteristic of religion than of science" (Hull, 1952, pp. 153–54). Taking up an interest in Gestalt psychology, Hull as a young professor at Wisconsin managed to get Kurt Koffka to visit for a year. However, Koffka's "strikingly negative" attitude toward Watson paradoxically convinced Hull "not that the Gestalt view was sound" but that Watson's behaviorism needed improvement along the mathematical lines Hull was already inclined to follow: "Instead of converting me to *Gestalttheorie,* [I experienced] a belated conversion to a kind of neo-behaviorism—a behaviorism mainly concerned with the determination of the quantitative laws of behavior and their deductive systematization" (Hull, 1952, p. 154). In 1929, Hull moved to Yale University, where he embarked on a most influential career as the preeminent experimental psychologist of his day.

Hull's program had two components. First, as we have seen, Hull was fascinated by machinery and was convinced that machines could think, so he attempted to build machines capable of learning and thinking. The first description of such a machine came in 1929, representing, as he put it, "a direct implication of the mechanistic tendency of modern psychology. Learning and thought are here conceived as by no means necessarily a function of living protoplasm than is serial locomotion" (Hull & Baernstein, 1929). The other component of Hull's theoretical ambition represented a continuation of the geometric spirit of Hobbes and the associationism of Hume, whom

Hull thought of as the first behaviorist. Around 1930, Hull says, "I came to the definite conclusion … that psychology is a true natural science" whose task is the discovery of "laws expressible quantitatively by means of a moderate number of ordinary equations" from which individual and group behaviors might be deduced as consequences (Hull, 1952, p. 155). Given Hull's mechanistic and mathematical interests, it is unsurprising to learn that he contracted a bad case of physics envy and fancied himself the Newton of behavior. In the mid-1920s, he read Newton's *Principia,* and it became a sort of bible for him (Smith, 1986). He assigned portions of it to his seminars and placed it on his desk between himself and visitors; it represented for him the very pinnacle of scientific achievement, and he strove to emulate his hero.

The goals of building intelligent machines and of formalizing psychology according to a mathematical system were not incompatible; Newtonians had conceived of the physical universe as a machine governed by precise mathematical laws: Hull simply aimed to do the same thing for allegedly mental phenomena and behavior. During the early 1930s, Hull pursued both formal theory and learning machines in tandem, publishing increasingly mathematical treatments of complex behaviors such as the acquisition and assembling of simple S-R habits, and promising the production of "psychic machines" capable of thought and useful as industrial robots (Hull 1930a,b, 1931, 1934, 1935). However, as the 1930s wore on, Hull's psychic machines played a less and less prominent place in his work. It appears that he feared that his preoccupation with intelligent machines would appear "grotesque" to outsiders, and that his work on them would be suppressed, as university authorities had suppressed his earlier work on hypnosis (Smith, 1986). At the same time, like Tolman and most other psychologists, Hull came under the influence of logical positivism. Its insistence on formalism and the reduction of the mental to the physical was quite consistent with Hull's own philosophy of science, so that he found increased emphasis on formal, mathematical theory to be most useful as "propaganda" by which to advance his cause (Smith, 1986).

Hull's turn from the pursuit of psychic machines and formal theories to the exclusive pursuit of the latter may be conveniently dated to 1936, the year in which he was president of the APA, and he described in his presidential address his ambitions for theoretical psychology. In his talk, Hull tackled the central problem of behaviorism: accounting for mind. He noted the same outward sign of mind as Tolman did: purposive, persistent behavior in the striving for goals. However, he proposed to account for them in a completely different way, as the outcome of mechanistic, lawful, principles of behavior: "The complex forms of purposive behavior [will] be found to derive from … the basic entities of theoretical physics, such as electrons and protons." Hull recognized that traditionally such a mechanistic position had been only philosophical, and he proposed to make it scientific by applying what he took to be scientific procedure. Science, Hull stated, consisted of a set of "explicitly stated postulates" (as did Euclid's geometry) from which, "by the most rigorous logic," predictions about actual behaviors would be deduced. Just as Newton had derived the motions of the planets from a small set of physical laws, so Hull proposed to predict the motions of organisms from a (rather larger) set of behavioral laws set forth in his paper. The virtue of the scientific method, Hull claimed, was that its predictions could be precisely tested against observations, while the nebulous claims of philosophy, whether idealistic or materialistic, could not be.

Using his set of proposed postulates, Hull tried to show that purposive behavior could be accounted for mechanistically. Finally, he asked, "But what of consciousness?" and in answering this question articulated his own version of methodological behaviorism. Psychology could dispense with consciousness, Hull said, "for the simple reason that no theorem has been found as yet whose deduction would be facilitated in any way by including" a postulate referring to consciousness. "Moreover, we have been quite unable to find any other scientific system of behavior which ... has found consciousness necessary" (p. 31) to deduce behavior. As did Tolman, Hull set conscious experience, the original subject matter of psychology, outside the bounds of psychology as behaviorists viewed it. Hull, like Watson, attributed continued interest in consciousness among psychologists to "the perseverative influences of medieval theology," claiming that "psychology in its basic principles is to a considerable degree in the thrall of the middle ages, and that, in particular, our prevailing systematic outlook in the matter of consciousness is largely medieval." But, concluded Hull, "fortunately the means of our salvation is clear and obvious. As ever, it lies in the application of scientific procedures.... For us to apply the methodology, it is necessary only to throw off the shackles of a lifeless tradition" (p. 32).

Reference to purposive robots was relegated to a footnote in which Hull mentioned "a kind of experimental shortcut to the determination of the ultimate nature of adaptive behavior." If one could build "from inorganic materials ... a mechanism which would display" the adaptive behaviors derived from his postulates, then "it would be possible to say with assurance and a clear conscience that such adaptive behavior may be 'reached' by purely physical means" (p. 31). During his actual presentation to the APA, Hull demonstrated for the audience one of his learning machines, and they were deeply impressed by its performance (Chapanis, 1961). Since Hull rarely mentioned his "psychic machines" again, his statement of the central thesis of cognitive science has gone unnoticed or has been dismissed as peripheral to Hull's thinking. In fact, it is obvious that mechanical simulation of thought was central to Hull's thinking, and it gave rise to the formal theory for which he became famous and through which he became influential.

We have already seen how in the mid-1930s Tolman began to articulate his psychology with the terminology of logical positivism; the same happened to Hull. After 1937, he identified his system with "logical empiricism" and applauded the "uniting" of American behavior theory with Viennese logical positivism, which was producing "in America a behavioral discipline which will be a full-blown natural science" (Hull, 1943a). From then on, Hull bent his efforts to the creation of a formal, deductive, quantitative theory of learning and largely left his psychic machines behind, though they continued to play a heuristic, unpublished role in Hull's thinking (Smith, 1986). Adoption of positivist language obscured Hull's realism, as it did Tolman's. Hull, of course, did not believe in purposes and cognitions, as Tolman did, but he was a realist in believing that the postulates of his theories described actual neurophysiological states and processes in the nervous systems of living organisms, human or animal.

He set forth his postulate systems in a series of books. The first was *Mathematico-Deductive Theory of Rote Learning* (Hull et al., 1940), which offered a mathematical treatment of human verbal learning. The book was praised as "giving a foretaste of what psychology will be like when it reaches systematic, quantitative, precision" (Hilgard, 1940). The rote learning theory was a "dress rehearsal" for his major work,

Principles of Behavior (Hull, 1943b), the expression of "the behavior system … which I had gradually been developing throughout my academic life," and which had formed the basis of his APA presidential address. Upon publication, the *Psychological Bulletin* accorded it a "special review" in which *Principles of Behavior* was praised as "one of the most important books published in psychology in the twentieth century" (Koch, 1944). The book promised to unify all of psychology under the S-R formulation, and to perform needed "radical surgery" on the "withering *corpus* of social science," saving it for real science. Hull revised his system twice more (Hull, 1951, 1952a), but it was *Principles* that fulfilled his ambition of making a permanent name for himself in the history of psychology.

Tolman vs. Hull

Tolman's purposive behaviorism inevitably came into conflict with Hull's mechanistic behaviorism. Tolman always believed that purpose and cognition were real, although his conception of their reality changed over time. Hull, on the other hand, sought to explain purpose and cognition as the result of mindless mechanical processes describable in logico-mathematical equations. During the 1930s and 1940s, Tolman and Hull engaged in a sort of intellectual tennis match: Tolman would attempt to demonstrate that purpose and cognition were real, while Hull and his followers patched up the theory or tried to show that Tolman's demonstrations were flawed.

Let us consider an example of an experiment that contrasts the cognitive and S-R views. It was actually reported in 1930 (Tolman, 1932), well before the Hull-Tolman debates really got under way, but it is a simpler version of more complex experiments described in Tolman's (1948) "Cognitive Maps in Rats and Men," meant to differentially support Tolman's theory. The maze is shown in Figure 7-1. Rats were familiarized with the entire maze by forcing them to run each path in early training. Having learned the maze, a rat coming out of the start box into the choice point must pick one of the paths. How does the rat do this?

A Hullian analysis may be sketched. The choice point presents stimuli (S) to which three responses (Rs) corresponding to each path have been conditioned during initial training. For a variety of reasons, most obviously the different amounts of running that must be done in each alley, Path 1 is preferred to Path 2, which is preferred to Path 3. That is, connection $S{\to}R_1$ is stronger than $S{\to}R_2$, which is stronger than $S{\to}R_3$. Such a state of affairs may be notated.

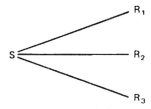

This is called a *divergent habit family hierarchy*. Now, should a block be placed at Point 1, the rat will run into it, back up, and choose Path 2. The connection $S{\to}R_1$ is weakened by the block, so that $S{\to}R_2$ becomes stronger and is acted on. On the other hand, if the second block is placed, the rat will retreat to the choice point and again choose Path 2 as $S{\to}R_1$ is again blocked, and $S{\to}R_2$ becomes stronger. However, the

FIGURE 7-1 Tolman-Honzik Maze.

block will be met again, S→R₂ will weaken, and finally S→R₃ will be strongest and Path 3 will be chosen. This is the Hullian prediction.

Tolman denied that what is learned is a set of responses triggered to differing degrees by the stimuli at the choice point. Instead, he held that the rat learns a mental map of the maze that guides its behavior. According to this view, the rat encountering the first block will turn around and choose Path 2, as in the S-R account, because Path

2 is shorter than Path 3. However, if it encounters Block 2, the rat will know that the same block will cut off Path 2 as well as Path 1. Therefore the rat will show "insight": It will return and choose Path 3, ignoring Path 2 altogether. A map displays all aspects of the environment and is more informative than a set of S-R connections. The results of the experiment supported Tolman's cognitive theory of learning over Hull's S-R account.

While Hull and Tolman differed sharply on their specific accounts of behavior, we should not forget that they shared important assumptions and goals. Both Tolman and Hull wanted to write scientific theories of learning and behavior applying to at least all mammals, including human beings. They pursued their mutual goal by experimenting on and theorizing about rats, assuming that any difference between rat and human was trivial, and that results from laboratories represented naturalistic behavior as well; they followed Herbert Spencer's formula for psychology. Both Tolman and Hull rejected consciousness as the subject matter of psychology and took the description, prediction, and control of behavior as psychology's task; they were behavioralists—specifically, methodological behaviorists. Finally, both were influenced by, and seemed to endorse, logical positivism.

Psychologists have tended to assume that Tolman and Hull were slavish adherents of logical positivism, and that they personally set the positivist style of modern psychology. However, such a judgment does them a disservice, obscures their independence, and depreciates their creativity. Tolman and Hull reached their conceptions of science, psychology, and behavior quite independently of logical positivism. When they encountered logical positivism in the 1930s, each found he could use this prestigious philosophy to more powerfully state his own ideas; but we must not forget that their ideas were their own. Unfortunately, because they did adopt positivist language and because positivism quickly came to be psychologists' philosophy of science, the real programs of Tolman and Hull were obscured or forgotten, resulting in some fruitless controversies in the 1950s, as we shall see in Chapter 10.

Although both Tolman and Hull were honored and influential, there is no doubt that Hull was very much more influential than Tolman. At Berkeley, Tolman filled students with enthusiasm for psychology and a healthy disrespect for scientific pomposity. He wrote lively papers and took a zestful approach to science, saying that "in the end, the only sure criterion is to have fun. And I have had fun" (Tolman, 1959). He was never a systematic theorist and had finally to confess to being a "crypto-phenomenologist" who designed his experiments by imagining what he would do if he were a rat, being gratified to find that rats were as clever and commonsensical as he was, being no machines. Unfortunately, this all meant that while Tolman could inspire students, he could not teach them a systematic viewpoint with which to evangelize psychology. Tolman had no disciples.

Hull, however, did. Instead of valuing having fun, Hull valued the long, arduous labor of constructing postulates and deriving theorems from them. Though tedious, this gave Hull an explicit set of ideas with which to infect his students for spreading throughout the discipline. Moreover, Hull's institutional situation was ideal for building discipleship. Besides the department of psychology at Yale, Hull was strategically placed at Yale's Institute of Human Relations (IHR), which attracted bright minds from many disciplines eager to learn the rigors of science for application to their fields and to the problems of the world. We will later see how social learning theory emerged from Hull's seminars at the IHR. Hull found someone to continue his program in Kenneth Spence (1907–1967). Spence collaborated on Hull's great books, continued his rigorous theorizing into the 1950s, created a truly positivist version of neobehaviorism, and trained many leading experimental psychologists of the 1950s and 1960s: Hull's intellectual grandchildren. And, of course, Hull's rigorous theoretical system, pristinely mechanistic and eschewing any mysticism about purpose and cognition, was perfectly in tune with the naturalistic-positivistic *Zeitgeist* of American psychology after World War I.

Studies during the 1950s therefore consistently found Hull's impact on psychology to be much greater than Tolman's. For example, as late as the 1960s, a study of which psychologists were most often cited in the leading journals of psychology (Myers, 1970) found that the most-cited psychologist was Kenneth Spence, with Hull himself at eighth place. This is especially remarkable considering that Hull had been dead since 1952, and that his theory had been subjected to scathing criticism since the early 1950s. Despite the fact that many psychologists saw a cognitive "revolution" taking place in the 1960s, E. C. Tolman, the purposive, cognitive behaviorist, did not place in the top 60.

CONCLUSION: WE'RE ALL BEHAVIORISTS NOW

Hull's colleague Kenneth Spence observed in 1948 that few psychologists "ever seem to think of themselves, or explicitly refer to themselves as behaviorists," because behaviorism was "a very general point of view which has come to be accepted by almost all psychologists." Spence noted one exception to his conclusion: Tolman protested perhaps too much that he was a good behaviorist. Spence also recognized that behaviorism took many forms, so that the term "behaviorism" was rather slippery. Still, behaviorism had made progress, Spence thought, because all the neobehaviorisms sharply separated themselves from Watson's early, rather crude formulation of classical behaviorism. Spence tried to tidy up the Babel of behaviorisms by formulating a behaviorist metaphysics along logical positivist lines. He hoped to create a common creed on which all behaviorists might agree. As we shall see in Chapter 10, his hope was misplaced, as the Tolmanians refused to assent.

On the horizon of experimental psychology lay a newly formulated radical behaviorism that after World War II would challenge and then replace all other behaviorisms. B. F. Skinner, a writer turned psychologist, had begun in 1931 to work out a behaviorism in the radical spirit of Watson, but with a new set of technical concepts. Skinner's influence lay in the future, when after the war psychologists would again lose confidence in their enterprise and begin to look for a new Newton. Before the war, however, Skinner was not taken too seriously. E. R. Hilgard (1939) said of Skinner's first major theoretical statement, *Behavior of Organisms,* that its narrow conception of psychology would greatly limit its influence.

During the years when academic psychologists came to accept behavioralism as the only legitimate approach to the problems of scientific psychology, other psychologists were beginning to tackle the problems of society. Psychology experienced its greatest growth not in experimental psychology, but in applied psychology.

NOTE: The Bibliography for this chapter is incorporated in Chapter 9.

REFERENCES

Angell, J. R. (1913). Behavior as a category of psychology. *Psychological Review, 20,* 255–270.

Bode, B. H. (1918). Consciousness as behavior. *Journal of Philosophy, 15,* 449–453.

Bridgman, P. (1927). *The logic of modern physics.* New York: Macmillan.

Brush, S. G. (1980). The chimerical cat: Philosophy of quantum mechanics historical perspective. *Social Studies of Science, 10,* 394–447.

Buckley, K. (1984). *Mechanical man: John B. Watson and the beginnings of behaviorism.* Westport, CT: Guildford Press.

Calkins, M. W. (1913). Psychology and the behaviorist. *Psychological Bulletin, 10,* 288–291.

Calkins, M. W. (1921). The truly psychological behaviorism. *Psychological Bulletin, 28,* 1–18.

Chapanis, A. (1961). Men, machines and models. *American Psychologist, 16,* 113–131.

Cohen, D. B. (1979). *J. B. Watson: The founder of behaviorism.* London: Routledge and Kegan Paul.

Dashiell, J. F. (1939). Some rapprochements in contemporary psychology. *Psychological Bulletin, 36,* 1–24.

Haggerty, M. E. (1913). The laws of learning. *Psychological Review, 20,* 411–422.

Harris, B. (1979). Whatever happened to Little Albert? *American Psychologist, 34,* 151–160.

Hilgard, E. R. (1939). Review of B. F. Skinner, *Behavior of organisms. Psychological Bulletin, 36,* 121–124.

Hilgard, E. R. (1940). Review of Hull et al. *Psychological Bulletin, 37,* 808–815.

Holton, G. (1978). *The scientific imagination: Case studies.* Cambridge, England: Cambridge University Press.

Hull, C. (1917). The formation and retention of associations among the insane. *American Journal of Psychology, 28,* 419–435.

Hull, C. L. (1920). Quantitative aspects of the evolution of concepts. *Psychological Monographs, 28,* no. 123.

Hull, C. L. (1930a). Simple trial and error learning: A study in psychological theory. *Psychological Review, 37,* 241–256.

Hull, C. L. (1930b). Knowledge and purpose as habit mechanisms. *Psychological Review, 37,* 511–525.

Hull, C. L. (1931). Goal attraction and directing ideas conceived as habit phenomena. *Psychological Review, 38,* 487–506.

Hull, C. L. (1934). The concept of the habit-family-hierarchy in maze learning. *Psychological Review, 41,* 33–54, 131–152.

Hull, C. L. (1935). The conflicting psychologies of learning: A way out. *Psychological Review, 42,* 491–516.

Hull, C. L. (1937). Mind, mechanism and adaptive behavior. *Psychological Review, 44,* 1–32.

Hull, C. L. (1938). The goal-gradient hypothesis applied to some "field-force" problems in the behavior of young children. *Psychological Review, 45,* 271–300.

Hull, C. L. (1943a). The problem of intervening variables in molar behavior theory. *Psychological Review, 50,* 273–288.

Hull, C. L. (1943b). *Principles of behavior.* New York: Appleton-Century-Crofts.

Hull, C. L. (1951). *Essentials of behavior.* New Haven: Yale University Press.

Hull, C. L. (1952a). *A behavior system.* New Haven: Yale University Press.

Hull, C. L. (1952b). Clark L. Hull. In E. G. Boring, H. S. Langfeld, H. Werner, & R. M. Yerkes (Eds.). *A history of psychology in autobiography,* Vol. 4. Worcester, MA: Clark University Press.

Hull, C. & Baernstein, H. (1929). A mechanical parallel to the conditioned reflex. *Science, 70,* 14–15.

Hull, C., Hovland, C., Ross, R., Hall, M., Perkins, D., & Fitch, F. (1940). *Mathematico-deductive theory of rote learning: A study in scientific methodology.* New Haven: Yale University Press.

Hunter, W. S. (1922). An open letter to the anti-behaviorists. *Journal of Philosophy, 19,* 307–308.

Hunter, W. S. (1923). Review of A. A. Roback, "Behaviorism and psychology." *American Journal of Psychology, 34,* 464–467.

Hunter, W. S. (1925). Psychology and anthroponomy. In C. Murchison (Ed.). *Psychologies of 1925.* Worcester, MA: Clark University Press.

Jastrow, J. (1927). The reconstruction of psychology. *Psychological Review, 34,* 169–195.

Jones, A. H. (1915). The method of psychology. *Journal of Philosophy, 12,* 462–471.

Koch, S. (1941). The logical character of the motivation concept. *Psychological Review, 48,* 15–38, 127–154.

Koch, S. (1944). Hull's Principles of behavior: A special review. *Psychological Bulletin, 41,* 269–286.

Kuo, Z. Y. (1928). The fundamental error of the concept of purpose and the trial and error fallacy. *Psychological Review, 35,* 414–433.

Langfeld, H. S. (1943). Fifty years of the *Psychological Review. Psychological Review, 50,* 143–155.

Lashley, K. S. (1923). The behavioristic interpretation of consciousness. *Psychological Review, 30,* Part 1: 237–272, Part 2: 329–353.

MacDougall, R. (1925). Men or robots? In C. Murchison (Ed.), *Psychologies of 1925.* Worcester, MA: Clark University Press.

McComas, H. C. (1916). Extravagances in the motor theory of consciousness. *Psychological Review, 23,* 397–406.

McGeoch, J. A. (1931). The acquisition of skill. *Psychological Bulletin, 28,* 413–466.

Myers, C. R. (1970). Journal citations and scientific eminence in psychology. *American Psychologist, 25,* 1041–1048.

Pepper, S. (1923). Misconceptions regarding behaviorism. *Journal of Philosophy, 20,* 242–245.

Perry, R. B. (1921). A behavioristic view of purpose. *Journal of Philosophy, 18,* 85–105.

Samelson, F. (1980). J. B. Watson's Little Albert, Cyril Burt's twins, and the need for a critical science. *American Psychologist, 35,* 619–625.

Samelson, F. (1981). Struggle for scientific authority: The reception of Watson's behaviorism, 1913–1920. *Journal of the History of the Behavioral Sciences, 17,* 399–425.

Schneider, S. M. & Morris, E. K. (1987). A History of the term Radical Behaviorism: From Watson to Skinner. *The Behavior Analyst, 10,* 27–39.

Skinner, B. F. (1938). *Behavior of organisms.* New York: Appleton-Century-Crofts.

Smith, L. J. (1986). *Behaviorism and logical positivism: A revised account of the alliance.* Stanford, CA: Stanford University Press.

Spence, K. (1948). Postulates and methods of "behaviorism." *Psychological Review, 55,* 67–78.

Stevens, S. S. (1935a). The operational basis of psychology. *American Journal of Psychology, 43,* 323–330.

Stevens, S. S. (1935b). The operational definition of psychological concepts. *Psychological Review, 42,* 517–527.

Stevens, S. S. (1939). Psychology and the science of science. *Psychological Bulletin, 36,* 221–263.

Titchener, E. B. (1914). On "Psychology as the behaviorist views it." *Proceedings of the American Philosophical Society, 53,* 1–17.

Tolman, E. C. (1920). Instinct and purpose. *Psychological Review, 27,* 217–233.

Tolman, E. C. (1922). A new formula for behaviorism. *Psychological Review, 29,* 44–53.

Tolman, E. C. (1923). A behavioristic account of the emotions. *Psychological Review, 30,* 217–227.

Tolman, E. C. (1925). Behaviorism and purpose. *Journal of Philosophy, 22,* 36–41.

Tolman, E. C. (1926). A behavioristic theory of ideas. *Psychological Review, 33,* 352–369.

Tolman, E. C. (1932). *Purposive behavior in animals and men.* New York: Century.

Tolman, E. C. (1935). Psychology vs. immediate experience. *Philosophy of Science.* Reprinted in Tolman (1951/1966).

Tolman, E. C. (1936). Operational behaviorism and current trends in psychology. In Tolman (1951/1966).

Tolman, E. C. (1948). Cognitive maps in rats and men. *Psychological Review, 55,* 189–209.

Tolman, E. C. (1951/1966). *Behavior and psychological man.* Berkeley: University of California Press.

Tolman, E. C. (1952). Edward Chace Tolman. In E. G. Boring, H. S. Langfeld, H. Werner, & R. M. Yerkes, (Eds.). *A history of psychology in autobiography,* Vol. 4. Worcester, MA: Clark University Press.

Tolman, E. C. (1959). Principles of purposive behaviorism. In S. Koche (Ed.), *Psychology: A study of a science,* Vol. 2. New York: McGraw-Hill.

Warren, H. (1938). Howard C. Warren. In C. Murchison (Ed.). *A history of psychology in autobiography,* Vol. 1. Worcester, MA: Clark University Press.

Watson, J. B. (1913a). Psychology as the behaviorist views it. *Psychological Review, 20,* 158–177.

Watson, J. B. (1913b). Image and affection in behavior. *Journal of Philosophy, 10,* 421–428.

Watson, J. B. (1916a). The place of the conditioned reflex in psychology. *Psychological Review, 23,* 89–116.

Watson, J. B. (1916b). Behavior and the concept of mental disease. *Journal of Philosophy, 13,* 589–597.

Watson, J. B. (1930). *Behaviorism.* 2nd ed. New York: Norton (1st ed., 1925).

Watson, J. B. & Rayner, R. (1920). Conditioned emotional reactions. *Journal of Experimental Psychology, 10,* 421–428.

Weiss, A. P. (1924). Behaviorism and behavior. *Psychological Review, 31,* Part 1:32–50, Part 2:118–149.

Wheeler, R. W. (1923). Introspection and behavior. *Psychological Review, 30,* 103–115.

Wickens, D. D. (1938). The transference of conditioned extinction from one muscle group to the antagonistic muscle group. *Journal of Experimental Psychology, 22,* 101–123.

Williams, K. (1931). Five behaviorisms. *American Journal of Psychology, 43,* 337–361.

Woodworth, R. S. (1924). Four varieties of behaviorism. *Psychological Review 31,* 257–264.

Yerkes, R. M. (1913). Comparative psychology: A question of definition. *Journal of Philosophy 10:* 581–582.

CHAPTER 8

Applied Psychology and the Problems of Society
Psychologists in Social Controversy (1913–1950)

INTRODUCTION

As psychologists began to concern themselves with the problems of American society, they naturally became involved in wider social, political, and intellectual controversies outside academia. Three issues attracted more attention than others: the apparently depressing picture of American intelligence revealed by the army intelligence tests; the revival of eugenics, caused in part by the test results; and the need to rethink the functions of the family, caused by the revolt of the Flaming Youth of the 1920s. Finally, all this public attention turned psychology into something of a popular fad in the dozen years following the Great War.

Entrance into World War I marked the end of two decades of profound social change, transforming the United States from a rural country of island communities into an industrialized, urbanized nation of everywhere communities. The United States became a great power that could project military might across the Atlantic Ocean and decide the outcome of a European war. Progressive politicians saw in the war a welcome chance to achieve their goals of social control, creating a unified, patriotic, efficient nation out of the mass of immigrants and scattered groups created by industrialization. Led by President Wilson, they also saw a chance to bring Progressive, rational control to the whole world. As one Progressive exclaimed, "Long live social control; social control, not only to enable us to meet the rigorous demands of the war, but also as a foundation for the peace and brotherhood that is to come" (quoted by Thomas, 1977, p. 1020).

But the Great War to End All Wars frustrated and then shattered the Progressives' dreams. The government created bureaucracies whose watchword was efficiency and whose aims were standardization and centralization, but they accomplished nothing. The horrors of the war, in which many European villages lost their entire male populations for a few feet of foreign soil, brought Americans face to face with the irrational and left many Europeans with lifelong depression and pessimism. After the war the victorious powers fell to dividing up the spoils of war like vultures, and Wilson became little more than a pathetic idealist ignored at Versailles and then at home, unable to bring America into his League of Nations. World War I did nothing but lay the groundwork for World War II.

Intellectuals and social and political leaders learned the lesson that reason was not enough to achieve social control. In the aftermath of war, the lesson was underlined by the revolt of the Flaming Youth of the 1920s and the seeming breakdown of the families that had raised them. Convinced of the wisdom of science, however—for scientism still ran strong in America—American leaders turned to social science, especially psychology, to solve the problems of the postwar world, to give them the tools by which to manage the irrational masses, to reshape the family and the workplace. As Philip Rieff (1966) put it, the Middle Ages, with faith in God, ruled through the church; the progressive nineteenth century, with faith in reason, ruled through the legislature; the twentieth century, with faith in science tempered by recognition of the irrational, rules through the hospital. In the twentieth century, then, psychology would become one of the most important institutions in society; no wonder that psychologists' ideas became more widely applied, the latest scientific marvel read by leaders for clues to social control, and by the masses for insights into the springs of their own behavior.

FOUNDING APPLIED PSYCHOLOGY
(1896–1915)

In 1892, William James wrote: "The kind of psychology which could cure a case of melancholy, or charm a chronic insane delusion away, ought certainly to be preferred to the most seraphic insight into the nature of the soul." James identified a tension in modern psychology—especially modern American psychology—that has steadily increased throughout the twentieth century: the tension between the psychologist as scientist and the psychologist as practitioner of a craft. The tension has been most evident in the history of the American Psychological Association (APA), founded in

1892. It was founded to advance the cause of psychology as science, but very quickly its members turned to the application of their science, and the APA found itself embroiled in largely unwanted problems concerned with defining and regulating the practice of psychology as a technological profession. There was, however, especially in America, no going back on the development of professional applied psychology: Psychology's social circumstances and the ideology of pragmatism and functionalism required it.

In nineteenth-century Germany, the academicians who controlled the gates of admission to the great universities had needed to be convinced of psychology's legitimacy as a discipline. Their leading academicians were the philosophers; and in their Mandarin culture, pure knowledge was valued above technology. Naturally, Wundt and the other German psychologists founded a discipline strictly devoted to "seraphic insights into the nature of the soul." In the United States, things were very different. American universities were not institutions controlled by a few academicians working for the central state; they were a variegated collection of public and private schools subject more to local whim than central control. As de Tocqueville observed, Americans valued what brought practical success and sought social and personal improvement rather than pure knowledge. So the tribunal that would pass on psychology's worthiness in America was composed of practical men of business and industry interested in techniques of social control. Naturally, then, psychologists came to stress the social and personal utility of their discipline instead of its refined scientific character.

As with phrenology, American psychology wanted to be recognized as a science, but especially as a science with practical aims. On the occasion of the twenty-fifth anniversary of the APA, John Dewey (1917) denounced the concept, characteristic of Gall or Wundt, of the mind as a creation of nature existing before society. By placing mind beyond society's control, such a view acted as a bastion of political conservatism, Dewey held. He offered his pragmaticist conception of mind as a social creation as the proper foundation for experimental psychology. Since in Dewey's view mind was created by society, it could be deliberately molded by society, and psychology, the science of the mind, could take as its goal social control, the scientific management of society. Such a psychology would fall in with Progressivism and give American psychology the social utility Wundt's psychology lacked.

American psychologists thus offered a science with pragmatic "cash value." Pragmatism demanded that ideas become true by making a difference to human conduct; so, to be true, psychological ideas would have to show that they did matter to individuals and society. Functionalism argued that the role of mind was to adjust the behavior of the individual organism to the environment. Naturally, then, psychologists would come to be interested in how the process of adjustment played itself out in American life, and they would then move to improve the process of adjustment to make it more efficient and to repair the process of adjustment when it went awry. Since adjustment was the great function of mind, every sphere of human life was opened to the psychological technologist: the child's adjustment to the family; parents' adjustments to their children and to each other; the worker's adjustment to the workplace; the soldier's adjustment to the army; and so on through every aspect of personality and behavior: No aspect of life would finally escape the clinical gaze of professional psychologists.

Interest in these matters appeared as soon as psychology reached America. Central to the first applications of psychology was Cattell's invention of the "mental test" in 1890. At the Columbian Exposition of 1893, psychology first came to the public's attention when people entered an exhibit and took psychological tests. The first "psychological clinic" was opened in 1896 by Lightner Witmer, and many others sprang up in the ensuing years. These clinics used tests to diagnose children with school problems but generally offered no treatment. A related development was the child guidance clinic; the first such clinic was attached to a juvenile court in Chicago in 1909. There psychologist Grace Fernald gave tests to children brought before the court. The earliest tests used with retarded children were "tests" made up using the standard brass instruments of the psychological laboratory, such as mental chronoscopes and sensory test apparatus, but these were soon replaced by the more sophisticated Binet test. The center of this activity was the Vineland Training School opened in 1905; its director, Henry Goddard, introduced the Binet test to the United States. In 1908, Clifford Beers, a former mental patient, started the mental hygiene movement with a book, *A Mind That Found Itself,* endorsed by William James himself. The aim of the movement was the prevention of psychological problems, and it provided a further impetus to the child guidance clinics, which began to look for problems before they developed. At the McLean Hospital, mental patients were tested and became subjects of investigations by psychologists. Finally, psychology was applied to business and industry, first to advertising by Walter Dill Scott, who gave a talk on the psychology of advertising in 1901, eventually becoming professor of advertising at Northwestern University in 1915. In the same year, psychologists began to use tests to pick workers for particular jobs.

Just before the United States entered World War I, then, psychologists were actively applying their ideas and techniques—especially tests—to a wide range of social problems. Their efforts, however, were scattered and small scale. When the war came, psychologists enlisted to apply themselves to a truly massive task: the evaluation of men for fitness to serve in the U.S. Army. One year later, psychology had become a permanent part of the intellectual landscape of American life, and its terminology had become part of the American vocabulary.

THE USES OF INTELLIGENCE TESTING

Psychology Enters Public Consciousness: Psychologists in the Great War

Psychologists, like Progressives, saw the Great War as an opportunity to show that psychology had come of age as a science and could be put to service. The organizer of psychology's efforts to serve the nation at war was Robert Yerkes, the comparative psychologist. With pride he explained in his presidential address to the APA, just months after the war began, how

> In this country, for the first time in the history of our science, a general organization in the interests of certain ideal and practical aims has been effected. Today, American psychology is placing a highly trained and eager personnel at the service of our military organizations. We are acting not individually but collectively on the basis of common training and common faith in the practical value of our work. (p. 85)

Just as Progressives used the war to unify the country, Yerkes exhorted psychologists to "act unitedly in the interests of defense," bringing psychologists together "as a professional group in a nation-wide effort to render our professional training service-able."

On April 6, 1917, only two days after the United States declared war, Yerkes seized the opportunity of a meeting of Titchener's "Experimentalists" to organize psychology's war efforts. Following a whirlwind of activity by Yerkes and some others—including a trip to Canada to see what Canadian psychologists were doing in their war—the APA formed twelve committees concerned with different aspects of the war, ranging from acoustic problems to recreation. Few young male psychologists were left uninvolved; but in this war, unlike the next, only two committees really accomplished anything: Walter Dill Scott's APA committee on motivation, which became the Committee on Classification of Personnel of the War Department; and Yerkes's own committee on the psychological examination of recruits, which concentrated on the problem of eliminating the "mentally unfit" from the U.S. Army. There was considerable tension between Yerkes and Scott from the outset. Yerkes came from experimental psychology and brought research interests to the job of testing recruits, hoping to gather data on intelligence as well as serve the needs of the military. Scott's background was industrial psychology, and he brought a practical management perspective to military testing, aiming above all at practical results, not scientific results. At the wartime organizational meeting of the APA at the Walton Hotel in Philadelphia, Scott said that he "became so enraged at [Yerkes's] points of view that I expressed myself very clearly and left the [APA] council" (von Mayrhauser, 1985). Scott believed Yerkes to be making a power play to advance his own interests in psychology, and he accused Yerkes of concealing self-interest behind sham patriotism. The upshot of the quarrel was that Yerkes and Scott went their own ways in applying tests to the examination of recruits. Yerkes (who had always wanted to be a doctor) set up under the Surgeon General's office in the Sanitary Corps, and Scott under the Adjutant General's office.

Insofar as concrete results welcomed and used by the military were concerned, Scott's committee was the more effective of the two. Drawing on his work in personnel psychology at the Carnegie Institute of Technology, Scott developed a rating scale for selecting officers. By himself, Scott convinced the army of the scale's utility, and he was allowed to form his War Department committee, which quickly became involved in the more massive undertaking of assigning the "right man to the right job" in the army. By the end of the war, Scott's committee had grown from 20 to over 175 members, had classified nearly 3,500,000 men, and had developed proficiency tests for 83 military jobs. Scott was awarded a Distinguished Service Medal for his work.

Yerkes's committee did virtually nothing for the army—he won no medal—but it did a great deal to advance professional psychology. In this respect, its most obvious achievement was to invent the group test of intelligence. Heretofore intelligence tests, the most important of which was Binet's, had been administered to individual subjects by clinical psychologists. Obviously, individual tests could not be administered to millions of draftees, so in May 1918, Yerkes assembled leading test psychologists at the Vineland Training School to write an intelligence test that could be given to groups of men in brief periods of time. Initially, Yerkes believed that group tests of intelligence were unscientific, introducing uncontrolled factors into the test situation, and wanted to test each recruit individually; but associates of Scott's at Vineland persuaded him that individual testing was just impossible under the circumstances (von Mayrhauser, 1985). Yerkes's group designed two tests, the Army Alpha test for literate recruits, and the Army Beta test for presumed illiterates who did badly on the Alpha. Recruits were graded on a letter scale from A to E, just like in school; "A" men were likely officers, "D" and "E" men were the unfit (see Figure 8-1).

Overcoming considerable skepticism, and following a trial period of testing at one camp, in December 1917 the Army approved general testing of all recruits. Throughout the war, Yerkes's work was met with hostility and indifference by army officers, who saw Yerkes's psychologists as meddlers having no business in the army, and by army psychiatrists, who feared psychologists might assume some of their roles within the military. Nevertheless, 1,175,000 men were tested before the program was ended in January 1919. With the invention of the group test, Yerkes and his colleagues had devised a tool that greatly expanded the potential scope of psychologists' activities, and multiplied by many times the numbers of Americans who might be scrutinized by the profession.

In concluding his presidential address, Yerkes "looked ahead and attempted to prophesy future needs" for psychology. "The obvious and significant trend of our psychological military work is toward service ... the demand for psychologists and psychological service promises, or threatens, to be overwhelmingly great." Yerkes foresaw better than he knew; while speaking only of psychological service in the military, Yerkes's words describe the most important change in institutional psychology in the twentieth century. Before the war, applied psychologists had worked in relative obscurity in isolated settings around the country; during the war, they touched millions of lives in a self-conscious, organized professional effort to apply psychology to a pressing social need; after the war, psychology was famous, and applied psychology grew by leaps and bounds, concerning itself with the "menace of the feeble-minded," with immigrants, with troubled children, with industrial workers, with advertising, with problems of the American family. Applied psychology had arrived as an important actor on the American social scene, and its influence has never ceased to grow in the seventy-five years since Yerkes called psychologists to military service.

Is America Safe for Democracy?
Impact of Army Intelligence Testing

Progressives believed with E. L. Thorndike (1920) that "in the long run it has paid the masses to be ruled by intelligence." But the results of the Army Alpha and Beta tests suggested that there were alarmingly few intelligent Americans—"A" men—and rather too many feebleminded Americans—"D" and "E" men. Yerkes's massive report on the results of the army tests recorded a mean American mental age of 13.08. Terman's work on translating and standardizing the Binet test had set the "normal" average intelligence at a mental age of 16. Henry Goddard had coined the term "moron" to denote anyone with a mental age of less than 13, so that nearly half of the drafted white men (47.3 percent) would have to be considered morons. Performance by recent immigrant groups and blacks was even worse. Yerkes (1923) told readers of *Atlantic Monthly* that "racial" differences in intelligence were quite real. Children from the older immigrant stock did quite well on the army tests. Draftees of English

From *The Camp Sherman News*

FIGURE 8-1 That psychological examination, 1918. In retrospect, we can see that the army tests of intelligence were remarkably silly. This cartoon, from *The Camp Sherman News*, reprinted in *Psychological Bulletin,* 1919, expresses the ordinary soldier's experience of the tests. Groups of men were assembled in rooms and given pencils and response sheets. They had to obey shouted orders to do unfamiliar things and answer strange questions. The test items that the unfortunate recruit in the cartoon has to answer are but slight exaggerations of the real items. Stephen Jay Gould gave the Beta test to Harvard undergraduates, following the exact procedures used in the war, and found that although most students did well, a few barely made "C" level. Gould's students, of course, were greatly experienced with standardized tests, in contrast with raw draftees under great stress, many of whom had little or no education. One can only imagine how puzzled and confused the average testee was, and can sympathize with the hapless soldier at Camp Sherman.

descent ranked first, followed by the Dutch, Danish, Scots, and Germans. Descendants of later-arriving immigrants did badly. At the bottom of the distribution of intelligence were Turks, Greeks, Russians, Italians, and Poles. At the very bottom were African-Americans, with a mental age on the army tests of just 10.41.

The results appalled people who agreed with Galton that intelligence is innate. In his book's title, psychologist William McDougall (1921) asked, *Is America Safe for Democracy?* and argued that unless action were taken, the answer was no: "Our civilization, by reason of its increasing complexity, is making constantly increasing demands upon the quality of its bearers; the qualities of those bearers are diminishing or deteriorating, rather than improving" (p. 168, italics deleted). Henry Goddard, who had helped construct the army tests, concluded that "the average man can manage his affairs with only a moderate degree of prudence, can earn only a very modest living, and is vastly better off when following direction than when trying to plan for himself" (Gould, 1981, p. 223). The Galtonian alarmists were convinced that individual and racial differences were genetic in origin and consequently incapable of being erased by education. For example, Yerkes (1923) noted that African-Americans living in northern states outscored those living in the southern states by a wide margin, but he claimed that this was because smarter blacks had moved North, leaving the feeble-minded behind. He could, of course, have noted that African-Americans were more likely to receive an education in the North than in the South, but he did not even consider such a possibility.

There were critics of the tests and their alleged results, but for a long time, the critics were ignored. The most insightful critic was the political writer Walter Lippmann, who published a devastating critique of the alarmist interpretation of the army results in the *New Republic* in 1922 and 1923 (reprinted in Block and Dworkin, 1976). Lippmann argued that the average American cannot have a below-average intelligence. Terman's figure of a "normal" mental age of 16 was based on a reference norm of a few hundred schoolchildren in California; the army results were based on over 100,000 recruits. Therefore it was more logical to conclude that the army results represented average American intelligence than to stick with the California sample and absurdly conclude that the American average was below average. Moreover, the classification of men into A, B, C, D, and E categories was essentially arbitrary, reflecting the needs of the army, not raw intelligence. For example, the alarmists were alarmed that only 5 percent of the recruits were "A" men; but Lippmann pointed out that the tests were constructed so that only 5 percent *could* be "A" men, since the army wanted to send 5 percent of the recruits to Officer Training School. Had the army only wanted half the number of officers, the tests would have been designed to yield 2.5 percent "A" men, and the alarmists would have been even more alarmed. In short, Lippmann showed, there wasn't anything in the army results to get excited about. But despite his cautions, many people did get excited about the army tests. The Galtonian alarmists pressed for political action to do something about the supposed "menace of the feebleminded," and as we shall shortly see, they got it.

Another and more enduring legacy of the army tests was the enhanced status given to mental tests by their application to war work. Lewis Terman, whose interest in human measurement had begun at age ten when his "bumps" were read by an itinerant phrenologist, was elected president of the APA, and in his presidential address (Terman, 1924) argued that mental tests were equal to experiments in scientific value and that, moreover, they were capable of addressing "one of the most important [issues] humanity faces," the relative contributions of nature and nurture to intelligence. Later Terman (1930) predicted the widespread use of tests in schools, in vocational and educational guidance, in industry, politics, and law, and even in "matrimonial clinics," where tests would be given to couples before they decided to wed. The goals of the phrenological Fowlers would be realized in Terman's world. Another leading test psychologist, Charles Spearman, grandiosely described the results from intelligence tests as having supplied the "long missing genuinely scientific foundation for psychology, ... so that it can henceforward take its due place along with the other solidly founded sciences, even physics itself" (quoted by Gould, 1981). Test psychologists were as prone to physics envy as experimental psychologists.

Terman's vision appeared to be well on its way to fulfillment. In his report on the army results, Yerkes spoke of "the steady stream of requests from commercial concerns, educational institutions, and individuals for the use of army methods of psychological examining or for the adaptation of such methods to special needs" (quoted in Gould, 1981). With Terman, Yerkes foresaw a bright future for applied psychology based on mental tests. He (Yerkes, 1923) called psychologists to answer the "need for knowledge of man [which] has increased markedly in our times." Since "man is just as measurable as a bar or a ... machine," psychologists would find that "more aspects of man will become measurable ... more social values appraisable," resulting in psychological "human engineering." In the "not remote future," applied psychology would be as precise and effective as applied physics. The goals of Progressive social control would have been reached with the tools of psychology.

Making America Safe for Democracy: Immigration Control and Eugenics

> We can have almost any kind of a race of human beings we want. We can have a race that is beautiful or ugly, wise or foolish, strong or weak, moral or immoral.
>
> This is not a mere fancy. It is as certain as any social fact. The whole question lies in what we can induce people to *want*. Greece wanted beautiful women and got them. Rome did the same thing. The Dark Ages wanted ugly men and women and got them.... We want ugly women in America and we are getting them in millions. For nearly a generation ... three or four shiploads have been landing at Ellis Island every week. If they are allowed to breed the future "typical American," then the typical future American is going to be as devoid of personal beauty as this vast mass of humanity, the majority of which has never learned to love or understand woman's beauty nor man's nobility of form. And the moment we lose beauty we lose intelligence.... Every high period of intellectual splendor has been characterized by "fair women and brave men." The nobility of any civilization can, to a considerable extent, be measured by the beauty of its women and the physical perfection of its men....
>
> [N]o man can travel over America and not be impressed with the association between a high type of womanly beauty and a high type of art and culture....
>
> As I have said, it is all a question of ideals. We can breed the race forward or backward, up or down.
>
> Albert Edward Wiggam,
> *The Fruit of the Family Tree*, pp. 262–63

Galtonians regarded recent immigrants and blacks as Prospero regarded Caliban in Shakespeare's *The Tempest:* as "a devil, a born devil, on whose nature, nurture can never stick." The army tests demonstrated their irredeemable stupidity, fixed in the genes, which no amount of education could improve. Since education was helpless to improve the intelligence, morality, and beauty of Americans, they concluded, something would have to be done about the stupid, the immoral, and the ugly, were America not to commit "race suicide." Specifically, according to Galtonians, inferior stock would have to be prevented from immigrating to America, and those Americans already here but cursed with stupidity or immorality would have to be prevented from breeding. Galtonians sought, therefore, to restrict immigration to what they regarded as the better sort of people, and to implement negative eugenics, the prevention from reproduction of the worst sort of people. Although they were only occasionally leaders in the politics of immigration and eugenics, psychologists played an important role in support of Galtonian aims.

The worst Galtonians were outright racists. Their leader was Madison Grant, author of *The Passing of the Great Race* (1916). He divided the supposed "races" of Europe into the Nordic, Alpine, and Mediterranean, the first of which, blond and Protestant, were self-reliant heroes more intelligent and resourceful than other races. The Nordics, Grant and his followers said, had founded the United States but were in danger of being swamped by the recent influx of immigrants from other racial groups. Yerkes (1923) himself endorsed Grant's fantastic racism, calling for selective immigration laws designed to keep out the non-Nordics, and so fend off the "menace of race deterioration" in the United States. Yerkes wrote the forward for psychologist Carl Brigham's *A Study of American Intelligence* (1923), which used the army results to show that due to immigration—and, worse, "the most sinister development in the history of the continent, the importation of the negro"—"the decline of American intelligence will be ... rapid ... [unless] public action can be aroused to prevent it. There is no reason why legal steps should not be taken which would insure a continuously progressive upward evolution.... Immigration should not only be restrictive but highly selective" (Gould, 1981, p. 230).

Galtonians pressed for action from Congress to stanch the flow of inferior types of people in the United States. Broughton Brandenburg, president of the National Institute of Immigration, testified, "It is not vainglory when we say that we have bred more than sixty million of the finest people the world has ever seen. Today, there is to surpass us, none. Therefore any race that we admit to our body social is certain to be more or less inferior" (Haller, 1963, p. 147). The most effective propagandist for the Galtonian, racist view of immigrants was A. E. Wiggam, author of *The New Decalogue of Science* and *The Fruit of the Family Tree*. Following Galton, Wiggam preached race improvement as almost a religious duty, and his popular books spread his pseudoscientific gospel to thousands of readers. The passage previously quoted reveals the crass racism and intellectual snobbery pervading the whole Galtonian movement in the United States. Wiggam's cant and humbug derive not from Darwin or Mendel, but from blind prejudice. In a scientist age, bigotry adopts the language of science, since the language of heresy will no longer do.

The Galtonian arguments were fallacious, and Brigham recanted in 1930, acknowledging the worthlessness of the army data. Nevertheless, in 1924, Congress passed an immigration restriction act—altered in the 1970s and again in 1991—that limited the number of future immigrants to a formula based on the number of immigrants from each country in 1890, before the flow of non-"Nordic" immigrants increased. Racism won a great battle in a nation that 148 years before had pledged its sacred honor to the thesis that "all men are created equal." No longer would the poor huddled masses yearning to breathe free—Polish or Italian, Mexican or Vietnamese— find free entry into the land of the free.

But what could be done about the "cacogenic"—genetically undesirable—people already in the United States? The army tests did much to further the cause of eugenics in the United States. British eugenics, as we saw in Chapter 4, was concerned with class rather than race, with positive rather than negative eugenics, and had no real success in obtaining eugenics legislation. American eugenics, however, was obsessed with race, proposed aggressive programs of negative eugenics, and was remarkably successful at getting them written into law.

Eugenics in the United States began just after the Civil War. At John Humphrey Noyes's Oneida Community, one of several socialist-Utopian "heavens on earth" created in the nineteenth century, a program called "stirpiculture" was begun in 1869. Based on Noyes's interpretations of Darwin and Galton, the program involved planned matings between the most "spiritually advanced" members of the community; not surprisingly, Noyes fathered more stirpiculture babies than anyone else (Walters, 1978). In the 1890s, the sexual reformer and feminist Victoria Woodhull preached that the goal of the emancipation of women and sexual education was "the scientific propagation of the human race."

Noyes and Woodhull followed Galton in advancing voluntary positive eugenics as the best application of evolution to human betterment. The turn to negative eugenics and to compulsory control of so-called cacogenic people began with the biologist Charles Davenport. With money from the Carnegie Institution, he established a laboratory at Cold Spring Harbor, New York, in 1904, which, with the addition of his Eugenics Records Office, became the center of American eugenics. Davenport was determined to "annihilate the hideous serpent of hopelessly vicious protoplasm" (quoted in Freeman, 1983), and popularized his views with *Eugenics: The Science of Human Improvement by Better Breeding* (1910) and *Heredity in Relation to Eugenics* (1911). Davenport believed that alcoholism, feeblemindedness, and other traits were based on simple genetic mechanisms, and that they in turn caused ills such as pauperism and prostitution. Prostitutes, for example, were morons who were unable to inhibit the brain center for "innate eroticism," and so turned to a life of sex. Committed to a belief that various ethnic groups were biologically distinct races, Davenport's writings are full of derogatory ethnic stereotypes supposedly rooted in the genes: Italians were given to "crimes of personal violence"; Hebrews were given to "thieving." Davenport claimed that if immigration from southeastern Europe were not halted, future Americans would be "darker … smaller … and more given to crimes of larceny, kidnapping, assault, murder, rape, and sex-immorality." Davenport wanted to place "human matings … upon the same high plane as that of horse breeding."

The leading eugenicist among psychologists was Henry Goddard, superintendent of the Vineland, New Jersey, Training School for Feeble-Minded Boys and Girls. Galton had drawn up family trees of illustrious men and women; with help from Davenport's Eugenics Records Office, Goddard drew up a family tree of stupidity, vice, and crime, *The Kallikak Family: A Study in the Heredity of Feeblemindedness*. Goddard presented the Kallikaks as the "wild men of today," possessing "low intellect but strong physiques." To support his description Goddard included photographs of

Kallikaks doctored to make them look subhuman and sinister (Gould, 1981). Like Davenport, Goddard believed that "the chief determiner of human conduct is a unitary mental process which we call intelligence ... which is inborn ... [and] but little affected by any later influences" (quoted by Gould, 1981). Goddard held that "the idiot is not our greatest problem. He is indeed loathsome," but he is unlikely to reproduce on his own, so "it is the moron type that makes for us our great problem." Precisely because these "high grade defectives" can pass for normal, getting married and having families, Goddard feared their influence on American intelligence. Their numbers would swamp the relatively few offspring of the well-to-do, natural American aristocracy.

Davenport, Goddard, and other Galtonian alarmists proposed various eugenics programs. One was education, aimed to promote positive eugenics. For example, in the 1920s, state fairs featured Fitter Families contests, sometimes in a "human stock" show, while eugenicists set up charts and posters showing the laws of inheritance and their application to humans. Some eugenicists favored contraception as a means of controlling cacogenics, but others feared it would promote licentiousness and be used mainly by intelligent people able to make plans—that is, the sort of people who should breed more, not less. McDougall (1921) wanted to encourage the fit to breed by giving them government subsidies to support their children. Goddard favored the segregation of morons, idiots, and imbeciles in institutions like his own, where they could live out happy lives in a setting suited to their feeblemindedness, barred only from having children.

The solution favored by Davenport and most other eugenicists was compulsory sterilization of the cacogenic. Voluntary methods were likely to fail, they feared, and permanent institutionalization was rather expensive. Sterilization was a one-time procedure that guaranteed nonreproduction of the unfit at small cost to the state. Sterilizations without legal backing had begun before the turn of the century in the Midwest; H. C. Sharp invented the vasectomy and performed hundreds on mental defectives in Indiana. Compulsory sterilization laws had also been introduced before the Great War. The first legislature to consider one was Michigan's, in 1897, but it failed to pass. In 1907, Indiana passed the first sterilization law, but it was overturned by the state supreme court in 1921 and was replaced with an acceptable law in 1923. After the war, state after state passed compulsory sterilization laws, until by 1932, over 12,000 people had been sterilized in thirty states, 7,500 of them in California. The conditions warranting sterilization ranged from feeblemindedness (the most common ground) to epilepsy, rape, "moral degeneracy," prostitution, and being a drunkard or "drug fiend."

The constitutionality of the compulsory sterilization laws was upheld with but one dissenting vote by the U.S. Supreme Court in 1927 in the case of *Buck* v. *Bell,* arising in the state of Virginia, second to California in the number of sterilizations performed. Carrie Buck was a black "feebleminded" girl living in the state colony for the feebleminded, who bore an allegedly feebleminded daughter out of wedlock. She was sterilized by court order, and she then sued the state of Virginia. The majority opinion was written by Oliver Wendell Holmes, a justice noted for his sympathy with Progressivism and his willingness to listen to expert scientific opinion in deciding cases. He wrote: "It is better for all the world, if instead of waiting to execute degenerate offspring for crime, or to let them starve for their imbecility, society can prevent those who are manifestly unfit from continuing their kind.... Three generations of imbeciles are enough" (Landman, 1932).

There were critics of eugenics and especially of human sterilization. Humanists such as G. K. Chesterton denounced eugenics as a pernicious offspring of scientism, reaching toward "the secret and sacred places of personal freedom, where no sane man ever dreamed of seeing it." Catholics condemned eugenics for "a complete return to the life of the beast," seeing people as primarily animals to be improved by animal means, rather than as spiritual beings to be improved by virtue. Leading biologists, including most notably those who synthesized Darwin and Mendel, condemned eugenics as biologically stupid. For example, since 90 percent of all subnormally intelligent children are born to normal parents, sterilizing the subnormal would have little effect on national intelligence or the rate at which subnormal children were born. Moreover, the "feebleminded" could have normal children. Carrie Buck's child, initially called feebleminded, proved later to be normal, even bright. Civil libertarians such as Clarence Darrow denounced eugenic sterilization as a means by which "those in power would inevitably direct human breeding in their own interests." In the social sciences, the attack on eugenics was led by anthropologist Franz Boas and his followers. Boas argued that differences between human groups were not biological but cultural in origin, and he taught the "psychic unity of mankind." His teachings inspired psychologist Otto Klineberg to empirically test eugenicists' claims. He traveled to Europe and tested pure Nordics, Alpines, and Mediterraneans, finding no differences in intelligence. In the United States, he showed that northern blacks did better on intelligence tests by virtue of getting more schooling, not because they were more intelligent. In 1928, Goddard changed his mind, arguing that "feeble-mindedness is *not incurable*" and that they "do not generally need to be segregated in institutions" (Gould, 1981).

By 1930, eugenics was dying. Thomas Garth (1930), reviewing "Race Psychology" for the *Psychological Bulletin,* concluded that the hypothesis that races differ on intelligence and other measures "is no nearer being established than it was five years ago. In fact, many psychologists seem practically ready for another, the hypothesis of racial equality." The leading spokesmen for eugenics among psychologists, Brigham and Goddard, had taken back their racist views. The Third International Conference of Eugenics attracted fewer than one hundred people. But what finally killed eugenics was not criticism but embarrassment. Inspired by the success of eugenics laws in the United States, the Nazis began to carry out eugenic programs in deadly earnest. Beginning in 1933, Hitler instituted compulsory sterilization laws that applied to anyone, institutionalized or not, who carried some allegedly genetic defect. Doctors had to report such people to Hereditary Health Courts, which by 1936 had ordered a quarter-million sterilizations. The Nazis instituted McDougall's plan, subsidizing third and fourth children of the Aryan elite, and providing S.S. mothers, married or not, with spas at which to bear their superior children. In 1936, marriages between Aryans and Jews were forbidden. In 1939, inmates of asylums with certain diseases began to be killed by state order, including all Jews, regardless of their mental condition. At first, the Nazis' victims were shot; later they were taken to "showers" where they were gassed. The final solution to the Nazis' eugenics desires was of course the Holocaust, in which six million Jews perished by order of the state. The Nazis enacted the final, logical conclusion of negative eugenics, and Americans, sickened by the results, simply ceased to preach and enforce negative eugenics. Many of the laws remained on the books, however. It was not until 1981 that Virginia amended its eugenics laws, following the revelation of state hospital records detailing the many instances of court-ordered sterilization. Moreover, eugenics continues as genetic counseling, in which bearers of genetically based diseases, such as sickle-cell anemia, are encouraged not to have children, or to do so under medical supervision, so that amniocentesis can be used to diagnose any undesirable condition, permitting abortion of "unfit" human beings.

PSYCHOLOGY AND EVERYDAY LIFE

Psychologists at Work

Aside from advertising psychology, which affects everyone with a radio or TV, more people have been affected by industrial psychology—the applications of psychology to business management—than by any other branch of applied psychology. As we have seen, the beginnings of industrial psychology lay before the war; but as with the rest of applied psychology, its efflorescence occurred after the war.

The goal of Progressives, in business as in government, was efficiency, and the path to efficiency in every case was thought to be through science. The first exponent of scientific management in business was Frederick Taylor (1856–1915), who developed his ideas around the turn of the century and published them in *Principles of Scientific Management* in 1911. Taylor studied industrial workers at work and analyzed their jobs into mechanical routines that could be performed efficiently by anyone, not just by the masters of a craft. In essence, Taylor turned human workers into robots, mindlessly but efficiently repeating routinized movements. Taylor was not a psychologist, and the shortcoming of his system was that it managed jobs, not people, overlooking the worker's subjective experience of work and the impact of the worker's happiness on productivity. Nevertheless, Taylor's goal was that of scientific psychology: "[U]nder scientific management arbitrary power, arbitrary dictation ceases; and every single subject, large and small, becomes the question for scientific investigation, for reduction to law." And when these laws were understood, they could be applied in the pursuit of greater industrial efficiency.

Gradually, managers recognized that it was not enough to manage jobs; efficiency and profits could be improved only if workers were managed as people with feelings and emotional attachments to their work. After the war, in the wake of psychologists' apparent success with the large-scale personnel problems posed by the army, industrial psychology became increasingly popular in American business. Perhaps the most influential piece of research demonstrating the usefulness of applying psychology to industry—management via feelings—was carried out in the early 1920s by a group of social scientists led by psychologist Elton Mayo at the Hawthorne plant of the Western Electric Company.

The "Hawthorne Effect" is one of the best known of psychological results. It seemed to demonstrate the importance of subjective factors in determining a worker's industrial efficiency. Although the experiments carried out were complex, the results from the relay assembly room are central to defining the Hawthorne Effect. A group of female workers assembling telephone relays were chosen for experimentation. The scientists manipulated nearly every aspect of the work situation, from the schedule of rest pauses to the amount of lighting. They found that virtually everything they did increased productivity, even when a manipulation meant returning to the old way of doing things. The researchers concluded that the increases in productivity were caused not by changes to the workplace, but by the activity of the researchers themselves. They felt that the workers were impressed by the fact that management cared about their welfare, and the workers' improved feelings about their jobs and about the company translated into improved output. Following a Populist line of thought already articulated by John Dewey's prescriptions for education, Mayo (1933, 1945) thought that because of industrialization, workers had become alienated from society, having lost the intimate ties of preindustrial life that bound people together in the insular communities of the past. Unlike the nostalgic Populists, however, Mayo, like Dewey, saw that the agrarian world was irretrievably lost, and he urged business to fill the void by creating communities of workers who found meaning in their work. Various measures were instituted to meet workers' apparent emotional needs; one of the first and most obviously psychological was the creation of "personnel counseling." Workers with complaints about their jobs or about how they were being treated by their employers could go to psychologically trained peer counselors to whom they could relate their frustrations and dissatisfactions. Such programs slowly grew in numbers over the following decades.

Recently, the Hawthorne results have been reanalyzed, resulting in the disconcerting finding that the Hawthorne Effect is a myth (Bramel & Friend, 1981). There is no firm evidence that the workers in the relay room ever felt better about the company as a result of the experiments, and much evidence to suggest that the workers regarded the psychologists as company spies. The improved productivity of the relay assembly team is easily explained as a result of the replacement, in the middle of the experiment, of a disgruntled, not very productive worker by an enthusiastic, productive worker. More broadly, a radical critique of industrial psychology (Baritz, 1960; Bramel & Friend, 1981) argues that industrial psychology produces happy robots, but robots nonetheless. Mayo's personnel counselors were to "help people think in such a way that they would be happier with their jobs"; one counselor reported being trained to "deal with attitudes toward problems, not the problems themselves" (Baritz, 1960). By using psychological manipulation, managers could deflect workers' concerns from objective working conditions, including wages, and turn them instead to preoccupations with feelings, to their adjustment to the work situation. Workers would still carry out the robotic routines laid down by Taylor, but they would do so in a happier frame of mind, prone to interpret discontent as a sign of poor psychological adjustment rather than as a sign that something was really wrong at work.

When Psychology Was King

The psychology of introspection held no fascination for the ordinary American. Margaret Floy Washburn, a student of Titchener's, described in her APA presidential address (1922) the reaction of an intelligent janitor to her psychological laboratory: "This is queer place. It somehow gives you the impression that the thing can't be done." By the 1920s, however, psychology had gone behavioral and was proving—in industry, in schools and courts, and in war—that psychology could be done. Contemporary observers remarked on the tremendous popularity of psychology with the public. The first historian of the 1920s, Frederick Lewis Allen (1931, p. 165), wrote: "Of all the sciences it was the youngest and least scientific which most captivated the general public and had the most disintegrating effect upon religious faith. Psychology was king.... [O]ne had only to read the newspapers to be told with complete assurance that psychology held the key to the problems of waywardness, divorce, and crime." Grace Adams, another student of Titchener's, who had abandoned psychology for journalism and who had become quite critical of psychology, called the period from 1919 to 1929 the "Period of the Psyche." Humorist Stephan Leacock wrote in 1923 of how "a great wave of mind culture has swept over the community."

Psychology achieved its special place in public attention because of the intersection of the revolution in morals led by Flaming Youth (Ostrander, 1968) with the final triumph of scientism. "The word science," Allen said, "had become a shibboleth. To preface a statement with 'Science teaches us' was enough to silence argument." Religion seemed on the verge of destruction. Liberal theologian Harry Emerson Fosdick wrote: "Men of faith might claim for their positions ancient tradition, practical usefulness, and spiritual desirability, but one query could prick all such bubbles: Is it scientific?" (Allen, 1931). The faithful responded in two ways: Modernists such as Fosdick strove to reconcile science with the Bible; fundamentalists (the word was coined by a Baptist editor in July 1920) strove to subordinate science, especially Darwinism, to the Bible. Many other people, of course, simply lost all faith. Watson, for example, had been raised as a strict Baptist in Greenville, South Carolina, and had (like 71 percent of early behaviorists [Birnbaum, 1964]) chosen the ministry as his vocation, only to give it up on his mother's death. In graduate school he had a nervous breakdown and abandoned religion completely.

Science undermined religion; scientism bid to replace it. The Flaming Youth of the 1920s were the first generation of Americans to be raised in the urban, industrial, everywhere communities of twentieth-century life. Cut off from the traditional religious values of the vanishing island communities, they turned to modern science for instruction in morals and rules of behavior. Postwar psychology, no longer preoccupied with socially sterile introspection, was the obvious science to which to turn for guidance concerning living one's life and getting ahead in business and politics.

Popular psychology simultaneously accomplished two apparently contradictory things. It provided people with a sense of liberation from the outdated religious morality of the past; this use was stressed by Flaming Youth and their sympathizers yearning for the sexual freedom of a tropical isle. At the same time, it provided new, putatively scientific techniques for social control; this use was stressed by Progressives. As one popularizer, Abram Lipsky, wrote in *Man the Puppet: The Art of Controlling Minds:* "We are at last on the track of psychological laws for controlling the minds of our fellow men" (Burnham, 1968). Ultimately, the liberating and controlling effects of psychology were not at odds. While Flaming Youth liberated themselves from old values, they chose new, psychological ones, and psychological techniques of control were used to enforce them.

The first wave of popular psychology, and what the general public thought of as the "new psychology" (Burnham, 1968), was Freudianism, used to dissolve Victorian morals. Under the microscope of psychoanalysis traditional morals were found to be neurosis-breeding repressions of healthy biological needs, primarily sex. Youth concluded (falsely) from psychoanalytic doctrine that "The first requirement for mental health is an uninhibited sex life. As Oscar Wilde wisely counseled, 'Never resist temptation!' " (Graves & Hodge, 1940). Lady Betty Balfour, addressing the Conference of the British Educational Association in 1921, expressed the popular view of proper Freudian child rearing: She was "not sure that the moral attitude was not responsible for all the crime in the world." Children, vulgar Freudians believed, should be reared with few inhibitions, so they might grow up unrepressed, happy, and carefree, like Mead's notional Samoans.

The second wave of popular psychology in the 1920s was behaviorism, which the general public sometimes confused with psychoanalysis. Robert Graves and Alan Hodge, literate observers of the English scene, nevertheless described psychoanalysts as viewing people as "behaviouristic animals." The leading popularizer of behaviorism was Watson himself. He had turned to psychoanalysis in the wake of his nervous breakdown and, while impressed with Freud's biological emphasis, came to regard analytic psychology as "a substitution of demonology for science." The "unconscious" of psychoanalysis was a fiction, Watson held, representing no more than the fact that we do not verbalize all the influences on our behavior. If we do not talk about stimuli, we are not aware of them and so call them unconscious, according to Freudian jargon, but there is no mysterious inner realm of mind whence come hidden impulses (Watson, 1926c). According to Watson, there was "too little science—real science—in Freud's psychology" for it to be useful or enduring, and he offered behaviorism as the new claimant for popular attention (Watson, 1926a).

Watson described behaviorism as representing "a real renaissance in psychology," overthrowing introspective psychology and substituting science in its place. Watson consistently linked introspective psychology to religion and railed against both. Behaviorists "threw out the concepts of mind and of consciousness, calling them carryovers from the church dogma of the Middle Ages.... Consciousness [is] just a masquerade for the soul" (Watson, 1926a). "Churchmen—all medicine men in fact—have kept the public under control" by making the public believe in unobserved mysteries such as the soul; science, says Watson the philosopher, is "blasting" through the "solid wall of religious protection" (1926b). Having disposed of the traditional past, both social and psychological, Watson offered strong opinions and advice on the issues of the day.

Watson attacked eugenics. Belief in human instincts, he wrote, has been "strengthened in the popular view by the propaganda of the eugenists," whose programs for selective breeding are "more dangerous than Bolshevism." Watson maintained that there are no inferior races. Taking note of American racism, Watson said that Negroes had not been allowed to develop properly, so that even if a Negro were given a million dollars a year and sent to Harvard, white society would be able to make him feel inferior anyway (1927b). A human being, Watson told readers of *Harper's*, is "a lowly piece of protoplasm, ready to be shaped ... crying to be whipped into shape" (1927b) and promised that the behaviorist "can build any man, starting at birth, into any kind of social or asocial being upon order" (1926a).

Since there were no human instincts, and human beings could be built to order, Watson naturally had much advice to give to parents eager for scientific child-rearing techniques. Watson took a strong line, denying any influence of heredity on personality and maintaining that "the home is responsible for what the child becomes" (1926a). Homemaking, including child rearing and sexual technique, should become a profession for which girls ought to be trained. Their training would brook no nonsense about loving children, cuddling them, or putting up with their infantile demands. Watson viewed the traditional family (and the new affectionate family of other family reformers) with scorn. According to Watson, a mother lavishes affection on children out of a misplaced "sex-seeking response." Her own sexuality is "starved," so she turns to cuddling and kissing her child; hence the need for training in sex.

Watson's (1928b, pp. 81–87) advice on how to raise children is brutally behavioristic:

> There is a sensible way of treating children. Treat them as though they were young adults. Dress them, bathe them with care and circumspection. Let your behavior always be objective and kindly firm. Never hug and kiss them, never let them sit in your lap. If you must, kiss them once on the forehead when they say good night. Shake hands with them in the morning.... Try it out.... You will be utterly ashamed of the mawkish, sentimental way you have been handling it....
>
> Nest habits, which come from coddling, are really pernicious evils. The boys or girls who have nest habits deeply imbedded suffer torture when they have to leave home to go into business, to enter school, to get married.... Inability to break nest habits is probably our most prolific source of divorce and marital disagreements....
>
> In conclusion won't you then remember when you are tempted to pet your child that mother love is a dangerous instrument? An instrument which may inflict a never healing wound, a wound which may make infancy unhappy, adolescence a nightmare, an instrument which may wreck your adult son or daughter's vocational future and their chances for marital happiness.

Watson's book (written with the assistance of Rosalie Rayner Watson, his second wife) *Psychological Care of Infant and Child,* from which this advice comes, sold quite well. Even Carl Rogers, founder of client-centered therapy and later a leader of humanistic psychology, tried to raise his first child "by the book of Watson." Occasionally, Watson so despaired of the ability of a mother to raise a happy child—he dedicated the child-care book to the first mother to do so—that he advocated taking children away from their parents to be raised by professionals in a creche (Harris and Morawski, 1979), the solution proposed by Skinner in his utopian novel *Walden II.*

"The behaviorist, then," wrote Watson (1928a), "has given society ... a new weapon for controlling the individual.... If it is demanded by society that a given line of conduct is desirable, the psychologist should be able with some certainty to arrange the situation or factors which will lead the individual most quickly and with the least expenditure of effort to perform that task." In his second career as an advertising executive, Watson had an opportunity to demonstrate the power of behavioral social control by manipulating consumers. Expelled from academia for his affair with and subsequent marriage to Rosalie Rayner, Watson was hired by the J. Walter Thompson advertising agency, which was looking for the scientific principles that would control the minds of men and women.

Central to Watson's schemes for social control was using the word as a whip to the human emotions. In evangelical preaching, words were used as whips to stir up hearers into an emotional conversion experience that would move them to Christ. To give a famous Puritan example, Jonathan Edwards's sermon, "Sinners in the Hands of an Angry God," which described people as suspended over hellfire like a spider on a single, silken thread, was constructed to appeal to his parishioners' hearts, not to their intellects. Watson was named after, and taught the views of, John Albert Broadus, a leading Baptist evangelist. Broadus taught that reason was not a secure base for morals, so that preaching had to exploit fear and anger as the emotional bases of the habits of good Christian living, and he praised Edwards's sermon. In "The Heart or the Intellect," Watson (1928a) described the need to condition the emotions in order to effect social control. The head, Watson said, cannot control the guts, making imperative the use of classical conditioning techniques to build in the habits demanded by modern society.

As evangelists had stressed fear in the training of children, so Watson's child-rearing advice always ran to the punitive. He said that people don't use their talents to the full because they have not been pushed hard enough: "The stuff [talent] is there crying out to be whipped into shape. It is a cry for getting some kind of shock or punishment ... which will force us to develop to the limits of our capabilities" (Watson, 1927b). He repeatedly held up Little Albert B. (Albert Broadus?) (Creelan, 1974) as a model of proper emotional training. In adult humans, language could be used as Edwards and Broadus used it, to manipulate emotions in order to bring about some desired behavior. For example, in setting up an advertising campaign for baby powder, Watson used statements by medical experts to make mothers feel anxious about their infant's health and uncertain about their own competence to look after their child's hygiene. Feelings of anxiety and insecurity would then make mothers more likely to purchase a product endorsed by experts. At the same time, although Watson may not have meant to teach this message, his advertising made parents feel more dependent on experts to teach them how to raise their children. In this way, advertising helped to reinforce social scientists' message that society needed professional social scientists to solve its problems.

It is not surprising, then, that Progressives embraced Watson's behaviorism. In the New York *Herald Tribune,* Stuart Chase, who later coined the phrase "New Deal," exclaimed that Watson's *Behaviorism* was perhaps "the most important book ever written. One stands for an instant blinded with a great hope" (quoted by Birnbaum, 1955). As Watson (1928a) had said, behaviorism gave society "a new weapon for controlling the individual," and Progressives were eager to wield it in pursuit of their dreams of social control. Watson, they thought, had correctly described the laws of conditioning governing the masses of humankind. Progressives, however, were pleased to place themselves among the "very few" individuals endowed with "creative intelligence," exempt from the laws of conditioning, and able to use them as tools to escape "the voice of the herd" and to manage the herd toward Progressive ends. The "great hope" of Progressivism was always that an elite of scientific managers might be empowered to run society, and behaviorism seemed to provide exactly the techniques Progressives needed to control the behavior, if not the minds, of men. Watson himself, it should be said, did not fall in with the Progressives' schemes. He insisted that the laws of conditioning applied to everyone, whether or not their ancestors had come over on the *Mayflower,* and that anyone could be trained to use behavioral techniques for self-control or the control of others (Birnbaum, 1964).

While Watson's popularized behaviorism was welcomed by many, others found it disturbing or shallow. Joseph Jastrow (1929) felt that psychology was degraded by

Watson's popularization of himself in magazines and newspapers. What was valuable in behaviorism—the study of behavior—"will survive the 'strange interlude' of ... behaviorism" and Watson's public antics. Grace Adams ridiculed Watson's behaviorism for sharing "most of the appealing points of psychoanalysis with few of its tedious difficulties," the resulting shallow system being "a cheering doctrine, surely—direct, objective, and completely American." Warner Fite (1918), already depressed by the experimental psychology of 1912, regarded behaviorism as the logical end product of scientism, or, as he put it, in "behavioristic psychology we behold the perfected beauty of the scientific prepossession." According to behaviorists, "Mind, in the sense of an inner, personal, spiritual experience, must be laid away, along with the immortal soul, among the discarded superstitions of an unscientific past.... According to them, your behavior is simply and solely what other persons are able to observe; and how you look, not to yourself, but to the world—that is all there is of *you*" (pp. 802–03). Lumping together the effects of psychoanalysis and behaviorism, Fite foresaw the psychological society of the later twentieth century: "Doubtless the time is coming, before we are through with the [scientific] prepossession, when all domestic and social intercourse will be made luminous and transparent by the presence of expert psychologists. In those fair days social intercourse will be untroubled by falsehood or insincerity, or even by genial exaggeration" (p. 803).

By 1930, the fad for psychology had run its course. After the crash of 1929, the popular press had more pressing economic matters to consider, and the volume of pieces written on psychology diminished noticeably. Grace Adams hoped that its influence was finished, but in fact psychology was only in retrenchment (Sokal, 1983). Psychology continued to grow and expand its areas of application throughout the 1930s, albeit at a slower rate than in the glory years after World War I. Its reemergence on the popular stage awaited another cue of war.

Flaming Youth and the Reconstruction of the Family

> I learned to my astonishment that I had been involved in a momentous debauch; the campus reeked of a scandal so sulphurous it hung over our beanies for the rest of the academic year. In blazing scareheads the Hearst Boston *American* tore the veil from the excesses tolerated at Brown University dances. At these hops, it thundered, were displayed a depravity and libertinism that would have sickened Petronius, made Messalina hang her head in shame. It portrayed girls educated at the best finishing schools, crazed with alcohol and inflamed by ragtime, oscillating cheek to cheek with young ne'er-do-wells in raccoon coats and derbies. Keyed up by savage jungle rhythms, the *abandonnes* would then reel out to roadsters parked on Waterman Street, where frat pins were traded for kisses under cover of darkness.... [T]he writer put all his metaphors into one basket and called upon outraged society to apply the brakes, hold its horses, and retrieve errant youth from under the wheels of the juggernaut.
> S. J. Perelman
> "Cloudland Revisited: Sodom in the Suburbs," pp. 239–40

Youth was in revolt during the 1920s—it was the Jazz Age and the day of the flapper—and, of course the older generation, led by Hearst leader writers, were aghast. Youth seemed to embody the chaos of modernism described by William Butler Yeats in the poem "Second Coming." Confused and bewildered, the parents of the 1920s *Flaming Youth*—the title of a best-selling novel pandering to parents' fears, and object of Perelman's satiric pen—tried to understand what had gone wrong with their children; and, more importantly, they tried to learn what to do about it. The apparent crisis of the family and its youth created an opportunity for social scientists, including psychologists, to extend the realm of their concern, and of scientific social control, from the public arena of politics and business into the intimate circle of the family.

As social scientists saw it, families as traditionally conceived and organized were out-of-date in the modern world. Families had been economic units, in which father, mother, and child had distinct and productive roles to play. In the industrialized world, however, work was leaving the home, so that individuals, not families, were the economic units. Children should not be permitted to work, since they needed to be in school learning the values and habits of urbanized American society. Women were "following their work out of the home" to factories and businesses. The labor of men was likewise apart from the home, being just an eight-hour job, not a way of life. The family was no longer a socially functional unit. Progressive Deweyites considered the family selfish because a parent's concern was for his or her own child, whereas in the modern, urban world it was necessary to be equally concerned for all children. The crisis of Flaming Youth was but a symptom, social scientists said, of a deeper social crisis.

The family would have to be remade, then, by professional social scientists bringing their expertise to bear on problems of family adjustment. Raising children could no longer be thought of as something anyone could do without help. The state, through professional social scientists, was to have the leading role in child rearing. As one reformer wrote: "The state is but the coordinated parentage of childhood ... compel[ling] co-partnership, co-operation, corporate life and conscience" (Fass, 1977). In a phrase, motherhood must become "mothercraft," a profession requiring education and training. Making a profession of raising children advanced the cause of professional social science, providing an ideology that justified intervening in family life with "expert" advice not possessed by ordinary people.

Since the traditional family's role as economic unit no longer existed, social scientists had to provide the new family with a new function: "The distinguishing feature of the new family will be affection. The new family will be more difficult, maintaining higher standards that test character more severely, but will offer richer fruit for the satisfying of human needs." "It does not seem probable that the family will recover the functions it has lost. But even if the family doesn't produce thread and cloth and soap and medicine and food, it can still produce happiness" (Fass, 1977). In the view of reformers, the function of the family was to produce emotional adjustment to modern life. The modern parent, then, was to become something of a psychotherapist, monitoring children's emotional states and intervening when necessary to adjust their states of mind. The ideas of the parent as professional and the family as the producer of emotional happiness were mutually reinforcing. Parents would need, at the very least, training in their new therapeutic roles, and they would probably also need a cadre of experts to call on for advice and to fall back on when acute difficulties arose. Applied psychologists would naturally find a fertile field for professional application of psychology to child rearing, child guidance, and child psychotherapy.

Meanwhile, youth were constructing a new set of values and a new social control system for themselves. As parents lost control of their children, youth found in the culture of their peers a new center for life apart from the family. Youth set their own values, their own style, their own goals. Central to the youth culture of the 1920s was having a "good personality," learning to be "well-rounded," and fitting in with other youth. Youth valued self-expression and sociability, attending to personal satisfaction instead of the production of objective accomplishments. Groups such as fraternities and sororities enforced conformity to the new rules of personality with therapeutic tricks of their own. Deviant youth were forced to participate in "truth sessions" in which their "objectionable traits" and weaknesses were identified and analyzed. Then the offender would make amends, since "the fraternity's group consciousness is the strongest thing. One doing wrong not only disgraces oneself but his fraternity group" (Fass, 1977).

Parents and youth, then, were not so far apart, despite the ravings of Hearst's leader writers. Both were being remade by the "triumph of the therapeutic," the modern tendency to define life in psychological terms. Parents were learning that their function was therapeutic, producing emotionally well-adjusted children. The youth culture similarly valued emotional adjustment and tried to achieve it through therapeutic techniques of its own. The central values of the twentieth century were formed during the 1920s: being true to one's "real" self, expressing one's "deepest" feelings, "sharing" one's personality with a larger group.

Just as the new family and the youth culture were struggling toward a redefinition of life as centered on self, not accomplishment, an anthropologist and psychologist, Margaret Mead, came back from the South Seas bearing witness to an idyllic society in which people had little work to do and led peaceful lives of perfect adjustment, harmony, and sexual fulfillment. As in the Enlightenment, when philosophes had felt themselves emerging from centuries of religious repression, there was a longing for the free and easy life—especially the sexual life—apparently to be found in Tahiti. Committed to environmentalism, the philosophers had thought that Tahitian paradise could be constructed in Europe through social engineering. As twentieth-century intellectuals reacted against Victorian sexual morality and the excesses of eugenics, they felt themselves on the verge of a "new Enlightenment" or, as Watson put it, of a "social Renaissance, a preparation for a change in mores" (Freeman, 1983). So they were as fascinated by Margaret Mead's (1928) *Coming of Age in Samoa* as eighteenth-century readers had been by the first travelers' tales of the Pacific Islands. One reviewer of Mead's book wrote, "Somewhere in each of us, hidden among our more obscure desires and our impulses of escape, is a palm fringed South Seas island … a langorous atmosphere promising freedom and irresponsibility.… Thither we run to find love which is free, easy and satisfying" (Quoted by Freeman, 1983, p. 97).

Margaret Mead was a young psychologist and anthropologist who had studied under the founder of modern American anthropology, Franz Boas, whose opposition to eugenics we have already noted. Boas and his followers were convinced, with John Dewey, that human nature was, in Dewey's words, a "formless void of impulses" shaped by society into a personality. They agreed with Dewey that mind was a social construction owing nothing to nature and everything to culture. Similarly, culture was just "personality writ large," according to Ruth Benedict, another student of Boas: Personality, being entirely shaped by culture, imaged culture in the historical individual, and culture, the molder of personality, was the personality of a society. If eugenicists went to one extreme, denying nurture any influence over nature, Boasians went to the other, regarding culture as "some kind of mechanical press into which most individuals were poured to be molded." Agreeing with Watson at his most extreme, Mead wrote how the "almost unbelievably malleable" raw material of human nature was "moulded into shape by culture."

Mead traveled to American Samoa, conducted rather sloppy fieldwork, and returned with a description of a society that at once seemed to support the Deweyite and Boasian conception of an infinitely plastic human nature, and to offer the ideal form of the happy society, in which people experienced "perfect adjustment" to their surroundings, their society, and each other. Mead limned a society that knew no Flaming Youth in stressful revolt against their parents, a society with no aggression, no war, no hostility, no deep attachment between parent and child, husband and wife, no competition, a society in which parents were ashamed of the outstanding child, and proud of the slowest, who set the pace for the development of every other child. Most alluring was the idea that the Samoans, far from regarding sex as a sin, thought sexual relations "the pastime *par excellence*," a "fine art," making "sex [into]-play, permissible in all hetero- and homosexual expression, with any sort of variation as an artistic addition." The Samoan avoidance of strong feelings and deep attachments extended to love: "Love between the sexes is a light and pleasant dance.... Samoans condone light love-affairs, but repudiate acts of passionate choice, and have no real place for anyone who would permanently continue ... to prefer one woman or one man" (Freeman, 1983, p. 91). Samoans regarded jealousy as a sin and did not regard adultery as very serious, Mead reported. Before marriage, Mead said, adolescents experienced a free and easy promiscuity, each boy and girl engaging in many light sexual dalliances of no deep moment. There were no Flaming Youth because what Flaming Youth wanted, condemned by fuddy-duddy Hearst writers, was approved, even encouraged, by Samoan society. Samoans also lived the superficial lives of conformity to the group and average well-roundedness that Flaming Youth defined as its norm. Putting it in scientistic terms, one commentator on Mead's book remarked on "the innocent, strangely impersonal, naively mechanistic-behavioristic sexing of the light-hearted youths of far-off Samoa."

Mead's Samoans promised to resolve the nature–nurture disputes of the 1920s against the eugenicists and in favor of the Boasians. Mead's work also lifted up a vision of a new Utopia of sexual freedom and perfect happiness, a vision that outraged Hearst's Boston *American* but became the foundation for the *hedonistic* philosophy of the 1960s. Finally, it gave psychologists the central role in constructing the new society. Commenting upon the work of Boas and his students, Bertrand Russell, who had earlier endorsed Watson's behaviorism, asserted that "the scientific psychologist, if allowed a free run with children" could "manipulate human nature" as freely as physical scientists manipulated nature. Psychologists and other social scientists could ask, even dream, no more than this: to be the architects of a new Western civilization, well adjusted and harmonious, emotionally open and sexually liberated, warm and supporting and not in neurotic pursuit of excellence. Mead's Samoa, a culture entirely outside the traditions of the West, became the social scientists' Holy Grail, a blueprint for them to follow in constructing the New Man of Deweyite, Progressive idealism.

The reality behind the Flaming Youth and Samoan society was different, however, from both the Hearst writer's ravings and Mead's more prosaic depictions. Perelman's "orgy" was in fact "decorous to the point of torpor": "I spent the evening buffeting about the stag line, prayerfully beseeching the underclassmen I knew for permission to cut in on their women ... [frequently] retiring to a cloakroom with several other blades and choking down a minute quantity of gin, warmed to body heat, from a pocket flask. Altogether, it was a strikingly commonplace experience, and I got to bed without contusions" (p. 239). Derek Freeman (1983) has shown that Samoa, far from being the sexual paradise described by Mead, was obsessed with virginity, and rife with rape, aggression, competition, and deep human feelings.

NOTE: The Bibliography for this chapter is incorporated in Chapter 9.

REFERENCES

Allen, F. L. (1931). *Only yesterday: An informal history of the 1920s.* New York: Harper & Row.

Baritz, L. J. (1960). *The servants of power: A history of the use of social science in American industry.* Middletown, CT: Wesleyan University Press.

Beers, C. (1968/1953). *A mind that found itself.* New York: Doubleday.

Birnbaum, L. T. (1955). Behaviorism in the 1920s. *American Quarterly, 7,* 15–30.

Birnbaum L. T. (1964). Behaviorism: John Broadus Watson and American social thought 1913–1933. Unpublished doctoral dissertation, University of California, Berkeley.

Brigham, C. (1923). *A study of American intelligence.* Princeton, NJ: Princeton University Press.

Block, N. J. & Dworkin, G. (Eds.), (1976). *The I.Q. controversy: Critical readings.* New York: Pantheon.

Bramel, D. & Friend, R. (1981). Hawthorne, the myth of the docile worker, and class bias in American psychology. *American Psychologist, 36,* 867–878.

Buckley, K. W. (1982). The selling of a psychologist: John Broadus Watson and the application of behavioral techniques to advertising. *Journal of the History of the Behavioral Sciences, 18,* 207–221.

Burnham, J. C. (1968). The new psychology: From narcissism to social control. In J. Braeman, R. H. Bremner, & D. Brody (Eds.), *Change and continuity in twentieth-century America: The 1920's.* Columbus, OH: Ohio State University Press.

Creelan, P. G. (1974). Watsonian behaviorism and the Calvinist conscience. *Journal of the History of the Behavioral Sciences, 10,* 95–118.

Dewey, J. (1917). The need for social psychology. *Psychological Review, 24,* 266–277.

Fass, P. (1977). *The damned and the beautiful: American youth in the 1920's.* Oxford: Oxford University Press.

Fite, W. (1918). The human soul and the scientific prepossession. *Atlantic Monthly, 122,* 796–804.

Freeman, D. (1983). *Margaret Mead and Samoa: The making and unmaking of an anthropological myth.* Cambridge, MA: Harvard University Press.

Garth, T. R. (1930). A review of race psychology. *Psychological Bulletin, 27,* 329–356.

Gould, S. J. (1981). *The mismeasure of man.* New York: W. W. Norton.

Graves, R. and Hodge, A. (1940). *The long week-end: A social history of Britain 1918–1939.* New York: W. W. Norton.

Haller, M. (1963). *Eugenics: Hereditarian attitudes in American thought.* New Brunswick, NJ: Rutgers University Press.

Harris, B. & Morawski, J. (1979). *John B. Watson's predictions for 1979.* Paper presented at the 50th annual meeting of the Eastern Psychological Association, Philadelphia, April 1979.

Jastrow, J. (1929). Review of J. B. Watson, Ways of behaviorism, psychological care of infant and child, battle of behaviorism. *Science, 69* (April 26), 455–457.

Landman, J. H. (1932). *Human sterilization: The history of the sexual sterilization movement.* New York: Macmillan.

Mayo, E. (1933). *The human problems of an industrial civilization.* Cambridge, MA: Harvard University Press.

Mayo, E. (1945). *The social problems of an industrial civilization.* Cambridge, MA: Harvard Graduate School of Business Administration.

McDougall, W. (1921). *Is America safe for democracy?* New York: Scribner's. Reprint ed. New York: Arno Press, 1977.

Mead, M. (1928). *Coming of age in Samoa.* New York: Morrow.

Napoli, D. S. (1981). *Architects of adjustment: The history of the psychological profession in the United States.* Port Washington, NY: Kennikat Press.

Ostrander, G. M. (1968). The revolution in morals. In J. Bracman, R. H. Bremner, & D. Brody (Eds.), *Change and continuity in twentieth-century America: The 1920s.* Columbus, OH: Ohio State University Press.

Perelman, S. J. (1958). Sodom in the suburbs. In S. J. Perelman, *The most of S. J. Perelman.* New York: Simon & Schuster.

Rieff, P. (1966). *The triumph of the therapeutic.* New York: Harper & Row.

Sokal, M. M. (1983). James McKeen Cattell and American psychology in the 1920s. In Josef Brozek (Ed.), *Explorations in the history of psychology in the United States.* Lewisburg, PA: Bucknell University Press.

Taylor, F. (1911). *Principles of scientific management.* New York: Harper Brothers.

Terman, L. M. (1924). The mental test as a psychological method. *Psychological Review, 31,* 93–117.

Terman, L. M. (1930). Lewis M. Terman. In C. Murchison (Ed.), *A history of psychology in autobiography,* Vol. 2. Worcester, MA: Clark University Press.

Thomas, J. L. (1977). Nationalizing the Republic. In Bailyn, B., Davis, D., Donald, D., Thomas, J., Wieber, R., & Wood, W. S. *The Great Republic.* Boston: Little, Brown & Co.

Thorndike, E. L. (1920). Intelligence and its uses. *Harper's Magazine, 140,* 227–235.

von Mayrhauser, R. T. (1985). *Walking out at the Walton: Psychological disunity and the origins of group testing in early World War I.* Paper presented at the annual meeting of Cheiron, the Society for the History of the Behavioral Sciences, Philadelphia, June 14.

Walters, R. G. (1978). *American Reformers 1815–1860.* New York: Hill and Wang.

Washburn, M. F. (1922). Introspection as an objective method. *Psychological Review, 29,* 89–112.

Watson, J. B. (1926a). What is behaviorism? *Harper's Magazine, 152,* 723–729.

Watson, J. B. (1926b). How we think: A behaviorist's view. *Harper's Magazine, 153,* 40–45.

Watson, J. B. (1926c). Memory as the behaviorist sees it. *Harper's Magazine, 153,* 244–250.

Watson, J. B. (1927a). The myth of the unconscious. *Harper's Magazine, 155,* 502–508.

Watson, J. B. (1927b). The behaviorist looks at the instincts. *Harper's Magazine, 155,* 228–235.

Watson, J. B. (1928a). The heart or the intellect. *Harper's Magazine, 156,* 345–352.

Watson, J. B. (1928b). *Psychological care of infant and child.* New York: W. W. Norton.

Wiggam, A. E. (1924). *The fruit of the family tree.* Indianapolis, IN: Bobbs-Merrill.

Yerkes, R. M. (1918). Psychology in relation to the war. *Psychological Review, 25,* 85–115.

Yerkes, R. M. (1923). Testing the human mind. *Atlantic Monthly, 131,* 358–370.

CHAPTER 9

Reshaping Psychology:
Psychologists in Professional Controversy

TENSION BETWEEN ACADEMIC AND APPLIED PSYCHOLOGY
- **Divorce: The Clinicians Walk Out**
- **Reconciliation in the Crucible of World War II**
- **Redefining Clinical Psychology**

OPTIMISM IN THE AFTERMATH OF WAR
- **Contending for Respectability and Money at the Dawn of Big Science**
- **Psychologists Look Ahead to the Psychological Society**
- **Values and Adjustment**

TENSION BETWEEN ACADEMIC AND APPLIED PSYCHOLOGY

Divorce: The Clinicians Walk Out

After the war, psychologists in increasing numbers began practicing applied psychology. At the time it was called, inappropriately, "clinical" psychology, because of its roots in Witmer's psychological "clinic." In fact, the "clinical" psychology of these years bore little resemblance to today's clinical psychology. The term has come to mean primarily the practice of psychotherapy by psychologists, but before World War II, "clinical" psychology had mostly to do with giving tests to various populations: children, soldiers, workers, mental patients, and occasional individual clients.

In any event, "clinical" psychologists rarely performed research and were often employed outside universities, working for companies or on their own as psychological consultants. The old guard of scientific psychologists who had founded the APA, for all their apparent commitment to useful psychology, were made uncomfortable by the increasing numbers of "clinical" psychologists. The APA, after all, had been founded to "advance psychology as a science," and it was not at all clear that clinicians were advancing scientific psychology, because they did no research. Moreover, clinicians were predominantly women, and male psychologists had a hard time taking women seriously as anything more than psychological dilettantes.

During the 1920s and 1930s, the APA vacillated in its treatment of applied psychologists. Entry to the association had for some time depended on having published articles in scientific journals; then a class of associate members was created for the nonscientists, who enjoyed only limited participation in the association. These "clinical" psychologists, whose numbers rapidly swelled, naturally resented their second-class status. During the same period, the APA recognized that, as the official organization of psychologists, it bore some responsibility for assuring the competence of practicing psychologists, being deeply concerned about charlatans and frauds passing themselves off as genuine psychologists and tarnishing the honor of the science in the eyes of the public. So for a time the APA issued expensive certificates, badges of authenticity, to applied—or, as they were officially called, "consulting"—psychologists. The experiment was short-lived, however. Few psychologists bothered to apply for the certificates. The academicians of the APA also were unwilling to exert themselves to attain the proper ends of professionalization by enforcing standards and taking legal action against psychological frauds.

Gradually, applied psychologists got fed up with the APA. They realized that their interest, the creation of a socially accepted and defined practice of psychology on a par with physicians, lawyers, engineers, and other professional practitioners of a craft, could not be realized in an association devoted exclusively to psychology as an academically based science. As early as 1917, applied psychologists tried to form their own association, but the enterprise was controversial and died when the APA agreed to the creation of a clinical section within the association. In 1930, a group of applied psychologists in New York formed a national organization, the Association of Consulting Psychologists (ACP). The ACP pressed states (beginning with New York) to establish legal standards for the definition of "psychologist," wrote a set of ethical guidelines for the practice of psychology, and began its own journal, the *Journal of Consulting Psychology,* in 1937. Despite pleas by professional psychologists for the APA to get involved in defining and setting standards for practitioners of the psychological craft (for example, Poffenberger, 1936), the association continued to fail them. So in 1938, the unhappy psychologists of the clinical section of the APA left the parent organization and joined with the ACP to create the American Association for Applied Psychology (AAAP).

During the years between the world wars, applied psychologists groped for an identity distinct from traditional, scientific psychology. The interests of academic and professional psychologists were different and to some extent incompatible—the advancement of research versus the advancement of the legal and social status of clinicians. Academic psychologists feared—and still fear—the growing numbers of applied psychologists, worrying that they might lose control of the association they founded. Yet the applied psychologists remained inextricably linked to academic psychology. They received their training in university departments of psychology and traded on the claim of psychology to be a scientific discipline. So, while applied psychologists established a professional identity by founding the AAAP, the absolute divorce of scientific and applied psychology would, this time, be short-lived.

Reconciliation in the Crucible of World War II

As it had just twenty-four years earlier, world war would profoundly affect psychology. The Great War to End All Wars had transformed a tiny, obscure academic discipline into an ambitious, visible profession. World War II provided an even greater opportunity for psychologists to act together in pursuit of social good and their own professional interests. Along the way the war caused psychology to grow at a faster rate than ever, to reunify into a single academic-applied profession, and to invent a new professional role—the psychotherapist—which quickly threatened to become the role that defined American psychologists. After the war ended, psychology fought unsuccessfully to be included among the sciences supported by federal research money. As a profession, however, psychology was more successful. The government found itself in need of mental health professionals and embarked on a program to recruit and train a new psychological profession, requiring that psychology define itself anew and set standards for its practitioners.

In the 1930s, as we have seen, psychology was racked by deep divisions. Professional psychologists had formed their own organization, the American Association of Applied Psychologists (AAAP), breaking with the APA in 1938. Another dissident group was the Society for the Psychological Study of Social Issues (SPSSI), formed by left-wing psychologists in 1936. Although affiliated with the APA, SPSSI psychologists aimed, in contrast to the traditional academicians of the APA, to use psychology to advance their political views. For example, SPSSI psychologists marched in New York's May Day parade carrying banners that read "Adjustment comes with jobs" (it was the depth of the Depression) and "Fascism is the world's worst behavior problem!" (Napoli, 1981). The older APA, devoted as it was to pure research and scholarly detachment, had a hard time finding a place for either the AAAP or SPSSI.

However, it seemed to many psychologists, such as Robert Yerkes and Ernest Hilgard, that the institutional divisions within psychology could and should be overcome. After all, the professionals of the AAAP received their educations in academic departments of psychology, and it was the scientific principles of psychology that SPSSI wished to apply to pressing social problems. So, in the years following the break between the AAAP and the APA, informal negotiations were carried on with the aim of reunifying psychologists under a single banner.

The process was greatly accelerated by the coming of World War II. In 1940, even before the United States entered the war, the APA had assembled an Emergency Committee to plan for the inevitable involvement of the United States and its psychologists in the global conflict; in 1941, several months before the Japanese attack on Pearl Harbor, the *Psychological Bulletin* devoted a whole issue to "Military Psychology." In the same year, the APA moved to remove the greatest bar to full participation by applied psychologists in the association. At the annual meeting of the APA in September, the requirement that a prospective member have published research beyond the dissertation was replaced with a requirement that to join the APA one had to present either publications or a record of five years' "contribution" to psychology as an associate, the class of membership to which AAAP psychologists had belonged.

Once the war began, changes came at a faster pace. The annual meetings were abandoned in response to government calls to conserve vital fuels. A Committee on

Psychology and War was formed, planning not only for war activities by psychologists, but for a significant postwar social role for psychology as well. The committee noted that in view of the coming world conflict psychology should be unified, as it had been in the last war, and to this end it proposed creation of a "general headquarters" for psychology. Such headquarters came into existence as the Office of Psychological Personnel (OPP) located in Washington, DC.

Creation of the OPP as a "general headquarters" for psychology was a major event in the history of institutional psychology in the United States. Prior to 1941, the APA had no permanent central office: The APA was located in the professorial offices of whoever was its secretary in a given year. The OPP, however, became the central office of the American Psychological Association, located in Washington—fount of funding and locus of lobbying—ever since. Psychologists at the OPP saw an opportunity both to reunify psychology and to advance psychology's role in American society. In 1942, Leonard Carmichael, psychology's representative on the National Research Council, reported to the APA Council that "this office [the OPP] may well mark the initiation of a central agency for psychologists which will have an important and growing effect upon the psychological profession." The head of the OPP, Stuart Henderson Britt (1943), defined the job of the OPP as more than doing useful war work, serving in addition *the advancement of psychology as a profession* (italics in original) and promoting "sound public relations for psychology."

There was much war work to be done. Psychologists were in great demand by the military. Uniquely among the social sciences, psychology was listed as a "critical profession" by the War Department. A survey of psychologists in December 1942, just one year after Pearl Harbor, turned up 3,918 psychologists (not all of them APA members), of whom about 25 percent were engaged full time in war-related activities. Many other psychologists served the war effort indirectly. E. G. Boring, for example, wrote a text on military psychology called *Psychology for the Fighting Man,* which in turn became a textbook used at West Point (Gilgen, 1982). As in World War I, psychologists served in many specialized capacities, ranging from test administration to studying the psychological demands made on human performance by new and sophisticated weapons, to the biological control of guided missiles. The war made human relations in industry more important, emphasizing the role of the psychologist in efficient industrial management. Industry faced two problems psychologists could help solve. Producing war material required vastly increased rates of production, while at the same time regular factory workers were drafted into the military, being replaced with new, inexperienced workers, especially women, who began for the first time to enter the work force in large numbers. The War Production Board, alarmed by problems of low productivity, absenteeism, and high turnover, appointed an interdisciplinary team headed by Elton Mayo to apply social science techniques to retaining workers and improving their productivity. The business community came to recognize that "the era of human relations" was at hand, since "the factors that 'make a man tick' can be described and analyzed with much of the precision that would go into the dies for … a Sherman tank" (Baritz, 1960).

Even as the war raged, psychologists prepared for the postwar world by setting their own house in order. The Emergency Committee set up the Intersociety Constitutional Convention, a meeting of representatives of the APA, the AAAP, SPSSI, and other psychological groups, such as the National Council of Women Psychologists. The convention created a new APA along federal lines. The "new" APA was to be an organization of autonomous divisions representing the various interest groups within psychology. New bylaws were written, including, in addition to the APA's traditional purpose of the advancement of psychology as a science, the advancement of psychology "as a profession, and as a means of promoting human welfare." Robert Yerkes, who did more than anyone else to create the new APA, laid out the goals of the organization to the convention: "The world crisis has created a unique opportunity for wisely planned and well directed professional activities. In the world that is to be, psychology will play a significant role, if psychologists can only unite in making their visions realities" (paraphrased by Anderson, 1943, p. 585). In the gloomiest year of the war, psychologists began to glimpse a rosy future.

In 1944, the memberships of the APA and AAAP were polled to ratify the new bylaws. In the APA, members—the traditional academic psychologists—approved the new APA by 324 votes to 103 (out of 858 eligible voters), while among the associates (likely members of the AAAP), the vote was 973 to 143 in favor (out of 3,806 eligible to vote). Although the endorsement of the new APA, especially among its traditional members, was short of ringing, nevertheless the new bylaws were approved. The OPP became the office of the executive secretary of the APA, now permanently housed in Washington. A new journal, *The American Psychologist,* was created to serve as the voice of the new united psychology.

In this new APA there was a young and growing segment, almost entirely new: the clinical psychologist as psychotherapist.

Redefining Clinical Psychology

"It seems as if the ivory tower had literally been blown out from under psychology" (Darley & Wolfle, 1946). Before the war, psychology had been controlled by the academicians of the APA, despite complaints from and concessions to the AAAP. The war, however, drastically altered the social role of psychologists, and the balance of political power in psychology, primarily by inventing a new role for applied psychologists to fill in quickly growing numbers. During the 1930s, applied psychologists continued as they had in the 1920s, serving primarily as testers, evaluating employees, juvenile offenders, troubled children, and people seeking guidance about their intelligence or personality. However, the war created a pressing demand for a new kind of service from psychologists: psychotherapy, previously the preserve of psychiatrists.

Of all the varied jobs psychologists performed in wartime the most common one, as in World War I, was testing—testing of recruits to determine for what military job they were most suited or testing soldiers returning from the front to determine if they needed psychotherapy. As late as 1944, Robert Sears could describe the role of the military psychologist in these traditional terms. However, the soldiers returning from the front needed more psychological services than anyone had anticipated or the existing psychiatric corps could provide. By the end of the war, of 74,000 hospitalized veterans, about 44,000 were hospitalized for psychiatric reasons. Psychologists had heretofore performed diagnostic duties as part of military medical teams, but faced with the overwhelming need to provide psychotherapy, psychologists—however ill-trained—began to serve as therapists, too. Even experimental psychologists were pressed into service as therapists. For example, Howard Kendler, fresh from Kenneth

Spence's rigorously experimental program at the University of Iowa, wound up doing therapy at Walter Reed Army Hospital in Washington.

As the war wound down, it became clear that the desperate need for psychological services among veterans would continue. In addition to the hospitalized veterans, "normal" veterans experienced numerous adjustment difficulties. At the very least, men who had been wrenched from their prewar jobs, towns, and families desired counseling about how to make new lives in the postwar world; 65 percent to 80 percent of returning servicemen reported interest in such advice (Rogers, 1944). Others suffered from the World War II equivalent of the posttraumatic stress syndrome of the Vietnam veterans of the 1970s. Secretary of War Stimson wrote in his diary about "a rather appalling analysis of what our infantrymen are confronting in the present war by way of psychosis. The Surgeon General tells us the spread of psychological breakdown is alarming and that it will affect every infantryman, no matter how good and strong" (Doherty, 1985, p. 30). Upon return to the United States, veterans felt a "sense of strangeness about civilian life," were often bitter about how little people at home appreciated the horrors of combat, and experienced restlessness, disturbed sleep, excessive emotionality, and marital and family disturbances. Finally, many veterans were handicapped by wounds and needed psychological as well as physical therapy (Rogers, 1944).

The Veterans Administration (VA) acted to provide the services veterans needed. To meet the need for vocational guidance, the VA established guidance centers at universities, where GIs were receiving college educations paid for by the GI bill. Psychologists working at these counseling centers continued the development of prewar applied psychology on a larger scale than before, and their activities by and large define the job of today's counseling psychologist. More disturbed veterans, especially those in VA hospitals, needed more than simple advice; and the VA set out to define a new mental health professional, the clinical psychologist, who could provide psychotherapy to the thousands of veterans who needed it. In 1946, the VA set up training programs at major universities to turn out clinical psychologists whose job would be therapy as well as diagnosis. Because it was the largest employer of clinical psychologists, the VA did much to define the job of the clinical psychologist and how he or she would be trained.

Spurred by the VA, the newly reunified APA, now fully emerged from the ruined ivory tower of academe, undertook the tasks it had avoided for decades: defining the professional psychologist and setting up standards for his or her training. These tasks have not proved easy, and to this day there is widespread disagreement among psychologists about the proper nature of training for the professional psychologist. Since World War II, the APA has established many panels and commissions to look into the matter, but no proposal has satisfied everyone, and controversy about the nature of clinical psychology has been chronic.

The most obvious model of professional training was rejected by the committees appointed after the war to set up professional training in psychology. Typically, schools that train the practitioners of a craft are separate from the scientific discipline to which they are related. Thus physicians are trained in medical schools, not biology departments, and chemical engineers are trained in engineering schools, not chemistry departments. Of course, physicians are not ignorant of biology and chemical engineers are not ignorant of chemistry, but their schooling in basic science is considered quite distinct from their training in the crafts to which they aspire. Psychologists, however, needed to separate themselves from their very close rivals, the psychiatrists, who from the first appearance of "clinical" psychology before World War I had feared that psychologists might usurp their therapeutic duties. So, rather than define themselves as merely practitioners of a craft springing from science, as physicians had, clinical psychologists decided to define themselves as *scientist-practitioners*. That is, graduate students training to become clinical psychologists were to be taught to be scientists first—carrying out research in scientific psychology—and professionals—practitioners of a craft—second. It was as if physicians were to be trained first as biologists and only secondarily as healers. The appeal of the scheme was that it preserved for clinicians the prestige of being scientists while allowing them to fill the many jobs the VA had open for psychotherapists (Murdock & Leahey, 1986). The model of the clinical psychologist as scientist-professional was enshrined by the Boulder Conference of 1949. As we shall see in Chapter 15, the Boulder model has not been without its detractors, and periodically the APA has been called upon to rethink its approach to professional training. Additionally, from the very first (for example, Peatman, 1949), academic psychologists have been afraid that their discipline would be taken over by professionals and that they would become the second-class citizens of the APA.

Whatever the trials and tribulations surrounding the redefinition of clinical psychology, it grew rapidly, becoming in the public mind the primary function of the psychologist. In 1954, during the annual meeting of the APA, Jacob Cohen and G. D. Wiebe asked the citizens of New York who "the people with the badges" were. Of the interviewees, 32 percent correctly identified them as psychologists, although almost as many, 25 percent, thought they were psychiatrists. When asked what the people with the badges did, 71 percent said it was psychotherapy, work scarcely done by psychologists before 1944; 24 percent said "teachers," leaving 6 percent "other" (the percentages are rounded). The founders of the APA had prided themselves on being scientists and had formed their organization to advance the cause of psychology as a science. By 1954, just sixty-two years later, scientific psychology had largely ceased to exist in the public mind, replaced by an applied discipline with, given what even the best scientific minds in psychology—Hull, Tolman, Thorndike, Watson—had accomplished, a remarkably shallow foundation.

OPTIMISM IN THE AFTERMATH OF WAR

Contending for Respectability and Money at the Dawn of Big Science

Allied victory in World War II depended in many respects on the successful employment of science, primarily physics, in the pursuit of war aims. During the war, federal spending on scientific research and development went from $48 million to $500 million, from an 18 percent share in overall research spending to 83 percent. When the war ended, politicians and scientists recognized that the national interest demanded continued federal support of science, and that control of research monies should not remain a monopoly of the military. Congress, of course, never allocates money without debate, and controversy over the proposed vehicles by which research dollars would be allocated centered on two problems concerning who would be eligible to apply for it.

The first problem has rarely concerned psychology, but is important to understanding how research funds are doled out in the modern era of Big Science, in which huge amounts of money can be awarded to only a few of the investigators who would like to have their research supported. The problem is this: Should money be given to only the best scientists, or should it be parceled out on some other basis, perhaps allocating a certain amount of funds for each state? Progressive New Deal politicians such as Wisconsin Senator Robert La Follette pushed the latter scheme, but they were defeated by elitists in the scientific ranks and their conservative political allies who saw to it that applications for research money would be strictly competitive. As the system has evolved, most research money is "won" by a few elite institutions of higher education, while researchers at universities of lesser prestige are pressured to compete for grants they are in little position to gain. Universities value their scientists' winning grants because they get "overhead money"—money ostensibly to be spent on electricity, janitors, and other laboratory maintenance—which they in fact spend for new buildings, more staff, copiers, and many other things they would not otherwise be able to afford. In 1991, it was discovered that several universities had illegally channeled research overhead money to use for entertainment and other illegitimate purchases (Cooper, 1991). In this system of grants, scientists are not employees of their university; rather, they are its means of support. Scientists, in turn, are compelled to direct their research not to the problems they think are important, but to those the federal funding agencies think are important. Thus scientists spend much of their time and talent trying to second-guess bureaucrats, who themselves are implementing vague congressional directives.

Of direct importance to psychology was whether or not the funding agency to be created, the National Science Foundation (NSF), should support research in the social sciences. Old Progressives and New Deal liberals included a Division of the Social Sciences in the original NSF bill, but it was opposed by natural scientists and conservative legislators. A leading supporter of the original bill, Senator J. William Fulbright of Arkansas, argued that the social sciences should be included because they "could lead us to an understanding of the principles of human relationships which might enable us to live together without fighting recurrent wars." Opponents argued that "there is not anything that leads more readily to isms and quackeries than so-called studies in social science unless there is eternal vigilance to protect."

In debate, even Senator Fulbright found little good to say about social science, conceding that "there are many crackpots in the field, just as there were in the field of medicine in the days of witchcraft." He was unable to give an adequate definition of social science and wound up quoting a natural scientist who said that "I would not call it a science. What is commonly called social science is one individual or group of individuals telling another group how they should live." In a letter to Congress, leading physical scientists opposed the Division of Social Science. The original bill mollified them by including special controls "to prevent the Division of Social Sciences getting out of hand," as Fulbright put it on the floor of the Senate. He also said, "It would surprise me very much if the social sciences' division got anything at all" because the NSF board would be dominated by physical scientists. The upshot of the debate was a vote of 46 to 26 senators to remove the Division of Social Sciences. As sciences, the social sciences did not command universal respect (social scientists might feel that with a friend like Fulbright they did not need enemies), however much their concrete services, such as counseling, psychotherapy, and personnel management, might be needed.

Although the government was not yet sympathetic to supporting psychology and the other social sciences, a new foundation, the Ford Foundation, was. For decades, private research foundations, most notably the Rockefeller Foundation, had made modest grants to support social science. After the war, the Ford Foundation was established as the world's largest foundation, and it decided to fund the behavioral sciences—it has been said that John Dewey coined the term, but the Ford Foundation minted it—in a big way. The foundation staff saw the behavioral sciences as the bright hope for the future because they might be used to end war and ameliorate human suffering, and they proposed to use Ford's immense resources to give as "equal [a] place in society" to "the study of man as [to] the study of the atom." At the top levels of the foundation, the staff's proposal met the same kind of resistance found in the Senate. The president, Paul Hoffman, said that social science was "a good field to waste billions" in, and his adviser, Robert Maynard Hutchins, president of the University of Chicago, said that the social science research he had seen—and Chicago had the first school of social science—"scared the hell out of me." Nevertheless, the Ford staff, led by lawyer Rowman Gaither, who had helped start the Rand Corporation, pushed ahead with their ambitious plan and got it approved. At first, the foundation tried to give the money away as grants; but since this didn't get rid of the money fast enough (but did take it out of their control), they set up the Center for Advanced Studies in the Behavioral Sciences in California. This center was a place where elite social scientists could go for a few years at a time and, freed from academic pressures, pursue theorizing and research in a congenial climate, sharing their ideas with colleagues from every field.

Psychologists Look Ahead to the Psychological Society

By the end of the war, it was clear to psychologists that their ivory tower had indeed been destroyed. Psychology's links to its ancient roots in philosophy—to "long-haired" philosophers (Morgan, 1947)—were irrevocably severed, and for the good of psychology, according to the newest generation of American psychologists. At an APA symposium on "Psychology and Post-War Problems," H. H. Remmers observed, but did not mourn, psychology's loss of its "philosophical inheritance":

> Our philosophical inheritance has unfortunately not been an unmixed blessing. Deriving from that relatively sterile branch of philosophy known as epistemology and nurtured by a rationalistic science which tended to exalt thought at the expense of action and theory over practice, psychology has too frequently ensconced itself in the ivory tower from which pedants descended upon occasion to proffer pearls of wisdom, objectivity, and logical consistency to their charges without too much concern about the nutritional adequacy of such a diet. (p. 713)

Clifford T. Morgan made the same point more bluntly at a 1947 conference on "Current Trends in Psychology" by observing that "biggest of them all is that in the past thirty years psychology has shortened its hair, left its alleged ivory tower, and gone to work." Clearly, the world in the making demanded that psychologists be concerned less with abstruse, almost metaphysical, questions inherited from philosophy, and be concerned more with questions about how to achieve human happiness.

Psychologists entered their brave new world with anxious hope. Wayne Dennis, speaking at the Current Trends conference, proclaimed that "psychology today has unlimited potentialities" [sic]. At the same time, he worried that psychology had not yet achieved the "prestige and respect" needed to earn a "successful existence as a profession. We cannot function effectively as advisers and consultants, or as researchers in human behavior, without holding the confidence and good opinion of a considerable part of the population." His worries were not misplaced, as the Senate's debate on the Division of Social Sciences in the NSF demonstrated. Dennis spoke for many when he advocated further professionalization of psychology as the means of achieving public respect. Psychologists, he said, should set their own house in order, tighten requirements for training in psychology, persecute pseudopsychologists, and establish certification and state licensing standards for professional psychologists.

Despite such temporary worries, psychologists saw for themselves a secure and powerful place in the postwar world. Remmers, reflecting the views of many psychologists, defined psychology's new, postphilosophical job: "Psychology in common with all science must have as its fundamental aim the service of society by positive contributions to the good life … knowledge for knowledge's sake is at best a by-product, an esthetic luxury." In colleges, psychology should be "placed on a par with the other sciences," and its role should be to teach the undergraduate how "to assess himself and his place in society." More broadly, psychology should help construct a "science of values" and learn to use "journalism, radio, and in the near future, television" to achieve "culture control." Psychology should be more widely used in industry, education—"the most important branch of applied psychology"—gerontology, child rearing, and the solution of social problems such as racism. Remmers failed only to mention psychological psychotherapy among the potential contributions of psychology to human happiness. Psychologists were at last prepared to give people what William James had hoped for in 1892: a "psychological science that will teach them how to *act.*"

Values and Adjustment

There was an unremarked irony in psychology's postwar position. The old psychology of Scottish commonsense philosophy had proudly taken as its ultimate mission the training and justification of Christian religious values. The new psychology of brass-instrument experiments had, in challenging the old psychology, proudly cast off moral, especially religious, values in the name of science. With scientism becoming the new religion of the modern age, however, by 1944 Remmers could envision psychology as a "science of values." Psychology had come full circle—from serving the Christian God and teaching his values, to becoming itself, as John Burnham (1968) put it, a *"deus ex clinica"* representing the values of scientism.

What were the new values? Sometimes psychology seemed, in keeping with the value-free pose of science, only to offer tools for social control. Watson, for example, saw conditioning as a technique by which psychology might inculcate society's values, whatever they might be, in its citizens. As Remmers put it, the "good life" to be furthered by psychology was "the homeostasis of society"; psychology would keep people from unpleasantly rocking the boat. Watson, Remmers, and other control-minded psychologists would have agreed with the motto of the 1933 World's Fair: "Science Finds, Industry Adopts, Man Conforms" (Glassberg, 1985). Emphasis on techniques of social control is symptomatic of the psychology of adaptation's deep relationship with political Progressivism, and it laid applied psychologists open to Randolph Bourne's criticism of Progressive politicians. Once a Progressive himself, Bourne came to realize that Progressives held no clear values of their own: "They have, in short, no clear philosophy of life except that of intelligent service. They are vague as to what kind of society they want, or what kind of society America needs, but they are equipped with all the administrative attitudes and talents to attain it" (Abrahams, 1985, p. 7).

On the other hand, psychology sometimes held up a positive value of its own, the cult of the self. Psychology's object of study and concern is the individual human being, and its central value became encouraging the never-ending growth of individuals. As Dewey had said, "Growth itself is the only moral end." The contradiction between pretending to have no values and holding the value of individual growth was not noticed by American psychologists because their central value was so American as to be transparent. From the time of de Tocqueville, Americans had sought self-improvement more than anything else. Continuing growth and development seem as natural and necessary to Americans as God-centered stasis, the never-changing ideal divine order, had seemed to Europeans of the Middle Ages. In our world of self-made individuals, psychological techniques that fostered continual growth and change appeared value-free: What American society and psychology wanted was individualism.

However, the value of individualism had undergone important changes since the nineteenth century. *Character* was the concept by which people understood the individual in the nineteenth century. Emerson defined character as "moral order through the medium of individual nature," and the words used to describe character included "duty," "work," "golden deeds," "honor," "integrity," and "manhood." In his or her character, then, a person had a certain relationship, good or evil, to an encompassing and transcendent moral order. Aspiring to good character demanded self-discipline and self-sacrifice; popular psychologists such as the phrenologists offered guides to the diagnosis of one's own and others' character and gave advice on how to improve one's character. In the twentieth century, however, the moral concept of *character* began to be replaced by the narcissistic concept of *personality,* and self-sacrifice began to be replaced by self-realization. The adjectives used to describe personality were not moral: fascinating, stunning, magnetic, masterful, dominant, forceful. Having a good personality demanded no conformity to moral order, but instead fulfilled the desires of the self and achieved power over others. Character was good or bad; personality was famous or infamous. Psychologists, having shed the religious values that defined character, aided the birth of personality. Self-growth meant realizing one's potential, not living up to impersonal moral ideals—and potential, that which has not yet become actual, can be bad as often as good. Some potential is for doing bad things. Developing everyone's full potential, then, can be bad for society. Thus psychology's cultivation of individual growth was at odds with its claim to provide society with tools of social control.

This same essentially moral conflict exists between the psychology of developing potential and the most important concept of the psychology of adaptation, adjustment. Everything in twentieth-century psychology has revolved around the concept of adjustment. In experimental psychology, psychologists of learning studied how the mind and, later, behavior adjusted the individual organism to the demands of its environment. In applied psychology, psychologists developed tools to measure a person's adjustment to his or her circumstances, and should the adjustment be found wanting, tools to bring the child, worker, soldier, or neurotic back into harmony with society. In the psychological conception, sin was replaced with behavior deviation and absolute morality was replaced with statistical morality (Boorstin, 1973). In more religious times, one had a problem if one offended a moral norm standing outside oneself and society; now one had a problem if one offended society's averages as determined by statistical research. In theory, psychology placed itself on the side of individual expression, no matter how eccentric. In practice, by offering tools for social control and by stressing adjustment, it placed itself on the side of conformity.

A new Hellenistic Age was in the making. In the first Hellenistic Age, the natural sciences flourished at Alexandria, supported by the state. People's first desire was personal happiness—*ataraxia*—and they sought out teachers who promised a recipe by which one might find freedom from disturbance. In the modern Hellenistic Age, the natural sciences would again flourish with government support. People's first desire would again be personal happiness—adjustment—and they would seek out psychologists for recipes by which they might find fulfillment, sex, and the right job, things without which the modern person would be greatly disturbed. In both Hellenistic Ages, there remained a deep hunger for more transcendent truths, but in neither were they forthcoming.

BIBLIOGRAPHY FOR CHAPTERS 7, 8, and 9

For a general account of American history for the years 1912 to 1950, see John L. Thomas, "Nationalizing the republic" (for the period 1912–1920), and Robert H. Wiebe, "Modernizing the republic" (for the period 1920 and after), both in Bernard Bailyn et al., *The Great Republic* (Boston: Little, Brown, 1977). For a general account of the period with an emphasis on social history, including shrewd observations on the role of the social sciences as shapers of modern morality, see Daniel Boorstin (1973), for an emphasis on politics, see Eric F. Goldman, *Rendezvous with destiny: A history of modern American reform,* 3rd ed. (New York: Vintage, 1977).

The period between the wars has been studied a great deal, with emphasis on the 1920s. The first book on the 1920s was Allen (1931); for a more recent interpretation, see Geoffrey Perrett, *America in the twenties: A history* (New York: Touchstone, 1982). Ostrander (1968) provides a brief account of changes in morals in the 1920s. For American religion during these years, see George M. Marsden, *Fundamentalism and American culture: The shaping of twentieth-century evangelicalism 1870–1925* (Oxford: Oxford University Press, 1980). Graves and Hodge (1940) provide a wonderfully well written account of the British scene between the wars.

Several important studies of the social movements are discussed in Chapters 8 and 9. On eugenics, the standard history is sure to become Daniel J. Kevles, "Annals of eugenics: A secular faith," which appeared in *The New Yorker,* October 8, 15, 22, and 29, 1984, and as a book, *In the name of eugenics: Genetics and the uses of human heredity* (New York: Knopf, 1985);

quotations in the eugenics section are from Kevles unless otherwise noted. Gould (1981) contains useful accounts of American hereditarian attitudes, as well as a critique of intelligence testing and an account of immigration restriction upon which I relied and borrowed quotations. On the sterilization movement, the indispensable first source is Landman (1932), which contains valuable detail on sterilization legislation and court decisions; Landman was sympathetic to the ideals of the negative eugenicists, but quite critical of their practices. For the applications of social science to industry and other social problems, see Baritz (1960), who focuses on industrial social science, and Napoli (1981), who discusses applied psychology in all its varied roles. On Flaming Youth, see Fass (1977), from whom the quotations in the text are drawn, who presents the problems of youth in the 1920s from the perspectives of the youth themselves, popular commentators, and social scientists. A related source is Christopher Lasch's *Haven in a heartless world: The family besieged* (New York: Basic Books, 1977), which concentrates on social scientists' views of the family. An excellent book that touches on many subjects, including American hereditarianism, the reaction against it by American social scientists, and changing conceptions of the ideal family is Derek Freeman (1983), who dismantles Margaret Mead's romantically naive portrait of the Samoans, first by setting it in its historical context, and then by contrasting it to his own more intimate and prolonged fieldwork. My account of the change from "character" to "personality" is based on Warren I. Susman, " 'Personality' and the making of twentieth-century culture," in J. Higham & P. Conkin (Eds.), *New directions in American intellectual history* (Baltimore: Johns Hopkins University Press, 1979). Finally, the situation of American science after World War II may be found in Daniel J. Kevles, *The physicists: The history of a scientific community in America* (New York: Knopf, 1978); while Kevles obviously concentrates on physics, he provides a general account of the controversy surrounding creation of the NSF.

Moving on to works specifically on psychology, Sokal (1983) and Burnham (1968) offer good broad accounts of psychology in the 1920s, focusing on psychology's social relations, especially in the case of Burnham. For the period after World War II, with some prewar background, consult Gilgen (1982). On behaviorism in particular, see Birnbaum's works (1955, 1964) as well as David Bakan, "Behaviorism and American urbanization," *Journal of the History of the Behavioral Sciences* (1966, *2:* 5–28); John C. Burnham, "On the origins of behaviorism," *Journal of the History of the Behavioral Sciences* (1968, *4:* 143–52); and Paul Creelan (1974). For the application of intelligence tests to World War I recruits, see Daniel J. Kevles, "Testing the Army's intelligence: Psychologists and the military in World War II," *Journal of American History* (1968, *55:* 565–81); and Franz Samelson, "Putting psychology on the map: Ideology and intelligence testing," in Allan R. Buss (Ed.), *Psychology in social context* (New York: Irvington, 1979), who draws on archival sources to demonstrate how psychologists were affected by the social and political context of the World War I and postwar years. The sources and results of the clash between Yerkes and Scott are told by von Mayrhauser (1985), part of his doctoral dissertation at the University of Chicago. There are several useful histories of clinical psychology. The broadest is John M. Reisman, *The development of clinical psychology* (New York: Appleton-Century-Crofts, 1966). More attention to professional issues is provided by Robert I. Watson, "A brief history of clinical psychology," *Psychological Bulletin* (1953, *50:* 321–46); and Virginia Staudt Sexton, "Clinical psychology: An historical survey," *Genetic Psychology Monographs* (1965, *72:* 401–34). An insider's account of the growth of clinical psychology during and immediately after World War II is given by E. Lowell Kelly, "Clinical psychology," in Dennis (1947). A brief overview of clinical psychology training issues is found in Leonard Blank, "Clinical psychology training, 1945–62: Conferences and issues," in Leonard Blank & Henry David (Eds.), *Sourcebook for training in clinical psychology* (New York: Springer, 1964).

Psychologists themselves have provided periodic treatments of their immediate history. For the period in question, the broadest and most detailed treatment is given by Jerome S.

Bruner and Gordon W. Allport, "Fifty years of change in American psychology," *Psychological Bulletin* (1940, *37*: 757–76), which provided the basis for Allport's APA presidential address, "The psychologist's frame of reference," *Psychological Bulletin* (1940, *37*: 1–28). Earlier relevant surveys include Robert Davis & Silas E. Gould, "Changing tendencies in general psychology," *Psychological Review* (1929, *36*: 320–31); Florence L. Goodenough, "Trends in modern psychology," *Psychological Bulletin* (1934, *31*: 81–97); and Herbert S. Langfeld, "Fifty volumes of the Psychological Review," *Psychological Review* (1943, *50*: 143–55). Later accounts looking back to the period in question are Kenneth E. Clark, "The APA study of psychologists," *American Psychologist* (1954, *9*: 117–20); W. A. Kaess & W. A. Bousfield, "Citation of authorities in textbooks," *American Psychologist* (1954, *9*: 144–48); Russell Becker, "Outstanding contributors to psychology," *American Psychologist* (1959, *14*: 297–98); and Kenneth Wurtz, "A survey of important psychological books," *American Psychologist* (1961, *16*: 192–94).

The narrative account of psychology's preparation for and participation in World War II, including reunification of the APA and AAAP and planning for psychology's postwar role, is based on careful reading of all the *Psychological Bulletins* for the relevant years. The reference to Carmichael (1942) is to his oral report to the meeting of the APA Council (the association did not meet because of the war) in New York on September 3, 1942, beginning in the *Bulletin* at page 713.

Finally, a contemporary account of psychology's place in the postwar competition for research funds is given by Robert Leeper, "An analysis of science legislation in the last Congress," *American Psychologist* (1947, *2*: 127–35). For the debate in the Senate itself, see the *Congressional Record;* Leeper's page references to the *Record* are unaccountably mistaken: One should look up bill S-1805 in the Index for 1946; the quotations in the text are from p. 8048, while other brief considerations on the social sciences may be found throughout the entire, oft-interrupted, debate. My account of the founding of the Ford Foundation and its interest in behavioral science is based on an Invited Address to Cheiron, the Society for the History of the Behavioral Sciences, June 13, 1985, by Arnold Thackray, "Inventing behavioral science."

REFERENCES

Abrahams, E. (1985, May 12). Founding father of the New Republic. Review of D. W. Levy, "Herbert Croly of the *New Republic:* The life and thought of an American Progressive." *Washington Post Book World, 7.*

Adams, G. (1934). The rise and fall of psychology. *Atlantic Monthly, 153,* 82–90.

Anderson, J. E. (1943). Outcomes of the Intersociety Constitutional Convention. *Psychological Bulletin, 40,* 585–588.

Beers, C. (1968/1953). *A mind that found itself.* New York: Doubleday.

Boorstin, D. J. (1973). *The Americans: The democratic experience.* New York: Vintage.

Braeman, J., Bremner, R. H., & Brody, D. (Eds.), (1968). *Change and continuity in twentieth-century America: The 1920's.* Columbus, OH: Ohio State University Press.

Britt, S. H. (1943). The Office of Psychological Personnel—Report for the second six months. *Psychological Bulletin, 40,* 436–446.

Burnham, J. C. (1968). The new psychology: From narcissism to social control. In J. Braeman, R. H. Bremner & D. Brody (Eds.), *Change and continuity in twentieth-century America: The 1920's.* Columbus, OH: Ohio State University Press.

Cohen, J. & Wiebe, G. D. (1955). Who are these people? *American Psychologist, 10,* 84–85.

Cooper, K. J. (1991, May 6). Universities' images stained by improper charges to government. *Washington Post,* A 13.

Darley, J. & Wolfle, D. (1946). Can we meet the formidable demand for psychological services? *American Psychologist, 1,* 179–180.

Dennis, W. (Ed.), (1947). *Current trends in psychology*. Pittsburgh: University of Pittsburgh Press.

Doherty, J. C. (1985, April 30). World War II through an Indochina looking glass. *Wall Street Journal, 30*.

Gilgen, A. R. (1982). *American psychology since World War II: A profile of the discipline*. Westport, CT: Greenwood Press.

Glassberg, D. (1985). *Social science at the Chicago World's Fair of 1933–1934*. Paper presented at the annual meeting of Cheiron, the Society for the History of the Behavioral Sciences, Philadelphia, June 15.

Leacock, S. (1923). A manual of the new mentality. *Harper's Magazine, 148*, 471–480.

Morgan, C. T. (1947). Human engineering. In W. Dennis (Ed.), *Current trends in psychology*. Pittsburgh: University of Pittsburgh Press.

Murdock, N. & Leahey, T. H. (1986, April). Scientism and status: The Boulder model. Paper presented at the annual meeting of the Eastern Psychological Association, New York.

Napoli, D. S. (1981). *Architects of adjustment: The history of the psychological profession in the United States*. Port Washington, NY: Kennikat Press.

Ostrander, G. M. (1968). The revolution in morals. In J. Braeman, R. H. Bremner, & D. Brody (Eds.), *Change and continuity in twentieth-century America: The 1920's*. Columbus, OH: Ohio State University Press.

Peatman, J. G. (1949). How scientific and how professional is the American Psychological Association? *American Psychologist, 4*, 486–489.

Poffenberger, A. T. (1936). Psychology and life. *Psychological Review, 43*, 9–31.

Remmers, H. H. (1944). Psychology—Some unfinished business. *Psychological Bulletin, 41*, 713–714.

Rogers, C. (1944). Psychological adjustments of discharged service personnel. *Psychological Bulletin, 41*, 689–696.

Sears, R. R. (1944). Clinical psychology in the military services. *Psychological Bulletin, 41*, 502–509.

Sokal, M. M. (1983). James McKeen Cattell and American psychology in the 1920s. In Josef Brozek (Ed.), *Explorations in the history of psychology in the United States*. Lewisburg, PA: Bucknell University Press.

PART IV

ECLECTIC PSYCHOLOGY (1950–1960)

World War II transformed psychology from a relatively staid science to a profession increasingly concerned with human welfare. Clinical psychology as we know it today—doing psychotherapy—was created by the need for psychological services for returning war veterans. Psychology experienced explosive growth after the war, especially in its applied branches. Scientific psychology grew, too, but at a much slower pace. Growth led to fragmentation. Psychologists divided along professional lines into clinicians, counselors, industrial psychologists, experimental psychologists, and others. In 1988, professional lines became fault lines, and academic psychologists split from the APA to form the American Psychological Society.

Theoretically, the divisions of the past continued and new ones were invented. Radical behaviorism was added to the behaviorisms of the 1930s and 1940s. Mediational behaviorism developed out of Hullian behaviorism. Cognitive psychology began in the 1950s, matured into cognitive science in the 1970s, and was challenged in the 1980s by a new paradigm, "connectionism."

Psychology has become a major institution in modern American life. It is accepted in every college and university as a popular study. Psychologists work in business and industry, and troubled people consult psychologists for help with their problems. Psychological language has become part of everyday life. Some critics say that ours has become the psychological society. Psychology's tremendous growth and increasing influence, along with changes in scientific behavioral psychology, will occupy us in Chapters 10 and 11.

CHAPTER 10

Behaviorism's Indian Summer
After the Golden Age

ECLECTIC PSYCHOLOGY: THE 1950s

Following the crises and turmoil of the war years, psychology settled into comfortable eclecticism. Psychologists were all behavioralists now, and different behavioral theories existed side by side in relative peace. The various species of self-styled behaviorism included commonsense theories about attitudes and beliefs in social psychology, and behaviorist and nonbehaviorist theories of cognition. While much theoretical debate existed among the various positions, there was relatively little of the stridency that had marked the birth of behaviorism. Three important developments took place in the harmonious environment of eclectic psychology. First was the growing influence of B. F. Skinner's radical behaviorism in experimental psychology and then in its application to human thought and behavior. The second major development, which occurred primarily outside psychology, was the founding of the field of artificial intelligence. This field eventually gave birth to cognitive psychology, cognitive science, and a renaissance in the philosophy of mind. Finally, clinical and applied psychology continued to grow, threatening to turn the APA into more of a professional trade organization than a scientific association. With this came the laying of the first barely visible foundations of the psychological society of the 1970s and 1980s.

TROUBLES WITH BEHAVIORISM (1950–1954)

The most consciously troubled area in psychology after the war was the core of traditional scientific psychology, experimental psychology, which by 1950 meant primarily the study of learning. Sigmund Koch, already becoming an effective gadfly to the pretensions of scientific psychology, wrote (1951a, p. 295) that "psychology seems now to have entered an era of total disorientation." In another (1951b) paper, Koch asserted that "since the end of World War II, psychology has been in a long and intensifying crisis ... its core seems to be disaffection from the theory of the recent past. Never before had it seemed so evident that the development of a science is not an automatic forward movement." Koch located two causes of the "crisis" in experimental psychology, one internal and one external. Within experimental psychology, Koch saw a decade-long stagnation in the development of the prewar theoretical systems of learning theory. Outside, clinical and applied psychology were bidding for "social recognition" by abandoning theory for useful practices so they could take on "social responsibilities." In the rush toward social usefulness, theoretical psychologists had become depressed and were looking for a "new wave" to excite them again.

Koch was not a cranky prophet alone in his dissatisfaction with the state of experimental psychology, for signs of dissatisfaction abounded. In 1951, Karl Lashley, at one time Watson's student, attacked the standard S-R chaining theory of complex behaviors, originally proposed by Watson himself. Lashley argued on physiological grounds that chaining was impossible because of the relatively slow transmission of nervous impulses from receptor to brain and back to effector. He proposed instead that organisms possess central planning functions that coordinate sets of actions as large units, not as chains. He specifically argued that language was organized this way, raising a problem that would increasingly bedevil behaviorism. On another front in 1950, Frank Beach, a student of animal behavior, decried experimental psychologists' increasing preoccupation with rat learning. He questioned whether psychologists were interested in a general science of behavior or in only one topic, learning, in only one species, the Norway rat. Without studies of other behaviors and species, he argued, the generality of laboratory findings must remain suspect. He also pointed out the existence of species-specific behaviors such as imprinting that are not the exclusive result of either learning or instinct. Such behaviors escape all existing learning theories, which sharply divide the learned from the unlearned and then study only the latter. Problems of comparative psychology would increasingly plague the psychology of learning in the 1950s and 1960s.

Philosophical Behaviorism

Psychological behaviorism arose out of the problems of animal psychology and in revolt against introspective mentalism. Consequently, behavioristic psychologists never addressed one of the more obvious difficulties that might be raised against their movement—namely, that ordinary people believe they possess mental processes and consciousness. There exists a folk psychology of mind that deserves attention from any psychological program departing from it. It may fairly be asked why, if there are no mental processes—as behaviorists seem to maintain—ordinary language is so rich in descriptions of mind and consciousness? Philosophical behaviorists addressed the problem of reinterpreting commonsense mentalistic psychology into acceptable "scientific" behavioristic terms as part of their more general program of linking claims about unobservables with observables.

As it is usually presented, philosophical or "logical behaviorism is a semantic theory about what mental terms mean. The basic idea is that attributing a mental state (say thirst) to an organism is the same as saying that the organism is disposed to behave in a certain way (for example to drink if there is water available)" (Fodor, 1981, p. 115). According to logical behaviorists, when we attribute a mental statement to a person, we're really just describing their actual or likely behavior in a given circumstance, not some inner mental state. In principle, then, it would be possible to eliminate mentalistic concepts from everyday psychology and replace them with concepts referring only to behavior. As stated, logical behaviorism is rather implausible. For example, according to logical behaviorism, to believe that ice on a lake is too thin for skating must mean that one is disposed not to skate on the ice and to say to others that they ought not skate on the lake. However, things are not so simple. If you see someone you thoroughly dislike about to skate out on the ice, you may say nothing, hoping that your enemy will fall through the ice and look a fool. Should you harbor real malice toward the skater—if, for example, he is blackmailing you—you may say nothing, hoping he will drown; indeed, you may direct him to the weakest ice. So the mental statement "believing the ice is thin" cannot be simply and directly translated into a behavioral disposition, because how one is disposed to behave depends on other beliefs that turn on still others—for example, that the skater *is* the blackmailer—making any direct equation of mental state and behavioral disposition impossible.

The difficulties of logical behaviorism are relevant to experimental psychology because its doctrines are the application of operationism to ordinary psychological terms. For logical behaviorism's equation of mental state and behavior or behavioral disposition provides operational definitions of "belief," "hope," "fear," "being in pain," and so on. The example of the thin ice shows that one cannot give an operational definition of "believing the ice is thin," and failure to "operationalize" so simple and straightforward a concept casts doubt on the whole enterprise of operationism in psychology. The British philosopher G. E. Moore, following Ludwig Wittgenstein, refuted the logical behaviorist, operationist treatment of mental terms more bluntly: "When we pity a man for having toothache, we are not pitying him for putting his hand to his cheek" (Luckhardt, 1983).

Logical behaviorism is so obviously false that it makes an admirable straw man for philosophers of other dispositions, but it is not clear that anyone has actually held the position just sketched. It is typically attributed to Rudolph Carnap, Gilbert Ryle, and Ludwig Wittgenstein, but in fact these philosophers held different and more interesting views on the nature of mentalistic folk psychology. We discussed Carnap's "behaviorism" in Chapter 11 in connection with E. C. Tolman, who was for a time under Carnap's influence. Carnap came closest to holding the position of logical behaviorism, but we should bear in mind that for him it was just a temporary way station on the road to interpreting mentalistic language as talk about brain states. As we shall see in Chapter 15, Carnap's physicalistic view is fraught with difficulties; but it is possible to separate the idea that mental terms refer to behavioral dispositions from the idea that they refer to brain states.

In *The Concept of Mind* (1949), the English philosopher Gilbert Ryle attacked what he called "the dogma of the Ghost in the Machine" begun by Descartes. Descartes had defined two worlds—one material and including the body, the other mental, a ghostly inner stage on which private mental events took place. Ryle accused Descartes of making a huge "category mistake," treating mind as if it were a distinct thing opposed to the body and somehow lying behind behavior. Here is an example of a category mistake: A person is taken on a tour of Oxford University and sees its college buildings, its library, its deans, its professors, and its students. At the end of the day the visitor asks, "You've showed me all these things, but where is the university?" The mistake is in supposing that since there is a name "Oxford University," it must apply to some object separate from the buildings and so on, yet be like them in being a thing. So Ryle claimed that Cartesian dualism is a category mistake. Cartesians describe behaviors with "mental" predicates such as "intelligent," "hopeful," "sincere," "disingenuous," and then assume that there must be a mental thing behind the behaviors that makes them intelligent, hopeful, sincere, or disingenuous. Here, says Ryle, lies the mistake, because the behaviors *themselves* are intelligent, hopeful, sincere, or disingenuous; no inner ghost is needed to make them so. Moreover, inventing the Ghost in the Machine accomplishes nothing, because if there were an inner ghost, we would still have to explain why its operations are intelligent, hopeful, sincere, or disingenuous. Is there a Ghost in the Ghost? And a Ghost in the Ghost in the Ghost? The Ghost in the Machine, far from explaining mental life, vastly complicates our efforts to understand it.

So far, one might, as Ryle feared, put him down as a behaviorist claiming that mind *is* only behavior. But Ryle held that there is indeed more to mental predicates than simple descriptions of behavior. For example, when we say birds are "migrating," we see them flying south, and a behaviorist might say that "migration" is just "flying-south behavior." However, as Ryle pointed out, to say that birds are "migrating" is to say much more than that they are flying south, since the term "migration" implies a whole story about why they are flying south, how they will return later, how it happens every year, and theories about how they navigate. So to say birds are "migrating" goes *beyond* saying that they are flying south, but it does not go *behind* saying that they are flying south. Similarly, to say a behavior is "intelligent" does more than simply describe some behavior, since it brings in the various criteria we have for saying a course of action is intelligent—for example, that it is appropriate to the situation and that it is likely to be successful. But saying a person is acting intelligently does not go behind the behavior to some ghostly inner calculations that make it intelligent, however much it goes beyond a behaviorist's description of what the person is doing. While Ryle rejected dualism, and while his analysis of mind had some similarities to behaviorism, it was rather different from either psychological behaviorism or logical, philosophical behaviorism.

A difficult and subtle analysis of ordinary psychological language was made by the Viennese (later British) philosopher Ludwig Wittgenstein. Wittgenstein argued that Cartesian philosophers had led people to believe that there are mental objects (for example, sensations) and mental processes (for example, memory), whereas in fact there are neither. As an example of a mental object, consider *pain*. Quite clearly, the behaviorist is wrong in asserting that pain is behavior. The behaviorist error is in thinking that first- and third-person uses of "pain" are symmetrical. If we see someone moaning and holding his head, we say, "He is in pain"; but I do not say, "I am in pain" because I observe myself moaning and holding my head, as strict operationism requires. So the sentence "I am in pain" does not describe behavior; nor, held Wittgenstein, does it describe some inner object. An object can be known, so we can say true things about it—for example, "I know this book, *Wittgenstein*, costs $5.95." But a statement of knowledge only makes sense if we can doubt it—that is, if some other state of affairs may be true than the one we think. So one can sensibly say, "I don't know if *Wittgenstein* costs $5.95." Now, "I know I'm in pain" seems to make sense and point to an inner object of description, but the statement "I don't know that I'm in pain" is simply nonsense; of course, one can have experienced bodily damage and not feel pain, but one cannot meaningfully say, "I don't know if I'm in pain." Another problem with thinking of pain as an object concerns how pains are located. Should I hold a piece of candy between my fingers and then put my fingers in my mouth, we would agree that the candy is in my mouth as well as my hand. But suppose I have a pain in my finger and put my finger in my mouth. Is the pain *in* my mouth? It seems odd to say so; pains are therefore not assigned location as we assign locations to ordinary objects. Wittgenstein concluded that pain is not some inner object that we know at all, and that statements about pain (or joy, or ecstasy) are not descriptions of anything. Rather they are expressions. Moaning expresses pain, it does not describe pain. Wittgenstein maintained that sentences such as "I am in pain" are learned linguistic equivalents of moaning, expressing but not describing the state of pain. Pain is perfectly real; it is not, however, a ghostly mental object.

Luckhardt (1983) introduces a useful analogy to clarify Wittgenstein's point. A painting expresses an artist's conception through the physical medium of paint on canvas. We find it beautiful (or ugly) as we interpret it. Behaviorists are like paint salespeople who point out that since the painting is made of paint, its beauty is identical with the arrangements of the paints on the canvas. However, this is obviously absurd, since a painting venerated for its beauty among academic painters and audiences in 1875 is likely to be considered tacky kitsch by modernists and their audience. Beauty depends on an interpretation of paint on canvas and is not identical with it. The painting is, again, a physical expression by an artist that is in turn interpreted by its viewers. So "I am in pain," like moans and grimaces, is a physical expression by a person that must be interpreted by those who hear it.

Likewise, mental processes do not consist in any *thing*, either, argued Wittgenstein. Consider memory. Obviously, we remember things all the time, but is there an inner mental process of remembering common to all acts of memory? Wittgenstein thought not. Malcolm (1970) gives the following example: Several hours after you put your keys in the kitchen drawer, you are asked, "Where did you put the keys?" You may remember in any of several ways:

1. Nothing occurs to you, then you mentally retrace your steps earlier in the day and have an image of putting the keys in the drawer, and say, "I left them in the kitchen drawer."

2. Nothing occurs to you. You have no images, but ask yourself, "Where did I put the keys?," then exclaim, "The kitchen drawer!"

3. The question is asked while you are deep in conversation with another person. Without interrupting your talk, you point to the kitchen drawer.

4. You are asked while writing a letter. Saying nothing, you walk over to the drawer, reach in, and hand over the keys, all the while composing the next sentence in the letter.

5. Without any hesitation or doubt, you answer directly, "I put them in the kitchen drawer."

In every case, you remembered where the keys were, but each case is quite unlike the others. The behaviors are different, so there is no essential behavioral process of remembering; there is no uniform mental accompaniment to the act of remembering, so there is no essential mental process of remembering; and since there is no common behavior or conscious experience, there is no essential physiological process of remembering. In each case, there is behavior, there are mental events, and there are physiological processes, but no one of them is the same, so there is no uniform *process* of memory. We group these events together under "memory" not because of some essential defining feature of each episode, the way we define "electrons" in terms of uniform defining features, but because they share what Wittgenstein called a "family resemblance." The members of a family resemble one another, but there is no single feature all members possess. Two brothers may share similar noses, a father and son similar ears, two cousins similar hair, but there is no essential defining feature shared by all. Wittgenstein argued that terms referring to mental processes are all family-resemblance terms, having no defining essence that can be captured. "Remembering," "thinking," "intending" are not processes, but human abilities. To the Wittgensteinian the Würzburg psychologists' efforts to lay bare the processes of thinking had to end in failure, for there are no processes of thought to be found. Thinking, like remembering, is just something people *do* (Malcolm, 1970).

If Wittgenstein is right, the consequences for psychology are profound. Wittgenstein (1953) had a poor opinion of psychology: "The confusion and barrenness of psychology is not to be explained by calling it a 'young science....' For in psychology there are experimental methods and *conceptual confusion*" (*Philosophical Investigations,* II, Sec. XIV). Psychology's conceptual confusion is to think there are mental objects and mental processes when there are not, and then to seek for explanations of the fictitious objects and processes.

> I have been trying in all this to remove the temptation to think that there "*must be*" a mental process of thinking, hoping, wishing, believing, etc., independent of the process of expressing a thought, a hope, a wish, etc.... If we scrutinize the usages which we make of "thinking," "meaning," "wishing," etc., going through this process rids us of the temptation to look for a peculiar act of thinking, independent of the act of expressing our thoughts, and stowed away in some particular medium. (Wittgenstein, 1958, pp. 41–43)

Wittgenstein's point here is related to Ryle's: There is nothing behind our acts; there is no Ghost in the Machine. Behind the point about psychology there is a broader point about science: Explanations stop somewhere (Malcolm, 1970). It is no good asking a physicist why an object once set in motion will travel in a straight line forever unless acted on by another force, because this is a basic assumption that allows physics to explain other things. No one has seen an object move that way and the only apparently undisturbed objects we can observe moving, the planets, move (roughly) in circles; indeed, the ancients assumed that an object in space set in motion would naturally move in a circle. Similarly, a physicist cannot explain why quarks have the properties they do, only how, given those properties, their behavior can be explained. Psychologists have all along supposed that thinking, memory, wishing, and so on required explanations, but Ryle, and especially Wittgenstein, claim that they do not. They are human abilities, and thinking, remembering, and wishing are things we just *do* without there being some "inside story," mental or physiological, although they are not just behaviors, either. Psychologists went wrong when they framed their question as: "What is the process of thinking?" —naturally coming up with theories about mental processes. As Wittgenstein remarks:

> We talk of processes and states and leave their nature undecided. Sometimes perhaps we shall know more about them—we think. But that is just what commits us to a particular way of looking at the matter. For we have a definite concept of what it means to learn to know a process better. The decisive movement in the conjuring trick has been made, and it was the very one that we thought quite innocent. (Wittgenstein, 1953, *Philosophical Investigations* I, paragraph 308)

To Wittgenstein, we cannot scientifically explain behavior, but we can understand it. To understand people's behavior, and the expressions of their thoughts, we must take into consideration what Wittgenstein called human "forms of life." "What has to be accepted, the given, is—so one could say—*forms of life*" (Wittgenstein, 1958). In discussing Luckhardt's painting metaphor, we pointed out that the beauty of a painting lies in its interpretation. How we interpret the painting depends on the immediate and overall context in which we meet it. The gallery-goer may have read art history and criticism, and this knowledge will shape her appreciation of the picture. She will see Frank Stella's latest canvas against the background of Stella's previous work, the works by other artists arranged in the show, and her knowledge of the history, ambitions, and techniques of modern and postmodern painting. Simply as paint on canvas the painting has no meaning and is neither beautiful nor ugly; it takes on meaning only in the eye of an interpretive viewer. All this context is a "form of life," the form of life of modernism and postmodernism in the arts. Observe that a person who knows nothing of modernism is likely to find a Stella work literally without meaning, because that person does not participate in the appropriate form of life. Should he take modern art history classes, he can learn a new form of life and the painting will become meaningful.

Wittgenstein's point is that human action is meaningful only within the setting of a form of life. An untutored Westerner is likely to find practices of another culture, or another historical time, without meaning in the same way the naive gallery-goer finds the Stella painting meaningless. The reverse is true: Some African tribesmen came to a city for the first time and were deeply shocked when in a tall building they saw two men go into a box and emerge a few seconds later as three women. (They saw an elevator.) If Wittgenstein's claim is correct, then not only can psychology not be a science because there are no mental processes and objects for it to study and explain, but psychology and the other social sciences cannot be sciences because there are no historically permanent and cross-culturally universal principles for understanding human thought and behavior. Psychology, he says, should give up the "craving for generality" and "the contemptuous attitude to the particular case" it has picked up from natural science (Wittgenstein, 1953) and accept the modest goal of explicating forms of life and explaining particular human actions within their historically given forms of life.

Are Theories of Learning Adequate?

Hull and Tolman were not professionally raised on logical positivism and operationism, but the succeeding generation of experimental psychologists, coming into professional maturity after World War II, was. Many of the new generation believed with Sigmund Koch that the theoretical debates of the 1930s and 1940s had led nowhere, that the problems of the psychology of learning—the heart of the adjustment process—were not being solved. So in the later 1940s and through the early 1950s, theoretical psychologists engaged in earnest self-scrutiny, applying the tools of logical positivism and operationism to developing tactics of theory construction in psychology, and applying the criteria of positivism and operationism to the theories of Hull and Tolman.

Central to much of the metatheoretical discussion of the period was the status of what Tolman had called "intervening variables," the theoretical concepts such as cognitive map and habit strength that Hull and Tolman employed to explain behavior. The terms of the debate were framed in 1948 by Kenneth MacCorquodale and Paul Meehl, who distinguished between intervening variables and "hypothetical constructs." Although it was meant to be a dimension along which psychological concepts might be arrayed, in practice their distinction was used dichotomously, and theoretical analysts tended to write about intervening variables *vs.* hypothetical constructs. Intervening variables were concepts defined purely operationally, as mere shorthand descriptions for experimental procedures or measurements. Hypothetical constructs, on the other hand, possessed, perhaps in addition to operational meaning, "surplus meaning" over and above procedures and measurements. It was usually argued that hypothetical constructs were temporary expedients aiding creativity in the early stages of scientific development. Failure to "purify" hypothetical constructs into intervening variables was described as a "practice that cannot be scientifically defended," since "valid intervening variables ... are the only kinds of constructs admissible in sound scientific theory" (Marx, 1951).

No one was very clear on what the surplus meaning of hypothetical constructs consisted in. Sometimes it seemed to mean no more than the idiosyncratic associations its proposer might have for it (Kendler, 1952); sometimes it seemed to refer to hypothetical neural mechanisms thought to underlie behavior (Marx, 1951); and sometimes it seemed to refer to more abstract models of behavior (Tolman, 1949). Whatever surplus meaning was, however, everyone save Tolman and his associates (Tolman, 1949; Krech, 1949) agreed that it was bad and should be purged from psychological theory as soon as possible.

An important and illustrative example of the fight over the meaning and status of hypothetical constructs is the controversy between Tolmanians and neo-Hullians over what is learned, which had continued since the 1930s. Neo-Hullians maintained that when an animal learns how to run a maze, it has learned a series of responses to be executed at different points in the maze. Tolmanians continued to maintain that the animal learns a cognitive map representation of the maze. A huge number of experiments had been done to resolve these two points of view, but by 1950, no progress had been made in determining which was correct. In 1952, Howard Kendler, a student of Spence's, argued that the dispute between Tolmanians and neo-Hullians was a pseudodispute. Applying operational criteria, Kendler tried to show that there was no real difference between the two camps. Since "the only meaning possessed by … intervening variables is their relationship to both independent and dependent variables," any theory of learning is only about responses to given choice points in a maze. Kendler accused the Tolmanians of committing "the fallacy of reification" by believing that cognitive maps are more than shorthand descriptions of maze behavior. Since theoretical concepts must be defined operationally—in terms of behaviors occurring under specified conditions—differences between Hull's and Tolman's positions were no more than differences "between personal thought processes leading to the invention of theoretical constructs."

Kendler's very influential paper illustrates how logical positivism and operationism blinded psychologists of the period to other ways of doing science, even when those other ways were practiced by dominant figures such as Hull and Tolman. Hull and Tolman were both *realists;* that is, they believed their constructs referred to some real object or process occurring within living organisms. In Hull's case, these processes were physiological; but Kendler dismissed Hull's commitment to the physiological reality of his concepts as an "individual's intuitive conception," not to be mixed up with the operational definition of the concepts, which alone are scientifically meaningful. With respect to Tolman, Kendler entirely failed to consider that Tolman's constructs might refer to *psychologically* real entities. Kendler, advocate of operationism and the pure intervening variable, was a nominalist, defining terms only in terms of their use, failing to see that theoretical constructs might refer to something besides behavior. Tolman's colleague Benbow Ritchie (1953) tried to point out Kendler's mistake, but the tide of operationism was too strong. Psychologists by and large accepted Kendler's judgment that there was no real difference between Hull and Tolman, and they went on to other things.

Kendler's paper also reaffirms that operationism is a species of idealism rather than materialistic realism. Notice that intervening variables do not actually intervene. As just "shorthand descriptions," they have no reality in the organism and so play no causal role in intervening between stimulus and response. Intervening variables do no more than organize the scientist's experience of others' behavior. Thus direct experience is, for operationism, the ultimate reality, and operationism is therefore a form of idealism.

At the Dartmouth Conference on Learning Theory held in 1950, the new generation of learning theorists evaluated learning theories in the light of the logical positivism they assumed, and thought their teachers had accepted. Hull's theory, as the one they believed most closely shared their positivist standards of theory construction, came in for the most devastating criticism. Sigmund Koch, the author of the report on Hull, said, "We have done what may be construed as a nasty thing. We have proceeded on a literal interpretation of some such proposition as: 'Hull has put forward a hypothetico-deductive theory of behavior.' " Proceeding on that interpretation, Koch showed that, judged by positivistic criteria, Hull's enterprise was a total failure. Koch's rhetoric was damning: Hull's theory suffered from "horrible indeterminancy" and "manifold inadequacies" in the definition of its independent variables; it was "empirically empty" and a "pseudoquantitative system"; and it failed to progress from the 1943 formulation to the ones of the early 1950s: "It may be said with confidence that with respect to most of the issues considered ... there has been no evidence of constructive advance since 1943." The other theories, including those of Tolman, B. F. Skinner, Kurt Lewin (a Gestalt psychologist), and Edwin R. Guthrie (another behaviorist), were variously criticized for failure to meet positivist criteria for good theory.

Clearly, the older theories of learning were not adequate, at least as judged by the standards of logical positivism. But were the logical positivist's standards necessarily right? At Dartmouth it was noticed that B. F. Skinner's brand of behaviorism failed to live up to logical positivistic principles because it did not try to. Skinner had set his own standards of theoretical adequacy, and judged by them, his theory did well. Perhaps, then, change was called for in psychologists' goals, rather than in their continued pursuit of goals set by abstract philosophy. Were theories of learning needed at all?

ARE THEORIES OF LEARNING NECESSARY? RADICAL BEHAVIORISM (1938–1958)

Radical Behaviorism

Define
And thus expunge
The *ought*
The *should*
* * *
Truth's to be sought
In *Does* and *Doesn't*
　　　B. F. Skinner, *For Ivor Richards* (1971)

By far the best known and most influential of all the major behaviorists is Burrhus Frederick Skinner (1904–1990), whose radical behaviorism, if accepted, would constitute a momentous revolution in humanity's understanding of the human self, demanding as it does no less than the complete rejection of the entire intellectual psychological tradition that we have considered in this book with the exception of the neo-realists. It would replace this tradition with a scientific psychology grounded in neo-Darwinian evolutionary theory, which looks outside humans for the causes of behavior. Virtually every psychological thinker we have considered, from Wundt, James, and Freud to Hull and Tolman, intended psychology to be an explication of internal processes, however conceived—processes that produce behavior or conscious phenomena. Skinner followed Watson in placing responsibility for behavior squarely in the environment, however. A person does not act at the behest of moral values, the "ought" and "should," the highest guides to action for Plato. For Skinner, people deserve neither praise nor blame for anything they "do" or "don't." The environment controls behavior so that both good and evil, if such exist, reside there, not in the person. To paraphrase Shakespeare's Julius Caesar: "The fault, dear Brutus, lies in our contingencies of reinforcement, not in ourselves."

The heart of radical behaviorism may best be approached by looking at Skinner's attitude to Freud in his paper "A Critique of Psychoanalytic Concepts and Theories." For Skinner, Freud's great discovery was that much human behavior has unconscious causes. However, to Skinner Freud's great mistake was in inventing a mental apparatus—id, ego, superego—and its attendant mental processes to explain human behavior. Skinner believed that the lesson taught by the unconscious is that mental states are simply irrelevant to behavior. We may observe that a student shows a neurotic subservience to her teachers. The Freudian might explain this by asserting that the student's father was a punitive perfectionist who demanded obedience, and that his child incorporated a stern father image that now affects her behavior in the presence of authority figures. Skinner would allow us to explain the current servility by reference to punishments at the hand of a punitive father, but he would insist that the link be direct. The student cowers now because as a child she received punishment from a similar person, not because there is any mental image within her of her father. For Skinner, the inference to an unconscious father image explains nothing that cannot be explained by simply referring current behavior to the consequences of past behavior. The mental link adds nothing to an account of behavior, according to Skinner, and in fact complicates matters by requiring that the mental link itself be explained. Skinner has extended this criticism of mental entities to encompass all traditional psychologies, rejecting equally the superego, apperception, habit strength, and cognitive maps. All are unnecessary to the proper scientific explanation of behavior.

Although radical behaviorism represents a sharp break with any traditional psychology, whether scientific or commonsense, its intellectual heritage can be located. It stands clearly in the empiricist camp, especially with the radical empiricism of Renaissance philosopher Francis Bacon and German physicist Ernst Mach. As a young man, Skinner read Bacon's works, and he often referred favorably to the great inductivist. Like Bacon, Skinner believed that truth is to be found in observations themselves, in "does" and "doesn't," rather than in our interpretations of our observations. Skinner's first psychological paper was an application of Mach's radical descriptive positivism to the concept of the reflex. Skinner concluded that a reflex is not an entity inside an animal, but merely a convenient descriptive term for a regular correlation between stimulus and response. This presaged his rejection of all hypothetical entities.

Skinner's account of behavior is also heir to Darwin's analysis of evolution, as Skinner himself often suggested. Darwin argued that species constantly produce variant traits and that nature acts on these traits to select those that contribute to survival, eliminating those that do not. Similarly, for Skinner, an organism is constantly producing variant forms of behavior. Some of these acts lead to favorable consequences—are reinforced—while others do not. Those that do are strengthened, for they contribute to the organism's survival and are learned. Those that are not reinforced are not learned and disappear from the organism's repertoire, just as weak species become extinct. Both Skinner's analysis of behavior and his values were Darwinian, as we shall see.

Like many innovative scientific thinkers, Skinner received little early training in his discipline. He took his undergraduate degree in English at Hamilton College, intending to be a writer, studying no psychology. However, a biology teacher called his attention to works by Pavlov and the mechanist physiologist Jacques Loeb. The former taught him a concern for the total behavior of an organism, and the latter impressed him with the possibility of careful, rigorous, scientific research on behavior. He learned of Watson's behaviorism from some articles by Bertrand Russell on Watson, whom Skinner then read. After failing to become a writer, Skinner turned to psychology filled with the spirit of Watsonian behaviorism. He initiated a systematic research program on a new kind of behavior, the operant.

The Experimental Analysis of Behavior

The basic goal guiding Skinner's scientific work was stated in his first psychological paper and was inspired by the success of Pavlov's work with conditioned reflexes. Wrote Skinner in "The Concept of the Reflex" (1931): "Given a particular part of the behavior of an organism hitherto regarded as unpredictable (and probably, as a consequence, assigned to non-physical factors), the investigator seeks out the antecedent changes with which the activity is correlated and establishes the conditions of the correlation" (1931/1972, p. 440). The goal of psychology is to analyze behavior by locating the specific determinants of specific behaviors, and to establish the exact nature of the relationship between antecedent influence and subsequent behavior. The best way to do this is by experiment, for only in an experiment can all the factors affecting behavior be systematically controlled. Skinner thus called his science "the experimental analysis of behavior."

A behavior is explained within this system when the investigator knows all the influences of which the behavior is a function. We may refer to the antecedent influences acting on a behavior as *independent variables,* and the behavior that is a function of them we may call the *dependent variable.* The organism can then be thought of as a *locus of variables.* It is a place where independent variables act together to produce a behavior. There is no mental activity that intervenes between independent and dependent variables, and traditional references to mental entities may be eliminated when independent variables have been understood. Skinner assumed that physiology would ultimately be able to detail the physical mechanisms controlling behavior, but that analysis of behavior in terms of functional relationships among variables is completely independent of physiology. The functions will remain even when the underlying physiological mechanisms are understood.

Thus far, Skinner's account closely followed Mach. Scientific explanation is nothing more than an accurate and precise description of the relationship between observable variables; for Skinner, these are environmental variables and behavior variables. Just as Mach sought to exorcise "metaphysical" reference to unobserved causal links in physics, so Skinner sought to exorcise "metaphysical" reference to causal mental links in psychology. In his early work, Skinner emphasized the descriptive nature of his work, and it is still sometimes called *descriptive behaviorism.* We may note here the mirror-image nature of Skinnerian and Titchenerian psychology. Titchener also followed Mach by seeking only to correlate variables analyzed within an experimental framework, but of course he wanted a description of consciousness, not behavior. Skinner sometimes conceded the possibility of such a study, but he dismissed it as irrelevant to the study of behavior, as Titchener had dismissed the study of behavior as irrelevant to the psychology of consciousness.

What separated Titchener and Skinner, besides their subject matters, was the importance of control for Skinner. Skinner was Watsonian in wanting not just to describe behavior but to control it. In fact, for Skinner, control was the ultimate test of the scientific adequacy of observationally determined functions between antecedent variables and behavior variables. Prediction alone is insufficient, for prediction may result from the correlation of two variables causally dependent on a third, but not on each other. For example, children's toe size and weight will correlate very highly: The bigger a child's toe, the heavier he or she is likely to be. However, toe size does not "cause" weight, or vice versa, for both depend on physical growth, which causes changes in both variables. According to Skinner, an investigator can only be said to have explained a behavior when in addition to being able to predict its occurrence she can also *influence* its occurrence through the manipulation of independent variables. Thus an adequate experimental analysis of behavior implies a technology of behavior, wherein behavior may be engineered for specific purposes, such as teaching. Titchener always vehemently rejected technology as a goal for psychology, but it was a concern of Skinner's that became increasingly pronounced after World War II.

The experimental analysis of behavior is without doubt the closest psychology has come to a normal science research program. It began with Skinner's first psychological book, *The Behavior of Organisms* (1938). This work contains most of the important concepts of the experimental analysis of behavior, and Skinner wrote in 1977 that *The Behavior of Organisms* "has long been out of date ... but I am continually surprised at how little of the book is actually wrong or no longer relevant." We would expect this in a document that created a successful paradigm and research program: It laid out the "hard core" of the program, as well as some specific hypotheses in the "protective belt." What is out of date are only the latter; the hard core remains relevant.

In *Behavior of Organisms,* Skinner distinguished two kinds of learned behavior, each of which had been studied before but not clearly differentiated. The first category Skinner called *respondent* behavior, or learning, studied by Pavlov. This category is properly called *reflex* behavior, for a respondent is a behavior *elicited* by a definite stimulus, whether unconditioned or conditioned. It loosely corresponds to "involuntary" behavior, such as the salivary responses studied by Pavlov. The second category Skinner called *operant* behavior or learning, which corresponds loosely to "voluntary" behavior. Operant behavior cannot be elicited but is simply emitted from time to time. However, an operant's probability of occurrence may be raised if its emission is followed by an event called a *reinforcer;* after reinforcement, it will be more likely to occur again in similar circumstances. Thorndike's puzzle boxes define an operant learning situation: The imprisoned cat emits a variety of behaviors; one of which, such as pressing a lever, leads to escape, which is *reinforcing.* With the cat placed back in the box, the probability of the correct response is now higher than before; the operant response, lever-pressing, has been strengthened. These three things—the setting in which the behavior occurs (the puzzle box), the reinforced response (lever-pressing), and the reinforcer (escape)—collectively define the *contingencies of reinforcement.* The experimental analysis of behavior consists of the systematic description of contingencies of reinforcement as they occur in all forms of animal or human behavior.

These contingencies are analyzed in Darwinian fashion. Emitted behavior is parallel to random variation in species' traits. Reinforcement from the environment follows some operants and not others; the former are strengthened and the latter are extinguished. The environment's selection pressures select favorable responses through the process of operant learning, just as successful species flourish while others become extinct. Skinner considered the experimental analysis of behavior to be part of biology, concerned with explaining an individual's behavior as the product of the environment resulting from a process analogous to that which produces species. There is no room in either discipline for vitalism, mind, or teleology. All behavior, whether learned or unlearned, is a product of an individual's reinforcement history or his or her genetic makeup. Behavior is never a product of intention or will.

Skinner's definition of the operant and its controlling contingencies distinguished him from other behaviorists in three frequently misunderstood ways. First, operant responses are never elicited. Suppose we train a rat to press a lever in a Skinner box (or "experimental space," as Skinner called it), reinforcing the bar-press only when a certain light is on above the bar. The rat will soon come to bar-press whenever the light comes on. It may appear that the stimulus of the light elicits the response—but according to Skinner, this is not so. It merely sets the occasion for reinforcement. It enables the organism to discriminate a reinforcing situation from a nonreinforcing situation, and is thus called a *discriminative stimulus.* It does not elicit bar-pressing as an unconditioned stimulus or a conditioned stimulus elicited salivation in Pavlov's dogs. Thus Skinner denied that he was an S-R psychologist, for that formula implies a reflexive link between a response and some stimulus, a link that exists only for respondents. Watson adhered to the S-R formula, for he applied the classical conditioning paradigm to all behavior. The spirit of radical behaviorism is so clearly Watsonian that many critics mistake Watson's analysis of behavior for Skinner's.

There is a second way in which Skinner is not an S-R psychologist. He said that the organism may be affected by controlling variables that need not be considered stimuli. This is clearest with respect to motivation. Motivation was seen by Hullians and Freudians as a matter of drive-stimulus reduction: Food deprivation leads to unpleasant stimuli associated with the hunger drive, and the organism acts to reduce them. Skinner sees no reason for the drive-stimuli. They are examples of mentalistic thinking that may be eliminated by directly linking food deprivation to change in behavior. Depriving an organism of food is an observable procedure that will affect an organism's behavior in lawful ways, and there is no gain in speaking of "drives" or their associated stimuli. A measurable variable, although not conceived in stimulus terms, may be causally linked to changes in observable behavior. The organism is truly a locus of variables, and whether or not the variables are stimuli of which the organism is aware is irrelevant, which renders the S-R formulation less applicable to Skinner.

The third important aspect of the operant concerns the definition. Behavior for Skinner was merely movement in space, but Skinner was careful not to define operants as simple movements. To begin with, an operant is not a response; it is a class of responses. The cat in the puzzle box may press the escape lever in different ways on different trials. Each is a different *response* in that its form is different at each occurrence, but all are members of the same *operant,* for each response is controlled by the same contingencies of reinforcement. Whether the cat butts the lever with its head or pushes it with its paw is unimportant—both are the same operant. Similarly, two otherwise identical movements may be instances of different operants if they are controlled by different contingencies. You may raise your hand to pledge allegiance to the flag, to swear to tell the truth in court, or to wave to a friend. The movements may be the same in each case, but each is a different operant, for the setting and reinforcement (the contingencies of reinforcement) are different in each case. This proves to be especially important in explaining verbal behavior: "Sock" is at least two operants controlled either by (a) a soft foot covering or (b) a punch in the nose. Earlier behaviorists such as Hull tried to define responses in purely physical terms as movements and were criticized for ignoring the meaning of behavior. A word, it was argued, is more than a puff of air; it has meaning. Skinner agreed, but he placed meaning in the contingencies of reinforcement, not the speaker's mind.

These are the most important theoretical ideas that guide the experimental analysis of behavior. When Skinner asked "Are theories of learning necessary?" and answered "No," he did not intend to eschew all theory. What he rejected was theory that refers to the unobserved hypothetical entities he considered fictions, be they ego, cognitive map, or apperception. He did accept theory in the Machian sense as being a summary of the ways in which observable variables correlate, but no more. But Skinner was additionally guided by theoretical assumptions at the level of the disciplinary matrix, and it is those we have just reviewed.

Skinner also defined an innovative and radical methodology, or shared exemplar, in his *Behavior of Organisms*. First, he chose an experimental situation that preserved the fluidity of behavior, refusing to chop it up into arbitrary and artificial "trials." An organism is placed in a space and reinforced for some behavior that it may make at any time. The behavior may be closely observed as it continuously changes over time, not as it abruptly changes with each trial. Second, the experimenter seeks to exert maximal control over the organism's environment, so that the experimenter may manipulate, or hold constant, independent variables and thus directly observe how they change behavior. Third, a very simple, yet somewhat artificial response is chosen for study. In Skinner's own work, this was typically either a rat pressing a lever or a pigeon pecking a key to obtain food or water. Choosing such an operant makes each response unambiguous, easily observed, and easily counted by machines to produce a cumulative record of responses. Finally, Skinner defined rate of responding as the basic datum of analysis. It is easily quantified; it is appealing as a measure of response probability; and it has been found to vary in lawful ways with changes in independent variables. Such a simple experimental situation stands in contrast to the relative lack of control found in Thorndike's puzzle boxes or Hull's and Tolman's mazes. The situation is capable of defining precise puzzles for the investigator, since it imposes so much control on the organism. The investigator need only draw on previous research to select what variables to manipulate and observe their effects on response rate. There is minimal ambiguity about what to manipulate or measure. Skinner provided a well-defined exemplar shared by all who practice the experimental analysis of behavior.

A final methodological point also set Skinner apart from the other behaviorists. Skinner completely dispensed with statistics or statistically dictated experimental design. He believed statistics are necessary only for those who infer an inner state from behavior. Such researchers see actual behavior as indirect measures of the inner state, contaminated by "noise," and thus they must run many subjects and treat data statistically to get measures of this hypothetical state. Skinner studied behavior itself, so there can be no "noise." All behavior is to be explained; none may be explained away as irrelevant or as "error variance." His experimental paradigm gives such clear-cut results and allows such control that "noise" does not occur. As a result, those who practice the experimental analysis of behavior run only a few subjects (often for long periods) and do not use statistics. The statistics are unnecessary, for one can see in graphic records of behavior how response rate changes as variables are altered; no inference is necessary.

The research that resulted from these guiding assumptions had a clear normal science cast. Skinner asserted that his and his followers' research tested no hypotheses but simply extended the experimental analysis of behavior piece by piece into new territory. For Kuhn, the puzzle-solving rather than hypothesis-testing character of normal science was one of its defining features, for normal science research extends the paradigm rather than tests it. The appeal of well-defined normal science is attested by the fact that the experimental analysis of behavior has many practitioners, so many that it has its own division in the APA.

Skinner had his own clear picture of the experimental analysis of behavior's paradigm. In commenting on graduate training, he remarked that his students would be ignorant of learning theory, cognitive psychology, and most of sensory psychology or mental measurement. On the methodological side, they would "never see a memory drum" (Evans, 1968). Scientific training such as this would surely produce the Kuhnian normal scientist we described in Chapter 1. (Interestingly, such a training program was instituted for a while at Columbia University after World War II [Krantz, 1973].)

It should be noted that the practice of a unique normal science within the larger body of psychology exacts a price. The experimental analysts have established their own journals, one in 1958 *(Journal of the Experimental Analysis of Behavior),* and one in 1967 *(Journal of Applied Behavioral Analysis).* A study of citations in articles appearing in the first has shown that from 1958 to 1969 writers in *JEAB* cited their own journal more and more, and others less and less, indicating a growing isolation of the experimental analysis of behavior from psychology as a whole (Krantz, 1973). The establishment of their own division in the APA underscores this isolation. Like Freud, Skinner undoubtedly viewed this isolation with equanimity, for he, just as Freud, felt he was on the correct track toward a scientific psychology while everyone else remained trapped in the prescientific past.

Interpreting Human Behavior

In his *Behavior of Organisms,* Skinner carefully articulated his experimental analysis of behavior as a paradigm for animal research. In the 1950s, while other behaviorists were liberalizing their brands of behaviorism, Skinner began to extend his radical behaviorism to human behavior without changing any of his fundamental concepts. Skinner viewed human behavior as animal behavior not significantly different from the behavior of the rats and pigeons he had studied in the laboratory.

His most important undertaking was to interpret language within the framework of radical behaviorism. As a would-be writer, Skinner was naturally interested in language, and some of his earliest, albeit unpublished, research was on speech perception. His ideas on language were set forth in a series of lectures at Harvard

University and then in a book, *Verbal Behavior* (1957). At the same time, Skinner was also concerned with using his radical behaviorism and experimental analysis of behavior as bases for the construction of a utopian society and the reconstruction of existing society. His first extended treatment of these problems came in *Walden II* (1948) and *Science and Human Behavior* (1953).

Although "most of the experimental work responsible for the advance of the experimental analysis of behavior has been carried out on other species ... the results have proved to be surprisingly free of species restrictions ... and its methods can be extended to human behavior without serious modification." So wrote Skinner in what he considered his most important work, *Verbal Behavior* (p. 3). The final goal of the experimental analysis of behavior is a science of human behavior using the same principles first applied to animals. Extension of his analysis to human behavior increasingly preoccupied Skinner after World War II.

The scope and nature of the extension is well conveyed in an interesting paper, "A Lecture in 'Having' a Poem," about how he came to write his only published poem, partially quoted at the beginning of this chapter. In this paper, he draws an analogy between "having a baby" and "having a poem": "A person produces a poem and a woman produces a baby, and we call the person a poet and the woman a mother. Both are essential as loci in which vestiges of the past come together in certain combinations" (p. 354). Just as a mother makes no positive contribution to the creation of the baby she carries, so "the act of composition is no more an act of creation than 'having' the bits and pieces" that form the poem. In such cases, something new is created, but there is no creator. Again we see the hand of Darwin: A baby is a random combination of genes that may be selected for survival or may die. A poem is a collection of bits and pieces of verbal behavior, some of which are selected, some of which are rejected, for appearance in the poem. As Darwin showed that no divine Mind was necessary to explain the production and evolution of natural species, so Skinner sought to show that it is not necessary to invoke a nonmaterial mind even to explain language—man's unique possession, according to Descartes.

His argument was worked out in most detail in *Verbal Behavior*. It is a complex and subtle book that defies easy summary. Only a few salient points may be discussed here. It is a work of interpretation only. Skinner reported no experiments and sought only to establish the plausibility of applying his analysis to language, not its reality. Further, to say he was analyzing language is misleading; the title of his book is *Verbal Behavior,* behavior whose reinforcement is mediated by other persons. The definition includes an animal behaving under the control of an experimenter, who together form a "genuine verbal community." It excludes the listener in a verbal interchange, except insofar as the listener reinforces speech (for example, by replies or compliance with demands) or acts as a discriminative stimulus (one speaks differently to one's best friend and to one's teacher). The definition makes no reference to the process of communication we usually assume takes place during speech. Skinner's account may be contrasted with that of Wundt, who excluded animals from consideration, examined the linguistic processes of both speaker and listener, and attempted to describe the communication of a *Gesamtvorstellung* from the mind of a speaker to the mind of a hearer.

Nevertheless, *Verbal Behavior* is basically about what we ordinarily consider language, or more accurately speech, for Skinner analyzed only real utterances spoken in analyzable environments, not the hypothetical abstract entity "language." Skinner introduced a number of technical concepts in his discussion of verbal behavior. To show the flavor of his analysis, we will briefly discuss his concept of the "tact," because it corresponds roughly to the problem of universals, and because Skinner considered it the most important verbal operant.

We apply the three-term set of contingencies of reinforcement, stimulus, response, and reinforcement. A *tact* is a verbal *operant response* under the *stimulus control* of some part of the physical environment, and correct use of tacts is reinforced by the verbal community. So a child is reinforced by parents for emitting the sound "doll" in the presence of a doll (Skinner, 1957). Such an operant "makes contact with" the physical environment and is called a *tact*. Skinner reduced the traditional notion of reference or naming to a functional relationship between a response, its discriminative stimuli, and its reinforcer. The situation is exactly analogous to the functional relation holding between a rat's bar-press in a Skinner box, the discriminative stimulus that sets the occasion for the response, and the food that reinforces it. Skinner's analysis of the tact was a straightforward extension of the experimental analysis of behavior paradigm to a novel situation.

Skinner's radical analysis of tacting raises an important general point about Skinner's treatment of human consciousness, his notion of private stimuli. Skinner believed that earlier methodological behaviorists such as Tolman and Hull were wrong to exclude private events (such as mental images or toothaches) from behaviorism simply because such events are private. Skinner held that part of each person's environment includes the world inside her or his skin, those stimuli to which the person has privileged access. Such stimuli may be unknown to an external observer, but they are experienced by the person who has them, can control behavior, and so must be included in any behaviorist analysis of human behavior. Many verbal statements are under such control, including complex tacts. For example: "My tooth aches" is a kind of tacting response controlled by a certain kind of painful inner stimulation.

This simple analysis implies a momentous conclusion. For how do we come to be able to make such statements as the private tact? Skinner's answer was that the verbal community has trained us to observe our private stimuli by reinforcing utterances that refer to them. It is useful for parents to know what is distressing a child, so they attempt to teach a child self-reporting verbal behaviors. "My tooth aches" indicates a visit to the dentist, not the podiatrist. Such responses thus have Darwinian survival value. It is these self-observed private stimuli that constitute consciousness. It therefore follows that human consciousness is a product of the reinforcing practices of a verbal community. A person raised by a community that did not reinforce self-description would not be conscious in anything but the sense of being awake. That person would have no self-consciousness.

Self-description also allowed Skinner to explain apparently purposive verbal behaviors without reference to intention or purpose. For example, "I am looking for my glasses" seems to describe my intentions, but Skinner (1957) argued: "Such behavior must be regarded as equivalent to *When I have behaved in this way in the past, I have found my glasses and have then stopped behaving in this way*" (p. 145). Intention is a mentalistic term Skinner has reduced to the physicalistic description of one's bodily state.

The last topic discussed in *Verbal Behavior* is thinking, the most apparently mental of all human activities. Skinner continued, however, to exorcise Cartesian mentalism by arguing that "thought is simply *behavior*." Skinner rejected Watson's view that thinking is subvocal behavior, for much covert behavior is not verbal, yet can still control overt behavior in a way characteristic of "thinking": "*I think I shall be going* can be translated *I find myself going,*" (p. 449) a reference to self-observed, but nonverbal, stimuli.

The extreme simplicity of Skinner's argument makes it hard to grasp. Once one denies the existence of the mind, as Skinner did, all that is left is behavior, so thinking must be behavior under the control of the contingencies of reinforcement. The thought of B. F. Skinner was, in his terms, simply "the sum total of his responses to the complex world in which he lived." "Thought" is simply a tact that we have learned to apply to certain forms of behavior, a tact Skinner asked people to unlearn, or at least not teach to our children. For Skinner did not merely wish to describe behavior, human or animal, he wanted to control it, control being a fundamental part of the experimental analysis of behavior. Skinner believed that current control of human behavior, based as it is on mental fictions, is ineffective at best and harmful at worst.

During World War II, Skinner worked on a behavioral guidance system for air-to-surface missiles called "Project Orcon" for *Or*ganic *Con*trol. He trained pigeons to peck at a projected image of the target that the missile they were imprisoned in was to seek out. Their pecking operated controls on the missile so that it followed its target until it struck the target, destroying target and pigeons alike. Skinner achieved such complete control of the pigeons' behavior that they could carry out the most difficult tracking maneuvers during simulated attacks. The work impressed him with the possibility of a thorough control of any organism's behavior. Skinner's superiors found the project implausible, and no pigeon-guided missiles ever flew. Shortly afterward, however, Skinner wrote his most widely read book, *Walden II,* a utopian novel based on the principles of the experimental analysis of behavior.

In the book, two characters represent Skinner: Frazier (an experimental psychologist and founder of Walden II, an experimental utopian community) and Burris (a skeptical visitor ultimately won over to membership in Walden II). Near the end Frazier speaks to Burris: "I've had only one idea in my life—a true *idée fixe*.... The idea of having my own way. 'Control' expresses it, I think. The control of human behavior, Burris" (p. 271). Frazier goes on to describe Walden II as the final laboratory and proving ground of the experimental analysis of behavior: "Nothing short of Walden II will suffice." Finally Frazier exclaims: "Well, what do you say to the design of personalities? the control of temperament? Give me the specifications and I'll give you the man! ... Think of the possibilities! A society in which there is no failure, no boredom, no duplication of effort.... Let us control the lives of our children and see what we can make of them" (p. 274).

We have met the *idée fixe* of control before in the history of behaviorism. Frazier's claim to custom-make personalities recalls Watson's claim to custom-make the careers of infants. We have seen how important the desire for social control in Progressivism was to the favorable reaction to Watson's behaviorism. Skinner was heir to the Progressive desire to scientifically control human lives in the interest of society, more specifically the survival of society, the ultimate Darwinian and Skinnerian value. He was also heir, and consciously so, to the tradition of Enlightenment optimism about human progress. Skinner asked people, in an otherwise disillusioned age, not to give up Rousseau's utopian dream, but to build a utopia on the principles of the experimental analysis of behavior. If pigeons' behavior can be controlled so that the birds guide missiles to their death, so a human being, whose behavior is likewise determined, can be controlled to be happy and productive and to feel free and dignified. *Walden II* was Skinner's first attempt to describe his vision.

NOTE: The Bibliography for this chapter is incorporated in Chapter 11.

REFERENCES

Evans, R. I. (1968). *B. F. Skinner: The man and his ideas.* New York: Dutton.

Fodor, J. A. (1981). The mind-body problem. *Scientific American, 244,* 114–122.

Kendler, H. H. (1952). "What is learned?"—A theoretical blind alley. *Psychological Review, 59,* 269–277.

Koch, S. (1951a). The current status of motivational psychology. *Psychological Review, 58,* 147–154.

Koch, S. (1951b). Theoretical psychology 1950: An overview. *Psychological Review, 58,* 295–301.

Krantz, D. L. (1973). Schools and systems: The mutual isolation of operant and non-operant psychology. In M. Henle, J. Jaynes, & J. Sullivan (Eds.), *Historical conceptions of psychology.* New York: Springer.

Krech, D. (1949). Notes toward a psychological theory. *Jounal of Personality, 18,* 66-87.

Lashley, K. S. (1951). The problem of serial order in behavior. In L. A. Jeffress (Ed.), *Cerebral mechanisms in behavior.* New York: John Wiley.

Luckhardt, C. G. (1983). Wittgenstein and behaviorism. *Synthese, 56,* 319–338.

MacCorquodale, K. & Meehl, P. E. (1948). On a distinction between hypothetical constructs and intervening variables. *Psychological Review, 55,* 95–107.

Malcolm, N. (1970). Wittgenstein on the nature of mind. *American Philosophical Quarterly Monograph Series,* Monograph 4: 9–29.

Marx, M. (1951). Intervening variable or hypothetical construct? *Psychological Review, 58,* 235–247.

Ritchie, B. F. (1953). The circumnavigation of cognition. *Psychological Review, 60,* 216–221.

Ryle, G. (1949). *The concept of mind.* New York: Barnes & Noble.

Skinner, B. F. (1931). The concept of reflex in the description of behavior. *Journal of General Psychology, 5,* 427–458. Reprinted in *Cumulative Record,* 3rd ed. Englewood Cliffs NJ: Prentice-Hall, 1972.

Skinner, B. F. (1938). *The behavior of organisms.* Englewood Cliffs, NJ: Prentice-Hall.

Skinner, B. F. (1948). *Walden II.* New York: Macmillan.

Skinner, B. F. (1953). *Science and human behavior.* New York: Macmillan.

Skinner, B. F. (1954). A critique of psychoanalytic concepts and theories. Reprinted in *Cumulative Record,* 3rd ed. Englewood Cliffs, NJ: Prentice-Hall, 1972.

Skinner, B. F. (1957). *Verbal behavior.* Englewood Cliffs, NJ: Prentice-Hall.

Skinner, B. F. (1971). *A lecture on having a poem.* Reprinted in *Cumulative Record,* 3rd ed. Englewood Cliffs, NJ: Prentice-Hall, 1972.

Skinner, B. F. (1977). Herrnstein and the evolution of behaviorism. *American Psychologist, 32,* 1006–1012.

Tolman, E. C. (1949). Discussion. *Journal of Personality, 18,* 48–50.

Wittgenstein, L. (1953). *Philosophical investigations,* 3rd ed. New York: Macmillan.

Wittgenstein, L. (1958). *The blue and brown books.* New York: Harper Colophon.

CHAPTER 11

Seeds of Change
Toward Cognitive Science and Social Unrest

INFORMAL BEHAVIORISM

EARLY THEORIES IN COGNITIVE PSYCHOLOGY

   Genetic Epistemology

   Cognitive Dissonance

   The "New Look" in Perception

   The Study of Thinking

THE MECHANIZATION OF THOUGHT

   Artificial Intelligence

   Simulating Thought

PSYCHOLOGY AND SOCIETY (1950–1958)

INFORMAL BEHAVIORISM

While Skinner's radical behaviorism continued the Watsonian tradition of rejecting all inner causes of behavior, behaviorists, with Hull and Tolman, did not. After World War II, one class of inner cause, cognitive processes, received increasing attention. Psychologists treated cognition from a variety of perspectives, including neo-Hullian "liberalized" or informal behaviorism, and a variety of unrelated theories proposed by American and European psychologists. In the long run, the most important approach to cognition grew out of mathematics and electrical engineering and had little or nothing to do with psychology and its problems. This was the creation of the field of *artificial intelligence* by the invention of the modern digital computer during World War II.

Few behavioralists were willing to agree with Skinner that organisms were "empty," that it was illegitimate to postulate, as Hull had, mechanisms taking place within the organism linking together stimulus and response. As Charles Osgood (born 1916) put it, "Most contemporary behaviorists [can] be characterized as 'frustrated empty boxers' " (Osgood, 1956). They were aware of the pitfalls of "junkshop psychology," in which mental faculties or entities were multiplied as fast as the behaviors to be explained. Yet they increasingly believed that behavior, especially "the phenomena of meaning and intention, so obviously displayed in human language behavior, entirely escape the single-stage conception" of black-box S-R psychology (Osgood, 1957). It was obvious to psychologists concerned with the human higher mental processes that people possess "symbolic processes," the ability to represent the world internally, and that human responses were controlled by these symbols, instead of being directly controlled by external stimulation. Their problem was avoiding "junkshop psychology": "What is the least amount of additional baggage needed to handle symbolic processes?" (Osgood, 1956).

They solved it by building on Hull's concepts of the r_g-s_g mechanism and the "pure stimulus act."

The r_g-s_g mechanism, or *fractional anticipatory goal response,* was proposed to handle a special type of error made by rats that had learned a maze. Hull observed that these animals often turned into blind alleys before arriving at the last choice point before the goal. The error was always to make the correct response too soon, and with increasing likelihood as the goal was approached. So, for example, if the last correct turn was to the right, the rat's error was most likely to be a right turn one choice point before the one leading to the goal. Hull explained his findings by arguing that animals had experienced Pavlovian (classical) conditioning while eating in the goal box on earlier trials, so that the goal box stimuli produced a salivary response. By generalization, the stimuli at the last, correct, choice point also elicited salivation, and by further generalization, so did other stimuli in the maze. Therefore, as a rat moved down the maze, it increasingly salivated in anticipation of the food, and the stimuli produced by salivating acted to prod the animal to turn right (in the example). Therefore, the animal would be more and more likely to turn into a blind alley before the last alley to the goal box was reached. Since the salivary response was covert (unobserved) rather than overt, Hull noted it with a small r, the salivary stimulus it caused by a small s. Since the salivary response was triggered by maze stimuli and had an effect on behavior, it could be viewed as part of an S-R behavior chain:

$$S \longrightarrow r_{salivation} \longrightarrow s_{salivary\ stimuli} \longrightarrow R.$$

The second of Hull's concepts leading to mediation theory was the *pure stimulus act.* Some behaviors, Hull noted, did not act on the environment, and he speculated that they occur to provide stimulus support for another behavior. For example, if you ask people to describe how they tie their shoes, they will typically go through the finger motions of shoe-tying while verbally describing what they are doing. Such behavior is an example of Hull's pure stimulus act. It is not too hard to imagine these acts occurring internally, without any outward show. For example, if asked, "How many windows do you have at home?" you will likely walk through a mental house and count the windows. Such processes *mediate* between external stimuli and our responses to them. The neo-Hullian psychologists conceived of human symbolic processes as internal continuations of S-R chains:

$$S \longrightarrow (r \longrightarrow s) \longrightarrow R$$

An external stimulus elicits an internal mediating response, which in turn has internal stimulus properties; and it is these internal stimuli, rather than external ones, that actually elicit overt behavior. "The great advantage of this solution is that, since each stage is an S-R process, we can simply transfer all the conceptual machinery of single-stage S-R psychology into this new model without new postulation" (Osgood, 1956, p. 178). So cognitive processes could be admitted into the body of behavior theory without giving up any of the rigor of the S-R formulation, and without inventing any uniquely human mental processes. Behavior could still be explained in terms of S-R behavior chains, except that now some of the chains took place invisibly within the organism. Behavioralists now had a language with which to discuss meaning, language, memory, problem solving, and other behaviors apparently beyond the reach of radical behaviorism.

The approach described by Osgood had many practitioners. Osgood applied it to language with especial reference to the problem of meaning, which he tried to measure behaviorally with his semantic differential scale. Irving Maltzman (1955) and Albert Goss (1961) applied it to problem solving and concept formation. The broadest program of human psychology in the liberalized vein was social learning theory, led by Neal Miller (born 1909). Miller and others at Hull's Institute for Human Relations at Yale tried to construct a psychology that would do justice to Freud's insights into the human condition, but remain within the objective realm of S-R psychology. They downplayed the axioms and quantification of Hull's animal work in order to incorporate humans within the S-R framework, and they added in mediation as a way of talking about mental life in terms more precise than Freud's. Miller's (1959) description of his brand of behaviorism, including the whole neo-Hullian mediational camp, as "liberalized S-R theory" is apt. Social learning theorists did not abandon S-R theory; they only loosened its restrictions in order to be able to encompass human language, culture, and psychotherapy. Howard and Tracy Kendler (1962, 1975), for example, applied mediation theory to human discrimination learning, showing that differences in discrimination learning patterns between animals, children, and adult humans could be explained by claiming that animals rarely developed mediating responses, and that the ability to form them developed in middle childhood.

The concept of mediation was a creative response by neo-Hullian behaviorists to the challenge of explaining human thought. However, mediationists did not leave S-R psychology intact because they had to modify Hull's strong versions of peripheralism and phylogenetic continuity to produce a theory capable of doing justice to the human higher mental processes. Hull had envisaged the fractional anticipatory goal response and the pure stimulus act as actual, if covert, motor responses that could enter into behavior chains; the mediationists, by contrast, conceived of mediation as taking place centrally, in the brain, giving up Watsonian and Hullian muscle-twitchism. Hull had wanted a single set of laws of learning to cover all forms of at least mammalian behavior; mediationists scaled back his ambition, accepting that while in a general way S-R theory might be universal, special allowances had to be made for species and developmental differences. Nevertheless, changes wrought by neo-Hullians were evolutionary, not revolutionary: Neal Miller was correct in asserting that they had liberalized S-R theory, not overthrown it.

While it was a major—perhaps *the* major—theoretical position in the 1950s, mediational behaviorism ultimately proved to be a bridge linking the inferential behavioralism of the 1930s and 1940s to the inferential behavioralism of the 1980s: cognitive psychology. The diagrams of mediational processes quickly became incredibly cumbersome (see, for example, the Osgood papers already cited). More importantly, there was no very good reason to think of processes one couldn't see as little chains of r's and s's. The mediationalists' commitment to internalizing S-R language resulted primarily from their desire to preserve theoretical rigor and avoid the apparent unscientific character of "junkshop psychology." In essence, they lacked any other language with which to discuss the mental processes in a clear and disciplined fashion and took the only course they saw open to them. However, when a new language of power, rigor, and precision came along—the language of computer programming—it proved easy for mediational psychologists to abandon their r-s life raft for the ocean liner of information processing.

EARLY THEORIES IN COGNITIVE PSYCHOLOGY

Not all psychologists interested in cognition worked within the framework of neo-Hullian mediational psychology. In Europe, cognitive development had been studied by the Swiss psychologist Jean Piaget (1896–1980) since the 1920s. In the United States, social psychologists had abandoned the concept of the group mind in the first decades of the twentieth century, gradually defining it as it is today—the study of people in groups. During the war, social psychologists had been concerned to study attitudes, how persuasion and propaganda change attitudes, and the relation of attitudes to personality. After the war, social psychologists continued to develop theories about how people form, integrate, and act on beliefs. Finally, Jerome Bruner studied how personality dynamics shape people's perceptions of the world, and how people solve complex problems.

Genetic Epistemology

Although European psychology in the early twentieth century was quiescent, it was by no means extinct. Piaget was a most important European psychologist. Piaget, like Freud and Wundt before him, had begun with purely biological interests, but he eventually found himself practicing an innovative psychology. In Piaget's case, the influences that drew him away from biology were threefold. First, he maintained a strong interest in the questions of epistemology, although he believed traditional philosophies to be too speculative and unscientific. Second, he experienced psychoanalysis with one of Freud's pupils and studied with Jung's mentor, Bleuler, at Zurich. Third, he worked with Alfred Binet's collaborator, Theophile Simon, administering intelligence tests to children. Out of this eclectic background Piaget formulated a unique cognitive psychology. The traditional problems of epistemology are important: What is knowledge, and what are people that they may have knowledge? To Piaget, these questions should admit of a scientific answer based on sound theory and empirical research. In particular, Piaget felt it should be possible to trace the psychological growth of knowledge in children as they grow up by studying their reactions to intellectual situations, as in intelligence tests, followed up by probing questions, as in psychoanalysis. Finally, Piaget's biological orientation shone through in his conception of knowledge as a set of cognitive structures that enable a child to adapt to the environment. Piaget calls his field of study *genetic epistemology*, the study of the origins of knowledge in child development.

As one would expect with a European psychologist, Piaget showed strong Kantian influences. The titles of many of his works are the names of Kant's transcendental categories: *The Child's Conception of Space, The Child's Conception of Number, The Child's Conception of Time,* and many more. In other ways, too, Piaget was distinctly European. Like Wundt, Piaget was interested in the general human mind, which Piaget calls the *epistemic subject,* not in individuals or their unique lives. Also like Wundt, Piaget was less interested in applied aspects of his work than are Americans, although he sometimes wrote on education. The question of whether training can accelerate the course of cognitive growth Piaget called "The American Question," for it was not asked in Europe. In true pragmatic fashion, Americans wanted to know how to get knowledge faster and more efficiently.

Piaget began his studies of children's knowledge in the 1920s, but—after a brief flurry of interest—his work was largely ignored in the United States. It was only in the 1960s that his work was rediscovered, in a context to be discussed in Chapter 13. From 1930 to 1960, Piaget's thought was clearly out of step with American behaviorism, and his works consequently went largely unread and untranslated.

The details of Piaget's theory are complex, but Piaget was no behaviorist. Genetic epistemology is concerned with human knowledge, not human behavior, and Piaget's theory explicitly attempted to characterize the mental structures that guide a child's knowledge of the world. Furthermore, he rejected associationism and atomism in favor of *structuralism,* a European philosophy that explains human behavior by reference to unobserved, abstract, mathematically describable structures.

During his long intellectual lifetime, Piaget systematically pursued his own research program, paying only occasional attention to behaviorism. Thus, although he was little read before 1960, Piaget and his genetic epistemology constituted a sophisticated alternative to behaviorism ready to be picked up when behaviorism faltered. After 1960, as young psychologists became disenchanted with behaviorism, Piaget would be increasingly read, translated, and researched by students of cognitive development.

Cognitive Dissonance

Social psychology is the study of the person as a social being, and so it has roots going back to the Greek political thinkers and to Hobbes's first political science. We have said little about it before because as a field it is exceedingly eclectic, unified by no coherent vision of humanity. It draws our attention now because during the 1940s and 1950s it continued to employ mental concepts of a commonsense sort. We will briefly consider one theory widely influential in the 1950s and early 1960s, Leon Festinger's (1919–1989) theory of cognitive dissonance.

Festinger's theory is about a person's beliefs and their interaction. It holds that beliefs may agree with one another, or they may clash. When beliefs clash, they induce an unpleasant state called *cognitive dissonance,* which the person tries to reduce. For example, a nonsmoker who is persuaded that cigarettes cause lung cancer will feel no dissonance, for her or his belief that smoking causes cancer agrees with and supports her or his refusal to smoke. However, a smoker who comes to believe smoking causes cancer will feel cognitive dissonance, for the decision to smoke clashes with this new belief. The smoker will act to reduce the dissonance, perhaps by giving up smoking. However, it is quite common to manage dissonance in other ways. For example, a smoker may simply avoid antismoking information in order to avoid dissonance.

Festinger's theory provoked much research. One classic study appeared to challenge the law of effect. Festinger and a collaborator, J. Merrill Carlsmith, devised some extremely boring tasks for subjects to perform, such as turning screws for a long time. Then the experimenter got the subject to agree to tell a waiting subject that the task was fun. Some subjects were paid $20 for telling the lie; others were paid only $1. According to the theory, the $20 subjects should feel no dissonance: The large payment justified their little lie. However, the $1 subjects should feel dissonance: They were telling a lie for a paltry amount of money. One way to resolve this dissonance would be to convince oneself that the task was in fact fun, for if one believed this, telling another subject that it was fun would be no lie. After the whole experiment was over, another experimenter interviewed the subjects and discovered that the $1 subjects voted the task significantly more enjoyable than the $20 subjects, as Festinger's theory predicted. The finding appears inconsistent with the law of effect, for we might expect that a $20 reward for saying the experiment was fun would change one's report about the enjoyability of the experiment more than a $1 reward.

What is most important about the theory of cognitive dissonance for historical purposes is that it was a cognitive theory—a theory about mental entities, in this case about a person's beliefs. It was not an informal behaviorist theory, for Festinger did not conceive of beliefs as mediating responses, but in commonsense terms, as controlling behavior. In the 1950s, the theory of cognitive dissonance and other cognitive theories in social psychology constituted a vigorous cognitive psychology outside the orbit of strict behaviorism. Festinger's (1957) book *A Theory of Cognitive Dissonance* made no reference to behaviorist ideas. Social psychologists rarely challenged behaviorism, but their field was an alternative to it.

The "New Look " in Perception

Shortly after the war, a new approach to the study of perception arose. Dubbed the "New Look" in perception, it was led by Jerome S. Bruner (born 1915). The New Look arose from an attempt to unify several different areas of psychology—perception, personality, and social psychology—and from a desire to refute the prevalent conception, going back at least to Hume and strongly present in S-R behavior theory, that perception was a passive process by which a stimulus impressed (Hume's term) itself on the perceiver. Bruner and his colleagues proposed a view of perception in which the perceiver takes an active role, rather than being a passive register of sense data. Bruner and others did a variety of studies to support the idea that a perceiver's personality and social background play a role in affecting what the perceiver sees. The most famous and controversial of these studies concern perceptual defense and raise the possibility of subliminal perception. Bruner and others in the New Look movement presented words to subjects for brief intervals, as had Wundt in his studies of the span of consciousness. However, these modern researchers varied the emotional content of the words: Some were ordinary or "neutral" words, others were obscene or "taboo" words. Bruner and his associates found that longer exposures are required for a subject to recognize a taboo word than to recognize a neutral word. It appears that subjects somehow unconsciously perceive the negative emotional content of a taboo word and then attempt to repress its entry into awareness. Subjects will see the word only when the exposure is so long that they cannot help seeing it.

Research on perceptual defense was extremely controversial for many years, some psychologists arguing that subjects see taboo words as quickly as neutral words, falsely denying the experience as long as possible to avoid embarrassment. The controversy grew heated and has never been fully resolved. What is significant for us is that the New Look in perception analyzed perception as an active mental process involving both conscious and unconscious mental activities intervening between a sensation and a person's response to it. The idea of perceptual defense is much closer to psychoanalysis than to behaviorism, a fact in part responsible for the controversy surrounding Bruner's findings. In any event, the New Look was a cognitive alternative to behaviorism.

The Study of Thinking

Concern with perception and his demonstrations that mind and personality actively shape it led Bruner to a study of the old "higher mental processes" (Bruner, Goodnow, and Austin, 1956). Although he was not a mediational theorist and placed his own theorizing in the psychodynamic tradition, Bruner linked his own interest in cognitive processes to the new mediational S-R theories and identified a revival interest in and investigation of the cognitive processes. In the landmark book *A Study of Thinking,* Bruner investigated how people form concepts and categorize new stimuli as members of different conceptual categories. Bruner and his colleagues presented subjects with arrays of geometrical figures defined along many dimensions: shape, size, color, and the like. The subject was then asked to figure out what concept the experimenter had in mind by choosing, or being presented with, examples and nonexamples of the experimenter's concept. For example, the concept to be discovered might be "all red triangles," and the experimenter might begin by pointing out to the subject a large red triangle as an example of the concept. The subject would then choose other stimuli from the array and be told whether each was or was not a member of the concept class. If the subject chose a large red square, the subject would be told "No"; and if the subject chose a small red triangle, he or she would be told "Yes." The subject would choose instances until he or she was prepared to guess the definition of the experimenter's concept.

Bruner, Goodnow, and Austin did not view the process of concept learning in terms of learning implicit mediational responses, although some informal behaviorists did. Rather, they looked on concept formation as an active, not reactive, process in which the subject's choices are guided by some strategy constructed to solve the problem. Again, the details of the theory are not important for our purposes. What is important is the mentalistic nature of Bruner's theory. The subject was not seen as a passive connector between S and R or even as linking S-r-s-R, or as a locus of variables. Instead, concept formation was conceived as an active intellectual process in which a subject constructs and follows certain strategies and decision procedures that guide (or fail to guide) the subject to the correct concept.

The investigations and theories of the mediational behaviorialists, Piaget, Festinger, and Bruner, demonstrated psychologists' revived interest in human cognitive processes following the war. However, while these research programs were vigorous, their theories were due to be assimilated and eclipsed by a different kind of cognitive psychology, whose roots and conceptions lie almost entirely outside the field of psychology altogether. For during World War II there appeared the thinking machine.

THE MECHANIZATION OF THOUGHT

Artificial Intelligence

Ever since Descartes, philosophers of the mind and psychologists had been attracted and repelled by the similarity of human and machine. Descartes thought that all human cognitive processes save thinking were carried out by the machinery of the nervous system, and he based his divisions of human being vs. brute and mind vs. body on his conviction. Pascal feared that Descartes was wrong, since it seemed to him his calculator could think, and he turned to the human heart and its faith in God to separate people from machines. Hobbes and La Mettrie embraced, and de Sade reveled in, the idea that people are no more than animal-machines, alarming the romantics who, with Pascal, sought the secret essence of humanity in feeling rather than intellect. Leibniz dreamed of a universal thinking machine, and the English engineer Charles Babbage tried to build one. William James worried about his automatic sweetheart, concluding that a machine could not feel and so could not be human. Watson, with Hobbes and La Mettrie, proclaimed that humans and animals are machines and that human salvation lay in accepting that reality and engineering a perfect future, limned by Skinner in *Walden II*. Science fiction writers and filmmakers began to explore the differences, if any, between human and machine in *Rossum's Universal Robots* and *Metropolis*. But no one had yet built a machine that anyone could even hope would emulate human thinking. Until World War II.

Since the time of Newton, the trend of science has been the mechanization of the world picture. As we have seen, in the twentieth century, psychologists had wrestled with the last refuge of teleology—purposive animal and human behavior. Hull tried to give a mechanical account of purpose; Tolman first left it in behavior as an observable, but later put it in the organism's cognitive map room; and Skinner tried to dissolve purposes into environmental control of behavior. None of these attempts to deal with purpose was entirely convincing, but Tolman's failure is the most revealing about the behaviorist enterprise. Tolman could be fairly criticized for committing the Cartesian category mistake and building a homunculus (or, in the case of a rat, a ratunculus) into a person's head, and explaining that person's behavior as the outcome of the homunculus's decision making. For a map implies a map reader; there really was a Ghost in Tolman's machine. Psychologists seemed to be on the horns of a trilemma: (1) They could try to explain purposive behavior by reference to inner events, as Tolman did; but this risked inventing a mythical inner Ghost whose behavior was as mysterious as the outer behavior science wanted to explain to begin with. (2) They could try to explain away behavior as purely mechanical, as Hull had, or as subtle and mislabeled environmental control of behavior, as Skinner did; but, while suitably scientific and tough-minded, this seemed to deny the obvious fact that behavior is goal directed. (3) Or, following Brentano and Wittgenstein, they could accept purpose as an irreducible truth of human action, neither requiring nor needing explanation; but this denied that psychology could be a science of the same sort as physics, a conclusion unthinkable to psychologists in the grip of physics envy.

Out of scientific work in World War II came the modern high-speed digital computer, bringing with it concepts that made the first alternative more attractive than it had ever been, because they seemed to offer a way around the bogey of the Ghost in the Machine. The most important of these concepts were the idea of *informational feedback* and the concept of the computer *program*. The importance of feedback was grasped immediately; the importance of the idea of programming took longer to be realized, but it eventually gave rise to a new solution to the mind-body problem called *functionalism*. What made the concepts of feedback and programming impressive, even commanding, was their association with real machines that seemed to think.

Given the contemporary rivalry between information-processing psychology and radical behaviorism, there is irony in the fact that the concept of feedback, and hence modern cognitive psychology, arose out of the same war problem that Skinner had worked on in his Pelican project. Project ORCON had aimed at the ORganic CONtrol of missiles. Mathematicians and computer scientists aimed at the mechanical control of missiles and other weapons, inventing the modern digital computer. In 1943, three researchers described the concept of informational feedback that lay behind their solution to guiding devices to targets: They showed how purpose and mechanism were not incompatible. In fact, feedback had been used by engineers since at least the eighteenth century. The achievement of Rosenblueth, Wiener, and Bigelow (1966) was making feedback a scientific concept and describing it in general terms. A good example of a system using feedback is a thermostat and a furnace. You give the thermostat a goal when you set the temperature at which you want to keep your house. The thermostat contains a thermometer that measures the house temperature, and when the temperature falls below the set point, the thermostat turns on the furnace. As the furnace warms the room, the thermometer registers the change and the thermostat turns the furnace off when the correct temperature is reached. Here is a feedback loop of information: The thermostat is sensitive to the state of the room, and based on the information received by its thermometer, it takes action. The action in turn changes the state of the room, which feeds back to the thermostat, changing its behavior, which in turn influences the room temperature, and so on in an endless cycle.

In a simple way, the thermostat and the furnace constitute a purposive organism. Their goal is to maintain a constant temperature, and they are able to respond appropriately to changes in the environment. And there is, of course, no Ghost in the Thermostat. In older times, there would have been a servant who read a thermometer and stoked the furnace when necessary; but he has been replaced by a mere machine, and a simple one at that. The promise of the concept of feedback is that it might be possible to analyze all purposive behavior as instances of feedback: The organism has some goal (for example, to get food), is able to measure its distance from the goal (for example, it's at the other end of the maze), and behaves so as to reduce and finally eliminate that distance. The Ghost in the Machine, or Tolman's cognitive map reader, could be replaced by complex feedback loops. Practically, too, servants and industrial workers might be replaced by machines capable of doing what before only people could do.

So, machines could be purposive. Were they then intelligent, or at least capable of becoming intelligent? Could they emulate human intelligence? Whether computers were or could be intelligent became the central question of cognitive science, and the question was raised in its modern form by the brilliant mathematician A. M. Turing (1912–1954), who had contributed much to the theory of computers during the war. In 1950, Turing published a paper in *Mind,* "Computing Machinery and Intelligence," that defined the field of artificial intelligence and established the program of cognitive science. "I propose to consider the question, Can machines think?," Turing began. Since the meaning of "think" was so terribly unclear, Turing proposed to set his question more concretely "in terms of a game which we call the 'imitation game.' " Imagine an interrogator talking via computer terminal to two respondents, another human and a computer, without knowing which is which. The game consists in asking questions designed to tell which respondent is the human and which is the computer. Turing proposed that we consider a computer intelligent when it can fool the interrogator into thinking it is the human being. Turing's imitation game has since become known as the Turing Test, and it is widely taken to be the criterion of artificial intelligence (AI). Workers in the field of AI aim to create machines that can perform many of the same tasks previously done only by people, ranging from playing chess to assembling automobiles to exploring the surface of Mars.

Simulating Thought

We have already seen that some psychologists, most notably Hull, had tried to construct learning machines. There were naturally some psychologists, therefore, who were drawn to the computer for a model of learning and purposive behavior. In conversation with Harvard psychologist E. G. Boring, Norbert Wiener asked what the human brain could do that electronic computers could not, moving Boring (1946) to ask the same question as Turing: What would a robot have to do to be called intelligent? After reviewing human intellectual faculties and psychologists' early attempts to mimic them with machines, Boring (1946, p. 192) formulated his own version of the Turing Test: "Certainly a robot whom you could not distinguish from another student would be an extremely convincing demonstration of the mechanical nature of man and the unity of science." For Boring, a thinking robot could carry much metaphysical baggage, since it would vindicate La Mettrie's declaration that man is a machine and promised to secure psychology a place among the natural sciences. Boring's hopes have become the expectations of contemporary cognitive scientists.

In the early 1950s, various attempts were made to create electronic or other mechanical models of learning and other cognitive processes. The English psychologist J. A. Deutsch (1953) built an "electro-mechanical model ... capable of learning mazes and discrimination ... [and insightful] reasoning." Similar models were discussed by L. Benjamin Wyckoff (1954) and James Miller (1955). Slack (1955) used the similarities between feedback and Dewey's reflex arc to attack Hullian S-R theory.

Another English psychologist, Donald Broadbent (1957), proposed a mechanical model of attention and short-term memory in terms of balls being dropped into a Y-shaped tube representing various sensory "channels" of information. Broadbent argued that psychologists should think of the input to the senses not as stimuli but as *information*. Information-processing concepts were applied to human attention and memory by George Miller in a now classic paper, "The Magical Number Seven, Plus or Minus Two: Some Limits on Our Capacity for Processing Information" (1956). Miller was moving away from an eclectic behaviorist position on human learning and would emerge as one of the leaders of cognitive psychology in the 1960s. In the 1956 paper, he drew attention to limitations on human attention and memory and set the stage for the first massive wave of research in information-processing psychology, which concentrated on attention and short-term memory.

In all of these early papers attempting to apply computer concepts to psychology, there was some confusion about what was actually doing the thinking. Encouraged by the popular phrase for the computer, "electronic brain," there was a strong tendency to think that it was the electronic device itself that was thinking, and that psychologists should look for parallels between the structure of the human brain and the structure of electronic computers. For example, James Miller (1955) envisioned a "comparative psychology ... dealing not with animals but with electronic models," since the actions of computers are "in many interesting ways like living behavior." However, the identification of neural and electronic circuitry was much too simple. As Turing said in his 1950 paper, computers are general-purpose machines (the theoretically ideal general-purpose computer is called a *Turing machine*). The actual electronic architecture of a computer is unimportant, because what makes a computer behave as it does is its *program,* and the same program may be run on physically different machines and different programs run on the same machine. Turing pointed out that a man in a room with an infinite supply of paper and a rulebook for transforming input symbols into output symbols could be regarded as a computer; in such circumstances, his behavior would be controlled only trivially by his neurology, since his answers to questions would be dictated by the rulebook, and if one changed the rulebook, his behavior would change. The distinction of computer and program was crucial to cognitive psychology, for it meant that cognitive psychology was not neurology, and that cognitive theories of human thinking should talk about the human mind—that is, the human program—rather than the human brain. A correct cognitive theory would be implemented by the human brain and could be run on a properly programmed computer, but the theory would be in the program, not in the brain or the computer.

What began to emerge in the 1950s was a new conception of the human being as machine, and a new language in which to formulate theories about cognitive processes. People could be described, it seemed, as general-purpose computing devices, born with certain hardware and programmed by experience and socialization to behave in certain ways. The goal of psychology would be the specification of how human beings process information; the concepts of stimulus and response would be replaced by the concepts of information input and output, and theories about mediating r-s chains would be replaced by theories about internal computations and computational states. This new conception of psychology was clearly stated by Allan Newell, J. C. Shaw, and Herbert Simon in 1958 in "Elements of a Theory of Problem

Solving." Since the early 1950s, they had been at work on writing programs that would solve problems, beginning with a program that proved mathematical theorems, the Logic Theorist, and moving onto a more powerful program, the General Problem Solver (GPS). They had previously published their work primarily in computer engineering journals, but writing now in *Psychological Review,* they defined the new cognitive approach to psychology:

> The heart of [our] approach is describing the behavior of the system by a well-specified program, defined in terms of elementary information processes....
>
> Once the program has been specified, we proceed exactly as we do with traditional mathematical systems. We attempt to deduce general properties of the system from the program (the equations); we compare the behavior predicted from the program (from the equations) with actual behavior observed ... [and] we modify the program when modification is required to fit the facts.

Newell, Shaw, and Simon claimed special virtues for their approach to psychological theorizing. Computers are "capable of realizing programs," making possible very precise predictions about behavior. Additionally, in order to actually run on a computer, programs must provide "a very concrete specification of [internal] processes," ensuring that theories be precise, never vague and merely verbal. The Logic Theorist and the General Problem Solver represent, Newell, Shaw, and Simon conclude, "a thoroughly operational theory of human problem solving."

Newell, Shaw, and Simon make stronger claims for their problem-solving programs than Turing made for his hypothetical AI program. Researchers in artificial intelligence wanted to write programs that would behave like people without necessarily thinking like people. So, for example, they write chess-playing programs that play chess but use the brute-force number-crunching ability of supercomputers to evaluate thousands of moves before choosing one, rather than trying to imitate the human chess master who evaluates many fewer alternatives, but does so more cleverly. Newell, Shaw, and Simon, however, moved from artificial intelligence to *computer simulation* in claiming that not only did their programs solve problems, but they solved problems in the same way human beings did. In a computer simulation of chess (of which there are a few), the programmer would try to write a program whose computational steps are the same as those of a human master chess player. The distinction between AI and computer simulation is important because pure AI is not psychology. Efforts in AI may be psychologically instructive for suggesting the kinds of cognitive resources humans must possess to achieve intelligence, but specifying how people actually behave intelligently requires more.

While apparently breaking with the past in giving up altogether on S-R theory of any form, GPS was really a continuation of the Hullian impulse in psychology. Like Hull, Newell, Shaw, and Simon wanted a theory that was fundamentally mathematical, precise, and well specified; that could predict behavior in detail as deductions from the theory; and that was thoroughly operational. The theory of the General Problem Solver hews to the ideal of Newton's *Principia Mathematica* as much as Hull could have wished, and Hull could have fairly seen the implementation of the program on a computer as justification and fulfillment of his own preoccupation with building a learning machine. Newell, Shaw, and Simon are simply bringing to the Hullian impulse much better tools with which to theorize and a much richer language in which to frame behavioralist theories. Computers were invented by electrical engineers and mathematicians, not psychologists; the concept of programming general-purpose machines was mathematician John von Neuman's and Turing's, not any psychologist's; Newell, Shaw, and Simon were from Carnegie-Mellon University, a university outside the circle of leading academic universities at which behaviorism held sway, and closely connected with business, industry, and engineering; and Simon was more an economist than a psychologist, winning the Nobel Prize for economics in 1978 for his theory of "satisficing." Their work, like that of Broadbent, Miller, and the other pioneers in cognitive science, assimilated a powerful tool invented outside psychology to the central program of behavioralism: the description, prediction, and control of human behavior.

PSYCHOLOGY AND SOCIETY (1950–1958)

American psychologists—and by the 1950s, psychology had become an American science (Reisman, 1966)—entered the 1950s with a confidence in the future shared by most other Americans. The war had ended, the Depression was only an unpleasant memory, the economy and the population were booming. To Fillmore Sanford (1951), secretary of the APA, the future of psychology lay with professional psychology, and that future was bright indeed, because a new era had dawned, "the age of the psychological man":

> Our society appears peculiarly willing to adopt psychological ways of thinking and to accept the results of psychological research. American people seem to have a strong and conscious need for the sorts of professional services psychologists are … equipped to give.… [T]he age of the psychological man is upon us, and … psychologists must accept responsibility not only for having spread the arrival of this age but for guiding its future course. Whether we like it or not, our society is tending more and more to think in terms of the concepts and methods spawned and nurtured by psychologists. And whether we like it or not, psychologists will continue to be a consequential factor in the making of social decisions and in the structuring of our culture. (p. 74)

Sanford argued that psychologists had an unprecedented opportunity to "create a profession the like of which has never before been seen, either in form or content … the first *deliberately designed* profession in history."

By every quantitative measure, Sanford's optimism was justified. Membership in the APA grew from 7,250 in 1950 to 16,644 in 1959; the most rapid growth occurred in the applied divisions, and psychologists, by establishing various boards and committees within the APA, did deliberately design their profession, as Fillmore hoped. Despite skirmishes with the other APA, the American Psychiatric Association (which was loath to give up its monopoly on mental health care and opposed the legal recognition of clinical psychology), states began to pass certification and licensing laws covering applied—primarily clinical and counseling—psychologists, defining them legally and, of course, acknowledging them as legitimate professionals (Reisman, 1966). Psychology in industry prospered as industry prospered, businesspeople recognizing that "we need not 'change human nature,' we need only to learn to control and to use it" (Baritz, 1960). Popular magazine articles on psychology began to appear regularly, often telling people how to choose genuine clinical psychologists from psychological frauds. Psychologists basked in the favorable series on psychology appearing in *Life* by Ernest Havemann in 1957: They gave him an award for his series.

Certain troubles remained, however. Within psychology, traditional experimental and theoretical psychologists were becoming unhappy with the increasing numbers and influence of applied psychologists. In 1957, a committee of the Division of Experimental Psychology polled its membership's attitudes to the APA. They found that although 55 percent approved of the APA, 30 percent were opposed to it; and they noted a growing, though still minority, desire by the experimentalists to secede from the APA (Farber, 1957). The first claims were made that clinical psychologists (and psychiatrists) could effectively neither diagnose (Meehl, 1954) nor treat (Eysenck, 1952) their patients. Divided among themselves, psychologists were also divided from the mainstream of American thought in the 1950s. Surveying the social attitudes of twenty-seven leading psychologists, Keehn (1955) found that they were far more liberal than the country as a whole. Compared to most Americans, psychologists were nonreligious or even antireligious (denying that God exists, that survival of bodily death occurs, and that people need religion), were opposed to the death penalty, believed that criminals should be cured rather than punished, and supported easier divorce laws.

Amid the prosperity and general good feelings of the 1950s there was a small but growing disturbing current, felt faintly within psychology itself and more strongly in the larger American culture: an unhappiness with the ethos and ethic of adjustment. Robert Creegan (1953) wrote in *American Psychologist* that "the job of psychology is to criticize and improve the social order ... rather than to adjust passively ... [and] grow fat." Sociologist C. Wright Mills deplored the application of psychology to industrial social control "in the movement from authority to manipulation, power shifts from the visible to the invisible, from the known to the anonymous. And with rising material standards exploitation becomes less material and more psychological" (Baritz, 1960). Psychoanalyst Robert Lindner (1953) attacked the ideology of adjustment as a dangerous "lie" that had reduced human beings to a "pitiful" state and threatened "to send the species into the evolutionary shadows." Lindner blamed psychiatry and clinical psychology for preserving the myth of adjustment by regarding neurotics and other unhappy humans as "sick" when in fact, according to Lindner, they were in healthy but misdirected rebellion against a stifling culture of conformity. The goal of therapy, Lindner wrote, should not be conforming the patient to a sick society but working "to transform the negative protest and rebellion of the patient into positive expression of the rebellious urge."

Outside psychology rebellion against adjustment was more widespread and grew with the decade. In sociology, David Riesman's *The Lonely Crowd* (1950) and William H. Whyte's *The Organization Man* (1956) dissected and attacked the American culture of conformity. In politics, Peter Viereck praised *The Unadjusted Man: A New Hero for America*. Novels such as J. D. Salinger's *Catcher in the Rye* (1951), Sloan Wilson's *The Man in the Grey Flannel Suit* (1955), and Jack Kerouac's *On the Road* (1957) expressed the unhappiness of people caught in a gray world of adaptation and conformity, yearning for lives less constrained and more emotional. The movie *Rebel Without a Cause* portrayed the tragic fate of one whose anxiety and unhappiness found no constructive purpose. And the fierce, restless energy of the young—whose numbers were growing rapidly—exploded in rock and roll, the only creative outlet it could find.

At the end of the decade, sociologist Daniel Bell wrote about the exhaustion of ideas during the 1950s. The beliefs of the past were no longer acceptable to young thinkers, and the middle way of adjustment was "not for [them]; it is without passion and deadening." Bell identified a "search for a cause" moved by "a deep, desperate, almost pathetic anger." The world, to many young minds, was gray and unexciting. In psychology, eclecticism could be boring, for there were no issues to fight over, no battles to be fought as before, when psychology had begun, or when functionalist had battled structuralist and behaviorist had battled introspectionist. Psychology was thriving, but to no clear end, apparently happy in its work of adjustment.

All this was about to change.

BIBLIOGRAPHY FOR CHAPTERS 10 AND 11

Accessible discussions of logical behaviorism may be found in Fodor (1981); Arnold S. Kaufman, "Behaviorism," *Encyclopedia of the social sciences,* Vol. 1 (New York: Macmillan, 1967), pp. 268–73; Arnold B. Levison, (Ed.), *Knowledge and society: An introduction to the philosophy of the social sciences* (Indianapolis: Bobbs-Merrill, 1974), Ch. VI; and Norman Malcolm, *Problems of mind: Descartes to Wittgenstein* (New York: Harper Torchbooks, 1971), Ch. III. Ryle's *Concept of mind* (1949), is well written, even witty, and quite readable even by someone with no previous knowledge of philosophy. Wittgenstein, on the other hand, is a notoriously difficult philosopher to understand. For our present purposes, his most important works are *The blue and brown books* (1958), a published version of Cambridge lectures delivered in 1933 and 1934, which formed the preliminary studies for the posthumously published *Philosophical investigations* (1953). Wittgenstein wrote in a sort of dialogue style, arguing with an unnamed interlocutor and, like Plato, tended to develop arguments by indirection rather than outright statement. Further difficulty understanding his philosophy arises from the fact that in an important sense he had nothing positive to say, aiming like Socrates at clearing up misconceptions instead of offering his own conceptions. As Malcolm put it in the book cited above, "Philosophical work of the right sort merely unties knots in our understanding. The result is not a theory but simply—no knots!" So one should not tackle Wittgenstein without guidance. The best book-length introduction is Anthony Kenny's *Wittgenstein* (Cambridge, MA: Harvard University Press, 1973). The best treatment of Wittgenstein's philosophy of mind is Malcolm (1970). Luckhardt (1983) is also helpful and clear, especially concerning Wittgenstein's attitude to behaviorism.

Papers expounding the positivistic view of psychological theory construction nearly filled the pages of the *Psychological Review* in the late 1940s and early 1950s. Some of them, including Kendler's, are collected in Melvin Marx (Ed.), *Theories in contemporary psychology* (New York: Macmillan, 1963). A witty reply to Kendler from the realist perspective was given by Tolman's colleague Benbow F. Ritchie, "The circumnavigation of cognition," *Psychological Review* (1953, *60:* 216–21). Ritchie likens Kendler to an operationist geographer who defines problems of navigation purely in terms of the procedures for getting from one point to another on the earth's surface, thereby dismissing the dispute between the "flat-earth theorists" and the "ball theorists" as a pseudoissue, since both theories are operationally reducible to statements about movement on the earth's surface, rendering irrelevant any "surplus meaning" concerning the shape of the earth. The "what is learned" debate has been insightfully studied by philosopher Ron Amundson, "Psychology and epistemology: The place versus response controversy," *Cognition* (1985, *20:* 127–55). If you are interested in the many experiments done concerning "what is learned," you should consult reviews found under the heading "Learning" in the *Annual review of psychology,* which began publication in 1950. Also useful is Ernest R. Hilgard's (later coauthored by Gordon Bower) text, *Theories of learning,* whose first edition appeared in 1948 (New York: Appleton-Century-Crofts). For an account of the broader issues raised by operationism, see Thomas H. Leahey, "Operationism and ideology," *Journal of Mind and Behavior* (1983, *4:* 81–90).

The works of B. F. Skinner are fully listed in the Chapter 10 References. The best single book of Skinner's to read is *Science and human behavior* (New York: Macmillan, 1953), because there he discussed his philosophy of science, explained his scientific work, and went on to criticize society in light of his conclusions, offering behaviorist remedies for social ills. His autobiography, in three volumes, has been completed and published by Knopf (New York): *Particulars of my life* (1976), *The shaping of a behaviorist* (1979), and *A matter of consequences* (1983). Richard Evans has conducted two interviews with Skinner: *B. F. Skinner: The man and his ideas* (New York: Dutton, 1968) provides a good introduction to Skinner, and *A dialogue with B. F. Skinner* (New York: Praeger, 1981) provides an update. Paul Sagal discusses *Skinner's philosophy* (Washington, DC: University Press of America, 1981). Some of Skinner's later works are cited in Chapter 15.

Miller (1959) provides a good general introduction to informal, "liberalized" behavioralism, although he focuses on his own research and neglects the many other mediational behaviorists, such as Osgood, who were important figures in the 1950s. Miller and his associates, particularly John Dollard, developed their social learning theory over many years and in many publications, beginning with John Dollard, Leonard Doob, Neal Miller, O. Hobart Mowrer, and Robert Sears, *Frustration and aggression* (New Haven, CT: Yale University Press, 1939). Their most important books were Neal Miller and John Dollard, *Social learning and imitation* (New Haven, CT: Yale University Press, 1941); and John Dollard and Neal Miller, *Personality and psychotherapy* (New York: McGraw-Hill, 1950). As the title of the last book implies, Miller and Dollard were pioneers in behavioral psychotherapy, and an excellent summary of their therapeutic methods and comparison with other systems may be found in Donald H. Ford and Hugh B. Urban, *Systems of psychotherapy: A comparative study* (New York: McGraw-Hill, 1963). The Kendlers presented their mediational theory of reversal shift learning in many publications, but the classic paper was Howard Kendler and Tracy Kendler, "Vertical and horizontal processes in problem solving," *Psychological Review* (1962, *69:* 1–16). Their cited 1975 paper provides a retrospective on their work and shows how it turned gradually into information-processing psychology.

Jerome Bruner and George S. Klein provide an account of the beginnings and guiding concepts of the New Look in perception in "The functions of perceiving: New Look retrospect," in B. Kaplan & S. Wapner (Eds.), *Perspectives in psychological theory: Essays in honor of Heinz Werner* (New York: International Universities Press, 1960). Jean Piaget wrote many books, most of them very difficult. A comprehensive statement of his theory for the period in question is his *The psychology of intelligence* (Totowa, NJ: Rowman & Littlefield, 1948). Piaget's *Six psychological studies* (New York: Random House, 1964) collects some of his more accessible papers. Secondary sources include Alfred Baldwin, *Theories of child development,* 2nd ed. (New York: John Wiley, 1980); John Flavell, *The developmental psychology of Jean Piaget* (New York: Van Nostrand, 1963); Herbert Ginsberg & Sylvia Opper, *Piaget's theory of intellectual development* (Englewood Cliffs, NJ: Prentice-Hall, 1969); and Thomas H. Leahey & Richard J. Harris, *Human learning* (Englewood Cliffs, NJ: Prentice-Hall, 1985). Finally, Howard Gruber and Jacques Voneche have compiled *The essential Piaget* (New York: Basic Books, 1977), a comprehensive anthology of extracts from all Piaget's major works, including some rare adolescent pieces, and have added their own penetrating commentary. Chapter 13 includes references to later works by Piaget and critical secondary sources.

Boring (1946) is the first paper I know of to address the meaning of the World War II computer revolution for psychology, and it includes a comprehensive listing of the prewar mechanical models, including Hull's. For Turing, see Alan Hodge, *Alan Turing: The enigma* (New York: Simon & Schuster, 1983). Broadbent (1958) is useful for comparing information-processing and S-R theories. Finally, a book that doesn't fit well anywhere but that documents the revival of interest in cognition in the early 1950s is Bruner et al. (1957), a collection of papers given at the University of Colorado Symposium on Cognition in 1955. The meeting was attended by leading psychologists of cognition, including mediation theory (Charles Osgood), social psychology (Fritz Heider), psychoanalysis (David Rapaport), and Bruner himself. Only one approach was missing: artificial intelligence. Its omission demonstrates that the computer revolution had not yet hit psychology, as well as how the field of AI developed entirely separately from the psychology of thinking.

A brief survey of general historical developments during the 1950s may be found in the relevant sections of Bernard Bailyn, David Davis, David Donald, John Thomas, Robert Wiebe, and Gordon Wood, *The great republic* (Boston: Little, Brown, 1977). Emphasis on the social, cultural, and intellectual history of the period is in Jeffery Hart, *When the going was good: American life in the fifties* (New York: Crown, 1982). For psychology in the 1950s, see Reisman (1966) and Albert R. Gilgen, *American psychology since World War II: A profile of the discipline* (Westport, CT: Greenwood Press, 1982). If one is interested in the conflict between the two APAs, psychological and psychiatric, one should read the professional journal of the APA, the *American Psychologist.* The year of maximum conflict appears to have been 1953, when the journal was filled with articles, letters, and notes on the struggle of psychologists to win legal approval of their profession over the protests of the psychiatrists. Lindner's (1953) work should be regarded as a symptom of some psychologists' unhappiness with the ideology of adjustment rather than as offering a sound set of analyses or arguments in itself. It depends on a dubious reading of Freud and Darwin, advocates negative eugenics, and is, in general, rather hysterical in its treatment of modern life.

REFERENCES

Baritz, L. J. (1960). *The servants of power: A history of the use of social science in American industry.* Middletown, CT: Wesleyan University Press.

Beach, F. A. (1950). The snark was a boojum. *American Psychologist, 5,* 115–124.

Bell, D. (1960). *The end of ideology: On the exhaustion of political ideas in the fifties.* Glencoe, IL: The Free Press.

Boring, E. G. (1946). Mind and mechanism. *American Journal of Psychology, 59,* 173–192.

Broadbent, D. E. (1957). A mechanical model for human attention and immediate memory. *Psychological Review, 64,* 205–215

Broadbent, D. E. (1958). *Perception and communication.* Elmsford, NY: Pergamon Press.

Bruner, J. S., Brunswik, E., Festinger, E., Heider, F., Muenzinger, K. F., Osgood, C. E., & Rapaport, D. (1957). *Contemporary approaches to cognition.* Cambridge, England: Cambridge University Press.

Bruner, J. S., Goodnow, J., & Austin, G. (1956). *A study of thinking.* New York: John Wiley.

Creegan, R. (1953). Psychologist, know thyself. *American Psychologist, 8,* 52–53.

Deutsch, J. A. (1953). A new type of behavior theory. *British Journal of Psychology, 44,* 304–318.

Estes, W., Koch, S., MacCorquodale, K., Meehl, K., Mueller, C., Schoenfeld, W., & Verplanck, W. (1954). *Modern learning theory.* New York: Appleton-Century-Crofts.

Eysenck, H. J. (1952). The effects of psychotherapy: An evaluation. *Journal of Consulting Psychology, 16,* 322–324.

Farber, I. E. (1957). The division of experimental psychology and the APA. *American Psychologist, 12,* 200–202.

Festinger, L. (1957). *A theory of cognitive dissonance.* Stanford: Stanford University Press.

Festinger, L. & Carlsmith, J. M. (1959). Cognitive consequences of forced compliance. *Journal of Abnormal and Social Psychology, 58,* 203–210.

Goss, A. E. (1961). Verbal mediating responses and concept formation. *Psychological Review, 68,* 248–274.

Keehn, J. D. (1955). The expressed social attitudes of leading psychologists. *American Psychologist, 10,* 208–210.

Kendler, H. H. (1952). "What is learned?"—A theoretical blind alley. *Psychological Review, 59,* 269–277.

Kendler, H. H. & Kendler, T. S. (1962). Vertical and horizontal processes in problem solving. *Psychological Review, 69,* 1–16. Reprinted in R. Harper (Ed.), (1964). *The cognitive processes: Readings.* Englewood Cliffs, NJ: Prentice-Hall.

Kendler, H. H. & Kendler, T. S. (1975). From discrimination learning to cognitive development: A neobehavioristic odyssey. In W. K. Estes (Ed.), *Handbook of learning and cognitive processes,* Vol. 1. Hillsdale, NJ: Erlbaum.

Krech, D. (1949). Notes toward a psychological theory. *Journal of Personality, 18,* 66–87.

Lashley, K. S. (1951). The problem of serial order in behavior. In L. A. Jeffress (Ed.), *Cerebral mechanisms in behavior.* New York: John Wiley.

Lindner, R. F. (1953). *Prescription for rebellion.* London: Victor Gollancz.

MacCorquodale, K. & Meehl, P. E. (1948). On a distinction between hypothetical constructs and intervening variables. *Psychological Review, 55,* 95–107.

Maltzman, I. (1955). Thinking: From a behavioristic point of view. *Psychological Review, 62,* 275–286.

Meehl, P. E. (1954). *Clinical vs. statistical prediction: A theoretical analysis and review of the evidence.* Minneapolis: University of Minnesota Press.

Miller, G. A. (1956). The magical number seven, plus or minus two: Some limits on our capacity for processing information. *Psychological Review, 63,* 81–97.

Miller, J. G. (1955). Toward a general theory for the behavioral sciences. *American Psychologist, 10,* 513–531.

Miller, N. (1959). Liberalization of basic S-R concepts. In S. Koch (Ed.), *Psychology: Study of a science,* Vol. 2. New York: McGraw-Hill.

Newell, A., Shaw, J. C., & Simon, H. A. (1958). Elements of a theory of problem solving. *Psychological Review, 65,* 151–166.

Osgood, C. E. (1956). Behavior theory and the social sciences. *Behavioral Science, 1,* 167–185.

Osgood, C. E. (1957). A behavioristic analysis of perception and language as cognitive phenomena. In Bruner et al. (Eds.), *Contemporary approaches to cognition.* Cambridge, England: Cambridge University Press.

Reisman, J. M. (1966). *The development of clinical psychology.* New York: Appleton-Century-Crofts.

Rosenblueth, A., Wiener, N., & Bigelow, J. (1966). Behavior, purpose, and teleology (1943). Reprinted in J. V. Canfield (Ed.), *Purpose in nature.* Englewood Cliffs, NJ: Prentice-Hall.

Sanford, F. H. (1951). Across the secretary's desk: Notes on the future of psychology as a profession. *American Psychologist, 6,* 74–76.

Simon, H. A. (1956). Rational choice and the structure of the environment. *Psychological Review, 63:* 129–138.

Slack, C. W. (1955). Feedback theory and the reflex-arc concept. *Psychological Review, 62,* 263–267.

Turing, A. M. (1950). Computing machinery and intelligence. *Mind, 59,* 433–460.

Viereck, P. (1956). *The unadjusted man: A new hero for modern America.* New York: Capricorn Books.

Wyckoff, L. B. (1954). A mathematical model and an electronic model for learning. *Psychological Review, 61,* 89–97.

PART V

YEARS OF TURMOIL (1960–1970)

By the mid-1950s, behavioralism had settled down into a comfortable eclecticism. Skinnerians, neo-Hullians, and broadly cognitive theorists lived together with disagreement but without serious division. The situation was reminiscent of the years just before World War I, when functionalists, Titchenerians, Wundtians, and others lived together in relative harmony as the new psychologists. In 1913, Watson shattered the atmosphere of eclectic harmony, even though he did not really create the behavioralistic direction American psychology was already taking. Nevertheless, in his wake, there was a period of stress and self-inspection. Psychologists grappled with the challenge of behaviorism and came to a conscious redefinition of their field by the 1930s. Similarly, in the late 1950s, angry voices challenged the eclectic status quo and set off a new period of self-examination and inflamed rhetoric. Whether or not psychology was taken in a revolutionary direction after 1960 any more than it was after 1913 is a question to which we will have to return.

CHAPTER 12

Doubt and Challenge
Behaviorism Under Fire

CHALLENGES TO BEHAVIORISM
   Humanistic Psychology
   Cartesian Linguistics
EROSION OF THE FOUNDATIONS
   The Disappearance of Positivism
   Constraints on Animal Learning
   Awareness and Human Learning

CHALLENGES TO BEHAVIORISM

Humanistic Psychology

Although humanistic psychology did not take off until the late 1950s, its immediate historical roots lay in the post-World War II period. Its most important founders are Carl Rogers (1902–1987) and Abraham Maslow (1908–1970). While both were initially attracted to behaviorism, both became aware of its limitations and staked out similar alternatives. Rogers developed his *client-centered psychotherapy* in the 1940s and used it with soldiers returning to the United States. Client-centered psychotherapy is a phenomenologically oriented technique in which the therapist tries to enter into the world-view of the client, and help the client work through his or her problems so as to live the life the client most deeply desires. Rogers's client-centered therapy offered a significant alternative to the psychoanalytic methods used by psychiatrists, and thus it played an important role in the establishment of clinical and counseling psychology in the postwar period. Because of his emphasis on empathic understanding, Rogers came into conflict with behaviorism, which treated human beings just as it treated animals—as machines whose behavior could be predicted and controlled, without any attention being paid to subjective consciousness. In 1956, Rogers and Skinner began a series of debates about the relative adequacy of their points of view (Rogers & Skinner, 1956).
   Phenomenological psychology is especially appealing to the clinician, for the clinician's stock in trade is empathy, and phenomenology is the study of subjective

experience. Rogers distinguishes three modes of knowledge. The first is the objective mode, in which we seek to understand the world as an object. The second and third modes of knowing are subjective. One is each person's own subjective knowledge of personal conscious experience, including each person's intentions and sense of freedom. The other mode of subjective knowledge is the attempt to understand another person's subjective inner world. The clinician, of course, must master this last mode of knowing, for in Rogers's view, it is only by understanding the client's personal world and subjective self that the clinician can hope to help the client. Rogers believed that personal beliefs, values, and intentions control behavior. He hoped that psychology would find systematic ways to know the personal experience of other people, for then therapy would be greatly enhanced.

Rogers argued that behaviorism limits itself exclusively to the objective mode of knowledge, and so constrains psychology within a particular set of allowable techniques and theories. It treats human beings exclusively as objects, not as experiencing subjects in their own right. In specific contradistinction to Skinner, Rogers put great emphasis on each person's experienced freedom, rejecting Skinner's purely physical causality. Said Rogers (1964): "The experiencing of choice, of freedom of choice … is not only a profound truth, but is a very important element in therapy." As a scientist, he accepted determinism, but as a therapist, he accepted freedom: The two "exist in different dimensions" (p. 135, in discussion transcript).

Abraham Maslow was humanistic psychology's leading theorist and organizer. Beginning as an experimental animal psychologist, he turned his attention to the problem of creativity in art and science. He studied creative people and concluded that they were actuated by needs dormant and unrealized in the mass of humanity. He called these people self-actualizers because they made real—actualized—their human creative powers, in contrast to most people, who work only to satisfy their animal needs for food, shelter, and safety. Maslow concluded that creative geniuses were not special human beings, but that everyone possessed latent creative talents that could be realized if it were not for socially imposed inhibitions. Maslow's and Rogers's views come together in that they both sought ways to jolt people from comfortable but stultifying psychological ruts and move them to realize their full potential as human beings.

In 1954, Maslow created a mailing list for "people who are interested in the scientific study of creativity, love, higher values, autonomy, growth, self-actualization, basic need gratification, etc." (Sutich & Vich, 1969, p. 6). The number of people on Maslow's mailing list grew quickly, and by 1957, it became clear that more formal means of communication and organization were needed. So Maslow and his followers launched the *Journal of Humanistic Psychology* in 1961 and the Association for Humanistic Psychology in 1963.

Humanistic psychologists deserve the name because, in agreement with the ancient Greek humanists, they believe that "the values which are to guide human action must be found within the nature of human and natural reality itself" (Maslow, 1973, p. 4). But humanistic psychologists could not accept the naturalistic values of the behaviorists. Behaviorists treated human beings as things, failing to appreciate their subjectivity, consciousness, and free will. In the view of humanistic psychologists, behaviorists were not so much wrong as misguided. Behaviorists applied a perfectly valid mode of knowledge—Rogers's objective mode—to human beings, who could only be partially encompassed by this mode of knowing, by ordinary science. Most especially, humanistic psychologists were distressed by behaviorists' rejection of human free will and autonomy. Where Hull, "a near saint of pre-breakthrough [that is, prehumanistic] psychology" treated human beings as robots, humanistic psychologists proclaimed that "Man is aware.... Man has choice.... Man is intentional" (Bugental, 1964, p. 26).

Humanistic psychologists thus sought not to overthrow behaviorists (first-force psychology), or psychoanalysts (second-force psychology), but to build on their mistakes and go beyond them. "I interpret this third psychology [humanistic psychology] to include the first and second psychologies.... I am Freudian and I am behavioristic and I am humanistic" (Maslow, 1973, p. 4). Humanistic psychology, then, while offering a critique of and an alternative to behaviorism, tended still to live with the eclectic spirit of the 1950s. While it thought behaviorism was limited, it thought behaviorism nevertheless valid within its domain, and humanistic psychologists sought to add to behaviorism an appreciation of human consciousness that would round out the scientific picture of human psychology. A more strident, consciously revolutionary voice came from outside psychology, from the field of linguistics.

Cartesian Linguistics

If anyone played Watson to the eclectic peace of the 1950s, it was the linguist Avram Noam Chomsky (born 1928). Chomsky was radical in both politics and linguistics, the study of language. In politics, Chomsky was an early and outspoken critic of the war in Vietnam and of the United States' support of Israel in the Middle East. In linguistics, Chomsky revived what he took to be Descartes's rationalistic program, proposing highly formal accounts of language as the organ by which reason expresses itself and resurrecting the notion of innate ideas. Because Chomsky regarded language as a uniquely human, rational possession, he was brought into conflict with behavioral treatments of language.

THE ATTACK ON VERBAL BEHAVIOR

Since the time of Descartes, language has been seen as a special problem for any mechanistic psychology. Hull's student Spence suspected that language might render inapplicable to humans laws of learning derived from animals. In 1955, the informal behaviorist Osgood referred to the problems of meaning and perception as the "Waterloo of contemporary behaviorism" and in response attempted to provide a mediational theory of language, applicable only to human beings (Osgood, 1957). The philosopher Norman Malcolm (1964), sympathetic to behaviorism, regarded language as "an essential difference between man and the lower animals."

B. F. Skinner, however, was a dissenter from the Cartesian view, shared in part even by fellow behaviorists. The whole point of *Verbal Behavior* was to show that language, while it is a complex behavior, could be explained by reference to only the principles of behavior formulated from animal studies. Skinner therefore denied that there is anything special about language, or verbal behavior, or that there is any fundamental difference between humans and the lower animals. Somewhat as the empiricist Hume raised Kant from his dogmatic slumbers to a defense of the transcendental mind, Skinner's Humean treatment of language roused a rationalist counterattack that said behaviorism was not merely limited, but completely wrong. Further, a rationalist account of language was offered in its place. In the next section, we will look at the new psycholinguistics; here we will summarize the rationalist attack on *Verbal Behavior*.

In 1959, the journal *Language* carried a lengthy review of Skinner's *Verbal Behavior* by a young and obscure linguist named Noam Chomsky. Chomsky attacked not only Skinner's work, but also empiricist ideas in linguistics, psychology, and philosophy generally. He regarded Skinner's book as a *"reductio ad absurdum* of behaviorist assumptions" and wanted to show it up as pure "mythology" (Jakobovits & Miron, 1967). These are the words of an angry revolutionary, and Chomsky's review is perhaps the single most influential psychological paper published since Watson's behaviorist manifesto of 1913.

Chomsky's basic criticism of Skinner's book was that it is an exercise in equivocation. Skinner's fundamental technical terms—stimulus, response, reinforcement, and so on—are well defined in animal learning experiments but cannot be extended to human behavior without serious modification, as Skinner claims. Chomsky argued that if one attempts to use Skinner's terms in rigorous technical senses, they can be shown not to apply to language, while if the terms are metaphorically extended, they become so vague as to be no improvement on traditional linguistic notions. Chomsky systematically attacked each of Skinner's concepts, but we will consider only two examples: his analysis of stimulus and reinforcement.

Obviously, to any behaviorist proper definitions of the stimuli that control behavior are important. The difficulty of defining "stimulus," however, is a notorious one for behaviorism, noted by Thorndike and even some behaviorists. Are stimuli to be defined in purely physical terms, independent of behavior, or in terms of their effects on behavior? If we accept the former definition, then behavior looks unlawful, for very few stimuli in a situation ever affect behavior; while if we accept the latter definition, behavior is lawful by definition, for then the behaviorist only considers those stimuli that do systematically determine behavior. Chomsky raised this problem and others specific to Skinner's *Verbal Behavior.* First, Chomsky pointed out that to say each bit of verbal behavior is under stimulus control is scientifically empty; for given any response, we can always find *some* relevant stimulus. A person looks at a painting and says, "It's by Rembrandt, isn't it?" Skinner would assert that certain subtle properties of the painting determine the response. Yet the person could have said, "How much did it cost?" "It clashes with the wallpaper," "You've hung it too high," "It's hideous!" "I have one just like it at home," "It's forged," and so on, virtually *ad infinitum.* No matter what is said, *some* property could be found that "controls" the behavior. Chomsky argued that there is no prediction of behavior, and certainly no serious control, in this circumstance. Skinner's system is not the scientific advance toward the prediction and control of behavior it pretends to be.

Chomsky also pointed out that Skinner's definition of stimulus becomes hopelessly vague and metaphorical at a great remove from the rigorous laboratory environment. Skinner speaks of "remote stimulus control," in which the stimulus need not impinge on the speaker at all, as when a recalled diplomat describes a foreign situation. Skinner says the suffix "-ed" is controlled by the "subtle property of stimuli we speak of as action in the past." What physical dimensions define "things in the past"? Chomsky argued that Skinner's usage here is not remotely related to his usage in his bar-pressing experiments, and that Skinner has said nothing new about the supposed "stimulus control" of verbal behavior.

Chomsky next considered reinforcement, another term easily defined in the usual operant learning experiment in terms of delivered food or water. Chomsky argued that Skinner's application of the term to verbal behavior is again vague and metaphorical. Consider Skinner's notion of automatic self-reinforcement. Talking to oneself is said to be automatically self-reinforcing: That is why one does it. Similarly, thinking is also said to be behavior that automatically affects the behaver and is therefore reinforcing. Also consider what we might call "remote reinforcement": A writer shunned in his own time may be reinforced by expecting fame to come much later. Chomsky (1959/1967) argued that "the notion of reinforcement has totally lost whatever meaning it may ever have had.... A person can be reinforced though he emits no response at all [thinking], and the reinforcing 'stimulus' need not impinge on the 'reinforced person' [remote reinforcement] or need not even exist [an unpopular author who remains unpopular]" (p. 153).

Chomsky's attitude toward Skinner was contemptuous: He was not prepared to accept Skinner's *Verbal Behavior* as a plausible scientific hypothesis and regarded *Verbal Behavior* as hopelessly muddled and fundamentally wrong. His acute and unrelenting criticism, coupled with his own positive program, was aimed at the overthrow of behaviorist psychology—not its liberalization, as called for by Miller, or its transcendence, as called for by Rogers. For Chomsky, behaviorism could not be built upon, could not be transcended; it could only be replaced.

Adopting a rationalist, Cartesian perspective (Chomsky, 1966), Chomsky believes no behaviorist approach to language can cope with its endless creativity and flexibility. He argues that creativity can be understood only by recognizing that language is a rule-governed system. As part of their mental processes, persons possess a set of grammatical rules that allows them to generate new sentences by appropriately combining linguistic elements. Each person can thus generate an infinity of sentences by repeated application of the rules of grammar, just as a person can generate numbers infinitely by repeated application of the rules of arithmetic. Chomsky argues that human language will not be understood until psychology describes the rules of grammar, the mental structures that underlie speaking and hearing. A superficial behaviorist approach, which studies only speech and hearing but neglects the inner rules that govern speech and hearing, is necessarily inadequate.

As part of his effort to revive Cartesian rationalism in the twentieth century, Chomsky has advanced a nativist theory of language acquisition to accompany his formal, rule-governed theory of adult language. Chomsky (e.g., 1959, 1966) proposes that children possess a biologically given language acquisition device that guides the acquisition of their native language between the ages of about two and twelve years. Thus, for Chomsky as for Descartes, language is a possession unique to the human species. In one respect, Chomsky's thesis is even more nativist than Descartes's. Descartes proposed that humans have language because they can—alone among the animals—think and express themselves in language; while Chomsky believes that language itself, not the more general ability to think, is a human species-specific trait. Soon after Chomsky propounded his view, behavioralist psychologists revived La Mettrie's old project of teaching language to apes via sign-language, computer-language, or a system of plastic tokens. The success of the projects remains a source of intense controversy (see Leahey & Harris, 1989, for a review), but at present, it appears that although apes can learn crudely to communicate their desires through signs, they are unable to acquire anything remotely like human language.

Chomsky's ideas were enormously influential in psycholinguistics, rapidly and completely eclipsing behaviorist approaches, whether mediational or Skinnerian. Many psychologists became convinced that their behaviorist views were wrong and committed themselves to a renewed study of language along Chomskian lines. Chomsky's technical system, described in *Syntactic Structures* (which appeared in 1957, the year of *Verbal Behavior),* provided a new theory around which to design research. Study after study was done, so that in only a few years Chomsky's ideas had generated much more empirical research than had Skinner's. The study of child language was similarly stimulated by Chomsky's controversial nativism. Chomsky's impact was nicely described by George Miller. In the 1950s, Miller had adhered to a behaviorist picture of language, but personal contact with Chomsky convinced him the old paradigm had to be abandoned. By 1962, he was writing: "In the course of my work I seem to have become a very old-fashioned kind of psychologist. I now believe that mind is something more than a four letter, Anglo-Saxon word—human minds exist, and it is our job as psychologists to study them" (p. 762). The mind, exorcised by Watson in 1913, had returned to psychology, brought back by an outsider, Noam Chomsky. Chomsky's emphasis on the rule-governed nature of language helped shape later information-processing theories that claim all behavior is rule-governed.

EROSION OF THE FOUNDATIONS

Just when humanistic psychologists were challenging behaviorism's dominance in their own way, some of the fundamental working assumptions of behaviorism, and even of behavioralism, were coming into question. Combined with the attacks of critics, doubts thrown on these assumptions helped open the door for the formulation of new theories, some in the tradition of behavioralism, some more radical.

The Disappearance of Positivism

In the 1930s, logical positivism had provided a philosophical justification for behaviorism, helping to redefine psychology as the study of behavior rather than mind. Positivism modified at least the formulation of the leading learning theories of the era and completely captured the allegiance of young experimental psychologists who hitched their stars to operationism, using it as an analytical tool to define which problems were worth studying and which were blind alleys.

However, the methodological view of science became increasingly suspect in the late 1950s and beyond. Since its founding, logical positivism had undergone continuous change that took it further and further away from the simple logical positivism of the 1920s. For example, in the 1930s, it was recognized that theoretical terms cannot be neatly linked to observations by the single step of operational definition, a fact some psychologists acknowledged without abandoning the jargon of operationism. Younger philosophers, though, were less inclined to accept the positivist paradigm even in principle, so that during the 1960s, the movement became moribund.

It began to be called "the Received View," like a dead theology, and a symposium on "The Legacy of Logical Positivism" was published in 1969.

Although many criticisms of "the Received View" were offered, perhaps the most fundamental was that its explication of scientific practice was false. Historically oriented philosophers of science, such as Thomas Kuhn and Stephen Toulmin, showed that the supposed objectivity of science was a myth (see Chapter 1). Positivism's postmortem dissection of science as a logically coherent system consisting of axioms, theorems, predictions, and verifications was shown to distort and falsify science as a lively, fallible human enterprise.

Kuhn's views themselves became popular with many psychologists. As cognitive psychology seemed to replace behaviorism in the later 1960s, references to scientific revolutions and paradigm clashes abounded. Kuhn's doctrines seemed to justify a revolutionary attitude: Behaviorism must be overthrown; it cannot be reformed. Many psychologists adopted a kind of scientific revolutionary radical chic paralleling the widespread revolutionary radical political chic of the 1960s. Using *The Structure of Scientific Revolutions* to justify a scientific revolution raises an interesting problem in social psychology. Could the perception of revolution have been a self-fulfilling prophecy? Would there have been a so-called revolution against behaviorism without Kuhn's book? Or, more subtly, could belief in Kuhn's ideas have created the appearance of revolution where there was really only conceptual evolution?

We shall return to these questions in the next chapter, when we again ask, "Was there a revolution?" What is important at present for the fate of behaviorism was that by the later 1960s few, if any, philosophers of science believed positivism to be a credible philosophy of science. Many rejected the social psychological approach of Kuhn, but it was clear that positivism was no longer a viable alternative. Positivism had simply disappeared, and along with it, behaviorism's philosophical foundation.

Constraints on Animal Learning

At the other end from philosophy, behaviorism was anchored by empirical studies of animal behavior. Watson began his career as an animal psychologist, and Tolman, Hull, and Skinner rarely studied human behavior, preferring the more controlled situations that could be imposed on animals. Animal experiments were expected to yield general behavioral laws applicable to a wide range of species, including humans, with little or no modification. Tolman spoke of cognitive maps in rats and persons, Hull of the general laws of mammalian behavior, and Skinner of the extension of animal principles to verbal behavior. It was believed that the principles that emerged from artificially controlled experiments would illuminate the ways in which all organisms learn, regardless of their evolutionary conditioning. The assumption of generality was crucial to the behaviorist program, for if laws of learning are species-specific, studies of animal behavior are pointless for understanding humanity.

Evidence accumulated in the 1960s, however, that the laws of learning uncovered with rats and pigeons are not general, and that serious constraints exist on what and how an animal learns, constraints dictated by the animal's evolutionary history. This evidence came from both psychology and other disciplines. On the one hand, psychologists discovered anomalies in the application of learning laws in a variety of situations, while on the other hand, ethologists demonstrated the importance of innate factors in understanding an animal's behavior in the natural environment its ancestors evolved in.

In developing the pigeon-guided missile, Skinner worked with a young psychologist, Keller Breland, who was so impressed by the possibilities of behavior control that he and his wife became professional animal trainers. As Skinner put it in 1959: "Behavior could be shaped up according to specifications and maintained indefinitely almost at will ... Keller Breland is now specializing in the production of behavior as a saleable commodity." Skinner's claim for Breland resembles Frazier's boast in *Walden II* of being able to produce human personalities to order.

However, in the course of their extensive experience in training many species to perform unusual behaviors, the Brelands found instances in which animals did not perform as they should. In 1961, they reported their difficulties in a paper whose title, "The Misbehavior of Organisms," puns on Skinner's first book, *The Behavior of Organisms*. For example, they tried to teach pigs to carry wooden coins and deposit them in a piggy bank. Although they could teach behaviors, the Brelands found that the behavior degenerated in pig after pig. The animals would eventually pick up the coin, drop it on the ground and root it, rather than deposit it in the bank. The Brelands report that they found many instances of animals "trapped by strong instinctive behaviors" that overwhelm learned behaviors. Pigs naturally root for their food, and so they come to root the coins that they have been trained to collect to get food reinforcers. Breland and Breland (1961/1972) conclude that psychologists should examine "the hidden assumptions which led most disastrously to these breakdowns" in the general laws of learning proposed by behaviorism. They are clearly questioning behaviorism's paradigmatic assumptions in the light of experimental anomalies.

They identified three such assumptions: "That the animal ... [is] a virtual *tabula rasa*, that species differences are insignificant, and that all responses are about equally conditionable to all stimuli." These assumptions are fundamental to empiricism, and statements of them have been made by the major behaviorists. Although limits on these assumptions had been suggested before, the Brelands's paper seemed to open the floodgates to discoveries of more anomalies under more controlled conditions.

We may mention one such line of research, conducted by John Garcia (Garcia, McGowan, & Green, 1972) and his associates. Garcia was a student of Krechevsky, Tolman's major pupil. Garcia studied what he called "conditioned nausea," a form of classical conditioning. Standard empiricist assumptions, enunciated by Pavlov, held that any stimulus could act as a conditioned stimulus, which through conditioning could elicit any response as a conditioned response. More informally, any stimulus could be conditioned to elicit any response. Empirical studies further indicated that the conditioned stimulus and unconditioned stimulus had to be paired within about a half-second of each other for learning to take place.

Using a variety of methods, Garcia let rats drink a novel-tasting liquid and then made the rats sick over an hour later. The question was whether rats would learn to avoid the place they were sick, the unconditioned stimulus immediately connected with their sickness, or the solution they drank, although it was remote in time from the unconditioned response. The latter uniformly occurred. The usual laws of classical conditioning did not hold. Garcia argued that rats know instinctively that nausea must be due to something they ate, not stimuli present at the time of sickness. This makes good evolutionary sense, for sickness in the wild is more likely to be caused by drinking tainted water than by the bush under which a rat was sitting when it felt sick. Connecting taste with sickness is more biologically adaptive than connecting it with visual or auditory stimuli. It appears, therefore, that evolution constrains what stimuli may be associated with what responses.

Garcia's research was initially greeted with extreme skepticism and was refused publication in the major journal devoted to animal behavior. However, studies by other researchers demonstrated that for many behaviors, an animal's evolutionary inheritance places distinct limits on what it can learn. Garcia's studies are now considered classics.

In 1961, the Brelands stated that ethological work had done more to further understanding of animal behavior than behaviorist laboratory studies. By the 1970s, some animal psychologists proclaimed that a revolution had occurred in the study of animal learning in which the old paradigm was shattered (Bolles, 1975). Although such an assessment was premature, the existence of books and symposia in the 1970s on constraints on learning indicated that the field of animal learning was in disarray, that the old security of the rat lab and the anchor of general learning laws were gone.

This particular crisis revealed an interesting fact about the influence of Darwin on American psychology. Both functionalists and behaviorists viewed mind and behavior as adaptive processes, adjusting the organism to its environment. We have seen that Skinner's analysis of learning is squarely and consciously based on an extension of natural selection. Yet behaviorism adopted the empiricist assumptions of the Spencerian paradigm of the *tabula rasa* and species-general laws of learning and ignored the contribution of evolution to behavior. This was the product of another behaviorist assumption, peripheralism. Behaviorists of course recognized that a dog cannot respond to a tone it cannot hear; nor can it learn to fly. These constraints, however, are only on the organism's peripheral sensory and motor abilities. Since behaviorism denied that central processes exist, it could not recognize evolutionary limits on them. Therefore it had to assume that as long as an organism could sense a stimulus, it could be associated with any response it could physically make.

However, many of the puzzling phenomena uncovered by researchers such as the Brelands and Garcia seemed to involve either tastes or sights or sounds an animal could sense, yet could not associate with behavior. Such findings seemed to indicate central control over learning—central control that is at least partly determined by heredity. Therefore, although behaviorism, following functionalism, adopted the theory of natural selection as a conceptual tool, it denied the species-oriented implications of evolution because it denied centralism.

We may note, finally, that behaviorism's extreme empiricism denied already established constraints on learning. For example, Thorndike himself found great differences in how easily cats learned to escape from different puzzle boxes. In particular, they had a difficult time learning to lick their paws in order to escape. Such a behavior is not naturally connected to escape, and so cats were slow to discover the connection. Similarly, early students of animal behavior from Darwin to the ethologists had described biologically determined behavior patterns. All of this is consistent with the extension of a normal science paradigm. Certain anomalies are quietly ignored or put down to bad method (for example, the anecdotal method) until they become too serious to ignore, as they did in the 1960s in animal learning.

Awareness and Human Learning

Logical positivism and the assumption that the laws of learning discoverable with rats and pigeons were applicable without serious exception to all other species, including human beings, were fundamental assumptions of the behaviorist form of behavioralism that had been formulated in the 1930s. Behavioralism rested on a different assumption, that consciousness was of marginal importance in explaining behavior, including human behavior. The motor theory of consciousness and neorealist theories of consciousness viewed consciousness as an epiphenomenon that might at best report some of the determiners of behavior—and not do that very well—but played no role in the actual determination of behavior. Münsterberg, Dewey, and the functionalists placed the determinants of behavior in the environment and in physiological processes, seeing consciousness as merely floating over brain and body, reporting what it saw. Psychology, then, became the study of behavior, not consciousness, although consciousness might be consulted for its occasionally apt insights on why its owner behaved as he or she did. Within this broad framework behaviorists developed their research programs, using positivism to buttress the behavioralist disdain for consciousness, and turning to rigorous, experimental study of animal learning to find the answer to behavioralism's basic question, What causes behavior?

In its behaviorist form, the causal impotence of consciousness was asserted by the doctrine of the automatic action of reinforcers. The doctrine was contained in Thorndike's Law of Effect in the phrase "stamped in": Reward automatically "stamps in" an S-R connection; it does not lead consciousness to a conclusion upon which action is taken. In 1961, the automatic action of reinforcers was forcefully and dogmatically stated by Leo Postman and Julius Sassenrath (1961, p. 136): "It is an outmoded and an unnecessary assumption that the modification of behavior must be preceded by a correct understanding of the environmental contingencies." While a subject might report contingencies accurately, this only meant that consciousness had observed the causes of the changed behavior, not that consciousness had itself caused behavior to change.

Some experiments seemed to support the view. For example, Greenspoon (1955) was interested in nondirective psychotherapy, in which the therapist merely says "um-hum" periodically during a session. From the behaviorist perspective, this situation could be analyzed as a learning situation. The patient emits behaviors, some of which are reinforced by "um-hum." Therefore the patient should come to talk about those things that are reinforced, and not others. Greenspoon took this hypothesis to the laboratory. Subjects were brought to an experimental room and induced to say words. Whenever the subject said a plural noun, the experimenter said "um-hum." After a while, extinction was begun; the experimenter said nothing. At the end of the session, the subject was asked to explain what had been going on. Only ten of seventy-five subjects could do so and, interestingly, Greenspoon excluded their data from analysis. His results showed that production of plural nouns increased during training and then decreased during extinction—exactly as operant theory predicts—and in the apparent absence of subjects' awareness of the connection between plural nouns and reinforcement. Experiments similar to Greenspoon's found similar results.

In the 1960s, however, various researchers disenchanted with behaviorism, and often under Chomsky's influence, challenged the validity of the "Greenspoon effect," or learning without awareness. They argued that Greenspoon's method was inadequate. The questions probing awareness were vague, and they were asked only after extinction, by which time subjects who had been aware of the response-reinforcement contingency could have concluded they had been wrong. Replication of the Greenspoon procedure showed that many subjects held technically incorrect hypotheses that nevertheless led to correct responses. For example, a subject might say "apples" and "pears" and be reinforced, concluding that fruit names were being reinforced. The subject would continue to say fruit names and be rewarded, yet when the subject told the hypothesis to the experimenter, the subject would be called "unaware" (Dulany, 1968).

Those who doubted the automatic action of reinforcers carried out extensive experiments to show the necessity of awareness to human learning. One extensive research program was conducted by Don E. Dulany (1968), who constructed a sophisticated axiomatic theory about types of awareness and their effects on behavior. His experiments seemed to show that only subjects aware of the contingencies of reinforcement could learn, and that subjects' confidence in their hypotheses was systematically related to their overt behavior.

By 1966, the area of verbal behavior was in an apparent state of crisis that called for another symposium. The organizers of the meeting had optimistically hoped that they could gather psychologists from different backgrounds together to work out a unified S R theory of verbal behavior. They called together mediationists such as Howard Kendler, workers in the Ebbinghaus verbal learning tradition, colleagues of Noam Chomsky, and rebellious thinkers such as Dulany. Instead of unanimity the symposium discovered dissent and disenchantment, ranging from mild displeasure with the current state of verbal learning to a formal proof of the inadequacy of the S-R paradigm's theories of language. In closing the book in which the conference papers were published, the editors' comments reflected the growing influence of Kuhn, identifying behaviorism as a paradigm in crisis (Dixon & Horton, 1968). The last sentence in the book was: "To us, it appears that a revolution is certainly in the making."

NOTE: The Bibliography for this chapter is incorporated in Chapter 13.

REFERENCES

Beach, F. (1960). Experimental investigations of species-specific behavior. *American Psychologist, 15,* 1–18.

Bolles, R. C. (1975). Learning, motivation, and cognition. In W. K. Estes (Ed.), *Handbook of learning and the cognitive processes,* Vol. 1. Hillsdale, NJ: Erlbaum.

Breland, K. & Breland, M. (1961). The misbehavior of organisms. *American Psychologist, 16,* 681-684. Reprinted in Seligman & Hagar (1972).

Brewer, W. F. (1974). There is no convincing evidence for operant or classical conditioning in normal, adult, human beings. In W. Weimer and D. Palermo (Eds.), *Cognition and the symbolic processes.* Hillsdale, NJ: Erlbaum.

Bugental, J. F. T. (1964). The third force in psychology. *Journal of Humanistic Psychology, 4,* 19–26.

Chomsky, N. (1957). *Syntactic structures.* The Hague: Mouton.

Chomsky, N. (1959). Review of B. F. Skinner's Verbal behavior. *Language, 35,* 26–58. Reprinted in Jakobovits & Miron (1967).

Chomsky, N. (1966). *Cartesian linguistics.* New York: Harper & Row.

Dixon, T. R. & Horton, D. C. (Eds.), (1968). *Verbal behavior and general behavior theory.* Englewood Cliffs, NJ: Prentice-Hall.

Dulany, D. E. (1968). Awareness, rules, and propositional control: A confrontation with S-R behavior theory. In T. R. Dixon & D. C. Horton (Eds.), *Verbal behavior and general behavior theory.* Englewood Cliffs, NJ: Prentice-Hall.

Garcia, J., McGowan, B. K., & Green, K. F. (1972). Constraints on conditioning. In M. E. P. Seligman & J. L. Hager (Eds.), *Biological boundaries of learning.* New York: Appleton-Century-Crofts.

Greenspoon, J. (1955). The reinforcing effect of two spoken sounds on the frequency of two behaviors. *American Journal of Psychology, 68,* 409–416.

Jakobovits, L. & Miron, M. (Eds.), (1967). *Readings in the psychology of language.* Englewood Cliffs, NJ: Prentice-Hall.

Leahey, T. H. & Harris, R. J. (1989). *Human learning.* 2nd ed. Englewood Cliffs NJ: Prentice-Hall.

Malcolm, N. (1964). Behaviorism as a philosophy of psychology. In T. W. Wann (Ed.), *Behaviorism and phenomenology: Contrasting bases for modern psychology.* Chicago: Chicago University Press.

Osgood, C. (1957). A behaviorist analysis of perception and language as cognitive phenomena. In J. Bruner et al., *Contemporary approaches to cognition.* Cambridge: Harvard University Press.

Postman, L. & Sassenrath, J. (1961). The automatic action of verbal rewards and punishments. *Journal of General Psychology, 65,* 109–136.

Rogers, C. (1964). Toward a science of the person. In T. W. Wann (Ed.), *Behaviorism and phenomenology: Contrasting bases for modern psychology.* Chicago: Chicago University Press.

Rogers, C. R. & Skinner, B. F. (1956). Some issues concerning the control of human behavior: A symposium. *Science, 124,* 1057–1065.

Seligman, M. E. P. & Hager, J. L. (Eds.), (1972). *Biological boundaries of learning.* New York: Appleton-Century-Crofts.

Skinner, B. F. (1959). A case history in scientific method. In S. Koch (Ed.), *Psychology: Study of a Science.* New York: McGraw-Hill.

Sutich, A. J. & Vich, M. A. (1969). Introduction. In A. J. Sutich & M. A. Vich (Eds.), *Readings in humanistic psychology.* New York: The Free Press.

Wann, T. W. (Ed.), (1964). *Behaviorism and phenomenology: Contrasting bases for modern psychology.* Chicago: Chicago University Press.

CHAPTER 13

Continuity in Change
"Revolutions" in Psychology and Society

THE COGNITIVE "REVOLUTION"

Because of the attacks on behaviorism and the weakening of its supporting assumptions, cognitive psychology, which had never disappeared, was reinvigorated and attracted more attention and adherents than ever before. Precisely because the situation in experimental psychology was confused and in great flux, several forms of cognitive psychology emerged and vied for center stage. The two most important were structuralism and information processing. Structuralism was associated with the more radical cognitive psychologists, who sought a clear break with the past in American psychology; in particular, they looked to European psychology and continental European traditions in philosophy, psychology, and the other social sciences. Information-processing psychology was more conservative. While it rejected behaviorism, it nevertheless remained within the behavioralistic tradition of American psychology in the twentieth century. It adopted and adapted the approaches and procedures of artificial intelligence and cognitive simulation to forge a new language in which to cast psychological models from which behavior might be predicted and controlled.

The New Structuralism

The first form of cognitive psychology to emerge was *structuralism*. This was not a continuation of Titchener's system, with which it shares nothing but the name, but it was an independent movement of continental European origin. Structuralism hopes to be a unifying paradigm for all the social sciences, and its adherents range from philosophers to anthropologists. Structuralists believe that any human behavior pattern, whether individual or social, is to be explained by reference to abstract structures, frequently believed to be logical or mathematical in nature. In the realm of social behavior, the leading exponent of structuralism is Claude Lévi-Strauss, who seeks to explain everything from a culture's myths to its cooking practices by describing a small set of logical structures that underlie these myths and cooking practices.

In psychology, the leading structuralist was Jean Piaget. Piaget was originally trained as a biologist, but his interests shifted to epistemology, to which field he applied his scientific method. He criticized philosophers for remaining content with armchair speculations about the growth of knowledge when the questions of epistemology could be empirically investigated. Genetic epistemology was his attempt to chart the development of knowledge in children. Piaget divided the growth of intellect into four stages, in each of which occurs a distinct kind of intelligence. Piaget believed intelligence does not grow quantitatively, but undergoes widespread qualitative metamorphosis, so that the five-year-old not only knows less than the twelve-year-old, but also thinks in a different way. Piaget traced these different kinds of intelligence, or ways of knowing the world, to changes in the logical structure of the child's mind. Piaget attempted to describe the thinking of each stage by constructing highly abstract and formal logical models of the mental structures he believed guide intelligent behavior.

Some other psychologists are at least partially structuralists. It is sometimes held that Freud was a structuralist because he attempted to describe the structure of personality, but he lived long before the movement became self-conscious. Noam Chomsky may be regarded as a structuralist for trying to explain language in terms of its formal grammatical structure. In this, Chomsky follows the lead of the French linguist Ferdinand de Saussurre (1857–1913), who many think provided the inspiration for structuralism as a movement.

Structuralism has had enormous influence in continental European philosophy, literary criticism, and social science, including psychology. The leading exponents of structuralism, Lévi-Strauss, Michel Foucault, and Piaget, were French-speaking and carried on the Platonic-Cartesian rationalist attempt to describe the transcendent human mind. Piaget, for example, limited his interest to "the epistemic subject," the person as abstract knower. He disclaimed all interest in the "completely American" topic of individual differences. Also, like Wundt, he cared little for application. He spoke humorously of "the American question," a question never asked of him in Europe: namely, how can the stages of intellectual development be accelerated by training? Piaget felt it was best not to try, preferring to let natural development take its course.

As one might expect, given the European rationalist background of structuralism, its impact on American psychology has been limited. Americans have paid great attention to Piaget since 1960, and his theory has generated a good deal of research.

However, few American psychologists have adopted his structuralism. His logical models are generally viewed as too abstruse and far removed from behavior to be of any value. Americans are impressed by his findings, but frequently explain them in other terms. Additionally, Americans are interested in individual differences and the effects of experience or training on cognitive development and do not care greatly about Piaget's idealized "epistemic subject." As happened with Wundt, Americans have taken what they value from a rationalist psychology but have remained securely empiricists.

Chomsky's transformational grammar has suffered a similar fate. After an initial flurry of interest, psychologists came to feel that Chomsky's formal grammar, like Piaget's logical models, had little psychological reality, but merely gave overly complex formal descriptions of behavior. His nativist theory of language acquisition also gained initial acceptance, to be followed only by retreat to more empiricist accounts. After 1965, psycholinguists were prepared to declare themselves separate from, and perhaps superior to, formal linguists.

Man the Machine: Information Processing

In 1957, Herbert Simon, coauthor of the General Problem Solver (GPS), prophesied "that within ten years most theories in psychology will take the form of computer programs" (Dreyfus, 1972). But GPS exerted little influence on the psychology of problem solving during the 1960s. In 1963, Donald W. Taylor reviewed the research area of thinking and concluded that while computer simulation of thinking shows "the most promise" of any theory, "this promise, however, remains to be justified." Three years later Davis (1966) surveyed the field of human problem solving and concluded, "There is a striking unanimity in recent theoretical orientations to human thinking and problem solving ... that associational behavioral laws established in comparatively simple classical conditioning and instrumental conditioning situations apply to complex human learning"; Davis relegated GPS to one of three other minor theories of problem solving. Ulric Neisser, in his influential text *Cognitive Psychology* (1967), dismissed computer models of thinking as "simplistic" and not "satisfactory from the psychological point of view." On the tenth anniversary of his prediction, Simon and his colleagues quietly abandoned GPS (Dreyfus, 1972).

Yet it was acknowledged by everyone, including its opponents, that cognitive psychology was booming during the 1960s. In 1960, Donald Hebb, one of psychology's recognized leaders, called for the "Second American Revolution" (the first was behaviorism): "The serious analytical study of the thought processes cannot be postponed any longer." In 1964, Robert R. Holt said that "cognitive psychology has enjoyed a remarkable boom." The boom extended even to clinical psychology, as Louis Breger and James McGaugh (1965) argued for replacing behavioristic psychotherapy with therapy based on information-processing concepts. By 1967, Neisser could write that "A generation ago a book like this one would have needed at least a chapter of self-defense against the behaviorist position. Today, happily, the climate of opinion has changed and little or no defense is necessary."

Attempts to turn psychology into a branch of computer science had failed but had brought about a renaissance in cognitive psychology as psychologists accepted "the familiar parallel between man and computer" (Neisser, 1967). It was easy to think of people as information-processing devices that receive input from the environment (perception), process that information (thinking), and act upon decisions reached (behavior). While attempts to write running programs to emulate thought seemed rather boring to psychologists, the general image of human beings as information processors was immensely exciting. So while Simon was wrong in predicting that psychological theories would be written as computer programs, the broader vision of artificial intelligence and computer simulation had triumphed by 1967, having far more influence than either of its rivals, structuralism and mentalism.

The reason for the simultaneous failure of computer programs to become the new wave in psychological theory and the success of the general information-processing perspective may be found by continuing the quotations from Hebb and Neisser. Hebb: "The serious analytical study of the thought processes cannot be postponed any longer.... The mediational postulate ... is a powerful tool, and the time has come to use it" (1960, p. 743). Neisser: "Today, the climate of opinion is changed and little or no defense is necessary. Indeed, stimulus-response theorists themselves are inventing hypothetical mechanisms with vigor and enthusiasm and only faint twinges of conscience. The basic reason for studying the cognitive processes has become as clear as the reason for studying anything else: because they are there" (1967, p. 5).

It is important to remember the large community of psychologists who fell into the mediational tradition of psychology, whether neo-Hullian or neo-Tolmanian. These psychologists already accepted the idea of processes intervening between stimulus and response, and they had throughout the 1950s "invented hypothetical mechanisms," mostly in the form of mediating r-s links holding together observable S-R connections. During the 1950s, neobehaviorist human psychology flourished (Cofer, 1978). Ebbinghaus's study of memory had been revived in the field called "verbal learning," and, independently of computer science, verbal learning psychologists had begun by 1958 to distinguish between short-term and long-term memory. The field of psycholinguistics—an interdisciplinary combination of linguistics and psychology—had begun in the early 1950s under the auspices of the Social Science Research Council. The Office of Naval Research had since the end of World War II funded conferences on verbal learning, memory, and verbal behavior. A Group for the Study of Verbal Behavior was organized in 1957. It began, like Maslow's group of humanistic psychologists, as a mailing list; it became, again like the humanist group, a journal, the *Journal of Verbal Learning and Verbal Behavior*, in 1962.

These groups were interconnected, and all the psychologists involved with verbal behavior and thinking took the mediational version of S-R theory for granted. For example, in psycholinguistics, the "grammars [of the pre-Chomsky linguists] and mediation theory were seen to be variations of the same line of thought" (Jenkins, 1968). While as late as 1963 Jenkins (Gough & Jenkins, 1963) could discuss "Verbal Learning and Psycholinguistics" in purely mediational terms, it was clear by 1968 that Chomsky had "dynamited the structure [of mediational psycholinguistics] at the linguistic end" (Jenkins, 1968). Chomsky convinced these psychologists that their S-R theories, even including mediation, were inadequate to explain human language. So they looked for a new language in which to theorize about mental processes and were naturally drawn to the language of the computer, information processing. The "S" of the S-r-s-R formula could become "input," the "R" could become "output," and the "r-s" could become "processing." Moreover, information-processing language could be used, even without writing computer programs, as a "global framework within which precisely stated models could be constructed for many different … phenomena and could be tested in quantitative fashion" (Shiffrin, 1977, p. 2). Shiffrin is describing the landmark paper of the information-processing, non–computer-programming tradition, "Human Memory: A Proposed System and Its Control Processes" (Atkinson & Shiffrin, 1968), from which virtually all later accounts of information processing descend.

Information-processing language gave mediational psychologists exactly what they needed. It was rigorous, up to date, and at least as quantitative as Hull's old theory, without having to make the implausible assumption that the processes linking stimulus and response were just the same as single-stage learning processes in animals. Psychologists could now talk about "coding," "search sets," "retrieval," "pattern recognition," and other information structures and operations with every expectation that they were constructing scientific theories. Information-processing psychology met psychologists' physics envy better than Hull's had, for information-processing psychologists could always point to computers as the working embodiment of their theories. The theories might not *be* computer programs, but they were *like* computer programs in regarding thinking as the formal processing of stored information. Thus, while information-processing theories were independent of computational theories in artificial intelligence, they were conceptually parasitic on them, and cognitive psychologists hoped that at some future point their theories would be programs. Simon's prophecy failed, but his dream remained.

THE SOCIAL "REVOLUTION"

Funding Social Science

The political relations of the social sciences, including psychology, went from disaster to apparent triumph during the 1960s. The disaster was Project Camelot, the largest social science project ever conceived, under which the United States Army, together with the CIA and other intelligence agencies, gave up to $6 million to social scientists at home and abroad to pinpoint potential political trouble spots (for example, incipient guerrilla wars) and to use social scientific expertise to formulate remedies (for example, counterinsurgency actions). However, when in 1965 Project Camelot ceased to be secret, social science was thrown under a cloud. Foreign governments viewed Project Camelot as American meddling in their internal affairs. Their complaints led to a congressional investigation and to the termination of Project Camelot in July 1965. The image of social science was tarnished because social scientists participating in Project Camelot appeared to be tools of the American government rather than disinterested investigators of social phenomena.

However, out of the Camelot debacle social science was able to finally break through to a place at the federal research grant trough. As American cities exploded with race riots and street crime in the mid-1960s, and President Lyndon Johnson launched the War on Poverty, members of Congress were moved to ask if social science could do something about race hatred, poverty, crime, and other social problems. Psychologist Dael Wolfle, an experienced observer of relations between science and government, wrote in *Science* in 1966a (p. 1177) that "a call for large scale support of the social sciences was a recurring theme of the 25–27 January meeting of the House of Representatives Committee on Science and Technology." Wolfle thought that the time "may be ripe for special support of the social sciences," especially in view of recent advances in "quantitative and experimental methodology," so that "within a reasonable time, these disciplines can offer substantially increased help in meeting pressing social problems." As late as 1966, out of $5.5 billion spent by the federal government on scientific research, only $221 million (less than 5 percent) went to social science; but by 1967, the mood in Congress "was to do something generous for the social sciences" (Greenberg, 1967).

What Congress would do, however, remained unclear (Carter, 1966; Greenberg, 1967). In the Senate, liberal Democrats were eager to give social scientists money and to make them into social planners. Fred Harris, perhaps the most liberal person in the Senate and soon to attempt a (doomed) run for the Democratic presidential nomination in 1968, introduced a bill, S. 836, to the 90th Congress, authorizing the establishment of a National Social Science Foundation (NSSF) modeled on the National Science Foundation (NSF). Walter Mondale, heir to Hubert Humphrey's liberal Democratic mantle, introduced S. 843, the "Full Opportunity and Social Accounting Act," whose leading provision was the establishment in the president's Executive Office of a "Council of Social Advisers" who would carry out the "social accounting," using their presumed expertise to advise the president on the social consequences of government's action and to rationally plan America's future. In the House, Emilio Q. Daddario proposed a more conservative way to "do something generous for the social sciences" by rewriting the charter of the NSF. The NSF had been mandated to support the natural sciences, but had been permitted to support "other sciences" as well, and had in fact given small amounts to support social science ($16 million in 1966 [Carter, 1966]). Daddario's bill, H.R. 5404, charged the NSF to support social as well as natural science and to include social scientists on its governing body.

Organized psychology paid great attention to the Senate bills. *American Psychologist,* the official organ of the APA, devoted a special issue to the Harris and Mondale proposals; and Arthur Brayfield, executive secretary of the APA, submitted a long statement to Congress in support of S. 836. However, individual psychologists and other social scientists had mixed reactions to the proposal to set up an NSSF. On the positive side, an NSSF would give social scientists a federal funding source under their own control and would acknowledge their importance to the country, enhancing their social prestige. On the negative side, an NSSF might create a social science ghetto, stigmatizing social science by the act of setting it off from the "real sciences" in the NSF, and it might at the same time give social science too much visibility; Project Camelot had given social scientists more publicity and controversy than they were prepared to handle. Among the psychologists who testified before Harris's committee considering the NSSF bill, two (Brayfield and Ross Stagner) were enthusiastic, two (Rensis Likert and Robert R. Sears) supported it with reservation, and one (Herbert Simon) opposed it. Wolfle, in an editorial in *Science* (1966b), supported Simon's position. There was one point of loud universal agreement among all witnesses: Social science deserved a lot more federal money than it was getting; Sears, for example, said that regardless of what agency gave it, social science funding should go up "many times" the current level.

Social scientists got their money but not the NSSF or the "Council of Social Advisers." Mondale's bill, like his 1984 candidacy for president, went nowhere. Harris's bill never got out of committee. Daddario, however, got his bill to rewrite the NSF charter through the House and enlisted the support of liberal Senator Edward Kennedy, who drafted a revised version of the new NSF bill that was accepted by Daddario, passed by the Senate, and finally signed into law by President Johnson on July 18, 1968, as Public Law 90–407. The NSF, wanting to keep its control over American science and therefore ready as always to respond to the desires of Congress (the director, Leland J. Haworth, had assured Harris that the NSF *wanted* to support social science), promised to infuse new funds into social science. While psychologists might still suffer physics envy, hoping for federal grants took away some of the sting.

As it turned out, psychology gained nothing from the NSF's increased funding of social sciences. From 1966 to 1976, NSF spending on social sciences except psychology rose 138 percent, while spending on psychology *declined* 12 percent. Moreover, not only did NSF continue to spend more on the natural sciences than on the social sciences, the rate at which spending on the natural sciences increased was faster than that for the social sciences; for example, spending on physics and chemistry, the most traditional fields of natural science, rose 176 percent between 1966 and 1976. Why psychology fared so poorly remains unclear (Kiesler, 1977).

Professional Psychology

In contrast to experimental psychology, where an exciting change from behaviorism to cognitive psychology seemed to be taking place, during the decade 1958 to 1968 professional psychology seemed to be adrift. As Nevitt Sanford (1965) wrote: "Psychology is really in the doldrums right now.... The revolution in psychology that occurred during World War II ... has been over for some time."

There was no doubt that while psychology was growing faster than any other profession (Garfield, 1966), clinical and applied psychology were growing even faster. At the 1963 meeting of the APA there were 670 openings in clinical psychology for only 123 applicants (Schofield, 1966). The membership in the academic divisions of the APA had grown at a 54 percent rate between 1948 and 1960, while the professional divisions had grown at a 149 percent rate and the mixed academic/professional divisions had grown 176 percent (Tryon, 1963). The relative success of the professional as opposed to the traditional scientific branches of psychology led to increased tension between the two classes of psychologists (Shakow, 1965; Chein, 1966, who coined the labels "scientist" and "practitioner" for the two sides in what he saw as an "irrational" and "destructive" division among psychologists). Echoing the debates of the 1930s, Leonard Small (1963) said that the greatest task facing psychology was "to obtain recognition for its competence," and he hinted that if the APA did not assist professional psychologists in achieving this, they would organize separately.

However, while professional psychology was experiencing tremendous growth, professional psychologists were still somewhat uncertain as to their social and scientific roles. The Boulder Conference on clinical psychology had said that clinical psychologists were supposed to be both scientists and practitioners, but it was becoming obvious that few clinicians were becoming scientists, opting instead for the private or institutionalized practice of psychotherapy (for example, Blank & David, 1963;

Shakow, 1965; Garfield, 1966; Hoch, Ross, & Winder, 1966). The Boulder model was increasingly challenged, and psychologists began to think about training psychologists purely as professionals, along the lines of physicians' training (Hoch, Ross, & Winder, 1966), and to reflect on their aims as both scientists and professionals (Clark, 1967).

Amid all this self-searching, professional psychologists had reason to worry about their public image. The use of psychological tests in education, business, industry, and government had mushroomed since World War II, including not just intelligence tests, but also instruments designed to measure personality traits and social attitudes. Many people began to feel that these tests—inquiring as they often did into sexuality, parent-child relations, and other sensitive areas—were invasions of privacy, products of the morbid curiosity of psychologists and susceptible to abuse by employers, government, or anyone looking for tools of social control. In 1963, psychologists were upset by the popularity of *The Brain Watchers,* a book by journalist Martin Gross, which assailed the use of personality and social tests by government and industry. The antitest movement culminated in 1965, when some school systems burned the results of personality tests administered to children, and Congress investigated the use of personality tests by the federal government to screen possible employees, resulting in restrictions on their use. By 1967, psychologists were probably not surprised to learn that their prestige was pretty low. When parents were asked which of six professions they would most like their child to enter, they ranked them as follows, from most preferred to least: surgeon, engineer, lawyer, psychiatrist, dentist, psychologist. Most galling was the finding that parents preferred the clinical psychologist's archenemy, the psychiatrist, by 54 percent to 26 percent (Thumin & Zebelman, 1967).

Values

In 1960, psychiatrist Thomas Szasz began an effective assault on the entire mental health establishment by analyzing *The Myth of Mental Illness* (Szasz, 1960a,b). Szasz pointed out that the concept of mental illness was a metaphor based on the concept of physical illness, a bad metaphor with pernicious consequences. Szasz's analysis draws upon Ryle's analysis of the concept of mind. Ryle had argued that the mind was a myth, the myth of the Ghost in the Machine. Szasz simply drew attention to the conclusion that if there is no Ghost in the human machine, the Ghost—the mind—can hardly become ill. Just as we (falsely) attribute behaviors to an inner Ghost who causes them, so, Szasz said, when we find behaviors annoying, we think the Ghost must be sick and invent the (false) concept of mental illness: "Those who suffer from and complain of their own behavior are usually classified as 'neurotic'; those whose behavior makes others suffer, and about whom others complain, are usually classified as 'psychotic.' " So, according to Szasz, "Mental illness is not something a person has [he has no inner, sick Ghost], but is something he does or is" (p. 267).

Belief in mental illness has evil consequences, Szasz thought. To begin with, psychiatric diagnoses are stigmatizing labels that ape the categories of physical illness, but in reality function to give political power to psychiatrists and their allies in mental health. People labeled "mentally ill" can be deprived of their freedom and locked up for indeterminate periods of time, even though they may have committed no crime; while locked up, they can be given drugs against their will, something that may not be done even to convicted felons in prison: "There is no medical, moral, or legal justification for involuntary psychiatric interventions. They are crimes against humanity" (p. 268). In a deeper sense, the concept of mental illness undermines human freedom, belief in moral responsibility, and the legal notions of guilt and innocence deriving from human freedom and moral responsibility. Instead of treating a human being who may have offended us or committed a crime as an autonomous agent, we treat him or her as a diseased thing with no will. Because the myth of mental illness is a conspiracy of kindness—we would like to excuse and help people who have done wrong—a person categorized as mentally ill, and therefore not responsible for his or her behavior, will likely come to accept his or her supposed helplessness, ceasing to view himself or herself as a morally free actor. And by contagion, as science sees all action as determined beyond self-control, everyone may cease to believe in freedom and moral responsibility. Hence the myth of mental illness strikes at the very heart of Western civilization, committed as it is to human freedom and responsibility for one's actions.

Szasz is not saying that everything called "mental illness" is a fiction, only that the concept of "mental illness" itself is a fiction. It is obviously possible for a brain to be diseased and cause bizarre thoughts and antisocial behavior. However, in such a case, there is no mental illness at all, but a genuine bodily disease. But, Szasz held, most of what are called "mental illnesses" are "problems of living," not true diseases. Problems of living are quite real, of course, and a person suffering from them may need professional help working them out, so that psychiatry and clinical psychology are legitimate professions: "Psychotherapy is an effective method of helping people— not to recover from an 'illness,' but rather to learn about themselves, others, and life" (pp. xv–xvi). Conceived medically, psychiatry is a "pseudoscience"; conceived educationally, it is a worthy vocation.

Szasz's ideas were, and remain, highly controversial. To orthodox psychiatrists and clinical psychologists he is a dangerous heretic whose "nihilistic and cruel philosophies … read well and offer little except justification for neglect" of the mentally ill (Penn, 1985). But to others his ideas are attractive, offering an alternative conception of human suffering that does not needlessly turn an agent into a patient. Szasz and his followers in the "antipsychiatry movement," as it is sometimes called, have had some success in changing the legal procedures by which people can be involuntarily committed to mental hospitals. In many states, such commitments are now hedged about with legal safeguards; no longer is it possible in most places to carry off someone to the local mental ward merely on the say-so of a single psychiatrist, as it was in 1960 when Szasz wrote.

As American society became more troubled in the 1960s, by the struggle for civil rights, by riots and crime, and above all by the Vietnam War and the controversies attending upon it, the value of adaptation—conformity—was decisively rejected by increasing numbers of Americans. The roots of the discontent lay in the 1950s, as we have seen, but in the 1960s criticism of conformity became more open and widespread.

In social science, for example, Snell and Gail J. Putney attacked conformity in *The Adjusted American: Normal Neuroses in the Individual and Society* (1964). In *Civilization and Its Discontents,* Freud had argued that civilized people are necessarily a little neurotic, the psychological price paid for civilization, so that psychoanalysis could do no more than reduce neuroses to ordinary unhappiness. According to Putney and Putney, however, "normal neuroses" are not just ordinary unhappiness but are real neuroses that can and ought to be cured. Adjusted Americans, the Putneys said, have learned to conform to a cultural pattern that deceives them about what their real needs are. Because "normalcy ... [is] the kind of sickness or crippling or stunting that we share with everybody else and therefore don't notice" (Maslow, 1973), adjusted Americans are ignorant of their deepest yearnings and try to satisfy culturally prescribed rather than real human needs, consequently experiencing frustration and pervasive anxiety. The Putneys rejected the value of adjustment, replacing it with the value of "autonomy, [meaning] the capacity of the individual to make valid choices of his behavior in the light of his needs." Maslow (1961) thought that such views were held by most psychologists: "I would say that in the last ten years, most if not all theorists in psychology have become antiadjustment," and he endorsed the value of autonomy—self-actualization—as a replacement for adjustment.

Autonomy could be gained, humanistic psychologists said, through psychotherapy. Chief exponent of this view was Carl Rogers. His client-centered psychotherapy tried to take clients on their own terms and lead them not to adjustment to the regnant norms of society, but to insights into their real needs, and thence to an ability to meet them. A client who had been through successful psychotherapy became a Heraclitean human. By the end of successful client-centered therapy, Rogers (1958) said, "The person becomes a unity, a flow of motion ... he has become an integrated process of changingness." Rogers's therapy centered on feelings. The person who came for help, the client (like Szasz, Rogers rejected the metaphor of mental illness and refused to call those he helped "patients"), suffered above all from inability to properly experience and fully express his or her feelings. The therapist worked with the client to open up and experience feelings fully and directly, and to share these feelings with the therapist. So the "flow of motion" within the healthy human was most importantly a flow of feelings immediately and fully experienced. In the Rogerian conception, then, the unhealthy individual was one who controlled and withheld feelings; the healthy person—Maslow's self-actualizer—was one who spontaneously experienced the emotions of each moment and expressed emotions freely and directly.

Rogers, Maslow, and the other humanistic psychologists proposed the new values of growth and authenticity for Western civilization. Values concern how one should live one's life, and what one should treasure in life. Humanistic psychologists proposed that one should never become settled in one's ways, but instead be always in flux: the Heraclitean human. They taught that one should treasure feelings. Both values derive from psychotherapy as Rogers practiced it.

The value humanistic psychologists called "growth" was the openness to change Rogers hoped to bring about in his clients. A therapist naturally wants to change the client because, after all, the client has come seeking help to improve his or her life. Humanistic psychotherapists make change a basic human value, the goal of all living, whether within or without therapy. Humanistic psychologists agreed with Dewey that "growth itself is the only moral end."

The other new value—authenticity—concerned the open expression of feelings characteristic of the person who had been through Rogerian therapy. Maslow (1973) defined authenticity as "allowing your behavior and your speech to be the true and spontaneous expression of your inner feelings." Traditionally, people had been taught to control their feelings and to be careful in how they expressed them. Proper behavior in business and among acquaintances—manners—depended on not expressing one's immediate feelings, and on telling little lies that oiled public social intercourse. Only with one's most intimate circle was free, private, emotional expression allowed, and even then, only within civilized bounds. But humanistic psychologists opposed manners with authenticity, teaching that emotional control and deceptive emotional expression—Maslow called it "phoniness"—were psychological evils, and that people should be open, frank, and honest with each other, baring their souls to any and all as they might with a psychotherapist. Hypocrisy was regarded as a sin, and the ideal life was modeled on psychotherapy: The good person (Maslow, 1973) was unencumbered by hangups, experienced emotions deeply, and freely shared feelings with others.

Humanistic psychologists were clear that they were at war with traditional Western civilization and were trying to make a moral as well as a psychological revolution. Maslow (1967) denounced being polite about the drinks served at a party as "the usual kind of phoniness we all engage in" and proclaimed that "the English language is rotten for good people." Rogers (1968) closed an article on "Interpersonal Relationships: U.S.A. 2000" by quoting "the new student morality" as propounded at Antioch College: [We deny] "that nonaffective modes of human intercourse, mediated by decency of manners, constitute an acceptable pattern of human relations."

Rogers's ideas were, of course, not new in Western civilization. Valuing emotional feeling, trusting intuition, and questioning the authority of reason can be traced back through the romantics to the Christian mystics, and to the cynics and skeptics of the Hellenistic Age. Rogers, Maslow, and the others, however, gave expression to these ideas within the context of a science, psychology, speaking with the authority of science. The humanistic psychologists' prescription for *ataraxia*—feeling and sharing began to be put into practice in the modern Hellenistic Age. As the troubles of civilization mounted, ordinary life became intolerable for many; and as people had in the ancient Hellenistic world, they sought for new forms of happiness outside the accepted bounds of culture.

Humanistic psychology, a product of the modern Academy, advocated a modern form of skepticism. Maslow (1962) described the "innocent cognition" of the self-actualized person this way:

> If one expects nothing, if one has no anticipations or apprehensions, if in a sense there is no future ... there can be no surprise, no disappointment. One thing is as likely as another to happen.... And no prediction means no worry, no anxiety, no apprehension, no foreboding.... This is all related to my conception of the creative personality as one who is totally here-now, one who lives without the future or the past. (p. 67)

Maslow here captured the recipe for *ataraxia* of the Hellenistic skeptics, to form no generalizations, and hence be undisturbed by what happens. The humanistic self-actualizer, like the ancient skeptic, accepts what is without disturbance, "goes with the flow," and is carried without trouble down the constantly flowing stream of change of modern American life.

A much more visible manifestation of the new Hellenism were the hippies, who, like the ancient cynics, dropped out of the conventional society they scorned and rejected. Like humanistic psychologists, they were at war with their culture, distrusted reason, and valued feeling, but they carried their anti-intellectualism and contempt for manners to greater extremes, attempting to actually live lives that were Heraclitean flows of feeling, unconstrained by intellect or manners. The hippie movement began around 1964 and quickly became a powerful cultural force, described variously as "a red warning light for the American way of life," "a quietness, an interest—something good," or "dangerously deluded" (Jones, 1967). To explore and express their feelings hippies turned to drugs. Few had heard of Carl Rogers or Abraham Maslow, though the hippies shared their values; but they had heard of another psychologist, Timothy Leary. Leary was a young, ambitious, and successful Harvard psychologist whose personal problems drove him inward, to his feelings. He began to use drugs, at first peyote and then LSD, on himself and others to attain the Heraclitean state of being, the "integrated process of changingness" open to new experience and intensely aware of every feeling. The hippies followed Leary into the "psychedelic," mind-expanding world, using drugs (as had Coleridge and other young romantics) to erase individual discursive consciousness (Kant's *Verstand*) and replace it with rushes of emotion, strange hallucinations, and alleged cosmic, transcendental insights (*Vernunft*). For the hippies, as for the post-Kantian idealists, the ultimate reality was mental, not physical; and they believed drugs would open the "doors of perception" to the greater, spiritual world of mind. Even without drugs, hippies and humanistic psychologists were not quite of this world. In a letter, Maslow wrote: "I live so much in my private world of Platonic essences ... that I only *appear* to others to be living in the world" (Geiger, 1973).

By 1968, the hippie movement, and the associated movement of protest against the war in Vietnam, was at its height. The Age of Aquarius was at hand, an age of skepticism and cynicism—the new Hellenistic Age—which we have not yet passed through.

CONCLUSION: REVOLTS BUT NO REVOLUTIONS

Satirist Tom Lehrer once described Gilbert and Sullivan's famous patter songs as "full of sound and fury, signifying absolutely nothing." The 1960s were full of sound and fury, and 1968 was perhaps the worst year of all: the assassinations of Martin Luther King and Robert F. Kennedy, violent eruptions from the ghettos of every major American city, the growing antiwar movement. Never were the words of Yeats's "Second Coming" more true: Things seemed to be falling apart, America's youth lacked all conviction—the hippies dropped out of "straight" society—or were full of passionate intensity against their parents and their nation—the Weather Underground wanted to overthrow the government with bombs and terrorism. Many citizens wondered what rough beast was slouching toward Bethlehem to be born. In its "Prairie Fire Manifesto," the Weather Underground proclaimed, "We live in a whirlwind; nonetheless, time is on the side of the guerrillas." In psychology, the humanistic psychologists were at war with the culture of intellect, siding with and inspiring the hippies and their political wing, the Yippies, while cognitive psychologists cried for a Kuhnian revolution against Hull, Spence, and Skinner. But was there anything more to the 1960s than sound and fury?

No.

From Yippie to Yuppie

While humanistic psychology fancied that it offered a radical critique of modern American society, it was at heart profoundly conservative, even reactionary. In his concept of self-actualization, Maslow did no more than refurbish—tarnish might be a better word—Aristotle's *scala naturae* with modern psychological jargon. In its cultivation of feeling and intuition, humanistic psychology harked back to the romantic rejection of the Scientific Revolution but was never honest enough to say so. Humanistic psychologists, including Maslow and Rogers, always counted themselves scientists, ignoring the deep conflict between science's commitment to natural law and determinism and their own commitment to the primacy of human purpose. Humanistic psychology is therefore a sort of fraud trading on the good name of science to push ideas entirely at variance with modern science. In the nineteenth century, Dilthey and others of the authentic romantic tradition offered reasons for setting the human sciences—the *Geisteswissenschaften*—apart from physics, chemistry, and the other *Naturwissenschaften,* but humanistic psychologists could only offer barely articulate protests against scientistic imperialism. If a case is to be made against the natural scientific, reductionistic image of human beings, it must come from a different, more intelligent, source.

Similarly, the hippies and their followers, far from providing a radical critique of "Amerika," as they were wont to spell it, embodied every contradiction of the American past. They worshiped simple, preurban lives, yet mostly lived in cities (which were more tolerant of deviance than small towns) and focused their lives on drugs and electronic music, products of the industrial world they feigned to reject. With the humanistic psychologists, they valued feelings and openness to new experience, echoing the romantic poet Blake's cry, "God save us from single vision and Newton's sleep." As humanistic psychology failed to displace behavioralism, so did the hippie movement fail to overthrow straight society. In 1967, a theologian at the University of Chicago said that the hippies "reveal the exhaustion of a tradition: Western, production-oriented, problem-solving, goal-oriented and compulsive in its way of thinking" (Jones, 1967). As late as 1986, during the second term of the Reagan administration, in the years of the compulsively fit, compulsively successful Yuppies, it was obvious that problem solving and goal achievement were not exhausted. In 1967, the Eastern imports America feared were Zen, Buddhism, and the Maharishi Mahesh Yogi; today they are Nissans, Sonys, and Fujis. All that remains of the humanistic revolt is "feeling good about yourself."

Nor were the hippies and the humanistic psychologists the great nonconformists they made themselves out to be. The hippies lived strange lives, but they demanded conformity to their nonconformism. For them the great sin was to be "straight," to hold to the values of one's parents and one's natal culture, to work hard, to achieve, to be emotionally "closed." A song by a pioneer rock band, Crosby, Stills, Nash, and Young, depicted a member of the counterculture resisting the temptation to cut his hair. Humanistic psychologists did not shed adaptation as a virtue. Maslow (1961) described his utopia, Eupsychia, as a place where "there would be no need to hang onto the past—people would happily adapt to changing conditions." The great therapeutic breakthrough of the humanistic psychologists was the encounter group, in which people supposedly learned to be open and authentic. As Rogers describes it, members were coerced into being authentic:

> As time goes on, the group finds it unbearable that any member should live behind a mask or a front. The polite words, the intellectual understanding of each other and relationships, the smooth coin of tact and cover-up … are just not good enough…. Gently at times, almost savagely at others, the group *demands* that the individual be himself, that his current feelings not be hidden, that he remove the mask of ordinary social intercourse. (Zilbergeld, 1983, p. 16)

Humanistic psychologists, like the hippies, did not really question the value of adaptation and social control; they just wanted to change the standards to which people had to adapt.

From Mediation to Information Processing

By 1968, it was clear that of the claimants to cognitive psychology, the most influential and widely held was information-processing psychology. And by 1968, it was also becoming clear that just as humanistic psychology and the counterculture represented no radical break with the past, information-processing psychology was a continuation of behavioralism, not its revolutionary replacement. There was, to be sure, revolutionary sound and fury in the 1960s, supported by citations of Kuhn's *Structure of Scientific Revolutions* (e.g., Palermo, 1971); but closer examination of the leading ideas of the information-processing psychologists reveals that they were not about to become mentalists.

Despite the fact that he wrote about "Imagery: The Return of the Ostracized," Robert R. Holt (1964) unwittingly linked the new cognitive psychology to its behavioralist forebearers. He acknowledged that the concept of mediation had already brought cognitive concepts into behaviorism, and he set out the goal of cognitive psychology in terms Hull could have endorsed: constructing "a detailed working model of the behaving organism." Indeed, for Holt an attractive feature of information-processing models was precisely that with them one could "construct models of the psychic apparatus in which there can be processing of information without consciousness." Marvin Minsky (1968), the leader of artificial intelligence at MIT, was eager to show that AI could find "mechanistic interpretations of those mentalistic notions that have real value," thereby dismissing mentalism as prescientific.

Herbert Simon, one of the founders of modern information-processing psychology, betrays the continuity of information processing with behavioralism, and even its affinity with behaviorism, very well in his *Sciences of the Artificial* (1969, p. 25), writing: "*A man, viewed as a behaving system, is quite simple. The apparent complexity of his behavior over time is largely a reflection of the complexity of the environment in which he finds himself.*" Simon, like Skinner, views human beings as largely the products of the environment that shapes them, since they themselves are simple. In the same work, Simon followed Watson in dismissing the validity of mental images, reducing them to lists of facts and sensory properties associatively organized. Simon also argued that complex behaviors are assemblages of simpler behaviors. Information-processing psychologists share many important behaviorist assumptions: atomism, associationism, and empiricism. On the philosophical side, information processing espouses materialism, holding that there is no independent Cartesian soul, and positivism, continuing to insist on operationalizing all theoretical terms (Simon, 1969). Proponents of this position are made uncomfortable by Chomsky's nativism and his abstract analysis of language. They believe his linguistics confuses formal logical description of grammar with the concrete psychological processes that in fact produce grammatical speech.

Information-processing psychologists reject peripheralism. They believe complex processes intervene between stimulus (input) and response (output). Unlike Watson or Skinner, information-processing cognitive psychologists are willing to infer central mental processes from observable behavior. However, although peripheralism was part of Watson's and Skinner's behaviorisms, it was not shared by Hull, Tolman, or informal behaviorism. The information-processing adherents do not believe central processes are covert versions of S-R associations, but their theory is not far removed from Hull's or Tolman's, except in complexity and sophistication.

Information-processing psychology is a form of behavioralism. It represents a continuing conceptual evolution in the psychology of adaptation, for it views cognitive processes as adaptive behavioral functions and is in a sense a reassertion of earlier American functionalism. The functionalists saw the mind as adaptive but were trapped by the limited metaphysics of the nineteenth century into espousing at the same time a strict mind-body parallelism, engendering a conflict exploited by Watson in establishing behaviorism. The cybernetic analysis of purpose, and its mechanical realization in the computer, however, vindicated the functionalist attitude by showing that purpose and cognition were not necessarily mysterious, and need not involve dualism.

Watson's and Skinner's behaviorisms were extreme statements of the psychology of adaptation that attempted to circumnavigate the inaccessible—and therefore potentially mythical—reaches of the human mind. The information-processing view follows in the steps of William James, Hull, and Tolman in seeing, beneath behavior, processes to be investigated and explained. Behaviorism was one response by the psychology of adaptation to crisis; information processing is another; but in both we see a deeper continuity under the superficial changes. Perhaps to those involved, the revolt against S-R psychology was a scientific revolution; but viewed against the broader framework of history, the revolt is a period of rapid evolutionary change, not a revolutionary jump.

BIBLIOGRAPHY FOR CHAPTERS 12 AND 13

For histories of humanistic psychology, see Anthony J. Sutich, "Introduction," *Journal of Humanistic Psychology* (1961, *1*:vii–ix); and Sutich & Vich (1969). There are two good collections of articles from the various facets of humanistic psychology: James F. T. Bugental, *Challenges of humanistic psychology* (New York: McGraw-Hill, 1967); and Sutich & Vich (1969). Rogers (1964) is considered by humanistic psychologists to be a representative work (Sutich & Vich, 1969); and Maslow (1973) offers a varied selection of his papers.

The most accessible of Noam Chomsky's books is *Language and mind*, enlarged ed. (New York: Harcourt Brace Jovanovich, 1972).

For constraints on animal learning, see Seligman & Hager (1972), who reprint the most important papers of the period and add useful commentary. Garcia discusses the troubles he had publishing his taste-aversion work in "Tilting at the papermills of academe," *American Psychologist* (1981, *36*: 149–58). The occasion of the address is ironic, since it was given upon Garcia's acceptance of a prestigious APA award for his initially rejected work. A similar experience of frustration followed by fame is reported by a pair of other taste-aversion researchers, Paul Rozin and James Kalat, "This week's citation classic: Specific hungers and poison avoidance as adaptive specializations of learning," *Psychological Review* (1971, *78*: 459–86), *Current Contents; Social and Behavioral Sciences* (August 4, 1980, *31*: 14).

Without question, the best guide to the awareness and learning literature is Brewer (1974).

Collections of the leading research in artificial intelligence and computer simulation for both ends of our period are available in E. A. Feigenbaum & J. Feldman (Eds.), *Computers and thought* (New York: McGraw-Hill, 1963); and M. Minsky (Ed.), *Semantic information processing* (Cambridge: MIT Press, 1968); Feigenbaum and Feldman also reprint Turing's classic paper. Hubert L. Dreyfus (1972) provides a history and penetrating critique of work in AI and computer simulation. Cofer (1978) is a valuable history of the activities of the mediational behaviorists from World War II to 1962. Neisser's *Cognitive psychology* (1967) is viewed by many psychologists as having created cognitive psychology in its modern form.

A complete "autopsy" of Project Camelot and the ensuing political fallout may be found in a special issue of *American Psychologist* (1966, *21*, no. 5, May). Good accounts of the maneuvering around the founding of an NSSF as opposed to including social science in the NSF are given by Carter (1966) and Greenberg (1967). The *American Psychologist* special issue on the Harris and Mondale bills was 1967, *22* (no. 11, November). It reprints both bills, articles by their sponsors (Mondale's has the earnest but mushy and soporific qualities of his presidential campaign speeches), and the testimony given before the committees considering each bill. Digests of the testimony on the NSSF bill may be found in *Transaction* (1968, *5*, no. 1, January–February: 54–76). For the legislative histories of the bill, the place to go is the *Congressional Record* for the 90th Congress, Session 2. Mondale's bill is introduced and never heard from again. Harris's bill was discussed on the floor of the Senate, mostly by a cosponsor, Senator Ralph Yarborough, but otherwise languished in committee. Representative Daddario's bill to revise the NSF is fully discussed in an excellent but anonymously written report entered in the *Record* on pages 14889–95, including complete background on the establishment of the NSF, a legislative history of Daddario's bill, and an accounting of all the changes to NSF that it made. It is interesting to observe the support of liberal Democrats for social science. Charles G. McClintock and Charles B. Spaulding, "Political affiliation of academically affiliated psychologists," *American Psychologist* (1965, *20*: 211–21), showed that until after World War II psychologists had voted with the rest of the public—Republican before F.D.R. and Democratic afterward—but they had, unlike the rest of the voting populace, continued to become more Democratic after the war. In the 1952 and 1956 elections, American voters as a whole had supported the liberal and rather intellectual Adlai Stevenson against Eisenhower by only 44 percent and 42 percent, while psychologists had voted for Stevenson by margins of 63 percent and 68 percent. By 1960, a bare majority of voters voted for John Kennedy, while 79 percent of psychologists did so. Psychologists, like their supporters in the Senate, were more liberal than the country as a whole, and social scientists benefited greatly from the rise of political liberalism from 1965 to 1980.

In 1963, *American Psychologist* (*18*) devoted two special issues to the problems of clinical psychology, no. 6 (June) and no. 9 (September). Alarm over Martin Gross's *The brain watchers* is found in various "Comments" in the August (no. 8) issue of the same year. Political controversies over the use and abuse of tests led to a special issue devoted to "Testing and public policy" in 1965 (*20*, no. 11, November). The whole fuss was humorously captured by satirist Art Buchwald in a column published in the *Washington Post* (Sunday, June 20, 1965), in which he made up his own personality test. Since 1965, Buchwald's test has been widely circulated among psychologists, many of whom are ignorant of its origin.

Szasz's views were first presented in his book (Szasz 1960a) and elaborated in many books and articles since. While Ryle's *Concept of mind* is in Szasz's bibliography, he does not in fact derive his own argument from Ryle; nevertheless, the affinity of the two analyses is clear. For a contemporary "straight" view of the hippie movement, see Jones (1967). However, the movement is best appreciated through its art and music, of which the most lasting has proved to be the music: the Grateful Dead and the Jefferson Airplane in particular made records still likely to be accessible. Also illuminating is the New Journalism that came out of and at first depended on the movement. My own favorites are Tom Wolfe's *The electric Kool-Aid acid test* (New York: Bantam, 1968) and anything by Hunter S. Thompson, but most relevantly *Fear and loathing in Las Vegas: A savage journey into the heart of the American dream* (New York: Popular Library, 1971). Wolfe's book is especially interesting in the present context, as it centered on the quintessential hippie group, the Merry Pranksters of Ken Kesey, author of a brilliant antipsychiatric novel, *One flew over the cuckoo's nest* (New York: New American Library, 1963). Wolfe became the outstanding observer of the new psychological Hellenistic Age.

For a more detailed argument that no cognitive revolution took place, see T. H. Leahey, "The mythical revolutions of American psychology," *American Psychologist* (1992, *47*, 308–318).

REFERENCES

Atkinson, R. M. & Shiffrin, R. M. (1968). Human memory: A proposed system and its control processes. *Psychology of Learning and Motivation, 2,* 89–195. Reprinted in Bower (1977).

Blank, L. & David, H. (1963). The crisis in clinical psychology training. *American Psychologist, 18,* 216–219.

Bower, G. (Ed.), (1977). *Human memory: Basic processes.* New York: Academic Press.

Breger, L. & McGaugh, J. L. (1965). Critique and reformulation of "learning-theory" approaches to psychotherapy and neurosis. *Psychological Bulletin, 63,* 338–358.

Carter, L. J. (1966). Social sciences: Where do they fit in the politics of science? *Science, 154,* 488–491.

Chein, I. (1966). Some sources of divisiveness among psychologists. *American Psychologist, 21,* 333–342.

Clark, K. (1967). The scientific and professional aims of psychology. *American Psychologist, 22,* 49–76.

Cofer, C. N. (1978). Origins of the Journal of Verbal Learning and Verbal Behavior. *Journal of Verbal Learning and Verbal Behavior, 17,* 113–326.

Collier, R. (1964). Selected implications from a dynamic regulatory theory of consciousness. *American Psychologist, 19,* 265–269.

Davis, G. (1966). Current status of research and theory in human problem solving. *Psychological Bulletin, 66,* 36–54.

Dixon, T. R. & Horton, D. C. (Eds.), (1968). *Verbal behavior and general behavior theory.* Englewood Cliffs, NJ: Prentice-Hall.

Dreyfus, H. L. (1972). *What computers can't do: A critique of artificial reason.* New York: Harper & Row.

Garfield, S. L. (1966). Clinical psychology and the search for identity. *American Psychologist, 21,* 343–352.

Geiger, H. (1973). Introduction: A. H. Maslow. In A. Maslow, *The farther reaches of human nature.* New York: Viking/Esalen.

Gough, P. B. & Jenkins, J. J. (1963). Verbal learning and psycholinguistics. In M. Mary (Ed.), *Theories in contemporary psychology.* New York: Macmillan.

Greenberg, D. S. (1967). Social sciences: Progress slow on House and Senate bills. *Science, 157,* 660–662.

Hebb, D. O. (1960). The second American Revolution. *American Psychologist, 15,* 735–745.

Hoch, E., Ross, A. O., & Winder, C. L. (1966). Conference on the professional preparation of clinical psychologists. *American Psychologist, 21,* 42–51.

Holt, R. R. (1964). Imagery: The return of the ostracized. *American Psychologist, 19,* 254–264.

Jakobovits, L. & Miron, M. (Eds.), (1967). *Readings in the psychology of language.* Englewood Cliffs, NJ: Prentice-Hall.

Jenkins, J. J. (1968). The challenge to psychological theorists. In T. R. Dixon & D. C. Horton (Eds.), *Verbal behavior and general behavior theory.* Englewood Cliffs, NJ: Prentice-Hall.

Jones, R. (1967, July 7). Youth: The hippies. *Time,* 18–22.

Kiesler, S. B. (1977). Research funding for psychology. *American Psychologist, 32,* 23–32.

Marx, M. (Ed.), (1963). *Theories in contemporary psychology.* New York: Macmillan.

Maslow, A. H. (1961). Eupsychia—The good society. *Journal of Humanistic Psychology, 1,* 1–11.

Maslow, A. H. (1962). Notes on being-psychology. *Journal of Humanistic Psychology, 2,* 47–71.

Maslow, A. H. (1967). Self-actualization and beyond. In J. F. T. Bugental (Ed.), *Challenges of humanistic psychology.* New York: McGraw-Hill.

Maslow, A. H. (1973). *The farther reaches of human nature.* New York: Viking/Esalen.

Miller, G. (1962). Some psychological studies of grammar. *American Psychologist, 17,* 748–762. Reprinted in Jakobovits and Miron (1967).

Minsky, M. (1968). Introduction. In M. Minsky (Ed.), *Semantic information processing.* Cambridge: MIT Press.

Neisser, U. (1967). *Cognitive psychology.* New York: Appleton-Century-Crofts.

Palermo, D. (1971). Is a scientific revolution taking place in psychology? *Science Studies, 1,* 135–155.

Penn, I. N. (1985, June 24). The reality of mental illness (letter to the editor). *The Wall Street Journal, 33.*

Putney, S. & Putney, G. J. (1964). *The adjusted American: Normal neuroses in the individual and society.* New York: Harper Colophon.

Rogers, C. R. (1958). A process conception of psychotherapy. *American Psychologist, 13,* 142–149.

Rogers, C. (1968). Interpersonal relationships: U.S.A. 2000. *Journal of Applied Behavioral Science, 4,* 265–280.

Sanford, N. (1965). Will psychologists study human problems? *American Psychologist, 20,* 192–198.

Schofield, W. (1966). Clinical and counseling psychology: Some perspectives. *American Psychologist, 21,* 122–131.

Seligman, M. E. P. & Hager, J. L. (Eds.), (1972). *Biological boundaries of learning.* New York: Appleton-Century-Crofts.

Shakow, D. (1965). Seventeen years later: Clinical psychology in the light of the 1947 committee on training in clinical psychology report. *American Psychologist, 20,* 353–367.

Shiffrin, R. M. (1977). Commentary on "Human memory: A proposed system and its control processes." In G. Bower (Ed.), *Human memory: Basic processes.* New York: Academic Press.

Simon, H. (1969). *The sciences of the artificial.* Cambridge, MA: MIT Press.

Skinner, B. F. (1959). A case history in scientific method. In S. Koch (Ed.), *Psychology: Study of a science.* New York: McGraw-Hill.

Small, L. (1963). Toward professional clinical psychology. *American Psychologist, 18,* 558–562.

Szasz, T. S. (1960a). *The myth of mental illness.* New York: Harper Perennial Library. Rev. ed. 1974.

Szasz, T. S. (1960b). The myth of mental illness. *American Psychologist, 15,* 113–119.

Taylor, D. W. (1963). Thinking. In M. Marx (Ed.), *Theories in contemporary psychology.* New York: Macmillan.

Thumin, F. J. & Zebelman, M. (1967). Psychology and psychiatry: A study of public image. *American Psychologist, 22,* 282–286.

Tryon, R. C. (1963). Psychology in flux: The academic-professional bipolarity. *American Psychologist, 18,* 134–143.

Wann, T. W. (Ed.), (1964). *Behaviorism and phenomenology: Contrasting bases for modern psychology.* Chicago: Chicago University Press.

Wolfle, D. (1966a). Social problems and social science. *Science, 151,* 1177.

Wolfle, D. (1966b). Government support for social science. *Science, 153,* 485.

Zilbergeld, B. (1983). *The shrinking of America: Myths of psychological change.* Boston: Little, Brown.

PART VI

CONTEMPORARY PSYCHOLOGY (1970–TODAY)

Historians avoid writing about the present or the recent past because they believe perspective improves with distance. Only the passage of time reveals which ideas and events had lasting influence, and which were mere fads. On the other hand, one of the most important motives for writing history is using the past to illuminate the present, and our journey through psychology's scientific history would be incomplete without a look at psychology today and a guess about tomorrow.

The core of scientific psychology—experimental psychology—was fragmented in the 1960s into behaviorist and cognitive camps. Today, excepting a gallant regiment of radical behaviorists, experimental psychology has reunified around the information-processing approach from cognitive science. Nonetheless, some psychologists and philosophers harbor doubts about the viability of cognitive science as the general theory of behavior for which psychologists yearned in the Golden Age of Theory. Just recently, a new brand of cognitive science—connectionism—has come along to challenge the hegemony of the information-processing approach. Whether connectionism will supplant or supplement information processing remains to be seen. Complicating the picture are more radical thinkers who question the very possibility of scientific psychology.

On the professional front, psychology is a huge success. Phil Donohue remarked on television one morning that you can't go on television anymore without a clinical psychologist. Professional psychologists have become ubiquitous explainers of unusual behavior, from outright psychosis to supposed love addictions. At the same time, the tension between academic and professional psychologists has grown to the point that another divorce has occurred; this time the academics walked out of the APA to start their own psychological society. Finally, some writers—including some psychologists—wonder if perhaps the influence of psychology on modern culture has not grown too great.

Chapters 14 and 15 describe psychology's last two decades, and wonder about what happens next.

CHAPTER 14

Cognitive Science
From Triumph to Trouble

THE RISE OF COGNITIVE SCIENCE

The Triumph of Information Processing

During the 1960s and early 1970s, information-processing theory gradually replaced mediational theory as the language of cognitive psychology. By 1974, the venerable *Journal of Experimental Psychology* contained articles by proponents of only two theoretical orientations, information processing and radical behaviorism, the former substantially outnumbering the latter. In 1975, the journal was divided into four separate journals, two concerned with human experimental psychology, one with animal psychology, and one with long, theoretical-experimental papers; and the human journals were controlled by the information-processing point of view. During the same years, information-processing psychologists launched their own journals, including *Cognitive Psychology* (1970) and *Cognition* (1972); and the new cognitive view spread to other areas of psychology, including social psychology (Mischel & Mischel, 1976), social learning theory (Bandura, 1974), developmental psychology

(Farnham-Diggory, 1972), animal psychology (Hulse, Fowler, & Honig, 1978), psycho-analysis (Wegman, 1984), and psychotherapy (Mahoney, 1977; Meichenbaum, 1977; founding of the journal *Cognitive Therapy and Research* [1977]), and even philosophy of science (Rubinstein, 1984). Mediational behaviorism ceased to exist, and the radical behaviorists were confined to a sort of publications ghetto comprising three journals: *Journal of the Experimental Analysis of Behavior, Journal of Applied Behavior Analysis,* and *Behaviorism.*

The fields of artificial intelligence and computer simulation psychology began to merge in the late 1970s into a new field distinct from psychology, called *cognitive science.* Cognitive scientists launched their own journal, *Cognitive Science,* in 1977 and held their first international conference a year later (Simon, 1980). Cognitive science defined itself as the science of what George Miller named *informavores* (Pylyshyn, 1984). The idea was that all information-processing systems—whether made of flesh and blood, like human beings, or silicon and metal, like computers, or of whatever materials might be invented or discovered—operated according to the same principles and therefore constituted a single field of study, cognitive science, "converging around the information processing paradigm" (Simon, 1980).

The proponents of cognitive science were confident that their position was secure as the only respectable scientific game in town. Herbert Simon (1980), writing about the behavioral and social sciences for the centenary issue of *Science* declared that "Over the past quarter-century, no development in the social sciences has been more radical than the revolution—often referred to as the information processing revolution—in our way of understanding the processes of human thinking." Simon dismissed behaviorism as "confining" and "preoccupied with laboratory rats" and praised information-processing theory for helping psychology achieve "a new sophis-tication" and for creating a "general paradigm, the information processing paradigm," which preserved behaviorism's "operationality" while surpassing it "in precision and rigor."

As defined by Simon, the "long-run strategy" of human cognitive science had two goals, each of which is reductionistic in its own way. First, "human complex performance"—the old " 'higher mental processes' "—would be connected with "the basic elementary information processes and their organization." In other words, cognitive science, like behaviorism, aimed to show that complex behavior could be reduced to assemblages of simpler behaviors. Second, "we cannot be satisfied with our explanations of human thinking until we can specify the neural substrates for the elementary information processes of the human symbol system." In other words, like the strict behaviorism of Karl Lashley and A. P. Weiss, cognitive science aimed to show that human thinking could be reduced to neurophysiology.

In 1979, Lachman, Lachman, and Butterfield attempted in their often-cited *Cognitive Psychology and Information Processing* to describe information-processing cognitive psychology as a Kuhnian paradigm. They claimed that "Our [cognitive] revolution is now complete and the atmosphere is one of normal science" (p. 525). They defined cognitive psychology in terms of the computer metaphor discussed in the last chapter: Cognitive psychology is about "how people take in information, how they recode and remember it, how they make decisions, how they transform their internal knowledge states, and how they translate these states into behavioral outputs. The analogy is important. It makes a difference whether a scientist thinks of humans as if they were laboratory animals or as if they were computers" (p. 99). Our choices seem to rest entirely between viewing people as rats or as computers; we may not think of them as human beings. Behavioralism began when psychologists refused to anthropomorphize human beings; the information-processing "paradigm" wants to "computermorphize" them.

In discussing an example of "cognitive behavior" [sic], Lachman, Lachman, and Butterfield presuppose that people *must* process information, thereby legitimating information-processing psychology's answers to questions about why people behave as they do. When you drive a car, you *must* "perceive each familiar landmark anew each time," "have represented the landmark's appearance in your memory," "match up your current perception of the landmark to its stored representation," and so on, though "decid[ing] repeatedly when to shift gears" and where to park (p. 7). Wittgenstein pointed out that how we frame questions about human behavior determines a great deal—probably more than the empirical facts—about the answers we get from our investigations. Lachman, Lachman, and Butterfield's analysis of driving is a splendid example of this process at work; when they say we *must* do the things they claim—even if they are out of awareness, as they concede—information-processing psychology is forced on us, and the only possible answers to the question of how we drive or do anything else become information-processing ones. The form of the question dictates the answer.

Lachman, Lachman, and Butterfield's explication of the information-processing "paradigm" makes clear that information-processing psychology is a form of behavioralism with strong affinity to all but radical behaviorism. Speaking of "cognitive behavior," for example, shows that information processing is the latest form of behavioralism. Their dismissal of introspection as "unreliable and impoverished" and their evaluation of mentalistic introspective psychology as having "reached a dead end" by 1913 are consistent with behavioral views on the psychology of consciousness. They identify the study of consciousness with the study of attention as a stage in information processing, a narrow view of consciousness that Wundt would have rejected. Lachman, Lachman, and Butterfield themselves recognize that information processing took over much from neobehaviorism: nomothetic explanation, empiricism, focus on the laboratory, operationism, and "the rational canons of natural science." In short, although Lachman, Lachman, and Butterfield specifically deny it, information processing adopted a modified logical positivism from neobehaviorism. This becomes clearest at the end of the book, when the authors become confused about the existence of the information processes they have discussed for five hundred pages. They would clearly like to assert that information processes are real processes that actually take place inside an organism. Yet these processes are generally observable to neither the person who is having them nor to a neuroscientist watching the brain. Information-processing psychology is then forced to define its theoretical terms operationally: "Flowcharts, in a way, have the same status for us that operational definition had for our predecessors" (Lachman, Lachman, & Butterfield, 1979, p. 125). But, as we learned from Howard Kendler's operational analysis of the "What is learned?" controversy of the 1950s, operationism is antirealistic, treating theoretical terms simply as convenient fictions. The tension between realism and operationalism is manifest in the last pages of *Cognitive Psychology and Information Processing,* but its authors do not seem to feel it, lamely concluding that it is too early to tell if human information processes are real or not.

The convergence of artificial intelligence and cognitive psychology into the field of cognitive science, and the grandiose claims of cognitive scientists, already stated by Simon, one of the first cognitive psychologists, are repeated by the Research Briefing Panel on Cognitive Science and Artificial Intelligence (Estes & Newell, 1983). According to the panel, cognitive science addresses a "great scientific mystery, on a par with understanding the evolution of the universe, the origin of life, or the nature of elementary particles" and is "advancing our understanding of the nature of mind and the nature of intelligence on a scale that is proving revolutionary."

An important part of the optimism of cognitive scientists, and the conceptual basis of the merger of cognitive psychology and artificial intelligence, was the computer metaphor of mind:body:: program:computer, known as *functionalism*. For it is functionalism that allows cognitive scientists to regard people and computers as essentially similar, despite their material differences.

The New Functionalism

The basic thesis of functionalism derives from the activity of computer programming. Suppose I write a simple program for balancing my checkbook in a programming language such as BASIC. The program will specify a set of *computational functions:* retrieving my old balance from memory, subtracting checks written, adding deposits made, and comparing our results to the bank's. Ignoring minor formatting differences, I can enter and run this program on many different machines: an Apple, an Atari, an IBM PC, a PC clone, or a mainframe computer. In each case, the same computational functions will be carried out, although the physical processes by which each computer will perform them will be different, because the internal structure of each machine is different.

To be able to predict, control, and explain the behavior of a computer, it is unnecessary to know anything at all about the electronic processes involved; all one needs to understand is the higher-level computational functions in the system. I am composing these words on a program called AmiPro, and because I understand the programmed functions of AmiPro, I can use it effectively—that is, I can predict, control, and explain my computer's behavior. I know absolutely nothing about the lower-level computational functions that compose higher-level functions, such as moving paragraphs about, nor do I know anything about how my PC's hardware works; but such knowledge is not necessary to use any properly programmed computer.

Functionalism simply extends the separation of program and computer to include human beings. Computers use hardware to carry out computational functions, so functionalism concludes that people use "wetware" to do the same things. When I balance my checkbook by hand, I carry out exactly the same functions as my BASIC computer program does. My nervous system and my PC's Intel 386 microchip are materially different, but we instantiate the same program as we each do my accounts. So, functionalism concludes, my mind is a set of computational functions that runs my body in exactly the same way that a computer program is a set of computational functions that controls a computer: My mind *is* a running program. In this way, psychologists can hope to predict, control, and explain human behavior by understanding the human "program" and without understanding the nervous system and brain. Cognitive psychologists are thus like computer programmers asked to study an alien computer. They dare not fool with the machine's wiring, so they attempt to understand its program by experimenting with its input-output functions.

Behind functionalism is an important assumption. A computer program can be written to carry out any activity that can be completely described as a set of formal rules. Balancing a checkbook can be described as a formal procedure in which certain rules are applied to various numerical quantities. The claim that a computer can do activity X assumes that X is a formalizable task. To claim that a computer can play chess assumes that chess is a formal rule-governed activity. And likewise with composing music, deciding whether or not to have an abortion, getting married, deciding to get married, playing poker, seducing an attractive person. If a computer is to do any of these things, or to imitate how people do them (obviously a computer can't get married—yet), it must be the case that each activity can be formalized as a precise set of rules that can be captured in the computational functions of a program.

The attraction of functionalism and information processing is that they offer a solution to the behaviorist's problem: how to explain the intentionality of behavior without any residue of teleology. Within behavioralism there were two basic approaches. Pure mechanists such as Hull tried to describe humans and animals as machines that blindly responded to whatever stimuli they happened to encounter. E. C. Tolman, after abandoning his early realism, opted for a representational strategy: Organisms build up representations of their world that they use to guide overt behavior. Each strategy was flawed and finally failed. Tolman was able to show, contrary to Hull, that animals do not simply respond to their environment. Rather, they learn about it and base their behavior on more than just the currently operative stimuli, using representations stored away from earlier experience as well. Tolman's approach, however, ran into the homunculus problem: He implicitly postulated a little rat in the head of a real rat, who read the cognitive map and pulled the levers of behavior. In short, he created a Ghost in the Machine, failing to explain purpose and pushing the problem onto the mysterious Ghost. The mediational neo-Hullians tried to combine Hull's mechanistic S-R theory with Tolman's intuitively plausible representationalism by regarding mediating r-s mechanisms as representations, an interpretation countenanced by Hull's concept of the "pure stimulus act." But the mediational compromise rested on the counterintuitive notion that the brain's r-s connections follow exactly the same laws as overt S-R connections.

Functionalism preserves the virtues of Hull's and Tolman's approaches while seeming to avoid their vices by invoking the sophisticated processes of computer programs instead of little r-s links. Computers carry out their computational functions upon internal representations; in the checkbook example, the program directs the computer to manipulate representations of my previous balance, my checks, my deposits, and so on. Yet my PC contains no little accountant bent over ledger books doing arithmetic: There is no ghostly accountant in the machine. Rather, the machine applies precisely stated formal rules to the representations, carrying out the computations in a completely mechanistic fashion. From the perspective of functionalism, both Hull and Tolman were right, but it remained for the computational approach to put their insights together. Hull was right that organisms are machines; Tolman was right that organisms build up representations from experience. According to functionalism, computer programs apply Hullian mechanistic rules to Tolmanian representations, and, if functionalism is correct, so do living organisms.

As Lachman, Lachman, and Butterfield (1979) state, "Information processing psychology is fundamentally committed to the concept of representation." Brentano recognized that intentionality is the criterion of mentality. Mental states such as beliefs possess "aboutness": They refer to something beyond themselves, which neurons cannot do. Tolmanian representations possess intentionality: A cognitive map is about, is a representation of, a maze. What kinds of representations do computers use?

Although the concept of representation seems straightforward enough, it is fraught with difficulty, as Wittgenstein pointed out. Suppose I draw a stick figure, like so:

What does it represent? At first glance, you might take it to be a man walking with a walking stick. But I might be using it to represent a fencer standing at rest, or to show how one ought to walk with a walking stick, or a man walking backward with a stick, or a woman walking with a stick, or many other things. Another example: No matter how much you might look like a portrait of Henry VIII, it remains a representation of Henry, not of you. Of course, I might use it to represent you if someone asks what you look like and you are not around. So representations don't represent by virtue of their appearance. Exactly what does make a representation a representation is a matter of debate, but functionalism has a distinctive strategy for handling the problem.

Any representation has both semantics and syntax. The semantics of a representation is its meaning; its syntax is its form. If I write the word DESK, its meaning (semantics) lies in its reference to certain items of furniture, and its syntax is the actual structure and arrangement of the letters D, E, S, and K. From a scientific, materialistic standpoint, the mysterious thing about representations is their meaning, their intentionality; that was the original point of Brentano's concept of intentionality, showing that meaning could not be reduced to physical processes. But, as previously remarked, the goal of functionalism is to demystify intentionality, bringing behavior and mental processes within the scope of mechanistic science. It tries to do this by reducing semantics to syntax.

When I typed DESK a moment ago, did the computer understand its meaning? No; it treated those letters purely syntactically, storing them as a set of 0s and 1s in its binary machine language. However, I can ask AmiPro to do what appear to be intelligent things, couchable in mentalistic language, with the word DESK. So I can ask it to find every occurrence of DESK in a given file, and it will find both occurrences of DESK and of "desk." I could ask it to substitute CHAIR for every occurrence of DESK. AmiPro can check the spelling of DESK, or consult a thesaurus to provide words of similar meaning. Yet although the computer could do all these things with the word DESK, it could not be said to possess the semantic component of DESK. For in every case the computer would operate by looking for the unique machine code of 0s and 1s into which it encoded DESK, and then carrying out my specified operation on that register. The computer operates only on the syntax of a representation, although its behavior may be consistent with its knowing the meaning of the representation. Although from its behavior it may seem to know the semantic meaning of DESK, all it really knows is the syntax of 0s and 1s.

Another way of expressing this difficult but important point is to borrow some terminology from Daniel Dennett (1978), one of the creators of functionalism. When we play chess with a computer, we are likely to treat it as a human being, attributing to it mental dispositions: It *tries* to develop its queen early, it *wants* to capture my queen's pawn, it's *afraid* I will seize control of the center of the board. Dennett calls this adopting the *intentional stance*. We naturally adopt the intentional stance toward people, sometimes toward animals, and toward machines in certain cases. But what is going on inside the computer is not intentional at all. The layout of the pieces on the chessboard is represented internally as a complex pattern of 0s and 1s in the computer's working memory. Then the computer finds a rule that applies to the current pattern and executes the rule, changing the content of a memory register, which is displayed on a video screen as the move of a chess piece. Next an input command—your chess move—alters the pattern of 0s and 1s, and the computer again applies the applicable rule to the new pattern, and so on. The program does not *try, want,* or *fear*; it simply carries out formal computations on patterns of 0s and 1s, and you regard that as intentional behavior.

In an interview with Jonathan Miller, Dennett (1983, pp. 77–78) summarizes the computational approach to intentionality this way (the dialogue is somewhat compressed):

> The basic idea is that you start at the top with your whole intelligent being, with all its beliefs and desires and expectations and fears—all its information. Then you say: "How is all that going to be represented in there?" You break the whole system down into subsystems, little homunculi. Each one is a specialist, each one does a little bit of the work. Out of their cooperative endeavors emerge the whole activities of the whole system.
> But isn't this another way of being unscientifically mentalistic?
> Yes, you do replace the little man in the brain with a committee, but the saving grace is that the members of the committee are stupider than the whole. The subsystems don't individually reproduce the talents of the whole. That would lead you to an infinite regress. Instead you have each subsystem doing a part; each is less intelligent, knows less, believes less. The representations are themselves less representational, so you don't need an inner *eye* to observe them; you can get away with some sort of inner process which "accesses" them in some attenuated sense.

So while we attribute intentionality to the chess-playing computer, in fact it is only a collection of nonintentional, stupid subsystems carrying out blind computations on syntactically defined representations, following mechanistic rules.

Where does this leave people? Margaret Boden, a popularizer and philosophical exponent of AI, thinks it leaves people as they are; she sees AI as entirely compatible with humanistic treatments of people as creators and users of meaning (Boden, 1977, 1979). Other philosophers, however, take the computational metaphor more seriously and reach a different conclusion. Stephen Stich (1983) has forcefully argued that the only scientifically acceptable theories in human cognitive psychology will eventually have to be syntactic theories, which treat human information processing just like a computer's, as mechanical computation on syntactically defined representations. Dennett (1978) tries to straddle these two views, acknowledging that in science we must ultimately treat people as machines, but that the "folk psychology" of belief and desire may be retained as an instrumental calculus for everyday use. Stich replies that, in the end, scientific truth must prevail as it always has: "The general conception of the cosmos embedded in the folk wisdom of the West was utterly and thoroughly mistaken.... Nor is there any reason to think that ancient camel drivers would have greater insight or better luck when the structure at hand was the structure of their own minds rather than the structure of matter or of the cosmos" (pp. 229–30). This is the attitude of scientistic imperialism: "If our science is inconsistent with the folk precepts that define who and what we are, then we are in for rough times. One or the other will have to go" (p. 10). "Deprived of its empirical underpinnings, our age old conception of the universe within will crumble just as certainly as the venerable conception of the external universe crumbled during the Renaissance" (p. 246). Stich finds the prospect cheering.

It is well to take the computational argument seriously. Although as Lachman, Lachman, and Butterfield (1979) point out, most cognitive psychologists use information processing as a language and do not write computer programs, still the final "cash value," to use William James's phrase, of information processing lies in the promise to turn information-processing theory into computational theory. As Ulric Neisser (1984), a frequent critic of information processing, nevertheless admits, "Models that actually run on real computers are more convincing than models that exist only as hypotheses on paper." The inspiring thing to psychologists about artificial intelligence was, as George Miller (1983) says, that when behaviorists said that talk of mind was "moonshine," cognitive psychologists could point to AI: "It can't be moonshine if I can build one."

Moreover, cognitive science draws its scientific respectability from the promise of writing computational theories. In a briefing for federal officials such as the president's science adviser, the Research Briefing Panel on Cognitive Science and Artificial Intelligence wrote:

> The hypothesis that links artificial intelligence and human cognition together, providing the frame within which scientific inquiry proceeds, holds that all intelligence, including human intelligence, arises from the ability to use symbols. By symbols, we mean physical symbol systems, as first understood in computer science. Without this stipulation the hypothesis would constitute only another version of the long-held view that symbols are important in human mental life. But with the notions of symbol and symbol system firmly connected to the physical world via the realization in computers, the hypothesis anchors the study of all the higher processes of mind to the same scientific world of mechanism as all other natural sciences. (Estes & Newell, 1983, p. 24)

In their briefing, the panel works hard to establish the scientific status of cognitive science—the briefing very soberly presents cognitive science as serious basic science—and the claim that "symbolic behavior can be realized in a physical system" distances cognitive science from psychology's unscientific moonshine by pushing it toward physics and Newtonian mechanism. Clark Hull made the same move, but he lacked the means to convincingly turn his theories into working machines.

Ultimately, information-processing theories must be turned into formal computational theories, because if they are not, there will be no more reason to think of people as computers than as animals. And perhaps a good deal less. After all, computers are composed of silicon and metal, humans and animals are made of flesh and blood; computers are designed and manufactured, humans and animals evolved; computer minds spring into full-blown existence when the machine is started, humans and animals develop from infancy to adulthood; computers do not actively interact with the world through bodies, humans and animals do. On a less physical level, computers have no society, no culture, nor do they live in groups; humans and some animals live in groups, and only humans live in culture, a world they themselves create. The similarity of human and computer is really rather slight, and we should worry if it is the only game in town. Lachman, Lachman, and Butterfield say that it matters which analogy we follow, animal or computer. The analogy does, indeed, matter. But which analogy is right? Is either?

DOUBTS ABOUT COGNITIVE SCIENCE

When in 1957 Herbert Simon prophesied that by 1967 psychological theories would be written as computer programs, he also foresaw that "within ten years a digital computer will be the world's chess champion" and that "within ten years a digital computer will discover and prove an important new mathematical theorem." In 1965, Simon predicted that "machines will be capable, within 20 years, of doing any work that a man can do" (Dreyfus, 1972). By 1986, none of Simon's forecasts had come to pass. More important, some psychologists and philosophers had begun to wonder if they *could* come to pass. The issue is not Simon's credibility as a prophet—others in artificial intelligence made similar claims (Dreyfus, 1972)—but the credibility of the information-processing, computational approach to psychology. For if it should turn out that computers in principle cannot do "any work that a man can do," then treating people as computers would be bad psychological theory.

In 1981, James J. Jenkins, who had experienced the transition from mediational behaviorism to information processing, asserted that "there is a malaise in cognitive psychology, a concern with trivia, a lack of direction." He asked, and seemed to answer in the negative, "Is the field advancing as we feel sciences are supposed to advance? ... Is the field developing and deepening our understanding of cognitive principles, processes, or facts that can contribute to the solution of real problems and generate answers to relevant questions?" While Jenkins did not doubt that "human beings are universal machines" and was able to find "some [better] directions for cognitive psychology," he pictured a field adrift. In the same year, the editors of *Cognition,* then celebrating its tenth birthday, fretted that "in cognitive psychology, progress is [not] obvious," that since 1971 there had been in the field no "major development," that "little has really changed" (Mehler & Franck, 1981).

Even more dissatisfied with the state of cognitive psychology was Ulric Neisser, the man who had helped establish it and the information-processing approach in his *Cognitive Psychology* of 1967. In 1976, he wrote a new text, *Cognition and Reality,* which "destroyed my reputation as a mainstream cognitive psychologist" (Goleman, 1983). In the new book, Neisser said, "The actual development of cognitive psychology in the last few years has been disappointingly narrow," wondered "whether its overall direction is genuinely productive," and said he had come to "realize that the notion of *information processing* deserves a closer examination." Neisser began to argue that cognitive psychology should "take a more 'realistic' turn." Subsequently, Neisser's unhappiness with cognitive psychology has not diminished: "The upshot of so much effort has been disappointing. There is little sense of progress" (Neisser, 1982). The "information processing approach remains somehow unsatisfying as an account of human nature" (Neisser, 1984). Neisser urges that the information-processing approach be replaced with an "ecological approach" that studies cognition in natural contexts instead of in the narrow confines of experiments invented to meet the needs of the laboratory.

While such disgruntled views may not be typical of cognitive psychologists, Jenkins, Mehler, Franck, and Neisser are acknowledged leaders in the field, and their unhappiness is surely a symptom of something wrong. But what?

Is Information Processing a Paradigm?

In their eagerness to rebel against behaviorism, cognitive psychologists embraced Thomas Kuhn's analysis of science and rushed to proclaim information processing a new scientific "paradigm" for psychology (for example, Lachman, Lachman, & Butterfield, 1979). However, most "Kuhnian" analyses of psychology tended to overlook an important component, perhaps the most important component, of a paradigm as described by Kuhn. Kuhn claimed that a paradigm has two parts, the disciplinary matrix, a set of philosophical assumptions, and the shared exemplar, a visibly successful research achievement providing a model for investigations of nature conducted within the paradigm. Psychologists' analyses of information processing and its rivals focused on the rather nebulous disciplinary matrix and neglected the shared exemplar (again see Lachman, Lachman, & Butterfield, 1979; for a later example, see Brewer & Nakamura, 1984).

But, as Kuhn recognized, much—perhaps most—of a paradigm's puzzle-solving power derives from the shared examplar, because it defines the puzzles. Pavlov's research program furnishes an instructive example. While Pavlov clearly had philosophical assumptions about psychology, more important to the brilliance of his research was his *experimental* paradigm, the shared exemplar of all classical conditioning research: pairing US with CS. Pavlov's experimental setup allowed him to pose concrete, answerable questions, such as, What happens if I alter the temporal relationship of US and CS? Or if there is more than one CS? Or if I present CS without US? No matter what one's philosophical prejudices, one cannot do research without a concrete model, and a scientific community's research cannot accumulate toward a common goal without a *shared* exemplar.

Perhaps cognitive psychologists neglect the shared exemplar because information-processing psychology does not offer one. The first to identify the problem (though without the Kuhnian terminology) was Allen Newell (1973) of the original Newell, Shaw, and Simon GPS team. Newell's paper was one of the first to express unhappiness with information processing, and it is often cited by other dissidents. In commenting on the papers at a cognitive psychology symposium, Newell said that "half of me is half distressed and half confused. Half of me is quite content and clear on where we are going." Newell's happy half applauded the fine technical achievements of the research presented at the symposium. The distressed half looked at all the fine research at hand, anticipated more fine research yet to come, but asked, *"Where will psychology then be? Will we have achieved a science of man adequate in power and commensurate with his complexity?"* (pp. 283–84). The problem Newell saw was that cognitive psychologists were investigating a myriad of specific phenomena—he listed fifty-nine and implied there were more—but that it was impossible to "put them all together." As he tried to put them all together, "[i]t became less and less clear to me that all these papers were cumulating."

While cognitive psychologists share the disciplinary matrix of information processing, they have no shared exemplar around which to organize their collective research, so that the papers cannot accumulate. Nor is there reason to think things have changed since 1973. Both Jenkins (1981) and Neisser (1982) echo Newell's complaint.

Lack of a shared exemplar affects theory construction. Because each cognitive scientist is concerned with his or her own phenomenon, small-scale theories of specific tasks proliferate, while the goal of constructing a general cognitive theory is neglected. Jenkins (1981) complains that these small theoretical models are "not models of the mind, but rather models of the task being performed by the subjects." Precisely because human beings have such general and flexible intelligence, when they are asked to do a laboratory task, they take on the characteristics of the task, so that a theoretical model of subjects' behavior reflects the demands of the task and captures no general aspect of mental functioning.

The task-modeling approach is encouraged by the computational metaphor of artificial intelligence. In AI, a programmer who wants a computer to accomplish some task examines the task very closely and writes a program that allows the computer to succeed. Workers in cognitive psychology seem to do the same thing: They analyze a task and ask what a person (rather than the AI programmer's computer) must be doing to solve the task. In AI, this approach poses no problems, because the programmer's goal is simply to write a successful program. In cognitive psychology, however, the goal ought to be different: to discover how people do in fact accomplish what they do. Focusing on the task in an AI manner leads psychologists to study what information processing says people must logically be doing and may obscure what they really are doing. Morever, theories generated by logical task analysis may be amply confirmed by experiment without revealing anything significant about human nature. Because human beings are the most general-purpose computers that exist, when placed in an experiment, they become the sort of device needed to solve the problem with which they are presented, and so they act as the cognitive theory predicts. However, the theory only describes an evanescent moment in subjects' lives, not their enduring cognitive architecture (Jenkins, 1981).

A further obstacle to theorizing in information-processing psychology is that its disciplinary matrix, to continue using Kuhn's terms, is too vague and ill-defined to demand rigorous theorizing. This is especially true when information processing is used as a metaphor without specific commitment to producing a computational version of a theory. About all the information-processing metaphor says is that people take in input, represent and process it internally, and produce output. Since the constraints of the approach are so vague, it is little wonder that cognitive psychologists analyze and theorize about tasks rather than people; at least a task specifies and constrains how one should theorize and for what one should account. As a result, there is no shared agreement on the enterprise of cognitive psychology. Speaking of memory, the most widely investigated of the cognitive processes, Endel Tulving (1979), one of the field's leaders, argued that "After a hundred years of laboratory-based study of memory, we still do not seem to possess any concepts that the majority of workers would consider important or necessary." Tulving's contention is supported by the findings of White (1985). White examined seven leading textbooks in cognitive psychology published in 1979–1980 and found widespread disagreement on important ideas. Of 3,246 publications cited in all the books, only 19 (0.6 percent) were cited by every author. Only 146 (4.5 percent) were cited in as many as three texts. Examination of the texts' content showed that few phenomena were discussed in all of them, and that even frequently occurring concepts were often discussed under different names. White's findings were confirmed in a study by Robert Dale of five leading textbooks from the late 1980s. Again, only 19 works were cited by all authors. Dale concurred with White's conclusion that cognitive psychology had a long way to go to become a normal science (Adler, 1990).

Clearly, despite claims to the contrary from Lachman, Lachman, and Butterfield (1979) and others, information-processing psychology is not a Kuhnian paradigm. There is no widely shared exemplar or even set of exemplars. There is no tightly woven disciplinary matrix of pretheoretical assumptions constraining the forms theories take. Information processing is, as Lachman, Lachman, and Butterfield say, a metaphor; but it is no more than that. The metaphor of information processing provides only an *approach* to psychology within the behavioralist tradition.

Was There a Revolution?

Like the citizens of the United States, France, and the Soviet Union, cognitive scientists share a myth of revolutionary origin. Proponents of information processing believe that information processing constitutes a Kuhnian paradigm, that behaviorism constituted another, and that in the 1960s a Kuhnian scientific revolution occurred during which information processing overthrew behaviorism. We have already learned that neither information processing nor behaviorism was a paradigm, so it is reasonable to doubt that there was a revolution. Information processing is best viewed as the latest form of behavioralism, with strong affinities to historical forms of behaviorism. Mentalism was the study of conscious experience as such; behavioralism is the study of behavior. What attitude does information processing take to consciousness and introspection?

In an influential paper on the introspectability of information processes, Richard E. Nisbett and Timothy Wilson (1977) describe the characteristic information-processing account of consciousness: that it is the *result* of thinking, not the process of thinking, that appears in consciousness as a result, not a cause, of information processing. Nisbett and Wilson then elaborate on the information-processing view, reviewing evidence "consistent with the most pessimistic view concerning people's ability to report accurately about their cognitive processes." They conclude that people have "little or no direct introspective access to higher order cognitive processes," and that when people are asked to describe the processes that caused their behavior, "they do not do so on the basis of any true introspection. Instead, their reports are based on a priori, implicit, causal theories"—that is, on folk theories about their behavior. Reports will be true when folk theories are true, false when folk theories are false; but in any case, it is not from introspection of information processes that people derive accounts of their own behavior.

Wundt would not have been surprised at Nisbett and Wilson's findings, because their experiments were quite like those of the Würzburg psychologists whose work Wundt denounced. In both the Nisbett-Wilson and Würzburg experiments, people performed some more or less complex task and were then asked why they behaved as they did. For example, after performing the task of choosing the best pantyhose from a display, subjects talked about superior color and texture. In fact, each pair of pantyhose was identical; subjects tended overwhelmingly to choose the pair that was last on their right. Wundt was quite aware, and argued in his critique of the Würzburg school's experiments, that this sort of retrospective accounting of mental process can yield no scientific data.

The real issue lying between Wundt and Nisbett and Wilson shows that it is not their respective evaluations of Würzburg-type experiments that has changed, but rather the meaning they give their interpretations. Nisbett and Wilson do not doubt that their subjects knew what was going on in consciousness during the experiments, but they argue that conscious content did not reflect underlying cognitive processes. Thus, for them, verbal reports of consciousness may be safely ignored in explaining behavior. In other words, Nisbett and Wilson are behavioralists whose scientific aim is the prediction and control of behavior. Like Ralph Barton Perry, they argue that while one knows more about oneself than anyone else, one's mind is nevertheless in principle open to complete scrutiny from outside. Wundt, however, was a mentalist. What bothered him about the Würzburg results was that their descriptions of conscious content were so variable. He had no interest in behavior; for him, the subject matter of psychology was conscious experience in itself and for itself, without regard to how it predicted or explained behavior. Nisbett and Wilson have no interest in consciousness unless it helps them predict, explain, and control behavior; when they find it cannot, they throw it out altogether.

Nisbett and Wilson's analysis has not escaped criticism, but the critics still operate within the framework of behavioralism. Nisbett and Wilson concluded that introspective reports "may have little value" in trying to construct cognitive explanations of behavior. Critics tend to argue that Nisbett and Wilson's conclusion is just a little too bleak: Sometimes people's introspective reports have scientific value. The most important of the more optimistic accounts of verbal reports was that of K. Anders Ericsson and Herbert Simon (1980). Ericsson and Simon began by stating information-processing psychology's goal in a way that would have cheered Clark Hull or John Watson: "We would like to have processing models so explicit that they could actually produce the predicted behavior from the information in the stimulus." In their account of information processing, one frequently important stage of processing involves placing material in short-term memory (STM), either during processing as a way station or at the end of processing when a response is produced. "Within the context of this general model, verbalization processes produce (externalize) information that is in STM." Thus, under the right conditions (typically violated in the Nisbett & Wilson studies), verbal reports of information-processing activity can be accurate, as reports of one stage of information processing.

The Ericsson and Simon view of introspection differs only in emphasis from Nisbett and Wilson and from behaviorism. Nisbett and Wilson think that verbal reports of cognitive processes are only very rarely accurate; Ericsson and Simon think that they are accurate about certain aspects of information processes, but certainly not all. Nisbett and Wilson implicitly urge that verbal reports be entirely discarded from cognitive science; Ericsson and Simon argue that when used properly, as "subject behavior," they may be of service to the cognitive scientist—the view that seems to have become the consensus (Klatzky, 1984). Ericsson and Simon recognize that their account is not very different from Watson's. Watson abjured introspection but thought that having subjects talk aloud while solving problems might reveal their thought processes, and Ericsson and Simon agree. Since Watson believed thinking was talking to yourself, talking aloud would, by definition, reveal thought. Ericsson and Simon, however, regard thinking as unconscious data processing, so their use of talking is more confused and confusing than Watson's. Nevertheless, the point stands: The information-processing account of awareness is little different from the behaviorist account.

Behavioralists wanted to predict, control, and explain behavior. Some behavioralists were willing to theorize about processes linking environment and behavior, and to use verbal reports as evidence concerning mediating processes. Other behavioralists rejected inner processes (radical behaviorism), and some rejected introspective reports (methodological behaviorism). Information-processing cognitive scientists are not radical behaviorists, since they are happy to theorize about mediating processes, but they disagree about how useful verbal reports are in finding out about them. Neither behaviorism nor information-processing psychology is interested in consciousness for its own sake: Both are forms of behavioralism.

Exactly what is it, from the information-processing standpoint, that subjects are supposed to detect by introspection? It is admitted that subjects know of what they are conscious, and no one claims that people might introspect the states of their brain. Of what, then, are they supposed to be aware? Nisbett and Wilson quote a researcher who said, "I don't remember any subject who ever described anything like the process of [cognitive] dissonance reduction that we knew to have occurred." Wittgenstein observed much of what Nisbett and Wilson observed: When people remember something—where they left their keys, for example—the conscious processes they experience are infinitely different from case to case. He concluded from this that there was no process called "memory." Information-processing psychologists find the same thing, and conclude that people do not know the unconscious process called "memory." The information-processing view rests on an assumption: There are processes that *must* have occurred, whether or not anyone observed them. Yet these processes, at least for the most part, do not occur in consciousness, where they might be observed, nor would one see them if one opened up the brain—"dissonance reduction" is not a brain process. While Wittgenstein's conclusion that there are no cognitive processes may seem strange, the information-processing view is also strange, perhaps stranger. They assert that there *must be* information processes taking place in people who are not aware of them, processes that cannot be observed by a neuroscientist or by people in whom the processes are taking place. Instead of taking people's inability to report these processes as evidence that they do not exist, as Wittgenstein did, information-processing psychologists impugn people's awareness of the reasons for their actions.

Here we again see the AI model of cognitive psychology at work. Cognitive psychologists take a task and analyze it from the information-processing perspective, working out what a computer program would have to do to accomplish it. Then they assume that something very similar *must* be happening in humans doing the same task. Should subjects verbally report similar processes, cognitive psychologists will be pleased at the support for their model. Should subjects report something different, it does not matter, because subjects do not always understand their own minds. In either event, the logical analysis of the task dictates the psychological theory, just as it does in AI. What subjects say will be taken seriously only when it supports the model, and will be dismissed as erroneous folk theorizing when it does not.

These considerations return us to a problem that troubled Lachman, Lachman, and Butterfield (1979). Do the information processes postulated by cognitive psychology really occur in human thinking, or are they only convenient fictions that help cognitive scientists predict, control, and explain behavior? If information processes are neither consciously experienced events nor brain events, it becomes difficult to say what they might be other than theoretical conveniences. Some cognitive scientists, most notably John Anderson (1978, 1981), have concluded that radical behaviorism is correct in claiming that there is no way of knowing what processes take place between stimulus and response. Since more than one information-processing model is compatible with any set of behavioral data, and since the processes may not be directly observed, there is no sure way of deciding between competing models. In other words, there is no point in claiming psychological reality for any information-processing model. Theoretical models are useful insofar as they help predict, describe, and control human behavior: "Lack of unique identifiability [of one model of behavior over another] is no reason not to postulate internal structure and representation.... [G]o ahead and get on with the business of science: Postulate some set of internal structures and processes that are consistent with the data and don't worry about unique identifiability" (Anderson, 1981). While Anderson's views are not typical of cognitive scientists (see Hayes-Roth, 1979; Pylyshyn, 1979), they do reveal the difficulties of postulating information processes that are neither introspectible conscious contents nor identifiable brain states.

The debate over the psychological reality of information processes repeats the "What is learned?" debate among behaviorists of the 1950s. Then, too, there were realist theorists such as Tolman and Hull, asserting the reality of cognitive maps and habit strengths. And there were also nominalists such as Howard Kendler, asserting that theoretical terms must be regarded as useful fictions only. In its attitudes to consciousness, introspection, and verbal reports, and in its theoretical debates, information-processing psychology is updated, high-tech behavioralism, differing from behaviorism only in theoretical language, not in substance. Information-processing psychologists would have little trouble subscribing to the creed of behaviorism laid out by John B. Watson in the first paragraph of his 1913 behaviorist manifesto.

Cognitive scientists believe in a revolution because it provides them with an origin myth, an account of their beginnings that helps legitimize their practice of science (Brush, 1974). Kuhn provided the language of paradigm and revolution, Chomsky provided the angry voice crying for change, and the sound and fury of the alienated 1960s provided an exciting backdrop for the shift from mediational behaviorism to information processing. But there was no revolution: Behavioralism continued with a new language, a new model, and new concerns directed to its familiar end: the description, prediction, and control of behavior (Leahey, 1981, 1992).

Myths of revolution usually turn out on close examination to be misleadingly simple. The revolution of the thirteen colonies against England was mainly an assertion of traditional English liberties, not a revolution at all. The French Revolution began in the name of Reason, drowned in blood, and unleashed Napoleon on Europe. The Russian Revolution traded Oriental despotism for totalitarian tyranny. The cognitive revolution was an illusion.

Is the Turing Test Valid?

Imagine that you are seated at a table in an empty room. On the table before you are a book and a supply of paper, and in the wall in front of the table are two slots. Out of the left-hand slot come pieces of paper on which are written Chinese characters. You know nothing about Chinese. When you receive a slip of paper, you examine the string of symbols on it and find the corresponding string in the book. The book tells you to copy out a new set of Chinese figures on one of your pieces of paper and pass it out the right-hand slot. You can do this for any string of characters that comes in the left slot. Unknown to you, Chinese psychologists on the other side of the wall are feeding into the left slot Chinese stories followed by questions about the stories, and they receive answers out of the other slot. From their point of view, the machine beyond the wall understands Chinese, because they are able to carry on a conversation with the machine, receiving plausible answers to their questions. They conclude that the machine beyond the wall understands Chinese and has passed the Turing test.

Of course, you know that you understand nothing—you are just writing down one set of meaningless squiggles by instructed response to another set of meaningless squiggles. John Searle (1980), whose thought experiment this is, points out that you are functioning in the "Chinese Room" exactly as a computer functions. The computer accepts machine code input (patterns of 0s and 1s), applies syntactic rules to transform these representations into new representations (new patterns of 0s and 1s), and generates output. It is the computer user alone who calls what the computer is doing "understanding stories," "playing chess," "simulating an atomic strike," or whatever, just as it is the Chinese psychologists who say that the room "understands Chinese." Searle's argument shows that the Turing test is not an adequate measure of intelligence, because the Chinese Room passes the Turing test without understanding anything, and its mode of operation is exactly the same as a computer's.

Searle goes on to point out an important peculiarity about cognitive simulation compared to other kinds of simulation. Meterologists construct computer simulations of hurricanes, economists of U.S. foreign trade activity, and biologists of photosynthesis. But their computers do not develop 100 mph winds, multi–billion-dollar trade deficits, or convert light into oxygen. Yet cognitive scientists claim that when and if they simulate intelligence—that is, a program passes the Turing test—their machine will *really be* intelligent. In other fields, simulation and real achievement are kept separate, and Searle regards it as absurd to ignore the distinction in cognitive science.

Searle distinguishes between *weak AI* and *strong AI*. Weak AI would be maintaining the distinction between simulation and achievement, and using computers as other scientists do, as wonderfully convenient calculating devices with which to use and check theories. Strong AI is the claim—refuted by the Chinese Room thought experiment—that simulation of intelligence *is* intelligence. Searle believes that strong AI can never succeed, for the same reason that a computer cannot perform photosynthesis: It's made out of the wrong materials. In Searle's view, it is the natural biological function of certain plant structures to photosynthesize, and it is the natural biological function of brains to think and understand. Machines have no natural biological functions and so can neither photosynthesize nor understand. Computers may provide tools to help investigate photosynthesis and understanding, but they cannot, Searle concludes, ever actually do either one. Searle's argument is similar to a point made by Leibniz:

> And supposing there were a machine, so constructed as to think, feel, and have perception, it might be conceived as increased in size, while keeping the same proportions, so that one might go into it as into a mill. That being so, we should, on examining its interior, find only parts which work one upon another, and never anything by which to explain a perception. (Gunderson, 1984, p. 629)

Is Formalism Plausible?

There is in cognitive science no small amount of scientistic hubris. According to the Briefing Panel of Cognitive Science, because computers engage in "*symbolic* behavior" (precisely what Searle's argument denies), "we ourselves can program computers to deal with many things—anything to which we set our mind." (The panel has apparently forgotten the grandiose claims made in the 1950s that never came to fruition.) Hidden underneath the panel's claim is the assumption of *formalism.* Computers can do anything that can be written as a computer program, and the panel, following Simon in claiming that computers can be programmed to do "anything a man can do," "anything to which we set our mind," implicitly asserts that anything people do is a formal procedure. Formalism in psychology represents the final development of the mechanization of the world picture. Just as physical science succeeded by analyzing nature as a machine, cognitive science hopes to succeed by analyzing human beings as machines (Dreyfus, 1972). However, Searle's Chinese Room already challenges mechanistic formalism by showing that formal processing of symbols does not yield understanding of language. Other challenges have also arisen, the greatest of which is the *frame problem,* because it challenges not only the ability of computers to imitate human intelligence, but the very possibility of achieving machine intelligence at all.

Daniel Dennett (1984, pp. 129–30) asks us to consider the following story:

> Once upon a time there was a robot, named R_1 by its creators. Its only task was to fend for itself. One day its designers arranged for it to learn that its spare battery, its precious energy supply, was locked in a room with a time bomb set to go off soon. R_1 located the room, and the key to the door, and formulated a plan to rescue its battery. There was a wagon in the room, and the battery was on the wagon, and R_1 hypothesized that a certain action which it called PULLOUT (WAGON, ROOM) would result in the battery being removed from the room. Straightaway it acted, and did succeed in getting the battery out

of the room before the bomb went off. Unfortunately, however, the bomb was also on the wagon. R_1 *knew* that the bomb was on the wagon in the room, but didn't realize that pulling the wagon would bring the bomb out along with the battery. Poor R_1 had missed that obvious implication of its planned act.

Back to the drawing board. "The solution is obvious," said the designers. "Our next robot must be made to recognize not just the intended implications of its act, but also the implications about their side effects, by deducing these implications from the descriptions it uses in formulating its plans." They called their next model the robot-deducer, R_1D_1. They placed R_1D_1 in much the same predicament that R_1 had succumbed to, and as it too hit upon the idea of PULLOUT (WAGON, ROOM) it began, as designed, to consider the implications of such a course of action. It had just finished deducing that pulling the wagon out of the room would not change the color of the room's walls, and was embarking on a proof of the further implication that pulling the wagon out would cause its wheels to turn more revolutions than there were wheels on the wagon—when the bomb exploded.

Back to the drawing board. "We must teach it the difference between relevant implications and irrelevant implications," said the designers, "and teach it to ignore the irrelevant ones." So they developed a method of tagging implications as either relevant or irrelevant to the project at hand, and installed the method in their next model, the robot-relevant-deducer, or R_2D_1 for short. When they subjected R_2D_1 to the test that had so unequivocally selected its ancestors for extinction, they were surprised to see it sitting, Hamlet-like, outside the room containing the ticking bomb, the native hue of its resolution sicklied o'er with the pale cast of thought, as Shakespeare (and more recently Fodor) has aptly put it. "Do something!" they yelled at it. "I am," it retorted. "I'm busily ignoring some thousands of implications I have determined to be irrelevant. Just as soon as I find an irrelevant implication, I put it on the list of those I must ignore, and …" the bomb went off.

R_1 and his descendants are caught in the frame problem. How is it possible to formalize human knowledge and problem-solving skills as a set of computerized rules? It is quite obvious that people do not do what the R robots do: Somehow we just solve problems rapidly and with little conscious thought, just as the Würzburg psychologists discovered. If we did work the ways the Rs did, we, like they, would have died long ago. Rather than working computationally, humans seem to work intuitionally: Solutions to problems just occur to us without thinking; adaptive behaviors happen without thought. We do not have to think to ignore all the absurdities that R_2D_1 had to work at ignoring, because the absurd and irrelevant implications of our behavior just do not occur to us. But a computer, being a formal system, must work out all the implications of its acts and then ignore them.

Empirical evidence also implies that people's behavior is not formalizable. Hubert and Stuart Dreyfus's (1988) study of expert performance—for example, flying fighter planes—shows that only novices apply rules to guide their behavior, while experts just fly. Eleanor Rosch's (1977) studies of human concepts show that they are not based on tidy, computerlike lists of defining attributes, but are centered on stereotypical prototypes surrounded by fuzzy boundaries. Consider, for example, the problem of differentiating among *glass, cup,* and *mug* (Leahey & Harris, 1992). Each term conjures up an ideal prototype, but setting the boundaries among them is problematic. The prototype of the cup has a handle on it, but we call paper cups *cups,* not glasses. One might say it's because they are not made of glass, but would one call a glass something that is shaped like a teacup but is made of glass? If mugs have handles but are thicker than cups, is there a minimum thickness a cup must have to become a mug? Does the name of the moment depend on what a vessel holds? Is a paper cup filled with beer a "cup of beer"? If we fill a typical glass with coffee, do we call it a "glass of coffee" as we offer it to a visitor? If we fill a mug with water, is it a "mug of water"? Our intuitions are troubled by these borderline cases, suggesting that we do not use formal rules to distinguish among *glass, cup,* and *mug.* If such homely concepts cannot be formalized, it is wildly improbable that computers can be programmed to do anything we set our minds to, including morality, justice, politics, art, drama, poetry, or even the everyday encounters of social life.

Conclusion: The Symbolic Paradigm in Trouble?

Increasingly, workers in cognitive science acknowledge limitations on their achievements and shy away from the pretensions of the past (Waldrop, 1984; Rose, 1985). Most believe that in time the AI approach to cognition will be vindicated: There will be intelligent machines and human behavior will be explicable in terms of computational information processing. But even these scaled-down ambitions are best regarded as hopes. If Dreyfus, Searle, and other critics of cognitive science are correct, human beings will remain exceptions to the mechanized world picture.

THE NEW CONNECTIONISM

A New Game in Town

For all the doubts and difficulties of the symbol-manipulation paradigm in cognitive science, it remained for two decades "the only game in town," as philosopher Jerry Fodor liked to put it. If thinking wasn't the manipulation of formal symbols following formal rules, what else could it be? Since there was no answer to this question (except from ghettoized Skinnerians and a few other marginal dissidents such as Wittgensteinians), cognitive psychologists remained, perforce, in the information-processing camp. However, in the early 1980s, a rival game set up shop under the name "connectionism," recalling to us (but not to connectionists) the older connectionism of E. L. Thorndike.

A measure of the impact and importance of connectionism was the reception accorded the publication in 1986 of a two-volume exposition of its views and achievements, *Parallel Distributed Processing: Explorations in the Microstructure of Cognition.* The senior author and leader of the PDP (for parallel distributed processing, another name for connectionism) Research Group was David E. Rumelhart, formerly one of the leaders of symbolic paradigm AI. These volumes sold six thousand copies the day they went on the market (Dreyfus & Dreyfus, 1988). Six thousand copies may not sound like much, but in the academic world, where five hundred copies is a respectable sale for a technical book, it's enormous. Shortly afterward, Rumelhart won a MacArthur foundation "genius grant." Soon connectionism was being hailed as the "new wave" in cognitive psychology (Fodor & Pylyshyn, 1988).

In important respects, connectionism represents the resuscitation of traditions in both psychology and AI that seemed long dead. In psychology, there is a connectionist tradition running from Thorndike to Hull and neo-Hullian mediational theorists

(Leahey, 1990). All of them banished symbols and mentalistic concepts from their theories and attempted to explain behavior in terms of the strengthening or weakening of connections between stimuli and responses: This is the central idea of Thorndike's Law of Effect and his and Hull's habit family hierarchies. Mediational psychologists introduced internal processing to Hull's connectionistic ideas by inserting covert connections—the little r-s connections—between external stimulus and overt response.

In AI, connectionism revives a minority tradition in computer science that competed with the symbol manipulation paradigm in the 1950s and 1960s. The symbol manipulation computer architecture is designed around a single processing unit performing one computation at a time. Traditional computers gain their power from the ability of CPUs to perform sequential computations at enormous speeds. From the beginnings of computer science, however, there has always existed the possibility of a rival architecture built around multiple processors all hooked up together. With multiple processors working at once, sequential processing of information is replaced by *parallel processing*. Sequential architecture machines must be programmed to behave, and this is also true for many parallel processing machines. However, some designers of parallel processing computers hoped to build machines that could learn to act intelligently on their own by adjusting the strengths of the connections between their multiple processors according to feedback from the environment. The most important example of such a machine was Frank Rosenblatt's Perceptron machine of the 1960s.

Obviously, parallel-processing computers are potentially much more powerful than single CPU machines, but for a long time obstacles stood in the way of constructing them. Parallel machines are more physically complex than sequential machines, and they are vastly more difficult to program, since one must somehow coordinate the work of the multiple processors in order to avoid chaos. With regard to self-programming machines, there is the special difficulty of figuring out how to get feedback information about the results of behavior to interior ("hidden") units lying between input and output units. Since sequential machines were great successes very early on, and the power of the parallel architecture seemed unnecessary, work on parallel-processing computers virtually ceased in the 1960s. The funeral of early connectionist AI seemed to come in 1969 when Marvin Minsky and Seymour Papert, leaders of the symbolic AI school, published *Perceptrons,* a devastating critique of Rosenblatt's work, seeming to prove mathematically that parallel machines could not learn even the simplest things.

In the 1980s, however, developments in both computer science and psychology converged to revive the fortunes of parallel-processing architectures. Although serial processors continued to gain speed, designers were pushing up against the limits of how fast electrons could move through silicon. At the same time, computer scientists were tackling jobs demanding ever greater computing speed, making a change to parallel processing desirable. For example, consider the problem of computer vision, which must be solved if robots like R_2D_2 are to be built. Imagine a computer graphic made up of 256×256 pixels (dots of light on a monitor). For a serial computer to recognize such an image, it would have to compute one at a time the value of $256 \times 256 = 65,536$ pixels, which might take hours. On the other hand, The Connection Machine, a parallel-processing computer containing 256×256 interconnected processors, can assign one to compute the value of a single pixel and so can process the graphic in a tiny fraction of a second (Hillis, 1987). Along with developments in hardware such as The Connection Machine came developments in programming making it possible to coordinate the activity of independent processors, and in the case of self-modifying networks, to adjust the behavior of hidden units (Tank & Hopfield, 1987).

In psychology, continued failings of the symbolic paradigm made parallel, connectionist processing an attractive alternative to the old game. In addition to the difficulties with functionalism we have already discussed, two issues were especially important for the new connectionists. First of all, traditional AI, while it had made advances on tasks humans find intellectually taxing, such as chess playing, was persistently unable to get machines to perform the sorts of tasks that people do without the least thought, such as recognizing patterns. Perhaps most importantly to psychologists, the behavior that they had most intensively studied for decades—learning—remained beyond the reach of programmed computers, and the development of parallel machines that could actually learn was quite exciting.

The other shortcoming of symbolic AI that motivated the new connectionists was the plain fact that the brain is not a sequential computing device. If we regard neurons as small processors, then it becomes obvious that the brain is much more like The Connection Machine than like a PC or an Apple. The brain contains thousands of massively interconnected neurons, all of which are working at the same time. As Rumelhart and the PDP group announced in their book, they aimed to replace the computer model in psychology with the brain model. The interconnected processors of connectionist models function like neurons: Each one is activated by input and then "fires," or produces output, depending on the summed strengths of its input. Assembled properly, such a network will learn to respond in stable ways to different inputs just as organisms do: Neural nets, as such processor assemblages are often called, learn.

The Subsymbolic Paradigm

At present, connectionist theory is too new and too diverse to be described in detail or evaluated fairly. But we can address what some observers regard as the deepest issue raised by connectionism: the role of rules in explaining human behavior (Dreyfus & Dreyfus, 1988; Smolensky, 1988).

Since the time of Newton, central to scientific explanation has been the positing of laws—rules—followed by objects in nature. But the notion of rules following behavior is ambiguous: Is behavior actually the result of being governed by rules, or the result of nonrulelike causal processes that can be described as rules? Consider, for example, the orbit of the moon around the earth. Its orbiting behavior can be described as consistent with the rules of Newtonian physics, but clearly the moon is not itself following those rules: It's simply affected by gravity and centrifugal force.

Now consider a simple human example. If I show you a drawing of an unfamiliar animal and tell you it's a "wug," and then show you a picture of two of them, I know you'll say without instruction that there are now two "wugs." Your behavior is consistent with the grammatical rule that in English plurals are formed by adding /s/. But did you follow the rule consciously? If not, did you follow it unconsciously? In this case, you might be tempted to say that you learned the rule consciously as a child, and now apply it unconsciously as an adult. To throw doubt on this hypothesis, consider that you pronounced "wugs" as "wugz," while if I had told you the animal was a "wuk," you would have said two of them were "wuks," pronouncing the final /s/ hissingly. In this case, your behavior would be consistent with the phonological English rule to say final /s/ unvoiced following unvoiced consonants and voiced (that is, as /z/) following voiced consonants. But it is unlikely that you were ever taught this rule or used it consciously even in childhood.

A traditional computer is unlike the moon: Not only can its behavior be described as if it's following rules, we know that inside it's actually using rules, the ones we programmed into it. The assumption of traditional cognitive science has been that people are like serial processing computers: We learn and then apply rules, at first consciously and then unconsciously. Connectionist neural networks, however, do not apply rules to representations; they just modify excitation strengths between their units in accord with feedback about their behavior from the environment. So we now face the question, "Are human beings more like traditional computers or like neural nets?" If the former proposition is false, then traditional cognitive science must collapse.

More is at stake, however, than the fate of traditional information-processing psychology. For if we are not rule-followers like traditional computers, then the ancient and dominant tradition in philosophy going back to Plato and extending to the present is false (Dreyfus & Dreyfus, 1988). Traditionally, philosophy has assumed that having knowledge is knowing rules, and that rational action consists in the following of rules. Human intuition—the key to the frame problem—has been deprecated as at best following rules unconsciously, and at worst as irrational impulses. So psychology has been constituted as the search for the rule-governed springs of human behavior, and we are advised that morally right behavior is that which follows moral rules. But connectionism could vindicate human intuition as the secret of human success and rehabilitate a dissident tradition in philosophy—represented, for example, by Friedrich Nietszche—that scorns being bound by rules as an inferior way of life. As is so often the case, what appears to be merely a technical dispute among scientists touches the deepest questions about human nature and human life.

At present, though, whatever issues hinge on the acceptance or rejection of traditional AI or connectionism, it is too early to tell which will triumph. Nevertheless, there is a new game in psychology's town, and we are in for a time of excitement and ferment unseen since the 1960s.

NOTE: The Bibliography for this chapter is incorporated in Chapter 15.

REFERENCES

Adler, T. (1990, April). Different sources cited in major cognitive texts. *APA Monitor, 8.*

Anderson, J. R. (1978). Arguments concerning representations for mental imagery. *Psychological Review, 85,* 249–277.

Anderson, J. R. (1981). Concepts, propositions, and schemata: What are the cognitive units? In J. H. Flowers (Ed.), *Nebraska symposium on motivation 1980* (Vol. 28): Cognitive processes. Lincoln: University of Nebraska Press.

Bandura, A. (1974). Behavior theory and the models of man. *American Psychologist, 29,* 859–869.

Boden, M. (1977). *Artificial intelligence and natural man.* New York: Basic Books.

Boden, M. (1979). The computational metaphor in psychology. In N. Bolton (Ed.), *Philosophical problems in psychology.* London: Methuen.

Brewer, W. F. & Nakamura, G. V. (1984). The nature and functions of schemas. In R. S. Wyer & T. K. Srull (Eds.), *Handbook of social cognition.* Hillsdale, NJ: Erlbaum.

Brush, S. G. (1974). Should the history of science be rated 'X'? *Science, 183,* 1164–1172.

Dennett, D. (1978). *Brainstorms.* Cambridge, MA: MIT/Bradford.

Dennett, D. (1983). Artificial intelligence and the strategies of psychological investigation. In J. Miller, *States of mind.* New York: Pantheon.

Dennett, D. (1984). Cognitive wheels: The frame problem of AI. In C. Hookway (Ed.), *Minds, machines, and programs.* New York: Cambridge University Press.

Dreyfus, H. (1972). *What computers can't do: A critique of artificial reason.* New York: Harper & Row.

Dreyfus, H. L. & Dreyfus, S. E. (1988). Making a mind vs. modeling the brain: Artificial intelligence back at a branchpoint. In S. R. Graubard (Ed.), *The artificial intelligence debate: False starts, real foundations.* Cambridge, MA: MIT Press.

Ericsson, K. A. & Simon, H. (1980). Verbal reports as data. *Psychological Review, 87,* 215–251.

Estes, W. K. & Newell, A. (Co-chairs). (1983). Report of the Research Briefing Panel on Cognitive Science and Artificial Intelligence. In *Research Briefings 1983.* Washington, DC: National Academy Press.

Eysenck, H. J. (1952). The effects of psychotherapy: An evaluation. *Journal of Consulting Psychology, 16,* 319–324.

Farnham-Diggory, S. (Ed.), (1972). *Information processing in children.* New York: Academic Press.

Flowers, J. H. (Ed.), (1981). *Nebraska symposium on motivation 1980* (Vol. 28): Cognitive processes. Lincoln: University of Nebraska Press.

Fodor, J. A. & Pylyshyn, Z. W. (1988). Connectionism and cognitive architecture: A critical analysis. In S. Pinker & J. Mehler (Eds.), *Connections and symbols.* Cambridge, MA: Bradford Books/MIT Press.

Goleman, D. (1983, May). A conversation with Ulric Neisser. *Psychology Today, 17,* 54–62.

Gunderson, K. (1984). Leibnizian privacy and Skinnerian privacy. *The Behavioral and Brain Sciences, 7,* 628–629.

Hayes-Roth, F. (1979). Distinguishing theories of representation. *Psychological Review, 86,* 376–382.

Hillis, W. D. (1987, June). The Connection Machine. *Scientific American, 256,* 108–115.

Hookway, C. (Ed.), (1984). *Minds, machines, and programs.* New York: Cambridge University Press.

Hulse, S., Fowler, H., & Honig, W. (Eds.), (1978). *Cognitive processes in animal behavior.* Hillsdale, NJ: Erlbaum.

Jenkins, J. J. (1981). Can we find a fruitful cognitive psychology? In J. H. Flowers (Ed.), *Nebraska symposium on motivation 1980* (Vol. 28): Cognitive processes. Lincoln: University of Nebraska Press.

Kasschau, R. A. & Kessel, F. S. (Eds.), (1980). *Psychology and society: In search of symbiosis.* New York: Holt, Rinehart & Winston.

Klatzky, R. (1984). *Memory and awareness: An information-processing perspective.* San Francisco: W. H. Freeman.

Lachman, R., Lachman, J., & Butterfield, E. (1979). *Cognitive psychology and information processing.* Hillsdale, NJ: Erlbaum.

Leahey, T. H. (1981). *The revolution never happened: Information processing is behaviorism.* Paper presented at the 52nd annual meeting of the Eastern Psychological Association, New York, New York, April 23.

Leahey, T. H. (1990). *Three traditions in behaviorism.* Paper presented at the Annual Meeting of the American Psychological Association, Boston, August.

Leahey, T. H. (1992). The mythical revolutions of American psychology. *American Psychologist, 47,* 308–318.

Leahey, T. H. & Harris, R. J. (1992). *Human learning,* 3rd ed. Englewood Cliffs, NJ: Prentice-Hall.

Mahoney, M. J. (1977). Reflections on the cognitive-learning trend in psychotherapy. *American Psychologist, 32,* 5–13.

Mehler, J. & Franck, S. (1981). Editorial. *Cognition, 10,* 1–5.

Meichenbaum, D. (1977). *Cognitive behavior modification: An integrative approach.* New York: Plenum.

Miller, G. A. (1969). Psychology as a means of promoting human welfare. *American Psychologist, 24,* 1063–1075.

Miller, G. A. (1972). *Psychology: The science of mental life.* New York: Harper & Row.

Miller, G. A. (1983). The background to modern cognitive psychology. In J. Miller, *States of mind.* New York: Pantheon.

Miller, J. (1983). *States of mind.* New York: Pantheon.

Minsky, M. & Papert, S. (1969). *Perceptrons: An introduction to computational geometry.* Cambridge, MA: MIT Press.

Mischel, W. & Mischel, H. (1976). A cognitive social learning approach to morality and self-regulation. In T. Lickona (Ed.), *Moral development and behavior.* New York: Holt, Rinehart & Winston.

Neisser, U. (1976). *Cognition and reality.* San Francisco: W. H. Freeman.

Neisser, U. (1982). Preface; Memory: What are the important questions? In U. Neisser (Ed.), *Memory observed: Remembering in natural contexts.* San Francisco: W. H. Freeman.

Neisser, U. (1984). Toward an ecologically oriented cognitive science. In T. M. Schlecter & M. P. Toglia (Eds.), *New directions in cognitive science.* Norwood, NJ: Ablex.

Newell, A. (1973). You can't play 20 questions with nature and win. In W. G. Chase (Ed.), *Visual information processing.* New York: Academic Press.

Nisbett, R. E. & Wilson, T. D. (1977). Telling more than we can know: Verbal reports on mental processes. *Psychological Review, 84,* 231–259.

Pylyshyn, Z. W. (1979). Validating computational models: A critique of Anderson's indeterminacy claim. *Psychological Review 86:* 383–405.

Pylyshyn, Z. W. (1984). *Computation and cognition: Toward a foundation for cognitive science.* Cambridge, MA: MIT/Bradford.

Rosch, E. (1977). Human categorization. In N. Warren (Ed.), *Studies in cross-cultural psychology.* London: Academic Press.

Rose, F. (1985). The black knight of AI. *Science, 85,* 46–51.

Rubinstein, R. A. (1984). *Science as a cognitive process.* Philadelphia: University of Pennsylvania Press.

Rumelhart, D. E., McClelland, J. L., & the PDP Research Group (1986). *Parallel distributed processing: Explorations in the microstructure of cognition,* 2 vols. Cambridge, MA: Cambridge University Press.

Searle, J. (1980). Minds, brains, and programs. *The Behavioral and Brain Sciences, 3,* 417–424.

Simon, H. (1980). The social and behavioral sciences. *Science, 209,* 72–78.

Smolensky, P. (1988). On the proper treatment of connectionism. *The Behavioral and Brain Sciences, 3,* 417–424.

Stich, S. P. (1983). *From folk psychology to cognitive science: The case against belief.* Cambridge, MA: MIT/Bradford.

Tank, D. W. & Hopfield, J. J. (1987, December). Collective computation in neuron like circuits. *Scientific American, 257,* 104–115.

Tulving, E. (1979). Memory research: What kind of progress? In L. G. Nilsson (Ed.), *Perspectives on memory research.* Hillsdale, NJ: Erlbaum.

Waldrop, M. M. (1984). The necessity of knowledge. *Science, 223,* 1279–1282.

Wegman, C. (1984). *Psychoanalysis and cognitive psychology.* New York: Academic Press.

White, M. G. (1985). On the status of cognitive psychology. *American Psychologist, 40,* 116–119.

CHAPTER 15 _____

Psychology Divided, Psychology Ascendant
An Uncertain Field
in a Psychological Land

THE STRANGE DEATH OF RADICAL BEHAVIORISM

While it is true that radical behaviorism has been somewhat ghettoized, it would be false to assert, as many have, that it is dead. For the radical behaviorists' ghetto is lively indeed. They have their own successful journals, as noted earlier; their own division within the APA (Division 25); and their own society, the Association for Behavior Analysis, which runs a fourth journal, *The Behavior Analyst*. Radical behaviorists continue to pursue their own research, to develop the conceptual foundations of their discipline, to grapple with cognitive science, and to offer proposals for remaking society.

Beyond Freedom and Dignity

In *Walden II* and *Science and Human Behavior,* Skinner first described his ideal society and its rationale. Against the backdrop of the 1960s, Skinner returned to the problems of society, and again offered radical behaviorism and its technology of behavior as cures for the ills of the modern world. During the 1970s and 1980s, Skinner became preoccupied with spreading his social message, in talk after talk (for example, Skinner, 1985b) and at greatest length in his book *Beyond Freedom and Dignity* (1972). Skinner argued that it is a great mistake to assume, as everyone does, that people possess free will, and hence moral responsibility and dignity; most psychologists assume, as Skinner did, that humans are not free—after all, cognitive scientists think humans are machines—but few of them talk about (at least in public, as Skinner did) the ethical consequences of determinism. Nor was Skinner depressed by determinism, because he found in the technology of behavior ways to improve human life and attacked those who stand in the way of its use.

The consequences of a rigorous determinism for understanding human nature are profound. In general, our own experience and the teachings of our culture tell us there is free will, although from time to time philosophers such as Spinoza have argued otherwise. It appears that one chooses to lift one's arm, that one chooses a profession, that one chooses for whom to vote. To accept a rigorous determinism and apply it to one's own behavior is extremely difficult, requiring the overthrow of a lifetime's habits of thought. Yet such a revolution is required when radical behaviorists ask that we give up the traditional notions of freedom and dignity.

As early as his first paper, Skinner (1931) wrote of the "*preconceptions of freedom*" that hinder the scientific understanding of behavior. Skinner assumed that all behavior is determined, and that consequently a notion such as freedom is nonsense. In his view, a desire for freedom is always a response to punishment. Skinner drew an important distinction between positive reinforcement and punishment. Positive reinforcement effectively controls behavior without undesirable consequences, since it lets you do essentially what you want. Punishment, on the other hand, is generally ineffective and produces unfortunate side effects, since organisms react emotionally to punishment. Organisms seek to avoid—that is, to be free from—punishment but do not avoid positive reinforcement, which is by definition desirable. Historically, governments have tried to control behavior through punishment. One is told what *not* to do, not what to do. As an emotional reaction to punishment, a "literature of freedom" has grown up demanding freedom from punishment, but it has also fostered a belief in freedom as a characteristic of life, a false belief according to the scientific assumption of determinism. Now that the early aims of the literature of freedom have been attained in constitutions and so forth, the illusory notion of freedom stands in the way of further progress, for it resists the control of behavior by positive reinforcement as well as by punishment.

Skinner argued that if humanistic goals, the goals of human happiness, are to be reached, it will be done only by controlling behavior through positive reinforcement, for scientific control is more efficient than the haphazard control exerted by the current social environment. It is important to remember again that Skinner assumed all behavior is always completely determined, that there is never freedom of choice. Therefore Skinnerians propose that we substitute deliberate, systematic control for inefficient control. If the goal is happiness, it will be reached faster if we apply methodical control, and this cannot be done without first abandoning belief in freedom, which prohibits such control.

The concept of dignity, Skinner argued, depends on belief in free will. We believe that one deserves praise for freely chosen good acts and deserves blame for freely chosen wrong acts. However, Skinner, accepting the logic of determinism, argued that both praise and blame are equally irrational, since all behavior is determined for Skinner by the contingencies of reinforcement, not by an individual's free will. We do not blame the rain for getting us wet or praise the sun for warming our skin (although ancient religions did); we accept each as a natural occurrence beyond the will of any person. Skinner asked us to view human behavior as we have other natural phenomena, not religiously, but scientifically, recalling Watson's linkage of religion and mentalism. The poet is not to be praised for "having a poem," for the poet is merely the site at which external variables operate. A criminal is not to be blamed for "having a crime," for the criminal, too, is a locus of variables that converge on an act society condemns. Desirable behaviors should be strengthened by positive reinforcement, while undesirable behaviors will not be learned, at least in a properly engineered society such as Walden II. Both freedom and dignity are outmoded concepts, Skinner concluded, inconsistent with scientific determinism, and therefore stand in the way of an effective control of human behavior.

To what end are we to be controlled? Skinner's answer is Darwinian. A culture is an experiment in survival, just as a species is an experiment in survival. The ultimate biological value is survival, for the "good" species is the one that survives. Similarly, the "good" society will be the one that survives. Skinner argues that the chances our society will survive will be greatly enhanced should it adopt the methods of the experimental analysis of behavior in pursuit of life, liberty, and the pursuit of happiness. Scientific control is our surest guarantee against both unhappiness and extinction. The technology of behavior must be used, Skinner argues, if humanity is to survive. The old mentalistic scheme of freedom and dignity is outmoded and must be replaced by his science of behavior. Skinner (1972) wrote: "The ease with which mentalistic explanations can be invented on the spot is perhaps the best gauge of how little attention we should pay to them.... It is science or nothing."

Skinner's thought stands clearly in the tradition of those who would improve humans by improving their environment. He feels an affinity for Jean-Jacques Rousseau, who, although he believed humans are free, located their faults in the environment: "Man is born free but he is everywhere in chains." In *Emile*, Rousseau proposes that a teacher's student will be happiest if the student feels free but is kept under the teacher's subtle control. Skinner's *Walden II* is a Rousseauian utopia. Control is benign and hidden, so feelings of freedom and dignity remain, even though they have no referents beyond those feelings.

Skinner was, finally, a humanist, although not a humanistic psychologist. For Skinner, the human being, at least as scientifically understood, is the measure of all things. Reason and logic are arbitrary verbal behaviors whose truth lies only in the contingencies of reinforcement, not in a realm of Ideas. Freedom and dignity are verbal operants, not linguistic expressions of enduring values. The crisis Skinner set for the modern person is the crisis set for ancient Greeks by the Sophists, and by the Marquis de Sade for eighteenth-century Europeans. Is there anything of value in human affairs beyond feelings, if freedom and dignity mean nothing else? To what can we cling if all tradition is thrown into doubt, if the old center cannot hold? Skinner answers: "the experimental analysis of behavior." He says, "I am all for *feelings* of causal adequacy as I am for feelings of freedom and dignity. I want people to be adequate, unhampered, successful, and aware of the fact that they are so, and I have suggested ways in which that may be brought about—by changing their environment" (Skinner, 1984a, p. 507).

Critique of Cognitive Science

Skinner, of course, was critical of theories referring to unobserved internal states that cause behavior. Although he always scorned cognitive science as a "magical term" (1984a) whose popularity "is largely due to the freedom to use a lay vocabulary, not the discovery of an alternative science of comparable rigor to the experimental analysis of behavior" (1984b), until 1985 he had not responded to it in detail (see, for example, Skinner 1974), but he later accused it of many shortcomings (Skinner, 1985a).

Skinner accused cognitive science of reviving and resting upon two (to him) obnoxious doctrines: the copy theory of perception—cognitive science's central concept of mental representations; and the commonsense idea that mental states cause behavior—the concept of the inner person. Against representations Skinner reasserted his familiar perceptual realism: "What is seen is [a] presentation, not a representation" of an object. Skinner went on to reject the idea that representations are "stored" in a "memory" from which they are "retrieved." Skinner (1985a) said these notions depend on a misleading analogy to physical records:

> When physical records are stored, the records continue to exist until they are retrieved, but is that true when people "process information"? A storage battery would be a better model of a behaving organism. We put electricity into a battery and take it out when needed, *but there is no electricity in the battery*. When we "put electricity in," we change the battery, and it is a changed battery that "puts out electricity" when tapped. Organisms do not acquire behavior as a kind of possession; they simply come to behave in various ways. The behavior is not in them at any time. (pp. 294–95)

Skinner here in his own way stated a criticism of information-processing theory that we have met before: Exactly where does information processing take place? We observe and respond to the environment, we have sensations and thoughts in consciousness, and neuroscientists will one day be able to observe the brain processes behind thought and behavior; but the information-processing psychologists have invented a nonphysical—to Skinner, a fictitious—level of discourse between consciousness and the brain. If there are no representations, and no storage and retrieval of representations, then there is no information processing and no inner person making decisions on the basis of stored representations. Skinner (1984b) simply denied the validity of the human-computer analogy: "Information processing was devised for, and is useful for formulating, systems which are not analogous to the human organism."

Skinner accused cognitive science of being bad science, and at the same time showed that he was less scientific than they. He said, "We need a language of feelings and states of mind in our daily lives. It is the language of literature and most of philosophy. Clinical psychologists use it to learn many things about the histories of their clients that they could not discover any other way." But Skinner insisted such mental talk has no place in a *science* of behavior. Skinner (1985a) concluded with strong language:

> *I accuse* cognitive scientists of misusing the metaphor of storage....
>
> *I accuse* cognitive scientists of speculating about internal processes [of which] ... they have no appropriate means of observation....
>
> *I accuse* cognitive scientists of emasculating the experimental analysis of behavior....
>
> *I accuse* cognitive scientists of reviving a theory in which feelings and states of mind ... are taken as the causes of behavior....
>
> *I accuse* cognitive scientists, as I would psychoanalysts, ... of inventing explanatory systems which are admired for a profundity which is more properly called inaccessibility.
>
> *I accuse* cognitive scientists of relaxing standards of definition and logical thinking and releasing a flood of speculation ... inimical to science. (p. 300)

Finally, Skinner cried out against radical behaviorism's confinement to a ghetto: "Let us bring behaviorism back from the Devil's Island to which it was transported for a crime it never committed, and let psychology become once again a behavioral science" (p. 300).

Skinner's plea may be answered, for there appear to be grounds for reconciliation between one form of cognitive science, Neisser's (1984) "ecological psychology," and radical behaviorism. Like the radical behaviorist, the "ecological cognitive psychologist [begins] ... with a careful description of the environment and people's ordinary activities within it." Like the radical behaviorist, the ecological cognitive scientist "tak[es] the environment seriously." Like the radical behaviorist, "ecological psychologists are generally reluctant to construct models or to postulate hypothetical mental events." Like the radical behaviorist, the ecological psychologist believes that "introspection does not reveal [the] structures" in the environment to which people respond. Neisser does not discuss the parallels between his description of ecological psychology and radical behaviorism, but they are there.

CHALLENGES TO SCIENTIFIC PSYCHOLOGY

From Psychology's Occult Doubles

One of psychology's leaders in the first decades of the twentieth century, Joseph Jastrow, was annoyed by being constantly asked about psychic phenomena, and by the implicit confusion between psychology and psychical research. Today psychologists are still embarrassed by their links to "occult" disciplines and marginal sciences. Part of the embarrassment stems from psychology's social success. People today look to psychology for advice on all sorts of personal and social problems, so that some practitioners of occult crafts have come to cast their work in a psychological mold. Astrology, for example, is often defended as a means of reading character and a source of advice in love and business, rather than as a prophetic science, its original claim. The clichéd opening line "What's your sign?" is based on the notion that people born under certain signs have certain personalities and will get along well or ill with those born under certain other signs. There is nothing to the claim, but there is a strong parallel to psychological tests that purport to reveal character and suggest interpersonal strategies. In fact, *Teacher* magazine carried an article in 1978 suggesting that pupils be grouped by astrological sign, a purpose for which psychological tests had long been used. In supermarket tabloids, "spiritual healers" and "advisers" tout themselves as counselors on "love, health, alcohol, business"—subjects shared with professional psychologists and psychiatrists.

Experimental psychologists, too, have their occult doubles in the field of psychical research, whose newer name, parapsychology, helps tie the fields together in the public mind. Like experimental psychologists, parapsychologists have their own journals and associations. Their work sometimes appears on the program of APA meetings under the auspices of the Division of Humanistic Psychology, and parapsychologists are active in the new transpersonal psychology movement, which bills itself as a "fourth force" in psychology, going beyond humanism to a more cosmic, transcendental psychology.

Mainstream psychologists have a problem differentiating themselves from what they regard as pseudosciences without seeming dogmatically intolerant. Scientifically minded psychologists, which includes not only experimentalists but the vast majority of professional psychologists, try to separate themselves from pseudoscience on formal methodological grounds. In fact, the APA has refused to create a Division of Transpersonal Psychology, despite petitions to APA Council to do so. However, as we saw in Chapter 1, formal "demarcation criteria" do not work very well. The rejection of parapsychology and, *a fortiori,* spiritualism and astrology rests on their violation of the substantive content of science, not on their violation of its methods. For parapsychologists do follow the methodological canons of science. They conduct carefully controlled research, they use statistics, they are on the watch for fraud, they replicate their studies more than mainstream psychologists do, and they are outraged when such hard work fails to gain them recognition as scientists.

Occult science has failed to gain scientific recognition because it does not fit in with the content of science. To begin with, psychologists have a hard enough time explaining how people understand natural language, so they get annoyed when parapsychologists badger them about telepathy and clairvoyance. To borrow Kuhnian language, a scientific community recognizes as scientists those who might be able to contribute to solving current puzzles, and it dismisses researchers concerned with bizarre anomalies as cranks. It might turn out in the future that the cranks were on to something, but scientific research is an orderly process focused on current problems, not speculative possibilities. An instructive parallel occurred in the flurry of interest a few years ago in the claim by a science journalist that a human being had been cloned. Biologists dismissed the assertion as wild and ludicrous— not because a human could not in principle be cloned, but rather because it was absurd to attempt it now, and they regarded anyone trying for a human clone as a crank. Scientists accept only their own breed of science as scientific. Method will not save your reputation if your topic of research does not come within the boundaries currently accepted by science.

The real problem with parapsychology is that it violates the oldest and deepest of science's substantive commitments, the commitment to naturalism: to explain happenings in the universe in natural terms. The founders of psychical research and parapsychology were frank in challenging naturalism by hoping to turn the scientific method against scientific content. They hoped to prove with statistics and experiment that spiritual powers and spiritual life existed, that life continued after death. But science in the twentieth century is firmly committed to naturalism and materialism. Naturalism is science's central dogma, without which it could not function, and anyone who challenges this dogma has little hope of gaining a hearing from science.

Some parapsychologists have attempted to steer around these objections by dropping the quasi-religious claims that animated the psychical researchers and by adopting up-to-date scientific vocabulary. Thus some parapsychologists try to explain psychical wonders in the Alice-in-Wonderland terms of modern quantum physics, while others cast their research and theories in information-processing terms. Their attempt to finally naturalize the supernatural seems to have little chance of success, but it is instructive to ask what would happen if they did succeed. Parapsychology might gain the ear of science, but it would very likely lose the ear of the public. Science has been accepted by many as a substitute religion—but most still want religion, even under the parapsychological guise of science. In a world where religion falls back on "creationist science" to defend faith, which is by definition unscientific, all the borderlines are fuzzy indeed.

Ordinary people do not go to spiritualistic séances, write to psychic advisers, and read astrology books to learn about information-processing mechanisms and ESP (Tart, 1978). They want some sense of how to live their lives. For many more moderns than Frederic Myers, the Old World sustenance of traditional religion fails to sustain faith in the age of science: of nuclear war, the space shuttle, and the ironies of doctors heroically struggling to perform *in utero* surgery on one fetus only to abort another of the same age. Science has accomplished so much, it seems natural to turn to it for answers to ancient moral and religious questions. But it cannot give them. Science gives us the techniques to diagnose fetal abnormalities, and even ways to operate on some of them before the baby is born; it gives us ways to abort fetuses early and late. But it is helpless to tell us which choice to make, to tell us when the fetus becomes a human being, to decide between right and wrong.

Psychology, more than any science, occupies treacherous ground between *is* and *ought*. Physical science reveals the workings of impersonal nature; and while it can harm and benefit humankind, it is unreasonable to ask that its laws tell us how to use them. Yet psychology is the science of human behavior. It purports to reveal the springs of human action, and consequently it seems on the surface not unreasonable to ask it how to act, how to make sense of our lives. Certainly, psychology writers from Aristotle to Bentham to Skinner have moved from science to morality, pretending to describe the perfect, scientifically engineered community and to prescribe the laws of the land as dictated by human nature. But this urge to ask a science for moral guidance is not legitimate. Operant psychology may help me control my child's behavior, but it cannot tell me how she should behave. Cognitive psychology may help me construct lessons that my students remember, but it cannot tell me what my students should learn. Science deals with facts, not morals.

Occult psychology—parapsychology, spiritualism, astrology—is the clearest manifestation of the confusion of science and values that pervades all of psychology. Each occult system takes on the trappings of science in order to borrow its authority and uses that authority to promote various moral and religious values. Practitioners of occult psychology have not been loath to satisfy humankind's spiritual needs. Practitioners of mainstream psychology, however much they try to distance themselves from their occult doubles, have also not been loath to prescribe to troubled humans: in clinical and counseling practices, in industrial psychology, in advertising psychology. We see, then, that psychology, whether mainstream or occult, has been used to meet human needs that science cannot meet. People need to know how they ought to act—they need ethics and morality. People need to find meaning in their lives—they need a form of life, a structure within which to live. Science can meet neither need, and the deepest fraud of psychology's occult doubles is pretending that science can do so. Mainstream psychology itself sits awkwardly astride science and morality. Psychology calls itself a science, yet, with its occult neighbors, it is tempted to become a new religion (Albee, 1977a). Psychological science, like any science, may encompass means, but it can never encompass ends.

From Biology

Depression is the most common psychological disorder of our time (Klerman, 1979). It has long been treated by psychotherapy, but it now seems likely that long-term, nonsituational depression, called *endogenous* depression, is caused by deficiencies of certain neurotransmitters in the brain (Snyder, 1980), not by early childhood experiences or any other psychological cause. People who suffer from endogenous depression can be effectively treated with antidepressant drugs: After a few weeks, they stop feeling depressed. Therefore it may be that "much of the by now entrenched psychodynamic theory is irrelevant or misleading," that treating biological depression psychologically is "tragic … since a large fraction of the 30,000 suicides a year in the United States are probably committed by people with [endogenous] depressions" (Wender & Klein, 1981). Faced with this challenge to their practice, clinical psychologists respond by asserting that psychotherapy may nevertheless be useful in helping depressives (and others with biochemical disorders), even if they are also treated with drugs (Peele, 1981). Nevertheless, a challenge remains: A psychological state, depression, has been shown to have a biological cause. A piece of psychology has been reduced to biology. Perhaps psychology will be "cannibalized" by biology, as biologist E. O. Wilson (1975) has predicted.

REDUCTIONISM

The idea that one science can reduce another derives from the positivist notion, now called the "unity of science" (Putnam, 1982), that all the sciences can be arranged in a hierarchy from highest to lowest, with each science reducible to a more basic science, until we arrive at physics, the most basic science. According to this theory, psychology is more basic than sociology and can reduce its social concepts to psychological concepts of individual behavior. Psychology's concepts and laws of individual behavior can in turn be reduced to the concepts and laws of neurophysiology, which describes the functioning of individuals' bodies. It has become generally agreed that such reduction is implausible. Functionalists, for example, argue that mental states are defined by what they do—their function—rather than by the material that performs the function. Thus two people might be engaging in the psychological function of "thinking of Paris," but it is highly unlikely that exactly the same cells in their brains are firing.

The clearest refutation of unity-of-science reductionism comes from Donald Davidson's (1980) "anomalous monism." Davidson rejects Cartesian or religious dualism, but he defends a form of materialism in which the psychological concepts of folk psychology cannot be reduced to the laws of neurophysiology, even though every mental event is identical with some brain event. If we accept materialism, then we accept that every mental event is also a brain event. However, for psychology to be reduced to neurophysiology, it must be the case that psychological concepts, not just psychological events, must correspond to neurophysiological concepts. When we explain a person's speech or actions psychologically, we do so against a background of assumed beliefs and desires. Most importantly, we assume that a person is rational, that his or her beliefs are reasonably coherent and consistent. If a man says things that are blatantly contradictory, if his actions are inconsistent with his beliefs, we conclude that he is irrational, give up trying to explain his behavior psychologically, and may banish him from human society. Davidson concludes: "But in inferring this system [of interconnected beliefs and desires] from the evidence, we necessarily impose conditions of coherence, rationality and consistency. These conditions have no echo in physical theory, which is why we can look for no more than rough correlations between psychological and physical phenomena" (p. 231). In short, there is no danger that neurophysiology can reduce psychology. Psychological theory is autonomous.

SOCIOBIOLOGY

E. O. Wilson, who said that biology would "cannibalize" psychology (and all the social sciences), had in mind as the cannibal the division of biology he named sociobiology. Sociobiology is the study of the biological basis of social behavior, and it represents the application of the neo-Darwinian theory of evolution to behavior. The basic idea of sociobiology is that behavioral traits as well as morphology are shaped by natural selection. Since aggression, group living, cooperation, parenting, and sexual behavior help determine whether an animal succeeds or fails in growing up and having offspring, it seems highly probable that evolution has shaped these social behaviors in different ways in different species in different ecological circumstances. Work on the evolutionary, biological basis of social behavior in animals was well advanced when Wilson summarized it in his text *Sociobiology* in 1975. The book became the center of a ferocious and often bitter controversy when in his last chapter Wilson speculatively extended his biological perspective to human beings, claiming that social science and psychology would disappear into biology.

A few psychologists found Wilson's ideas stimulating (for example, Campbell, 1975), but naturally, most were alarmed (among them Wispé & Thompson, 1976; Wyers et al., 1980). The field most likely to be absorbed into sociobiology was the study of animal behavior, and while many psychologists resist it (Wyers et al., 1980), there are signs that absorption is taking place (Fox, 1983). The field of comparative psychology had been in crisis for some time (Hodos & Campbell, 1969; Lockard, 1971; Wasserman, 1981; Gottlieb, 1984), seeming not to have progressed since the time of Beach's 1950 critique (Lown, 1975; Porter, Johnson, & Granger, 1981), and so could be revitalized and redirected by the fresh approach of sociobiology.

The alarm of human psychologists was based on a misunderstanding of evolutionary biological explanations. Their deep misunderstanding of sociobiology was visually portrayed on the cover of *Time* for August 1, 1977: "Why you do what you do: SOCIOBIOLOGY: A new theory of behavior." The cover showed a young man and woman in a partial embrace; their expressions were blank and their limbs were connected to strings that rose out of the picture into the hands of an unseen puppeteer, presumably their genes. Human psychologists feared that sociobiology might displace psychology as an account of human behavior. So, for example, a sociobiologist might explain that Bill Smith cheated on his wife because mammalian males have a desire for sexual variety. However, contrary to the claims of some sociobiologists themselves, sociobiology does not and cannot explain individual behavior, which is the province of psychology. Sociobiology can explain why the members of a species have certain dispositions, why they find some things easy to learn and others hard to learn. To continue the example, males have a disposition toward sexual variety because males can fertilize many females, and if they do so they will achieve evolutionary success, having many offspring. Females are less disposed to sexual variety because the number of offspring they can have is much smaller, so that they are better off concentrating on one fit male, rather than risking pregnancy by unknown males of questionable fitness. Thus sociobiology may explain why Bill Smith feels a desire for sex with women other than his wife—but no more. A man may feel such desire but refuse to act on it because he believes adultery to be immoral; in a different culture, polygyny may be normal, so Bill could take a new wife without qualms. Thus how an individual behaves is not determined by biology, but by the forces of his or her own individual life, including learning, culture, and moral beliefs. Psychology is the study of the individual, and while it can learn about human dispositions from evolutionary biology, the explanation of human action remains its exclusive preserve. Sociobiology is an insightful colleague, but it is a toothless cannibal (Symons, 1987).

CONCLUSION: ELIMINATION OF SCIENTIFIC PSYCHOLOGY?

Psychology is not about to be devoured by either neurophysiology or sociobiology. However, considerations from each context suggest a different and, to some, more disturbing conclusion. Perhaps psychology cannot be a science at all.

Paul and Patricia Churchland (for example, P. M. Churchland, 1985; P. S. Churchland, 1986) have argued that neurophysiology will replace and eliminate rather than reduce psychology. From their perspective, Davidson's anomalous monism provides no defense against their claims but instead supports them (Rosenberg, 1983, 1984). The Churchlands claim that folk psychology, and along with it all forms of intentional, representational psychology such as functionalism, are scientifically false in the same way that Ptolemaic astronomy was false. The failure of psychological concepts to map onto neurophysiology shows that psychological concepts are false, and so they must be replaced by neurophysiological ones. Anomalous monism admits that every mental event is identical with some brain event, claiming only that psychology organizes its talk about mental events in ways irreducible to physical science. The Churchlands urge us to drop psychology altogether and talk only about brain events and the laws of neurophysiology. Precisely *because* "considerations of rationality, coherence and consistency … have no echo in physical theory," they should be eliminated.

The Churchlands' crusade represents scientism at its imperialistic worst. They (like Stephan Stich) want people to give up talking about hopes, beliefs, desires, and so on, merely because such concepts have no place in science. But their view is like the paint seller's view of art. Obviously, the aesthetic properties of a painting depend upon the physical qualities of its paint, and equally clearly they are logically independent of the paint's physical properties. Eliminative materialism is like saying that because we cannot map the aesthetic properties of paintings onto the physical qualities of the paint, we should give up aesthetics. If humans adopt the eliminative view, they will have to give up a lot: law (there is no physical difference between murder in self-defense and murder for gain); morality (whether a fetus should be aborted does not depend on physical properties); fiction (Shakespeare and Dickens make constant reference to intentions, beliefs, and so on—even "Star Trek" could not be understood neurophysiologically); politics (science cannot tell fascism from freedom); and, of course, everyday loves, hopes, fears, expectations, and interests.

The eliminativist views folk and intentional psychology as scientific theories and then regards them as false. The lesson to learn from this controversy is that folk psychology is no more a science than aesthetic theory is. Intentional psychology is not autonomous science, it is not a science at all, and as such it is quite ineliminable. The Churchlands may be right that scientific psychology will one day be purely neurophysiological. It is clear, however, that no human form of life can be built on physical science alone, precisely because science cannot tell right from wrong; and making that distinction, and making meaningful sense of life, is the essence of being human.

Related considerations from sociobiology reinforce the conclusion that human psychology is not and cannot be a science (Rosenberg, 1980; Hull, 1984; Leahey, 1982, 1984). Science searches for exceptionless general laws that apply to spatiotemporally unrestricted objects. So physics is not about our solar system, but about stars and planets anywhere and everywhere. It is about quarks and leptons, not chairs and books, though these are made of quarks and leptons. Chairs and books are not suited to scientific laws because they are spatiotemporally local, products of a particular culture in a particular time, and science is universal, applying to all times and places. Of course we can talk intelligibly about furniture, but such talk is not science. There is a craft, and even a practice, of furniture design and making, but a craft is not a science.

From the standpoint of evolution, species are not spatiotemporally unrestricted and so cannot fit into scientific laws. Every species is an individual, a product of a particular history, inhabiting a particular ecological niche. The laws of evolutionary biology apply across species: They should apply to any self-replicating organism anywhere, any time. So just as there cannot be scientific laws about just our sun or just our moon, there cannot be laws about particular species. Of course, there will be disciplined studies of the sun and the moon, of gerbils and dolphins, but these studies will produce facts about individual things and species, not general laws. But if there is no science of gerbils or dolphins, because they are individuals rather than general entities, so there is also no science of *Homo sapiens*. Psychology is a disciplined study of one species, but it will produce no spatiotemporally unrestricted laws, and so it cannot be a science.

In 1671, Elizabeth Knapp was declared a witch (Demos, 1982). A psychologist reading about her would conclude that she suffered from catatonic schizophrenia: She was alternately sane and insane, and when insane she would hold fixed poses and experience hallucinations and delusions. It is quite likely that a tendency to schizophrenia is a genetic, inherited disposition. A biologist, then, could explain her disease from the standpoint of evolution and genetics, and from the standpoint of neuroscience, but he or she could not tell the whole story. Even if one inherits a tendency to schizophrenia, certain individual experiences are required to cause the disease to actually manifest itself, and personal learning is the province of the psychologist. Moreover, Elizabeth Knapp's hallucinations and delusions centered on the devil: She seemed to see him, to speak in his voice, and she claimed to have signed a compact to serve him. The content of her hallucinations and delusions was determined by her culture, not by the abnormal state of her brain. A modern schizophrenic would be more likely to hallucinate space aliens and have delusions about the CIA. Neuroscience says that Elizabeth Knapp and a modern schizophrenic suffer from the same brain disease, and so it cannot explain why Elizabeth saw the devil while moderns see Martians. History, social science, and psychology can, and only they can. Physical science can explain, predict, and control the natural world, including the world of our bodies. Humans, however, live not just in the physical world, but "in a world we ourselves create." Our forms of life lie beyond science, but not beyond disciplined inquiry.

From the Humanities

Psychology and the other social sciences are, of course, not the only disciplines concerned with human beings. There are also the humanities. Although the humanities are often honored, the honor generally takes the form of lip service rather than sincere respect. In the modern world, science and technology are revered, and whatever does not fit their mold is deemed eccentric—interesting, perhaps, but decidedly second-rate. Psychologists are not the only people to suffer from physics envy. Hence, since the time of August Comte and John Stuart Mill, psychologists have acted on the assumption that, to quote Mill, "The backward state of the Moral Sciences [today's social sciences] can only be remedied by applying to them the methods of Physical Science, duly extended and generalized." After a hundred years of psychological physics envy, however, it is not at all clear that Mill was right. As Johann Herder said in the seventeenth century, "We live in a world we ourselves create," so the study of the human world—the object of the humanities—should be very different from the study of the physical world. The case of Elizabeth Knapp brings the point home. We may know all there is to know about the genetics and biochemistry of schizophrenia, and be able to cure it with sophisticated drugs, but to sympathize with her, to *understand* her predicament and what it meant to her and her neighbors, requires different tools from the ones science can give us. It requires *hermeneutics*.

Hermeneutics traditionally denotes the field of biblical exegesis: closely examining a text of the Bible and interpreting its meaning. Broadly speaking, it is what is done in the humanities. An English literary critic takes the text of *Macbeth* and tries to set forth and discuss its meaning—for Shakespeare, for Shakespeare's audience, for us, his modern audience. The critic does not care about the causal processes in William Shakespeare that caused him to write *Macbeth;* instead he or she tries to grasp the human meaning of the play. A historian considering the case of Elizabeth Knapp does much the same thing. He or she may find useful the scientific hypothesis that schizophrenia is a brain disease, but the historical interest lies in understanding what Elizabeth Knapp and her contemporaries made of her condition. Doing this requires not science, but understanding and the ability to enter into the world-view of another place and time, making rational sense of it, a sense that can then be set down for the historian's readers.

It is possible to regard psychology from a hermeneutical rather than a scientific standpoint. Take, for example, Freud's theory of dreams. One might regard it as a scientific account of how dreams come about in the night: Repressed ideas, released from the shackles of repression, filter up toward consciousness and are reworked as they go by dreamwork into a disguised form suitable for conscious expression. In this scientific account of dreams, it ought ideally to be possible to follow the moment-by-moment construction of a dream from repressed impulse in the brain stem to conscious experience in the visual and auditory centers of the cerebral hemispheres.

But the title of Freud's book was *Die Traumdeutung, (The Meaning of Dreams)*, or, as usually translated, *The Interpretation of Dreams*. If one disregards the theory of his last chapter, one finds that Freud treated dreams primarily as texts to be interpreted: He practiced hermeneutics (see Chapter 3). Like the critic studying *Macbeth,* Freud took a dream as a text, a meaningful expression of a person's unconscious neurotic problems. Used as a text examined for meaning, it is irrelevant if the dream was produced as the scientific theory describes, and the process of creation can be ignored much as the critic ignores the process by which Shakespeare wrote *Macbeth*. Working together, therapist and client can recover the underlying meaning of the dream and in so doing reveal something important about the client—and, they hope, relieve him or her of neurotic misery.

It is possible to take hermeneutics as a model for psychology and the social sciences. For we may regard not just dreams but all of behavior as texts to be scrutinized for meaning. Their meaning derives from the form of life we share as human beings in a historical culture—the historian and anthropologist deal with alien forms of life—and the job of the psychologist from the hermeneutical point of view is to *make sense* of human life in this time and place rather than to predict, control, and scientifically explain it. The hermeneuticist practices *Geisteswissenschaft*—human science—rather than *Naturwissenschaft*. As the word "science" is used today, hermeneutics is no science because it does not aim at universal, exceptionless causal laws. Because we live in a scientistic age, labeling something "unscientific" seems to consign it to a junk heap of useless and pointless oddities. If we can free ourselves from physics worship and scientism, however, we can see hermeneutics as only different from science, and value it on its own terms. Moreover, hermeneutics concerns itself with human life: with right and wrong, with love and hate, with what it means to be human rather than animal, and this concern is not obviously inferior to science.

PROFESSIONAL CONTROVERSIES

Clinical Psychology

Clinical psychology was invented just after World War II. By 1968, there were twelve thousand clinical psychologists in the world, and their ranks had swelled to over forty thousand by 1983—the overwhelming majority of them located in the United States (Zilbergeld, 1983). Although there was some concern that such rapid growth might be eroding the quality of therapists in training (Strupp, 1976), clinical psychologists could hardly doubt that theirs was a growth field. Nevertheless, clinical psychologists were not completely happy.

To begin with, the question of how best to train clinical psychologists would not go away. The 1950 Boulder model had laid down that clinical psychologists were to be trained as scientific psychologists first and as professional service providers second. However, it was clear that the Boulder model was honored more in the breach than in the observance. By and large, clinical students wanted to help people and learn how to practice therapy and regarded the scientific part of their training as a boring chore. Some clinical psychologists welcomed the seeming death of the Boulder model. George W. Albee (1970), for example, argued that it had been a mistake for clinical psychologists to model themselves on physicians to begin with, when in fact they should be agents of widespread social change. Other clinicians, of course, defended the Boulder model (for example, Shakow, 1976). Faced with change that seemed to be slipping out of organized psychology's control, the APA set up another conference on clinical training.

This one met in Colorado, too, at the resort of Vail in 1973. Despite dissension, it endorsed something that Boulder and other training conferences had rejected, the recognition of a new degree in clinical psychology, the Psy.D., for professionally oriented students. The Psy.D. program would reduce the scientific demands made on students in training and would frankly mint practitioners rather than academicians (Strickler, 1975). Naturally, the proposals proved controversial; some clinicians welcomed the idea (Peterson, 1976), while others (Perry, 1979) denounced the Psy.D. and a related development, the establishment of "freestanding" professional schools, so-called because they were not affiliated with a university. Despite the growth of Psy. D. programs and graduates in the 1980s, delegates to a national conference on clinician training in 1990 held that the scientist practitioner model was "essential" for psychology and "ideal" for practice (Belar & Perry, 1991).

Another problem that would not go away was clinical psychology's status anxiety. On the one hand, mainstream clinical psychologists wanted to assert their superiority over the growing horde of therapy providers who did not hold a Ph.D. or were not trained in psychology, such as clinical social workers, marriage counselors, and psychiatric nurses. The most psychologists could do about them was to keep out of the APA anyone without a Ph.D. On the other hand, clinical psychologists wanted to assert their virtual equality with psychiatrists, who felt disdain for clinical psychologists. Seymour Post (1985) called clinical psychologists and anyone else without an M.D. "barefoot doctors of mental health." "Amazingly," Post went on, "this group of laymen is now clamoring for all the privileges of being a physician, including the right to admit patients to hospitals under their direct management." Worse, "patients come to them with symptoms as they would to a general physician or internist. They are not competent to play such a role. Malpractice is the rule" (p. 21). Throughout the 1980s, organized psychiatry attempted to block the full therapeutic practice of psychologists, maintaining that psychologists are not fully competent to diagnose or treat mental disorders. One psychiatrist, AMA President Paul Fink, seemingly oblivious of the fact that compared to psychiatrists psychologists receive many more hours of therapy and diagnosis training, said that psychologists are "not trained to understand the nuances of the mind" (anonymous, 1988, p. 4).

Naturally, psychologists resent such attitudes. Bryant Welch, head of APA's Practice Directorate, undoubtedly spoke for many clinicians in saying "organized medicine and psychiatry are a veritable menage of monopolistic personality disorders" (anonymous, 1988, p. 1). Whatever the merits of Post's arguments, however, it is certainly true that clinical psychologists were clamoring for something approaching the legal status of psychiatrists. Clinical psychologists had won the right to be licensed by the state, despite some well-placed misgivings about whether licenses really served the public interest as opposed to the private interests of psychologists (Gross, 1978). On the other hand, when a hospital accreditation committee restricted clinical psychologists to hospital practice under an M.D., clinical psychologists were outraged (Dörken & Morrison, 1976). In the 1990s, clinical psychologists fought against psychiatric resistance for the right to prescribe psychoactive medication (Squires, 1990; Wiggins, 1992). The biggest dispute between clinical psychology and psychiatry, however, naturally involved money.

Who should pay for psychotherapy? Although the obvious answer is the client or patient, most medical treatment today is paid for by insurance companies or the government, and questions arise about whether or not psychotherapy should be included in third-party payment plans. A few psychiatrists and clinical psychologists (such as Albee, 1977b) agree with Szasz that there is no such thing as mental illness, and logically conclude that psychotherapy is not really therapy, and so should not be covered under third-party payment schemes. Medical therapy for actual disorders of the nervous system (such as endogenous depression) would be covered. In practice, however, most therapists recognize that if psychotherapy costs had to be borne by clients, their practices would bring in a lot less income. Psychiatrists and clinical psychologists therefore agree that third parties should pay for psychotherapy, but they disagree bitterly about who should be paid.

For many years, much to the resentment of clinical psychologists, insurance companies agreed with psychiatrists that only M.D.'s should be paid for medical procedures, and, with certain special limitations that did not apply to organic diseases, they covered psychotherapy only if performed by a psychiatrist. Clinical psychologists rightly viewed this as a monopoly, and they pressed for "freedom of choice" legislation in the states that would force insurance companies to pay clinical psychologists, too. Of course, psychologists wanted to share the monopoly, not destroy it outright. Already faced with rising costs, insurance companies allied with psychiatry to resist the encroachments of psychology and filed suit (the test case arose in Virginia) alleging improper interference with the practice of medicine and business. Ultimately, freedom of choice laws were upheld in the courts, but the battle was long, and fueled the long-standing hostility between the APA and the "other" APA, the American Psychiatric Association. The battle was refought in a new arena during the late 1970s and early 1980s, when the federal government considered passing national health insurance, died down during the Reagan and Bush administrations, only to revive with Bill and Hillary Clinton's ambitious schemes for national health policy.

Organized psychology also had to deal with another means of controlling health care costs: managed care. The phrase "managed care" encompasses a variety of schemes by which companies and government control patients' access to high-cost specialized care. The APA put forward its own concept of managed care for mental health, called "Paradigm II" (Welch, 1992). Central to Paradigm II is the direct marketing of psychological health care services to the companies who must buy health-care plans for their employees to ensure that psychologists are included. Moreover, psychologists and psychiatrists also must market their skills to individuals (Gelman & Gordon, 1987).

Squabbles over insurance and managed care, and the increased marketing of health care like any other product, raised a nasty question potentially embarrassing to psychiatrist and clinical psychologist alike: Does psychotherapy *work?* Private and public health plans do not pay for quackery, so treatments must be proven safe and effective. The first person actually to investigate the outcomes of psychotherapy was the English psychologist Hans J. Eysenck in 1952. He concluded that getting therapy was no better than just *waiting* for therapy for the same period of time—the "cure" rate for spontaneous remission was as good as for therapy. This implies that psychotherapy is a fraud. Since then, psychotherapists have challenged Eysenck's conclusion, and hundreds of psychotherapy outcome studies have been done. Naturally, mainstream clinical psychologists eagerly argue that psychotherapy, or at least their kind of psychotherapy, is effective, but the evidence is at best extremely mixed. There is a consensus that psychotherapy is probably better than doing nothing for a psychological problem, although the magnitude of improvement is not very great (Smith, Glass, & Miller, 1980; Landman & Dawes, 1982). However, many studies have concluded that professional psychotherapy with a trained therapist may be no more beneficial than amateur therapy or self-help (Prioleau, Murdock, & Brody, 1983; Zilbergeld, 1983). It is also not clear if psychotherapy is safe. Zilbergeld (1983) quotes estimates that most clinicians are not competent, and he describes numerous cases of people made worse by therapy.

In terms of numbers of practitioners and patients, clinical psychology is a success. But it remains riven by doubts about its identity, its status, and its effectiveness. Carl Rogers, who was the founder of clinical psychology if anyone is, said, "Therapists are not in agreement as to their goals or aims…. They are not in agreement as to what constitutes a successful outcome of their work. They cannot agree as to what constitutes a failure. It seems as though the field is completely chaotic and divided" (Zilbergeld, 1983, p. 114).

Divorced Again: The Academics Walk Out

The tensions between academic psychologists and practitioners that created the AAAP in 1938 were only papered over by the creation of the "new" APA in 1945. Indeed, tensions between the two communities got worse as the balance of practitioners to academics shifted decisively in favor of the former in the 1980s: In 1940, about 70 percent of APA members worked in academia, while by 1985, only about 33 percent did. By 1965, scientist-academics were pressing for some restructuring of the APA that would give them a greater voice and interest in an APA they viewed as increasingly devoted to guild interests of practitioners, such as getting insurance payments, the ability to write prescriptions for psychoactive drugs, and hospital privileges for clinical psychologists on a par with psychiatrists. Efforts to reorganize the APA gained momentum in the 1970s as various committees and commissions were set up to recommend changes in APA structure that would satisfy both academics and practitioners. Repeated failure of every proposal alienated academics, leading to their gradual defection from APA and increasing the urgency felt by the reforming academics who remained in APA.

The last attempt to reorganize came in February 1987, when an ambitious restructuring plan was rejected by the governing body of the APA, its Council. Academic reformers formed the Assembly for Scientific and Applied Psychology, whose acronym (ASAP) reflected their sense of the need for immediate change. APA Council created another reorganizing committee, the Group on Restructuring (GOR), chaired by APA past-president and ASAP member Logan Wright. For several months, GOR met in a series of meetings one member described later as the most unpleasant experience she had ever had. A clinical psychologist quit in the middle amid great acrimony and bitterness, and in December 1987, GOR approved a rather awkward restructuring scheme by a vote of 11–3.

The plan was debated by APA Council at its winter meeting in February 1988. The debate was emotional, marked by accusations of bad faith, conflict of interest, and insincerity. It was only due to backstage maneuvering that the plan was approved by Council 77–41, with a tepid recommendation to the membership to adopt it. Even the distribution of ballots became a source of controversy in the campaigns to win approval or defeat. In the end, at the close of summer 1988, the GOR plan was rejected 2–1 by 26,000 of APA's 90,000 members. In the same election, Stanley Graham was elected president of APA. Graham was a private practitioner who, despite having signed the reorganization document as a member of GOR, reversed his position and campaigned against ratification. The upshot was that many academics, in the words of Logan Wright, concluded that "APA has become a guild contolled by small-business people" (Straus, 1988).

ASAP then put into action its backup plan to form a new society dedicated to academic psychologists' concerns, the American Psychological Society (APS). Starting with the initial membership of ASAP of about five hundred, APS had over ten thousand members by February 1990. Rancor between the organizations was strong. Attempts were made in APA Council to oust APS members from APA governance positions on grounds of conflict of interest, but after spirited and bitter debate, nothing came of them. Various APS organizers quit anyway.

As the American Psychological Association celebrated its centennial in 1992, American psychology found itself divided again. The needs and desires of psychological practitioners for a professional society, and of academic scientists for a learned society, again proved incompatible. The first divorce of practitioners and scientists was reconciled during the heady patriotic days of World War II. Whether psychology will come together again in a single organization without such an external crucible is an open question. Perhaps psychology is simply too large and diverse a field to be unified.

PSYCHOLOGY AND SOCIETY

Giving Psychology Away

Against the background of turmoil and alienation of the late 1960s, psychology experienced an outbreak of "relevance" in 1969 (Kessel, 1980). Psychologists fretted that they were not doing enough to solve the problems of society. The most widely cited expression of psychologists' impulse to social relevance was George Miller's 1969 presidential address to the APA, in which he stated, "I can imagine nothing we could do that would be more relevant to human welfare, and nothing that could pose a greater challenge to the next generation of psychologists, than to discover how best to give psychology away." Miller asserted that "scientific psychology is one of the most potentially revolutionary intellectual enterprises conceived by the mind of man. If we were ever to achieve substantial progress toward our stated aim—toward the understanding, prediction, and control of mental and behavioral phenomena—the implications for every aspect of society would make brave men tremble." However, Miller said, despite continuous work by applied psychologists, on the whole psychologists "have been less effective than we might have been" in providing "intellectual leadership in the search for new and better personal and social relationships." In considering how to give psychology away, Miller rejected behavioral technology for psychology's playing a part in a broad mutation of human and social values: "I believe that the real impact of psychology will be felt not through … technological products … but through its effects on the public at large, through a new and different public conception of what is humanly possible and what is humanly desirable." Miller called for "a peaceful revolution based on a new conception of human nature" based on education: "Our scientific results will have to be instilled in the public consciousness in a practical and usable form."

Miller was riding the crest of the wave of public interest in psychology. In 1967, *Psychology Today* began publishing, and in 1969, *Time* inaugurated its "Behavior" department, so psychology was being almost given away in the popular media. Psychologists pushed social relevance as never before. The theme of the 1969 APA meeting was "Psychology and the Problems of Society," and the pages of *American Psychologist* began to fill with articles and notes on student activism, psychology's duty to social responsibility, and hip references to Bob Dylan, the musical poet of youth rebellion.

Not all psychologists eschewed psychological technology in solving social problems. Two years after Miller, Kenneth Clark (1971), in his APA presidential address, argued that political leaders should have "imposed" on them the "requirement" that "they accept and use the earliest perfected form of psychotechnological, biochemical intervention which would assure their positive use of power." In an article in *Psychology Today,* psychologist James McConnell (1970) proclaimed, "Somehow we've got to learn to *force* people to love one another, to *force* them to want to behave properly. I speak of psychological force." The technology was available, McConnell opined, by which society can "gain almost absolute control over an individual's behavior.… We should reshape our society so that we all would be trained from birth to want to do what society wants us to do." McConnell concluded, "Today's behavioral psychologists are the architects and engineers of the Brave New World."

McConnell was not alone in his eagerness to take over and reshape traditional social functions. Harriet Rheingold (1973) urged the creation of a new psychological profession, the "Scientists of [Child] Rearing," that "must be accepted as the highest in the land." Furthermore, "parents must be taught how to rear their children," and, like clinical psychologists themselves, "parents to be must be certified." Along similar lines, Craig T. Raimey (1974) called for organized psychology to push for "the establishment of adequate services to the children of this nation." Psychological professionals would play many roles in Raimey's utopian scheme, functioning on local advisory councils, in coordinating agencies, as referral resources, and above all in schools, which would play the central role in screening, assessing, and treating unfortunate children.

Ironically, the problems that psychology sought to cure in society erupted in the APA. A ferocious debate started in the 1970s about the social value, if any, of standardized tests, especially I.Q. tests. It had long been known that black children did much worse than white children on I.Q. tests. Arthur Jensen (1969) started an uproar when, in a seeming return to old eugenic positions, he argued that the difference was genetic; blacks were inherently inferior to whites, so that the Great Society's compensatory education programs were doomed to failure. Debate among Jensen, his critics, and supporters raged for several years. At the 1968 APA convention, the Black Psychological Association presented a petition calling for a moratorium on the use of I.Q. tests in schools, alleging widespread abuse, specifically that tests participated in the oppression of black children by relegating them to low achievement school tracks. The APA responded in typical academic-bureaucratic fashion: It appointed a committee. In 1975, it published its report (Cleary, Humphries, Kendrick, & Wesman, 1975), which predictably concluded, in standard academic-bureaucratic fashion, that while tests might be abused, they were basically sound.

The committee's finding was unsatisfactory to black psychologists. Speaking as chair of the Association of Black Psychologists, George D. Jackson (1975) called the report "blatantly racist" and concluded that "we need *more* than a moratorium now—we need government intervention and strict legal sanctions." The debate over testing has continued ever since, and in fact a few school systems have seriously curtailed the use of tests to track students. Nevertheless, there remains irony in organized psychology's inability to happily resolve problems very similar to those of the society it presumed to scientifically revolutionize.

Some Americans, especially conservative ones, did not want what psychologists were giving away. In a widely quoted speech, then Vice President Spiro Agnew (1972) blasted psychologists, especially B. F. Skinner and Kenneth Clark, for proposing "radical surgery on the nation's psyche." Agnew quoted John Stuart Mill: "Whatever crushes individuality is despotism," and added, "we are contending with a new kind of despotism." Conservative columnist John Lofton (1972) contributed to a special issue of *American Psychologist* concerned with the serious overproduction and underemployment of Ph.D. psychologists. From some informal interviews, Lofton concluded that the public believed, "The tight market for Ph.D's is a good thing. There are too many people with a lot of knowledge about unimportant things" (p. 364). People were unsympathetic to psychology, Lofton said, because they were concerned about abuses of behavior modification technology and tests, and felt traditional American resentment of "lordly Ph.D's, of whatever stripe." Academic psychology, including cognitive psychology, has been similarly castigated from outside: "The discipline continues to traffic in two kinds of propositions: those that are true but self-evident and those that are true but uninteresting.... [On] almost any issue that might be considered important for human existence ... it offers pitifully little that rises above the banal" (Robinson, 1983, p. 5).

Ten years after Miller's address, a symposium was held to see what progress had been made in giving psychology away. Most of the reports were rather gloomy; even the optimists thought little had been accomplished. Two authors were especially scathing. Sigmund Koch (1980) tore Miller's speech apart, revealing its fatuities, flabby thinking, and self-contradictions. He argued that, if anything, psychology was being given away too well in pop psychotherapy and a flood of self-help books. Koch said, "In sum, I believe the most charitable thing we can do is not to give psychology away, but to take it back." Michael Scriven (1980), a philosopher turned program evaluator, issued psychology a failing report card. Psychology failed for being ahistorical, for not applying to itself the standards it applied to others, for fancying itself value-free, and for continuing indulgence in the Newtonian fantasy. George Miller, who was there to introduce Koch and Scriven, was depressed: "Two men who I admire enormously have just destroyed my life."

The Turn to Service

Although Sigmund Koch and Michael Scriven complained about the quality of the psychology that was being given away, psychologists generally seemed to be heeding George Miller's appeal to get involved with the problems of society. For as the 1970s wore on, psychologists were less likely to be found in the haunts of scientific psychology's founders, the classroom and the laboratory, than in settings where they provided services. One of the major changes in the United States in the 1960s and 1970s was the change from a primarily industrial-productive economy to a service-information economy. Between 1960 and 1979, the total U.S. labor force grew by 45 percent, while the service sector grew by 69 percent. The greatest growth occurred in the social sciences, whose ranks grew by an incredible 495 percent; psychology grew by 435 percent.

Increasingly, psychologists were choosing specialties outside the old core area of experimental psychology. Between 1966 and 1980, the increase of new Ph.D.'s in experimental psychology averaged only 1.4 percent per year (the slowest growth of all specialty areas), while growth in applied areas was much greater: For example, clinical psychology grew about 8.1 percent per year, counseling 12.9 percent, and school psychology 17.8 percent. By 1980, applied psychologists made up about 61 percent of all doctoral psychologists, while traditional experimentalists constituted but 13.5 percent. And new psychologists were choosing to work outside academia. In 1967, 61.9 percent of new doctoral psychologists took work in colleges or universities; by 1981, the figure was down to 32.6 percent. The most rapidly growing employment setting was self-employment, as a privately practicing clinician or consultant. Self-employed psychologists were not even counted before 1970. In 1970, only 1.3 percent of new doctoral psychologists chose self-employment, but by 1981, 6.9 percent did so. Other rapidly growing employment settings were government, business, and nonprofit institutions. Even psychologists trained in research specialties were increasingly likely to be employed outside academic settings, although often nonacademic employment was forced on them by the limited number of university and college jobs. In 1975, 68.9 percent of new research specialty doctoral psychologists went into academic settings; in 1980, only 51.7 percent did so, for an average annual decline of 8 percent. There were offsetting increases in employment outside academia, so that there were few actually unemployed psychology Ph.D.'s.

Psychologists by 1985 could be found virtually everywhere, touching millions of lives. At the Educational Testing Service, psychologists continued to refine the Scholastic Aptitude Test (SAT), familiar to virtually every reader of this book, and pushed testing into new areas. You cannot become a golf pro without taking a multiple-choice ETS test (Owen, 1985). At the Stanford Research Institute, psychologists and others worked on an ambitious marketing program, the Values and Lifestyle Program (VALS). VALS used a technique called "psychographics" to break American consumers into several well-defined groups, such as "I-Am-Mes," "Belongers," and "Achievers." Companies and advertising agencies paid for VALS profiles to target their products to the most receptive groups and tune their pitches to the psychological makeup of their audiences (Atlas, 1984; Novak & MacEvoy, 1990). Clinical psychologists, despite some official misgivings from the APA, were running radio call-in shows on which people could air their problems and seek advice and comfort from a psychologist (Rice, 1981). Such shows started locally, but by 1985, a nationwide radio network, Talk Radio, devoted at least six hours a day to the "psych jockeys," and in 1986, the APA created a Division of Media Psychology. People were bringing their troubles to psychologists as never before: Between 1957 and 1976, the percentage of Americans who had consulted a mental health professional rose from 4 percent to 14 percent; among the college-educated, the change was from 9 percent to 21 percent. In fact, the number of people exposed to therapeutic techniques is very much greater, since many self-help organizations, such as those for losing weight and stopping smoking, use such techniques (Zilbergeld, 1983). Finally, bookshops have Psychology sections mostly filled with self-help psychology books, and we can add to these most of the books in the Family Life sections concerning sex, intimacy, and child rearing.

By 1985, psychologists were everywhere and were taking themselves seriously as a social force. Charles Kiesler (1979), executive officer of the APA, wrote: "I see psychology, then, as a national force for the future: as a knowledgeable force on scientific issues, on the delivery of human services, and on various human concerns about which we know something."

OUR PSYCHOLOGICAL SOCIETY

Ever since its beginnings in philosophy, psychology has perched awkwardly astride the dividing line between science and morals, between what is—how human beings really are—and what ought to be—how human beings should behave. Natural science can rest content with describing nature as it is, giving humans power for good or evil. The other social disciplines, or *Geisteswissenschaften,* describe what human beings have made of themselves across cultures and throughout history. Psychology, however, shares the Neoplatonic tragedy of humankind. People are at once animals, part of the natural world, and, in a sense, divine makers of social worlds, and psychology must come to grips with "*Homo sapiens* the animal" and "human being the creator" of forms of life. Psychology is perennially torn apart by its conflicting obligations, tempted on the one hand by the Newtonian dream of a natural science of humankind, yet likewise tempted to build a better form of life, to remake society in its own image.

Through it all, psychology has remained the study of the individual human being. The human species is studied by biology; human society is studied by sociology and anthropology. In our own time, psychology, as the avowed science of the individual person, has come to replace traditional ways of moralizing about human action, and to replace them with its own perspective centered on the self and on feelings. In Platonism and traditional religion, the rules by which people live their lives have been thought to come from outside, from a transcendent realm of the Good or from the transcendent world of God. However, as religious and metaphysical traditions have been eroded by mechanistic science, people have turned to science for moral guidance, and this has led them, inevitably, to psychology, the science of individual action. It is quite natural, then, that as transcendental norms fade they should be replaced by scientific ones, and the priest or shaman be replaced by the clinical psychologist. Psychology, as the study of the individual, must then decree that the rules by which we should live life come from within each one of us, rather than from outside, and that these new rules can be discovered by looking within ourselves, by finding out how we really feel about things. In our psychological society, we are told to buy products because if we do, we will "feel good" about them and, even more importantly, about ourselves. Similarly, we are encouraged to share our feelings freely with others—whether they want to hear them or not—because only in this way, psychology says, can we become real human beings.

Psychology, however much behaviorists and cognitive scientists might object, teaches introspection as the final judge of right and wrong and encourages people to undertake an inward journey in search of introspective certainty concerning their real feelings and their supposed secret selves. In the United States, at least, psychology has become a new religion establishing an inner quest for self where before there had been an outer quest for God. The most acute observer of modern America, Tom Wolfe (1977), described the psychological society this way: Americans "plunged straight toward what has become the alchemical dream of the Me Decade. The old alchemical dream was changing base metals into gold. The new alchemical dream is: changing one's personality—remaking, remodelling, elevating, and polishing one's very *self* ... and observing, studying, and doting on it. (Me!)" (p. 126, ellipses in original). The Me Decade, the Me Society, is the nearly inevitable result of scientism and psychology. If there is no transcendent truth outside nature, and if psychology is the science of the individual, then the only proper guide to life must come from scientific psychology, and that entails looking within for truth that cannot come from without.

For good or ill, we human beings of the West, especially the United States, live in a psychological society. We are raised according to the findings of child psychologists, and we raise our children following the newer findings of child psychologists. In business, we turn to psychologists to manage workers and help us sell our products; as consumers, we are vulnerable to appeals crafted by psychologists. When we fall in love, we find ourselves in a "relationship" to be scrutinized in terms of our feelings, and if we find trouble doing that, we phone or visit a psychologist to help us out. We have come to believe the Deweyan notion that there are no fixed rules, that growth is the only moral end. Since there are no outside goals to aim for, only inner ones, only growth and constant change are left to measure our self-worth and our love for each other. As Woody Allen, neurotic spokesman for the psychological society, complains in *Annie Hall,* "A relationship, I think, is like a shark; it has to constantly move forward or it dies."

BIBLIOGRAPHY FOR CHAPTERS 14 AND 15

The literature on cognitive science is vast. An excellent introduction to AI is John Haugeland, *Artificial Intelligence: The very idea* (Cambridge, MA: MIT Press/Bradford, 1985). The easiest introduction to functionalism is Jerry Fodor, "The mind body problem," *Scientific American* (1981, *244* [no. 1, January]: 114–23). There are two useful anthologies on foundations and criticisms of cognitive science. They are John Haugeland (Ed.), *Mind design* (Cambridge, MA: Bradford/MIT, 1981); and Douglas R. Hofstadter & Daniel C. Dennett (Eds.), *The mind's eye* (New York: Basic Books, 1981). The latter book is edited by two defenders of formalistic AI, and although they reprint papers critical of cognitive science, such as Searle (1980, also reprinted by Haugeland), they try to defend the AI approach throughout their commentary. It is therefore useful to also read Searle's review of *The mind's eye* in the *The New York Review of Books,* April 29, 1982. Waldrop (1984) provides a readable account of some of the latest work in AI expanded into a book, *Man made minds: The promise of artificial intelligence* (New York: Walker, 1987). Owen J. Flanagan, *The science of the mind* (Cambridge, MA: MIT Press, 1984), canvasses the field of cognitive psychology, including Freud, James, and Piaget, as well as information processing. An outstanding book on the promise and the limits of AI, including its moral implications, is Joseph Weizenbaum, *Computer power and human reason* (San Francisco: W. H. Freeman, 1976). Weizenbaum is an eminent MIT computer scientist who has become revolted by what he regards as "obscene" uses of computers—for example, to do psychotherapy. Finally, while there is no historical connection between modern functionalism and earlier functionalism, there are interesting parallels. For example, John Dewey, in "The realism of pragmatism," *Journal of Philosophy* (1905, 2:324–27), describes his instrumentalism as a representational theory of mind.

For the information-processing view of consciousness, see Klatzky (1985), and George Mandler, "Consciousness: Its function and construction," in *Cognitive psychology: A survey of cognitive science* (Hillsdale, NJ: Erlbaum, 1984); for the transpersonal psychology view, see Ronald S. Valle & Rolf von Eckatsberg (Eds.), *The metaphors of consciousness* (New York: Plenum, 1981); for a variety of scientific approaches, see Kenneth Pope & Jerome Singer (Eds.), *The stream of consciousness* (New York: Plenum, 1978). The article by Nisbett & Wilson (1977) provoked many replies, rebuttals, and elaborations. Two replies to Nisbett and Wilson I find especially interesting: John G. Adair & Barry Spinner, "Subject's access to cognitive processes: Demand characteristics and verbal report," *Journal for the Theory of Social Behavior* (1981, *11*:31–52); and John Sabini & Maury Silver, "Introspection and causal accounts," *Journal of Personality and Social Psychology* (1981, *40:* 171–79).

Connectionism has generated a lot of literature, most of it highly technical. A good general survey is William Bechtel & Adele Abrahamsen, *Connectionism and the mind* (Cambridge, MA: Basil Blackwell, 1990). Also useful is the collection of papers edited by Stephen Graubard (1988) *The artificial intelligence debate: False starts, real foundations* (Cambridge, MA: MIT Press). The papers were ostensibly written for outsiders and contain history, philosophy, and controversy relating to connectionism. The paper by Smolensky (1988) is wide-ranging and thoughtful and is the clearest discussion I've found of the foundational ideas of connectionism, but it is tough going. The standard symbolic paradigm critique of connectionism is Fodor & Pylyshyn (1988). Finally, one of the nice things about connectionist models is that one can get them and build one's own, using ordinary computers. The PDP folks have published J. L. McLelland & D. E. Rumelhart, *Explorations in parallel distributed processing: A handbook of models, programs and exercises* (Cambridge, MA: Bradford/MIT, 1988), complete with floppy disks containing most of the models presented in their main work. Using the models, however, requires a modest degree of programming skill. Easier to use are the menu-driven programs one can purchase with the program *Brainmaker,* published by California Scientific Software in 1988. It comes with easy-to-run prepackaged models, and it's relatively easy to build your own. Moreover, the program comes with not only a manual, but a little book, *Introduction to neural networks,* that's a good introduction to connectionism.

A truly excellent way to understand radical behaviorism and its relations to critics and rival views, especially cognitive science, is to read a special issue of *The Behavioral and Brain Sciences* (1984, 7 [no. 4, December]) devoted to the "Canonical Papers of B. F. Skinner." The issue reprints Skinner's most important papers, and follows them with critical commentary from dozens of philosophers and scientists, followed in turn by Skinner's replies. It should be pointed out that radical behaviorism is no longer Skinner's monopoly, and that others who call themselves behaviorists today formulate the field with different emphases. For instructive examples, see Willard F. Day, "Contemporary behaviorism and the concept of intention," in William J. Arnold (Ed.), *Nebraska symposium on motivation 1975 (Vol. 23): Conceptual foundations of psychology* (Lincoln: University of Nebraska Press, 1976); Charles P. Shimp, "Cognition, behavior, and the experimental analysis of behavior," *Journal of the Experimental Analysis of Behavior* (1984, *42*:407–20); or Gerald E. Zuriff, *Behaviorism: A conceptual reconstruction* (New York: Columbia University Press, 1985).

For psychology's occult doubles, see Thomas H. Leahey & Grace Evans Leahey, *Psychology's occult doubles: Psychology and the problem of pseudoscience* (Chicago: Nelson Hall, 1983); and Thomas H. Leahey & Grace Evans Leahey, "Occult muddles: Essay review of recent books on the occult," *Journal of the History of the Behavioral Sciences* (1986, *22*:220–25).

The references in the text provide a survey of reductionism. For sociobiology, there are many points of entry. Leahey & Harris (1985) have a one-chapter treatment of sociobiology. David Barash offers the best book-length treatments, including his text *Sociobiology and behavior,* 2nd ed. (New York: Elsevier, 1982), and his book on human sociobiology, *The whisperings within* (New York: Penguin, 1979). Michael Ruse, *Sociobiology: Sense or nonsense?* (Dordrecht, Holland: D. Reidel, 1979), is a wise introduction to and a balanced evaluation of the field. See also Chapter 15 of this text.

Hermeneutics is a sprawling, diverse field with many practitioners. It is primarily a European movement, though recently much interest has been shown in American philosophical and psychological circles. One way to begin to understand hermeneutics is through sources that explicitly contrast it with more familiar ways of thinking. The last part of Dreyfus (1972) contrasts European phenomenology, a branch of hermeneutics, with AI. Kenneth J. Gergen has recently criticized social psychology for not being a science, and his alternative "social construction," although not explicitly hermeneutic, is closely related. His most famous paper, which provoked both interest and outrage in social psychology, was "Social psychology as history," *Journal of Personality and Social Psychology* (1973, *26:* 309–20), expanded into a book, *Toward transformation in social knowledge* (New York: Springer-Verlag, 1982). His ideas have been vehemently rejected by mainstream social psychologists. Barry Schlenker reasserted the Newtonian values of the profession in his reply to Gergen's paper, "Social psychology and science," *Journal of Personality and Social Psychology* (1974, *29*:1–15). The editors of the *Personality and Social Psychology Bulletin* organized a symposium around the Gergen-Schlenker exchange, including new statements by the combatants, and it may be found in *Personality and Social Psychology Bulletin* (1976, *2*:371–444). Using a lively dialogue form, Gary Gutting contrasts hermeneutics with positivism and mainstream philosophy of science in "Paradigms and hermeneutics. A dialogue on Kuhn, Rorty, and the social sciences," *American Philosophical*

Quarterly (1984, *21*:1–15). The reference to Rorty is to philosopher Richard Rorty, who has incorporated hermeneutics into a reinvigorated pragmatism that has stirred up the same sort of storm in philosophy that Gergen did in social psychology. Rorty analyzes and rejects traditional philosophy and introduces hermeneutics in *Philosophy and the mirror of nature* (Princeton, NJ: Princeton University Press, 1980); he develops his view in *Consequences of pragmatism* (Minneapolis: University of Minnesota Press, 1982), which is briefly summarized in "The fate of philosophy," *The New Republic* (1982, *187* [no. 16, October 18]: 28–34). Several books about hermeneutics have been published, but the one I have found to be the clearest is Roy J. Howard, *Three faces of hermeneutics: An introduction to current theories of understanding* (Berkeley: University of California Press, 1982); Howard's book is especially helpful because he connects hermeneutics to English-speaking philosophy, particularly to the followers of Wittgenstein.

The references provide a survey of works on the applications of psychology. On the fuss over insurance, see three special issues of *American Psychologist* devoted to the topic, September 1977 and August 1983, in the "Psychology of the Public Forum" section, and February 1986. The literature evaluating psychotherapy is vast, difficult, and treacherous. Probably the best place to enter the literature is Prioleau, Murdock, & Brody (1983). They do a good job of discussing the complex issues involved in evaluating therapy outcomes, the "Peer Commentary" section gives ample voice to critics who disagree with the article's contention that therapy is ineffective, and the reference section lists all the important works. Zilbergeld (1983) also discusses this literature, more readably but less precisely. See also J. Berman & N. Norton, "Does professional training make a therapist more effective?" *Psychological Bulletin* (1985, *98*: 401–407).

My account of the split between the APA and the APS is based primarily on my own experience as substitute or regular representative on APA Council of Division 24 (Theoretical and Philosophical) from fall 1986 to winter 1989. I have also drawn on a variety of accounts appearing in the newsletter of the APA, the *APA Monitor,* and the APS newsletter, the *APS Observer.* See also S. C. Hayes, "The gathering storm," *Behavior Analysis* (1987, *22:* 41–45); C. Holden, "Research psychologists break with APA," *Science,* (1988, *241:* 1036); and C. Raymond, "18 months after its formation, psychological society proves its worth to behavioral-science researchers," *Chronicle of Higher Education* (June 27, 1990, *5:*9). I should state that I am one of the disgruntled academics of APA. While I was not a member of ASAP, and have not given up my APA membership, I am a charter member of APS, supporting its separation from APA.

The statistics in the "Turn to Service" section are drawn from Georgine M. Pion & Mark W. Lipsey, "Psychology and society: The challenge of change," *American Psychologist* (1984, *39:* 739–54). David Owen's (1985) book on the SAT should be read by everyone who has taken the SAT or is a parent of someone who will take the SAT. Owen really does "rip the lid" off an incredibly corrupt institution that serves no ends but its own and does significant social harm. Anyone who reads the book will agree with Jonathan Yardley of the *Washington Post* that the SAT "is a scam," and with Owen's conclusion that ETS should be abolished.

The outstanding impressionistic portrait of the psychological society is Wolfe (1977). Another, more sardonic, tourist is Shiva Naipul, who reports in "The pursuit of wholiness," *Harper's* (April 1981:20–27). The most scientific survey of the psychological society comes from pollster Daniel Yankelovich, "New rules in American life: Searching for self-fulfillment in a world turned upside down," *Psychology Today* (April 1981, 35–91). The term "psychological society" seems to have been coined by writer Martin L. Gross, *The psychological society: A critical analysis of psychiatry, psychotherapy, and the psychological revolution* (New York: Touchstone, 1978). Gross's book is quite good, if a little heavyhanded at times. Two related books are Peter Schrag, *Mind control* (New York: Delta, 1978), which is positively Orwellian in tone; and R. D. Rosen, *Psychobabble* (New York: Avon, 1979), which provides a witty tour of various pop psychotherapies. Several broad critiques of the psychological society exist, and

I will mention only those I find especially useful. First, there is an excellent but often overlooked book by Daniel Boorstin, *The image: A guide to pseudo-events in America* (New York: Harper Colophon, 1964). The first book I know of to specifically address psychology's contribution to a new moral order was Phillip Rieff, *The triumph of the therapeutic* (New York: Harper & Row, 1966). Concern with the psychological society and the therapeutic sensibility grew more intense in the 1970s, producing Richard Sennett, *The fall of public man* (New York: Vintage, 1976), my own favorite of these books; and Christopher Lasch, *The culture of narcissism* (New York: W. W. Norton, 1979), which has probably had the greatest impact. An excellent book, which focuses closely on the therapeutic sensibility encouraged by clinical psychology and psychiatry, is Zilbergeld (1983), with the unforgettable title *The shrinking of America*. Two related books bear mention. First is Alasdair MacIntyre, *After virtue: A study in moral theory* (Notre Dame, IN: University of Notre Dame Press, 1981), who takes a long view of the turn from exterior to interior standards of morality, extending back to the prephilosophic Greeks. Two recent books argue that popularized psychology has undermined traditional ideas of free will and moral responsibility: Wendy Kaminer, *I'm dysfunctional, you're dysfunctional: The recovery movement and other self-help fads* (Boston: Addison-Wesley, 1992); and Charles W. Sykes, *A nation of victims: The decay of the American character* (New York: St. Martin's Press, 1992); see also J. R. Dunlap [Review of Sykes] *American Spectator* (December 1992, *25:* 72–73). The best actual antidote to the language of feelings is Miss Manners: Judith Martin, *Miss Manners' guide to excruciatingly correct behavior* (New York: Warner Books, 1982).

REFERENCES

Agnew, S. (1972, January). Agnew's blast at behaviorism. *Psychology Today, 5,* 4, 84, 87.

Albee, G. W. (1970). The uncertain future of clinical psychology. *American Psychologist, 25,* 1071–1080.

Albee, G. W. (1977a). The Protestant ethic, sex, and psychotherapy. *American Psychologist, 32,* 150–161.

Albee, G. W. (1977b). Does including psychotherapy in health insurance represent a subsidy to the rich from the poor? *American Psychologist, 32,* 719–721.

Anonymous (1988, Summer). AMA and psychiatry join forces to oppose psychologists. *Practitioner Focus, 2,* 1, 4–5.

Atlas, J. (1984). Beyond demographics. *Atlantic Monthly* (October): 49–58.

Belar, C. D. & Perry, N. W. (Eds.), (1991). *Proceedings: National Conference on scientist-practitioner education.* Sarasota, FL: Professional Resource Exchange.

Campbell, D. T. (1975). On the conflicts between biological and social evolution and between psychology and moral tradition. *American Psychologist, 30,* 1103–1126.

Churchland, P. M. (1985). *Matter and consciousness.* Cambridge, MA: MIT/Bradford.

Churchland, P. S. (1986). *Neurophilosophy.* Cambridge, MA: MIT Press.

Clark, K. (1971). The pathos of power: A psychological perspective. *American Psychologist, 26,* 1047–1057.

Cleary, T., Humphries, L., Kendrick, S., & Wesman, A. (1975). Educational uses of tests with disadvantaged students. *American Psychologist, 30,* 15–91.

Davidson, D. (1980). *Essays on actions and events.* Oxford, England: Clarendon Press.

Demos, J. P. (1982). *Entertaining Satan: Witchcraft and the culture of early New England.* New York: Oxford University Press.

Dörken, H. & Morrison, D. (1976). JCAH standards for accreditation of psychiatric facilities: Implications for the practice of clinical psychology. *American Psychologist, 31,* 774–784.

Fodor, J. A. & Pylyshyn, Z. W. (1988). Connectionism and cognitive architecture: A critical analysis. In S. Pinker & J. Mehler (Ed.), *Connections and symbols.* Cambridge, MA: Bradford Books/MIT Press.

Fox, J. (1983). Debate on learning theory is shifting. *Science, 222,* 1219–1222.

Gelman, D. & Gordon, J. (1987, December 14). Growing pains for the shrinks. *Newsweek,* 70-72.

Gottlieb, G. (1984). Evolutionary trends and evolutionary origins: Relevance to theory in comparative psychology. *Psychological Review, 91,* 448–456.

Gross, S. J. (1978). The myth of professional licensing. *American Psychologist, 33,* 1009–1016.

Hodos, W. & Campbell, C. B. G. (1969). Scala naturae: Why there is no theory in comparative psychology. *Psychological Review, 76,* 337–350.

Hookway, C. (Ed.), (1984). *Minds, machines, and programs.* New York: Cambridge University Press.

Hull, D. L. (1984). Historical entities and historical narratives. In C. Hookway (Ed.), *Minds, machines, and programs.* New York: Cambridge University Press.

Jackson, G. D. (1975). On the report of the ad hoc committee on educational uses of tests with disadvantaged students. Another psychological view from the Association of Black Psychologists. *American Psychologist, 30,* 88–93.

Jensen, A. (1969). How much can we boost I.Q. and scholastic achievement? *Harvard Educational Review, 39,* 1–123.

Kasschau, R. A. & Kessel, F. S. (Eds.), (1980). *Psychology and society: In search of symbiosis.* New York: Holt, Rinehart & Winston.

Kessel, F. S. (1980). Psychology and society: In search of symbiosis. Introduction to the symposium. In R. A. Kasschau & F. S. Kessel (Eds.), *Psychology and society: In search of symbiosis.* New York: Holt, Rinehart & Winston.

Kiesler, C. A. (1979). Report of the Executive Officer 1978. *American Psychologist, 34,* 455–462.

Klatzky, R. (1984). *Memory and awareness: An information-processing perspective.* San Francisco: W. H. Freeman.

Klerman, G. L. (1979, April). The age of melancholy? *Psychology Today, 12,* 36–42, 88.

Koch, S. (1980). Psychology and its human clientele: Beneficiaries or victims? In R. A. Kasschau & F. S. Kessel (Eds.), *Psychology and society: In search of symbiosis.* New York: Holt, Rinehart & Winston.

Landman, J. T. & Dawes, R. (1982). Psychotherapy outcome: Smith & Glass conclusions stand up under scrutiny. *American Psychologist, 37,* 504–516.

Leahey, T. H. (1982). *Will psychology disappear? The new prospects for reductionism.* Paper presented at the annual meeting of the Eastern Psychological Association, Baltimore, Maryland, April.

Leahey, T. H. (1984). *Evolution, history and cognitive science: Psychology without science or science without psychology.* Paper presented at the annual meeting of the Eastern Psychological Association, Baltimore, Maryland, April.

Leahey, T. H. & Harris, R. J. (1992). *Human learning,* 3rd ed. Englewood Cliffs, NJ: Prentice-Hall.

Lockard, R. B. (1971). Reflections of the fall of comparative psychology: Is there a lesson for us all? *American Psychologist, 26,* 168–179.

Lofton, J. (1972). Psychology's manpower: A perspective from the public at large. *American Psychologist, 27,* 364–366.

Lown, B. A. (1975). Comparative psychology 25 years after. *American Psychologist, 30,* 858–859.

McConnell, J. V. (1970, April). Criminals can be brainwashed–Now. *Psychology Today, 3,* 14–18, 74.

Neisser, U. (1984). Toward an ecologically oriented cognitive science. In T. M. Schlecter & M. P. Toglia (Eds.), *New directions in cognitive science.* Norwood, NJ: Ablex.

Nisbett, R. E. & Wilson, T. D. (1977). Telling more than we can know: Verbal reports on mental processes. *Psychological Review, 84,* 231–259.

Novak, T. P. & MacEvoy, B. (June, 1990). On comparing alternative segmentation schemes: The List of Values (LOV) and the Life Styles (VALS). *Journal of Consumer Research, 17,* 105–109.

Owen, D. (1985). *None of the above: Behind the myth of scholastic aptitude.* Boston: Houghton Mifflin.

Peele, S. (1981). Reductionism in the psychology of the eighties: Can biochemistry eliminate addiction, mental illness, and pain? *American Psychologist, 36,* 807–818.

Perry, N. J. (1979). Why clinical psychology does not need alternative training models. *American Psychologist, 34,* 603–611.

Peterson, D. R. (1976). Need for the Doctor of Psychology degree in professional psychology. *American Psychologist, 31,* 792–798.

Porter, J., Johnson, S., & Granger, R. G. (1981, December). The snark is still a boojum. *Comparative Psychology Newsletter, 1,* 1–3.

Post, S. C. (1985, July 25). Beware the 'Barefoot doctors of mental health.' *The Wall Street Journal,* 21.

Prioleau, L., Murdock, M., & Brody, N. (1983). An analysis of psychotherapy versus placebo studies. *The Behavioral and Brain Sciences, 6,* 275–310.

Putnam, H. (1982). Reductionism and the nature of psychology. *Cognition, 2,* 131–146.

Raimey, C. T. (1974). Children and public policy: A role for psychologists. *American Psychologist, 29,* 14–18.

Rheingold, H. (1973). To rear a child. *American Psychologist, 28,* 42–46.

Rice, B. (1981, December). Call-in therapy: Reach out and shrink someone. *Psychology Today,* 39–44, 87–91.

Robinson, P. (1983, July 10). Psychology's scrambled egos. *Washington Post Book World, 13,* 5, 7.

Rosenberg, A. (1980). *Sociobiology and the preemption of social science.* Baltimore: Johns Hopkins University Press.

Rosenberg, A. (1983). Content and consciousness versus the intentional stance. *The Behavioral and Brain Sciences, 3,* 375–376.

Rosenberg, A. (1984). *Davidson's unintended attack on psychology.* Paper presented at the Conference on the Philosophy of Donald Davidson, New Brunswick, NJ, May 1.

Scriven, M. (1980). An evaluation of psychology. In R. A. Kasschau & F. S. Kessel (Eds.), *Psychology and society: In search of symbiosis.* New York: Holt, Rinehart & Winston.

Searle, J. (1980). Minds, brains, and programs. *The Behavioral and Brain Sciences, 3,* 417–424.

Shakow, D. (1976). What is clinical psychology? *American Psychologist, 31,* 553–560.

Skinner, B. F. (1931). The concept of reflex in the description of behavior. *Journal of General Psychology, 5,* 427–458.

Skinner, B. F. (1972). *Beyond freedom and dignity.* New York: Knopf.

Skinner, B. F. (1974). *About behaviorism.* New York: Knopf.

Skinner, B. F. (1984a). Some consequences of selection. *The Behavioral and Brain Sciences, 7,* 502–510.

Skinner, B. F. (1984b). Representations and misrepresentations. *The Behavioral and Brain Sciences, 7,* 655–667.

Skinner, B. F. (1985a). Cognitive science and behaviorism. *British Journal of Psychology, 76,* 291–301.

Skinner, B. F. (1985b). *What is wrong with everyday life in the Western world?* Paper presented at the annual meeting of the American Psychological Association, Los Angeles, California, August 26.

Smith, M. L., Glass, G. V., & Miller, T. I. (1980). *The benefits of psychotherapy.* Baltimore, MD: Johns Hopkins University Press.

Smolensky, P. (1988). On the proper treatment of connectionism. *The Behavioral and Brain Sciences, 3,* 417–424.

Snyder, S. H. (1980). *Biological aspects of mental disorder.* New York: Oxford University Press.

Squires, S. (1990, July 24). The quest for prescription privileges. *Washington Post, Health,* p. 7.

Straus, H. (1988, August 12). Psychology field finds itself of two minds: Private practice, research. *Atlanta Journal and Constitution.*

Strickler, G. (1975). On professional schools and professional degrees. *American Psychologist, 31,* 1062–1066.

Strupp, H. (1976). Clinical psychology, irrationalism, and the erosion of excellence. *American Psychologist, 31,* 561–571.

Symons, D. (1987). If we're all Darwinians, what's the fuss about? In C. Crawford, M. Smith, & D. Krebs (Eds.), *Sociobiology and psychology.* Hillsdale, N. J.: Erlbaum.

Tart, C. (1978). Information processing mechanisms and ESP. Invited address presented at the annual meeting of the American Psychological Association, Toronto, Canada, August 31.

Waldrop, M. M. (1984). The necessity of knowledge. *Science, 223,* 1279–1282.

Wasserman, E. A. (1981). Comparative psychology returns. *Journal of the Experimental Analysis of Behavior, 35,* 243–257.

Welch, B. L. (1992, September). Paradigm II: Providing a better model for care. *APA Monitor,* 42-43.

Wender, P. H. & Klein, D. F. (1981, February). The promise of biological psychiatry. *Psychology Today, 15,* 25–41.

Wiggins, J. G. (1992, September). Capitol Comments: Time is ripe to seek prescription authority. *APA Monitor,* 3.

Wilson, E. O. (1975) *Sociobiology: The new synthesis.* Cambridge, MA: Harvard University Press.

Wispé, L. G. & Thompson, J. N. (Eds.), (1976). The war between the words: Biological vs. social evolution and some related issues. *American Psychologist, 31,* 341–384.

Wolfe, T. (1977). The Me Decade and the third great awakening. In T. Wolfe, *Mauve gloves and madmen, clutter and vine.* New York: Bantam Books.

Wyers, E. J., et al. (11) (1980). The sociobiological challenge to psychology: On the proposal to "cannibalize" comparative psychology. *American Psychologist, 35,* 955–979.

Zilbergeld, B. (1983). *The shrinking of America: Myths of psychological change.* Boston: Little, Brown.

INDEX

Consciousness *(continued)*
  relational theory of, 170–73
Consciousness debate, 169–74
Constructive empiricists, 9
Contingencies of reinforcement, 264, 350
    (*See also* Behaviorism)
Control of behavior (*See* Behavioralism;
    Behaviorism; Social control)
Copy theories of knowledge/mind, 170,
    173–74, 176
Cultural parochialism, 70

D

Darrow, Clarence, 112, 223
Dartmouth Conference on Learning
    Theory, 260
Darwin, Charles, 107, 108, 109–13
    pragmatism and, 126
    Skinner and, 262, 268
Darwinian psychology, 115–18
Dashiell, John F., 196
Davenport, Charles, 221
Demarcation criterion, 7, 96
Dennett, Daniel, 329, 339
Dennis, Wayne, 245
Dependent variable, 199, 200, 263
Descartes, René, 6, 77, 118, 167–68, 174,
    255, 295
Descent of Man (Darwin), 115–16
Descriptive behaviorism, 263
Determinism, Skinner's view of, 349–50
Developmental psychology, 323
    cognitive psychology and, 323
Dewey, John, 142–45, 213, 232, 246
    education and, 142
    instrumentalism and, 149, 173–74
    reflex arc and, 149–50
Dignity, Skinner's view of, 349–51
Disciplinary matrix, 332–34
Discrimination, conditioned response and,
    167
Discriminative consciousness, 168
Discriminative stimulus, 265
Dissociative disorder, 70
DNA, 10, 108, 112
Donders, F.C., 35
Dora, Freud's case of, 87–88
Dreams, Freud on, 89–92, 360
Dualism, 3, 23, 31, 141, 170
Dulany, Don E., 301

Dunlap, Knight, 176
Dunton, Larkin, 141

E

Ebbinghaus, Hermann, 48, 160–61, 306
Eclectic psychology, 252
Ecological psychology, 352
Education, Progressivism and, 142
Educational Testing Service, 368
Edwards, Jonathan, 124, 228–29
Effect, law of, 163–64, 300, 342
Ego, 1, 78, 90
Ego instincts, 88
Ehrenfels, C., 55
Einstein, Albert, 7–8
Elements, Titchener's catalogue of, 53
Elements of Psychophysics (Fechner), 33,
    160
Ellis, Havelock, 79, 81
Elton, G.R., 18
Emerson, Ralph Waldo, 124
Emotions and the Will (Bain), 27
Empathy, 291
Empiricism/empiricists, 3, 23, 24, 31, 146,
    294
    animal behavior and, 297–99
Encounter groups, 315–16
Enlightenment, in America, 121–22, 142
Epistemic subject, 276, 304
Epistemology, 2
Ericsson, K. Anders, 335–36
Eros, 88–89
Erotogenic zones, 93
Essay on the Principle of Population
    (Malthus), 110
Ethics, psychology and, 2
Eugenics, 117–18
    in America, 219–24
    Nazi use of, 223–24
    Watson on, 227
Eugenics Records Office, 221
Eugenics Review, 118
Evangelical Christianity, American
    psychology and, 122
Evolution, 106–11 (*See also* Adaptation,
    psychology of)
Exercise, law of, 163–64
Experimental analysis of behavior, 263–71,
    350–51
Experimental introspection, 42–43

Greenspoon effect, 300–301
Group for the Study of Verbal Behavior,
    306
Group tests of intelligence, World War I
    U.S. Army, 215–19
  criticism of, 218
Growth, as humanistic value, 312
Grünbaum. Adolf, 96

H

Haeckel, Ernst, 72
Haggerty, M.E., 175, 186
Hall, G. Stanley, 60, 131, 139, 142
Harter, N., 152
Hawthorne Effect, 224–25
Hebb, Donald, 305, 306
Hegel, Wilhelm Friedrich, 15–16, 30
Hellenism, new, 313–14
Helmholtz, H. von, 31–32, 34–35, 38, 74
Heraclitus, 127, 146
Herbart, J.F., 30–31, 74
Hereditary Genius (Galton), 117
Hermeneutics, 359–60
  psychoanalysis and, 97–98
Hickock, Laurens Perseus, 125
Higher-order conditioning, 167
Hilgard, Ernest R., 238
Hippie movement, 313–14
  conservative/reactionary nature of,
      315–16
Historiography
  of psychology, 16–18
  of science, 16
History of Experimental Psychology
      (Boring), 16
Hitzig, E., 26, 148
Hobbes, Thomas, 276
Hobhouse, Leonard T., 119
Hoffman, Paul, 244
Holt, Edwin Bissel, 170, 171–72, 197
Holton, Gerald, 11–12
Hull, Clark Leonard, 9, 196, 197, 200–204,
      259, 260–61, 266, 279, 293, 317, 327
  computers and, 283
  on consciousness, 203
  mediational behaviorism and, 274
  vs. Tolman, 204–7
Humanistic psychology, 291–93, 312
  conservative/reactionary nature of,
      315–16

Human learning, awareness and, 300–301
Human Learning (Thorndike), 164
Hume, David, 23, 118, 124, 201, 293
Hunter, Walter, 188, 190–91
Hutchins, Robert Maynard, 244
Huxley, Thomas Henry, 109, 112
Hypothetical constructs, 259
Hysteria, 70–71, 82

I

Id, 78, 79
Ideal gas law, 10
Ideals of natural order, 6
Ideology/idealism, 28, 29–31
Imageless thought, 49–51, 58
Imitation game, 281
Immigration control, eugenics and,
      219–21
Independent variables, 199, 200, 263
Individual differences
  in Darwinian psychology, 117
  Gall's psychology of, 25
Individualism, 246
Individual question, evolutionary theory
      and, 107
Industrial psychology, 215, 284
Informal behaviorism, 272–75
Informational feedback, 280–81
Information processing, 303, 305–7
  as form of behavioralism, 316–17
  introspection and, 334–36
  as paradigm, 332–34
  theory, Skinner's critique of, 351–2
  triumph of, 323–31
Informavores, 324
Instincts, Freud on, 79–89
Institute for Human Relations (Yale), 274
Instrumentalism/instrumentalists, 149,
      173–74
Insurance issues, 362–63
Intelligence testing, 114–15
  in World War I U.S. Army, 215–19
  criticism of, 218
Intelligent consciousness, 168
Intentionality, 58, 60
Intentional stance, 329
Internalism-externalism, history of science
      and, 15
Interpretation of Dreams, The (Freud), 67,
      73–74, 89–92

V

Values, psychology as science of, 245
Values and Lifestyle Program (VALS), 368
van Frassen, B.C., 9
Vasectomy, 222
Verbal Behavior (Skinner), 268–70
Chomsky's attack on, 293–96
Verbal learning, 306
Veterans Administration (VA), 241
Vineland Training School, 214, 221
Vocational guidance, VA and, 241
Völkerpsychologie, 38, 43, 46–47
Voluntarism, 45

W

Walden II (Skinner), 228, 270, 279, 349, 350
Walden (Thoreau), 124
Wallace, Alfred Russell, 111
Ward, James, 160
Washburn, Margaret Floy, 225
Watson, John Broadus, 50, 79, 136, 151,
168–69, 191–93, 317, 336
behaviorism of, 182–88, 227–29
on eugenics, 227
radical environmentalism of, 191–92, 227
Watson, Robert I., 17
Weiss, Albert P., 188
Wertheimer, M., 56–57, 60
Whig history of science, 14–15
Wiener, Norbert, 281
Wiggam, Albert Edward, 219, 220
Will to system, 40–42
Wilson, E.O., 356
Wilson, Timothy, 334–36
Wish-fulfillment
dreams and, 90
religion and, 94

Witmer, Lightner, 214, 236
Wittgenstein, Ludwig, 254, 255–59, 280,
325, 328, 336
Wolf Man, Freud's case of, 97
Women
in psychology, 237, 239
role of, in early America, 123
Woodhull, Victoria, 221
Woodworth, Robert, 49, 50, 58, 190, 191
World War I, 38, 56, 136, 140, 211–12
psychology/psychologists in, 214–16
World War II, 60, 272, 279, 280
effect on psychology of, 238–40, 251
psychology's role in, 239
Wright, Chauncey, 126–27
Wundt, Wilhelm, 2, 9, 11, 21, 30, 31, 52,
160–61, 213, 268, 335
biographical data, 37–39
imageless thought and, 49–50
language and, 46–47
psychology of consciousness and, 40–47
psychological methods, 42–43
theory/research, 44–47
will to system, 40–42
Würzburg School, 48–52

Y

Yerkes, Robert, 168, 175, 186, 197, 238, 240
group tests of intelligence and, 215–16,
219
racist views of, 218, 220
Yippies, 314
Yuppies, 315

Z

Zeitgeist history, 15–16, 17